RT OF
TECTION

Protection Officer

ker

Universal Publishers
Boca Raton, Florida

The Fine Art of Executive Protection:
Handbook for the Executive Protection Officer

Universal Publishers
Boca Raton, Florida • USA
2008

ISBN-10: 1-58112-984-X
ISBN-13: 978-1-58112-984-7

www.universal-publishers.com

You are an Executive Protection Officer.

You provide professional protection and physical security to your Principal.

As an executive protection officer, you provide a high quality service with expertise and accuracy, and you are always ready to train and improve your skills by challenging any conventional methods.

You perform your duties with determination and professionalism, whether on national or international soil, always in accordance and harmony with the law.

You conduct your duties according to the highest standards of integrity, morality, honor, and loyalty.

You carry out your assignments of protection regardless of nationality, religion, or race, respecting your colleague officers with strict solidarity.

Your colleague officers are your brothers-in-arms, discipline and comradeship are your strength—courage, and loyalty are your virtues.

Your assignment to protect your Principal is sacred. You will carry it out until the end, at all costs and at the risk of your life.

In the line of duty, you will act without passion and without hate; you will respect the defeated, never abandon your dead or wounded, and never leave your post.

You will get your inspiration and commitment to excellence from our motto:

"SEMPER PROTECTAMUS"
Semper Paratus -Nec Aspera Terrent

To all those brave women and men, Security Guards, Dignitary and Executive Protection Officers, Law and Security Enforcement Personnel, which lost their lives to protect others.

To my Father

To Smokey

My gratitude and love to my dear wife Serran, for being on my side with her dedication, support, patience, and encouragement and for helping me to finish this project.

Violence, when there are other alternatives, is immoral.
Violence, when there are no alternatives, is survival.

"I do not know what it is like to hit a man twice."

Li Shu Wen (1864-1934)

Manchu Imperial Bodyguard

"Imagine what I could have done using a fistful of these warriors."
Napoleon Bonaparte (1769-1821)

Napoleon's bodyguard Roustan (Turkish = Rüstım)

"It is a fine thing to be honest, but it also very important to be right."
Winston Churchill (1874-1965)

Caesar Augustus' Praetorian Guard

"Chastity, Poverty, Obedience and Protection of the Pilgrims on their Journey"
Perpetual vow of the Knights Templar (1120-1312)

Knight Templar

*"The public good is in nothing more essentially interested, than in the
protection of every individual's private rights."*

William Blackstone (English Jurist, 1723-1780)

Swiss Guard (Pontifical bodyguards)

"Stand with anybody that stands right, stand with him while he is right and part with him when he goes wrong."
Abraham Lincoln

Toshizo Hijikata, Vice Commander of the *Shinsen-gumi*
(A Special Police Protection Unit, 1869)

A special thanks is reserved for Jeff Young and Rebekah Galy of Universal Publishers, which professional guidance and expertise helped me through the process of publishing this and my previous book.

The man who follows the crowd will usually get no further than the crowd.
The man who walks alone is likely to find himself in places no one has ever been.

Alan Ashley-Pitt

Bu'shi'do

Bushido–means "Way of the Samurai"–based on the "Seven Virtues".
Among the Chinese warriors, it is known as *Wu Shi Dao*-"The Way of the Warrior".

During the 9th and 12th centuries in Japan, the warrior class, known as *samurai*–also called *bushi* (meaning: knight or warrior)–raised from the provinces. They became the ruling class until their decline and later total abolition in 1876 during the *Meiji* Era.

These warriors were men who lived by the *bushido*, a philosophy and guide for the warrior. The samurai were trustworthy and honest, and their loyalty to the emperor and his overlord "*daimyo*" was unique.

They lived frugal lives with no interest in riches and material values, but rather in honor and pride. They were men of true valor, with no fear of death. They would enter any battle, no matter the odds. To die in battle would only bring honor to one's family and one's lord.

This code of honor and moral principles, transferred verbally to each generation of samurai, became the written known form of the Bushido.

An Executive Protection Specialist is a warrior, but much more so a guardian, believing and doing what duty demands; proud of his/her formidable skills, but never takes pleasure out of the resulting consequences.

Throughout history, there have always been people like us, whether Praetorians, Knights Templar, or samurai, who turned into implements of steel and armor, so others would not need to. They were willing to offer their lives so others could live safely. Protection was their watchword–protection their creed.

Using the *bushido* code and the outlined virtues as a reference provides a point for reflection to everybody interested in the profession of Executive Protection Specialist. These virtues are not only of the samurai but form the essence applicable to the conduct of a true *Guardian*.

Jin

Compassion

The meaning suggests that one should aid the poor and care for those in trouble–to develop a sympathetic understanding of people. Through intensive training and hard work, one acquires strength, agility, and sharp senses. You are not as most people; therefore, your power should serve for good. You have compassion. You help your comrades and those in need at every opportunity. If an opportunity does not arise, you reach out to find one.

Gi

Integrity

Be honest throughout your dealings with all people. Believe in justice, not from other people, but from you. Honesty, justice, and integrity must become one with your life and actions. This is about making the right move or the right decision, not because it is easy, but to preserve correct ethics and morals. No matter the outcome or result, one does not lose face by applying proper justice.

Chu ugi

Loyalty

These are the Japanese characters for "loyalty"–but they also contain the meaning of "being faithful and true." You should show loyalty to your commander. Warriors are responsible for everything that they have done and everything that they have said, no matter the consequences. They are loyal to all of those in their care. They remain fiercely true to everyone within their responsibility.

Yuu

Courage

It is important to display courage and bravery when facing Death. This does not mean that you should seek out death, but you must be vigilant in trying to ignore idle threats. Do not use courage blindly; be intelligent and wise. Do not hide in a shell like a turtle, but enjoy life smartly and be alert. Risk has to be in a perfect harmonic balance, so seek fulfillment in bravery.

Makoto

Honesty and Sincerity

Be truthful and honest not only to your commander, but also to yourself. When you have sworn to perform an action, it is as good as done. Nothing will stop you from completing what you have said–you have no need to "give your word", nor do you need to "promise"–because speaking and doing are the same action.

Meiyo

Honor

Honor means: showing great respect for yourself, other people, and the rules by which you live. When you are honorable, you keep your word. You do the right, re-gardless of what others think or are doing. Honor is a path of integrity. You have only one judge of honor and character, and this is yourself. The decisions you make and the way you carry them out, is a reflection of who you are.

Rei

Respect

We show respect by speaking and acting with courtesy. We treat others with dignity and honor the rules of our family, school, and nation. Respect yourself, and others will respect you. The true strength of a warrior becomes apparent during difficult times.

浪人　Ro'nin

Ronin–a Warrior without Master

In ancient Japan, a *Ronin* was a samurai who served no master. Regardless, these samurai lived by the code of their kinship. Loyalty, honor, courage, and integrity were not just words, but the path these warriors took throughout their lives. They often hired themselves to needy persons, who were unable to defend their lives and possessions from bandits, thieves, and murderers. Many times these lonely warriors received only food in return for risking their lives.

The most famous Ronin was *Musashi Miyamoto*. He was the original true bodyguard, a wanderer, loner, and arguably the best samurai who ever lived. Musashi was Japan's greatest swordsman, and his bravery and mastery of weapons is legendary, even today. He was one of the famous 47 Ronin.

Musashi Miyamoto

For reasons of simplicity, the designation *Executive Protection Officer* will appear abbreviated as EPO.

The Author

Mr. Hunsicker is a Security Enforcement and Personal Protection Specialist with more than 20 years of professional experience in the fields of physical security and close protection; namely threat and risk management, dignitary protection, advisory, and coordination for physical security.

He served as security coordinator and dignitary protection adviser in Asia, European and African countries, and the United States. His assignments included clients of the private and corporate sector, celebrities, governmental entities, and NGOs. He also frequently accepted *pro bono* assignments as consultant to educational and humanitarian entities.

His skills and knowledge gained from specialized military training, such as special operations, expert marksmanship, weapons instructor, Martial art training, and Martial art instructor became enriched by a great field experience. Whether as a team member, team leader, coordinator, or adviser for physical security and dignitary protection, his rich experience permitted him to instruct and to lecture security, intelligence, and risk management related topics at several international institutions.

Over the years, Mr. Hunsicker played a role in the training, planning, and organization of security enforcement units and training facilities of international, private, and corporate clients.

He was the founder and executive of an international security agency, which later expanded into an institute for international security studies, with a special department for counter-terrorism studies.

He held membership of professional organizations, such as the Airborne Law Enforcement Association and International Counter Terrorism Officers Association. He is actively associated with the International Association of Airport and Seaport Police, the Counter Terrorism Study Unit of ISIS, the German Military Police Association, and the Diplomatic and Executive Protection Officers Association. His affiliation extends to humanitarian organizations, such as UNICEF, UNDP, UNA, the Sovereign Military Hospitaller Order of Malta, the Hereditary Knights Templar of Britannia, and the Royal British Legion, among others.

Mr. Hunsicker is also the author of *Understanding International Counter Terrorism: A Professional's Guide to the Operational Art.*

Prologue

This manual contains information collected from training material and results based on and gained throughout my professional experience as Dignitary Protection Adviser and Security Enforcement Expert.

All reference material is quoted and respective sources are indicated. A wide variety of references and sources are listed for further reading.

Written material of this particular subject, personal protection and physical security in general has been excellently carried out by many instructors, professionals, and governmental entities. However, none has offered to the public an in-depth look into the operational aspects of the executive protection specialist.

The number of incidents and crimes carried out by terrorists, criminals, and gangs, such as physical threats, violent attacks, assassinations, kidnapping, and hostage situations are increasing by the minute worldwide. Each incident is a constant and ever-demanding challenge to the law enforcement and the personal security professionals in particular. A detailed but understandable manual for the Executive Protection Officer is a priority and the answer to those challenging situations.

Information about every aspect of executive protection is not only an important part of the professional's training curriculum, but it also plays a vital role for the client, who seeks protection. This manual will provide a clear view of all aspects, not only for the professional, but also for prospect clients. To make sure of this, all available training and study material, individual case studies, and real scenarios, combined with professional experience serve as a foundation for this specialist's manual.

Reasonable efforts have been made to provide reliable data and information, but one can only assume limited responsibility for any changes or the validity of all material because of the rapid path and ever changing patterns in this profession.

Table of Contents

The Advance

The Protective Duty at Home and Office

The Vehicle and Driving

Terrorism

Kidnapping and Bombs

First Aid

Legal Status

Appendix

Throughout history, legends, and mythology, we read about brave individuals, who apparently used their special skills to protect kings against assassins; castles against rivaling clans; villages against terrorizing tribes and/or foreign invaders. Alternatively, they simply fought against dragons and mythical beasts, which terrorized entire regions. These were the times where the strong were dominating the weak, and the weak would seek out to find a skilled and fearless fighter, a champion, and a protector. One who would volunteer and place his own life at risk to defend and protect the weak and oppressed. Every single chapter of our history is highlighted with instances of conflicts, revolutions, wars, invasions, vandalism, assassinations, conquests, and terrorism. No matter what excuses, reasons, or means are presented to justify those actions, whether such impulses were based on or because of a social and political statement or a religiously rooted motivation, such events marked and continue to influence the shape, progress, and development of our society. As time goes by, we are able to observe that the physical security and personal protection business has changed. Fearless sword-bearing fighters, which once defended the weak from their oppressors, transformed into well-equipped, high-tech mercenaries. Protectors of royalties and important public figures turned to modern day's bodyguards and close protection officers. The physical security and personal protection business has experienced such a boost over recent years, that one might wonder whether qualified personnel, if available, can in fact match such a demand.

Just watching the various news channels, national and international, provides us with a clear picture of what this business is about and what one should expect from the professional and from the client's point of view. Physical security and, especially, personal protection is a vital element for the one under threat. Any close protection officer should be fully trained and has to be fully apt to detect, target, and neutralize any unexpected security threat or breach. The knowledge and skills, gained in specialized training and on-the-job experience, must cover all possible areas. Any personal limitations about the required knowledge and skills or personal reasons represent failure, most likely with a fatal outcome. Let's have a closer look and analyze a few incidents in which EPOs directly or indirectly played a significant role:

Incident 1:

The Date: August 1997
The Location: Paris, France
The Principal: Diana Princess of Wales and Dodi al-Fayed

The Incident: Princess Diana and Dodi al-Fayed were ready to leave from Hotel Ritz. To defeat the waiting "paparazzi", a black Mercedes limousine and a green Range Rover were used as decoys; leaving the hotel at the same time. Meanwhile, Diana and Dodi left the hotel in a second black Mercedes with their driver Henri Paul and their bodyguard Trevor Rees-Jones. Reports and accounts of what happened then are still not clear and very contradicting. Chased by the paparazzi on bikes, Henri Paul sped the black Mercedes south on Rue Cambon toward the underpass of the Alma tunnel. A few minutes later, Paul Henri was trying to avoid a collision with another car and lost control over the black Mercedes, which ended in a tragic accident. Dodi and Henri Paul died instantly; Diana died later in the hospital, and the bodyguard was seriously injured.

The Analysis: There was no coordination between the bodyguard of the decoy cars and the principal's bodyguard. The driver's physical and psychological condition was not checked. Aware of the photographers outside the hotel, no effort was made to implement an alternative plan. There was no real plan in place for this situation; besides, the bodyguards could not execute their job properly because of personal reasons. The bodyguard was not in control of the situation, neither in the hotel, nor in the car. Both bodyguards resigned from their jobs after Rees-Jones' recovery.

Incident 2:

The Date: September 2002
The Location: Kandahar, Afghanistan
The Principal: President Hamid Karzai

The Incident: A gunman, wearing the uniform of the new Afghan National Army opened fire, wounding the Governor of Kandahar and an U. S. Special Ops Soldier (providing security for Karzai). The gunman, one of the president's bodyguard, and another person were killed.

The Analysis: The assigned protection personnel was not adequately positioned–allowing the crowd to close in on the principal's vehicle easily. Protection personnel were much too distracted. Windows on the president's car were open–permitting any attacker to make a direct approach (fortunately nobody had planned to throw a grenade!). Vehicles within the motorcade had not enough distance between each other to maneuver and evacuate effectively after the attack (the situation after the attack appeared to be extremely chaotic).

Incident 3:

The Date: October 2006
The Location: Ankara,Turkey
The Principal: Prime Minister Recep Tayyip Erdoğan

The Incident: The Prime Minister, on the way to a party meeting, fainted and collapsed in the back of his limousine. As an immediate, however panic-driven reaction, he was driven directly to a nearby hospital. Arrived at the hospital, the Prime Minister's aide rushed out of the car to call for assistance from the medical staff. The driver and the head of security "decided" to leave the car at the same time (almost simultaneously)–leaving an unconscious Prime Minister alone inside the car. None of those present could even imagine what would happen next–the limousine (a ballistic level 5 (CEN B6/B7) Mercedes Sedan) activated the automatic security system immediately and locked the now semi-conscious Prime Minister "safely" inside. The medical team arrived, but was of no help in face of this new situation. The driver and the head of security finally snapped out of an initial state of panic and after a few minutes of blaming each other, both decided to get the Prime Minister out of the car. After challenging the security system of the car and almost 2 hours of sledgehammer blows later, they finally managed to smash the car's rear window and take the Prime Minister out.

The Analysis: This is a classic case of a total screw-up. This incident might have been a perfect commercial for Mercedes, but it is a disaster for anybody of the executive protection business. This was not the only incident and analyzing each of them would fill another volume. So, forgive the skepticism about such professionalism. It is unacceptable that nobody of the protection team was aware of the physical condition of the Prime Minister. Nobody had knowledge of the contact details of his personal doctor. The security team probably never heard of CPR or First Aid procedures. A well equipped medical emergency unit was located right in the parliament building, which was a few minutes away from where the PM collapsed–the driver, behaving like a local taxi driver, took the PM to a distant hospital. Besides completing a list of mistakes, the head of security did not even bother to call and inform the hospital about the emergency, or the arrival of the PM.

Mind you, by attempting to analyze these particular incidents, the main purpose is to highlight errors and to improve the professionalism of the executive protection sector in general–not to criticize any particular person. In fact, this analysis has no intention to offend any person, entity, or authority under any circumstances.

Any professional, actively engaged within the executive protection field–whether in a team or as team leader–must be trained and apt to pinpoint even the most unexpected security concerns. The book contains carefully selected material, which for the professional provides all those ingredients that are essential for a successful mission. For the client as a prospect principal, it will provide all those important and sought for details, which will assure a lifesaving protection.

While every effort has been made to make this work as informative and practical as possible, there will still be plenty of room for that very personal experience, which one can only gain in the field. This work is offering the insights, the experience and considerations earned in training, on duty, by learning and exchange of knowledge and yes, from mistakes.

Always remember that the job of an executive protection officer is nothing compared with an action movie, nor does it provide a replay option as in most FPS (First Person Shooter) video games. We are talking about the real thing–real life action. You make a mistake and it's "Game Over". You will not have a chance to restart the mission or to pause and save at a given checkpoint.

This book has no intention to criticize or replace anything that has been published by other qualified executive protection professionals as a result of hard work. The content of this book provides the novice to this profession with tools and a clear inside view of what is expected when placed in a position of trust–entrusted with the responsibility, safety, and the life of another person.

The advanced professional, who has the skills and to whom the job has become second nature, will find in this book information that will help to expand and to refresh those skills. Alertness and awareness are disrupted and easily weakened by everyday routines. The material will assist to regain awareness and refresh the principles of close protection.

The person, who at some point in life is in need of protection and ultimately requires the service of an executive protection professional, will gain knowledge of what to expect from personal protection and what will keep him/her safe.

> "There is no security for any of us unless there is security for all."
> Howard Koch, U. S. Screenwriter (1901-1995)

The Threats

- **Stalking**

- **Kidnapping and Abduction**

- **Hostage Taking**

- **Assassination**

- **Terrorism**

Any person, whether as an individual or with family because of position, lifestyle, wealth, or public importance, is at a constant risk and can easily become a target for various threats. Such risks and threats must be detected by the smallest signs. Once aware of such a possible threat, it has to be dealt with immediately. To understand these threats and, more importantly, the person or group of people using these threats, we have to analyze the mechanisms and motivations.

Stalking

Stalking is a form of repeated invasion of a person's privacy. Such an invasion in a manner of repeated harassment causes fear to the target. The statutes may vary between jurisdictions of States and countries, but can include such acts as:

- Repeatedly following of the target/victim
- Unwanted forms of contact (by letter, phone, mail, or other electronic communications)
- Observation of a person's actions and routines up close for a certain extended period of time
- Inappropriate contact of the target's family, friends, colleagues, associates
- Stalking via the Internet

According to various statistics and researches conducted by government and law agencies, 1 out of 10 women and 1 out of 38 men will become a victim of stalking in their lifetime. This is not ruling out that some might even be the target of various stalkers at different times.

The Behavior of the Stalker

Stalking as such exists on a continuum of severity. The form of stalking might be subtle, so the victim is not aware of what is happening, and the perpetrator might not have any malicious intent. Some might even believe that the victim likes them or might build a wrong sense of need to help the victim. Stalking consists contrary to any other category of crime, not in one single action, but in a serious of actions. Some of such actions might appear at first glance to be legal, such as sending an e-mail, calling on the phone, or even sending gifts. Most stalking cases do not escalate to extreme violence and harassment, which might end in an abduction of the victim.

Stalkers often use manipulative behavior and legal actions to intimidate and manipulate the victim; sometimes the threat of committing suicide is used to force the victim to intervene, which will bring the victim closer to the stalker. Stalkers may also use violence to frighten the victim or engage in vandalism and damage property (like the victim's car, or killing the victim's pet).

The use of physical attacks, which might leave abrasions and bruises, is another form to scare the victim directly. Physical attacks, which leave serious injuries or which involve sexual assault are less common.

The Types of Stalkers

From the psychological view, we might group stalkers into two main categories:

- Psychotic
- Nonpsychotic

Many stalkers reveal preexisting psychotic disorders such as delusional disorder, schizophrenic disorder, or schizophrenia. However, most of these stalkers are of a nonpsychotic character and exhibit

Disorders, such as major depression, adjustment disorders, or dependency on substances. Others might show personality disorders, such as antisocial, dependency, paranoia, narcissism. In pursuing victims, the nonpsychotic stalker can be easily influenced by various psychological factors, including but not limited to anger, hostility, blame projection, obsession, denial, and minimization and jealousy. [1]

In "A Study of Stalkers", P. E. Mullen (et al) [2] identifies six distinct types of stalkers:

- The rejected stalker–pursues their victims to correct or reverse or avenge a rejection (separation, termination of a relationship, divorce)

- The resentful stalker–pursues a vendetta because of sense of grievance against the victim. Motivation is mainly driven by the desire to frighten and distress the victim.

- The intimacy seeker–seeks to establish a certain intimacy or even loving relationship with the victim. For those, the victim is representing the long sought-after soul mate, or they were meant to be together.

- The Eroto-manic stalker–believes the victim is in love with him/her. He/she reinterprets what their victim says or does to support the delusion, convinced that such an imagined romance will end in a permanent union. The targets are often celebrities, or persons of higher social status (however not all celebrities' stalkers are eroto-manics).

- The incompetent suitor–despite poor social/courting skills, this type possesses a sense of entitlement to an intimate relationship with those who have attracted their amorous interests and desires.

- The predatory stalker–is spying and observing the victim, as part of preparing and planning an attack (mostly sexual) on the victim.

- The terrorism stalker–commonly known as the political stalker, uses stalking as a tool to accomplish a political agenda. They use threats and intimidation to force their targets to refrain or to become part of their particular activity – regardless of the victim's consent.

Many stalkers will fit the categories with paranoid disorders. Intimacy-seeking stalkers often present delusional disorders, which are secondary to the preexisting psychotic disorders, such as schizophrenia. The continual clinging to a relationship by the rejected stalkers unites with the entitlement of the narcissistic personality and the persistent jealousy of the paranoid personality.

Male and Female Stalker

Even though most stalkers are male, female stalkers are not far behind. The demographic characteristic of male or female stalkers does not differ, although more male stalkers are reported with a history of criminal offenses and substance abuse. The psychiatric aspects between male and female stalkers do not differ otherwise. Female stalkers tend to target someone they have known once; they also tend to target female victims. Men, on the other hand, do not target other men.

Mullen, Pathé and Purcell in "A Study of Women Who Stalk," [3] conclude that the two psychiatric variables which differentiate female from male stalkers is motivation for stalking and the choice of victim. Female stalkers seek intimacy with the victim, who is usually someone they already know. The victim is often chosen from those who assume a profession of a helper, such as doctors, therapists, police officers, security guards. Female stalkers are as dangerous as male stalkers.

Stalking does not consist of a single incident, but is a continuous process. It can be a terrifying experience for the victims, placing them at the risk of long lasting psychological trauma and possible physical harm.

Stalking is a form of a mental assault, in which the perpetrator repeatedly, disruptively, and wanted or unwanted breaks the life, the intact world of the victim. This can be someone with whom he/she has or had a relationship. The separated acts, which form the intrusion, cannot cause the mental abuse by themselves, but in the whole.

The victim will suffer not only mental and emotional damage:

- Denial and doubt about themselves – the victim does not believe, that it is happening to them
- Self-blame
- Guilt, shame and embarrassment
- Frustration
- Loss of self-esteem
- Insecurity
- Shock and confusion
- Irritability
- Fear, anxiety, phobias and panic attack
- Anger toward the stalker and the legal process
- Depression
- Flashbacks and emotional numbness
- Disconnection from other people
- Hypervigilance
- Difficulties to concentrate and focus
- Tendency to suicide
- Problems with intimacy and loss of trust to other people, even the partner
- PTSD (post-traumatic stress disorder)

But will also suffer psychologically:

- Sleep disturbances and nightmares
- Sexual dysfunction
- Fatigue, weight fluctuations and gastrointestinal problems
- Dermatological eruptions and changes
- Headaches and dizziness
- Self-medication, drug and alcohol abuse
- Heart palpitation, sweating and shortness of breath

Seven Points to Remember

- Stalking is a crime–it is a course of conduct directed at a target person, which places the victim in fear of his/her safety. Stalking is against the law in all states of the U. S. A.; stalking across state borders is illegal and under the jurisdiction of the federal law. In many other countries, stalking does not get the full attention from the legal system, and victims are easily confronted with a justice system, which is not ready to respond properly.

- Many people are stalked–1 out of 10 women and 1 out of 38 men will become a victim of stalking in their lifetime.

- Stalking can be very dangerous – 75 percent of women killed by their intimate partners were stalked by these partners prior to the killing. All stalkers should be considered unpredictable and extremely dangerous.

- Stalking is intrusive and harmful to the victim–victims are losing time and their ability to focus on their work and might not even return to work, others are relocating because they still fear for their safety. Insomnia, depression, anxiety are typical results of stalker attacks.

- Anybody can be stalked–the vast majority of people stalked are ordinary people-not celebrities. Most stalkers are no strangers to their victims, but are known by them.

- Stalking can occur during, after, or in absence of a relationship–very often the stalking starts in the relationship, where the stalker keeps the victim under constant surveillance and threat. Others start stalking after a relationship has ended, which is motivated by certain desperation and the desire to regain control. Other stalkers become fixated on a target person without ever having a relationship or contact. Any form of stalking is unpredictable and therefore dangerous.

- Any type of technology can be useful for the stalker–technological innovations are very useful in our everyday life, but can become ideal tools for the criminal stalker. Computer, internet, cell phones, surveillance equipment are the favored gadgets of the stalkers.

Kidnapping and Abduction

Kidnapping

Kidnapping is any illegal capture or detention of a person against their will, regardless of age, for ransom or any other reason. The term *Abduction,* having the same meaning, is mostly used with kidnappings where a child and one of the parents is involved.

In criminal law, *kidnapping* is the taking away or the *asportation* of a person against the person's will, usually to hold the person in false imprisonment, or confinement without any legal authority. The *asportation* (carrying things away illegally) element can be interpreted in various ways and depends on the law of each state or country. Under common English law, for example, the asportation element requires that the victim is moved outside the boundaries of England or overseas to be considered the act as a "kidnapping". Kidnappings for ransom are a common thing in less developed and unstable countries, where the economic conditions are one of the motives for such a crime. The entire process of kidnapping with or without a demand, however, became a complete new meaning with the appearance of mass-kidnappings, hostage-takings, beheadings, and killings in Iraq, Afghanistan, and Palestine. The following are some of the kidnappings and abductions of people, public figures, and celebrities that made headlines:

- On October 19, 1928, William Hickman became the first American, tried and executed for kidnapping and murder of the 12-year old Marian Parker, daughter of an L. A. banker.

- 1932, Charles Lindbergh Jr., the aviator's two-year old son was kidnapped and killed. This was the most publicized kidnapping among celebrities.

- In 1933, Brooke Hart, the son of a California business was kidnapped and murdered. The kidnapper, after being arrested, was lynched by the public.

- In 1950 South Korean citizens were abducted by the North Korean officials.

- On September 28, 1953 the 6-year old Robert C. Greenlease Jr., was kidnapped and murdered by B. Heady and C. Hall. The kidnappers demanded a ransom of $600, 000 from the father, a wealthy car dealer. The money was never recovered–some sources indicate that more than half of the ransom was stolen by a corrupt police officer.

- In 1960, Adolf Eichmann (a Nazi war criminal) was abducted by the *Mossad* (Israeli Secret Service) in Argentine and brought to stand trial in Israel. He was convicted for crimes against humanity and hanged in 1962.

- In 1960, Eric Peugeot, the son of Raymond Peugeot, the automobile industry millionaire, was kidnapped at the age of four in Paris. He was returned after a ransom payment and his kidnappers were arrested a few years later.

- In 1970, James Cross, a British diplomat and Pierre Laporte, a provincial politician of Quebec, was kidnapped by the "Front de Libération du Quebec." Cross was later released, but Laporte was killed. This incident set off what became known as the "October Crisis."

- Karl Maria von Spret, West Germany's ambassador to Guatemala, was kidnapped in 1970 in Guatemala City. He was killed.

- In 1973, John Paul Getty III, grandson of J. Paul Getty, the American oil tycoon, at that time the world's richest man was kidnapped in Italy. His grandfather initially refused to pay a US $3 million ransom. To enforce the demand, one of the boy's ears was cut off and sent to a newspaper.

- Patty Hearst, the granddaughter William Randolph Hearst was kidnapped by the SLA (Symbionese Liberation Army) in 1974. Her father paid US $6 million in food to the poor of the Bay Area as ransom. Patty Hearst, however, was not released; instead, she joined her captor's group and was later convicted on bank robbery charges.

- From 1970-1980 a series of abductions of Japanese citizens was carried out by the North Korean officials.

- In 1977, Hanns-Martin Schleyer, a German business manager was kidnapped in Köln. His body was found near Mulhouse, France.

- In 1978, the former Italian Prime Minister Aldo Moro was kidnapped and killed by extremists.

- In 1985, the abducted Mexican-American DEA agent Enrique Camarena was found dead.

- In 1987, the Dutch company executive, Gerrit Heijn was kidnapped. He was killed by his kidnapper a few days later. The kidnapper pretended the victim was still alive and demanded ransom. He was arrested thanks to the registered banknotes.

- In 1989, the Belgian politician Paul Boeynants was kidnapped. He was released after one month in captivity in exchange for the ransom.

- In 1990, a small ten-year-old Japanese girl was kidnapped in Nigata. She was held captive for 9 years and 2 months.

- On August 1993, Lewis Lent, a janitor from Massachusetts confessed kidnaps of several victims: 12-year old Sara Wood, who disappeared on a quiet road near her home in Herkimer (New York). Lent confessed that he kidnapped, sexually assaulted, and killed Sara. He refused, however, to indicate the location where he buried the body. He also pled guilty to the kidnapping and murder of the 12-year old Jimmy Bernardo of Pittsfield, Massachusetts in 1990. Lent is suspected in several other child kidnappings–he was sentenced to life without parole for the Bernardo murder and 25 years to life for the Wood murder.

- In 1998, the son of the Hong Kong tycoon Li Ka Shing was kidnapped. He was released after a record ransom payment of 1 Billion HK dollars (approx. US $134 million) was delivered to the kidnapper. Despite his nickname "Big Spender", the kidnapper Cheung Chi Keung was not able to spend the ransom money. He was captured and executed in Guangzhou in 2000.

- Natascha Kampusch, a 10-year old Austrian girl was kidnapped in 1998 and held captive for 8 years. Fortunately for the victim, the kidnapper killed himself in 2006 and she could be freed by the police.

Abduction

(Latin: *abductio, abducere* = to lead away)

Abduction is a law term used to denote the forcible or fraudulent removal of a person, limited by custom to the case where a woman is the victim. For men or children, it has been usual to substitute it with the term *kidnapping*. The most common form of abductions in recent years is the abduction of children by one of the parents (multinational, multicultural origin).

The child abduction can be distinct as follows:

- A stranger removing a child for criminal or mischievous purposes
- A stranger removing a child (usually a baby) to replace a child loss and to bring up as that person's own child.
- A parent removes or retains a child from the other parent's care (often in the course of or after divorce proceedings and/or between multicultural parents).

Abduction by a Stranger

Though perhaps the most feared kind of abduction, the removal by a stranger is not the most common type. The stereotypical version of stranger abduction is the classic form of "kidnapping," exemplified by the Lindbergh kidnapping, in which the child is detained, transported some distance, held for ransom or with intent to keep the child permanently. These instances are rare. (In a study commissioned by the U. S. Department of Justice, the Office of Juvenile Justice and Delinquency Prevention revealed, that in 1999 were only approximately 115 stereotypical stranger abductions.)

The most common form of "stranger abduction" however, is the situation in which a child is abducted by a stranger, friend, or acquaintance for some purpose other than ransom and typically involves less force and is of a shorter duration.

According to the National Non-Family Abduction Report 2002, approximately 58, 000 of such child abductions took place in 1999 in the United States only. This report also revealed that the vast majority of these victims were teenagers; fifty-seven percent of the victims were missing for at least one hour; and nearly 50% suffered sexual assault or rape during that abduction.

Removal by Stranger to Raise as Own

A very small number of abductions result from (typically) women who kidnap babies (or other young children) to bring up as their own. These women are often unable to have children of their own and seek to satisfy their unmet psychological need by abducting a child, rather than by adopting. The crime is often premeditated, with the woman often simulating pregnancy to reduce suspicion when a baby suddenly appears in the household.

Parental Child Abduction

The most common kind of child abduction is the parental child abduction, which often occurs when the parents separate or begin their divorce proceedings. In those cases, a parent may remove or keep the child from the other, seeking to gain an advantage in the expected or pending child custody proceedings, or because that parent fears losing the child in those expected or pending child custody proceedings. A parent may refuse to return a child at the end of an access visit or may flee with the child to prevent an access visit. Parental child abductions may be within the same city, within the state region, or within the same country, or may be international.

This is considered as Child Abuse. (Several studies commissioned by the U. S. Department of Justice's, the Office of Juvenile Justice and Delinquency Prevention and the National Family Abduction Report of 2002 revealed that in 1999, 53% of family abducted children disappeared for less than one week. 21% disappeared for one month or more.)

Depending on the laws of the state and country in which the parental abduction occurs, this may or may not constitute a criminal offense. For example, removal of a child from the U. K. for a period of 28 days or more without the permission of the other parent (or person with parental responsibility) is a criminal offense. Many U. S. States are handling "interstate child abduction" as a crime, and the National Conference of Commissioners on Uniform State Laws is working on a project to draft an uniform state law which is mainly dealing with parental abductions.

International Child Abduction

Very serious problems can arise when a parental abduction is carried out and results in moving a child across an international border. The laws of the states are different, and a foreign child custody order may not be recognized.

The Hague Convention on the Civil Aspects of International Child Abduction is an international treaty and legal mechanism to recover children abducted to another country by one parent or a family member. Many nations signed this treaty, however the process of recognition, proceeding, and recovery is time-consuming and nerve-wracking, and the experience in many cases is of a disappointing and frustrating nature.

Unfortunately this treaty, as well as many others of similar nature and purpose, is also signed by nations where corruption is considered a part of the constitution—where child-slavery, torture, honor-killings and female circumcision are a common part of daily life.

Characteristics of Abduction

- Most international abductions occur post-custodial (custody order already exists). The most frequent pattern was an order of joint legal custody with physical custody to the parent who was then left behind.
- Nearly half of abductions occur during a court ordered visitation.
- About 48% of abductions occur within one year of the marital separation, whereas an additional 25% occur after more than three years.
- Abductors have social support for and assistance in their actions. About 87% of abductors are assisted by their families and about 65% are assisted by friends.

Abduction Planning Activities (Occurs in 35-70% of cases)

- Saved money or waited for expected cash payment
- Gathered, destroyed, or hidden legal documents and records
- Liquidated assets
- Quit or changed jobs
- Applied for a passport for child from the authorities or diplomatic mission
- Move to other residence
- Received visits from friends or family members from another country to assist with abduction
- Preparatory visit to country to which child will later be taken
- Applied for a visa for the child from diplomatic mission of another country

International Abductor Risk Profile

- Parents who have strong ties to another country are at risk of abducting their children, particularly when, in the context of separation and divorce, they:
  - Experience severe loss or humiliation
  - Idealize their own family, homeland and culture
  - Deprecate American society and culture
  - Rescind and dismiss the child's mixed heritage
  - Have offers of emotional/financial support from their homeland
- About 92% of parents who abduct to another country have one or more ties to that country. Therefore, in cases at risk for international child abduction, the country to which the child is likely to be abducted is highly predictable.
- Possible types of ties to destination country to which child is abducted:
  - 61% were nationals only of the country to which the child was abducted
  - 77% had family in the destination country
  - 65% had close friends in the destination country
  - the abductor speaks the language of the destination country
  - the abductor grew up mainly in the destination country
  - the abductor lived in the destination country as a child
  - 56% lived in the destination country as an adult
  - 49% had gone on visits to the destination country
  - the abductor shared the same race or ethnicity in the destination country
  - the abductor had employment or business interests in the destination country
  - the abductor has dual nationality; from the country of residence and the destination country

- In most cases, the abductor and the left behind parent are of different nationalities, ethnicities and religions.
- The left behind parent is more likely to have a higher income and to be employed compared to the abducting parent.
- Mothers and fathers are about equally likely to abduct their children. But there are differences based on cultural background and inter-marital patterns, which affect whether mothers or fathers are more likely to abduct to specific geographical areas (e. g. fathers more often abduct their child to an Islamic country, mothers more often abduct to a European country or country with Western culture).
- More than 50% of the abductors and left behind parents are in their thirties.
- Family violence is a characteristic of most of these families. Allegations of spouse abuse, child abuse and serious child neglect are frequent, with many having sought restraining orders or reporting abuse to the respective authorities.
- More than 80% of the left behind parents report that, prior to the abduction, the abductor threatened they would never see their children again.
- The left behind parents report that the abducting parent threatened their lives (60%), their children's lives (20%), and the lives of others (40%).

In case of child abduction, time is very precious and doing the right things is vital for the outcome of such a nerve-wracking and time-consuming situation. Every single hour wasted means valuable time saved and precious miles gained for the abductor. The following action plan is by far not perfect but might assist to get quick and positive results.

- **Contact local law enforcement without delay**
- File a missing person's report on the abducted child. Ask the local police to enter your child into the Missing Person File Records (in the U. S. it's the FBI's National Crime Information Center-Missing Person File (NCIC-MPF).
- Provide a complete description of your child, a birth certificate, and photos. It is **not** necessary to have a custody order to have your child entered into the NCIC, but a copy of it if you have one would be of use.
- Take note of the name, badge number, and phone number of the police officer who is taking the missing person report. Ask for a copy. Or, ask for the case report (or police report) number.
- Verify with local law enforcement that a Missing Person File Records (NCIC-MPF) entry has been made. Ask for a copy of the MPF printout. Or, ask for the record number (NCIC).

Be aware: Law enforcement officials are used to telling that they cannot do anything for 24 hours or that they cannot do anything at all without a custody order. These "excuses" and "justifications" are very common.

Laws and procedures regarding Missing Children/Persons may differ from country to country but should never permit a delay regarding the search, especially in an international abduction, where the abductor might try to cross the border at any moment.

In the U. S., Federal Law–the National Child Search Support Act (42 U.S.C. §§ 5779-5780)–prohibits waiting periods and does not require to have a custody order before law enforcement enters a missing child into the NCIC. Further, the FBI has authority to do so under the Missing Children Act (28 U.S.C. § 534).

- Ask the local law enforcement for immediate assistance to stop the abductor from leaving the country (or entering or exiting another).
- Call the local law enforcement directly and ask for their urgent attention to the abduction (whether international or national) in progress.
- Ask the local law enforcement to contact INTERPOL for immediate assistance.
- Notify seaport authority, police, and border authority at the nearest airports, bus depots, and train stations about the abduction in progress. Fax pictures and descriptions (if possible, passport details) of the abductor and child.
- Ask the local law enforcement to coordinate with the prosecutor to get a local court order authorizing the pick-up of the child. If the child is still within local and State boundaries and the State law is permitting such order.
- Find out from the local law enforcement or the local prosecutor if the abductor can be criminally charged under the local/State law. (If the destination country is a *Hague Convention* country, with a good track record of returning children to other member countries, it is important to consider the outcome. Criminal charges against the abductor might adversely affect a return proceeding under the *Hague Convention*.)

To get best results regarding the *Hague Convention* and related procedures, one should check whether the country of residence and the destination country of the abductor have signed the treaty and have a good track record. See "Countries of the Hague Convention".

- Find out if a passport has been issued to your child. If you have custody, put a hold on issuance of a passport.
- Ask if the abductor's passport is still valid, or has been renewed. Ask if the child's passport could be revoked. This could be particularly helpful if the child is taken to a non-Hague country.
- If you do not already have a passport, apply for one now in case you need to travel abroad.
- *Contact airlines the abductor would be likely to fly.*
- Explain the urgency of the situation. Ask if the airline has issued tickets or has booked reservations for the abductor and child. If the airline volunteers any pertinent information about the abductor's flight plans, notify the law enforcement at once! Ask the law enforcement get this information if you can't.
- *Contact the embassy or consulate of the destination country.*
- Tell embassy personnel the situation and ask if they can help.
- If the abductor is a national of that country, ask if the abductor's passport can be revoked.

It is very difficult to stop any abduction in progress. Often, it is too late–the abductor is long gone before the searching parent discovers what has happened. If the abductor's scheme is discovered while he or she is still in flight, government authorities local and abroad have a narrow window of opportunity to stop the abduction. They must act swiftly and in concert. It is up to the searching parent to set the rapid response in motion.

Despite media and popular use of the word hostage to describe various foreign nationals, and sometimes fellow-citizens, abducted in Lebanon, Colombia, and other nations around the world, these incidents like abductions are more often kidnappings. This is because there is no confrontation between authorities and abductors.

A kidnap victim is held hostage. The difference lies in knowing the whereabouts of the perpetrators and their victim in the latter instances, and their unknown whereabouts in the former.

Countries of the Hague

(Convention on the Civil Aspects of International Child Abduction)

Concluded: 25 October, 1980
Entered into force: 01 December, 1983

- Argentina
- Australia
- Austria
- Bahamas
- Belgium
- Belize
- Bosnia and Herzegovina
- Burkina Faso
- Canada
- Chile
- China
  - Hong Kong
  - Macau
- Colombia
- Croatia
- Cyprus
- Czech Republic
- Denmark
- Ecuador
- Finland
- France
- Germany
- Greece
- Honduras
- Hungary
- Iceland
- Ireland
- Israel
- Italy
- Luxembourg
- Macedonia
- Mauritius
- Mexico
- Monaco
- Netherlands
- New Zealand
- Norway
- Panama
- Poland
- Portugal
- Romania
- Slovak Republic
- Slovenia
- South Africa
- Spain
- St. Kitts and Nevis
- Sweden
- Switzerland
- Turkey
- United Kingdom
  - Bermuda
  - Cayman Islands
  - Falkland Islands
  - Isle of Man
  - Montserrat
- United States of America
- Venezuela
- Yugoslavia
- Zimbabwe

Hostage Taking

Persons who take hostages, whether in the course of a well-planned, well-thought out action or a spur-of-the-moment reaction, can be divided into four categories:

- Professional Criminals
- Inadequate Personalities
- Splintered Groups
- Structured Groups

Professional Criminals

Professional criminals make their livings (full or part-time) by robbery, burglary, and similar illegal activity. When they take a hostage, it means that the job has gone wrong. Usually, the crime in progress is a felony, and the criminal takes a hostage or hostages to escape. For the police, the professional criminal is, in the first moments of confrontation, the most dangerous type of hostage-taker. There is an initial period of panic that generates a fight or flight reaction, so called because the instinct of cornered animals is either to flee or turn and attack. In humans, the fight or flight reaction is that brief time during which the trapped person most wants to strike out at or flee from whatever is causing the panic. In this case, it is the police. The police tactic here is to carefully contain the professional criminal in the smallest practical area and give him time to think, rationalize, and generally consider all the options on the situation in which he finds himself. In containing the professional criminal, the officer (s) should find good cover that affords sufficient protection. Cover is not the same as concealment, since a curtain or cardboard box can conceal but not afford much protection. After the panic reaction period has subsided, usually in 10 to 30 minutes, the professional criminal becomes the easiest type of hostage-taker with whom the police deal. This is because, as a professional, the criminal realizes he has nothing to gain from keeping the hostages, much less harming or killing one of them.

Inadequate Personality

Inadequate personality is an individual who police officers in the street may refer to as a psycho. The more delicate designation is inadequate personality or emotionally disturbed person. This individual is a self-professed loner and loser for whom nothing goes right and the whole world is against. He wants to get attention, and taking someone hostage is just the way to do it. The last thing this type of hostage-taker wants is escape. He wants to keep the incident going because he is enjoying it. Newspaper and broadcast reporters have repeatedly established contact with such hostage-takers, provided a public forum for them, and, incidentally, almost invariably prolonged an agonizing incident for the hostages.

Splintered Groups (Prison inmates for example)

Splintered groups also use attracting attention as their primary intent. They may not even know what their actual wants are, but they will demand things such as better food, conjugal visits, and improved recreational facilities. The splintered group (this term is used because inmates usually are not organized into a tightly knit unit) is unique among hostage-takers. Therefore, the strategy in dealing with them is different. Rather than stretching out time as a tactic, it is appropriate early on in the incident, during that period called a "window of time," to use a show of force. This use of force can break down the least adequate of the hostage-takers involved in the splintered group. Since most prison takeovers are spontaneous, this early show of force can be effective. However, if there is information or other suspicions that it is a carefully planned takeover, the show of force tactic should be abandoned—unless it results in an immediate harm to the hostages. In addition, even if a prison takeover is spontaneous and hostages are involved, if the appropriate show of force is not effected almost immediately, that window of time is closed and the use of force no longer appropriate or effective. In this event, it is best to resort to using time delaying tactics because, in reality, the hostage-takers become a group of inadequate personalities. When in doubt, use time.

Structured Groups (Terrorists)

Structured groups who engage in hostage-taking, and this includes hijacking, are employing a tactic used primarily as a propaganda tool to maximize the effect of violence for political or economic gains. The selection of targets and victims is made with the aim of eliciting the maximum propaganda value from the incident. These incidents may be immediate reactions to world events, or an eruption in a long-standing feud or continuing animosity. Often, it is impossible to discern the motivation behind a particular hostage-taking incident. Terrorists, particularly in hostage situations, will often use multiple incidents in an effort to separate and disperse law enforcement resources. The primary defensive tactic is to cut the terrorists' lines of communication while the police keep and improve their own.

Hostage Incidents

Pueblo incident	North Korea	January	23, 1968	11 months
October Crisis	Quebec, Canada	October	5, 1970	60 days
Munich Massacre	Munich, Germany	September	4, 1972	a few hours
Norrmalmstorg Robbery	Stockholm, Sweden	August	23, 1973	5 days
Mayaguez Incident	Cambodian coast	May	12, 1975	3 days
Holland Train Hostage Case	Netherlands	December	4, 1975	7 days
Balcombe Street Siege	London, United Kingdom	December	6, 1975	5 days
Entebbe Airport Hostage Crisis	Entebbe Airport, Uganda	June	27, 1976	8 days
Japan Airlines JAL Flight 472 Hijacking	en route from Mumbai to Tokyo	September	28, 1977	5 days
Landshut Flight	Mogadishu, Somalia	October	13, 1977	5 days
Iran Hostage Crisis	Tehran, Iran	November	4, 1979	444 days
Siege of Masjid al Haram	Mecca, Saudi-Arabia	November	2, 1979	14 days
Dominican Embassy Siege	Bogotá, Colombia	February	27, 1980	61 days
Iranian Embassy Siege	London, United Kingdom	April	30, 1980	6 days
Achille Lauro Cruise-ship Hijacking	en route from Alexandria to Port Said	October	7, 1985	2 days
Palace of Justice Siege	Bogotá, Colombia	November	6, 1985	2 days
Ouvéa Cave Hostage Crisis	Ouvéa, New Caledonia	April	22, 1988	14 days
Supreme Court of Justice Hostage Crisis	San José, Costa Rica	April	26, 1993	4 days
Air France Flight 8969	Algiers to Marseilles	December	24, 1994	3 days
Budyonnovsk Hospital Hostage Crisis	Budyonnovsk, Russia	June	14, 1995	2 days
Japanese Embassy Hostage Crisis	Lima, Peru	December	17, 1996	126 days
Indian Airlines Flight 814	Kathmandu, Nepal	December	24, 1999	8 days
Bus 174 Hostage Taking	Rio de Janeiro, Brazil	June	12, 2000	a few hours
Moscow Theater Hostage Crisis	Moscow, Russia	October	23, 2002	2 1/2 days
Beslan School Hostage Crisis	Beslan, Russia	September	1, 2004	3 days

Why Hostages Are Taken

In the case of the professional criminal, hostages are seen as a possible means of escape from a difficult situation. Inadequate personalities use hostages as a means of getting attention. People will start talking to them, asking what's wrong. A disgruntled or dismissed employee then has the opportunity to air grievances in public. A jilted lover may want to prove his love is greater and somehow feels that by taking his ex-girlfriend hostage, he is expressing that love for all to see. For prisoners, hostages are used to give inmates the power to negotiate with prison officials. Terrorists use hostages to get the widest possible media coverage.

In all cases, however, the hostage-takers want to extract something from the authorities or the outside world. They cannot get what they want from the hostages, so it is not the hostages themselves who are the important factor; they merely allow the hostage-taker to make an announcement. This announcement may take the form of a telephone call to the police or news media by the perpetrator, or it could be a shouted warning to passersby or even gunshots fired into the air. If a bad guy took a hostage and no one knew, what would the hostage-taker accomplish? Even if he had all of his windows booby-trapped or had a well-written note or a prepared statement to make to the media, these preparations would be meaningless if no one was aware of the situation.

Assassination

Assassination is the deliberate killing of an important person, usually a political figure or other strategically important individual. Assassins, and particularly their "employers," usually follow an ideological or political agenda, and regard the target as an obstacle to furthering this agenda. Other motivations may be money, as in the case of a contract killing or simply revenge.

The Assassins (Arabic: حشّـــاشيــن, hashshāshīn), can be traced back to the 11th century. They were the creation of a dissident sect of Shi'a Islam–the Nizari Isma'ilis to be precise. The Assassins became known for their fearless assassinations and killings of local and foreign rulers, religious opponents and their significant involvement during the Crusades. There are many accounts and legends related to the Assassins, many of which are the results of medieval travelers and storytellers. The *Old Man of the Mountain*, Hasan-bin Sabbah (Persian: حسـن صـبـاح) [4], their mysterious leader, the gardens of paradise, the superlative skills of the assassins in disguise were part of stories, which were filling the literature in Europe and beyond. Marco Polo told in his diaries about the Old Man of the Mountain and the assassins:

> "The Old Man kept at his court such boys of twelve years old as seemed to him destined to become courageous men. When the Old Man sent them into the garden in groups of four, ten or twenty, he gave them hashish to drink. They slept for three days, then they were carried sleeping into the garden where he had them awakened. When these young men woke, and found themselves in the garden with all these marvelous things, they truly believed themselves to be in paradise. And these damsels were always with them in songs and great entertainment; they received everything they asked for, so that they would never have left that garden of their own will. And when the Old Man wished to kill someone, he would take him and say: 'Go and do this thing. I do this because I want to make you return to paradise'. And the assassins go and perform the deed willingly."

Hashish (Arabic: حشّـيـش hashīsh = dry herbage (or fodder)) was probably the substance of choice in those days. But it is definitely not the origin for the word assassin. As the story goes, many assassins were caught after they accomplished their missions, resulting in their own deaths and the promised immediate entry into paradise.

The Assassins changed their original Isma'ili doctrine [5] to something that might have given the impression that assassination is part of their religious duty. Their influence and power could be noticed in their expansion; strongholds were built all over Syria and Persia. According to historians, some were branching as far as Pakistan and India. [6] In those days, it was common and useful to have agents placed in the enemy's quarters, camps, and cities. The Assassins were contracted for their services because of their efficiency and secrecy–no one else was able to kill high ranking people in enemy territory. For a period of time, they were allies and within the direct services of the Crusaders–not because the Crusaders were sympathizing with them, but because of their common enemies.

Intense physical and special assassination tactics and techniques was the skill, religious education was the backbone and motivation of the assassins. When on a mission, they generally worked alone. Rarely were two or more assassins on the same target. They dressed up as merchants or religious men, spending a good deal of time in a city, in order to get well acquainted with the houses and streets, surroundings, and daily routines of their victim. The actual murder was performed in public with a dagger, a small piece of a robe or a scarf. Often such assassinations were performed inside a mosque on a Friday. Assassination in public had purpose, to spread the information about the deed, to make it well known, and to frighten the people. In most cases (not good publicity though), the Assassin himself was killed immediately after that by guards of the victim.

However, assassins of a more common background and less historical pedigree than the ones of the Alamut assassins can be found throughout history in any part of the world. Some of those actually became part of history; others made headlines because the targets they selected or they were assigned to assassinate where historical or important figures.

Assassinations and Assassination Attempts on U. S. Presidents

- Andrew Jackson
  January 30, 1835:
  At the Capitol Building, a man named Richard Lawrence aimed two pistols at the President. Both of the pistols misfired. Lawrence was apprehended after Jackson had beaten him with his cane. Lawrence was found not guilty by reason of insanity and confined to a mental institution until his death in 1861.

- Abraham Lincoln
  April 14, 1865:
  Attending the play *Our American Cousin* at Ford's Theater in Washington, D.C., Lincoln was shot by John W. Booth, a well-known actor and Southern sympathizer. Lincoln died the next morning. Booth was shot and killed by Boston Corbett while on the run, holed up in a northern Virginia barn. A number of others were implicated, four of them were hanged.

- James A. Garfield
  July 2, 1881:
  Garfield, accompanied by Secretary of State James G. Blaine, was waiting in the Baltimore-Potomac Railway station in Washington, D.C., when he was shot by Charles J. Guiteau. Guiteau, a mentally ill man, had previously petitioned the Garfield administration to be appointed ambassador to France (a post for which Guiteau was unqualified). Garfield died three months later, on the 19th of September. Guiteau was found guilty and hanged. This case prompted the passage of the Pendleton Civil Service Reform Act.

- William McKinley
  September 6, 1901:
  While attending the Pan-American Exposition in Buffalo, New York, President McKinley was shot by Leon Czolgosz, an anarchist. McKinley died on his wounds on 14 September, and Czolgosz was later executed by electrocution.

- Theodore Roosevelt
  October 13, 1912:
  Roosevelt, no longer president, was running for the Progressives. Roosevelt, while waiting to deliver his speech in Milwaukee, Wisconsin, was attacked by John Schrank. Schrank shot once with his revolver, but a 100-page speech folded over twice and an eye-glasses case in the breast pocket slowed the bullet and saved Roosevelt. Roosevelt insisted on giving his speech even with the bullet still lodged inside him. He later went to the hospital, but the bullet was never removed. Schrank defended himself, saying that William McKinley's ghost told him to avenge his assassination. Schrank was found legally insane and was institutionalized until his death in 1943.

- Franklin D. Roosevelt
  February 15, 1933:
  One month before being sworn in for his first term in office, Roosevelt's motorcade came under fire in Miami, Florida. Five shots were fired by Giuseppe Zangara, which left four people wounded and killed the mayor of Chicago, Anton Cermak. Zangara was found guilty of murder and was executed March 20.

- Harry S. Truman
  November 1, 1950:
  In Washington, D.C., Oscar Collazo and Griselio Torresola ambushed the Blair House where Truman was living temporarily while the White House was undergoing major renovations. Torresola was killed by guards, and Collazo was wounded. Collazo was found guilty of murder, assault, and attempted assassination of the president. He was sentenced to death. Truman reduced the sentence to life in prison. President Jimmy Carter freed Collazo in 1979.

- John F. Kennedy
  December 11, 1960:
  President-elect John F. Kennedy, while vacationing in Palm Beach, Florida, was threatened by the 73 year-old former postal worker Richard Paul Pavlick. Pavlick's plan was to crash his dynamite-laden 1950 Buick into Kennedy's vehicle. The plan, however, was disrupted when Pavlick saw Kennedy's wife and daughter waving a good-bye to him. Pavlick was arrested by the Secret Service three days later, after he was stopped for a driving violation—the dynamite still in his car. Pavlick spend the next six years in both federal prison and mental institutions. He was released in December, 1966.

  November 22, 1963:
  Dallas, Texas—touring in an open car with state governor John Connally and their wives, Kennedy was hit and killed and Connally wounded by a sniper's bullet. Lee Harvey Oswald was quickly charged with the Kennedy shooting, as well as that of a Dallas police officer J. D. Tippit. Oswald was shot and fatally wounded two days later by nightclub owner Jack Ruby. The Warren Commission concluded that Oswald was the sole assassin, but in the 1970s the House Select Committee on Assassinations concluded that at least two people were probably involved in the assassination, Oswald being one of them.

- Richard M. Nixon
  February 22, 1974:
  Samuel S. Byck attempted to kill Nixon by crashing a commercial airliner into the White House. On the plane, he was informed that the plane could not take off. He shot the pilot and co-pilot before killing himself.

- Gerald R. Ford
  September 5, 1975:
  Sacramento, California—Squeaky Fromme, a Charles Manson follower, pointed a .45 caliber Colt pistol at Ford while he was shaking her hand in the crowd. Four cartridges were in the pistol's magazine, but none in the firing chamber. She was restrained by a Secret Service agent. Fromme was sentenced to life in prison, where she remains.

  September 22, 1975:
  San Francisco, California-Sara J. Moore fired with a revolver at Ford from a distance of

14 m. The shot missed Ford, thanks to the bystander Oliver Sipple, who grabbed Moore's arm. Moore was sentenced to life in prison.

- Jimmy Carter
  May 5, 1979:
  Carter was about to speak at the civic center mall in Los Angeles, when Raymond Lee Harvey was arrested ten minutes earlier for carrying a pistol. He later told authorities that he and another man were hired to create a diversion so that Mexican hit men armed with sniper rifles could kill Carter.

- Ronald Reagan
  March 30, 1981:
  Washington, D. C.–John Hinckley Jr., fired at Reagan at close range six shots from a .22 caliber handgun. One bullet ruptured Reagan's lung and lodged close to his heart. Another bullet entered the brain of press secretary James Brady. A police officer and a Secret Service agent were also critically wounded. Hinckley was found not guilty because of insanity. He remains in St. Elizabeth's Hospital in Washington DC. Reagan was the first president in office to survive an assassin's bullet, and the fifth president overall to be shot.

- George H.W. Bush
  April 13, 1993:
  Sixteen suspected terrorists, contracted by Saddam Hussein's regime, smuggled a car bomb into Kuwait. The plan was to kill Bush during his speech at the Kuwait University. The plot was foiled when Kuwaiti officials found the bomb and arrested the suspected assassins. Bush had left office in January 1993. On June 26, 1993, the U. S. launched a missile attack targeting Baghdad intelligence headquarters in retaliation for the attempted attack against Bush.

- Bill Clinton
  October 29, 1994:
  Francisco Martin Duran fired from Pennsylvania Avenue with a semi-automatic rifle at least 29 shots at the White House. He thought that Clinton was among the men in dark suits standing there. Clinton was in the White House Residence watching a football game. No one was hurt and Duran was sentenced to 40 years in prison.

- George W. Bush
  May 10, 2005:
  Bush was giving a speech in the Freedom Square at Tbilisi, Georgia, when Vladimir Arutinian threw a live Soviet made RGD-5 hand grenade towards the podium. Bush was standing and Georgian President Mikhail Saakashvili, their wives and officials were seated. After hitting a girl the grenade landed in the crowd, 18 meters away from the podium. It did not detonate. Arutinian was arrested in July 2005 and admitted that he throw the grenade. He was convicted in January 2006, and was given a life sentence.

Assassinations by Countries

- Afghanistan
  - 1919, Habibullah Khan, Emir of Afghanistan
  - 1933, Mohammed Nader Shah, King of Afghanistan
  - 1978, Mohammed Daoud Khan, President of Afghanistan

- 1979,   Adolph Dubs,   U. S. Ambassador to Afghanistan
- 1979,   Nur Mohammad Taraki,   President of Afghanistan
- 1979,   Hafizullah Amin,   Prime Minister of Afghanistan
- 1996,   Mohammed Najibullah,   President of Afghanistan
- 2001,   Ahmed Shah Massoud,   Leader of the Afghan Northern Alliance
- 2001,   Abdul Haq,   Afghan Northern Alliance Commander
- 2002,   Abdul Qadir,   Vice President of Afghanistan
- 2002,   Abdul Rahman,   Afghan Minister for Civil Aviation and Tourism

♦ Algeria
- 117 BC, Hiempsal,   Co-ruler of Numidia
- 1942,   François Darlan,   Senior of the Vichy Regime
- 1957,   Maurice Audin,   Communist Mathematician
- 1963,   Mohamed Khemisti,   Algerian Foreign Minister
- 1987,   Mustafa Bouyali,   Islamic Fundamentalist
- 1992,   Mohamed Boudiaf,   President of Algeria
- 1993,   Youcef Sebti,   Poet
- 1993,   Kasdi Merbah,   Prime Minister of Algeria
- 1994,   Abdelkader Alloula,   Play-wrighter
- 1994,   Cheb Hasni,   Singer
- 1998,   Lounès Matoub,   Singer
- 1999,   Abdelkader Hachan,   Islamic Fundamentalist

♦ Angola
- 2002,   Jonas Savimbi,   Angolan Rebel Leader

♦ Antigua and Barbuda
- 1710,   Daniel Parke,   British Governor of the Leeward Islands

♦ Argentina
- 1870,   Justo José de Urquiza,   President of Argentina
- 1970,   Pedro Aramburu,   President of Argentina
- 1974,   Carlos Prats,   Chilean General
- 1976,   Zelmar Michelini,   Uruguayan Minister of Education
- 1976,   Héctor Gutiérrez Ruiz,   Speaker, Uruguayan House of Representatives

♦ Australia
- 1994,   John Paul Newman,   Minister of New South Wales
- 2004,   Ivens Buffett,   Deputy Chief Minister of Norfolk Island

♦ Austria
- 1916,   Karl von Stürgkh,   Minister President of Austria
- 1923,   Franz Birnecker,   Austrian Labor Representative
- 1934,   Engelbert Dollfuss,   Chancellor of Austria
- 1989,   Abdul Rahman Ghassemlou,   Dissident Kurdish-Iranian Political Leader

♦ Bangladesh
- 1975,   Mujibur Rahman,   President of Bangladesh
- 1975,   Tajuddin Ahmed,   Politician
- 1975,   Syed Nazrul Islam,   Politician

- 1975,   Mohammad Mansoor Ali,   Prime Minister
- 1975,   Khaled Mosharraf,   Coup Organizer
- 1981,   Ziaur Rahman,   President of Bangladesh

♦ Belgium
- 1950,   Julien Lahaut,   Chairman of the Communist Party of Belgium
- 1971,   Maximiliano Gómez,   Dominican Communist Leader
- 1990,   Gerald Bull,   Canadian Developer
- 1991,   André Cools,   Belgian Politician

♦ Bermuda
- 1973,   Sir Richard Sharples,   Governor of Bermuda

♦ Bhutan
- 1964,   Jigme Palden Dorji,   Prime Minister of Bhutan

♦ Bolivia
- 1865,   Manuel Isidoro Belzu,   President of Bolivia
- 1871,   Mariano Melgarejo,   President of Bolivia
- 1967,   Che Guevara,   Argentinian Revolutionary Leader
- 1976,   Juan José Torres,   President of Bolivia

♦ Brazil
- 1930,   João P. Cavalcânti de Albuquerque
- 1964,   Adib Shishakli,   Syrian Military Dictator
- 1988,   Chico Mendes,   Brazilian Environmental Activist
- 1992,   Daniela Perez,   Brazilian Actress
- 2005,   Dorothy Stang,   American Nun

♦ Bulgaria
- 1895,   Stefan Stambolov,   Prime Minister of Bulgaria
- 1923,   Aleksandar Stamboliyski,   Prime Minister of Bulgaria
- 1995,   Lambo Kyuchukov,   Minister of Education
- 1995,   Vasil Iliev,   Insurance CEO
- 1996,   Andrey Lukanov,   Prime Minister of Bulgaria
- 1998,   Ivo Karamanski,   Insurance Tycoon
- 1999,   Lyubomir Georgiev Penev,   Owner of *Nova Televizia TV*
- 2000,   Velichko Todorov,   Leader of the People's Party
- 2001,   Georgi Valkov Georgiev,   European Karate Champion
- 2002,   Nikolai Kolev,   Supreme Court Prosecutor
- 2003,   Todor Matov,   International Wrestling Referee
- 2003,   Iliya Pavlo,   President of *Multigroup Corporation*
- 2004,   Stoil Slavov,   Associate of *Interpetroleum and Partners*
- 2004,   Martin Elandzhiev,   National Kick-Boxing Champion
- 2005,   Shinka Manova,   Director of Customs
- 2005,   Emil Kyulev,   Banker
- 2005,   Georgi Stoyanov Vasilev,   Counselor of Sofia
- 2006,   Ivan Todorov,   Businessman

- Burkina Faso
  - 1987,   Thomas Sankara,   Head of State of Burkina Faso
  - 1991,   Clément O. Ouédraogo,   Opposition Leader
  - 1998,   Norbert Zongo,   Journalist

- Burma (Myanmar)
  - 1947,   Aung San,   Burmese Nationalist Leader

- Burundi
  - 1961,   Louis Rwagasore,   Prime Minister of Burundi
  - 1962,   Jean Nduwabike,   Trade Union Leader
  - 1964,   Gabriel Gihimbare,   Roman Catholic Bishop
  - 1965,   Pierre Ngendandumwe,   Prime Minister of Burundi
  - 1965,   Joseph Bamina,   Prime Minister of Burundi
  - 1965,   Paul Mirerekano,   Burundian Politician
  - 1965,   Gervais Nyangoma,   Politician
  - 1972,   Martin Ndayahoze,   Army Commander and Information Minister
  - 1975,   Ntare V,   King of Burundi
  - 1993,   Melchior Ndadaye,   President of Burundi
  - 2001,   Kassi Manlan,   World Health Organization Representative

- Cambodia
  - 1950,   Ieu Koeus,   Prime Minister of Cambodia

- Cameroon
  - 1958,   Ruben Um Nyobé,   Leader of Union of the Peoples of Cameroon (UPC)

- Canada
  - 1868,   Thomas D'Arcy McGee,   Canadian Father of Confederation
  - 1880,   George Brown,   Newspaper Editor and Senator
  - 1968,   Sergio Pérez Castillo,   Cuban Diplomat
  - 1970,   Pierre Laporte,   Quebec Minister of Labor
  - 1982,   Atilla Altıkat,   Turkish Diplomat
  - 1998,   Tara Singh Hayer,   Journalist

- Chad
  - 1975,   François Tombalbaye,   President of Chad

- Chile
  - 1970,   René Schneider,   Chilean General
  - 1973,   Victor Jara,   Singer
  - 1991,   Jaime Guzmán,   Chilean Senator

- China
  - 1323,   Sidibala,   Great Khan of the Mongol Empire, Emperor of Yuan China
  - 1849,   João M. Ferreira do Amaral, Portuguese Governor of Macau
  - 1909,   Ito Hirobumi,   Japanese Resident-General of Korea to Manchuria
  - 1928,   Zhang Zuolin,   Manchurian Warlord
  - 1939,   Chen Lu,   Foreign Minister of Wang Jingwei Government

- 1946,   Wen Yiduo,   Chinese Poet and Scholar

- ◆ Colombia
  - 1948,   Jorge Eliécer Gaitán,   Colombian Liberal Party Leader
  - 1989,   Luis Carlos Galán,   Colombian Presidential Candidate
  - 1990,   Bernardo Jaramillo Ossa,   Colombian Presidential Candidate
  - 1994,   Andrés Escobar,   Colombian International Football player
  - 1998,   Fernando Landazabal Reyes,   Colombian Defense Minister
  - 1999,   Jaime Garzón,   Colombian Journalist
  - 2006,   Elson Becerra,   Colombian International Football Player

- ◆ Congo
  - 1977,   Marien Ngouabi,   President of the Congo
  - 1977,   Émile Biayenda,   Archbishop of Brazzaville
  - 1961,   Patrice Lumumba,   Prime Minister of the Congo
  - 1961,   Maurice Mpolo,   Lumumba Associate
  - 2001,   Laurent Kabila,   President of the Democratic Republic of the Congo

- ◆ Cuba
  - 1935,   Antonio Guiteras,   Revolutionary Socialist Leader

- ◆ Cyprus
  - 1979,   Youssef El-Sebai,   Egyptian Writer
  - 2001,   Youcef Essalhi,   French Fundamentalist

- ◆ Czech Republic
  - 932,   Václav I (Saint Wenceslas),   Duke of Bohemia
  - 1306,   Václav III,   King of Bohemia
  - 1634,   Albrecht von Wallenstein,   Czech General
  - 1923,   Alois Rašín,   Minister of Finances of Czechoslovakia
  - 1942,   Reinhard Heydrich,   General of Nazi Paramilitary and Governor of the occupied Czechoslovakia
  - 1948,   Jan Masaryk,   Czech Politician

- ◆ Denmark
  - 1286,   Erik V Klipping,   King of Denmark

- ◆ Dominican Republic
  - 1899,   Ulises Heureaux,   President of the Dominican Republic
  - 1961,   Rafael Leónidas Trujillo,   Dominican Republic Dictator
  - 1967,   Orlando Mazara
  - 1968,   Flavio Suero
  - 1969,   Henry Segarra
  - 1970,   Amín Abel Hasbún
  - 1972,   Amaury Germán Aristy

- ◆ Ecuador
  - 1875,   Gabriel García Moreno,   President of Ecuador
  - 1999,   Jaime Hurtado,   Communist Legislators
  - 1999,   Pablo Tapia,   Communist Legislators

- Egypt
  - 48 BC, Pompey the Great, Roman Politician
  - 19 BC, Germanicus, Roman Military Leader
  - 1121, Al-Afdal Shahanshah, Vizier of Fatimid Egypt
  - 1130, Al-Amir, Fatimid Caliph
  - 1260, Qutuz, Mamluk Sultan of Egypt
  - 1293, Khalil, Mamluk Sultan of Egypt
  - 1800, Jean Baptiste Kléber, French General
  - 1910, Boutros Ghali, Prime Minister of Egypt
  - 1924, Sir Lee Stack, Governor-General of the Anglo-Egyptian Sudan
  - 1944, Walter Edward Guinness, UK's Minister Resident in the Middle East
  - 1945, Ahmed Maher Pasha, Prime Minister of Egypt
  - 1948, Mahmud Fahmi Nokrashi, Prime Minister of Egypt
  - 1949, Hassan al-Banna, Founder of the Muslim Brotherhood
  - 1981, Anwar Sadat, President of Egypt
  - 1990, Rifaat al-Mahgoub, Speaker of Egyptian Parliament
  - 1992, Farag Foda, Egyptian Politician and Intellectual

- El Salvador
  - 1913, Manuel Enrique Araujo, President of El Salvador
  - 1977, Osmín Aguirre, President of El Salvador
  - 1980, Oscar Romero, Archbishop of San Salvado
  - 1980, Ita Ford, Roman Catholic Nun
  - 1980, Maura Clarke, Roman Catholic Nun
  - 1980, Dorothy Kazel, Roman Catholic Nun
  - 1980, Jean Donovan, Roman Catholic Nun
  - 1983, Albert Schaufelberger, Senior U. S. Naval Representative
  - 1989, Ignacio Ellacuría, Roman Catholic Priest

- Finland
  - 1904, Eliel Soisalon-Soininen, Attorney General
  - 1904, Nikolai Ivanovich Bobrikov, Governor-General of Finland
  - 1922, Heikki Ritavuori, Minister of Interior of Finland

- France
  - 1354, Charles d' Espagne
  - 1407, Louis of Valois, Duke of Orléans
  - 1572, Gaspard de Coligny
  - 1589, Henri III, King of France
  - 1610, Henri IV, King of France
  - 1789, Jacques de Flesselles, Provost of Paris
  - 1793, Jean-Paul Marat, Revolutionary
  - 1894, Marie François Sadi Carnot, President of France
  - 1914, Jean Jaurès, Politician
  - 1914, Gaston Calmette, Editor of the *Le Figaro*
  - 1923, Marius Plateau, Secretary of Action Française
  - 1932, Paul Doumer, President of France
  - 1934, Louis Barthou, Foreign Minister
  - 1938, Ernst vom Rath, German Diplomat

- 1944,	Constant Chevillon,	Leader of FUDOFSI
- 1961,	Camille Blanc,	Mayor of Evian
- 1965,	Mehdi Ben Barka,	Moroccan Socialist Leader
- 1973,	Outel Bono,	Chadian Physician
- 1978,	José M. Beñaran Ordeñana,	Basque Leader
- 1980,	Salah al-Din Bitar,	Syrian Baath Politician
- 1982,	Jean-Pierre Maïone-Libaude,	Right-Wing Activist
- 1983,	Pierre-Jean Massimi,	Secretary of the Département Haute-Corse
- 1985,	René Audran,	General
- 1986,	Georges Besse,	*Renault* Executive
- 1987,	André Mécili aka Ali Mécili,	Algerian Opposition Leader
- 1988,	Dulcie September,	African National Congress Representative
- 1991,	Shapour Bakhtiar,	Prime Minister of Iran
- 1995,	Abdelbaki Sahraoui,	Co-Founder of the Algerian Islamic Salvation Front
- 1998,	Claude Erignac,	Prefect of Corsica
- 2006,	Robert Feliciaggi,	Corsican Member of Parliament

♦ Georgia
- 1922,	Cemal Pasha,	Ottoman Minister to Tbilisi

♦ Germany
- 235,	Alexander Severus,	Roman Emperor
- 268,	Postumus,	Gallic Emperor
- 268,	Laelianus,	Gallic Emperor,
- 1208,	Philipp von Hohenstaufen,	Emperor
- 1225,	Engelbert I. von Köln,	Archbishop of Cologne
- 1233,	Konrad von Marburg,	Inquisitor
- 1356,	Johann Windlock,	Bishop of Constance
- 1833,	Kaspar Hauser	
- 1921,	Talat Pasha,	Ottoman Minister of Interior Affairs
- 1921,	Matthias Erzberger,	Politician
- 1922,	Walther Rathenau,	Industrialist and Politician
- 1934,	Dr Erich Klausener,	Minister of Police
- 1934,	Gustav von Kahr,	Politician
- 1934,	General Kurt von Schleicher,	Adviser to Reichspresident Paul von Hindenburg
- 1961,	Salah Ben Youssef,	Tunisian Politician
- 1970,	Belkacem Krim,	Algerian Politician
- 1974,	Günter von Drenkmann,	Berlin Chief Justice
- 1977,	Siegfried Buback,	German Attorney General
- 1977,	Jürgen Ponto,	CEO *Dresdner Bank*
- 1977,	Hanns-Martin Schleyer,	President of the German Employer's Union
- 1981,	Heinz-Herbert Karry,	Minister of Economy
- 1985,	Ernst Zimmermann,	Industrialist
- 1986,	Karl-Heinz Beckurts,	*Siemens* Executive
- 1986,	Gerold von Braunmühl,	Official in the German Foreign Ministry
- 1989,	Alfred Herrhausen,	CEO *Deutsche Bank*
- 1991,	Detlev Karsten Rohwedder,	Director Treuhandanstalt for Former East-Germany
- 1992,	Sadegh Sharafkandi,	Dissident Kurdish-Iranian Politician
- 1992,	Fattah Abdoli,	Dissident Kurdish-Iranian Politician

- 1992,　Homayoun Ardalan,　　Dissident Kurdish-Iranian Politician

♦ Greece
   - 514 BC,　Hipparchus,　　Tyrant of Athens
   - 461 BC,　Ephialtes,　　Leader of the Democracy Movement
   - 404 BC,　Alcibiades,　　General and Politician
   - 336 BC,　Philip II of Macedon,　　King of Macedon
   - 281 BC,　Seleucus I Nicator,　　Founder of the Seleucid dynasty
   - 272 BC,　Cleon of Sicyon,　　Tyrant of Sicyon
   - 1831,　Ioannis Capodistrias,　　President of Greece
   - 1913,　George I of Greece,　　King
   - 1983,　George Tsantes,　　U. S. Military Attaché to Greece
   - 1985,　Nikos Momferratos,　　Greek Newspaper Publisher
   - 1988,　William Nordeen,　　Tsantes' successor as U. S. Attaché
   - 1989,　Pavlos Bakoyannis,　　New Democracy Politician
   - 1997,　Costis Peratikos,　　Greek Shipowner
   - 2000,　Stephen Saunders,　　Brigadier and British Military Attaché to Greece

♦ Guatemala
   - 1898,　José María Reina Barrios,　　President of Guatemala
   - 1949,　Francisco Arana,　　Presidential Candidate
   - 1957,　Carlos Castillo Armas,　　President of Guatemala
   - 1970,　Karl von Spreti,　　German Ambassador to Guatemala
   - 1979,　Alberto Fuentes Mohr,　　Social Democratic Party Leader
   - 1979,　Manuel Colom Argueta,　　Mayor of Guatemala City
   - 1993,　Jorge Carpio Nicolle,　　Liberal Politician and Journalist
   - 1998,　Juan José Gerardi,　　Roman Catholic Bishop
   - 2006,　Mario Pivaral,　　UNE Congress

♦ Guyana
   - 1964,　Michael Forde,　　PPP Activist
   - 1978,　Leo J. Ryan,　　U. S. Congressman from San Mateo, California
   - 1980,　Walter Rodney,　　Guyanese Historian and Politician
   - 2006,　Satyadeow Sawh,　　Agriculture Minister

♦ Haiti
   - 1806,　Jean-Jacques Dessalines,　　Emperor of Haiti
   - 1993,　Antoine Izméry,　　Businessman
   - 1993,　Guy Mallory,　　Minister of Justice
   - 1994,　Jean-Marie Vincent,　　Roman Catholic Priest
   - 2000,　Jean Dominique,　　Journalist
   - 2005,　Jacques Roche,　　Journalist

♦ Honduras
   - 1966,　Maximiliano H. Martínez,　　President of El Salvador

♦ Hungary
   - 1918,　István Tisza,　　Premier of Hungary

♦ India
   - 1602,　Abul-Fazel,　　Vizier

- 1948, Mohandas Gandhi,   Independence Leader
- 1984, Indira Gandhi,   Indian Prime Minister
- 1991, Rajiv Gandhi,   Indian Prime Minister, son of Indira Gandhi
- 1995, Beant Singh,   Chief Minister of Punjab
- 2001, Phoolan Devi,   known as *Bandit Queen*,
                                   became Politician for the Lower Castes
- 2002, Abdul Ghani Lone,   Leader of Kashmiri Muslims

♦ Iran
- 465 BC, Xerxes I,   Persian King
- 423 BC, Xerxes II,   Persian King
- 423 BC, Sogdianus,   Persian King
- 238,   Khosrow I,   Armenian King
- 1092,   Nizam al-Mulk,   Persian Scholar and Vizier of the Seljuk Turks
- 1747,   Nader Shah,   Shah of Persia
- 1896,   Nasser-al-Din Shah,   Shah of Persia
- 1940,   Taghi Arani,   Communist
- 1947,   Qazi Muhammad,   Kurdish-Iranian Political Leader
- 1951,   Ali Razmara,   Prime Minister of Iran
- 1965,   Hassan Ali Mansur,   Prime Minister of Iran
- 1981,   Mohammad Ali Rajai,   President of Iran
- 1981,   Mohammad Javad Bahonar, Prime Minister of Iran

♦ Iraq
- 244,   Gordian III,   Roman Emperor
- 1958, Faisal II,   King of Iraq
- 1958, Nuri Pasha as-Said,   Iraqi Politician
- 1958, Ibrahim Hashim,   Prime Minister
- 1978, Abdul Razak al-Naif,   Prime Minister of Iraq
- 1996, Ali Garmaii,   Kurdish-Iranian Activist
- 1996, Mohammad Nanva,   Kurdish-Iranian Activist
- 2003, Aquila al-Hashimi,   Iraqi Governing Council Member
- 2003, Sérgio Vieira de Mello,   UN Special Representative to Iraq
- 2004, Waldemar Milewicz,   Polish Journalist
- 2004, Mounir Bouamrane,   Algerian-Polish TV Operator
- 2004, Hatem Kamil,   Deputy Governor of Baghdad
- 2004, Ezzedine Salim,   Chairman of the Iraqi Governing Council
- 2005, Barawiz Mahmoud,   Judge on the Iraqi Special Tribunal
- 2005, Dhari Ali al-Fayadh,   Iraqi MP
- 2005, Ihab al-Sherif,   Egyptian Envoy to Iraq

♦ Ireland
- 1882, Lord Frederick Cavendish, Chief Secretary for Ireland
- 1882, Thomas Henry Burke,   Permanent Under Secretary for Ireland
- 1922, Michael Collins,   President of the Provisional Government
- 1927, Kevin O' Higgins,   Irish Politician
- 1976, Christopher Ewart-Biggs, British Ambassador to Ireland
- 1981, Rev. Robert Bradford,   Unionist MP of Northern Ireland
- 1996, Veronica Guerin,   Irish Journalist

- ◆ Israel
  - 1134, Hugh II of Le Puiset, Count of Jaffa
  - 1174, Miles of Plancy, Regent of the Kingdom of Jerusalem
  - 1192, Conrad of Montferrat, King of Jerusalem
  - 1924, Jacob Israël de Haan, Pro Orthodox-Jewish Diplomat
  - 1933, Chaim Arlosoroff, Zionist Leader in the British Mandate of Palestine
  - 1948, Folke Bernadotte, Middle East Peace Mediator
  - 1957, Rudolf Kasztner, Hungarian Zionist Leader
  - 1981, Sheikh Hamad Abu Rabia, Member of the Knesset
  - 1995, Yitzhak Rabin, Prime Minister of Israel
  - 2001, Rehavam Zeevi, Israeli General and Politician

- ◆ Italy
  - 748 BC, Titus Tatius, Sabine King
  - 579 BC, Lucius Tarquinius Priscus, Etruscan King of Rome
  - 534 BC, Servius Tullius, Etruscan King of Rome
  - 133 BC, Tiberius Gracchus, Roman Tribune
  - 44 BC, Julius Caesar, Roman General
  - 43 BC, Cicero, Roman Orator
  - 41, Caligula, Roman Emperor
  - 54, Claudius, Roman Emperor
  - 69, Vitellius, Roman Emperor
  - 69, Galba, Roman Emperor
  - 96, Domitian, Roman Emperor
  - 192, Commodus, Roman Emperor
  - 193, Pertinax, Roman Emperor
  - 193, Didius Julianus, Roman Emperor
  - 212, Publius Septimius Geta, Roman Emperor,
  - 222, Elagabalus, Roman Emperor
  - 253, Volusianus, Roman Emperor
  - 253, Trebonianus Gallus, Roman Emperor
  - 1478, Giuliano de' Medici, Co-Ruler of Florence
  - 1848, Pellegrino Rossi, Minister of Justice
  - 1900, Umberto I of Italy, King
  - 1921, Said Halim Pasha, Ottoman Minister
  - 1924, Giacomo Matteotti, Italian Socialist Politician
  - 1925, Luigj Gurakuqi, Albanian Independence Leader
  - 1962, Enrico Mattei, Head of *Agip* Oil Company
  - 1975, Pier Paolo Pasolini, Italian Writer, Poet and Film Director
  - 1978, Aldo Moro, Prime Minister of Italy
  - 1978, Giuseppe Impastato, Anti-Mafia Activist
  - 1979, Emilio Alessandrini, Magistrate
  - 1979, Giorgio Ambrosoli, Lawyer
  - 1979, Cesare Terranova, Magistrate
  - 1979, Carlo Ghiglieno, *Fiat* Manager
  - 1979, Italo Schettini, Regional Councilor of Democrazia Cristiana
  - 1982, Carlo Alberto Dalla Chiesa, General of the Carabinieri
  - 1983, Rocco Chinnici, Magistrate
  - 1984, Leamon Hunt, U. S. Chief of the Sinai UN-MFOG

- 1988,	Antonio Saetta,	Judge
- 1990,	Giovanni Trecroci,	Vice Mayor of Villa San Giovanni
- 1992,	Giovanni Falcone,	Anti-Mafia Judge
- 1992,	Paolo Borsellino,	Anti-Mafia Judge
- 1992,	Salvatore Lima,	Mayor of Palermo
- 1993,	Pino Puglisi,	Priest
- 1999,	Massimo D' Antona,	Italian Labor Ministry Adviser
- 2002,	Marco Biagi,	Italian Labor Ministry Adviser

◆ Ivory Coast

- 2002,	Robert Guéi,	President of Côte d' Ivoire
- 2002,	Émile Boga Doudou,	Interior Minister
- 2003,	M. Ahmad al Rashid,	Saudi Ambassador

◆ Japan

- 592,	Emperor Sushun,	Emperor of Japan
- 1219,	Minamoto no Sanetomo,	Third Shogun of the Kamakura
- 1549,	Matsudaira Hirotada,	Feudal Ruler
- 1551,	Ouchi Yoshitaka,	Feudal Ruler
- 1557,	Oda Nobuyuki,	Samurai
- 1565,	Ashikaga Yoshiteru,	Feudal Ruler
- 1578,	Yamanaka Shikanosuke,	Samurai
- 1582,	Oda Nobunaga,	Samurai Warlord
- 1669,	Shakushain,	Ainu Chief
- 1858,	Shimazu Nariaki,	Feudal Ruler
- 1859,	Hashimoto Sanai,	Political Activist
- 1860,	Ii Naosuke,	Japanese Politician
- 1860,	Tokugawa Nariaki,	Feudal Ruler
- 1862,	Charles Lennox Richardson,	English Diplomat
- 1863,	Serizawa Kamo,	Chief of the Shinsen-gumi
- 1864,	Ikeuchi Daigaku,	Politician
- 1864,	Kusaka Gennai,	Politician
- 1864,	Sakuma Shozan,	Politician
- 1867,	Sakamoto Ryoma,	Japanese Author
- 1869,	Yokoi Shonai,	Political Activist
- 1878,	Okubo Toshimichi,	Prime Minister of Japan
- 1909,	Ito Hirobumi,	Prime Minister of Japan
- 1921,	Hara Takashi,	Prime Minister of Japan
- 1931,	Hamaguchi Osachi,	Prime Minister of Japan
- 1932,	Inukai Tsuyoshi,	Prime Minister of Japan
- 1936,	Takahashi Korekiyo,	Prime Minister of Japan
- 1943,	Isoroku Yamamoto,	Japanese Admiral
- 1960,	Inejiro Asanuma,	Chairman of Socialist Party of Japan
- 1991,	Hitoshi Igarashi,	Translator of *The Satanic Verses*
- 2002,	Koki Ishii,	Politician

◆ Jordan

| - 1951, | Abdullah I, | King of Jordan |
| - 1960, | Hazza al-Majali, | Prime Minister of Jordan |

- 1971,   Wasfi al-Tal,   Prime Minister of Jordan
- 2002,   Laurence Foley,   US-AID Official

- ◆ Kenya
  - 1965,   Pio Gama Pinto,   Politician
  - 1969,   Tom Mboya,   Politician
  - 1975,   Josiah Kariuki,   Politician
  - 1990,   Robert Ouko,   Foreign Minister of Kenya
  - 2000,   John Kaiser,   Missionary

- ◆ Korea
  - 304,   King Bunseo of Baekje,   King of Baekje
  - 1895,   Queen Min of Joseon,   Empress of Korea
  - 1979,   Park Chung Hee,   President of South Korea
  - 1974,   Yuk Yeong-su,   Wife of President Park Chung Hee
  - 1983,   Lee Bum Suk,   Foreign Minister of South Korea

- ◆ Lebanon
  - 1152,   Raymond II of Tripoli,   Count of Tripoli
  - 1270,   Philip of Montfort,   Lord of Tyre
  - 1950,   Sami al-Hinnawi,   Syrian Head of State
  - 1977,   Kamal Jumblatt,   Lebanese Leader
  - 1982,   Bachir Gemayel,   President of Lebanon
  - 1987,   Rashid Karami,   Prime Minister of Lebanon
  - 1989,   René Moawad,   President of Lebanon
  - 2002,   Elie Hobeika,   Lebanese Militia Leader
  - 2005,   Rafik Hariri,   Prime Minister of Lebanon
  - 2005,   Bassel Fleihan,   Minister of Economy and Commerce
  - 2005,   Samir Kassir,   Columnist at *An Nahar* (Daily Lebanese Newspaper)

- ◆ Liberia
  - 1980,   William R. Tolbert, Jr.,   President of Liberia
  - 1990,   Samuel Doe,   President of Liberia

- ◆ Madagascar
  - 1863,   Radama II of Madagascar,   King of Madagascar
  - 1975,   Richard Ratsimandrava,   President of Madagascar

- ◆ Malta
  - 1995,   Fathi Shakaki,   Leader of Islamic Jihad

- ◆ Mexico
  - 1913,   Francisco I. Madero,   President of Mexico
  - 1919,   Emiliano Zapata,   Revolutionary
  - 1920,   Venustiano Carranza,   President of Mexico
  - 1923,   Francisco "Pancho" Villa,   Revolutionary
  - 1924,   Felipe Carrillo Puerto,   Governor of Yucatán
  - 1928,   Álvaro Obregón,   President
  - 1929,   Julio Antonio Mella,   Cuban Revolutionary

- 1940,   Leon Trotsky,   Russian Communist Leader
- 1962,   Rubén Jaramillo,   Peasant Leader
- 1985,   Enrique Camarena,   Police officer
- 1993,   Juan Jesús Posadas Ocampo, Roman Catholic Cardinal of Guadalajara
- 1994,   Luis Donaldo Colosio,   Presidential Candidate
- 1994,   José Francisco Ruiz Massieu, Secretary-General of the P. R. I.
- 1999,   Paco Stanley,   Comedian
- 2001,   Digna Ochoa,   Human Rights Attorney

♦ Mozambique
- 1969,   Eduardo Mondlane,   Leader of the FRELIMO movement
- 2000,   Carlos Cardoso,   Journalist

♦ Nepal
- 2001,   Birendra, King of Nepal,   Queen Aiswary

♦ Netherlands
- 1296,   Count Floris V
- 1584,   William I of Orange,   Leader of the Dutch
- 1672,   Johan de Witt,   Politician
- 1672,   Cornelis de Witt
- 2002,   Pim Fortuyn,   Publicist and Politician
- 2004,   Theo van Gogh,   Film Director, Writer, Critic

♦ New Caledonia
- 1981,   Pierre Declercq,   Kanak Independence Leader
- 1985,   Éloi Machoro,   Kanak Independence Leader
- 1985,   Marcel Nonaro,   Kanak Independence Leader
- 1989,   Jean-Marie Tjibaou,   Kanak Independence Leader
- 1989,   Yéiwene Yéiwene,   Kanak Independence Leader

♦ Nicaragua
- 1912,   Benjamín Zeledón,   Liberal Revolutionary
- 1934,   Augusto César Sandino,   Nicaraguan Revolutionary
- 1956,   Anastasio Somoza García,   President of Nicaragua
- 1978,   Pedro Chamorro,   Newspaper Editor

♦ Niger
- 1999,   Ibrahim Baré Maïnassara,   President of Niger

♦ Nigeria
- 1966,   Sir Abubakar Tafawa Balewa, Prime Minister of Nigeria
- 1976,   Murtala Ramat Mohammed,   President of Nigeria
- 1986,   Dele Giwa,   Journalist
- 1995,   Ken Saro-Wiwa,   Activist
- 2001,   Bola Ige,   Justice Minister of Nigeria

♦ Norway
- 1973,   Ahmed Bouchiki,   Civilian (mistaken as *Ali Hassan Salameh*)

- ◆ Pakistan
  - 1951,   Liaquat Ali Khan,   Prime Minister of Pakistan
  - 1987,   Meena Keshwar Kamal,   Founder, Association of the Women of Afghanistan
  - 1989,   Abdullah Yusuf Azzam,   Militant Islamist
  - 1991,   Fazle Haq,   Governor of the Northwest Frontier Province
  - 1995,   Iqbal Masih,   Anti-Child Labor Activist
  - 2001,   Siddiq Khan Kanju,   Foreign Minister of Pakistan

- ◆ Palau
  - 1985,   Haruo Remeliik,   President

- ◆ Palestine
  - 2001,   Abu Ali Mustafa,   Leader of PFLP
  - 2002,   Salah Shahade,   Leader of Hamas' Military Wing
  - 2003,   Ibrahim al-Makadmeh,   Co-Founder of Hamas
  - 2004,   Sheikh Ahmed Yassin,   Leader and Founder of Hamas
  - 2004,   Abdel Aziz al-Rantissi,   Leader of Hamas
  - 2004,   Izz El-Deen Sheikh Khalil,   Hamas Operative

- ◆ Panama
  - 1955,   José A. Remón Cantera,   President of Panama

- ◆ Paraguay
  - 1980,   Anastasio Somoza Debayle,   President of Nicaragua
  - 1999,   Luis María Argaña,   Vice-President of Paraguay

- ◆ Peru
  - 1541,   Francisco Pizarro,   Spanish Conquistador
  - 1933,   Luis M. Sánchez Cerro,   President of Peru
  - 1935,   Antonio Miró Quesada,   Publisher of *El Comercio*

- ◆ Philippines
  - 1719,   Fernando M. de Bustamante,   Spanish Governor-General of the Philippines
  - 1763,   Diego Silang,   Revolutionary Leader
  - 1899,   Antonio Luna,   Leader of Filipino Army
  - 1935,   Julio Nalundasan,   Ilocos Congressman
  - 1949,   Aurora Quezon,   First Lady of the Philippines
  - 1949,   Ponciano Bernardo,   Mayor of Quezon City
  - 1980,   Joe Lingad,   Pampanga Governor
  - 1983,   Benigno Aquino Jr.,   Senator
  - 1984,   Cesar Climaco,   Mayor of Zamboanga City
  - 1986,   Evelio Javier,   Governor
  - 1987,   Rolando Olalia,   Head of the Kilusang Mayo Uno
  - 1987,   Lean Alejandro,   Student Activist Leader
  - 1987,   Jaime Ferrer,   Local Government Cabinet Secretary
  - 1989,   James N. Rowe,   U. S. Military Adviser
  - 2001,   Filemon' Ka Popoy' Lagman,   Founder, Buklurang Manggagawang Pilipino (BMP)
  - 2003,   Romulo Kintanar,   Leader of the New People's Army (NPA)

- 2004,   Arturo Tabara,   Leader of Revolutionary Workers' Party
- 2005,   Romeo Sanchez,   Politician
- 2005,   Abelardo Ladera,   Politician
- 2005,   William Tadena,   Cleric with the Philippine Independent Church
- 2006,   A. bin Muhammad Baraguir, Sultan of Maguindanao

♦ Poland
- 1079,   Stanisław Szczepanowski,   Bishop of Kraków
- 1922,   Gabriel Narutowicz,   President of Poland
- 1984,   Jerzy Popiełuszko,   Polish Priest
- 1998,   Marek Papała,   Chief of the Police

♦ Portugal
- 1355,   Inês de Castro,   Queen of Portugal
- 1483,   Fernando II,   Duke of Braganza
- 1484,   Diogo de Beja,   Duke
- 1908,   Carlos I of Portugal,   King
- 1908,   Luiz Filipe of Portugal,   Crown Prince
- 1918,   Sidónio Pais,   President
- 1965,   Humberto Delgado,   General and Presidential Candidate

♦ Qatar
- 2004,   Zelimkhan Yandarbiyev,   Separatist President of Chechnya

♦ Romania
- 1601,   Mihai Viteazul,   Ruler of Wallachia, Moldavia and Transylvania
- 1862,   Barbu Catargiu,   Prime Minister of Romania
- 1933,   Ion Duca,   Prime Minister of Romania
- 1938,   Corneliu Zelea Codreanu,   Politician
- 1939,   Armand Călinescu,   Prime Minister of Romania
- 1940,   Nicolae Iorga,   Prime Minister of Romania
- 1945,   Constantin Tănase,   Actor

♦ Rwanda
- 1985,   Dian Fossey,   Primatologist
- 1994,   Agathe Uwilingiyimana,   Prime Minister of Rwanda
- 1994,   Juvénal Habyarimana,   Rwandan Genocide

♦ Samoa
- 1999,   Luagalau Levaula Kamu,   Cabinet Minister

♦ Saudi Arabia
- 624,   Ka' b ibn al-Ashraf,   Chief of the Jewish Tribe of Banu Nadir
- 644,   Umar ibn al-Khattab,   Second Caliph
- 1975,   Faisal of Saudi Arabia,   King

♦ Slovakia
- 1999,   Ján Ducký

- Somalia
  - 1969,   Abdirashid Ali Shermarke,   President of Somalia
  - 1989,   George Adamson,   British Naturalist

- South Africa
  - 1828,   Shaka,   King of the Zulu
  - 1828,   Umthlangana,   Zulu Prince, brother of Shaka
  - 1966,   Hendrik Verwoerd,   Prime Minister of South Africa
  - 1974,   Onkgopotse Tiro,   South African Student Leader
  - 1977,   Steve Biko,   Anti-Apartheid Activist
  - 1982,   Ruth First,   Anti-Apartheid Scholar
  - 1985,   Vernon Nkadimeng,   South African Dissident
  - 1988,   Dulcie September,   Head of the African National Congress
  - 1993,   Chris Hani,   Leader of the South African Communist Party
  - 1995,   Johan Heyns,   Leader in the Dutch Reformed Church

- Soviet Union
  - 1762,   Peter III of Russia,   Tsar of Russia
  - 1801,   Paul of Russia,   Tsar of Russia
  - 1825,   Mikhail A. Miloradovich,   Military Governor of St. Petersburg
  - 1878,   Nikolay V. Mezentsev,   Executive Director
  - 1881,   Alexander II of Russia,   Tsar of Russia
  - 1902,   Dmitry Sipyagin,   Russian Interior Minister
  - 1904,   Vyacheslav Pleve,   Russian Interior Minister
  - 1905,   Grand Duke Romanov,   Governor-General of Moscow
  - 1911,   Peter Stolypin,   Russian Prime Minister
  - 1916,   Grigori Rasputin,   Priest
  - 1918,   V. Volodarsky,   Revolutionary
  - 1918,   Wilhelm Mirbach,   German Ambassador to Moscow
  - 1926,   Simon Petlyura,   Ukrainian Independence Leader
  - 1934,   Sergei Kirov,   Bolshevik Party Leader
  - 1994,   Giorgi Chanturia,   Georgian Opposition Leader
  - 1996,   Dzhokhar Dudayev,   Chechen Separatist President
  - 1998,   Galina Starovoitova,   Politician and Member of the Russian Duma
  - 1998,   Ruslan Chimayev,   Chechen Rebel Politician
  - 1998,   Otakhon Latifi,   Tajik Journalist
  - 1999,   Vasgen Sarkissian,   Prime Minister of Armenia
  - 1999,   Karen Demirchian,   Speaker of Armenian Parliament
  - 1999,   Leonard Petrossian,   Karabakh Politician
  - 2000,   Georgiy Gongadze,   Ukrainian Journalist
  - 2002,   Valentin Tsvetkov,   Governor of Magadan
  - 2003,   Sergei Yushenkov,   Russian Politician
  - 2003,   Yury Shchekochikhin,   Russian Journalist
  - 2004,   Georgy Tal,   Russian Businessman
  - 2004,   Paul Klebnikov,   Editor of the Russian *Forbes* magazine
  - 2004,   Akhmad Kadyrov,   Kremlin-backed President of the Chechen Republic
  - 2004,   Zelimkhan Yandarbiyev,   President of Separatist Chechnya
  - 2005,   Aslan Maskhadov,   President of Chechnya
  - 2005,   Elmar Huseynov,   Azerbaijani Journalist

- 2005,   Zhirgalbek Surabaldiyev,   Kyrgyz MP
- 2005,   Magomed Omarov,   Deputy Interior Minister of Dagestan
- 2005,   Bayaman Erkinbayev,   Kyrgyz MP
- 2006,   Abdul-Khalim Sadulayev,   President of Separatist Chechnya
- 2006,   Anna Politkovskaya,   Russian Journalist and Human Rights Campaigner

- ◆ Spain
  - 1870,   Juan Prim,   Prime Minister of Spain and Governor of Puerto Rico
  - 1897,   Antonio Cánovas del Castillo,   Prime Minister of Spain
  - 1912,   José Canalejas,   Prime Minister of Spain
  - 1921,   Eduardo Dato Iradier,   Prime Minister of Spain
  - 1936,   Federico García Lorca,   Spanish Poet and Dramatist
  - 1967,   Mohamed Khider,   Algerian Politician
  - 1968,   Melitón Manzanas,   Secret Police Officer
  - 1973,   Luis Carrero Blanco,   Prime Minister
  - 1985,   Ricardo Tejero Magro,   Director of the Central Bank
  - 1996,   Francisco Tomás y Valiente,   President of the Spanish Constitutional Court
  - 2000,   Fernando Buesa Blanco,   Basque Politician
  - 2000,   Ernest Lluch Martín,   Spanish Minister

- ◆ Sri Lanka
  - 1959,   S.n W. R. Dias Bandaranaike,   Prime Minister
  - 1975,   Alfred Duraiyapah,   Mayor of Jaffna
  - 1981,   A. Thiagarajah,   Member of Parliament
  - 1985,   V. Dharmalingam,   Member of Parliament
  - 1985,   K. Alalasunderam,   Member of Parliament
  - 1989,   A. Amrithalingam,   Member of Parliament, General Secretary of TULF
  - 1990,   T. Ganeshalingam,   Minister, Northeast Provincial Council
  - 1990,   Sam Tambimuttu,   Member of Parliament
  - 1990,   P. Kirubakaran,   Finance Minister
  - 1990,   K. Kanagaratnam,   Member of Parliament
  - 1991,   Ranjan Wijeratne,   Minister of Defense
  - 1993,   Ranasinghe Premadasa,   President of Sri Lanka
  - 1994,   Ossie Abeygunasekara,   Member of Parliament
  - 1994,   G. M. Premachandra,   Member of Parliament
  - 1994,   Gamini Disanayake,   Presidential Candidate, Member of Parliament
  - 1995,   Thomas Anton,   Deputy Mayor
  - 1997,   Mohammad Maharoof,   Member of Parliament
  - 1998,   Sarojini Yogeswaran,   Jaffna Mayor
  - 1998,   S. Shanmuganadan,   Member of Parliament
  - 1999,   Neelan Thiruchelvam,   Member of Parliament and TULF Leader
  - 2000,   C. V. Gunaratne,   Cabinet Minister
  - 2005,   Lakshman Kadirgamar,   Foreign Minister
  - 2006,   Vanniasingham Vigneswaran,   Tamil Rights Activist
  - 2006,   Parami Kulatunga,   Army General

- ◆ Sudan
  - 1973,   Cleo Noel Jr.,   U. S. Chief of Mission
  - 1973,   George Curtis Moore,   Deputy Chief ot Mission
  - 1973,   Guy Eid,   Belgian Chargé d' affaires

- ♦ Suriname
  - 1982,   Bram Behr,   Surinamese Journalist

- ♦ Sweden
  - 1436,   Engelbrekt Engelbrektsson,   Regent of Sweden
  - 1577,   King Eric XIV of Sweden
  - 1792,   King Gustav III of Sweden
  - 1810,   Axel von Fersen,   Grand Marshal of Sweden
  - 1975,   Andreas von Mirbach,   German Military Attaché to Stockholm
  - 1975,   Heinz Hillegaart,   German Diplomat
  - 1986,   Olof Palme,   Swedish Prime Minister
  - 2003,   Anna Lindh,   Swedish Minister of Foreign Affairs

- ♦ Switzerland
  - 1233,   Berthold von Helfenstein,   Bishop of Chur
  - 1308,   Albert I of Habsburg,   German King and Duke of Austria
  - 1375,   Guichard Tavelli,   Bishop of Sion
  - 1640,   Rudolf von Planta,   Judge of Lower Engadin
  - 1845,   Josef Leu,   Catholic Politician
  - 1898,   Elisabeth "Sissi",   Empress of Austria and Queen of Hungary
  - 1923,   Vaslav Vorovsky,   Soviet Diplomat
  - 1936,   Wilhelm Gustloff,   German Leader of the Swiss Nazi Party
  - 1990,   Kazem Rajavi,   Iranian Opposition Leader

- ♦ Syria
  - 246 BC, Antiochus II Theos,   Seleucid king
  - 223 BC, Seleucus III Ceraunus,   Seleucid king
  - 176 BC, Seleucus IV Philopator,   Seleucid king
  - 146 BC, Alexander Balas,   Seleucid king
  - 138 BC, Antiochus VI Dionysus,   Seleucid Heir to the Throne
  - 285,   Numerian,   Roman Emperor
  - 1146,   Zengi,   Ruler of Aleppo and Mosul, Founder of the Zengid Dynasty
  - 1940,   Abdul Rahman Shahbandar, Syrian Nationalist
  - 2005,   George Hawi,   Chief of Communist Party of Lebanon
  - 2005,   Gibran Tueni,   Journalist

- ♦ Tanzania
  - 1972,   Abeid Amani Karume,   President of Zanzibar, Vice-President of Tanzania

- ♦ Togo
  - 1963,   Sylvanus Olympio,   President of Independent Togo
  - 1992,   Tavio Amorin,   Socialist Leader

- ♦ Tunisia
  - 1988,   Khalil Wazir,   Military Leader of the PLO
  - 1991,   Salah Khalaf,   Deputy Leader of the PLO

- ♦ Turkey
  - 217,   Caracalla,   Roman Emperor

- 275, Aurelian, Roman Emperor
- 276, Florianus, Roman Emperor
- 1579, Mehmed Sokollu, Grand Vizier of Suleyman the Magnificent
- 1622, Osman II, Sultan of the Ottoman Empire
- 1913, Mahmud Sevket Pasha, Grand Vizier of the Ottoman Empire
- 1922, Azmi Bey, Ottoman Ittihat and Terakki Party Member
- 1929, Celal Pasha, Ottoman Minister of the Navy
- 1979, Abdi Ipekçi, Editor-in-Chief of the *Milliyet* newspaper
- 1980, Nihat Erim, Prime Minister of Turkey
- 1990, Bahriye Uçok, University Professor of Islam Studies
- 1990, Çetin Emeç, Journalist of the *Hürriyet* newspaper
- 1990, Turan Dursun, Author and Journalist
- 1992, Musa Anter, Dissident Kurdish-Turkish Activist and Writer
- 1993, Uğur Mumcu, Journalist of the *Cumhuriyet* newspaper
- 1999, Ahmet Taner Kışlalı, Politician, Professor at Ankara University
- 2006, Mustafa Yücel Özbilgin, Supreme Court Judge, Council of State (*Danıştay*)
- 2006, Fr. Andrea Santoro, Catholic Priest
- 2007, Hrant Dink, Journalists, Founder of the *Agos* newspaper

♦ Uganda
- 1972, Benedicto Kiwanuka, Chief Justice of Uganda
- 1977, Janani Luwum, Archbishop of Uganda, Rwanda, Burundi and Boga-Zaire

♦ United Kingdom
- 293, Carausius
- 946, King Edmund I, King of England
- 979, Edward the Martyr, King of England
- 1170, Thomas Becket, Archbishop of Canterbury
- 1567, Henry Stuart, 1st Duke of Albany
- 1570, James Stewart, 1st Earl of Moray, Regent of Scotland
- 1679, James Sharp, Archbishop of St. Andrews
- 1812, Spencer Perceval, Prime Minister of the United Kingdom
- 1882, Lord Frederick Cavendish, Chief Secretary for Ireland
- 1882, Thomas Henry Burke, Permanent Under Secretary for Ireland
- 1922, Sir Henry Hughes Wilson, British Field Marshal
- 1972, Paddy Wilson, SDLP
- 1975, Ross Mc Whirter, Co-Author of the *Guinness Book of Records*
- 1976, Christopher Ewart-Biggs, British Ambassador to Ireland
- 1977, Kadhi Abdullah al-Hagri, Prime Minister of Arab Republic of Yemen
- 1978, Georgi Markov, Bulgarian Dissident
- 1979, Airey Neave, British Conservative
- 1981, Sir Norman Stronge, Aristocrat and Northern Irish Politician
- 1981, James Stronge, Aristocrat and Northern Irish Politician
- 1981, Rev. Robert Bradford, Unionist MP in Northern Ireland
- 1990, Ian Gow, British Conservative
- 2006, Alexander Litvinenko, Ex-KGB

♦ United States
- 1844, Joseph Smith, Jr., Mormon Leader

- 1844,	Hyrum Smith,	Mormon Leader
- 1861,	Henry Heusken,	American Diplomat
- 1865,	Abraham Lincoln,	President of the United States
- 1868,	Thomas Hindman,	Confederate General
- 1868,	James Hinds,	U. S. Congressman
- 1873,	Edward Canby,	Union General, Leader of a Peace Conference
- 1877,	Crazy Horse,	Oglala Sioux Chief
- 1881,	James Garfield,	President of the United States
- 1890,	David Hennessey,	Police Chief of New Orleans
- 1893,	Carter Harrison, Sr.,	Mayor of Chicago
- 1900,	William Goebel,	Governor of Kentucky
- 1901,	William McKinley,	President of the United States
- 1905,	Frank Steunenberg,	Governor of Idaho
- 1926,	Don Mellett,	Editor and Campaigner against Organized Crime
- 1933,	Anton Cermak,	Mayor of Chicago
- 1935,	Huey P. Long,	Louisiana Senator and Governor
- 1955,	Curtis Chillingworths,	Judge
- 1963,	John F. Kennedy,	President of the United States
- 1963,	Lee Harvey Oswald,	alleged Assassin of John F. Kennedy
- 1963,	Medgar Evers,	U. S. Civil Rights Activist
- 1965,	Malcolm X	
- 1967,	George Lincoln Rockwell,	Founder of the American Nazi Party
- 1968,	Martin Luther King Jr.,	U. S. Civil Rights Activist
- 1968,	Robert F. Kennedy,	Presidential Candidate
- 1970,	Harold Haley,	Court Judge
- 1970,	Dan Mitrione,	FBI Agent
- 1976,	Orlando Letelier,	Chilean Ambassador to the United States
- 1978,	Harvey Milk,	Gay Rights Campaigner
- 1978,	George Moscone,	Mayor of San Francisco
- 1979,	John Wood,	U. S. Federal Judge
- 1980,	John Lennon,	British Musician, Ex-Beatle
- 1984,	Alan Berg,	Radio Talk show Host
- 1984,	Chiang Nan,	Taiwanese-American Writer
- 1986,	Alejandro González Malavé,	Undercover Police officer
- 1990,	Meir Kahane, Rabbi,	Founder of Jewish Defense League
- 1998,	Tommy Burks,	Tennessee State Senator
- 2001,	Thomas C. Wales,	Federal Prosecutor and Gun Control Advocate
- 2003,	James E. Davis,	New York City Council Member

♦ Uruguay

- 1868,	Bernardo P. Berro,	Uruguayan President
- 1868,	Venancio Flores,	Uruguayan President
- 1897,	Juan Idiarte Borda,	Uruguayan President

♦ Venezuela

- 1950,	Carlos Delgado Chalbaud,	Chairman of the Military Junta of Venezuela
- 2004,	Danilo Anderson,	State Prosecutor

♦ Vietnam

- 1947,	Hans Imfeld,	French Colonial Agent

- 1963,	Ngo Dinh Nhu,	Politician
- 1963,	Ngo Dinh Diem,	President of South Vietnam

- ◆ Yemen
  - 1948, Imam Yahya,   King of Yemen
  - 1977, Ibrahim al-Hamadi,   President of North Yemen
  - 1978, Ahmad al-Ghashmi,   President of North Yemen
  - 2002, Jarallah Omar,   Deputy Secretary-General of Yemeni Socialist Party

- ◆ Yugoslavia
  - 282, Probus,   Roman Emperor
  - 284, Carinus,   Roman Emperor
  - 1903, Aleksandar Obrenović,   King of Serbia
  - 1914, Franz Ferdinand,   Archduke of Austria and his wife Sophie
  - 1921, Milorad Drašković,   Yugoslav Interior Minister
  - 1934, Alexander I of Yugoslavia,   King of Yugoslavia
  - 1945, Sekula Drljević,   Montenegran Nationalist
  - 2000, Željko "Arkan" Ražnatović,   Serb Paramilitary Leader
  - 2000, Pavle Bulatović,   Defense Minister of Yugoslavia
  - 2000, Boško Perošević,   Premier of Vojvodina
  - 2000, Ivan Stambolić,   Serb Politician
  - 2003, Zoran Đinđić,   Prime Minister of Serbia

- ◆ Zambia
  - 1975, Herbert Chitepo,   Zimbabwean Nationalist Leader

- ◆ Zimbabwe
  - 1983, Attati Mpakati,   Left-Wing Malawian Politician

Hasan-bin-Sabbah

(حسـن صـبـاح)

Sheikh of the Mountains
Leader of the Assassins

Usama-bin-Laden

(أسـامة بـن محمـد بـن عـوض بـن لادن)

Sheikh of the (Afghan) Mountains
Leader of Al-Qaeda

Terrorists, unable to achieve their unrealistic goals by conventional means, attempt to send their ideological or religious messages by terrorizing the general public. Through the choice of their targets, often symbolic or representative of the targeted nation, terrorists attempt to create a high-profile impact on the public despite the limited material resources that are usually at their disposal. In doing so, they hope to demonstrate various points, that the targeted governments cannot protect their own citizens, or that by assassinating a specific victim they can teach the general public a lesson about espousing viewpoints or policies antithetical to their own. For example, by assassinating Egyptian President Anwar Sadat on October 6, 1981, a year after his historic trip to Jerusalem, the al-Jihad terrorists hoped to convey to the world, and especially to Muslims, the error that he represented. Another example, despite Arab protests, a British mandate is proclaimed in Palestine on September 11, 1922. September 11, 2001 was the date of the WTC attack.

This tactic is not new. Beginning in 48 AD, a Jewish sect called the Zealots carried out terrorist campaigns to force insurrection against the Romans in Judea. These campaigns included the use of assassins called "*Sicarii*", or dagger-men. They would infiltrate Roman controlled cities and stab Jewish collaborators or Roman legionnaires with a "*sica*" (dagger), kidnap members of the Staff of the Temple Guard to hold for ransom, or use poison on a larger scale. The Zealots' justification for their killing of other Jews was that these killings demonstrated the consequences of the immorality of collaborating with the Roman invaders, and that the Romans could not protect their Jewish collaborators.

Definitions of terrorism vary widely and are usually inadequate. Even terrorism researchers often neglect to define the term other than by citing the basic U. S. Department of State (1998) definition of terrorism: "premeditated, politically motivated violence perpetrated against noncombatant targets by sub-national groups or clandestine agents, usually intended to influence an audience."

Although an act of violence, generally regarded in the United States as an act of terrorism, may not be viewed so in another country. The type of violence that distinguishes terrorism from other types of violence, such as ordinary crime or a wartime military action can still be defined in terms that might qualify as reasonably objective. The social sciences researcher defines a terrorist action as the calculated use of unexpected, shocking, and unlawful violence against noncombatants (including, as well as civilians, off duty military and security personnel in peaceful situations); further, the attack on other symbolic targets perpetrated by clandestine members of a sub-national group or clandestine agent/s for the psychological purpose of publicizing a political or religious cause. And to intimidate or force a government or civilian population into accepting demands on behalf of the cause.

The Purpose of Terror

Terrorism for political purpose is usually a form of theatric performance and as such, there are a number of factors, which are almost universal in modern terrorist activities.

The use of violence to persuade, where bombings or other attacks are employed to "make a point" with target victims. The targeted victims are not necessarily those who are injured or killed. Rather, the attack may have been carried out to influence a government, or a group of governments, to take a certain course of action or perhaps to terminate or cease a course of action.

Selection of targets and victims for maximum propaganda value means choosing targets and victims, which will assure the heaviest possible media coverage. This consideration was particularly evident with terrorist attacks such as the World Trade Center bombing in New York City in 1993 and the hostage-taking of Israeli athletes during the 1972 Olympic Games in Munich. These were followed by terrorist activities including the bombing of the Murrah Federal Office Building in Oklahoma City, and the U. S. Embassies in Nairobi, Kenya and in Dar-Es-Salaam, Tanzania.

The use of unprovoked attacks, which, truth be told, is just about any terrorist attack—because they were "provoked" is only the convoluted rationale offered by the terrorists themselves.

Maximum publicity at minimum risk is the principle behind many terrorist actions, particularly those involving explosive devices. Bombings typically generate a good deal of publicity, depending on time and placement, so targets are usually selected for symbolic value, such as embassies, internationally known tourist attractions, and similar facilities.

The use of sophisticated timing elements allows detonation to be programmed well in advance, reducing the risk to the bomber or bombers, who can be long gone by the time the devices are discovered or exploded. Moving up on the list of favored terrorist activities, kidnapping or assaults and assassinations may generate greater or prolonged publicity, but they also present a higher risk for the attackers. There is something of a cyclical pattern to terrorist activities. That is, if there has been a rash of kidnappings, the public may become somewhat inured, and subsequent abductions may not generate the same degree of front-page coverage, television news exposure, or Internet hype. Bombings, just because they have been less frequent during the same period, may well produce more publicity than another kidnapping. A change in tactics, then, would produce more publicity than another kidnapping. Terrorists always want to remain in the forefront, so they will switch tactics to maximize publicity.

Use of surprise to circumvent countermeasures is one way terrorists try to attack hardened targets. Even though there are guards, detection devices, and increased perimeter security, the element of surprise can be employed to undermine the hardware and overwhelm the human factor in a fortified security system. Time is the terrorist's best friend. Even a well-protected and hardened target will experience slackened security measures during long periods of terrorist inactivity. Unless a suicide attack is planned, terrorists will wait to strike when security is relaxed.

Threats, harassment, and violence are tools terrorists use to create an atmosphere of fear. On occasion, terrorists have planted small bombs or incendiary devices in public locations, such as department stores and movie theaters. In recent years, anti-government terrorists in Egypt have attacked groups of tourists visiting the Pyramids and other monuments. To the public, there is no rhyme or reason to the time or placement of the devices, and soon the mere threat of such activity is enough to send waves of fear through the population.

Disregarding women and children as victims, often to the extent that locations with innocent victims are selected specifically to heighten the outrage, and fear, at the boldness of the terrorists' actions. This is yet another tactic to garner wider publicity and media coverage of the suffering and death of noncombatants. This characteristic differentiates the terrorist from a soldier or guerrilla. A soldier fights with the authority of a government for the protection of that government. A guerrilla fights the same kind of warfare as the soldier in technique and code of behavior, i.e. women and children are not specifically targeted. A terrorist, on the other hand, will focus on women and children, just to create a greater atmosphere of fear. Thus, the ethnic cleansing evidenced in Bosnia and Kosovo involving various population factions of the former Yugoslavia crossed the line from warfare to terrorism by militia.

Propaganda is used to maximize the effect of violence, particularly for economic or political goals. To carry out a particular operation without getting any publicity out of the action would be wasteful to a terrorist's cause. Thus, Black September, at the Olympic Games in Munich in 1972, and all those groups that mimicked that hostage-taking by claiming responsibility for attacks in other high-profile circumstances, wanted worldwide publicity for both political and economic goals. From a political standpoint, a group wants to show that it is a viable organization, a power to be reckoned with, and a force to be feared. On the economic level, the group shows sympathetic governments and others who support different terrorist groups that it, too, is worthy of funding. Even when terrorists do not publicly claim responsibility for an attack, many leave a signature or obvious clues during the action.

Loyalty to themselves or kindred groups is a common element of terrorist groups, existing among Armenians, Croatians, Kurds, Tamils, and Basques, to name a few. With these, and similar groups, the loyalty is so intense – distorted is not too strong a word – that the more radical elements of an otherwise peaceful movement will commit unspeakable criminal acts on behalf of that loyalty and associated cause. For the most part, however, second- and third-generation terrorists have diminished loyalty to the original cause, the sense of pride associated with it, and a reduced vision of the original goal. Many of them engage in terrorism as a form of gratification and perpetuate criminal activity as an end in itself. They have thus become nihilistic and interested primarily in financial remuneration for themselves. College-age individuals and educated political activists carried out the terrorism of the 1960s and 1970s for the most part. Now much of the low-intensity conflict and terrorist actions are being perpetrated by child soldiers, children, many of whom have not even reached puberty, who have become inured to violence and human emotion.

Stalking, Kidnapping, Abduction, Hostage Situations, Assassination, and Terrorism are the main threats waiting for the EPO to be unleashed. Considering, that an EPO will not have to face such threats frequently, he/she should be aware, prepared and ready for such incidents. A detailed study of any recorded case, involving these particular threats are the best source of information and constitute the best preparation for any professional. Case studies can reveal the why, how and when a perpetrator choose to operate in a particular pattern. Case studies can show how the threat affected the victims and how they reacted, what was done to deter or eliminate the threat, and the outcome of any actions.

If you know the enemy and know yourself, you need not fear the result of a hundred battles.

Sun Tzu - *The Art of War*

The Executive Protection Officer

- **The Requirements**

- **The Personality and Characteristics**

- **The Professional Conduct**

- **The EPO's Equipment**

- **The Weapons**

- **The Concealed Weapons**

- **The Self-Defense and Protection System**

- **The Body Armor**

- **The Protection Protocol**

- **The Relation with Press and Media**

- **The Operation with a Host Committee**

The individual's personality and character are very important when employing an executive protection officer. Obviously, it becomes part of the process to separate the most qualified ones from the "would be" officer candidates. Ideally, an EPO is selected from the most highly qualified professionals. For many executive protection agencies, a previous military and/or law enforcement experience is a preferred advantage, and often is it part of the requirements. College and university degrees (minimum bachelor degree) are another plus to be successful by many agencies. All these additional achievements are certainly a desirable asset, but should never be considered as a center part when seeking employment or for the client when seeking an EPO.

Many times, people interested in the EPO profession ask whether there are specific requirements regarding the physical appearance and size of an EPO– whether hairstyle, hair color and facial hair is of importance. Completing the picture, some people, obviously the more "practical" type, are keen to ask which choice of caliber and weapon/s would one have. Now, if one bothers to compare those questions with the content of the curriculum vitae submitted by the applicants, one might wonder whether they are applying for a movie casting, a job in an escort service, or a job as mercenary.

When watching the news and seeing the two meters and hundred and eighty kilograms of steroid-supplemented bouncers protecting one of those skinny pop-singers or the children of some movie star, one starts wondering. What might be the criteria the client used to select and employ them? Or, as many times reported, when so-called bodyguards are rampaging and engaging in close combat with photographers and fans, one can only shake the head in disbelief.

A specific requirement regarding physical appearance and size do not apply; however, the overall appearance of an EPO is extremely important, insofar that it sets the tone for the manner in which he is perceived. Some clients and employing agencies may have their own criteria regarding the height and weight. However, body weight should commensurate with the body height. Deploying a mix of tall, short, lean, stout and average-looking EPOs means that such a team is easily blending into the environment, like soldiers in their camouflage. Seeing but not being seen, that is the objective of the protective element. While on protective duty, never draw the attention to you.

Of course, there are more aspects and even more important characteristics to form an EPO suitable personality. Such personality is special because it is shaped from a sound judgment and a good strong moral character, with the ability to operate with all kind of people and under the most demanding conditions. Sometimes these conditions might stress the limits of physical endurance and demand a mental stress level beyond the acceptable.

Possessing certain personality characteristics and being of a sound mind and moral character form only a small portion of any basic requirements. The good EPO must also be able to manage his/her personal life and problems, never allowing those to interfere in the job, and above all preserve efficiency and professionalism.

The Requirements

The devastation and tragedy caused by the September 11 attacks, was followed by a wave of uncertainty and instability in the global business arena. The airline and travel industry felt the immediate impact and still today, like some of the other business sectors are struggling for a full recovery. Not so in the private security sector. September 11 revealed to be the magic key for everybody who was already or wanted to become involved in this particular field of business. The executive protection business in particular experienced a tremendous growth, never seen before. With terrorists on everyone's mind and high-paid employment waiting at almost every hot spot in the world, there has never been a better timing to enter these new dimensions of the executive protection world. Surely so, any police or military trained person would jump on such an opportunity to improve their living and to double or even triple the average income working as an EPO. However, the training, even specialized training and experience, that most of the law enforcement and/or military personnel receive is not necessarily the most adequate nor sufficient to qualify and to provide personal protection services.

In many U. S. states and in various countries, certain laws and regulations are made and apply specifically to security guards, which in most cases apply to bodyguards as well. The executive protection profession being a much more demanding activity is regulated by exactly the same laws. In many countries, incorporating a security company requires the same procedures and is ruled by the same regulations as those for a housecleaning company. So it is nothing surprising to see a cleaning company and a security services company under the same incorporation and ownership. Further, many countries do not issue licenses specifically for security guards, bodyguards, or EPOs–therefore it is most likely to find a security officer with a license type that is usually issued to private investigators. Fact is, most countries do not have the proper, detailed laws and regulations in place to monitor and to license the private security sector and/or related professional branches. Unfortunately, this applies not only to the areas of the security services providers and independent professionals, but also and more importantly to the area of training and education. Just as an example, in most U. S. states, security guards are required to have between 35 and 45 hours of mandated training. Further, they should receive fifteen hours of continuing education yearly, while in many countries nothing of this is required or even thought of.

We operated once in one particular country where laws and regulations were "specifically" made to meet the needs of the private security services and EPO professionals. These "model" laws and rules, however, revealed to be of such complexity, conflicting and contradicting in such a way that an application and issue of a license was impossible.

Other laws in some U. S. states regulate the services by different licenses. For example, only a licensed private patrol operator is allowed contract to perform security guard or bodyguard services to any person or business. This requires one to have a previous experience and pass a state test for qualification. A law enforcement officer on active duty, holding a *Guard ID* card and *Weapon Permit* for an exposed firearm, may perform armed security and bodyguard duties–but only as a security guard employee.

This might lead one to think that a person with military or law enforcement experience, by obtaining the proper license/s, would hold in his/her hands an unconditional guarantee for success. And, at the same time an opportunity to make more money, to have full control over his/her work, and eventually expand and reach for better things. Law enforcement and military personnel with the proper kind of executive protection training have a certain advantage and will find it easier to enter this very challenging and "well-paying" market, than someone from another professional background. Many law enforcement and special military skills can be an asset for the executive protection tasks (e. g. risk analysis, surveillance and counter-surveillance procedures, and physical security). But nevertheless, those skills will never be sufficient to cope with all those predictable and unpredictable challenges of the executive protection profession.

I am always amused when interviewing candidates for an EPO assignment. Succeeding in a 10-day, "intensive" executive protection or EPO-training, provided by a few accredited EP/EPO-schools, makes most candidates believe that they are sufficiently qualified to protect anybody anywhere in the world. If this is the general belief, then I have disappointing news–it is far from being the truth. Sometimes, I wonder whether believing in such a myth is caused by the candidate's own motivation and eagerness or simply because it is a suggestion induced by methods of training. After you've learned the first steps, never assume that you walk properly.

The qualities, training and skill characteristics of an EPO are of such a complexity that one cannot simply list them under "Job Description" or summarize as "Job Requirements". The executive protection training in its extent becomes part of an EPO's life. Therefore, in order succeed in the highly competitive and dangerous executive protection arena, one has to make the proper adjustments to one's lifestyle; especially when on long-term protection assignments.

Executive protection training should be focused on immediate protection, advance work, study of the various types of threats, the possible and actual risks that are applicable to one or to the principal. This form of study should become part of the EPO, transforming into a constant habit while traveling and/or scheduling anything that involves the EPO and the principal. Never think, that a back-up plan to the original plan should be enough—usually that is the moment when things tend to go really wrong.

Advance work, considered by most of the professionals a rather tedious exercise, is an important part of the EPO profession. An EPO with a "frequent traveler" as principal has all the advantages to become an expert in advance work. The complexity of the advance work is in the detailed study of factual and/or estimated information, the activities and/or arrangements made on one or several locations, which refer to the arrival, stay, and departure of the principal. This specific type of work requires a good amount of social skills and a refined sense for timing, planning, and organization. The fact that someone is familiar with the layout of a given region where he/she is planned to operate in does not necessarily mean the EPO knows how to advance a location properly. Good social skills, combined with knowledge of customer service procedures, will assure a smooth collection of data and information, which will be pertinent to the advance and the overall protection of the principal. It is a must to be organized first, before even considering practicing in the technique of advance work.

Further required for any protection program is the study, training, and mastering of a martial art. Let's leave the self-defense and protective aspects aside for a moment and focus on the benefit of mastering a martial art. Not every martial art is the ideal one for everybody. This is the main reason why so many different styles exist. While considering signing up with one of so many martial art schools, one should check the knowledge and teaching skills of the instructor and whether the martial art is appropriate. No matter which style or technique one selects, it is important that it provides the solid base for inner peace, mind-body control, and self-discipline. Now let's bring those abilities into our protection scenario and we will realize that one is able to react adequately and take control of a threat situation without risking any escalation. It does not matter how many years you are training at a specific art, whether you hold a black belt, or red sash, whether you're a qualified 2nd or 3rd Dan. What matters is your ability to stay fully in control of the situation. To apply your moves and techniques toward an opponent whenever necessary, to control your own fear and to protect your principal or the person you are assigned to.

What are the Requirements to Work as an EPO?

As mentioned before, the requirements for an EPO are more than just a handful of abilities and skills. The diversity and complexity of skills required from a prospect EPO cannot be presented in the form of a shopping list. Most clients, and even some of the executive protection training providers, may consider such a list as sufficient in order to select a candidate. In my point of view, even though professionally packaged, it will never satisfy the criteria for the selection of a good candidate.

Physical Condition is the most important asset of an EPO. A full medical check-up, which should include a full set of blood and urine analysis, x-rays, ECG, etc., should be made on a regular basis. Vaccines and immunization should be updated. Any excess of weight, or conditions like respiratory, heart and blood pressure should be taken care of immediately. A person with a pure health condition is not able to engage in such a strenuous and physically challenging activity of an EPO. The vision, if not 20/20, should be easily correctable. Although age should not form an obstacle, the expected age average is set between 21 and 55 (a top health condition must be assured). The age of the EPO is ruled by the physical condition, the training and above all the experience, which one only acquires over the years.

It is important that the EPO is in good physical condition. The physical conditioning has a lot of benefits, stimulating the mental awareness and confidence for example and to enable the EPO to respond and resolve an instantaneous conflict or problem. An EPO must be able to switch in a split of second between a relaxed state and a full readiness state. On the other hand, he/she might need to operate under vigorous physical condition for an extended period of time. For example, running beside the principal's car in a crowded street under the tropical heat of Central Africa or the humidity of a city in the Philippines.

Good physical fitness is as beneficial for appearance as it is for the endurance and good health. It is equally important for your physical condition to keep a good control on your meals and time of eating, as well as your sleep. We know that after we eat a large meal, we are not able to run fast or for long; we are unable to perform with full capacity. The same is true if we stay with an empty stomach. This applies to our sleep as well–an EPO will need to change from a normal sleeping habit to opportunistic sleeping. Most of the times, the EPO will not have a chance to get a full night's sleep at regular intervals. The best thing to do is to sleep whenever there is an opportunity–sometimes a 10 minute nap can be as refreshing as a full night's sleep.

Psychological Condition of the EPO is also of a prime importance. The EPO must be mature and precise in his/her ability, be able to quickly and correctly assess a situation, and respond in the proper manner as dictated by the situation at hand. He/she cannot allow to be ruled by an aggressive, hostile, or moody behavior, nor should he/she be slow in responding. The EPO must be able to correctly adapt to whatever quick changes and in whatever given situation or emergency. A high degree of dedication to duty and cause is a must for the successful EPO. The ability to perform under the most adverse and dangerous situations is mandatory for this job. *"Mens sana in corporae sanae"* (Latin= a healthy mind in a healthy body)

Self-Defense Skills gained from martial art training provides the EPO with the ability to defend him/herself and the principal. With disarming and defensive techniques, which are part of any martial art, the EPO is capable to defend him/herself and the principal in both armed and unarmed situations. At the same time, the EPO is able to keep control of a perpetrator until the proper authorities are notified and arrive.

Additional Skills training and practice in the following disciplines is mandatory for any EPO:

- Defensive tactics,
- Use and knowledge of improvised weapons,
- Use and knowledge of all types of firearms,
- Driving skills (evasive and defensive driving),
- First aid and CPR-techniques,
- Diving and Rescue Swimmer,
- Computer skills,
- Communication and language skills

To achieve adequate knowledge and skills, one does not need to attend an expensive Executive Protection School. One can easily find training facilities and course. Complete martial art courses take up much time (because of qualifications and ranking); enrolling in a basic self-defense course at a local martial art school might be an alternative. Any of these skills must be practiced until they become instinctive. A continuity of training even while off duty is most desirable. Already, the basic skills of these hands-on techniques will improve any individual's self-confidence. The magic words to achieve excellence in any skills are practice, practice and more practice.

The position of an EPO is indeed one of the most dangerous careers in the world. For that reason, only a few individuals have the necessary awareness and determination to succeed in the required skills, possessing the attitude and behavior to become competent in this position. Employment in the field of an EPO will be limited only by the required drive and determination that one possesses. The proper outfit, skills, approach and conduct will give the edge needed to belong to the elite and become an EPO.

The Personality and the Characteristics

The personality and character of an EPO is as important as his/her professional skills, and the valued personal qualities and characteristics of an EPO should include but not be limited to the following. An EPO should and is expected to be:

- self-confident, self-motivated, creative, innovative, enthusiastic
- resourceful, adaptable, flexible and able to improvise
- trustworthy and worthy of confidence, ethical, loyal
- ready and willing to take risks for the safety of others
- open-minded, disciplined and a team-player

He/she should have the ability to:

- analyze data and further developing a logical framework of strategic and tactical planning
- acknowledge the seriousness of assignments, possible risks and developing situations
- recognize the role each person plays in the overall mission and the organization
- appreciate, preserve and encourage whenever necessary the morale and productivity of colleague officers
- respond well to people of multiple and varying talents, motivations, interests, diverse ethnicities, multiple cultures and socio-economic status.
- communicate well on all levels orally and verbally
- conduct interviews, research, investigations
- work with high placed representatives of the political, social, scientific, and economical arena
- manage and support subordinates, support personnel, including the principal's staff and employees

Furthermore, the EPO should:

- be interested in continuing professional education and training and to develop a full potential of him/herself and colleague officers
- should be able to communicate verbally and in writing in one or two foreign languages
- posses basic knowledge of computers and word-processing (advanced skills are desirable)
- keep a helpful, friendly, and above all a professional attitude and conduct
- be able to respond disciplined and appropriate in emergency situations

Keep in your mind that each executive protection officer is unique, regardless of his total experience or ranking with or among other officers. The position of an EPO dictates however certain characteristics and abilities which are more of general nature and similar to those found in other profession.

Personality

Any EPO must have a personality, which allows them to relate well with other people, no matter which cultural, social, ethnical or religious background they might be. A certain amount of humor at the right moment can come in handy. He/she must be of an enthusiastic and expressive nature and capable of viewing a situation from various angles. EPOs demand as much of themselves as they do of others. As part of the job, an EPO must be able to communicate, give his/her directives and requirements clearly, unmistakably and effectively, and if required or questioned, be able to provide a clear and well-organized answer and explanations.

Awareness and Initiative

An EPO must know and recognize his limits, strengths, and weaknesses. The EPO is self-motivated and is able to set the standard, expecting the best of themselves and others. An EPO is constantly improving and refining his/her performance on the job, even when this means performing beyond the limits. EPOs are resourceful and capable of improvisation in order to solve any problems by themselves. In the event a situation develops and there are no instructions available, the EPO will act on his/her own initiative, not wait to be told what to do or how to respond. Passing the problem automatically to someone else is not an option. The EPO is able to motivate him/herself individually, completing any task that arises. He/she does not need a supervisor to explain every detail of the assignment explicitly and to direct how and when to respond. When the EPO sees a need, he/she jumps in to see that a condition is rectified. The EPO is constantly attempting to improve the protective curtain.

Psychological Agility

A well-trained and capable EPO must be able to resolve problems quickly. He/she must recognize a developing situation, analyze it, and resolve it in seconds. He/she must be able to think independently and have a good sense of self-direction. He/she cannot wait to ask for specific instructions at any or every instance.

He/she must be able to make their own decisions in whatever situation: Is the situation posing a threat? What are the possible alternatives? What are the consequences to the action or by lack of action? What action is the appropriate to be taken? Failure to see or recognize the complexities of a situation certainly leads to indecision and inaction. Experiencing uncertainty results in an inhibition of action; this could ultimately endanger a life or cause a terrible accident.

Emotional Stability

In a high-level area, such as that of executive protection, an officer must have the natural ability to remain calm and collected, no matter how chaotic, stressful, or demanding the situation appears. Once a conflict arises, he has to keep patience, calm, tact, and must be tolerant. He/she must assure that the overall performance on the job remains at the expected levels, even in pressure and stressful situations.

Placing blame on others, self-blame and self-pitying in the face of any disappointment or failure is not acceptable. Self-criticism and the desire to correct committed errors are encouraged. The EPO must be able to separate any private matters from the professional life. Family, wife, husband, children, even friends and neighbors have to be set aside, and everything will be controlled by and dedicated to his principal.

Patience

Boredom, as one will soon realize, is becoming one of the closest companions of an EPO. Patience is the necessary trait of the EPO. The EPO will need to operate for eight, twelve, and even more hours in shifts or solo. During those long hours, the EPO will need to deal with just sitting and waiting for a principal, or doing over-watch as a post assignment, which can become very boring. In order to avoid such boredom, a regular switching between stations every hour is a common routine. This is very helpful in relieving any stress, the sensation of boredom, and more importantly, it allows the eyes to refresh. Looking and focusing on things for a long period of time causes the eyes and brain to fail to recognize any even the slightest changes. Failing to see things or to recognize changes in patterns will lead to the wrong or a late reaction, which might be disastrous.

Decisiveness

It is further expected from an EPO to be able to make quick decisions and to accept the outcomes in any form. He/she must be able to make up his/her mind at once and on his/her own, without waiting for most likely unnecessary input from others, more so in crises or time-sensitive situations. The EPO must attempt to gain as much information as possible before forming any conclusion or decision, but he/she must be capable to decide as time allows or dictates.

Planning

The EPO's job is to plan and provide a secure environment surrounding a principal by analyzing the requirements, setting realistically acceptable goals, and seeing the plan to its conclusion. The EPO consistently prepares well-organized schedules, logistics, performs his duties in a timely fashion, ready to meet sensitive deadlines, even in the most difficult situations. An EPO must provide high-standard, high-quality services and a performance beyond what is expected.

Leadership

From principal to the service staff, once confronted with a difficult situation, everyone expects the EPO to take command and lead them out of it. Since an EPO is trained to handle such situations, he/she must set the standard so others will respond and follow. In a crisis situation, he/she remains calm, collected, and resourceful – ready to find the proper solution. The EPO must be able to create ideas, form a plan, and provide suggestions, without patronizing or making others feel inferior. He/she must speak with confidence and, if required, even disagree with people, while being able to sustain his/her argument with facts and clear reasoning. He must be able to retain the respect and the cooperation of others.

Always keep in your mind: *Respect is something one cannot demand—one has to earn it.*

Teamwork

The EPO does not always work solo, and in most job assignments he/she will join other EPOs to operate as an Executive Protection Team. This is the time when the EPO has to prove his/her teamwork abilities. In a team, every element works together for common purposes and outcomes. Each member performs his part for the best of the whole. Every EPO, as member of a team, should and can anticipate the movements, the thoughts of his/her partners. EPOs must be able to communicate, which is the magic spice in teamwork, through body signs. A slight move of the head, a finger or hand, unnoticed to others, can mean, "Check that person there," and as a team member, the EPO must be able to recognize those subtle signs.

Once the EPO is assigned a position on duty, it is mandatory that whoever is working in that position does not leave or stray into the area of responsibility of another officer. Neither can he/she just wander away. When leaving an assigned position, an area becomes vulnerable and is open, unavoidably weakening the total team effort. Team members always support each another. While assigned and concentrating on a given position, a team member is also aware of the positioning and developments around his colleague officers. He/she is responding to a need and will bring the appropriate assistance where and when needed. He/she must know the responsibilities of his colleague team members and therefore he/she should be capable to take over or fill in for another member.

The Professional Conduct

The professional conduct and image of the EPO are extremely important. Being photographed while protecting celebrities, heads of state and other VIPs, images that ultimately end up in newspapers, tabloid, or other media, is part of the EPO's existence. Since he/she is constantly being seen by the principal, staff members, visitors, contacts or the public, the EPO is measured and evaluated by all who can see him/her. His/her appearance and conduct might influence and determine the mindset of those observing. Consider the fact that there is always an outsider with the "urge" to compare and to take measure of the EPO.

The amount of respect, or lack of, earned by the EPO is directly correlated to his appearance and conduct. While operating with other agencies, law enforcement, and host committees it is much easier to earn cooperation if the EPO presents him/herself professionally and with a personal conduct above reproach. Professional appearance and personal conduct rules should never be compromised.

Education: It is more than clear by now, that an EPO must posses a good education and be trained in his/her specialty. But this is far away from being sufficient. He/she must be well read, informed, and educated in every and all areas. It is even more important to keep up-to-date with current events in the news. Depending on the activities and engagements of the principal, he/she might like to discuss regional, national, and international affairs, and replying in an informed and well-thought manner will definitely enhance the standing of the EPO. It is also extremely important to be current in history, geography, international affairs, and to know the importance of people that the principal might come in contact with.

Discipline: Discipline as such is a form of self-control. It is self-control that makes a person able to stand sentry in one place, sometimes for hours, or to be on time or not to respond in anger to a principal or team member. Self-control is that factor that makes us bring forth the extra effort, which is expected from us. It is this little internal control mechanism which enables us to stay awake and alert after hours on duty or when working without any sleep.

Perception: It is the ability to anticipate and instantly recognize a potential danger that would harm a principal. The EPO must also be perceptive for the needs and the concerns of and related to the principal. Being able to resolve the principal's concerns before they are expressed, gives the principal a peace of mind and the assurance that the EPO is well aware of all those conditions that might affect his/her secure environment.

Discretion, Honesty, Loyalty: Discretion plays a key role in an environment where situations are changing constantly. The meaning of discretion is freedom and capability to judge properly, especially in times when one cannot wait for someone else's advice and/or direction. In order to make adequate, rational decisions, we need to look at all options and alternatives. The final analysis is given to the good judgment of the EPO to select the proper direction and action. While working with other people, one has to extend the same clear judgment. It is equally important in good working relationships to solidify the foundation with respect–but with respect earned and through trust and discretion. The EPO's honesty and character should never be the center of doubt. He/she must be beyond and above any such doubt. The EPO must be worthy of confidence and trust, otherwise this is not the profession to choose. The principal must have the assurance the EPO can be entrusted with any type of secrets and/or to handle any type of valuables.

Don't ever take anything; don't ever lie; and do your job without questioning. The credibility, security, and confidence the principal must have in his/her EPO cannot be shaken or eroded by a lie, no matter how small or what importance it has. Loyalty is an integral part of the EPO's character, and this extends to employer, colleague officers, and principal. Loyalty is actually one of the few small things, with such a value, which cannot be bought or paid with money. If there is no loyalty, there will not be trust.

Sense of Dependability: The EPO should be the most reliable person that one can count on at every time–at any time. He/she must always be in the right position and readily responsive to any situation and capable of staying in control at all times. That is what the client or principal is looking for, that *his* or *her* executive protection officer can solve any situation and is always nearby for whatever needs and whenever necessary. It is good to know that an assignment or given task is carried out to full satisfaction and without any hesitation or lapse of confidence.

Cooperation: The EPO expects to have others cooperating with him/her, as much is it desired by others. An EPO should be able to cooperate with his colleague officers, host committee, and everybody else around. He/she must be equally able to solicit and to obtain the desired or needed cooperation from others. This is as simple as sharing–it works both ways. In the real world, an EPO might have to struggle with conflicting interests and purposes. For example, the hosting side might want the principal in the most glamorous exposure possible; whereas, the EPO side wants to limit the area of vulnerability to a minimum, automatically decreasing the effect of exposure. In such situations, the EPO will use his/her diplomatic abilities, accepting concessions in the interest of cooperation, showing flexibility toward the circumstances of the situation, but making sure that the secure environment of the principal is kept intact.

Alcohol and Drugs: These two must be at the very top of every EPO's NO-list. Never consume any alcohol, no matter what type within a fourteen hour range of the beginning of the assignment. The smell of alcohol is not only offensive, but it signals everybody that the EPO is not reliable and ultimately his/her judgment might be impaired–his/her reactions are not accurate. The physical demands of the job are strenuous enough that, under the use of alcohol, the total effectiveness would result in a less responsive and less effective EPO. This is a condition which is not acceptable. This is also valid for the use of prescription drugs, which might have certain undesirable and, for this type of job, unacceptable side-effects. Staying away from an assignment by explaining that one had a few drinks is much easier and acceptable. Accepting an assignment and explaining later to the authorities why an incident took place and why alcohol is in one's system is worse and unacceptable. Like in the case of Princess Diana, three totally independent tests were run on the body of Henri Paul, the driver in the tragic crash. All tests determined the driver had a high blood alcohol level. No matter what, Henri Paul will always be remembered as the drunk driver who caused Diana's death.

Appearance and Dress Code: Both are the ingredients, necessary for the EPO's presence and image of respect. He/she must be well-groomed and properly dressed for the respective occasion. The hair should be conservatively cut and styled in an acceptable fashion–radical and fancy styling or colors are not acceptable. Facial hair should be either shaved or neatly trimmed. Face and hands should be washed, fingernails cleaned, manicured for female EPO. The dress of the EPO is usually a business suit with matching shirt and matching tie. The color one chooses for the suit gives a certain aura to the person who wears it. A black suit, for example, besides representing in many cultures the color for mourning, has something sinister, while a dark blue suit shows seriousness and authority. A dark black suit with very thin pinstripes looks serene and professional. Based on my own experience, it will not hurt to consult with your principal directly, if you work independently. Otherwise consult with your team leader–sometimes principals demand a certain dress code for everyday duty and for receptions. Once, working on an assignment, the principal demanded us to wear a suit from a certain label only. While on another assignment in the Middle East, the entire team was dressed according to the regional customs. There is actually no exact directive for what one wears, but consulting with the boss will never hurt. With a perfect looking and good fitting suit one should wear a matching pair of comfortable and polished shoes. The basic rule for appropriate clothing is: know the itinerary of the principal, consult if necessary and dress according to the function or meeting.

Body Language: As a personality trait, the body language gives away what the person represents and feels, whether the person is confident, alert, enthusiastic, and totally capable and committed to being in control of any type of situation. It is this nonverbal communication of the body that will often signal to the observing public the relationship between the principal and his/her EPO. It might tell whether the EPO will go to extremes if necessary for his principal, or if the officer is with the principal only for the glamour and the money. These types of signals can spark a transgression toward the principal and cause the lack of respect for his/her protection.

Eating and Behavior: As an EPO on duty, never consume any food, beverages, not even chewing gum or cigarettes, in the presence of the principal or visible to the public–unless the situation allows or requires him/her to do so. An EPO walking along with the principal and carrying a soda bottle in his/her hands does not look professional–even if it might be the half-empty bottle from the principal. If the EPO would have called attention to this, before moving, the principal probably would have appreciated such concern.

If the principal is eating in a restaurant and the EPO is given the opportunity to eat as well, then he/she should make proper arrangements and take the meal at a different table. The EPO should easily observe from his/her table the surrounding area and the principal's table. Usually, there is time and it is part of the advance work to meet such arrangements prior to arrival. Order a simple meal that is ready in a short time and can be consumed before the principal is finished. The meal you choose should be according to the restaurant's terms–meaning that you would not order a *Burger King*-style hamburger with fried potatoes in a *Four-Forks*-class restaurant. But you might order *à la carte* or a *Bifteck Haché à la Lyonnaise* (French burger) with a butter sauce laced with thyme, sautéed vegetables and roasted potatoes, nicely served on a warm plate. Do not order any food that is messy, time consuming, and difficult to eat, such as spaghetti, lobster, or two-course meals. If by any chance the EPO is invited either by the host or spouse to join the meal, the EPO should politely decline or be as discrete as possible. It is important for any EPO to be knowledgeable beyond the basic table manners, in addition to those of foreign cultures.

Pay attention to the table setting. Use knives (meat-knife for meat, fish-knife for fish, butter-knife for bred or desert), forks (small fork for desert, larger one for the food), spoons (small one for desert, larger one for soup), plates and drinking glasses (water, wine) in their proper way.

Informal Table Setting *

Above the plate, from left to right:
- Bread and butter plate
- Butter knife
- Water/wineglass

Plate row from left to right:
- Napkin
- Salad fork
- Dinner fork
- Plate
- Dinner knife

* Slight variations may apply based on restaurant/hotel standards

Formal Table Setting *

Above the plate, from left to right:
- Salt and pepper
- Dessert fork and spoon
- Water and wineglasses

Plate row from left to right:
- Fish fork
- Dinner fork
- Salad fork
- Rim soup plate
- Plate
- Napkin
- Salad knife
- Dinner knife
- Fish knife
- Soupspoon

* Slight variations may apply based on restaurant/hotel standards

Never take large amounts of food to your mouth. Never dive for the food, but bring the food to your mouth. Do not hook the napkin into your collar and never wipe your mouth, but rather tip the corners of your mouth with the napkin. Do not place the used napkin on the table, but on your lap. Never overload your plate (even if it is the very first decent meal in several hours). Do not devour your food like it is to be the last meal. Take the food and eat it with a sense of good taste. Once you finish, excuse yourself politely and retreat to an area out of the public eye. Most of the time, the EPO will find ways to make it easier to arrange for meals. Whatever the occasion or event, make sure to carry a nutritious but not "heavy" sandwich or similar energy source in a pocket or emergency-pouch. Chewing gum, even though considered to be useful, for example to help to keep awake (or as an alternative for smoking), and smoking is not acceptable and should be avoided. If standing out of public sight and without being in direct contact with the principal, staff members, or visitors, chewing gum might be acceptable. Smoking, however, is a different issue. Especially when smoking in the dark, the EPO can easily be spotted, not to mention the smell, and the pile of cigarette butts on the ground, when staying at a post for several hours.

Attitude, Courtesy, Diplomacy: Of course, nobody likes somebody grouchy and impertinent. If this is the type of attitude of the EPO, then it is no wonder, he/she soon will realize, an alienation from colleagues and little cooperation and even less respect will be the result. Such attitude will reflect poorly on the principal and provoke a hostile environment. A professional EPO must be self-confident and assured, but friendly, helpful, and diplomatic. The proper manners and conduct reflect a good attitude and will help to gain respect and cooperation. "Please," "Thank you," "Yes Sir," "No Madam," and "Excuse me," are still the magic words and phrases in any language and are rewarded with equal attitude and respect. Addressing a man, a woman, a teenager properly with "Sir," "Madam," "Young lady," will equally be respected. Sometimes, those small details can give you access to many things. It also might happen after working for a principal for some time that he/she prefers to be addressed with their first name. This happens very often, most likely caused by the unavoidable close relationship between principal and EPO. This type of situation gives all too often a wrong impression and leads to wrong reactions; therefore, one should put a distance from such familiarity. Being polite and kind is not something from yesterday, and courtesy will always bring the deserved respect. While dealing with people, it is always the best approach to treat everybody with dignity and consideration.

Expressing kind words with a gentle manner is the foundation for authority and influence. In order to have people cooperate with us, we have to show them courtesy–the result is obvious; they will give us what we want, and we will also gain their respect. Working with service staff and especially with host committees is sometimes difficult task. After all, everybody's purpose is to make sure that their Boss is the center of attention and seen in the most favorable conditions. Goals and purpose of security, however, is under such conditions often directly conflicting. Satisfying both of the requirements takes a lot of tact and finesse. Diplomacy is the sophisticated art of convincing someone to believe, that it is their own idea to do what, in the end, we want the person to be done.

Service Rendering: It is in the best intention of the EPO to provide the best possible services to the client or the principal, no matter who they are. Only one type of service is acceptable–the utmost professional one. Being responsible for the health, well-being, safety, and life of an individual, private, or corporate entity and providing lousy and unprofessional service or conducting oneself in an improper and nonprofessional manner should not be accepted as an EPO. In many countries it is considered a criminal act when rendering poor services and, as result of negligence, a tragic incident results.

The Limits: The EPO should not ever take unnecessary risks. Times will come when a principal will expect a performance of an activity which is simply beyond the capability of the EPO. So what should the EPO do? If the consequences are clearly visible and by attempting such an activity the outcome would be injury, death, or legal action, then the answer is: do not do it. Sometimes the principal might insist–which leaves no options to the EPO. Since declining or discouraging the principal does not show the desired response, the EPO has nothing else to do but to resign from the job. There are times when it is physically impossible to work because of illness or fatigue. Recognize those limitations in due course and make arrangements for a replacement. Attempting to work while suffering with a fever or any other condition limits the ability to provide the proper service. Inadequate or impaired ability could result in miscalculations and mistakes, which can cause accidents, injury, or worse–death.

The EPO's Equipment

A very popular question from students and people interested in the executive protection profession is–what is an EPOs equipment and where does he/she put all that stuff? Apart from the weapon, every EPO has a small set of tools and useful items, which can be easily accessed. This multipurpose kit contains basic and essential items and is upgraded according to each officer's own needs.

The following list of equipment items will provide detailed information and specifications of each item contained in the multipurpose kit. The professionals among us are used to utilize their equipment of preference and might have some suggestions regarding the different makes or models. However, the client and new EPO, not so familiar with the equipment will have a closer look on the items contained in the kit and will find it useful to make an adequate selection. Referring to a specific brand or model in this context is a matter of personal preference and should assist with the indicated specifications to build a functional kit. It is not meant to standardize the multipurpose kit for EPOs. Let's not forget–your life and that of the principal depends on the right choice and performance of the selected equipment. The selection of lifesaving equipment should never be influenced by a budget factor.

The kit consists of:

Primary Items:

- ► 1 Weapon (primary and backup) and extra ammunition
- ► 1 Holster system, allowing to carry the firearm in a belt or shoulder holster
- ► 1 Baton (retractable autolocking) for self-defense or crowd control

- ▶ 1 Cellular phone (encrypted with military level cryptography)
- ▶ 1 Tactical folding knife (drop-point blade)
- ▶ 1 Tactical sunglasses (interchangeable lenses) with spare lenses
- ▶ 1 Double cuff restraints (nylon)
- ▶ 1 Radio (two-way) with throat mic or earbud with clip-on mic

Secondary Items:

- ▪ 1 Notebook computer (with tactical software, e. g. GPS, satellite imaging, surveillance, etc.)
- ▪ 6 Video Cameras (wide range, small, wireless, day and night capability)
- ▪ 1 Flashlight for search and emergency situations
- ▪ 1 Multiplier (multitask tool with screw drivers, wire cutter etc.)
- ▪ 1 Monocular (with nightvision capability)
- ▪ 1 First Aid/Medical (tactical trauma kit)
- ▪ 1 Tactical Vest
- ▪ 1 Rain jacket

Kit Content in detail:

- ▶ 1 Weapon (primary and backup) and extra ammunition

While operating in your own region/country, the weapon of choice as the primary and backup weapon will be the one you purchased and you are familiar with. If you operate outside your territory, and you are not able to take your own weapon on the assignment, you might have to choose, based on availability. Select a weapon which by caliber and specification is similar to yours. In this case, check the weapon and ammo carefully and demand to have some practicing with that weapon.

- ▶ 1 Holster *"Galco X-Project"* * system, allowing to carry the firearm in a belt-or shoulder holster

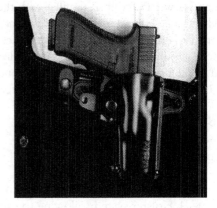

The X-Project Shoulder/Belt Holster System provides gun carriers with a unique, secure, dual-purpose holster that functions equally well as a comfortable and highly concealable shoulder system, or as a convenient and concealable belt holster.

The system consists of three major components: a holster with retention strap, a shoulder harness, and a belt attachment.

The holster quickly secures to the ambidextrous, fully adjustable shoulder harness by mushroom-shaped pins found on the oval harness plates, which allow the holster to be quickly attached and removed from the harness. The innovative design of the attachment pins offer the unique ability to wear the shoulder harness under a shirt, while the holster is attached outside the shirt.

---

* Indicating a specific brand name is a matter of personal preference. It is not intended to be or to set a standard for EPO equipment.

► 1 Baton (retractable auto-locking) *"Monadnock AutoLock"** for self-defense or crowd control

Specification:
- Size:
  16", 18", 21", 22", 26"
- Grips:
  Super Grip® and Foam Grip
- Tips:
  Safety Tip®, Power Safety Tip®,
  3xT Power Safety Tip
- Ball-bearing action with build-in safety future

---

* Indicating a specific brand name is a matter of personal preference. It is not intended to be or to set a standard for EPO equipment.

► 1 Cellular phone *"Sc-3200"** (encrypted with military level cryptography)

Buying a cell phone is easy; buying one to be useful for this type of activity is more complex. Let's be rational; what do we need a G3 cell phone with MP3 player, TV/FM radio receiver, megapixel camera and service provider contract for, when everybody can listen into our conversations of a sensitive and classified nature. What we really need is a 3-band GSM, highly encrypted cell phone, which is easily handled and operational everywhere. The Sc-3200 (in this case a rugged Nokia phone) comes with an ultra high encryption program, absolutely secure and unbreakable. It utilizes military level cryptography which disables all types of eavesdropping to calls between 2 or more sc-3200 devices. The devices work on the standard GSM telephony network. Calls made to other cellular devices, which don't have sc-3200 are the same as a normal cellular phone.

---

* Indicating a specific brand name is a matter of personal preference. It is not intended to be or to set a standard for EPO equipment.

► 1 Tactical folding knife *"Benchmade"** (drop-point blade)

Specification:
- Drop-Point Blade Shape with Clip-Point and ambidextrous thumb-studs
- Locking-Liner mechanism
- 440C Stainless Steel (58-60HRC)
- Length: 2.97"
- Open: 6.84"
- Weight: 3.4oz

* Indicating a specific brand name is a matter of personal preference. It is not intended to be or to set a standard for EPO equipment.

► 1 Tactical sunglasses *"ESS CDI"** (interchangeable lenses) with spare lenses

Specification:
- 2.2mm Lenses
- interchangeable Lenses
- ANSI-compliant
- Mil Spec, Color: Black
- Rx-Insert available prescription lenses easily fit into the RX-inserts

* Indicating a specific brand name is a matter of personal preference. It is not intended to be or to set a standard for EPO equipment.

► 1 Double cuff restraints *"Monadnock"** (nylon)

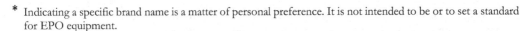
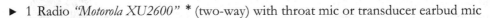

Specification:
- can be used on both wrists and ankles
- ½ inch wide plastic strip ensures it won't cut
- Color: black tactical

* Indicating a specific brand name is a matter of personal preference. It is not intended to be or to set a standard for EPO equipment.

► 1 Radio *"Motorola XU2600"** (two-way) with throat mic or transducer earbud mic

Specifications:
- two-way radio
- range up to 6 miles outdoors and 250, 000 sq. ft. or 20 floors indoors
- 2-watt technology provides up to four times the power of family radios
- multi-channel operation with 121 Interference Eliminator Codes (83 Digital and 38 Analog)
- voice-activated, hands-free operation (VOX) capability. No accessories required.

* Indicating a specific brand name is a matter of personal preference. It is not intended to be or to set a standard for EPO equipment.

▶ 1 Notebook *"Panasonic Toughbook-19"* * computer (with tactical software, e. g. GPS, satellite imaging, surveillance, etc.)

Specification:

- Intel® Centrino®Duo Mobile Technology
- 10.4" daylight-readable color LCD swivels for optimum visibility
- Simultaneous access to wireless WAN, wireless LAN, BluetoothTM and GPS
- Pressure-sensitive touch screen can be used with a stylus or the touch of a finger (also available with pen-only digitizer screen)
- 5 lbs, lightweight design
- Full magnesium alloy case with handle
- Moisture-and dust-resistant LCD, keyboard and touch pad
- Sealed port and connector covers
- Shock-mounted removable hard drive in stainless steel case

With one quick swivel, the wireless Toughbook 19 transforms from a fully-rugged maximum-performance notebook PC to a fully-rugged handwriting-friendly tablet PC. Take handwritten notes, mark and edit documents and draw diagrams. It even converts handwriting to printed text.

* Indicating a specific brand name is a matter of personal preference. It is not intended to be or to set a standard for EPO equipment.

▶ 6 Video Cameras 2.4 Ghz * (wide range, small, wireless, day and night capability)

Specification:
- Night-vision (>15 meters)
- Auto-scan between 4 selected channels
- High-quality wireless color camera with CMOS sensor: 628*582

- Transmission/Receiving frequency: 2.4GHz
- Transmission power: 10mW
- Built-in microphone
- Valid distance: 50m-150m
- Horizontal definition: 380TV line

Wireless cameras are a useful addition for any mobile surveillance job. Easy to set up with a laptop computer and suitable for any monitoring needs while on the road.

* Indicating a specific brand name is a matter of personal preference. It is not intended to be or to set a standard for EPO equipment.

► 1 Flashlight *"Streamlight Scorpion"** for search and emergency situations

Specification:
- Triple action tail cap switch (encases a spare bulb)
- Xenon gas filled bi-pin bulb
- Variable spot to flood focus
- 6, 500 candlepower tactical flashlight
- Variable spot to flood focus
- Includes two lithium batteries and spare bulb
- Unbreakable polycarbonate lens
- 4. 9 inches in length
- 4. 4 ounces with batteries
- Machined aluminum body, covered with a rubber armored sleeve for a sure grip

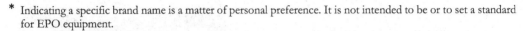

* Indicating a specific brand name is a matter of personal preference. It is not intended to be or to set a standard for EPO equipment.

► 1 Multiplier *"Gerber Diesel"** (multi-task tool with screw drivers, wire cutter etc.)

Specification:
- Tools lock for safety
- Blunt nose pliers
- Tool kit with adapter and six bits
- Overall Length: 6.56"
- Length Closed: 5"
- Weight: 11.1 oz.
- Handle Material: Stainless Steel
- Sheath: Ballistic nylon

- Components:
Blunt nose pliers, wire cutter, wire crimper, fine edge knife, serrated knife, cross point screwdriver, small, medium and large flat blade screwdrivers, lanyard ring, can opener, bottle opener, file, and ruler. Tool kit with six bits and adapter.

* Indicating a specific brand name is a matter of personal preference. It is not intended to be or to set a standard for EPO equipment.

► 1 Monocular *"N-Vision Pro"** (with nightvision capability)

Specification:
- Generation   2+
- Resolution   40+ lp/mm
- Field of View 15°
- Magnification 2.9x
- Dimensions, in 7.1 x 3.3 x 2.3
- Battery Type CR123 (1)
- Weight, lbs   1.5

Rugged and weather-proof body built with premium grade cast aluminum, 80mm objective lens, centrally positioned power control to suit left-handed as well as right-handed users, high-performance infrared illuminator with adjustable intense narrow "beam" and wide-angle "flood" modes, integrated tripod mount and N-Vision SLT (Super Light Transition) lens coating technology.

▶ 1 First Aid/Medical (tactical trauma kit)

Specification:
- Dimensions: 6 1/4" W x 9" H x 3 1/4" D
- Sam Splint 36
- CPR MicroShield
- NeoPro Exam Gloves
- Combat Application Tourniquet
- Space Blanket
- EMT Paramedic Shears, 5 1/2
- EMT Paramedic Shears, 7 1/4
- Lister Bandage Scissors, 4 ½
- Triangular Bandage, 37" x 37
- Swift Wrap Elastic Bandage, 2" x 5yds
- Swift Wrap Elastic Bandage, 3" x 5yds
- Swift Wrap Elastic Bandage, 4" x 5yds
- Multi-Trauma Dressing, 12" x 30
- Bloodstopper Trauma Dressing
- Multi-Trauma Dressing, 12" x 30
- Cloth Tape, 1" x 10yds

This is only a small list of items. Some of the kits on the market are very nicely assembled by professionals. So the best is, to get a ready assembled kit and add whatever a special situation or emergency might require.

▶ 1 Tactical Vest *"Web-Tex"** with belt

Specification:
- waterproof Cordura® nylon.
- adjustable pouches for magazines, flashlights and other items
- radio pouch
- cross-draw holster
- sniper shoulder and two internal pockets
- side lace adjustment

▶ 1 Rain jacket

The rain jacket should be black or dark blue, of a 100% waterproof/water-repellent material with a zip-out acrylic lining for isolation. The jacket should be of knee-length with two pockets outside and some storage compartments on the inside. The closure should be with Velcro® fastener (no buttons or zipper) for quick access. The material and look of the jacket should be suitable for any event appearance.

All these items are grouped by priority. The EPO will carry the primary items on the person, like the holster with the weapon and spare magazine/s, retractable baton, nylon restraints, tactical folding knife, sunglasses and cellular phone. The secondary items of no immediate use, such as flashlight with spare batteries, multiplier tool, spare lenses for sunglasses, binocular with spare batteries (if applicable), tactical vest, first aid kit, and rain jacket will be stored within range. They must be easy to access, stored in either a briefcase or a small tactical bag. Besides this type of equipment kit, the EPO will also need in his bag maps, photos, report forms, schedules, his/her filed folder with vital data, such as emergency contact telephone numbers. Always helpful on the road is a package of pain relievers (with a minimum of side effects), a few high calorie nutrients (liquid, capsule or bar). Further, extra writing utensils, small measuring tape, calculator, small digital camera, spare car keys. Disposable gloves, travel kit with razor and toothbrush, Band-Aids, insect repellent, travel sewing kit, paper clips, and safety pins and anything else that will assist the EPO in the job. Some items might need to be added according to the area of operation and time of year. Apart from all this, the EPO will need passport, national ID-Card, Driver's License (national and international), Weapons Permit (national and international) and EPO ID-Card with badge. Further an International Vaccination Certificate, business cards, pre-paid credit cards, pre-paid SIM cards for cellular phone and pre-paid calling card for public phones. Once everything is checked and packed, the EPO is ready for the assignment.

The Weapons

When choosing a personal-duty firearm, the EPO must consider several very important factors. The weapon must have the desired stopping power. Another of importance is the penetration force of the projectile through the human body. For example, if during a protective assignment, a weapon has to be fired, most likely this would be in crowded environment. Under such conditions, one cannot risk that any nearby person/s get possibly wounded or killed. The penetration force should be only enough that the bullet is stopping, but not passing through the intended target. A good selection is the hollow-point ammunition, which has much better stopping-power than the full-metal jacket or round-nose lead. This stopping-power (also called "knock-down power") refers to a particular bullet's ability to incapacitate an attacker. With other words, the greater the stopping-power, the less chances are the attacker will be able to continue shooting, stabbing, or beating after he is shot (see Fig. 1).

Contrary to what one sees in the movies, handguns are weak compared to rifles and shotguns, which because of their build and ammunition have stopping-power to spare. The vast majority of people shot with handguns survive (that is over 80%). Therefore, one must select the handgun load very carefully (see Fig. 2 and 3).

Hollow-point ammunition is NOT more lethal than *ball* (full-metal jacket) ammunition.[7] Hollow-point bullets usually expand and stop in the human body. Thus the attacker absorbs much more of the bullet's kinetic energy than if the bullet had merely zipped through him and left two small holes. Hollow-point ammunition, according to many, is considered safer for all parties concerned:

- The attacker is more likely to be incapacitated after one or two shots and thus unable to fire back, stab or use any other means of attack. The decreased likelihood of an attacker dying from a hollow-point bullet is saving from moral and legal complications one will experience by killing a man.

- Innocent by-standers are safer because hollow-point bullets are less likely to exit the attacker's body and travel on to injure anyone else nearby. The ricochet danger is also much lower than that of *ball*-ammunition. Furthermore, hollow-point bullets are less likely to penetrate walls or doors and strike any non-involved third parties. If an attacker is incapacitated quickly, he won't be able to endanger someone else.

- Lastly, the attacker is safer because he is far less likely to die of one or two hollow-point bullets. Most gunshot deaths occur from shock and loss of blood, and *ball*-rounds tend to make entry and exit wounds, whereas hollow-points go in and stay put. An attacker shot twice with *ball*-ammo will probably have four holes in him rather than two and is thus in far greater danger of death from blood loss. If one can avoid killing an attacker one should, for both moral and legal reasons.

The firearm, whether pistol or revolver must be accurate, of lightweight, easy to grip, handle and rest comfortable in the hand and concealable. Shooting in close quarters is an instinctive point and shoot technique, which does not require any specific sights. For night operations, however, the weapon should be equipped with Trijicon 3-Dot night sights. The ammunition should have a high stopping and disabling, such as the Hydra-Shok® bullet, which is the choice of law enforcement agencies nationwide. Federal's unique center-post design delivers controlled expansion, and the notched jacket provides efficient energy transfer to penetrate barriers while retaining stopping power. The deep penetration of this jacketed bullet satisfies even the FBI's stringent testing requirements.

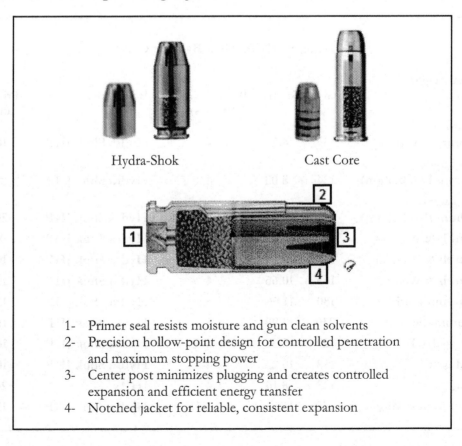

Hydra-Shok   Cast Core

1- Primer seal resists moisture and gun clean solvents
2- Precision hollow-point design for controlled penetration and maximum stopping power
3- Center post minimizes plugging and creates controlled expansion and efficient energy transfer
4- Notched jacket for reliable, consistent expansion

Fig. 1

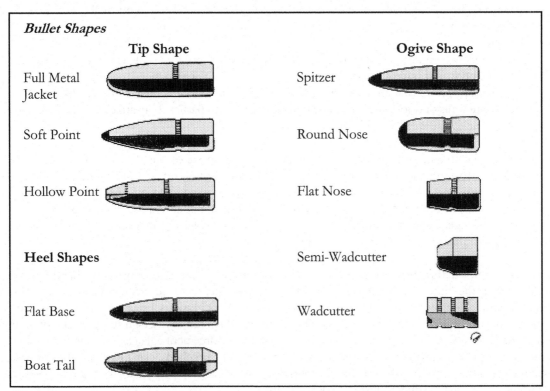

Bullet Shapes

Tip Shape	Ogive Shape
Full Metal Jacket	Spitzer
Soft Point	Round Nose
Hollow Point	Flat Nose
Heel Shapes	Semi-Wadcutter
Flat Base	Wadcutter
Boat Tail	

Fig. 2

Handgun-Hydra Shok Ballistic Chart

Bullet Weight Caliber	Grains	Grams	Barrel Length (Inches)	Bullet Style	Primer Number
32 Auto (7.65mm Browning)	65	4.21	4	Hydra Shok JHP	100
9mm Luger (9x19mm Parabellum)	124	8.03	4	Hydra Shok JHP	200
9mm Luger (9x19mm Parabellum)	147	9.52	4	Hydra Shok JHP	200
40 Smith & Wesson	180	11.66	4	Hydra Shok JHP	100
40 Smith & Wesson	155	10.04	4	Hydra Shok JHP	100
40 Smith & Wesson	165	10.66	4	Hydra Shok JHP	100
10mm Automatic	180	11.66	5	Hydra Shok JHP	150
45 Automatic	230	14.90	5	Hydra Shok JHP	150
38 Special + P	129	8.36	4-V	Hydra Shok JHP	100
357 Magnum	158	10.23	4-V	Hydra Shok JHP	100
357 Sig	125	8.10	4	JHP	200
44 Remington Magnum	240	15.55	6.5V	Hydra Shok JHP	150

Fig. 3

The 9mm Pistols:

The following are 9mm pistols, listed in three classes based on their reputation, experience and reliability to feed JHP properly. Even if the weapon of your choice is listed in Class III, does not necessarily mean it is unreliable–it may indeed feed hollow-point ammo. In this case I suggest to must fire at least 100-200 rounds of JHP carry load of you choice to determine if the pistol will feed those properly. Bear in mind, that these are only intended as a guideline.

Class I:

Pistols of this class are extremely reliable and high-quality new weapons, able to feed any hollow-point and tolerate +P loads without problems:
SIG/Sauer P220 series. *Czech* CZ75 and CZ85. *Walther* P5, P5C, and P88. *Heckler & Koch* USP and P7 series, all *Glock*-models. All *Ruger* 9mm pistols, *Taurus* PT-99, PT-92 and PT-92C, *Steyr* GB, *Beretta* 92 series. *Browning* BDM and Hi-Power (marked 'Portugal' on the slide), all *Smith & Wessons* with a four-digit model number (e. g. 5906, 3913) and the 900 series, Star M28, M30, M31.

Class II:

The pistols of this category are high quality weapons that may not feed all hollow-point types reliably. The *Remington* 115 gr. Hollow-point is recommended for the following makes:
Smith & Wesson with two or three digit model numbers (e. g. 39-2, 469, 59, 39), *Heckler & Koch* VP70, P9S, *Beretta* 'Brigadier' M1951 and its Egyptian copy, the *Interarms* 'Helwan'. *Colt* Series 70 Government Model and Series 70 Commander, *Astra* A-70, A-75 and A-100, *AMT* 'On Duty'. *Bersa* 'Thunder 9', *EAA* Witness, and all other CZ-75 copies (e. g. Tanfoglio, Tanarmi, Springfield Armory P9). *Taurus* PT-908, *Walther* P4, *Star* BK, BKM, Model B and 'Super', *Browning* Hi-Powers (without 'Portugal' on the slide), *Llama* Model 82, *IMI* 'Jericho' and 'Kareen'.

Class III:

These pistols should generally be loaded with ball for best reliability (experiment with the weapon extensively before carrying any JHP):
Walther P38, P4 or P1, *Luger*, *Llama*, *Maverick*, *MKS* Model JS, *Intratec* CAT-9, DC-9, KG-9, *SWD* Cobray Model 11/9 and similar models. *Scarab* Scorpion, *Kimel* AP-9, *Bryco Jennings* Model 59, All *KBI* Hungarian pistols (e. g. GKK, PJ9C, P9HK and other *FEG* products), Chinese *Tokarev* 'Norinco' or 'Sportarms', *Lahti*, *Radom*, *MAB* P15 and Model 1950.

EPOs that work for the private executive protection or security companies, contrary to government agencies, often carry their own weapons of choosing. This is a matter of preference and comfort. When operating as a team, however, the most appropriate is to select a handgun of the same make and caliber issued to all team members. In this way, full magazines can easily be exchanged among the members, in case one is running low on ammo, especially when a situation reveals to be a hairy one.

Today's demand is directed to more firepower and if available more magazine capacity. Many officers are using the *Glock* .40-caliber or 9mm. The compact and lightweight construction, accuracy and easy concealment is a certain advantage compared with other makes and models. This might be true, but it is also depending on each EPO's point of view. Agents of the U. S. Secret Service, for example, are issued the 9mm *SIG-Sauer* P228 with special ammunition. German agencies are using *Glock* and/or H&K 9mm pistols. In some cases, the available supply from national developers and manufacturers is the most decisive factor in selecting the model and make of the weapon, which is apart from essential factors (like reliability, accuracy, suitability and specific needs of a particular agency). On the other hand, this does not necessarily express, reflect, nor respond to the real demand and the needs of the officer in the field.

Beretta *Cougar* D

Technical Data

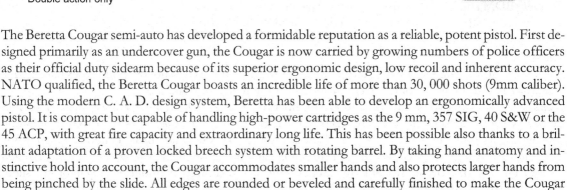

Manufacturer:	Beretta-Italy
Caliber:	357 SIG
Mag. capacity:	11
Overall length:	180 mm
Barrel length:	92 mm
Height:	140 mm
Width:	38 mm
Weight:	905 g
Sights:	3-dot sight, 3-dot tritium night
Trigger:	DAO *
Safety:	ambidextrous safety de-cocking lever, rotating firing pin striker, automatic firing pin block, chamber-loaded indicator

* Double action only

The Beretta Cougar semi-auto has developed a formidable reputation as a reliable, potent pistol. First designed primarily as an undercover gun, the Cougar is now carried by growing numbers of police officers as their official duty sidearm because of its superior ergonomic design, low recoil and inherent accuracy. NATO qualified, the Beretta Cougar boasts an incredible life of more than 30, 000 shots (9mm caliber). Using the modern C. A. D. design system, Beretta has been able to develop an ergonomically advanced pistol. It is compact but capable of handling high-power cartridges as the 9 mm, 357 SIG, 40 S&W or the 45 ACP, with great fire capacity and extraordinary long life. This has been possible also thanks to a brilliant adaptation of a proven locked breech system with rotating barrel. By taking hand anatomy and instinctive hold into account, the Cougar accommodates smaller hands and also protects larger hands from being pinched by the slide. All edges are rounded or beveled and carefully finished to make the Cougar virtually snag-proof and exceptionally easy to draw and conceal.

Beretta PX4 *Storm* F

Technical Data

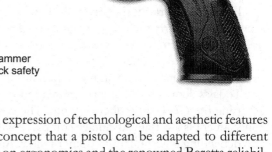

Manufacturer:	Beretta-Italy
Caliber:	9 x 19
Mag. capacity:	17
Overall length:	192 mm
Barrel length:	102 mm
Height:	140 mm
Width:	36 mm
Weight:	785 g
Sights:	Superluminova 3-dot
Trigger:	SA/ DA *
Safety:	ambidextrous manual safety on slide with hammer de-cocking function, automatic firing pin block safety

* Single action/ Double action

The new Beretta Px4 Storm pistol is the most advanced expression of technological and aesthetic features in a semiautomatic sidearm. Built around a modular concept that a pistol can be adapted to different needs and modes of operations, without compromising on ergonomics and the renowned Beretta reliability and performance, the Px4 Storm emphasizes power, ease of handling, performance and reliability. Initially manufactured in three calibers, the Px4 Storm uses an exclusive Beretta designed innovative locked-breech with rotating barrel system, the strongest action to date. The light yet durable frame employs modern thermoplastic technology through the use of technopolymer reinforced fiberglass.
Modular structure, ergonomics and interchangeability of parts make the Px4 Storm the ideal firearm for law-enforcement use, as well as personal defense. Available models and calibers: Px4 Storm F-9mmx19,

Px4 Storm G-9mmx19, Px4 Storm G-.40 S&W, Px4 Storm F-.40 S&W (45 ACP), Px4 Storm SD Type F-45 ACP. The high definition 3-dot sight system sports white indicators treated with Superluminova®, a special photosensitive material that makes them extremely visible even in darkness. A few minutes of exposure to light, even artificial light, are enough to ensure long lasting luminescence to the dots. The rear and front sights can be removed for replacement with other types.

Beretta 90 *two*

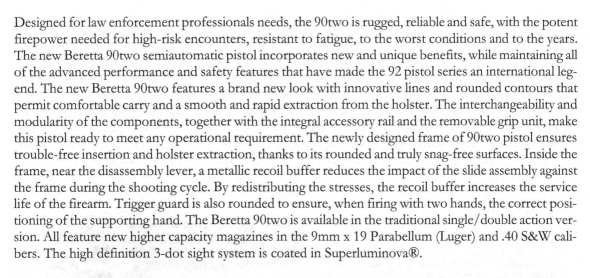

Technical Data

Manufacturer:	Beretta-Italy
Caliber:	9 x 19, .40 S&W
Mag. capacity:	10, 15, 17
Overall length:	216 mm
Barrel length:	125 mm
Height:	140 mm
Width:	38 mm
Weight:	920 g
Sights:	Superluminova 3-dot
Trigger:	SA/DA *
Safety:	ambidextrous manual safety on slide with hammer de-cocking function, automatic firing pin block safety.

* Single action/ Double action

Designed for law enforcement professionals needs, the 90two is rugged, reliable and safe, with the potent firepower needed for high-risk encounters, resistant to fatigue, to the worst conditions and to the years. The new Beretta 90two semiautomatic pistol incorporates new and unique benefits, while maintaining all of the advanced performance and safety features that have made the 92 pistol series an international legend. The new Beretta 90two features a brand new look with innovative lines and rounded contours that permit comfortable carry and a smooth and rapid extraction from the holster. The interchangeability and modularity of the components, together with the integral accessory rail and the removable grip unit, make this pistol ready to meet any operational requirement. The newly designed frame of 90two pistol ensures trouble-free insertion and holster extraction, thanks to its rounded and truly snag-free surfaces. Inside the frame, near the disassembly lever, a metallic recoil buffer reduces the impact of the slide assembly against the frame during the shooting cycle. By redistributing the stresses, the recoil buffer increases the service life of the firearm. Trigger guard is also rounded to ensure, when firing with two hands, the correct positioning of the supporting hand. The Beretta 90two is available in the traditional single/double action version. All feature new higher capacity magazines in the 9mm x 19 Parabellum (Luger) and .40 S&W calibers. The high definition 3-dot sight system is coated in Superluminova®.

Ceská CZ 75 B

Technical Data

Manufacturer:	Czech Ceská Zborjovka
Caliber:	9 mm Luger / 9 x 21 / .40 S&W
Mag. capacity:	16 / 16 / 10
Overall length:	206 mm
Barrel length:	120 mm
Height:	138 mm
Width:	~ 35 mm
Weight:	1000 g
Sights:	3-dot sight
Trigger:	SA/ DA *
Safety:	manual safety; safety stop on hammer; firing pin safety

* Single action/ Double action

Large capacity double-column magazine, comfortable grip in either hand, good results at instinctive shooting (without aiming), low trigger pull weight, high accuracy of fire, long service life and outstanding reliability -even when using various types of cartridges. The slide stays open after the last cartridge has been fired; the sights are outfitted with a three-dot illuminating system for better aiming in poor visibility conditions, suitable for combat-shooting. Versions differ in their caliber, size, weight, magazine capacity, trigger mechanism operation, safety elements, surface finish, grip panel types and other specific modifications. The pistols of the CZ 75 line are semi-automatic handguns with a locked breech principle.

Ceská CZ 75 SP-01 *Shadow*

Technical Data

Manufacturer:	Czech Ceská Zborjovka
Caliber:	9 x 19
Mag. capacity:	18
Overall length:	207 mm
Barrel length:	120 mm
Height:	147 mm
Width:	37 mm
Weight:	1180 g
Sights:	3-dot sight
Trigger:	SA/ DA *
Safety:	manual safety; safety stop on hammer
*	Single action/ Double action

This new generation of CZ 75 SP-01 pistol is especially adapted according to suggestions as proposed by users from Law Enforcement, Military and Police communities worldwide. The CZ 75 SP-01 *Shadow* features no firing pin block, which consequently helps to slightly reduce trigger pull weight and improves trigger travel properties. Pistol frame, which comes from a new mold, incorporates alterations such as recess beneath the trigger guard and beavertail to enable a higher grip of this handgun. Slightly "weaker" recoil spring originating from standard production CZ 75/85 pistols facilitates loading and enhances the shooting comfort. Sights consisting of fiber optics front sight and tactical "*Novak style*" rear sight to promote much easier, faster and more accurate target acquisition. Round off edges of magazine well, substantially improve reloading. This new generation of CZ 75 SP-01 Shadow pistol is appropriate for service use and self-defense.

Ceská CZ 85 B

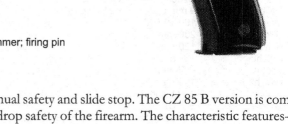

Technical Data

Manufacturer:	Czech Ceská Zborjovka
Caliber:	9 mm Luger / 9 x 21
Mag. capacity:	16
Overall length:	206 mm
Barrel length:	120 mm
Height:	138 mm
Width:	~ 35 mm
Weight:	1000 g
Sights:	3-dot sight
Trigger:	SA/ DA *
Safety:	manual safety; safety stop on the hammer; firing pin safety
*	Single action/ Double action

The CZ 85 B has ambidextrous control of the manual safety and slide stop. The CZ 85 B version is complemented with a firing pin safety to enhance the drop safety of the firearm. The characteristic features-a universal handgun for both left-and right-handers. The selective SA/DA firing mechanism, a large capacity double-column magazine, a comfortable grip and balance in either hand lead to good results at instinctive shooting (without aiming). Low trigger pull weight and high accuracy of fire. A long service life and outstanding reliability—even when using various types of cartridges. The slide stays open after the last cartridge has been fired, suitable for combat-shooting. The sights are fitted with a three-dot illuminating system for better aiming in poor visibility conditions. The combat-version features an adjustable rear sight by means of micrometer screws.

Ceská CZ 100

Technical Data

Manufacturer:	Czech Ceská Zborjovka
Caliber:	9 mm Luger / 9 x 21 / .40 S&W
Mag. capacity:	13 / 13 / 10
Overall length:	177 mm
Barrel length:	98 mm
Height:	130 mm
Width:	31 mm
Weight:	665 g
Sights:	solid or LPA
Trigger:	DAO *
Safety:	firing pin safety; DAO mode of fire

* Double action only

The CZ 100 belongs to a new range of high capacity semi-automatic pistols incorporating a locked breech. This pistol is distinguished by its modern conceptualization and the optimal combination of the frame with a high-impact plastic and steel slide. The consequently reduced weight significantly enhances the comfort of day-to-day carry. The trigger mechanism is a *DAO* type and incorporates a firing pin safety. The pistol is equipped with a single side slide stop and a magazine catch. Its operational and safety features justify ranking this handgun among the "load and forget" category. The characteristic feature, ergonomic shape, allows shooting with either hand. A comfortable grip and balance. Good results at instinctive shooting (without aiming). High accuracy of fire and a long service life. Outstanding reliability - even when using various types of bullets. Illuminated sights for aiming under poor visibility conditions. After each shot the firing pin returns to its rest position and is blocked there. The firing mechanism is uncocked, and the pistol is safe even when dropped. The wide trigger guard prevents snagging of the trigger by any objects, and any unintentional discharge during handling or dropping of the pistol. The slide can even be cocked with only one hand by positioning the rear sight or slide protrusion against any fixed edged object and levering against that point. The CZ 100 cal. 40 S&W is provided with compensator ports to reduce muzzle climb during firing.

Ceská CZ 110

Technical Data

Manufacturer:	Czech Ceská Zborjovka
Caliber:	9 mm Luger / 9 x 21 / .40 S&W
Mag. capacity:	13 / 13
Overall length:	180 mm
Barrel length:	98 mm
Height:	130 mm
Width:	31 mm
Weight:	665 g
Sights:	solid or LPA
Trigger:	SA/ DA *
Safety:	firing pin safety; loaded chamber indicator; cocking indication button; de-cocking lever

* Single action/ Double action

The CZ 110 belongs to a new range of high capacity semi-automatic pistols incorporating a locked breech. This pistol is distinguished by its modern conceptualization and the optimal combination of the frame with a high-impact plastic and steel slide. The consequently reduced weight significantly enhances the comfort of day-to-day carry. The pistol can be fired in either SA or DA modes of fire. Illuminated sights for aiming under poor visibility conditions. Its operational and safety features justify ranking this handgun among the "load and forget" category. This pistol is available in 9 mm Luger, 9x21, or .40 S&W calibers. The new CZ 110 pistol features a polymer frame, steel slide, high capacity magazine, extra accurate hammer-forged barrel, loaded chamber indicator, safety stop on the firing pin, de-cocking button, cocking indicator, accessory rail and SA/DA trigger mechanism.

Glock 28

Technical Data

Manufacturer:	Glock-Austria
Caliber:	.380 Auto
Mag. capacity:	10, 12, 15, 17, 19
Overall length:	160 mm
Barrel length:	88 mm
Height:	106 mm
Width:	30 mm
Weight:	529 g
Sights:	3-dot
Trigger:	SA *
Safety:	Trigger safety, firing pin safety, drop safety, load chamber indicator

*   Safe action firing mode

It employs innovative safety features, which makes the pistol easy to operate. It is exactly these characteristics that meet the requirements of police, special units, security services and the military. Whether strong masculine hands or delicate female hands, the pistol always feels as if it is made to measure. After comprehensive studies of the firing hand, a grip angle of 105% was chosen to provide best firing results. The grip design is based on the hand and equipped with a secure-grip profile. A secure weapon affording a secure grip. The Glock pistol is suitability for left and right-handed users alike. The special design of the operating elements, allows the index finger and thumb of left-handed person to assume the leading role for operation. The configuration of the operating elements for left and right-handed users also reduces the possibility of inadvertent firing. Small in dimensions and weight, it is great in performance when carried concealed. Because of the low-recoil firing characteristic of the .380 cartridge, it can be easily and accurately controlled. The standard magazine capacity of this balanced pistol of 10 rounds can be increased to 19 rounds when using optional magazines.

Glock 29

Technical Data

Manufacturer:	Glock-Austria
Caliber:	10mm Auto
Mag. capacity:	10, 15
Overall length:	172 mm
Barrel length:	96 mm
Height:	113 mm
Width:	32.5 mm
Weight:	700 g
Sights:	3-dot
Trigger:	SA *
Safety:	Trigger safety, firing pin safety, drop safety, load chamber indicator

*   Safe action firing mode

Superior versatility in the high-performance caliber 10mm: through reduced dimensions compared with the standard size Glock 20, the subcompact Glock 29 is also suitable for concealed carry. In addition to the use as backup weapon for hunting, more and more security personnel on patrol duty appreciate the comfortable firing characteristics and the grip ergonomics of the Glock 29 with a standard magazine capacity of 10 rounds.

Glock 31

Technical Data

Manufacturer:	Glock-Austria
Caliber:	. 357
Mag. capacity:	15, 17
Overall length:	186 mm
Barrel length:	114 mm
Height:	138 mm
Width:	30 mm
Weight:	660 g
Sights:	3-dot
Trigger:	SA *
Safety:	Trigger safety, firing pin safety, drop safety, load chamber indicator

* Safe action firing mode

The high-performance .357 is characterized by extremely high muzzle velocity and superior precision even at medium range. The Glock 31 is the optimum solution for all who are looking for these ballistic advantages in a reliable yet light pistol with large magazine capacity. Many law enforcement agencies have selected the Glock 31 as their official service weapon.

Glock 35

Technical Data

Manufacturer:	Glock-Austria
Caliber:	. 357
Mag. capacity:	15, 17
Overall length:	186 mm
Barrel length:	114 mm
Height:	138 mm
Width:	30 mm
Weight:	660 g
Sights:	3-dot
Trigger:	SA *
Safety:	Trigger safety, firing pin safety, drop safety, load chamber indicator

* Safe action firing mode

With its extended barrel and extended line of sight, the Glock 35 allows accurate hit patterns even with rapid firing. This has resulted in widespread distribution of the Glock 35 among the practical shooting community.

Glock 36

Six rounds of .45 Auto in a package that fits into the hands of any user. By using a single-stack magazine, the Glock 36 measures only a width of 28.5mm / 1.13 in. Together with the secure-grip design, this makes handling the pistol very easy. The pistol has 3-dot sights, SA-mode (safe action firing mode), trigger-, drop-, firing pin safety and loaded chamber indicator.

H&K P8

Technical Data

Manufacturer:	Heckler & Koch-Germany
Caliber:	9mm x 19
Mag. capacity:	15
Overall length:	194 mm
Barrel length:	108 mm
Height:	136 mm
Width:	38 mm
Weight:	720 g
Sights:	long glowing contrast points
Trigger:	DA/ DAO *
Safety:	reversed safety, de-cocker lever

* Double action/ Double action only

Upon exhaustive comparative trials, the Federal German Armed Forces selected the P8 as the service weapon. It differs from the USP particularly by the following features-the P8 specific arrangement of the safety and de-cocking lever, transparent magazine with special dust protection, barrel with lands-and grooves profile. The P8 system features are: the operation of the pistol, recoil operated weapon with locked breech and tilting barrel; braking of unlocking and buffer blow by a spring element. The grip made of glass fiber reinforced polymer with corrosion proof metal inserts; transparent magazine made of glass fiber reinforced polymer, magazine capacity 15 cartridges and open square notch rear sight with contrast points.

H&K P30

Technical Data

Manufacturer:	Heckler & Koch-Germany
Caliber:	9mm x 19
Mag. capacity:	15
Overall length:	194 mm
Barrel length:	108 mm
Height:	136 mm
Width:	38 mm
Weight:	720 g
Sights:	long glowing contrast points
Trigger:	DA/DAO *
Safety:	reversed safety, de-cocker lever

* Double action/ Double action only

The HK P30 pistol is the most recent creation of the famous German company Heckler und Koch Gmbh. It was announced in 2006; prototypes, initially known as HK P3000, were demonstrated during previous year. The P30 is a further evolution of the highly successful HK P2000 pistol; it is positioned by manufacturer as an ideal police pistol, but it also could make a very good self-defense weapon for civilians. HK P30 is technically similar to the HK P2000 pistol; the differences are in exterior appearance and ergonomics. P30 is available in several variants, which differ in the type of the trigger. The HK P30 pistol is short recoil operated, locked breech pistol that uses modified Browning-type locking. Frame of the pistol is made from impact-resistant polymer. Trigger unit is a separate module; several versions of the trigger unit are available, as described below. Other features of P30 include a double-stack magazine that holds 15 rounds of 9mm ammunition, with ambidextrous magazine release, ambidextrous slide release lever, and modular grip design. The grip shape can be tailored to the particular requirements of each shooter. This is achieved by replacing the removable backstraps and side grip panels (three sizes of either part are available). Front part of the frame, below the barrel, is shaped to form an integral Picatinny-type accessory rail.

H&K USP *Compact*

Technical Data

Manufacturer:	Heckler & Koch-Germany
Caliber:	9mm x 19, .45 AUTO, .40 S&W
Mag. capacity:	13, 12, 8
Overall length:	173 mm
Barrel length:	91 mm
Height:	127.5 mm
Width:	34 mm
Weight:	645 g
Sights:	long glowing contrast points
Trigger:	SA/ DA *
Safety:	reversed safety, de-cocker lever

* Single action/ Double action

The USP Compact is a narrow, compact pistol available in calibers 9 mm x19, .40 S & W and .45 AUTO. Based on the Standard USP Models, these handy pistols combine handy size with optimum accuracy. In the course of development, special emphasis has been placed on practical shooter requirements. This is why with the USP Compact the requirements of the police and military have been of decisive importance. The modular design gives the customer a choice among several trigger variants. In addition, the safety and de-cocking lever may simply be relocated for left handed shooters. Every shooter will thus find the weapon tailored to their specific requirement. Compared to some Subcompact pistols, the USP Compact has a handy grip with a selection of different, quickly interchangeable magazine floor plates. The USP is reliable, safe and accurate with the performances of a standard pistol and easy to carry in a concealed way. The modified browning operation is softened by a captive recoil spring and polymer absorbing bushing, which absorbs energy at the end of the slide's travel rearward (not quite as effective as the recoil system in the full-size USP). The Law Enforcement Modification (LEM) version provides Double Action Only (DOA) for consistent trigger pull (at two optional weight ranges), as preferred by some government agencies and police departments.

H&K P2000 SK

Technical Data

Manufacturer:	Heckler & Koch-Germany
Caliber:	9mm x 19
Mag. capacity:	10
Overall length:	163 mm
Barrel length:	83 mm
Height:	117 mm
Width:	32.5 mm
Weight:	606 g
Sights:	long glowing contrast points
Trigger:	CDA *
Safety:	reversed safety, de-cocker lever

* Combat Defense action

Compact, lightweight and handy. The new P2000 SubCompact combines all features expected for service use. The P2000 SK is based on the P2000. Irrespective of the small and lightweight design, no compromises to accuracy and reliability have been made. Thanks to its two inter-changeable backstrap inserts it may be adapted to hand-sizes of the individual users. The P2000 SK is a recoil operated weapon with locked breech and tilting barrel. The grip is made of glass fiber reinforced polymer with corrosion proof metal inserts and ambidextrous slide release. The interchangeable backstrap inserts are available in 2 different sizes (M and L). The pistol has an integrated support rail for aiming units and a magazine capacity of 10 cartridges. Sights consist of an open square notch rear sight with contrast points. The pistol has also an oversized recurved trigger guard for use with a gloved hand.

SIG-Sauer P220 *Crimson Trace*

Technical Data

Manufacturer:	SIG Sauer-Germany
Caliber:	. 45 ACP
Mag. capacity:	8
Overall length:	198 mm
Barrel length:	112 mm
Height:	143 mm
Width:	35 mm
Weight:	730 g
Sights:	contrast SIGlite-night sights
Trigger:	SA/DA/DAO *
Safety:	firing pin safety, de-cocker lever
*	Single action/ Double action/ Double action only

The P220 pistols are modern hand weapons complying with the latest technical advances in weapon design for military, police and sporting use. They operate on the principle of the mechanically locked, recoil-operated pistol with semi-automatic reloading. The automatic firing pin safety lock, safety notch on the hammer, de-cocking lever and the double-action trigger ensure safe carrying of the weapon and permanent, rapid firing readiness without actuating a manual safety lock. The de-cocking lever permits safe unlocking of the hammer in the safety notch without operation of the trigger. The firing pin remains locked during de-cocking by the automatic firing pin safety device. The distinctive contrast sights in conjunction with the ergonomically favorable grip design permit rapid, precision target acquisition and firing. The enclosed design prevents the penetration of dirt inside the weapon. SIG-Sauer pistols are available as Double-Action/Single-Action (DA/SA) as well as Double-Action-Only (DAO) models.
The DAO version has no de-cocking lever.

SIG-Sauer P220R *Carry*

Technical Data

Manufacturer:	SIG Sauer-Germany
Caliber:	. 45 ACP
Mag. capacity:	8
Overall length:	180 mm
Barrel length:	99 mm
Height:	139 mm
Width:	39 mm
Weight:	860 g
Sights:	contrast SIGlite-night sights
Trigger:	SA/DA/DAO *
Safety:	firing pin safety, thumb safety
*	Single action/ Double action/ Double action only

The P220R Carry is the latest step in the evolution of the P220. It is the most accurate out-of-the-box .45 and a perfect choice when it's time to carry the 'big caliber'. This "commander" sized pistol features a full-size frame with short slide and barrel, making it ideal for concealed carry. And like any P220, it performs above and beyond because the SIG-Sauer design allows for unparalleled performance regardless of bullet type or weight.

This 8+1 capacity pistol features a crisp 5-pound SAO trigger that breaks like glass and an ambidextrous thumb safety. The combination of SAO trigger, cold hammer forged barrel and near perfect lock-up offers shooters outstanding accuracy. This sets the P220 Carry apart from other 45s. The P220 Carry slide is machined from stainless steel bar stock and finished in a durable Nitron-finish. The lightweight alloy frame is hard-coat anodized and outfitted with a Picatinny rail for tactical versatility. The P220 Carry comes with either contrast or SIGLITE-night sights.

SIG-Sauer P226 *X-Five Tactical*

Technical Data

Manufacturer:	SIG Sauer-Germany
Caliber:	9mm only
Mag. capacity:	10, 15, 20
Overall length:	224 mm
Barrel length:	127 mm
Height:	136 mm
Width:	44 mm
Weight:	1319 g
Sights:	contrast SIGlite-night sights
Trigger:	SA/DA/DAO *
Safety:	firing pin safety, thumb safety
*	Single action/ Double action/ Double action only

The P226 X-Five Tactical utilizes a light-weight alloy frame with a Picatinny rail to provide the tactical edge. Features include ergonomic beavertail grip, standard single-action trigger w/ambidextrous thumb safety, post and dot contrast sights and polymer grips. The X-Five Tactical is nimble without sacrificing natural pointability and balance. The pistol is also available in a DA/SA configuration and can be outfitted with SIGLITE-night sights. The pistol comes with two 15 round magazines in 9mm.

SIG-Sauer SP2022

Technical Data

Manufacturer:	SIG Sauer-Germany
Caliber:	9mm, .357SIG, .40S&W
Mag. capacity:	10, 12, 15
Overall length:	188 mm
Barrel length:	99 mm
Height:	144 mm
Width:	36 mm
Weight:	860 g
Sights:	contrast SIGlite-night sights
Trigger:	SA/DA *
Safety:	firing pin safety, thumb safety
*	Single action/ Double action

The SP2022 is the latest version of our popular polymer framed pistol and features a durable, lightweight and wear-resistant polymer frame with the added tactical versatility of an M1913 Picatinny rail and comes with two interchangeable grips. The slide is machined from a solid block of stainless steel and protected by SIG's black Nitron-finish. The overall design is slightly different from earlier SIG-Sauer pistols such as P220 or P226, as there is no separate disassembly lever on the frame and the slide release lever looks quite different. The standard SIG does not have a manual safety but it does incorporate a de-cocking lever (lowers the hammer without striking the firing pin). A trigger-bar disconnect (disconnects the trigger when the slide is out of battery) and automatic firing pin lock (does not free the firing pin until the trigger is depressed). Further a hammer safety intercept notch (prevents the hammer from striking the rear of the firing pin until the trigger is depressed). Available in 9mm, .357 SIG and .40 S&W, the SP2022 can easily be converted from a Double-Action/Single-Action to a Double-Action Only configuration through a unique integral fire control unit. It also features the SIG-Sauer four-point safety system. The polymer framed pistols have earned an enviable reputation and proven track record of reliable performance in the hands of law enforcement professionals. In December of 2004 the U. S. Army Tank-automotive and Armaments Command at the Rock Island Arsenal awarded SIG a contract for 5, 000 SIG-Sauer SP2022 pistols chambered in 9mm.

Walther P99 AS

Technical Data

Manufacturer:	Walther-Germany
Caliber:	9mm x 19, .40 S&W
Mag. capacity:	10, 12, 15
Overall length:	181 mm
Barrel length:	102 mm
Height:	137 mm
Width:	32 mm
Weight:	605 g
Sights:	3-dot adjustable
Trigger:	SA/QA *
Safety:	de-cocking button, automatic safety

* Single action/ Quick action

The highly successful P99 Series was once again improved in conjunction with technical experts from a number of law enforcement agencies. The result is a state of the art product line, designed for use in modern police tactics. The P99 series offers the law enforcement professional a number of special features and various trigger mechanisms to meet the agencies needs. The line includes both full size and compact models for both uniform and undercover use. The P99 Series is the only hammerless pistol available to offer three trigger options. The P99AS-Anti-Stress has the traditional double action and single action modes, and the added feature of the anti-stress trigger position, which is engaged after reloading.

Walther P99 *Compact*

Technical Data

Manufacturer:	Walther-Germany
Caliber:	9mm x 19, .40 S&W
Mag. capacity:	10, 8
Overall length:	168 mm
Barrel length:	90 mm
Height:	110 mm
Width:	32 mm
Weight:	530 g
Sights:	3-dot adjustable
Trigger:	QA *
Safety:	de-cocking button, automatic safety

* Quick action

The P99 Compact is the ideal pistol for concealed carry. Today's trend is toward pistols that are compact in design and light in weight, yet have all of the features that the law enforcement professional is seeking. The P99 compact has the same highly advanced design features of the full size P99, but in a size that is designed for concealed carry. Just like the full size version, the compact P99 is available with same trigger variations including the QA, AS and DAO. The frame backstraps are interchangeable so that the pistol will fit in a wide variety of hand sizes. The pistol will not snag in clothing when it is drawn, thanks to rounded edges. The hammerless striker system and safety devices integral to the P99 are also available in the P99 compact. All the compact versions are delivered, as standard equipment, with a flat-bottom magazine butt plate and a finger rest magazine butt plate. The frame is molded with a weaver-style rail to accept lights and lasers. Perfect for concealed carry or as a backup weapon for law enforcement.

These handguns present just a small portion of EP-suitable weapons available on the market. An EPO, when working independently, should select a personal weapon always based on the need and the suitability regarding the assignment/s, work and environmental conditions, local regulations and laws.

Other Weapons

When dealing with the physical security of the principal residence, estate, ship or hangar, the EPO has to take in account the possibilities to protect and to defend all access points. The security posts outside the property (driveway, backyard, terrace, deck, tarmac, etc.), should be able to respond if the situation requires with adequate firepower. All security posts, on duty outside or inside the property should carry their personal weapon and a backup weapon. This backup weapon should meet the needs and be suitable for close-quarter confrontations. By selecting such weapon, one should take into consideration that the weapon must be suitable for close quarter combat–being small in size, with a good stopping power, and being effective on medium range targets. The preferred type for close-quarter needs is a semi- or full automatic weapon with a short barrel, collapsible stock, easy to carry and to handle and with a good magazine capacity.

Shotguns

The shotgun is, by far, the deadliest and most formidable, effective firearm ever created for short range personal defense. No other firearm will devastate, disable, or discourage an aggressor as reliably as a shotgun. Shotgun ammunition consists of three general types:

Buckshot Load
A shotgun shell loaded with large-diameter lead-pellets. It is used for big game hunting and for self-defense. For a standard 2 ¾ inch shell in 12 gauge, the number of pellets ranges from eight .36 inch in a "*000 buck*" to twenty-seven .24 inch pellets in a "*# 4 buck.*"
Note: "000 buck" and "00 buck" is pronounced as "triple ought buck" and as "double ought buck" respectively and NOT as "oh oh oh buck" or "zero zero buck."

Birdshot Load
A shotgun shell loaded with small-diameter pellets used for hunting game birds. Stopping power is poor, except when used at close range of between 7-10 m. It is only recommended for personal defense in the home, when adjacent properties might be affected by the use of buckshot loads.

Rifted Slug Load
A shotgun shell loaded with a solid lead-bullet. Slugs are huge hunks of soft lead, grooved on the sides to promote rotation and stability in flight. They have enormous stopping capability. Because slug loads must be carefully aimed like a rifle or handgun, their use ruins the shotgun's main advantage–superior hit probability.

The 12 gauge shotgun is the most devastating and lethal weapon yet devised for inflicting rack and ruin at close range. A safe bet for ammunition selection is to use the 2 ¾ inch 00 buckshot load. The impact of one of these shot shells is essentially equivalent to getting hit with a nine-round burst from a submachine gun. Controllability is important, and a standard 12 gauge shotgun shell has plenty of kick.

12 Gauge:
It has a one-shot stopping success of 81-96%
Some of the preferred and recommendable cartridges are:

Federal "Tactical"	2 ¾ inch	00 buck	96%
Winchester	2 ¾ inch	00 buck	94%
Federal	2 ¾ inch	00 buck	89%
Remington	2 ¾ inch	00 buck	88%

Slugs-fired from a 2 ¾ inch Federal, Remington, or Winchester shell, have a one shot stopping success of 98%. A deer-barrel with mounted rifle sights might be the appropriate platform for this round. It is not the best choice for self-defense because the aiming becomes a critical factor for an effective shot placement. Slugs also have ferocious recoil and tend to over-penetrate.

Birdshots-at close range can destroy a great deal of tissue, producing a gruesome wound. The depth of the injury, however, will likely be 150 mm or less. The possibilities to affect an assailant's heart or major cardio-vascular blood vessels are less. Because the wound trauma produced by birdshot is not decisively effective, a quick stop to deadly violence is not guaranteed.

Buckshots-on the other hand, will exhibit penetration on the order of 300 mm or so. A depth sufficient to intersect vital blood distribution structures and terminate aggression.

Some misconceptions may exist regarding the spread of shotgun pellets. It is not enough to merely point the shotgun in the general direction of an assailant and let fly. Birdshot or buckshot does not create a huge cone of death and destruction that devastates everything in its path. A defense- or riot-shotgun with a 450 to 510 mm open choked improved cylinder-barrel, the pellets will spread out about 25 mm for every meter of range traveled. Across a large room of 5 meters or so, the spread will only be about 150 mm-the size of a coffee cup saucer. At 15 meters, the spread will only be about 390 mm-approximate size of a large pizza. So it is obvious that a shotgun blast will not incapacitate multiple assailants at close range. The shotgun must be skillfully aimed and fired. Aiming is just not quite as precise as that required for a handgun or rifle to score multiple hits on an aggressor. The massive firepower of the shotgun however will most likely produce a favorable outcome in any self-defense encounter.

Mossberg 500

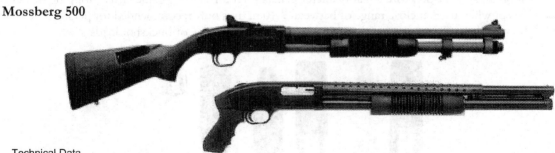

Technical Data

Manufacturer:	Mossberg-USA		Magazine:	6+1 rounds in underbarrel tube magazine
Type:	Rotary bolt, Pump action		Chamber:	76 mm
Gauge:	12		Barrel length:	469 mm
Overall length:	730 mm			
Weight:	3290 g			

The Mossberg 500 is a magazine fed, manually operated (pump action) smoothbore gun. The bolt carrier is operated via two action bars; chamber locking is achieved via tilting breechblock (bolt) into the barrel extension. The safety is located at the tang of the receiver and is fully ambidextrous. The receiver is made from aluminum alloys. Barrels are interchangeable without tools.

The Mossberg 500 is available in different hunting configurations, along with police models (usually with 469 mm barrels and cylinder bores). Stocks are polymer or wooden. Models with factory installed pistol grips are called "Cruisers." Sights can be rifle-type, ghost rings (rear peep sights) or a traditional hunting style bead. The Mossberg 500 is very popular because of quality and relatively low prices. However, the accuracy (for hunting) usually is not that outstanding making some models such as the Cruiser (and similar models) more suited to tactical or home defense use.

FN TPS (*Tactical Police Shotgun*)

Technical Data

Manufacturer:	FN Herstal-Belgium		
Type:	Rotary bolt, Pump action	Magazine:	7+1 rounds in underbarrel tube magazine
Gauge:	12	Chamber:	76 mm
Overall length:	879 mm, folded 984 mm	Barrel length:	457 mm
Weight:	3375 g		

FN Herstal has manufactured an entrant for the tactical shotgun market. Named the FN TPS and designed for police forces, it encompasses a range of features similar to most military assault rifles. Sleek, clean lines, modern composite materials, robust design. There is not much to dislike about the weapon. Perhaps consideration for a 10 round box magazine, and provision for a tactical light attachment would enhance it.

Benelli Nova *Tactical*

Technical Data

Manufacturer:	Benelli-Italy		
Type:	Rotary bolt, Pump action	Magazine:	4+1 rounds in underbarrel tube magazine
Gauge:	12	Chamber:	89 mm
Overall length:	1025 mm	Barrel length:	470 mm
Weight:	3005 g		

The Nova is the latest development in the pump action shotguns from the famous Italian Benelli Armi. It has been developed in the late 1990s and incorporates the latest in firearms design. Nova Tactical is a *Special Purpose* shotgun built to use the powerful 3 inch magnum shells.

The stock is equipped with an optional internal recoil reducer, which is an essential feature for such a light gun firing such powerful ammunition. The stock is in addition fitted with a rubber recoil pad. The Nova uses a rotating bolt with two lugs to lock the barrel. A tubular underbarrel magazine can hold up to four 3 inch shells in the standard version and up to 6 shells with a magazine extension installed. The Nova Tactical is available with rifle-type open or ghost ring (diopter) sights and with an optional accessory rail that mounts at the top of the receiver.

Benelli M4 *Super 90*

Technical Data

Manufacturer:	Benelli-Italy		
Type:	gas operated, semi-auto	Magazine:	6+1 rounds in underbarrel tube magazine
Gauge:	12	Chamber:	76 mm
Overall length:	886 mm (closed stock)	Barrel length:	470 mm
Weight:	3800 g		

Technically, the Benelli M4 Super 90 is a gas operated, smoothbore, magazine fed semi-auto shotgun. Barrel locking is achieved by rotating bolt with two lugs. The M4 Super 90 has dual gas cylinders, gas pistons and action rods for increased reliability. The gun can be field-stripped without any additional tools. The telescopic stock may be replaced by pistol grip or by a hunting-style stock without any tools. The barrel has internal screw-in choke system for increased versatility. Standard sights are ghost-ring rear and blade front. A weaver-style rail at the top of the receiver for scopes, laser illuminators, night-vision sights etc. The gun is designed to accommodate 3 inch and 2 ¾ inch (70 and 76 mm) shells of different power without any adjustments and in any combination. All surfaces are covered by nonreflective, wear-and-corrosion-resistant finish. The gun is very reliable in any weather conditions.

Submachine Guns

The submachine gun is an automatic or selective-fired shoulder weapon that fires pistol-caliber ammunition. The submachine gun, a light-weight and maneuverable fully automatic weapon is an effective and compact weapon for short-range and close quarter combat. Submachine guns can be easily silenced, making them a very useful weapon for a variety of special operations. The police, security forces and executive protection teams in need of compact-sized, massive short-range firepower select the submachine gun as a secondary weapon.

Laws and regulations for purchase, ownership, carrying and usage of shotguns and submachine guns are very complex from country to country, from state to state. In some countries, one can purchase a full automatic submachine gun, but cannot carry, nor use the weapon. In other countries, one is allowed to purchase a submachine gun, but has to have it modified to fulfill the laws and the requirements for the respective license. Shotguns can be purchased in some countries for hunting purposes only, but the owner has to bear a hunting license prior to purchase. There are also caliber and magazine capacity restrictions, as well as limitations to the full auto mechanism of a submachine gun. Further, in some countries a shotgun or submachine gun might be considered a weapon for self-defense and therefore easy to obtain and license. While in other countries, such weapons would only be granted the status of a collector's item with the requirement to be disabled from firing life ammo.

FN P90

Technical Data

Manufacturer:	FN Herstal-Belgium
Caliber:	5.7x28mm SS190
Mag. capacity:	50
Rate of fire:	900 round/min
Overall length:	500 mm
Barrel length:	263 mm
Weight:	2900 g
Sights:	Tritium illuminated reflex sight
Trigger:	selective fire
Safety:	breech block

The P90 is the ultimate system for operating in urban and other close-quarter combat scenarios. This system is built around FN's revolutionary 5.7x28mm ammunition. It utilizes the SS190 armor-piercing duty round, a dual-core projectile that destabilizes on impact to limit over-penetration. The P90 provides a compact, lightweight and completely ambidextrous platform for this ammunition. The compact 50-round box magazine runs horizontally along the top of the P90. Empty cases are ejected downward where they cannot interfere with the operator. The selective-fire P90 fires from a closed bolt, giving it outstanding accuracy and making it easy to keep rounds on target. It is the ideal personal defense weapon for armored vehicle or helicopter crews, executive protection, law enforcement and tactical entry teams.

The Standard P90 and P90 Triple Rail (TR) are also available in semi-automatic only models. The P90 system is offered in several selective-fire configurations including models with nonmagnifying black reticule reflex sights and with either visible or infrared laser target designation systems.

B&T MP 9

Technical Data

Manufacturer:	Brügger+Thomet-Swiss
Caliber:	9mm Parabellum
Mag. capacity:	15, 20, 25 and 30
Rate of fire:	900 round/min
Overall length:	523 mm (stock open)
	303 mm (stock closed)
Barrel length:	130 mm
Weight:	1400 g
Sights:	Ghost Ring Sight, fully Adjustable MIL-STD 1913 Picatinny Rail
Trigger:	selective fire
Safety:	Double Trigger Safety Drop safety

In 2001, Brügger & Thomet started to analyze the needs of military, police and security operators, who are in need of a shoulder fired 9mm support weapon. After completing this study B&T negotiated and purchased the TMP (Tactical Machine Pistol), including all patents, drawings and production rights. Based on the day-to-day needs and experience of professional users, taking in account all the other submachine gun types on the market, Brügger & Thomet redesigned the TMP-the result is the MP9-Tactical Machine Pistol. The super light recoil impulse and the easy, comfortable handling and maintaining make it a very user friendly weapon. A factor which is appreciated by many agencies.

This weapon is mission ready-it is lightweight, compact, ambidextrous, easy to use and fires the easy to find standard 9mm cartridge. An excellent choice for police, military and dignitary protection personnel.

H&K MP5K

Technical Data

Manufacturer:	Heckler&Koch-Germany
Caliber:	9 mm x 19
Mag. capacity:	15, 30
Rate of fire:	900 round/min
Overall length:	603 mm (stock open)
	325 mm (stock closed)
Barrel length:	115 mm
Weight:	2120 g
Sights:	open square notch
Trigger:	selective fire
Safety:	Ambidextrous Safety

The H&K MP 5 K variants are considered the ultimate in close quarters weapons. On the basis of their low weight and reduced overall length, they are easily concealed and carried. All MP5K Variants can be fitted with an optional folding buttstock. The MP-5K compact submachine gun (the "K" stands for the German "Kurz," which means "Short") has been developed Heckler & Koch for various counter-terrorism and security enforcement units, which needed a short-range weapon but with a serious fire-power. Thanks to its size, the MP-5K can be easily concealed under the clothes, in the glove compartment of a car or in the special carry/fire-case. It also allows a high mobility in confined and crowded spaces. The MP-5K is manufactured under license in Turkey and Iran and is widely used by various Law Enforcement and dignitary protection units worldwide. H&K developed in the mid-90s a variant of the MP-5K and called it HK MP-5K *PDW* (PDW= Personal Defense Weapon). The MP-5K PDW was intended to replace the pistol, which was issued to military personnel-it is much more compact than most of modern submachine guns, yet it offers much more firepower than any military pistol. The most negative and restraining factor to the popularity of the MP-5K PDW as replacement of the military sidearm, is the very limited penetration factor, helmets and body armor for example. This could be improved by using a 9x19mm Armor Piercing ammunition.

H&K HK MP7A1 *PDW*

Technical Data

Manufacturer:	Heckler&Koch-Germany
Caliber:	4.6x30mm HK
Mag. capacity:	20, 40
Rate of fire:	950+200 round/min
Overall length:	640 mm (stock open)
	420 mm (stock closed)
Barrel length:	180 mm
Weight:	1800 g
Sights:	open square notch
Trigger:	selective fire
Safety:	Trigger safety, separate firing pin safety

The HK MP7 personal defense weapon has the layout of a typical compact submachine gun (or perhaps a large pistol), with magazine being inserted into a pistol grip, with folding forward grip and telescopic buttstock. The result of the MP7A1 is somewhat unusual for a weapon of such small size. It is gas operated with a rotating bolt design, strongly resembling the mechanism of the HK-G36 assault rifle, but is suitably scaled down. The ambidextrous fire-mode selector and safety-switch allows semi-auto, 3-round burst and full-auto modes. The MP7A1 it designed to fire the special, high velocity ammunition, 4.6x30mm, which resembles a scaled down rifle round. This ammunition is unique to the MP7 and is also used for the HK UCP/P46 pistol.

The MP7A1 could be fired single-handed, or with both hands, either like a pistol or using a front grip. The telescopic buttstock can be extended to give additional stability. With buttstock and front grip retracted, the MP7 can be carried like any big pistol in the special holster, and can be effectively used in close quarter combat. The 4.6x30mm ammunition is loaded with pointed all-steel bullets in brass jacket. The bullet weight is 1.6 gram (25 grains) and the muzzle velocity is 725 m/s (ca. 2400 fps). The manufacturer claim a 100% penetration of the CRISAT body armor (1.6mm of Titanium plus 20 layers of Kevlar) at the distance of 200 meters. Other types of ammunition, including tracer, frangible, spoon-tip (rapid tumbling for use against unarmored human targets) are also available for the MP7A1.

When working for an agency or within a team, the selection of a personal weapon will become part of the assignment process, with little or no room for any personal preferences or selection. Unfortunately, not every thing in life is perfect, especially when good old Murphy is ruling the situation. As an independently operating EPO, you will find out at a very early stage of your career that an assignment might not turn out exactly as it was expected. And that the weapon/s you are used to operate with might not be in reach.

Assignments abroad and overseas, if not carefully prepared and planned, can prove to be filled with nasty surprises–staying cool and focused, being flexible and creative is, in such situations, the only key to succeed. Never think that anything similar to the following could not happen to you.

You signed a contract for a one-week assignment somewhere in Central Africa. Everything is perfectly prepared, you checked and double-checked each detail, your gear is packed, your documents are updated–you are ready to go. Departure procedures at the airport are going smoothly, your handgun has been processed according to the safety regulations–you can relax and enjoy the flight. You think about your new assignment, the money you will earn, the things you can pay off and still put some in savings. Arriving at your destination, your "dreams" come to a halt–you are face-to-face with naked reality. Airport authorities confiscate your treasured SIG P2022 (the caliber is illegal in this country). You try to solve the case and show your weapon permit or concealed weapon permit–neither does it impress the local authority, nor is it valid here. By now, you probably enter the second phase of Murphy's Law–every official might see and consider you a prime suspect, a foreign agent perhaps (good thing you shaved during flight, otherwise they might take you as a terrorist). Now you are passed on from one authority to the next, and if you still had a shred of hope, you realize that most of the officials have difficulty understanding your or any other version of English. Being held at the airport–your new promising assignment as an EPO is a complete disaster.

Fortunately, and after a few intense and nerve-wracking hours, your principal (to the local authorities, a well known personality) manages to clear you. Your principal, aware of and experienced with these types of set-backs, is sticking to the contract. In expectation that you might appreciate the efforts, he is using his local contacts and provides you with some firepower. Smiling and satisfied with his achievement, he presents a 1974 model of a P64, 9mm Makarov. Truly a collector's piece. He also has a piece of paper in the local language, indicating to be a temporarily but limited permit for a pistol. Giving the gun a closer look, you realize, the pistol is in very poor condition and the ammunition in similar state and reduced to a full magazine is posing a bigger danger to you than to a possible target.

A similar episode, however more colorful and with much more detail, actually happened in 1981 to an entire protection team. Thanks to a healthy team spirit, long years' experience, creativity, and a lot of organizational skills, the team accomplished the assignment with success. An associate of the principal was so impressed that he contracted the team a few months later for a longer term assignment.

Working independently and accepting assignments overseas, is like preparing for a SpecOps mission. The EPO must be in control of all aspects, especially regarding equipment, intel and planning at all times. Nothing can be left out; any single and even smallest detail must be checked and rechecked. As an experienced EPO, one has knowledge of the terrain, surrounding, culture, language and intel on the present situation prior to a new assignment. Further, one has contacts in or around the operation area, which must be flexible and able to supply whatever needed at a short notice. Never go on an assignment at the last day-rather depart one week prior to the beginning of the assignment, to have plenty of time to blend in with the environment, establish or renew contacts. Signing up for a job abroad requires the same detailed care as being assigned for advance duty. And remember, taking personal hardware on a trip will make things unnecessarily complicated (local and international airport security regulations, local laws and regulation at destination)–you need your mind free to focus fully on your assignment.

The Concealed Weapons

The EPO's personal weapon must be easily concealed-yet readily available. The proper fitting and the placing of the holster is very important. Selecting the type and material of the holster is as personal as it is to select the right weapon. Preferences as useful and functional as they are might be overruled by the need and the requirements and demands of the assignment. In all cases, a holster should perfectly conceal the weapon, fit snugly against the body, and allow an easy and quick draw of the weapon. The time one takes to clear, aim, and fire the weapon is a life saved. Most firearms manufacturers offer their own holsters for each of the manufactured models; other companies are specialized in custom made holsters. The ideal holster design should allow an easy one-handed insertion without looking at the holster, an audible indication that the handgun was locked in place and a quick one-handed withdrawal.

Carrying a concealed weapon requires a CCW License. In the U. S. each state has its own license requirements and not all permit the same choices of weapon. In many states, a CCW (carrying concealed weapon) license is valid for a firearm, edged weapon, or a stun gun (Taser), or multiple weapons. In other states, the license is valid only for a firearm–other weapons, chemical deterrents, and back-ups are illegal. These differences are important for licensees crossing state lines, despite reciprocity agreements. A licensee, therefore, is considered to have a constructive knowledge of all laws that apply to him/her.

It is extremely important for all concealed firearm permit holders to be aware of the requirements and laws of all reciprocating states. The permit issued by one state does not supersede any other state's laws or regulations. Legal conduct in one state may not be legal in another state. State firearms laws and reciprocity agreements are subject to frequent change, and further, are subject to court interpretation. One should always contact an attorney licensed to practice law for any legal advice.

Concealed Weapons Permit (U. S.)

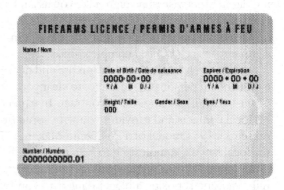

Firearms License (Canada)

While on assignments in other countries, such CCW licenses as issued under U. S. states criteria may not even exist and, therefore, have no legal recognition abroad. The same might happen with a weapon permit, or an international permit, which might not have any legal effect in the host country. When crossing several countries during an assignment, an issue like this can easily turn into a major problem. Therefore, it is of vital importance to check in due time and prior to any operation the legal aspects and possibilities regarding the carrying and use of firearms. Also, check the permitted caliber and types and the required paperwork for any temporary permit. Carrying firearms within the European Community for example requires a *European Firearms Pass*.

MEMBER STATE

EUROPEAN FIREARMS PASS
CARTÃO EUROPEU DE ARMAS DE FOGO
TARJETA EUROPEA DE ARMAS DE FUEGO
EUROPÆISK VÅBENPASS
EUROPÄISCHER FEUERWAFFENPASS
ΕΥΡΩΠΑΪΚΟ ΔΕΛΤΙΟ ΠΥΡΟΒΟΛΩΝ ΟΠΛΩΝ
CARTE EUROPÉENNE D'ARMES À FEU
CARTA EUROPEA D'ARMA DA FUOCO
EUROPESE VUURWAPENPAS
EUROOPAN AMPUMA-ASEPASSI
EUROPEISKT SKJUTVAPENPASS

European Firearms Pass

The Body Armor

As important as the EPO's sidearm is the body protection–a light-weight and flexible body armor, which withstands most calibers. Body armor has been in use from the commencement of recorded history. While it filled the practical purpose of protecting the wearer from the perceived threat, it has, on occasions, become a form of adornment as well (see Fig. 4). Armor has developed in response to increases in threat. Skin, bone, and wood gave way to leather, chain mail, and steel, and resulted in special fabrics, metals, and ceramics, which are in use today.

There are three forms of armor: covert, overt, and tactical. Covert armor is worn under the clothing and gives the EPO an element of surprise as well as protection when attacked (see Fig. 5). The attacker does not normally expect the victim to survive. Overt armor is worn when surprise has been lost and the threat is obvious to both sides. The main function is to protect (see Fig. 6). Tactical armor is worn in situations where surprise is lost and the EPO needs a form of protection, in addition to providing other practical functions, like the carrying of equipment, ammo, or identification (e. g. SECURITY). Overt armor, in much the same way as earlier armor, can be used to intimidate the opposition. The choice of color, the style of the armor, and the amount that is worn can give a distinct ascendancy to the EPO, as is evidenced by the appearance of a squad of fully protected SWAT-team or riot police. Overt or tactical armor is normally used when a high threat level exists.

Most EPOs choose not to wear body armor because it is considered to be a little bulky and restrictive in movement. It is the EPOs call whether he feels comfortable with or without it. The principal, however, should wear body armor when appearing in public.

A study by the United States Federal Bureau of Investigation has shown that wearing a protective vest increases a law enforcement officer's survivability chances by 40%.[8] This means wearing the vest at all times when on duty. Selecting the right armor is very important under these circumstances. The principles in selecting the right armor are the same, whatever your circumstances.

Fig. 4   Fig. 5   Fig. 6

Determine the level of threat. Is it knives, handguns, or rifles? Depending on the threat description, one needs a Level II or Level IIIA, for example (see Fig. 7). A major mistake is to select body armor at levels higher than the threat. Generally speaking and from experience–the higher the protection level selected, the more uncomfortable the armor becomes.

In addition, one needs to know the application of the vest, whether covert, overt, or tactical. If wearing it at all times, the usual would be a covert vest. Covert vests are mostly built to a maximum of Level IIIA, but can be upgraded for specific circumstances with small strike plates. Overt and tactical vests are normally capable of having full size strike plates inserted both front and rear, either permanently or for specific threats.

Vests are sometimes referred to as *OTV* (**O**uter **T**actical **V**est) or *BRV* (**B**ullet **R**esistant **V**est). One also needs to determine if any extras are needed for the armor; such as strike plates, collars, or groin protectors or pockets. Vests are available in a variety of colors and sizes. It is important to ensure that the vest will fit comfortably, provide the right level of protection, but still allow you to perform your duties effectively. Most vest providers and manufacturers will tailor the vest to a perfect fit.

Two of the major considerations when deciding on the level of protection required are:
- the common threats to one and the principal
- and that the threat level selected will defeat one's own firearm

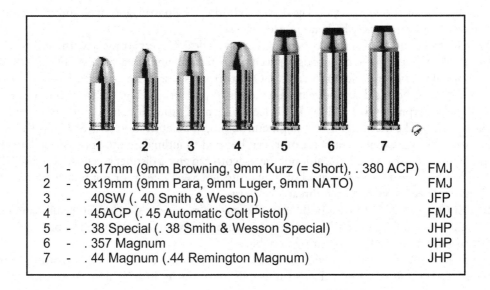

1	-	9x17mm (9mm Browning, 9mm Kurz (= Short), . 380 ACP)	FMJ
2	-	9x19mm (9mm Para, 9mm Luger, 9mm NATO)	FMJ
3	-	. 40SW (. 40 Smith & Wesson)	JFP
4	-	. 45ACP (. 45 Automatic Colt Pistol)	FMJ
5	-	. 38 Special (. 38 Smith & Wesson Special)	JHP
6	-	. 357 Magnum	JHP
7	-	. 44 Magnum (.44 Remington Magnum)	JHP

Ballistic Testing Rounds
Note: Check with supplier, foreign country standards might differ from those of the U. S.

Caliber	Bullet Type	Barrel Length inches	Velocity fps	mps
Threat Level I				
. 22 Cal.	40 Grain LR	6	1050	320
. 25 Cal.	Auto 50 Grain FMC	2	810	247
. 32 Cal.	Auto 71 Grain FMC	4	905	276
. 380 Cal.	Auto 88 Grain JHP	4	990	302
. 28 Cal.	Special Lead 158 Grain	6	850	259
. 38 Cal.	Special 158 Grain SWC	6	850	259
Threat Level II A				
. 22 Magnum	40 Grain Solid Point	6 ½	1180	360
. 38 Cal.	Special 125 Grain SJHP+P	6	1028	314
. 38 Cal.	Special 158 Grain Lead +P	6	1090	332
. 38 Cal.	Special 110 Grain JHP+P	6	1235	377
. 45 Cal.	Auto 230 Grain M.C.	5	810	247
. 357 Magnum	158 Grain JSP	4	1250	381
. 357 Magnum	158 Grain Lead	4	1250	381
. 357 Magnum	158 Grain Lead SWC	4	1253	382
. 41 Magnum	210 Grain Lead	8 3/8	1080	329
9MM	95 Grain JSP	4	1250	381
9MM	100 Grain JSP	4	1250	381
9MM	124 Grain FMJ	4	1090	332
9MM	115 Grain JHP	4	1160	354
9MM	147 Grain Subsonic JCE	5	1050	319
9MM	147 Grain JHP	5	1050	319
10MM	170 Grain JHP	5	1172	357
10MM	200 Grain Full Jacket TC	5	1072	327
Threat Level II				
. 41 Magnum	210 Grain SP	4	1300	397
. 44 Magnum	240 Grain SJSP	4	1180	360
. 44 Magnum	240 Grain Lead	4	1200	366
. 357 Magnum	125 Grain JHP	4	1450	442
. 357 Magnum	110 Grain JHP	4	1550	473
. 357 Magnum	158 Grain JSP	6	1395	425
. 357 Magnum	158 Grain JSP-Hornady	6	1445	441
. 357 Magnum	158 Grain Lead	8 3/8	1410	430
9MM	124 Grain FMJ	5	1175	358
9MM	Lapua 123 Grain FMC	4	1200	366
9MM	Norma 116 Grain FMJ	4	1150	351
9MM	Geco 123 Grain GMC	4	1200	366
9MM	Canadian 116	5	1250	381
9MM	Israli	4	1200	366
9MM	Cavim-FMJ	4	1110	339
Threat Level III A				
. 44 Magnum	240 Gr. SWC (Gas Checked)	6	1400	427
9MM	124 Grain FMJ	9 ½	1400	427
9MM	Canadian 116 Grain FMJ	16	1400	427
9MM	Norma 116 Grain FMJ	16	1325	404
9MM	Geco 123 Grain FMC	16	1310	400
9MM	Lapua 123 Grain FMC	16	1445	441
9MM	Israeli	16	1300	397
Threat Level III				
7.62 NATO	Ball 150 Grain FMJ (308)	28	2750	
30. 06	PSP 180 Grain	24	2700	
. 30	Carbine 110 Grain FMJ	18	1950	
12 Gauge	Rifled Slug	18	1550	
. 223	55 Grain FMJ (5.56 MM)	20	3075	
7.62 x 39	150 Grain FMJ	22	2400	
Threat Level IV				
30. 06	Armor Piercing 166 Grain	26	2850	

Fig. 7

The major developments in body armor production were the introduction of the *Kevlar* and *Spectra* products. Thanks to the combined efforts of ballistic science expertise and field experience, the development of new material combinations, it is possible to wear body armor that does not stick to the body (incorporated thermic system). New materials allow body armors to be light-weight and flexible, but with high protection against ammunition commonly used.

The Self-Defense Technique and Protection System

The need to defend and to protect the principal within medium and close range by using a self-defense technique is more common, than the use of a firearm. An EPO must be in control of a self-defense or close-combat method, which allows him/her a swift stopping action. The EPO must be able to control a possible attacker, whether this is a threat directed to the EPO or the principal. There are many good fighting styles and self-defense techniques out there, suitable for the needs of an EPO. This chapter is not intended to teach any martial art moves or techniques. But it shall highlight the vital areas, one should select for a straight attack (no fancy moves though), as well as the effects, such attacks can have on the attacker. As much as a possible blow may cause to the opponent, as much could a hit to the principal's body, even a seemingly innocent bumping into, could cause a delayed reaction and serious harm. When referring to medium-range combat means that two opponents are already within a touching distance. The body, well trained is an exceptional weapon-system, which by applying the right speed and combination of attacks can stop, paralyze, render unconscious and even kill. A head butt is also effective. But the delivery of the attacks, whether with a short punch and strikes with hands, fists, elbows, or kicks with legs and knees is only than effective, if the full energy is bundled in the attack and released on impact. This combination of body, attack and impact energy is known as "*Fa-Jing*." How does it work? Simply explained-it's the body which causes the fist or the knee for example to be thrust toward the target with a great speed and energy and not the fist or knee itself. Therefore it is not the pure muscles power, but the body as a whole which causes such an energy burst. Such a released energy is not only causing a surface impact, but has to reach deep inside the opponent. The energy released with a sneeze for example would be the ideal *Fa-Jing*-because the entire body reacts with it, not just part of it. When confronted with a threat situation, the entire body has to react and not only the part of the body which will be used to execute a defensive move or the attack. The brain, the command center will switch to pure combat/survival-mode and activate the entire body as a weapon-system.

An EPO uses his peripheral vision to evaluate the targets presented by the opponents, watching the principal and chooses the most vital target. He/she should be aggressive and concentrate the attacks on the opponent's vital points in order to end the fight quick.

Any EPO, in the execution of his job is often facing situations, where he or she is challenged to use the right amount of force in order to defend himself/herself and above all to protect the principal. But not always is force and impact affecting the adversary.

The following took place a couple of years back. A colleague and friend accepted a job at a foreign embassy. He was contracted as security adviser to the ambassador. One day, he was supervising his team on what appeared to be just another of those boring routine visits to a charity mission. At arrival however, the principal and the team were facing a small but unexpected mixed group of people, demonstrators, journalists and photographers. Still nothing to worry about-after all, these are the situations, which one is trained for and one has to be aware of. While leaving the cars, the team fully alert provided full cover for the principal. On the move, two members of the team had unavoidably some close contact with the demonstrators. The short but effective exchange of force executed by those two team members passed unnoticed. After a successful visit (which was not so boring after all) the party returned to the embassy without any further incident to report.

On the following day, one of team members reported sick, complaining about a severe headache and a blurry vision. He was taken to hospital for a full check-up (he was one of the two, which was engaged with the crowd). The examination and tests at the hospital could not provide any reasonable explanation for those symptoms and since he had no visible injury, he was discharged. When he reported back, my colleague evaluated the situation and considering the security officer's condition decided to question him regarding the previous day's incident again. The officer gave a full account of the incident. There was no doubt anymore about the origin of the presented symptoms-the security officer, unfortunately was hit with an elbow during the exchange (most likely without any precise area in mind). This elbow attack most certainly affected one or more pressure points at the impact area. The time of impact in relation to the affected points within the impact area caused a delayed reaction, which became only visible hours later (the next day). Based on this find, the officer could be treated accordingly and he was able to recover quick and without complications.

What happened to this security officer can happen to everybody. What initially appeared to be innocent and unintentional, can reveal to be an intentional attack with precise timing and specific impact, while not leaving a trace or markings-the target might experience a delayed reaction. In the above case, thanks to the knowledge and immediate reaction of the team leader, the security officer could be treated and recovered quickly. "*Never apply a poison, without having its antidote.*"

The Vital Targets

In order to localize and visualize the target areas, we divide the entire body into three sections. Each of these sections (see Fig. 8) contain vital body targets, nerve targets and body points (also known as acupuncture-or pressure points). (see Fig. 9-11) Always keep in mind, that your future client's body system might be the target of an attack.

The Upper Section

This section includes the head and the neck and is the most dangerous target area.

Head (top)
> The skull is weak where the frontal cranial bones join. A forceful strike causes trauma to the cranial cavity, resulting in unconsciousness and hemorrhage. A severe strike can result in death.[9]

Forehead
> A forceful blow can cause whiplash; a severe blow can cause cerebral hemorrhage and death.

Temples
> The bones of the skull are weak at the temple, and an artery and large nerve is found close to the skin. A powerful strike can cause unconsciousness and brain concussion. If the artery is severed, the resulting massive hemorrhage compresses the brain, causing coma and or death.

Eyes
> A slight jab in the eyes causes uncontrollable watering and blurred vision. A forceful jab or poke can cause temporary blindness, or the eyes can be gouged out. Death can result if the fingers penetrate through the thin bone behind the eyes and into the brain.

Ears
> A strike to the ear with cupped hands can rupture the eardrum and may cause a brain concussion.

Nose
> Any blow can easily break the thin bones of the nose, causing extreme pain and eye watering.

Below Nose

A blow to the nerve center, which is close to the surface under the nose, can cause great pain and watery eyes.

Jaw

A blow to the jaw can break or dislocate it. If the facial nerve is pinched against the lower jaw, one side of the face will be paralyzed.

Chin

A blow to the chin can cause paralysis, mild concussion, and unconsciousness. The jawbone acts as a lever that can transmit the force of a blow to the back of the brain where the cardiac and respiratory mechanisms are controlled.

Back of head (behind ears and base of skull)

A moderate blow to the back of the ears or the base of the skull can cause unconsciousness by the jarring effect on the back of the brain. However, a powerful blow can cause a concussion or brain hemorrhage and death.

Throat

A powerful blow to the front of the throat can cause death by crushing the windpipe. A forceful blow causes extreme pain and gagging or vomiting.

Neck (sides)

A sharp blow to the side of the neck causes unconsciousness by shock to the carotid artery,[10] jugular vein, and vagus nerve. For maximum effect, the blow should be focused below and slightly in front of the ear. A less powerful blow causes involuntary muscle spasms and intense pain. The side of the neck is one of the best targets to use to drop an opponent immediately or to disable him temporarily to finish him later.

Neck (back)

A powerful blow to the back of one's neck can cause whiplash, concussion, or even a broken neck and death.

The Middle Section

The middle section extends from the shoulders to the area just above the hips. Most blows to vital points in this region are not fatal but can have serious, long-term complications that range from trauma to internal organs to spinal cord injuries.

Shoulder muscles (front)

A large bundle of nerves passes in front of the shoulder joint. A forceful blow causes extreme pain and can make the whole arm ineffective if the nerves are struck just right.

Collarbone

A blow to the collarbone can fracture it, causing intense pain and rendering the arm on the side of the fracture ineffective. The fracture can also sever the brachial nerve or subclavian artery.

Armpits

A large nerve lies close to the skin in each armpit. A blow to this nerve causes severe pain and partial paralysis. A knife inserted into the armpit is fatal as it severs a major artery leading from the heart.

Biceps

A strike to the biceps is most painful and renders the arm ineffective. The biceps is an especially good target when an opponent holds a weapon.

Forearm muscles

The radial nerve, which controls much of the movement in the hand, passes over the forearm bone just below the elbow. A strike to the radial nerve renders the hand and arm ineffective. An opponent can be disarmed by a strike to the forearm; if the strike is powerful enough, he can be knocked unconscious.

Back of hand

The backs of the hands are sensitive. Since the nerves pass over the bones in the hand, a strike to this area is intensely painful. The small bones on the back of the hand are easily broken and such a strike can also render the hand ineffective.

Spine

A blow to the spinal column can sever the spinal cord, resulting in paralysis or in death.

Nipples

A large network of nerves passes near the skin at the nipples. A blow here can cause extreme pain and hemorrhage to the many blood vessels beneath.

Heart

A jolting blow to the heart can stun the opponent and allow time for follow-up or finishing techniques.

Solar plexus

The solar plexus is a center for nerves that control the cardio-respiratory system. A blow to this location is painful and can take the breath from the opponent. A powerful blow causes unconsciousness by shock to the nerve center. A penetrating blow can also damage internal organs.

Diaphragm

A blow to the lower front of the ribs can cause the diaphragm and the other muscles that control breathing to relax. This causes loss of breath and can result in unconsciousness because of respiratory failure.

Floating ribs

A blow to the floating ribs can easily fracture them because they are not attached to the rib cage. Fractured ribs on the right side can cause internal injury to the liver; fractured ribs on either side can possibly puncture or collapse a lung.

Kidneys

A powerful blow to the kidneys can induce shock and can possibly cause internal injury to these organs. A stab to the kidneys induces instant shock and can cause death from severe internal bleeding.

Abdomen (below navel)

A powerful blow to the area below the navel and above the groin can cause shock, unconsciousness, and internal bleeding.

The Lower Section

This section includes everything from the groin to the feet. Strikes to these areas are rarely fatal, but incapacitating.

Groin

A moderate blow to the groin can incapacitate an opponent and cause intense pain. A powerful blow can result in unconsciousness and shock.

Thighs (outside)

A large nerve passes near the surface on the outside the thigh about four finger-widths above the knee. A powerful strike to this region can render the entire leg ineffective, causing an opponent to drop. This target is especially suitable for knee strikes and shin kicks.

Hamstring

A severe strike to the hamstring can cause muscle spasms and inhibit mobility. If the hamstring is cut or ruptured, the leg is useless.

Thighs (inside)

A large nerve passes over the bone about in the middle of the inner thigh. A blow to this area also incapacitates the leg and can cause the opponent to drop. Knee strikes and heel kicks are the weapons of choice for this target.

Knee

Because the knee is a major supporting structure of the body, damage to this joint is especially harmful to an opponent. The knee is easily dislocated when struck at an opposing angle to the joint's normal range of motion, especially when it is bearing the opponent's weight. The knee can be dislocated or hyperextended by kicks and strikes with the entire body.

Calf

A powerful blow to the top of the calf causes painful muscle spasms and inhibits mobility.

Shin

A moderate blow to the shin produces great pain, especially a blow with a hard object. A powerful blow can possibly fracture the bone that supports most of the body weight.

Achilles

A powerful strike to the Achilles tendon on the back of the heel can cause ankle sprain and dislocation of the foot. If the tendon is torn, the opponent is incapacitated.

Ankle

A blow to the ankle causes pain; if a forceful blow is delivered, the ankle can be sprained or broken.

Instep

The small bones on the top of the foot are easily broken. A strike here will hinder the opponent's mobility.

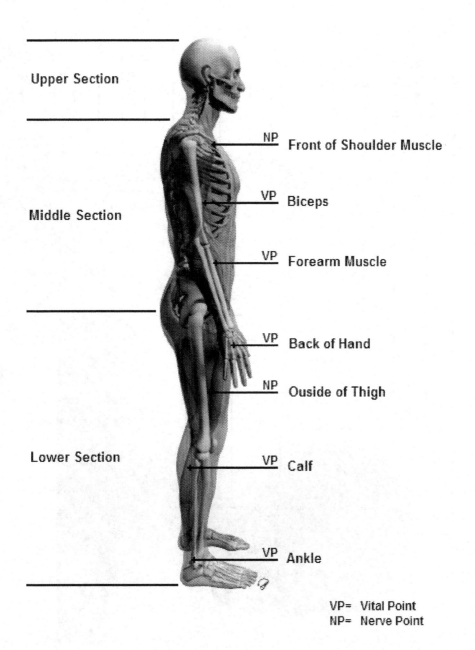

Upper Section

NP — Front of Shoulder Muscle

VP — Biceps

Middle Section

VP — Forearm Muscle

VP — Back of Hand

NP — Ouside of Thigh

Lower Section

VP — Calf

VP — Ankle

VP= Vital Point
NP= Nerve Point

Fig. 8

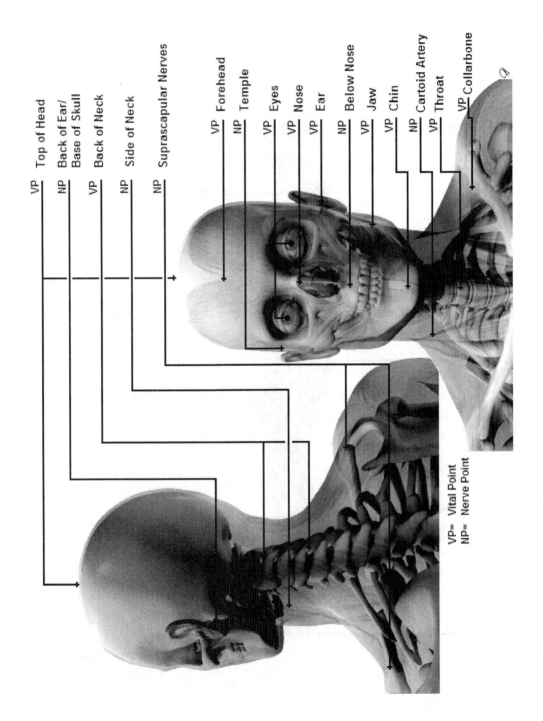

Top of Head — VP

Back of Ear/ Base of Skull — NP

Back of Neck — VP

Side of Neck — NP

Suprascapular Nerves — NP

Forehead — VP

Temple — NP

Eyes — VP

Nose — VP

Ear — VP

Below Nose — NP

Jaw — VP

Chin — VP

Cartoid Artery — NP

Throat — VP

Collarbone — VP

VP= Vital Point
NP= Nerve Point

Fig. 9

124

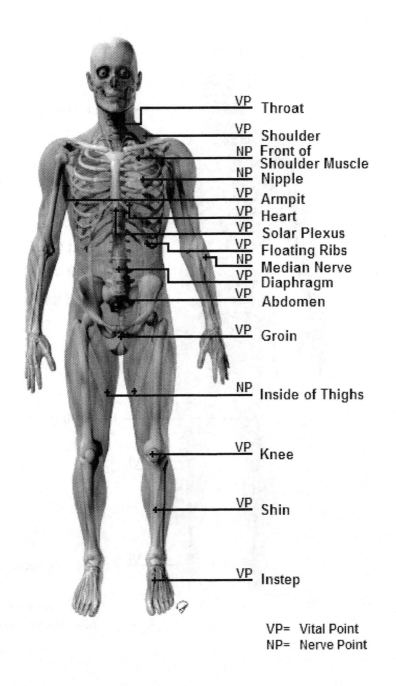

VP — Throat

VP — Shoulder

NP — Front of Shoulder Muscle

NP — Nipple

VP — Armpit

VP — Heart

VP — Solar Plexus

VP — Floating Ribs

NP — Median Nerve

VP — Diaphragm

VP — Abdomen

VP — Groin

NP — Inside of Thighs

VP — Knee

VP — Shin

VP — Instep

VP= Vital Point
NP= Nerve Point

Fig. 10

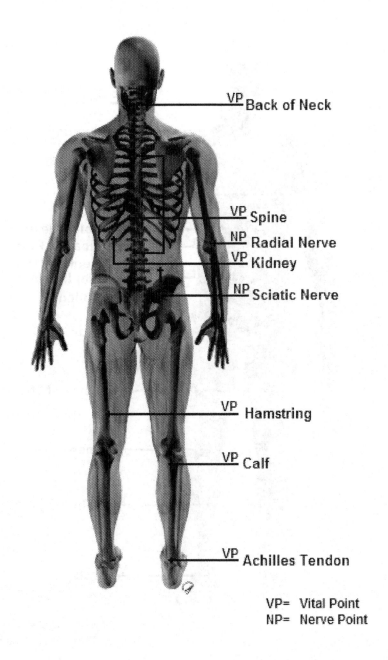

VP Back of Neck

VP Spine

NP Radial Nerve

VP Kidney

NP Sciatic Nerve

VP Hamstring

VP Calf

VP Achilles Tendon

VP= Vital Point
NP= Nerve Point

Fig. 11

126

The Nerve Centers

Knowing the target areas on the body, the effectiveness and action is not sufficient to achieve the success desired. An effective striking to the opponent's vital points is essential for a victorious outcome in a hand-to-hand combat. An EPO must be able to employ the principles of effective striking if he/she is to emerge as the victor or survivor in a fight to the death. The proper mental attitude is of primary importance in the EPO's ability to strike an opponent. In hand-to-hand combat, the EPO must have the attitude that he/she will defeat the attacker, protect the principal and complete the mission, no matter what. In a fight to the death, the EPO must have the frame of mind to survive above all else–the prospect of losing cannot be part of his/her mind. He/she must be committed to hit the opponent continuously with whatever it takes to drive the attacker to the ground or end any resistance. Any strike should be delivered in a way, that the target is hit and the "weapon" remains on the impact site for at least a tenth of a second. This will impart all the kinetic energy of the strike into the target area. It will produce a fluid shock-wave that travels into the affected tissue and causes maximum damage. It is imperative that all strikes to vital points and nerve motor points are delivered with this principle in mind. The strikes should be targeted at the opponent's vital points and nerve motor points. The results of effective strikes to vital points were described before. Strikes to nerve motor points cause temporary mental stunning and muscle motor dysfunction to the affected areas of the body. Mental stunning results when the brain is momentarily disoriented by overstimulation from too much input-a strike to a major nerve for example. Stunning completely disables an opponent for three to seven seconds and allows the EPO to finish off the opponent, gain total control of the situation. Sometimes, such a strike causes unconsciousness. A successful strike to a nerve motor center also renders the affected body part immovable by causing muscle spasms and dysfunction because of nerve overload.

The Jugular Notch

Located at the base of the neck just above the breastbone; pressure to this notch can distract and take away the opponent's balance. Pressure from fingers jabbed into the notch incurs intense pain that causes an opponent to withdraw from the pressure involuntarily.

The Suprascapular Nerve

This nerve is located where the trapezius muscle joins the side of the neck. A strike to this point causes intense pain, temporary dysfunction of the affected arm and hand, and mental stunning for three to seven seconds. The strike should be in a downward "knife-hand" or "hammer-fist" strike from behind.

The Brachial Plexus

This nerve motor center is on the side of the neck. It is probably the most reliable place to strike someone to stun them. Any part of the hand or arm may be applied-the palm heel, back of the hand, knife-hand, ridge-hand, hammer-fist, thumb-tip or forearm. A proper strike to the brachial plexus origin causes:

- Intense pain
- Complete cessation of motor activity
- Temporary dysfunction of the affected arm
- Mental stunning for three to seven seconds
- Possible unconsciousness

The Brachial Plexus Clavicle Notch

This area is behind the collarbone in a hollow about halfway between the breastbone and the shoulder joint. The strike should be delivered with a small-impact weapon or the tip of the thumb to create high-level mental stunning and dysfunction of the affected arm.

The Brachial Plexus Shoulder Joint

Located on the front of the shoulder joint, a strike to this point can cause the arm to be ineffective. Multiple strikes may be necessary to ensure total dysfunction of the arm and hand.

The Stellate Ganglion

The ganglion is at the top of the pectoral muscle centered above the nipple. A severe strike to this area can cause high-level stunning, respiratory dysfunction, and possible unconsciousness. A straight punch or hammer-fist should be used to cause spasms in the nerves affecting the heart and the respiratory system.

The Cervical Vertebrae

Located at the base of the skull, a strike to these particular vertebrae can cause unconsciousness or possibly death. The harder the strike, the more likely death will occur.

The Radial Nerve

This nerve motor point is on top of the forearm just below the elbow. Strikes to this point can create dysfunction of the affected arm and hand. The radial nerve should be struck with the hammer-fist or the forearm bones or with an impact weapon, if available. Striking the radial nerve can be especially useful when disarming an opponent armed with a knife or other weapon.

The Median Nerve

This nerve motor point is on the inside of the forearm at the base of the wrist, just above the heel of the hand. Striking this center produces similar effects to striking the radial nerve, although it is not as accessible as the radial nerve.

The Sciatic Nerve

A sciatic nerve is just above each buttock, but below the belt line. A substantial strike to this nerve can disable both legs and possibly cause respiratory failure. The sciatic nerve is the largest nerve in the body besides the spinal cord. Striking it can affect the entire body, especially if an impact weapon is used.

The Femoral Nerve

This nerve is in the center of the inside of the thigh. Striking the femoral nerve can cause temporary motor dysfunction of the affected leg, high-intensity pain, and mental stunning for three to seven seconds. The knee is best to use to strike the femoral nerve.

The Common Peroneal Nerve

The peroneal nerve is on the outside the thigh about four fingers above the knee. A severe strike to this center can cause collapse of the affected leg and high-intensity pain, as well as mental stunning for three to seven seconds. This highly accessible point is an effective way to drop an opponent quickly. This point should be struck with a knee, shin kick, or impact weapon.

Short and Precise Attacks (Hands)

During medium-range combat, punches and strikes are usually short because of the close distance between attacker and defender. Power is generated by using the entire body mass in motion behind all punches and strikes. The hands become the most lethal weapons. The knowledge of hand-to-hand combat provides the EPO another means to accomplish a mission. Well trained, hands can become as deadly as any other weapon when used by a skilled fighter.

Attack to solar plexus

The defender uses this attack for close-in fighting; when the opponent rushes or tries to grab. The defender puts the full weight and force behind the punch, maintaining however a steady stance at the moment of impact and hits the opponent in the solar plexus-knocking the breath out of his lungs. This attack can then be completed with a knee to the groin, or any other disabling blows to vital areas.

Strike to the throat

The defender uses the thumb-strike to the throat as an effective technique when an opponent is rushing or trying to grab. The defender thrusts his right (left) arm and thumb out and strikes his opponent in the throat-larynx area while holding his left (right) hand up for protection. He/she can follow up with a disabling blow to his opponent's vital areas.

Strike to the shoulder

The opponent tries to grab-the defender strikes the opponent's shoulder joint or upper pectoral muscle with his fist or thumb. This technique is painful and renders the opponent's arm numb. The defender then follows up with a disabling movement.

Strike to the face

The opponent makes an attack move-the defender counters by rotating his body in the direction of the opponent with quick strike with the hammer-fist to the temple, ear, or face. The defender follows up with kicks to the groin or hand-strikes to his opponent's other vital areas.

Strike to the side of the neck

The defender catches the opponent off guard, rotates at the waist to generate power, and strikes the opponent on the side of the neck (carotid artery) with a fist. This strike can cause muscle spasms at the least and may knock his opponent unconscious.

Hammer-fist to the pectoral muscle

When the opponent tries to grapple, the defender counters, striking the opponent with force in the pectoral muscle.[11, 12] This blow stuns the opponent. The defender immediately follows up with a disabling blow to a vital area of his opponent's body.

Punch to the solar plexus or floating ribs

The opponent tries to wrestle the defender to the ground. The defender counters with a short hook-punch to the opponent's solar plexus or to the floating ribs. A sharply delivered blow can puncture or collapse a lung or lacerate the liver.[13] The defender then follows up with a combination of blows to his opponent's vital areas.

Uppercut to chin

The defender steps between his opponent's arms and strikes with an uppercut-punch to the chin or jaw. Then he/she follows up with blows to his opponent's vital areas.

Strike to the side of the neck

The defender executes a knife-hand strike to the side of his opponent's neck the same way as the hammer-fist strike except he uses the edge of his striking hand.

Strike to the radial nerve

The opponent tries to strike the defender with a punch. The defender counters by striking the opponent on the top of the forearm just below the elbow (radial nerve) and uses a follow-up technique with other attacks to disable his opponent.

Strike to the chin

The opponent tries to surprise the defender by lunging at him. The defender quickly counters by striking the opponent with a palm-heel strike to the chin-using maximum force.

Strike to the solar plexus

The defender meets his opponent's rush by striking him with a palm-heel strike to the solar plexus. The defender then executes a follow-up technique to his opponent's vital organs.

Strike to the kidney

The defender grasps the opponent from behind by the collar and pulls him off balance. He quickly follows up with a hard palm-heel strike (single hand or both hands) to the opponent's kidney. The defender can then take down his opponent with a follow-up technique to the back of his knee.[14]

Short and Precise Attacks (Elbow and Knee)

The elbows are also formidable weapons. Tremendous striking power can be generated from them. The point of the elbow should be the point of impact. The elbows are strongest when kept in front of the body and in alignment with the shoulder joint-that is, never strike with the elbow out to the side of the body.

Elbow strikes

When properly executed, elbow strikes render an opponent ineffective. When using elbow strikes, execute them quickly, powerfully, and repetitively until the opponent is disabled. As much as using the elbow to attack, we can use the elbows in combined form to block and to counter-attack. Repetitive elbow strikes are very effective and disorienting to the opponent.

Knee strikes

The knees are especially potent weapons and are hard to defend or protect against. Great power is generated by thrusting the hips in with a knee strike. In order to attack effectively and avoid injury use the point of the knee as the impact surface. All knee strikes should be executed repetitively until the opponent is disabled. The following techniques are the most effective to overpower or disable an opponent.

Knee strike to the front

In case an opponent tries to grapple with the defender, the defender strikes his opponent straightforward in the stomach or solar plexus with his knee. This stuns the opponent and the defender can follow up with another technique.

Knee strike to the outside thigh

The defender delivers a knee strike to the outside the opponent's thigh (common peroneal nerve). This strike causes intense pain and renders the opponent's leg ineffective.

Knee strike to the inside thigh

This is an effective technique for close-in grappling. The defender delivers a knee-strike to the inside the opponent's thigh (peroneal nerve). The defender then executes a follow-up technique to a vital point.

Knee strike to groin

The knee strike to the groin is effective during close-in grappling. The defender gains control by grabbing his opponent's head, hair, ears, or shoulders and strikes him in the groin with his knee.

Knee strike to the face

The defender controls the opponent by grabbing behind his head with both hands and force-fully pushing his head down. At the same time, the defender brings the knee up and smashes the opponent in the face. When properly executed, the knee strike to the face is a devastating technique that can cause serious injury to the opponent.

The vital body targets and nerve targets are relatively easy to spot and to access, requiring less precision and any amount of force to strike. The body points are more difficult to access and require precision and an exact amount of force to attack. Like mentioned before, these specific types of attacks are even more dangerous, because if executed in a set time window to a certain point or combination of points with the precise amount of force, they can cause a delayed reaction. This might become only visible hours or days late.

The person hit might not show an immediate reaction or physical signs, but a few hours later can present all kinds of symptoms. Depending on the selected point/s, the person might die without any apparent sign or reason.

For example, when a sudden strike to the point *Ren* 14 (an acupuncture point belonging to the *Ren Mai* Channel, also known as *Conception Vessel*) is made, an increased parasympathetic stimulation is caused, which leads to knockout or cardiac arrest. The involuntary contraction of the diaphragm and abdominal muscles lead to breathing difficulty and damage to the left lobe of the liver, the pancreas, and the lower portion of the stomach. A sudden stimulation of the celiac plexus, which is located under the point Ren 14, causes severe pain, which is interpreted by the brain as coming from the internal organs.

The result is a sudden spasm of the diaphragm and abdominal muscles, which causes a person to feel like they cannot breathe. Because the left lobe of the liver, the pancreas, and part of the stomach are located under Ren 14, those organs can be directly damaged by a strong strike. When these organs are damaged, the pain is sensed by sympathetic nerves that are connected to a relay area called the celiac plexus. The pain is then transmitted to the spinal cord and brain. Thus, when the celiac plexus is directly "stimulated" by a strike to this area, intense pain is caused, that mimics damage to the pancreas, left lobe of liver, or the lower part of the stomach.

A precision blow to Ren 14 is also associated with sudden death–severe pain in the abdominal organs can cause vasovagal syncope (fainting caused by low blood pressure secondary to a low heart rate and dilated blood vessels). When the celiac plexus is struck with sufficient force, the stimulated pain in the abdominal organs can cause profound stimulation of the parasympathetic nervous system via the vagus nerve and cause cardiac arrest. This type of sudden death (commotio cordis) has been reported to occur during accidents, assaults, sports, and martial arts.[15] Because of the anatomy of this area, an impulse type of hit can be very effective at stimulating the celiac plexus.

The liver and pancreas have a large fluid content, which can transmit a shock wave. Since the relatively hard spine is located behind the celiac plexus, the energy of the shock wave is concentrated on the celiac plexus. The final effect is similar to a wave hitting a wall. A sudden snapping type of hit can cause a shock wave to travel through the liver and pancreas and stimulate the celiac plexus. Interestingly, contracted abdominal muscles actually facilitate this effect.

This type of precision attack is often used by martial art experts and is known as the *Dim Mak*. The following will provide a closer look at this "evil twin" of acupuncture.

Vital Point Striking (Dim Mak)

Dim Mak is often translated as "Death Touch." Less scary however is the much more adequate translation–"Vital Point Striking".

As detailed and instructive the content of this chapter might appear, it is intended as nothing other than to serve for information purposes only. As an additional study to the self-defense and protection system, the following should shed some light on what could happen if an exact point/area is hit and an immediate or delayed effect is triggered by an attack. However, this will not provide specific details on attack types and combinations necessary to provoke such effects.[16] Those interested in learning Dim Mak as an addition to their acquired martial art skills should consider a course in acupuncture/acupressure prior to anything else (unless you find a Dim Mak instructor with a TCM background).

The founders and grand masters of the mainstream Asian martial art styles realized early on that a fighting method is only as effective and precise as the target to which the attack has been delivered. A special training method was developed by which the hands, knuckles, and fingers had to be hardened (*Iron Palm Style*) and used as attack weapons. The locations of energy channels with their related and interrelated connection-, alarm-, and confluent-points used in acupuncture to restore the body energy were used as precision targets to block, delay, or disrupt the energy flow. This method, very well-balanced within the concept of yin and yang, became known to Chinese styles as *Dim Mak* and to the Japanese styles as *Kyusho Jitsu*. Dim Mak was conceived as an integral part of the main martial art styles; unfortunately, with the development and commercialization of new styles it became detached, altered and misused, in its concept over the years.

What makes Dim Mak so effective is the way one is able to deliver an attack, the range of effects it can have on the victim, immediately or days after, and in most cases without leaving any traces. Dim Mak is without a doubt the *evil twin* of Acupuncture.

To understand the path of energy channels and the exact location of the related points, it is necessary to become acquainted with the localization of the points and the method used to measure the distance between the points.

The following are the traditional finger measurements (the measurement is obtained from the size of the finger/s of the patient) used in TCM (Traditional Chinese Medicine) and Acupuncture. These measurements, *Cun* (pronounced 'Tsun') serve to establish the distances between the points (see Fig. 12 and 13).

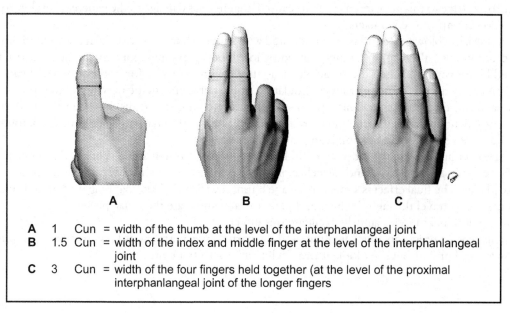

A	1	Cun = width of the thumb at the level of the interphanlangeal joint
B	1.5	Cun = width of the index and middle finger at the level of the interphanlangeal joint
C	3	Cun = width of the four fingers held together (at the level of the proximal interphanlangeal joint of the longer fingers

Fig. 12

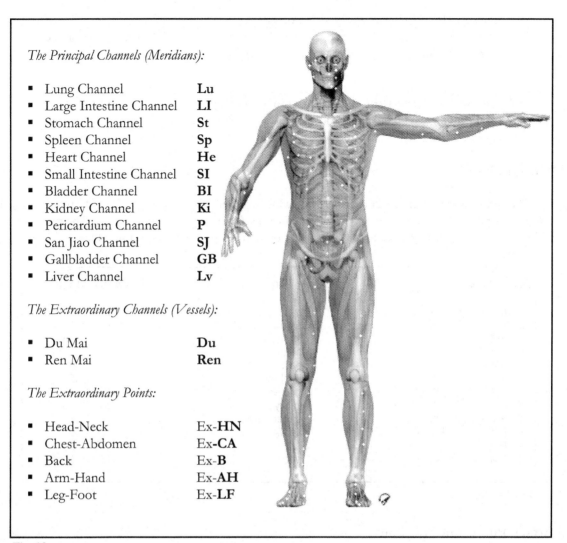

The Principal Channels (Meridians):

- Lung Channel **Lu**
- Large Intestine Channel **LI**
- Stomach Channel **St**
- Spleen Channel **Sp**
- Heart Channel **He**
- Small Intestine Channel **SI**
- Bladder Channel **Bl**
- Kidney Channel **Ki**
- Pericardium Channel **P**
- San Jiao Channel **SJ**
- Gallbladder Channel **GB**
- Liver Channel **Lv**

The Extraordinary Channels (Vessels):

- Du Mai **Du**
- Ren Mai **Ren**

The Extraordinary Points:

- Head-Neck Ex-**HN**
- Chest-Abdomen Ex-**CA**
- Back Ex-**B**
- Arm-Hand Ex-**AH**
- Leg-Foot Ex-**LF**

Fig. 13

The Point Categories:

- Shu-Points (*Bei Shu Xue*) (transporting points)
  - These points lay along the Bladder Channel on the back and have a segmental relation to one of the twelve organs

- Mu-Points (*Mu Xue*) (gathering points)
  - These points are located on the chest or abdomen along various channels. They have a segmental relation to one of the twelve organs.

- Qi-Points (*Yuan Xue*) (source points)
  - Each of the twelve primary channels possess a Qi or source point. On the Ying-Channel this point coincides with the third of the five Shu-points and is therefore always distally the third point. According to classical Chinese belief, these points should distribute the Qi-source along the channel.

- Connection Points (*Luo Xue*) (passage points)
  - Each of the twelve primary channels, the Du Mai, Ren Mai and the great Luo connection point of the Spleen has one connection point. At these points, are connecting the couples channels with each other.

- Confluent Points (*Ba Mai Jiao Hui Xue*) (tuning points)
  - Four points are located on the lower, and four on the upper extremities. These points develop their effect in relation to the eight extraordinary vessels.

The Qi Flow

The following is a time chart (see Fig. 14), which explains the flow of energy, Qi, throughout the body. Qi is passing through the body in a constant flow from one organ to the next. The time space in which Qi is flowing through a channel is the active time. It is also the time window which makes an attack more effective.

Active Time	Meridian	Active Point	
3 AM - 5 AM	Lung	Lu	8
5 AM - 7 AM	Large Intestine	LI	1
7 AM - 9 AM	Stomach	St	36
9 AM - 11 AM	Spleen	Sp	3
11 AM - 1 PM	Heart	He	8
1 PM - 3 PM	Small Intestine	SI	5
3 PM - 5 PM	Bladder	BI	66
5 PM - 7 PM	Kidneys	Ki	10
7 PM - 9 PM	Pericardium	P	8
9 PM - 11 PM	San Jiao	SJ	6
11 PM - 1 AM	Gallbladder	GB	41
1 AM - 3 AM	Liver	Li	1

Fig. 14

Attack Points and Antidote

The Lung Meridian (Lu)

Channel Pathway:
The **Lu** consists of 11 surface pathway points. The inner pathway begins in the central Sianjiao and descends the spine in order to connect to the large intestine. On the return pathway, it passes through the cardiac orifice of the stomach and traverses the diaphragm. On its path, the channel penetrates the lung, to which it belongs. It ascends the trachea and connects with the larynx and the pharynx, leaving the chest cavity beneath the clavicle at point Lu 1. The surface path of the lung meridian passes over the outer part of the inner upper arm to the elbow and runs over the radial area of the inner forearm and the thumb to the radial side of the thumbnail. Branch vessels run to the large intestine and the index finger at point Lu 7.

Lu 3
In medicine, this point is used for nosebleeds and asthma. Striking this point with force will cause an imbalance of energy between body and mind, resulting in extreme sadness, leading to a deep depression. Vertigo can be another effect resulting from a direct hit.
- Massaging the point with a mild pressure, inward toward the person.

134

Channel Pathway:

The **LI** consists of 20 surface pathway points. The channel begins at the radial side of the tip of the index finger, passes through the interspaces between the first and second metacarpal bones, through the anatomical snuffbox. Then over the superior part of the lateral aspect of the forearm to the lateral aspect of the elbow. The shoulder is reached via the lower part of the lateral aspect of the upper arm. From here, the channel branches behind the acromion to the seventh cervical vertebra (Du 14), and from there it runs on to the supraclavicular fossa. From the seventh cervical vertebra, the channel passes through the supraclavicluar fossa and enters the ribs, where it connects with the lung. After passing through the diaphragm, the channel reaches its organ, the large intestine.

The surface path leads laterally from the supraclavicular fossa, past the lower neck to the corners of the mouth, crossing the naso-labial groove opposite (LI 20). From this point, the meridian enters into contact with the branches of the stomach channel. At the corners of the mouth, two branches run off the pathway to the gums and the lower jaw.

LI 10

Striking this point with force and in a straight direction will cause the entire arm to become useless (dead arm) and cause spasms in the entire lower abdomen area.
- Massaging the whole outside of the forearm in a downward motion (away from the body) for some time will make the arm respond again. The spasm will stop–however some unpleasant sensation in the abdomen area might remain for a while.

LI 12

This point, if struck in a downward angle, will result in an energy drainage of the entire body.
- Massaging gently, but with deep penetration and toward the body will bring things back to normal.

The Stomach Meridian (St)

Channel Pathway:

The **St** has 45 surface pathway points. This pathway starts at the lateral side of the nostril and ascends the nose to the inner medial canthus, where it meets the bladder channel. From here, the channel runs to its first point on the lower edge of the eye socket and then perpendicular to the corner of the mouth. From this section, the channel branches to the gums of the upper jaw, circle the lips, and then meet the Extraordinary Vessel *Ren Mai* in the groove of the chin. From the corner of the mouth, the channel descends to the lower jaw and as a facial branch to the corner of the jaw. From here, it ascends via the zygomatic arch to the level of the temples and the region of St 8 in front of the ear.

A branch runs to Du 24 (Du Mai). The main pathway extends from the lower jaw over the side of the neck and cartoid artery to the upper clavicular fossa. Here the channel starts its inner path, which runs down from the diaphragm to its organ, the stomach and the spleen. Connections with the deeper layers of the points Ren 12 and Ren 13 are located there. From the upper clavicular fossa, the surface pathway runs over the chest and nipple to the abdomen, where it runs to the side of the straight abdominal muscle, passing the umbilicus to the groin.

An inner branch runs from the pyloric orifice of the stomach to St 30, near the groin. From there the channel continues to run superficially over the antero-lateral aspect of the upper thigh to the side of the patella. Then via the anterior aspect of the lower leg and foot dorsum, terminating at the lateral side of the second toenail. From St 36, below the knee, a branch descends via the antero-lateral aspect of the lower leg and foot dorsum to the lateral side of the third toe. From St 42, a branch meets with the spleen channel at the big toe.

St 15 and **St 16**

Striking any of these points in a downward direction with medium force will drain the energy and the heart will stop. Striking these points in an upward direction will cause an overload of qi-energy; consequently, the heart rate will lethally increase.

- Massaging H 1 and H 3 and CPR.

St 9 with Sp 21

Striking or strong pressure to these points in a combination will result in knockout, spleen damage, and lung failure.

- Massaging Sp 20 with Sp 21 in a downward direction together with direct moderate pressure to GB 20.

St 15 with GB 24

Striking these points with force will cause knockout and heart failure.

- Only CPR

The Spleen Meridian (Sp)

Channel Pathway:

The **Sp** channel pathway has 21 acupuncture points. The channel begins at the inside of the corner of the big toenail. It ascends in its surface path from here via the instep, at the border between the sole and dorsum, in front of the medial malleolus, to the lower leg. From here, the pathway continuous along the posterior border of the tibia and crosses below the knee in front of the liver channel. Continuing the upper leg over the antero-medial aspect of the inner thigh. Above the groin, the channel enters into its inner path to the deeper layers of the points Ren 3 and Ren 4. It then reaches the points Sp 14 and Sp 15 on the surface. From this stage it runs to the inner layer of Ren 10 and then the inner branch continues through the abdomen to its organ, the spleen, where it connects with the stomach. It ascends further via the diaphragm to the heart and connects with the heart channel.

The surface path of the channel in the abdomen leads from the dep layers of Ren 10 back to the point Sp 16, to the inside of the upper abdomen. From there it follows via the GB 24 and Lv 14 along the side of the chest to Sp 17 to Sp 20. At point Sp 20 in the 2nd ICS an inner branch leads via the dep layer of point Lu 1 along the throat to the root of the tongue base. From Sp 20 it raises again into the 6th ICS, below the armpit to the point Sp 21. This is where the *Great Spleen Network Vessel* starts.

Sp 20

Striking direct with force will cause numbness in entire arm and extreme liver failure.

- Pressing Liv 3 and/or Liv 14 inward will bring the arm back to life.

Sp 20 with Lv 14

Direct and strong pressure or hit to these points will cause severe numbness of the whole body and can lead to paralysis. Extreme pressure will cause heart and lung failure.

The Heart Meridian (He)

Channel Pathway:

The **He** channel path has 9 points on the surface. The inner channel pathway originates at the heart and the "heart system", with all its connections to the other organs. The descending part of the channel traverses the diaphragm and connects with the small intestine. The ascending part ascends along the esophagus, connects with the root of the tongue and the "eye system" (eyeball and accompanying tissues).

The main path of the channel runs through the lung and leaves the chest cavity from the side in the axilla at the point He 1. The surface pathway comes from the axilla and runs first to the medial aspect of the inner upper arm, the inside of the elbow joint and then to the antero-medial aspect of the inside of the lower arm. In the region of the wrist joint, the channel runs radially past the pisifom bone and via the palm of the hand to radial corner of the nail of the little finger.

He 3
Striking this point straight and hard results in external damage, nerve damage inside the upper arm, but most likely the heart will be affected (the person is not aware of it).
- Preventive measure is to squeeze H 9 each evening and morning during a few days.

He 5
Striking or pressing this point with force will drain the energy from the body and dangerously lower the blood pressure.
- Massaging gently H 5 toward the person and than H 3 straight inward.

The Small Intestine Meridian (SI)

Channel Pathway:
There are 19 points in the surface pathway of the **SI**. The small intestine channel originates at the ulnar corner of the nail of the little finger. It ascends in its surface over the outside aspect of the little finger and the hand at the dividing line between the skin of the dorsum and the palm, towards the region of the wrist. The meridian then ascends via the ulnar region of the outside of the lower arm, the Canalis nervi ulnaris, the posterior aspect of the outside of the upper arm, toward the posterior aspect of the shoulder joint. From here, it zigzags over the scapula and branches to connect with the seventh cervical vertebra (Du 14). From there, the inner pathway descends through the superior fossa of the clavicle and connects with the heart. Its further descent passes alongside the esophagus through the diaphragm, reaching the stomach and finally connects with its organ, the small intestine.
The surface path runs from the superior clavicular fossa, alongside the neck and over the lower jaw to the cheekbone (SI 18), branches to the inner corner of the eye (Bl 1) and connects with the bladder channel. Before reaching point SI 18, a branch runs from the cheek to the outer corner of the eye (GB 1) and finally enters the ear at SI 19.

The Bladder Meridian (Bl)

Channel Pathway:
The **Bl** consists of 67 points on the surface. The channel originates in its surface pathway at the inner canthus of the eye and ascends along the forehead to the *Du Mai* on the anterior hairline (Du 24). From there, the channel runs laterally to the points Bl 3 and Bl 4 and further over the skull. At the vertex, the channel runs from Bl 7 to the Du Mai (Du 20) and from there to Bl8. From the vertex it branches and enters the brain in the direction of the tip of the ear at point GB 8. From Bl 9, the channel returns to Du 16 and descends to point Bl 10. After crossing the skull, the channel separates at Bl 10 into its two principal branches along the spine. These pathways run almost parallel to the midline. The first branch runs over the seventh cervical vertebra (Du 14) and first thoracic vertebra (Du 13), from there it descends along the spine at 1. 5 cun lateral to the midline to the region of the sacrum, at the level of the fourth sacral foramen. From here, the channel returns cranially toward the midline, where it descends from the first sacral vertebra. Then via the sacral foramen, to the center of the buttocks, and at the end via the center of the posterior aspect of the thigh to the popliteal fossa at Bl 40. In the lumbar region (Bl 23 and Bl 52), the inner channel branches via the lumbar muscles into the interior, where it connects with the kidney and its organ, the bladder. The surface path of the second branch descends from Bl 10 and

paravertebrally from the second thoracic vertebra, but more distant to the midline, along the inner border of the scapula to the lumbar-sacral region (Bl 54). From here, it descends over the buttocks (GB 30) and the posterior aspect of the thigh to the popliteal fossa (Bl 40). Both channel branches meet at Bl 40 in the popliteal fossa and descend via the middle of the calf along the Achilles tendon to the heel. The channel circles the outer bones from behind and follows the fifth metatarsal bone on the border between dorsum and sole to end at the outer nail corner of the little toe.

Bl 6
A blow from back to front will drain all the energy from the body, causing extreme pain, dizziness and fainting.
- Sitting in a crouching position the attacked area must be massaged for a while in direction from back to the front of the head.

Bl 10
An indirect hit to this point will drain the energy from the kidney and the San Jiao, resulting in dizziness to unconsciousness. A straight hit will have a direct effect on the kidney, resulting in a possible kidney failure.
- Massaging point Ki 1 with a deep penetration using the thumb or knuckle.

The Kidney Meridian (Ki)

Channel Pathway:
The **Ki** channel incorporates 27 points in its surface pathway. The surface path of this channel originates at the underside of the little toe and ascends to point Ki 1 on the sole of the foot. From there, the channel traverses the arch of the foot to the navicular bone and the region inferior to the bone on the instep. The channel performs a loop, which reaches under the inner bone and ascends again to the posterior part of the inner side of the lower leg in front of the Achilles tendon. Point Ki 8 is located at the posterior border of the tibia, distal to the Sp 6, which is also traversed by the kidney channel. The channel then continues to ascend the leg to the medial side of the popliteal fossa and traverses the posterior aspect of the inner thigh to the region of the pubic symphysis.

The inner path of the channel begins at Ki 11, ascends over the spine before branching off to connect with its organ, the kidney, and connects with the bladder. Another branch runs from the kidney via the liver and diaphragm to the lung, where it connects with the heart and where other branches in the center of the chest lead to the pericardium channel. From the lung channel, ascending lateral to the larynx and pharynx to terminate at the root of the tongue.

The surface path ascends from the pubic symphisis to the lower and upper abdomen, where the channel runs parallel to the midline. It traverses the chest alongside the midline at a slightly greater distance from the same to the angle of the chest and clavicle joint. From Ki 25, a branch runs to the heart and lung.

Ki 5
Striking this point strongly in a downward direction with the heel for example will cause dizziness, disorientation. Hitting this point precision and depending on the impact force it will also damage the kidney—as result, blood will appear in the urine.
- Pressure by squeezing Ki 5 very gently, than massage Ki 1.

Ki 9
Striking this point with force in a downward direction will cause a confused state of the mind.
- Pressing Ki 1 and Ki 5 will help.

The Pericardium Meridian (P)

Channel Pathway:

The **P** channel has 9 acupuncture points on the surface pathway. Its inner path originates at the chest, where it serves its organ, the pericardium. The channel descends through the diaphragm to the abdomen and then connects with the upper, middle and lower *Jiao*.

The surface path emerges from the chest near the nipple at point P 1. From here, it ascends to the axilla and follows the antero-medial aspect of the upper arm, via the vessel-nerve street, to the cubital fossa. The channel ascends further on the middle of the antero-medial aspect of the lower arm. Precisely between the tendons of the palmaris longus and the flexor carpi radialis to the palm of the hand and the tip of the middle finger. One branch leads from P 8 to the tip of the ring finger and connects with the *San Jiao* channel.

The San Jiao Meridian (SJ)

Channel Pathway:

The surface pathway of the San Jiao channel consists of 23 points. The surface path originates at the ulnar corner of the nail of the ring finger. From there it ascends via the dorsum of the hand. Between the fourth and fifth metacarpal bone and the central part of the outer aspect of the lower arm between the ulna and the radius toward the tip of the ellbow. The channel continues via the posterior aspect of the upper arm and reaches the posterior aspect of the shoulder, traversing points of other channels (SI 12, GB 21). From the point GB 21, the channel continues first to the superior fossa of the clavicle and from there returns to the seventh cervical vertebra (Du 14). From the superior fossa of the clavicle, the inner pathway descends to the center of the chest, connects with the pericardium and traverses the diaphragm (connecting with all parts of its organ-the upper, middle and lower San Jiao).

From the seventh cervical vertebra, it ascends to the region behind the ear. It branches at point SJ 17 directly into the ear and leaves the ear in front of it at point SJ 21. From there, it connects with SJ 23 lateral of the eyebrow and the gallbladder channel lateral to the eye socket in the region of GB 1.

SJ 8
Striking this point in combination and followed by a hit to Du 24 will cause irreversible damage to the heart and the internal energy system. Delayed death will occur. If this point is hit alone, the blood pressure will raise dangerously.
- Massaging by pressuring the point P 6 toward the shoulder of the person on the inside of the arm.

SJ 12
Striking this point straight in will cause paralysis in the arm.
- Massaging SJ 12 toward the person.

The Gallbladder Meridian (GB)

Channel Pathway:

There are 44 points on the **GB** channel's surface. The surface pathway originates at the bony limit of the outer canthus and runs in front of the ear before ascending to the temple region. From there, it returns to the anterior part of the helix and passes the ear to the region of the mastoid process. It arches again from here over the temples to the forehead, before it returns at more slightly medial level over the skull, where it reaches the neck region at GB 20.

One branch of the principal channel departs from below GB 20, just below GB 12. It runs from there through SJ 17, through the ear and point SI 19 in front of the ear to GB 1. Another branch leads from GB 1 to the lower jaw at St 5, before it ascends to the cheek at SI 18 and descends back to St 6 at the corner of the jaw. From there, it runs to the superior clavicular fossa, where it reconnects with the main channel from GB 20. On its inner pathway, it winds from the superior clavicular fossa into the chest, traverses the diaphragm, connects with the liver and enters its organ, the gallbladder. Descending further down the flank, where it contacts with the deep layers of point Lv 13, before it enters the superficial layers in the region above the groin and descends past the hip to GB 30.

The further surface path of the channel reaches from GB 20 in the neck region via the seventh cervical vertebra (Du 14) to GB 21 on the descending aspect of the trapezius muscle. From there to the upper shoulder and point SI 12 to the superior clavicular fossa. The channel then zigzags over the axillar region to the side of the chest and flank to point Gb 29 in the hip region. From here, one branch runs to the sacral bone via points BL 31 and BL 34 before it reconnects with the inner branch at point GB 30. From here the channel descends alongside the middle region of the antero-lateral aspect of the thigh. It passes the outside of the knee to the middle part of the antero-lateral aspect of the lower leg. In front of the outside anklebone, via the dorsum, to the outside corner of the nail of the fourth toe. From point GB 41, on the dorsum of the foot, a branch runs between the first and second metatarsal bones to the big toe, where it connects with the liver channel.

GB 1

This point, when hit from a back to front movement, will cause nausea at the least and loss of memory followed by death at the very most.
- CPR will help, but a full recovery will occur with a combined massage of GB 1 in a backward motion and a light inward pressure to point GB 26.

GB 14

If a hit was made in an upward direction, the body will experience an energy (Yang) rush to the head, resulting in extreme dizziness, fainting, and eventual death. Actually, the same happens by extreme sunstroke.
- Apply pressure to GB 21 away from the neck toward the outer shoulder on both sides-Yang energy will be replaced by yin energy. Massage GB 20 in a downward manner toward the base of the neck. Additionally press Si 4 with a medium pressure (same treatment applies for sunstroke.) If it passes the stage of dizziness and fainting–use CPR at once.

GB 24

This point, when hit in a straightforward manner, will cause knockout by action of cartoid sinus. Depending on the force used by impact, the effect can be from debilitation to death.
- If uncontrollable shaking or knockout occurs, massage GB 20 on either side of the neck and CPR if required.

GB 24

Striking this point in a straightforward motion and with power will paralyze the leg.
- Massaging GB 31 will bring the leg back to normal.

The Liver Meridian (Lv)

Channel Pathway:
The **Lv** has 14 points in its surface pathway. The pathway originates at the outer corner and base of the nail of the big toe, between the first and second metatarsal bones, to the region of the inside anklebone. From here, it connects with Sp 6 and ascends via the center of the inside of the shinbone. The channel passes below the knee, crosses behind the spleen channel and runs inside, past the knee over the central aspect of the inside of the upper leg. From there further to the groin, where it passes over Sp 12

and Sp 13 before rounding the external genitalia and the pubic region over the abdomen in the region of Ren 3 and Ren 4. From there, the surface pathway ascends to the rib cage at point Lv 13 and ends at point Lv 14 below the nipple.

The internal path originates at point Lv 14, where it connects with the liver and the gallbladder. One branch traverses the diaphragm and ascends to the lung before it descends through the diaphragm again to the epigastrium. Another branch runs cranially alongside the side of the rib cage, touching the larynx and pharynx and ascends via the cheeks to the "eye system" (eyeball with all related structures). From there, a branch ascends to the apex and another descends to the corner of the mouth and circles the lips from within.

The Du Mai Vessel (Du)

Channel Pathway:

The **Du** Mai channel has 28 points on its surface path. The surface path originates in the region of the uterus/prostate and lower abdomen, where Ren Mai and Chong Mai also originate. In the region of the perineum, a mixture of the Qi of kidney and bladder channel takes place. On the inside of the spine, a branch leads to the kidney and from there ascends further alongside the inside of the spine to the apex, where it enters the brain. The second branch ascends from the abdomen to the umbilicus and heart. It ascends further via the region of the throat and the pharynx, where it contacts with Ren Mai and Chong Mai to the lower jaw and inferior border of the eye socket. Another branch ascends from the inner canthus to the apex.

The surface path of the channel leads from the perineum region via the Du 1 at the coccyx and sacrum and the entire spine to the region of the neck. Under the posterior nape of the neck at Du 16, a branch runs to the brain. At the skull, the channel descends via the midline and nose and philtrum to the frenum of the upper lip.

Du 4
This point in acupuncture is used to tonify the energy, especially the yang energy in the entire body. If struck hard and in a downward direction, it will drain the energy from the entire body, affecting small intestine and kidney.
- To restore the flow of qi, massaging the Du 26 with a gentle and light upward pressure. This point can be combined with Ren 1.

Du 4
If Ren 4 is hit with force and in an upward direction, it will result in an immediate increase of the blood pressure–lethal to someone whose pressure is high already.
- In this case, one has to massage Ren 4 in a constant downward move to cause the blood pressure to fall. Additionally St 9 can be used to tweak a reaction from the cartoid sinus.

Du 4
If Ren 4 is hit straight on the spot with force, the person will experience blackout and a total slow down of the qi energy–this is very dangerous, especially when the effect appears delayed.
- The person should be lying down and the top of the head at point Du 21 should be massaged together with the whole chest area in a downward direction.

Du 6
If hit with force, the blood pressure will raise immediately.
- Use the same technique as with Ren 4 for high blood pressure.

Du 14

This point, struck in a straight forward motion, is devastating. This is a heart-Mu point, which in medical terms is used to soothe the heart and to unbind the chest; the effect of a hit is lethal.
- Only CPR.

Du 14

If struck in a downward angle, the lungs will be shut off from energy.
- Only CPR

Du 14

If struck in an upward angle, external damage and an energy overload will occur, causing organs to overact and the heart rate to fall dangerously low.
- Use St 9 for a gentle massage until the heart rate is normalizing–remember this is a knockout point as well, so the massage has to be very careful.

Du 14 with Du 4

These points are hit straightforward and almost simultaneously–causing a sudden death if the strike is strong and knockout with long lasting damage if struck with less force.
- Only CPR

Du 17

An upward strike at this point will cause spasms in the lower abdomen and lower body.
- Applying pressure to the same point but in a downward motion.

Du 24

A strike from left to right (A) will cause nausea, vomiting, and blackout. A strike from right to left (B) will cause loss of balance and hearing.
- (A) Massaging the point Ren 4 in a small circles and in a counter-clockwise direction is helping. (B) Massaging the same point in small circles and in a clockwise direction brings help.

The Ren Mai Vessel (Ren)

Channel Pathway:

There are 24 points on the surface path of **Ren** Mai. The inner pathway originates at the uterus/prostate and the lower abdomen, where the *Du Mai* and *Chong Mai* also have their organs. This inner pathway intersects with the kidney channel and the Du Mai and ascends with the other two channels internally alongside the spine. From the source area, it runs to the perineum region.

The surface channel of the Ren Mai begins at the region of perineum at point Ren 1. The channel then ascends alongside the interior midline via the lower abdomen, umbilicus, ensiform process and the sternum to the jugular fossa. The channel traverses the midline in the region of the trachea and the larynx, where the contact with the Chong Mai, at the chin dimple is. Together with the Chong Mai, it branches from the region of the chin encircles the lips and ascends to the area below the eye socket.

Protective Action or Reaction

As mentioned earlier, self-defense and hand-to-hand combat is much more than a plain blocking and counter-attacking reactive behavior. When purchasing a firearm, one is expected to have an in-depth knowledge, not only about how to handle and fire the weapon, but also about the effect and damage the bullets can cause on impact. Learning a close-combat fighting method is not much different. One will acquire the knowledge and skill of hand-to-hand combat, but has to make certain that such knowledge includes everything related to the physical effects this fighting system might have on an opponent. Especially as an EPO, one might have to face situations where a close encounter is not avoidable and an immediate action is required. Knocking out an attacker in order to protect the principal is what the EPO is hired for–right? Wrong–it's not so simple. The type of threat, the required counter-measure/s, the use and amount of force necessary under given circumstances, and consideration of the legal aspects is what the EPO has to process before action.

The Protocol

There is a certain protocol that the EPO has to maintain while operating closely with a principal and his/her family. The EPO is only an observer, an invited guest in the principal's world, but is under no circumstances part of this world and its social circles. An EPO or EPO team working very closely with principal and family, spending a lot of time in the residence, traveling and being familiar with all events, will experience a natural tendency to become comfortable and at ease with everybody. It is like being at home. It is very natural that one becomes carried away, which might lead, in the end, to a certain excess of familiarity. There are certain indicators one has to be aware of in order to avoid that "trap".

The EPO has to remember at all times that he/she is not a personal friend, but an employee, like the maid and the cook (perhaps a bit more privileged, but that's about it). As an EPO and security expert, that status may be elevated compared to that of the maid, but at the end of the day, as an employee, the EPO can be replaced very easily and quickly. Being fired is probably easier and quicker than in the case of the maid (but I wouldn't dare to find it out). The EPO has to be conscious that he/she is replaceable.

- **Keeping a professional distance to the principal**

  The EPO's area of competence is that of security and protective policies. These are the only areas the EPO should provide advice and offer his/her services. If any advice or personal opinion is solicited in areas beyond security and protective procedures, the EPO should not attract attention by pretending to be an expert, but avoid any direct answer. Attempting to deflect the question in a diplomatic manner is more appropriate. Never should the EPO ask the principal for any advice, tip, or special favors, even if the initial offer comes from the principal. Asking for whatever information is related to the principal's security, such as itinerary, possible threats, suspicious people, and incidents, is part of the EPO's duty.

  An EPO should never use the principal's phone, fax, computer, office equipment, or any type of supplies for his/her personal reasons. The EPO should ask permission to use the phone, fax, or copier for service purposes only. Working as an EPO, the principal might permit many things and grant certain privileges denied to other employees–never abuse those privileges. Most clients take security and protection very seriously, which is reflected by their readiness to spend large amounts of money; others are not so generous with the spending and might even cut costs, when spending is needed most. It is the job of the EPO to consult and advise the client professionally and cost-effectively. It is his/her obligation to also be conscious about any expenses.

- **Treating the principal, family and staff professionally**

  Follow all the rules of good manners and etiquette and treat everybody with respect and dignity. Never become overly friendly or too personal with the principal, his/her family and/or the staff. By generating a shroud of mystery and secrecy, one can manage to keep this small distance and respect. The only things a principal needs to know is what is related to the job in a professional sense. The principal, family, staff, and other persons should always be addressed to as Sir, Madam, Miss, and so on. A person with title should be addressed with the respective honor, like Doctor, Your Excellency, Your Honor (it would be a good idea to get acquainted with titles and honors and how to address each of those properly). Working with a principal for some time and having earned trust and confidence, the principal might direct you to use his/her first name. This is the moment to show the ability of evasive but polite action–even if this is a well-intended offer, the EPO must turn it down in a nice manner. It is usually permissible, however, to address the principal's children by their first names, but in return they should address the EPO as Mister or Miss. It is also advisable to get familiar with the names of the principal's immediate staff and service personnel and to address them accordingly.

- **Respect and care for the principal's property**
As an EPO, one will have free access to all areas of a principal's property, which includes depending on the size and architectural build, swimming pool, green areas, flower arrangements, terraces, balconies, garages. Working independently is one thing; working with an entire team is something else. Whatever such working conditions are, one has always to make sure that everything is taken care of and respected as it would be one's own property. On night shift, it is almost inviting to take shortcuts via the flower beds, or over the freshly watered grass. Those small conveniences may cost the job and are not necessary. If you like conveniences and shortcuts, then this activity might not be the right one after all because you will never do your job thoroughly. If one is disrespecting and not caring about the client's property, how much respect should one expect then toward the principal.

There are a few other things one should keep in mind, even though that all this is part of everybody's good manners and education. Always make sure your shoe soles are clean. Some clients might insist on (in most cases the lady of the house) removal of the shoes at the door. If this is the case, make sure that the socks are intact. This brings us to another issue–in some countries it is custom to remove the shoes at the entrance. Many such customs might come in a surprise, so it's always good to do the homework. Expensive cars are another delicate issue–no matter what model or make, handle the principal's car like it is your own. Meaning: drive it carefully, without trying to find out how much horsepower you can handle or what a good driver you are. Remember, every single thing belonging to the client is part of the client's family. Treat everything properly.

Never touch anything which is of personal or private nature. Keep in mind, having access to the client's private papers, books, or personal items does not give you the right to put your nose in it. This all is part of the trust and confidence the client invests in the EPO; once this trust is slightly scratched, the principal will quickly lose trust and confidence in his/her security personnel. It is almost for certain that, at a certain stage, the principal will test his/her officers. He/she purposely will leave money, jewelry, or other valuables and sensitive papers in certain places–just to check if it has been removed or tampered with and if the EPO is reporting it.

- **Never discuss or mention any prior assignments**
When applying for a job, one should never use any previous client or contact or assignments as a reference. Assignments, clients, and related contacts are strictly confidential and must be treated as such at all times. Disclosing any previous training facility or seminar instructors is most welcome and should provide a full picture of your abilities and professional background. If there is a need to prove a specific point regarding security, then use an example in general terms without referring to any previous assignments. Never mention former clients' names, companies, or anything related to former jobs, which could give the wrong impression to the principal. After all, if one talks about former clients, then one might talk about the current principal as well. That is not professional at all. Everything the EPO sees and hears must remain confidential at all times (the same is valid for the spouse of the principal). The principal must rest assured and have fully confidence in the EPO.

• Conversations and comments

News and media people alike are always after some supplemental piece of information, which could become useful in their quest for headlines. A reporter would never neglect the opportunity to get hands on some extra information, which could spice-up a boring article, which otherwise would never make it to the front page. Such opportunity is in most cases provided free and effortlessly in the form of gossips, jokes, and remarks expressed by the personnel and staff members about the principal. This is obviously not done intentionally, and most media people are very proud about their professional abilities to obtain such "news".

And who could provide a closer view on the principal's private affairs—the maid, the cook, the gardener, or the secretary? Each of those could have something to comment about the principal's private affairs, but they have their limitations because of their working area. The EPO on the other hand, who can move freely and has unrestricted access (even into the bedroom if duty requires), would be the perfect source for this extra piece of fresh, untold "news". But the media are not the only ones the EPO has to be careful with, when commenting and/or expressing opinions. The principal and family members might be interested, too. The EPO must be very conscious about conversations, comments, and even jokes when talking to someone, because it can and will always be used against him/her. Never say anything (no matter positive or negative) about your assignment, the people you are working with, and in particular the people you are working for. Be loyal to your principal at all times. Always express your opinion in an affirmative and positive manner.

• Respect and good manners

When dealing with all kinds of situations, stress will give way to outburst and offensive language, or swearing or cursing. But whatever the cause, reason, or circumstances might be, never let yourself fall into an uncontrolled and bad mannered attitude. An EPO must always show good manners, no matter how much self-control might be necessary. Avoid any form of disturbances, such as loud laughter, loud talk or radio/TV in high volumes.

If smoking is the only bad habit—then do it in the open air, where the smoke will not offend anybody (it might be good opportunity, if not quitting, to decrease the number of cigarettes gradually). When finished with the cigarette, "recycle" what remains (tear the paper away, disperse the remaining tobacco, so that the wind can carry it away and drop the remaining paper with the filter in a waste bin). Do something afterward to freshen up your breath.

• The principal's personal routines

The EPO has to be silent and behave like a shadow. It is very important (unless certain circumstances demand the contrary) that the principal is able to keep a normal and relaxed lifestyle without changing any of his/her routines. The principal gives the itinerary and the indication of places to visit, and the EPO is responsible and makes certain that a secure environment around and within the principal's interests is established. The EPO has to learn the principal's personal habits and daily routines (when he/she is getting up in the morning, the time to leave for work, how long he/she stays at work, etc.). All the security has to be planned around those habits and routines. The principal should not change routines to fit the EPO's time schedule. Rather, it is the EPO who has to be flexible and to adapt to the lifestyle of the principal.

• Keeping a low profile

The EPO should dress and act appropriately and professionally. Even having a generous salary and the means to buy the latest in men's fashion, it would be foolish to wear something of the same or better style and class as the principal. It would draw the attention away from the principal. Some EPOs have lost their jobs because of such extravagant behavior.

- **Always keep a firm and professional reasoning**

  When dealing with security issues, the EPO should always keep a clear and professional tone and should never project a threat higher than the risk implies. This would frighten the principal, the family, and everybody else in the residence. The potential risk should be explained truthfully and straightforwardly, including the planned and projected steps to deal with it. Never over, neither underestimate any threat. The EPO must make this clear to the principal and keep him/her informed of all threats and the planned measures in place to handle a situation.

- **Be careful with spending and expenses**

  There might be occasions that the principal will invite the EPO for lunch or dinner. Or the EPO has to take the meal at the same time with the principal's party, or the principal is asks to take care of the payment. Whenever this happens, always bear in mind—never go overboard with spending other people's money. Always order something tasty, nutritious, not messy, within the principal's menu selection, and quick to eat.

  Never order anything you do not know, or a bigger portion or more expensive than the principal's choice. When taking care of the payment, and if allowed to tip, make sure that tipping is not included in the total mount. Be sure that the tip is not exaggerated (by average 10%-15%; in some foreign countries you should not tip at all). Never forget your good manners, whether you order, talk, eat, or pay.

- **Do not suffocate the principal**

  There is nothing more embarrassing than an over-protecting EPO. So many times we can observe those "fragile" celebrities almost being squashed by their bodyguards—a typical over-acting and over-reacting of insecure amateur bodyguards. The principal needs room to breathe, and he/she does not like their personal space invaded, unless a situation demands otherwise. The distance the EPO has to have to the principal varies with the situation. The closer the crowd, the closer is the EPO. But in situations where there is no or little threat or no crowd around, allow the principal more breathing space. When engaged in a phone call, a conversation, or any private or personal matter, the EPO should move discreetly away and allow the principal to have some privacy. If moving away is not possible because of space, then the EPO should turn discreetly away from the principal, but not diminish alertness.

The EPO must show good manners, professionalism and respect to the principal, the family members, staff, and related people. Staying above any doubt and causing a good impression at all times will assure a good standing and relationship with the principal and other entities directly or indirectly in connection with the assignment.

The Press and Media

The client—whether a celebrity, political figure, corporate executive, or renowned personality—can always be considered a newsworthy target. The principal makes a public appearance, gives a speech, or attends some reception; the news and media are not far behind and make sure to be very well represented. There are camera crews, reporters, photographers from networks, newspapers, magazines, local radio and television stations all over the place. All of those, professionals in their own rights, will be fighting for the best positions and angles for their cameras and questions. That is the moment the EPO is always anticipating, because media and security are operating on the same level but on a predefined collision course.

The media obviously wants to have unlimited and close-up access to the principal–the EPO's job is to assure the highest level of security and, therefore, keep the media at a safe distance. There is a small factor, which is very important in this balancing act–the principal and associates might need favorable attention from the media, but also seek full protection by security officers. This is a combination that makes the job worthwhile, because it is the EPO and the protection team's full responsibility to solve this problem with a good portion of common sense, compromise, and planning. The advance officer should anticipate all this and arrange defined locations for the media to meet. The best is, of course, to establish a specially marked area for the media. If possible, establish it based on the environment in the vicinity of the principal's arrival and departure and further at locations where the principal will hold a speech. That should be a location where the media can take their pictures and make their interviews or record any comments without being disrupted by spectators. The access point to the media area should be controlled by local police or by an EPO team member. Permission to access is granted only to credentialed media and credentialed members of the press. At access point everybody will be checked, credentials verified, camera, equipment bags and personal objects scanned. The EPO in charge of monitoring the media area entrance must keep vigilance on the area and the press in case someone or something was overlooked.

Members of the media are not the bad guys, if they are dealt with properly and given the right amount of respect. With the proper arrangements in place, the media will cooperate and they might even spot and point at an uncredentialed person within them. A very good tactic is to place the media in a position between the crowd (audience or spectators), the EPOs and the principal. In this way it forms a "buffer zone", preventing someone with bad intentions from approaching and getting near enough to achieve the intended purpose.

When working with the media remember:

- Members of the media and news are professionals in their fields and should be treated as such, with respect and dignity. Any questions, comments or remarks must be handled with diplomacy and tact. "No comment" is a simple statement, which can signify a lot to the receiver. Whatever the conditions are, no matter how far the media are pressing, never provide **any** information unless you have been specifically authorized and instructed. Always be polite and tactful. Whatever has to be disclosed, never compromise the principal or his security. The EPO has to make sure, that all inquiries are directed to one designated spokesperson. Most principals have a media liaison officer, who is responsible for all information released to the press; this will make sure that only complete and accurate information/statements are released.

- Never pose and attempt to avoid being in any photographs if possible. Any photograph taken from you or with the principal can be used as vital intelligence by anybody with the intention and planning to harm the principal. This could be used to identify the EPO and team members, as well as protective procedures. Never discuss anything about the principal, schedules, businesses, or anything else related to the assignment in presence of the media.

The following are examples of incidents, which were published in the press. A professional executive protection officer should always and at all costs: a) avoid such a negative exposure and b) be on top of any situation and anticipate any incident, before it comes to such an embarrassment. These type of incidents (whether justifiable or not) should not and cannot be tolerated by a principal. Incidents of that kind are leaving a very negative image of the EPOs-not mentioning, that such behavior is a disgrace to the entire EPO profession.

- January, 2005

  According to *FOX News*, Filmmaker Michael Moore's bodyguard was arrested for carrying an unlicensed weapon in New York's JFK airport. The Police took Patrick Burke, who says Moore employs him, into custody after he declared he was carrying a firearm at a ticket counter. Burke is licensed to carry a firearm in Florida and California, but not in New York. Burke was taken to Queens's central booking and could potentially be charged with a felony for the incident.

- March, 2006:

  According to *MSNBC*, three men hired to guard Britney Spears have filed a lawsuit, claiming they worked long hours and were not paid overtime. The lawsuit, filed in Superior Court, names three companies-Britney Brands Inc., Britney Touring Inc., and Team Tours Inc., as responsible for not properly compensating the former bodyguards L. Jones, R. Jones and S. Dukes. Together, the three men are seeking damages exceeding $25,000 for unpaid wages and benefits, their lawyer said. Jones and Dukes worked 12 to 16-hour shifts and were required to be on call 24 hours a day during trips with Spears, according to the lawsuit. L. Jones worked 12-hour shifts, the lawsuit said. The men claimed they were only paid a "straight salary," missed meals and didn't receive overtime pay. Hired in 2004, the men claim they were laid-off on November 2005, without receiving a final paycheck.

- November, 2006:

  According to *Reuters*, the Indian police detained three of Angelina Jolie's bodyguards on Friday. Parents complained, that the men had man-handled them and their children at an Islamic school in Mumbai where Jolie was filming a scene for "A Mighty Heart".
  M. H. Belose, the additional chief metropolitan magistrate, later that day freed the three identified bodyguards on bail and asked them not to leave the country for one week (must report to court every day for one week). Bail guarantees were set for $545 each. If convicted, the three can be jailed for up to three years. Witnesses said, the bodyguards pushed and shoved some of the parents. The Police prosecutor N. C. Tambe told the court that the three had upset people by calling them "bloody Indians" and "bloody Muslims".

- March, 2007:

  According to *BBC News*, two of the men who get paid to guard the body of Oscar-nominated actor Leonardo DiCaprio have been arrested after a scuffle near the Western Wall in Jerusalem. Reports state, that Leonardo DiCaprio was visiting the walled Old City in Jerusalem with his Israeli girlfriend Bar Refaeli when the incident with his bodyguards and a couple of photographers got ugly. A police spokesperson told the press that fists flew and that one photographer was slightly injured in the fight. According to reports two of Leonardo DiCaprio's guards were arrested after allegedly hitting some of the photographers. The guards arrested did not travel with the actor from the States, but were local guards hired through a private security company. The two guards were taken to the Jerusalem District police station and released later during the night after questioning with complaints filed against them.

- April, 2007:
  According to *Associated Press*, rap-singer Mystikal (real name: Michael Tyler) was sentenced together with his two bodyguards based on an incident in July 2002, were he confronted the hairdresser, accusing her of kiting $80, 000 worth of his checks. The rapper allegedly told her he wouldn't turn her into the police if she would have sex with him and bodyguards Leland "Pokie" Ellis and Vercy "V" Carter. Baton Rouge police later searched Mystikal's apartment and found a videotape of the sex acts. Last June, Mystikal reversed his initial plea of not guilty and struck a deal with prosecutors, averting a trial and a possible 10-year sentence (actually he got 6 years for sexual battery and 5 years probation for extortion). Ellis was sentenced to three years in prison, Carter to four years.

The Host Committee

When dealing with organizing and/or sponsoring organizations, events, fund-raisings or any other official place to which the principal is invited to, a person or group of officials in charge of such events is known as the "Host committee". This can be an engagement to deliver a speech, a charity dinner, a reception or political event. Whatever the function or the location is, there will always be a contact-person/group responsible for organizing that event.

This person/group will work with the EPO and provide assistance whenever necessary to the assigned security officers. The host is to be considered friendly and is interested to expose the principal to all the guests at the event. Such good intentioned enthusiasm of the host might easily become a security risk of serious concern for the EPO. For example, there might be situations, when there is no possibility to screen all the attending people, which the host might like to have the principal greet and meet. This "permission" to get close to a less shielded principal is the perfect chance for anybody who wants to harm the principal.

The EPO's priority is to check all the arrangements and plans of the host and if there is reason for a lack of a good protection, the EPO has to make sure, that changes are made to improve the security. In order to avoid a conflict, the EPO has to use tact and diplomacy to overcome any difficulty. It is always the best to find a platform of compromise for the host, but with emphasis on security.

The EPO has to work closely with the host, allowing the EPO to place and establish barriers, such as the placement of the tables, flowerpots and guest. All these factors must be taken in consideration to position the principal at the event. Whatever is suitable to place between the crowd, the EPO and the principal will prevent someone in the crowd from attacking the principal. A person assigned by the host should assist the security at the entrance door/s (checkpoint) by confirming the arriving people with the invitation/guest list and by screening the incoming guests.

The Executive Protection

- The Personal Protection Industry

- The Executive Protection Officer

- The Protection Concept

- The Principles of Protection

- Preparedness and Readiness

- Prevention

- The Target Hardening

- The Concept of the Concentric Circles

- Who needs Protection

The Personal Protection Industry

The private security, as a professional sector, contrary to general belief, is not a relatively modern development. Studying the history from the beginnings of mankind reveals, that the protection of life and property and the security in general has been one of the oldest tasks faced and undertaken by man.

Today, security transformed into a multifaceted and a very broad-based business sector, foundation for a profession with specialties and sub-specialties, which is employing more people than the public law enforcement sector. There are an estimated 1. 6 to 1. 9 million private security officers just in the USA, compared to total of 700, 000 law enforcement officers. By the year 2010, private "cops" will outnumber public police officers six to one-giving a whole new meaning to the notion of "protecting and serving". Private security officers are forming (for example in the USA) the largest protective resource. Financially speaking, it represents more than one percent of the entire gross national product of the United States with a projection of a continued growth. The private security as such has had an evolutionary growth deep-rooted in history, extending far back to antiquity.

The present day security companies are providing more complex services not only to private clients and corporations, but also to governmental organizations and state authorities. The times, where a security guard was related to banks and/or linked to money transports has long past. The security industry has diversified so much, that not only the business but also security personnel is classified by areas of activity and type of duty. For example: In-House Security, Contract Security, Public Security, Private Police, Security Police, Guard or Patrol.

The terms and titles used by the security industry to cover the variety of security personnel and positions range from Security Guard; Agent; Patrol; Security Officer; Safety Patrol Officer to Armed Security Agent. From Private Police Officer; Loss Prevention Officer; Bodyguard to Close Protection Agent and so on. As much controversy is generated toward the entire industry, especially in means of regulations and legal aspects, as much controversy exists regarding the job titles of their personnel.

The job title "Security Guard" for instance might be acceptable in some states, but might not be in accordance with local regulations in another. The use of job titles such as "Security Officer" or "Security Agent" can sometimes even be regulated like in various State and local governments (USA) by law. For example, California security licensees, according to the Business and Professions Code Section 7582.26 are forbidden to use certain words and/or phrases which could give the impression the person is connected in any way to the federal government. It would be unlawful for a security licensee to use the title Private Police or Special Agent California.

Every security officer is proud to use and to display his/her and most likely it also reflects the dedication and the amount of hours spent on special training and acquired skills. However, a title no matter how hard it is earned can cause more trouble to the bearer than good.

For example, security personnel are cautioned that identifying themselves as "Officer" to a person or the police, particularly in a threat-or tactical situation, can result in a mistaken identity-the result are charges for impersonating a police officer. While using the term "Guard", may prevent a potentially lethal confusion, especially when contacting with law enforcement personnel and dispatchers.

The laws and regulations regarding the security industry are in most cases too linear and not up-to-date with today's demands. For example in some states, applications for security related licenses are regulated and handled by the same entity, as those for bail enforcement (bounty hunters) or loss prevention and private investigators. We can observe that the security industry, including all possible and imaginable branches and specialties related to or interacting with security is expanding and developing. Such rapid expansion and development of the industry will require a thorough and well elaborated regulating law for their activities. Regulating the security industry according to the specific demands of private, corporate and government sectors is not only a matter for a local authority, but need to be considered and taken care of by a specialized entity. That entity must be able to regulate, enforce and over watch the vastness of this industry, in particular the areas of operation, training, specialization, level of access and clearance. Once fully regulated on a local, national level, it should be recognized on a global and international level as well.

Sed quis custodiet ipsos custodes? (Latin= Who watches the watchmen?)

The private security as we know it today has developed as the result of a multitude of ideas, concepts, historical events and identifiable individuals and personalities. Private security has become vital, essential and a strong ingredient of modern business, industry and society. The attack on the United States on September 11, 2001 triggered modifications and created such an enormous demand on the physical and protective security business worldwide never experienced before.

According to the industry research group *The Freedonia Group*[17], the world demand for private security services will grow 7.3 percent annually through 2010 based on rising urbanization and heightened fears of crime and terrorism.

The US will remain the largest market while developing regions will grow the fastest. This result was based on a study analyzing the $ 110 billion world security service industry. It presents historical demand data for 1995, 2000 and 2005 and forecasts to 2010 and 2015. The data are based on service type (e. g. personnel, alarm monitoring, prison management, consulting, private investigations, etc.), market sector, world region (e. g. North America, Western Europe, Asia/Pacific) and 23 individual major countries.

Based on this trend, any security oriented client is trying to get the best trained and globally deployable security personnel for his/her needs. Further, based on job offers worldwide, clients are seeking security personnel which they believe are licensed and operational wherever the client requires. That is not that simple. As mentioned earlier, licenses for security personnel and executive protection officers in particular are subject to local or national regulations. This means, that an officer with a valid California issued license, for example, is permitted to operate in the issuing state (it might be recognized by other US states). But this license is not valid to operate in another state or a foreign country.

Any client should make certain, that all the legal aspects on both sides are covered fully. Further the client has to take care of the legal paperwork at his/her end to avoid any legal surprises, which should be considered as part of the client's security. For short-term assignments, it is sometimes good to have a local EPO (holder of a local license) working conjoined with hired foreign EPOs. This might take care of the security license, but does not include a working permit for foreigners.

Numerous companies claim to issue international close protection/executive protection/bodyguard licenses or internationally recognized bodyguard certificates-there is no such thing. This type of highly condemnable promotion by many of the security industry has only one purpose-to attract students and gain some extra money. No matter, how fancy the certificate appears and the promises are tempting, remember-a license is only valid and permits to work within the local laws and requirements only. These local laws and regulations vary greatly from state to state and from country to country. Actually, in some states and/or countries the legal requirements are very simple and straight forward, without the need to prove previous law enforcement, military experience or special training. In fact most executive protection officers are working with a license, which is covers the activity of a security guard or a private investigator.

In the UK, the government body regulating the security industry, which includes the close protection, executive protection sector will issue specific executive protection licenses. This is one of the few specific close protection and executive protection licenses. For the license it requires proof of a minimum training in executive protection/close protection (recognition of foreign courses has to be checked) and/or professional experience to qualify for it. This license, like all the others will however only be recognized inside of the U. K.

The executive protection and specialist courses/seminars are meant to provide training in advanced procedures and techniques that usually are not employed by or applicable to security personnel, military and law enforcement units. Executive protection is a business for specialists, which requires and demands a specialized training. Most of the EPOs have a minimum of 5-10 years of experience and they are still learning.

The Executive Protection Officer

Over the years the profession of the personal and executive protection has followed the demand of the fast increasing number of clients, technology and world events. The industry of the personal protection has been submitted to constant changes, its personnel better trained and specialized, which ultimately reflects in the terms used to identify the professionals. What appears to be common in the business and as practiced in the entire security industry (accommodating regulating laws and requirements to obtain a license) reveals to be a problem. Particularly, when those terms are used in languages other than English, the image of the personal protection professionals becomes somehow confusing and conflicting. Despite the fact of higher professional qualifications and standards, when referring to personal and executive protection, most people immediately associate it with what is commonly known as "Bouncer" and "Bodyguard". In some countries a private investigator license includes a "bonus"-the bodyguard license.

The term "Bouncer" presents an image of someone who should physically break up fights and forcibly ejects undesirable people from a premise. Bouncers are often portrayed in the media as tough, thug-like guys who love to fight. Many nightclubs and discos foster that image by hiring over-sized individuals and bodybuilders to handle drunken and/or uncontrollable customers. Many of these bouncers have none or little experience and never received a specialized training. In India for example, bouncers are recruiting in gyms-a background check is done and that is it. Many of those employed are not even capable to express themselves sufficiently in the local language. Those inexperienced "professionals", when dealing with a crisis, besides having a communication problem, are forced to rely on their own common sense, physical instincts and whatever experience they have. Altogether not that much to solve a problem. What a scary concept.

The professional Bouncer is able to monitor and manage a crowd, makes sure that everyone is having a good time, behaves and follows the house-rules. As a professional, the Bouncer is friendly and polite, able to talk to people without appearing threatening or intimidating. This profession should not be restricted to male candidates only.

A "Bodyguard", "*Leibwächter*" (German), "*Livvagt*" (Danish), "*Garde du Corps*" (French), "*Guardia Personal*" (Spanish), "*Guarda Costas*" (Portuguese) or "*Yōjinbō*" (Japanese) is someone who escorts and protects a prominent person. A term easily translated into other languages triggers in most people images of starlets, pop stars and rap moguls rolling into nightclubs in LA and other places and surrounded by muscle-bound men in ill-fitting black suits. Actually none of those likes to be called "bodyguard" anymore (it sound so antiquated), so they prefer "VIP Protection" instead.

The term "bodyguard" quickly became replaced by a new title along with a new image, which is translating professionalism, training, and integrity. The "Executive Protection Expert" or "Executive Protection Officer" is a highly trained, well educated specialists. A professional who is as confident in a corporate environment and comfortable with diplomats, presidents and royalties as they are in the streets of a world full of violence. This new generation of personal protection officers provides security with excellence and expertise and keeping a "principal" safe and alive at all costs.

The Protection Concept

Executive protection in its basics can be traced back in time, when important and prominent people, mostly aristocrats and heads of states were in need of a personal protection. Experience based on time and events helped to improve this very basic protection arrangement and shaped it into a fully functional and most effective protection concept, as it is knows today. To give an exact date for the formation of today's protection concept would be as incorrect as mentioning a name of the one who created it first. The 1970s without a doubt was most likely the decade which provided more than sufficient reasons for a new concept of executive protection. It was the time, when most of the governmental agencies restructured their resources and established special branches and units with a unique purpose-to provide protective service to national officials and foreign dignitaries. What was once the job of military-and police units, depending on country and resources, was now the duty of especially selected and newly formed services. In the following decades the increasing numbers of incidents involving diplomats, politicians and the proliferation of terrorist fractions worldwide dictated immediate and effective changes of these newly structured and established agencies. Creating and providing assignment specific and mission realistic training programs to these new protection services shaped the elite concept of executive protection.

In the 1970s, the German *Bundespolizei* (Federal Police), *Bundesgrenzschutz* (Federal Border Police) and *Feldjäger* (Military Police) established their own *Personenschutz* (Personal/Dignitary Protection) branches. In 1974, Great Britain formed a *Diplomatic Protection Group* (DPG) under the responsibility of the Metropolitan Police Service. In 1975, the United States Secret Service established an uniform division, the *Executive Protection Service* for the protection of foreign embassies. In Hong Kong, the Hong Kong Police Force established the *VIP Protection Unit* (VIPPU), also known as the G4 (Section G, Division 4). In Canada during the 1950s and 1960s, members of the RCMP (Royal Canadian Mounted Police) were assigned to dignitary protection, but in the 1970s *Protective Policing Service* became an independent identifiable function of the RCMP. In Australia, in 1984, the Australian Federal Police established their *Australian Protective Service*.

The security industry aware of those changes, was eager to get hold of this new business opportunity, offering executive protection packages, an elite program of security to the wealthy and powerful. With the expansion of the private security sector over the years, the term executive protection was used and abused to its maximum. Executive protection served to install alarm systems, to mount closed circuit cameras and monitors and other technological gadgets in residences and/or corporate premises of executive, wealthy and prominent clients. For some companies, institutes and even licensed individuals, executive protection was the business term. It described everything from complex security systems to safeguard offices and/or buildings, surveillance and monitoring to bodyguarding and courses for defensive shooting and high-speed and evasive driving. As time passed by and business was going at its best, executive protection faced another stage of "enrichment". Executive protection, probably the phrase of the decade, became "enriched" by a variety of other security activities, such as risk management, physical security planning, threat assessment, etc..

No matter how innovative and plentiful those newly created services of the security industry are, the concept of executive protection is the essence of all known principles of protection:

- clear determination of the actual threats
- clear determination of potential vulnerabilities
- a careful analyzing and planning
- implementing a well conceived planning
- advance security arrangements
- total awareness and provision of a safe and secure environment

The term "executive protection" used by the industry, is misleading and its definition gave plenty of room to be misused and mistaken by the general public and professionals alike.

The concept as such is a security program designed around the lifestyle, the family and the environment of an individual, which is being protected. Executive protection is also a general term used to describe professionals providing close-proximity, personal security to a person, which most likely is or becomes targeted to an individual or a group of people intending to inflict harm.

Executive protection is a close-, personal protection, awareness and planning program, which is not limited to executives, but available and applicable to any person (group of persons) with the need for personal security. Never underestimate a threat, neither an enemy. A protection program can never provide the guarantee for an one-hundred-percent security, let's be conscious about that, but one is able to reduce the odds and risks for the person under protection with the implementation of effective protection programs. A full profile of the person/s to be protected, lifestyle and environment is as much important, as planning and execution of the programs. It is the EPO's responsibility to establish a profile, and get answers to certain questions which are fundamental in identifying certain dangers and to recommend the proper counter-measures. What kind of a person and character is the individual to be protected? Where should he/she be protected? What should he/she be protected from? Which will be the consequences and result of the protection? What type of protection should apply? Questions like these, answered in detail by the principal or the assigned representative should provide data for an initial security analysis. It must also include all the possible and imaginable areas of vulnerability. There are four main sectors, a principal is at risk:

Home -Work -Leisure -Travel

Based on the analysis a detailed security planning and an implementation of the program can be initiated. The planning of a security program should incorporate the entire living, working, leisure and travel environment of the person/s being protected. By providing the best possible security, the EPO must make certain to allow personal freedom and the least disruption of lifestyle possible.

The protection program's implementation starts with the principal's awareness of the potential hazards and his/her acceptance of the recommendations, which could be identified in the survey. The recommendations should be accompanied by an estimate of the costs, the program's advantages and disadvantages, as well as the equipment required for the program. It is very important, once the program is in place, that security briefings are held on a regular basis for all the personnel in contact with the principal. This includes the family members, household staff, secretaries, colleagues, friends, etc. Each of them must be aware of the dangers and potential risks and think effectively about security. The intended result of any executive protection is to reduce a threat or risk down to the minimum and to stop and discourage any possible attack whether from amateur-and/or professional enemies.

What are the threats?

Where are those good old days? Violence and crime in its most diversified and malicious form has spread and grown to terrifying dimensions. Terrorism, with its international ramifications covers the entire world. No matter how one observes the world of today and no matter how conclusive our analysis is, there are more than hundreds of reasons for a person to seek protection.

It might be true, chances to face a direct terrorist attack are most unlikely, but any other type of attack and violence is just around the corner. On the way out of the house, some drug addict in need of cash is threatening to kill you if he does not get what he wants. While you enjoy the day in the office, an employee unhappy with his sex life, starts shooting around with the newly purchased submachine guns. Your kids are having a good time in school, when suddenly a few of the students unpack their gear and start to recreate a trendy video game with real weapons and life ammo. You are a very popular singer, but some people might not like your music and wants to shut you up. Others, enjoying your music and desperately in love with your looks are willing to do everything to be close to you.

According to the Federal Bureau of Investigation's Uniform Crime Reports, the violent crime rate increased 1. 3% from 2004 to 2005 and the property crime rate decreased 2. 4% from 2004 to 2005. Those figures compared with those of 1996 indicate that crimes decreased. The UCR crime index includes seven offenses; homicide, forcible rape, robbery, aggravated assault, burglary, larceny-theft, and motor vehicle theft.

Reading the newspapers, one might conclude, that stalking, harassing, robbing, crime, vandalism, kidnapping and life threatening situations are the most likely scenarios a person should worry about nowadays. Those are the reasons to be concerned about personal security. No matter what type of danger and risk is out there, one should never underestimate the impact it might have on the security and safety of the person.

The principles, reasons and need of personal protection have not changed and remains the same since one person decided to protect another person. Protective service is the main principle and it embodies everything which is required to protect the principal from any and all potential threats and dangers and to reduce possible risks. It the EPOs full responsibility and duty to avoid and eliminate:

- Any intentional attack causing harm and/or injury
  - The inflicting of injuries and harm by means of an intentional attack executed by a person or a group of people, which is ready to commit an overt action in order to inflict a great injury or probably death to a selected target person. Intentionally attacking and injuring means also the use of force or violence to achieve the greatest possible damage (assassination or serious permanent injury) to the target person. An intentional attack can also be covered with an act of unintentional harm; what appears to be an unintentional mishap, can place the target person in serious danger. Safety measures and possible disrespect of safety regulations and similar issues have to be acknowledged and prevented. The EPO and the implemented security program has to recognize such situations and has to deal with it accordingly.

- Any unintentional provoked or caused harm and/or injury
  - Harm and injury can be caused unintentionally by an accidental step, a fall and even by a friendly guest or fan. A person, while being distracted by other things can slip, fall or trip. Best examples for such situations are microphone cables, loose carpets, unstable podiums, he combination of cocktail dress and high heels, or simply mother nature's rain, ice and snow. Besides causing a possible injury, it might also cause some headlines because these kind of incidents are the most anticipated by the media. The EPO has to make sure, that these even unexpected and unpredictable situations are under control and he/she is ready for a catch.

- Any negative exposure, embarrassment (public or otherwise)
  - Protect a person from negative exposure and/or embarrassment means that whatever the person intended to do should be in accordance with what he/she is standing for. Any contradicting situation he/she might get involved with or dragged into, should be avoided. For example, if the principal is known to be an advocate and defender of the unborn life, he/she should not be seen together with people vividly supporting abortion. It is the job of the EPO to keep the principal from public appearances, which might conflict with his/her beliefs and image, most likely demanding embarrassing explanations.

- Any non-authorized release of information on and about the principal
  - Protecting communications with and about the principal and keeping all communications confidential (including the itinerary and schedule) inspires trust and confidence. The EPO has to avoid any unauthorized disclosure of information about the principal. Any personal information being spread could have a negative effect on the principal. The EPO is also preventing that tactical information could get into the wrong hands, ultimately be harmful for the principal. The EPO assists the principal in keeping his/her schedule, eliminating any risk of late arrivals at planned events. It may also stop a planned or opportunistic attack by positioning the principal in an area of expectancy and elevated anticipation. As a result it will reduce the stress between several engagements. Principals expect from EPOs a total and unquestionable loyalty; privacy of personal information must be kept confidential at all times. Keeping information confidential is a very significant part of the principles, beliefs and reputation of the executive protection profession.

Safeguarding information for the principal, family members, associates and staff requires including electronic countermeasures, such as physical search for hidden audio and video devices, recording and transmission devices, telephone and wiretaps in the procedures. The identification and proposal of other means of safe communication is also part of the EPOs responsibility.

Preparedness and Readiness

Nothing else could summarize the content of this chapter better than the motto we adapted for our protection team:

Semper Paratus -Nec Aspera Terrent
(Latin= Always Prepared-Be Not Terrified by Adversity)

Security programs are conceivable with much more detail and perfection, thanks to the availability of technically advanced methods and the development of the security industry itself. With all these innovations and technologies at your fingertips, soon you discover there is a downside to it--cost-effectiveness and budget. Only combining common sense, knowledge and skills, the EPO is able to conceive and implement with the proper and cost-effective budget an executive protection package, tailored to the principal's security needs. Being always prepared for emergency situations, aware of any threatening situations and anticipating any and all types of danger is the exclusive responsibility of a professional EPO. Preparedness and readiness in any situation transmits the sense of confidence and anticipation to any protective defense. A protective shield, transpiring preparedness, readiness, confidence and alertness might reduce the risk of or deter any potential attack, whether such attack is planned or of opportunistic nature. An effective almost invisible protective shield-*The Shield (Defender) which shall not be seen* (א יראא ירא) (Motto of the **I**sraeli **S**ecurity **A**gency (ISA)).

Prevention

You will never know, until you fail.

That's what prevention in the protection program is all about. Prevention or deterrence is another very important ingredient in the complexity of executive protection, because the EPO will never know when an attack occurs or if an attack was avoided. An EPO can only be sure, that his/her assignment was a success, if the protection program was well planned and executed and no attack on the principal or to his/her environment took place. An attack can only succeed if there is a weakness in the protection program and its execution and if such weakness was exploited by a determined attacker.

Does the principal have sufficient protection? Is the security program covering all aspects? Should the principal be protected by one or more EPOs? A principal can easily be protected by one EPO, if this EPO is not used for any other duties. If the EPO is used for other duties, than the security arrangements can only be carried out partially; diminishing the effectiveness of the protection. An EPO, when assigned to protect the principal should never be used for other functions, not as driver, baggage carrier, shopping bag mule, or for any other job, usually carried out by staff personnel. Even though if nothing happens and the principal was not attacked, this is no reason to conclude that sufficient security was provided. If a principal is attacked, despite the fact that he/she is protected by a whole squad of Marines-could lead to conclude that the security program was not sufficient. Since executive protection cannot be measured by factors and units, any protection program to be implemented has to be very well balanced and should provide a complete security coverage.

While on assignments, the EPO will never be able to find out, whether his/her executive protection program is effective and successful. But an EPO will experience satisfaction, when the absence of incidents, is related to and caused by prevention and the deterring measures of the program. Prevention and deterrence is a very effective tool in protective detail. Failure is measurable by an actual attempt of an attack.

A final word to all security oriented clients, which have a protection program implemented; the absence of actual attacks and/or harmful incidents is not a reason to fire your EPO or EPO team.

The Target Hardening

Hardening the target is an indispensable part of the prevention process, which can be implemented in many ways. In simple terms, target hardening is a process, which makes a target more difficult to reach for any attacker, whether intentional or unintentional. The protection program is aimed to accomplish this task successfully by deterring an attack. Sometimes it does not need sophisticated technology to accomplish this. What, in some cases, a well elaborated security system with detection, monitoring, and alarming devices is not fully achieving can successfully by done with a simple change of schedule, routes and/or a low profile approach.

However, the result is in its complexity. It is the full integration and interrelation of its components, various measures, circumstances, people and the technology which makes it so effective. The process of target hardening is the constituted by:

People–Procedures–Technology

People
  - Includes the principal, family, staff personnel, executive board or management, company employees and the executive protection officers.
Procedures
  - Is in form of instructions and directives to provide guidance to those involved in the security process and protection program, outlining in detail the adequate response to any adverse activity or doubtable situation.
Technology
  - Includes everything in form of access controls, physical and psychological barriers, CCTV (closed-circuit television), lighting systems, intercoms, signs, and intrusion detection and alarm systems.

The Concept of the Concentric Circles

The concept of the concentric circles can be traced back in history. A perfect example of a concentric "walls-within-walls" design is the *Beaumaris Castle* (located in Anglesey-North Wales), which is considered the most technically perfect castle, which has few equals. The design involves no less than four successive lines of fortifications. It was state of the art for the late 13th century. (see Fig. 15)

Like in a castle, the same concept is also effective for the protection of the principal. The principal is surrounded by a number of concentric rings, providing a maximum of security not only to the principal but to his/her environment as well. (see Fig. 16) The center of the executive protection programs is focused on the person being protected-the principal and expand from there outward in a series of concentric rings. Under best conditions the program should consist of at least three protective rings.

The center circle involves the principal. The principal must be fully aware of the existence of criminals, with intentions to harm him/her or his family and/or to compromise the business and assets.

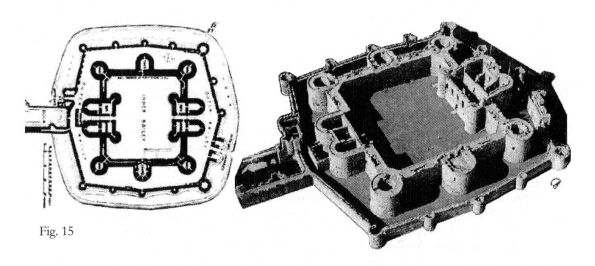

Fig. 15

Inside this circle are also those persons closest to the principal; family, friends, staff and protection personnel, which are working in close proximity to the principal. In many occasions a principal is resenting the established protective shield around him/her; most likely because it could avoid to move freely or infringes on the privacy. Many times the EPO will be confronted with a convincing "whatever happens, will happen", or he/she has to face the heroic type "if they really want me, than they have to stay in line". Obviously, those principals are difficult to work with (in many situations it showed, that spouses were more reasonable) and this reflects in their cooperation. A full understanding of the situation is required to receive the necessary cooperation and the EPO has the responsibility and duty to make certain that the principal is aware of this.

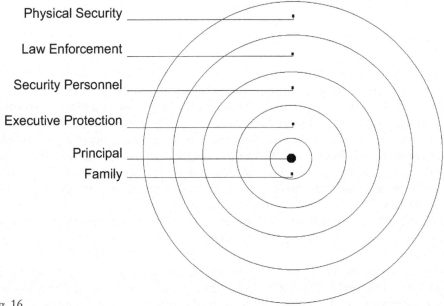

Physical Security

Law Enforcement

Security Personnel

Executive Protection

Principal

Family

Fig. 16

In the majority of situations, this type of principal did not contract a protective detail by his own, but has been assigned one because of his/her post and related regulations. Some business executives used to control whatever situation are belonging to this category as well. The majority of people receiving protection services are very cooperative; the ask for advise and follow the given instructions. The principal recognizes the necessity and the importance of the security and that whatever program is implemented is for his/her own benefit. The principal is the focus point of attention in his/her circle, followed only by a few trusted people, which includes the family members, staff and the EPO responsible for close-proximity protection. It is the main duty and responsibility of the inner circle security to protect the principal at all times at all costs.

The second concentric circle is the one of protection provided by the personnel, which is covering the principal from all sides. This full coverage is within arms reach of the principal. No matter to which direction the principal turns, there is always someone between the principal and the possible attacker or friendly people. It is the entire responsibility of this circle to keep a constant look-out for possible threats, suspicious persons, any furtive movements that might give away an attack, weapons, or "something" which appears to be out of place.

The protection program's third and fourth concentric circle incorporates security and law enforcement personnel (either plain or uniformed), which is responsible for control and check of access areas and for establishing surveillance points. This inner and outer perimeters of the principal's position is under a constant vigilance and shall permit access to authorized personnel only.

Physical security forms another circle and includes the environment and everything else. Applying psychological and physical barriers, alarm systems, CCTVs (closed-circuit televisions), reinforced doors, locks, hedges, fences, restricted areas and even strategically placed members of an audience or crowd are very effective to slow down and to deter any attack. In this context, the advance person can make arrangements and have small groups of people (previously cleared by security) or children (depending on the event) positioned between the principal and the remaining audience. This arrangement provides protection and a perfect image for the media.

All these circles are surrounded by knowledge and assessment. It is the awareness of and ability to identify every potential threat; the capability to identify, analyze and anticipate situations that would be disastrous to the protected person. It also incorporates the awareness of existing alternatives, options and secondary measures, which if required can instantaneously be activated and implemented to improve the protective program.

Who Needs Protection

There are no rules or formulae to determine, who is entitled or which group of people is requiring the services of an EPO more. Most likely and as a matter of cash flow, political figures, members of royal families, celebrities of all sorts, movie and television stars are the best known candidates. Unfortunately, this is giving us a wrong impression and sends the wrong message to those in need. An average person, even not having the financial means for a protection service, might get into a situation, that protection is required. A medic can be a target because of his scientific research, a tourist because he/she is traveling through a troubled nation. A woman, a victim of domestic violence, a witness to a crucial court case or an author can become a target. Everybody can once come in need to utilize the services of a professional trained EPO. It is the EPO's professional capability in the complexities of protection to keep a person safe from harm, injury, death or embarrassment. The service and tasks performed by the executive protection personnel, such as advance work, logistics, problem solving causes a sense of exaggerated importance to the principal.

Executive protection is an approach, using common sense, awareness, personnel, procedures, systems and advanced technology to protect an individual or group of people. The executive protection officer is responsible for the principal's security, safety, health and well-being. Preparation, anticipation and planning are the key factors which help to minimize the risk for the principal. Executive protection is not a confrontation driven program, but rather an anticipated and projected response to an unavoidable situation. Stopping an attack, avoid confrontation and keeping the principal out of danger and harm's way—that is the task of the EPO.

The fact that executive protection is very often used (not to say-abused) as a status symbol, gives a bitter taste to the protection industry. Taking in consideration the financial means and the status symbolic of executive protection, one should not be surprised to find on the Internet companies and individuals, offering protection services:

Example 1:

> *I am a 34 Yr Old former member of the British Royal Military Police. I served 16 yrs specializing in Close Protection Operations for British Royalty, British Government and Foreign and Commonwealth Diplomatic Staff and their families overseas. (Sierra Leone, etc) I have an extensive CV which is available when required. Make no mistake, I am a specialist in high threat CP Ops who can move seamlessly from Afghanistan/Iraq to Diplomatic Dinner parties. I am also an experienced CP and Conflict Management trainer. I am looking for employment in the Middle East (Saudi, Dubai, Qatar, UAE, Jordan etc). However all options will be considered. I am married and am willing to re-locate.*

> *Location: Middle East, Afghanistan, Bahrain, Dubai, Iran, Iraq, Israel, Jordan, Kuwait, Lebanon, Oman, Qatar, Saudi Arabia, Syria, United Arab Emirates, Yemen*
> *Budget: $ 120, 000-150, 000*

Example 2:

> *I have served in the Royal Navy for 6 years. I am looking for employment as soon as possible and I am willing to relocate anywhere in the world. I can supply a range of close protection officers to the client depending on the client's specifications. I have Management experience of 30+ personnel, Budget control, Project Management, Private Investigation and Surveillance, Debt Recovery agent, establishing links with national and international clients, Advertising and marketing, Strategy and implementation of Close Protection operations, Payroll of employees, Risk Consultancy, Security Consultancy, training and development of personnel and new applicants, Operations Management, Customer service and client satisfaction. Strategy and implementation of VIP and event security operations. Conflict Management, First Respondent, Para medicine, Protective Driving, Special Weapons & Tactics, and Pedestrian Escort and Attack on Principal Procedures, Venue Management and advanced Reconnaissance, Security Consultancy, Vehicle Management & Route Reconnaissance, Close Protection Protocol & Etiquette. I have also provided Private Security in the United Kingdom, France, Spain, Czech Republic, Ireland, Singapore, Dubai, Bahrain, Mombassa and South Africa*

> *Location: Oman, Qatar*
> *Budget: $ 70, 000-120, 000*

These offers are showing very clearly the direction the security industry is heading to. Let's take a closer look at these two offers. Leaving the professional experience aside, details which appear of no importance to the applicant, but extremely important for the client are completely absent and can be misleading:

- no mentioning of any foreign language skills
  (just wondering-does everybody speak English in Middle East, or did I always meet with the wrong people)
- no mentioning of any driver's license (type and classes/categories)
  (how about an international driver's permit)
- no mentioning of passport (visa and validity)

- roaming in the Middle-East is not that simple-a passport cannot have visa entries of certain Arab nations if one intends to enter Israel and vice-versa. Passports with less than 6 months of validity might be still good for traveling, but might not be good to stay in a country, etc., etc.
- no mentioning of working permit (in many countries foreigners cannot even obtain a working permit without having a residence permit)
- no mentioning of vaccination (types and certificate)
- no mentioning of firearms permit
- no mentioning of any First Aid/CPR/Paramedic/Lifeguard certification

A client or even an EPO, when recruiting for a team, should have similar questions and doubts, when presented with this type of offers and applications. According to these and similar offers, one is tempted to conclude that it is easier to hire a platoon of adventure driven, qualified mercenaries, than to find one suitable and qualified professional EPO.

Whether you are a client in need of protection or if you are an EPO seeking a job assignment, make always sure, that everything from professional and personal background to permits and ID papers is covered. Both parties, client and EPO can only reach an agreement, if both have taken care of all the legal issues related to the assignment. The success of an executive protection program is in the detail. Omissions regarding the EPO's personal and professional data or the client's personal background and legal status, no matter how insignificant it might appear, is not acceptable.

The Principal

- EPO and Principal Relationship

- Close Proximity

- Moving the Principal in a Crowd

- The Protective Team

- The Checkpoint

- The Security Posts

- The Observation Posts

- Special Duties

- The Command Post

EPO and Principal Relationship

The relationship between an EPO and a principal is a very close one-similar to that of a marriage. As much as a marriage is either blessed to succeed or condemned to fail, as much is the relationship with a principal. One important part in a relationship is the knowledge of the other one's likes and dislikes, moods and tempers, strength and weaknesses, physical abilities and condition, behavior and routines. Once the EPO is aware of all those details regarding the principal, he/she can start to work on the protection program itself. Having an incomplete picture of the principal is a risk to the entire protection program.

The EPO is only able to protect a principal with success, if he/she knows the person to protect in every aspect and detail. When accepting a protection assignment, the EPO has to ascertain that he/she is gathering as much information about the principal as possible. The principal, under normal circumstances will often provide a great amount of information or a designate staff member will be providing whatever information is necessary. Besides knowing the person and the personal preferences of the principal, it is equally important to know the routines, schedule/s, location/s of meetings and appointments. Also important are the names of family and staff members, contact phone numbers (24 hours a day), medical problems (heart conditions, allergies, disabilities, etc.), and medical contacts. Knowing the principal's blood type and allergic reaction to medications is lifesaving in an emergency.

Knowing the principal has to become part of the EPO. The better the EPO knows the principal, the easier and smoother is the relationship with the principal. The EPOs typical protection routine starts with the principal in the morning, than the EPO takes the principal to work, bring him/her home at the end of the day and watches over the principal during the night. In fact an EPO on an assignment is spending more time with the principal than with wife and family and this might be one of the reasons for divorced or single EPOs. Knowing the work and family environment of the principal is another important factor for the EPO and it is as much significant as to know the threat level of a potential risk. Knowing all these details makes it easier for the EPO to understand, anticipate, and neutralize the threat. If the EPO is aware of the principal's concerns and needs and is able to anticipate, the relationship will reveal to be friendly, cordial and rewarding. The same knowledge of personal details applies to other family members. It might not be appropriate to gather all the vital information at an initial meeting, which most likely tend to be nothing more than introduction. Following such an initial meeting, the EPO must make sure to gather all information necessary at the first opportunity, either first hand from the principal, wife or from a senior staff member. The obtained information is analyzed, recorded in a secure file and briefed to security personnel on a need-to-know basis.

The principal should equally know about the role of the EPO and how the reaction will be in case of an emergency. The principal has to be instructed to follow the leading EPO and to seek the EPO for guidance and direction in any situation of potential risk or harmful consequences. The principal should not only be aware, that the EPO's duty is to cover and evacuate, but that in case of emergency, such procedures could quickly become of a forceful and physical manner. Some principals might oppose to be handled with force and against their will, even if that will save their life. The EPO has to be professional, tactful and diplomatic and making clear to the principal, that such procedure is for his/her own good and it only applies if the situation is not permitting otherwise.

Close Proximity

The EPO's main responsibility is to protect the principal. Working close proximity, being immediate to the principal enables the EPO to provide full coverage and protection. This is the inner center of the concentric protective circles, which forms the secure environment. This might be considered as the most dangerous position, but in my point of view, there is no such rating regarding the EPO's position. Task or responsibility-every single aspect of the EPO's obligation is equally important or dangerous and if one of those responsibilities is executed in less detail and care, than the entire protection program fails.

The EPO working close proximity is usually within immediate reach of the principal. He/she is the one, who covers the principal in an emergency, during an harmful attack, with his/her own body and evacuates the principal to a safer location. Working close proximity, the EPO aware of an impending danger follows his/her procedures: *Cover* and *Protect-Evacuate* and *Extract*. The EPO's immediate reaction is to shield and to protect the principal from the danger and to evacuate the principal to a safer area, from where he/she can be extracted.

Receptions are the opportunity for a person to get closer to the principal. A reception renders the principal very vulnerable because a person can enter the reception line and try while shaking hands to grasp the principal's hand and expose him/her to a direct attack. The EPOs should be placed in positions, which permit to scan visually each and every person before they approach and shake hands with the principal. Positioned like this, the EPO is still able to respond and shield the principal in case of an harmful assault.

Reception Formation:

One EPO (2) is staying at an arms-length distance behind the principal (3). Additional EPOs (2) are positioned in a way that they can observe the guest approaching in the receiving line and passing the principal. The team leader or senior EPO (1) assumes a position near the receiving line in front of the principal. (see Fig. 17)

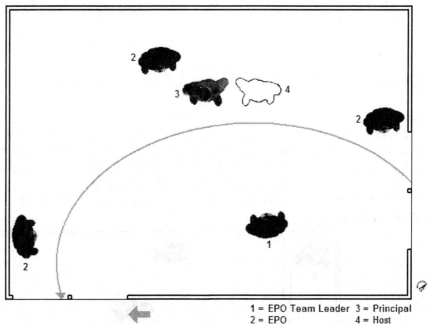

Fig. 17

Reception Formation

1 = EPO Team Leader	3 = Principal
2 = EPO	4 = Host

During an official dinner, banquet or delivering a speech on stage the EPOs should be positioned in formation of a ring around the principal. This allows the EPO to respond immediately to any potential problem. The selection and location of the table, or the location on stage where the principal will be seated or standing, becomes the center point for the formation. The evacuation route must be clear of any obstacles, like chairs, flowerpots, cables, etc.. The advance man has to check light switches, fuse box located within the environment and make sure, that those switches cannot be turned off accidentally. It wouldn't be the first time that a team evacuated a principal from an event because all of a sudden the environment was covered in darkness, thanks to someone who accidentally touched the wrong switch. Microphones also require special attention and should be checked right before the principal delivers his/her speech. Faulty connections or plugs may carry electrical current. Once the ring formation is in place and depending on the number of agents deployed, the team leader or senior EPO is the one usually positioned near the principal. He/she is responsible to cover and evacuate the principal.

Banquet Formation:

The team leader or senior EPO (1) is staying at an arms-length distance behind the principal (3) ready to respond to any action. One EPO (2) is seated at an adjacent table and one positioned at the entrance. Both are able to observe the guests (4) at the principal's table and the other tables, as well as the entrance. (see Fig. 18)

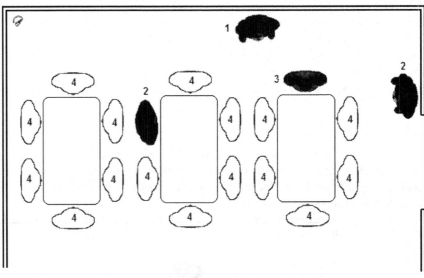

Fig. 18

Banquet Formation

1 = EPO Team Leader   3 = Principal
2 = EPO   4 = Guest

Stage Formation:

The team leader or senior EPO (1) is positioned on stage behind and near the principal (3). His/her responsibility is to monitor the entire room and staying alert for any threat indicators and to respond to the principal if needed. One EPO (2) is posted at the stage access (if a curtain at the back of the stage is present another EPO should be place there as well). Two additional EPOs will be posted in front of the stage scanning the entire audience for any signs of threat. (see Fig. 19)

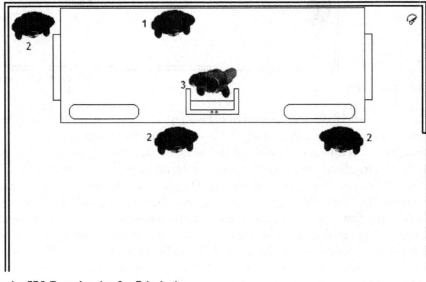

Fig. 19

Stage Formation

1 = EPO Team Leader   3 = Principal
2 = EPO

When on a visit or on the way to an event, the public appearance of the principal becomes equally important, than the event itself. In such situations, the principal might use the opportunity to wave to the crowd or to pose for photographers. In most cases he public is held at a safe distance either behind a fence-like barrier or other hindering objects. Whatever the precautions might be, the EPOs have to scan the crowd and keep a close eye on the principal and his/her moves.

Line Formation:

One EPO (2) precede the principal (3) along the fence line scanning for any potential threatening persons. The principal is closely followed by the EPO team leader (1). The EPO directly in front of the principal works very close to the principal looking at the eyes, faces and hands of those persons willing to touch or to shake hands with the principal. Another EPO trails along the line, while another EPO surveys the whole scenario from the rear. (see Fig. 20)

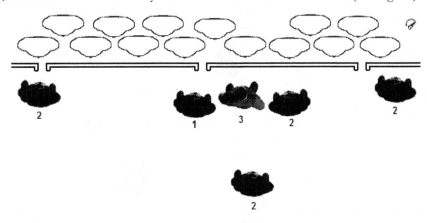

Fig. 20

Line Formation   1 = EPO Team Leader 3 = Principal
                    2 = EPO

The inner ring of EPOs (three to five officers) constantly surround the principal and form a shield to protect him/her from all directions. The EPOs do not leave the side of the principal, especially when in a crowd. In most circumstances, we can observe this very clearly with celebrities; the crowd tends to move closer to the principal–the closer the crowd gets, the closer the EPOs move to the principal. While on a free move from one location to another, the EPOs are at arms-length distance to the principal and the crowd is kept at a safe distance. The moment the crowd gets closer, the EPOs move in, nearly touching the principal.

Protective Formation:

Walking with a principal in a formation–the objective is to provide maximum coverage while remaining in a position to cover and evacuate the principal, regardless of the direction he walks, should he decide to change direction. (see Fig. 21, 22, 23)

Fig. 21

Protective Formation (one EPO)   1 = EPO
                                   2 = Principal

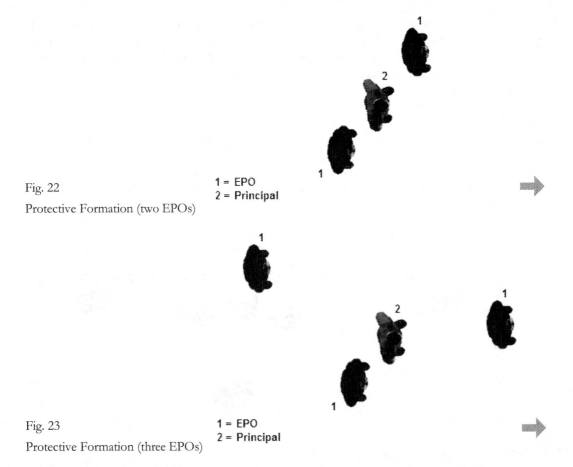

Fig. 22

Protective Formation (two EPOs)

1 = EPO
2 = Principal

Fig. 23

Protective Formation (three EPOs)

1 = EPO
2 = Principal

If a full security team is deployed, the principal will be surrounded with EPOs. One EPO, which is usually the senior EPO or a designated EPO team leader, is walking on the right side, a half step to the rear, but within an arms-length distance or even closer to the principal. He/she is able to communicate with the principal while they walk. He/she can whisper cautions or instructions to the principal. He/she is able to signal with one hand to the crowd to open a space, so that they can pass through and still be able to reach for the weapon, should that action be required. The free hand is close to the principal's back, so he/she is able to guide the principal if necessary. The EPO should however avoid touching the principal if possible. In this configuration, the EPO is in a position to cover the principal instantly. The EPO's field of vision is directed to the front and to the immediate right. Another EPO is in a similar position, but to the left side of the principal. This EPO's field of vision is directed to the front and to the left side. A third EPO walks in front at an arms-length distance. This officer's field of vision is to the front, left and to the right. A fourth EPO is at the rear, almost walking backward in order to protect the rear of the group. A fifth EPO is the designated point man (also called lead officer). This is usually the advance EPO, who knows the exact route, detours, obstacles, expected hazards, and other details. He/she is walking a few steps ahead, in front of the third EPO. His/her task is to open way and move the crowd, watching out for possible threats and leading the principal to the destination. This EPO is the one, who enters rooms, elevators, moves around corners first.

This formation of moving with the principal are the *Box-formation* and (see Fig. 24) the *Diamond-formation*. (see Fig. 25) Other formations are *Wedge-*, *Echelon-*and *V-formation*. From any of these formations, the principal is protected from all angles and sides. If the principal suddenly decides to change directions, for example to shake hands with a person, or to answer questions from the media, the EPO on that respective side simply becomes the leader. All other EPOs rotate with the principal, keeping always a close 360 degree coverage.

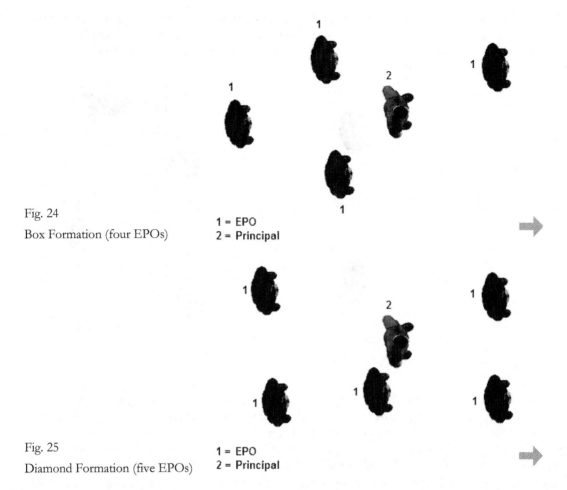

Fig. 24
Box Formation (four EPOs)

1 = EPO
2 = Principal

Fig. 25
Diamond Formation (five EPOs)

1 = EPO
2 = Principal

Rooms, elevators, doors, passages, corner bends are focus points for the protective team–especially for the advance EPO. Even though considered as good manners if one is opening a door for someone, or allowing someone to pass and enter first, this is not the case for the principal and the EPO. The EPO precedes the principal through a door and into the room. By proceeding so, the EPO quickly visually scans the room, checking for anything or looking for anyone, which could present an immediate threat.

The EPO is the first to enter an elevator, than the principal follows or depending on the situation both should enter almost simultaneously. By entering the elevator, the EPO should cover the sensors on the automatic door, preventing it from closing to quick and to allow the principal to get in smoothly (elevator standards and models vary in many countries). This procedure permits that in case of an emergency, for example during power failure, or an unexpected drop of the elevator, at least one EPO can be with the principal on the elevator.

Elevator Formation:

One EPO (2) precedes the principal (3) into the elevator. The principal steps directly to the side and toward the rear. The remaining officers encircle the principal, shielding him/her from onlookers. Exit from the elevator is made in the reverse order. The last EPO entering is the exiting. (see Fig. 26)

In situations, where only one EPO is with the principal, this officer, depending on whether he/she is right-or left-handed, should walk either on the left side or right side of the principal. If the EPO is left-handed he would walk on the left side of the principal, the right hand always near the principal's back and the left hand in a ready position to reach for the weapon if required. The right-handed agent would assume a similar position but on the right side of the principal. One hand near the principal's back, the EPO, in a situation of attack, can quickly and forcefully push the principal out of harm's way and step into the line of fire to protect the principal.

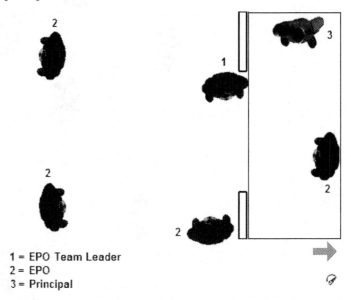

Fig. 26

Elevator Formation

1 = EPO Team Leader
2 = EPO
3 = Principal

In a situation that an object is thrown at the principal, the covering EPO, seeing the object will maneuver the principal out of its trajectory and proceed with cover and evacuate. Some are the opinion to bat a thrown object down or even to catch it. This is the most insane advise-never catch or try to bat it down it with the hands. Using the hands for a defensive action will be inaccurate and requires time-- lifesaving time. Any thrown or rolled object is considered a danger. One should always assume if in doubt, that it might be an explosive device-the covering EPO must get the principal out of harm's way. The procedures for explosive devices, such as grenades, and so on is the same as instructed by the military-the head covered and away from the explosive device (feet facing the direction of the explosive). The EPO places his/her own body between the expected explosion and the principal. If an explosion occurs, the EPOs should evacuate the principal, keeping their bodies between him/her and the source of the explosion. Covering the principal, the EPOs must be alert for any possible follow-up attack, which could originate from someone nearby with firearms. The EPOs must shield the principal and draw their own weapons for defense.

If the EPO sees a weapon (firearm, knife or similar), he/she will immediately face the threat and shout *Gun* or *Knife* and instantly takes required actions. He/she must immediately cover the principal or if necessary steps forward to protect and defend the principal. If the EPO is within reach of the attacker, he/she will attempt to divert the weapon downward and away from the principal. The other EPOs immediately cover and evacuate the principal. The principal has to be removed and evacuated to a safer location in case other attackers are waiting for the opportunity to attack.

To walk with the principal in public presents a whole assortment of challenges to the protective team. The protective formation has to change constantly and accordingly to the environment; if the people on the sidewalk are spread and not paying any attention to the principal, the protective formation can spread out and be wider. In this situation it is best not to draw any extra attention. If however the crowd is accumulating and getting closer, then the protective shield has to be closer of course. Besides the passersby, the EPO has to pay attention to the activity to vehicles on the street, watching people in windows and doorways, as well from above. Even if there is no encounter of some potential hazard is expected, any activity could turn at any moment toward the principal's presence. For example, while walking with the principal from the car to the office entrance a robbery could occur nearby, the robbers are on a run and without being aware of it, the principal could walk right into it. The principal could be shot or even taken hostage.

When on the move on foot with a principal, the EPOs must be more responsive and always scan the passersby, the environment and look for and detect any security or safety hazards. Any passing vehicles could present a serious threat. Vehicles can be used in a drive-by shooting, to throw an explosive device or as a get away in a kidnapping.

Keep constant alert at all times to irregular or unusual conditions and activities

Moving the Principal in a Crowd

The risk factors while moving and working a principal in a crowd is increasing greatly, the elements of potential danger are on a constant increase. The principal close to the crowd, may individually speak with as many people as possible, sign autographs, answer to the media, pose for photographers, or touch and shake hands with people. This makes the principal very exposed and vulnerable to any threat. Hands are reaching toward the principal, object like pens, notepads or autograph-books are handed to him/her, which could always hide a danger. Mothers holding babies and people with long coats could easily conceal a weapon or explosive device. Terrorists are known to deploy female suicide bombers; adhering to the Islamic dress code, wearing a standard *chador*, *niqab* or *burqa* (a large black cloak with head and face covering). Obviously, this type of garment does not allow any facial identification, nor does it reveal the danger, which might be hidden underneath. Not every professional, no matter how well they are trained have a photographic mind. Facial recognition can be very tricky and just simple things like glasses, beard, hat or head scarf are sufficient to make it more difficult to recognize someone especially in a crowd. Identification by means of facial recognition or iris scanning revealed to be, even for a computer, a difficult task. (see Fig. 27) Field reports show, that biometrics and related identification processes require a lot of "fine-tuning" in means of technology and even more, regarding the legal aspects. While a secure and safe way of identification is widely welcome, there are still groups of people which reject the idea. The constitutional guarantee of freedom of ethnicity and religion is in many cases abused for reasons to circumvent the established security related laws and regulations. In many cases this type of "misbehavior"

Identification Process

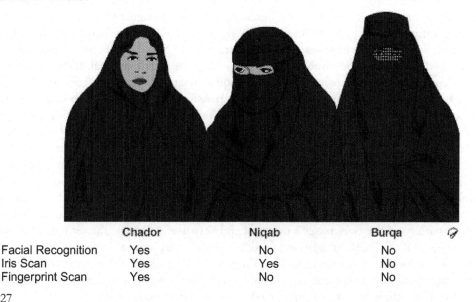

	Chador	Niqab	Burqa
Facial Recognition	Yes	No	No
Iris Scan	Yes	Yes	No
Fingerprint Scan	Yes	No	No

Fig. 27

caused political debates and gave origin to court hearings, where discrimination was used as a tool to undermine established laws. Security is everybody's concern and everybody should do the very best, to help in their own right to make sure of that and to maintain a secure environment.

Other factors the EPO has to be prepared for are camera flashes, which unexpectedly can go off near the face and eyes and can cause a momentarily blindness. If the principal is a famous and/or popular person, everybody likes to shake hands with him/her or touch him/her. This sometimes causes the crowd to press closer in to the principal and such situations leave only a small space for the EPOs to move. The protection circle is closing very tight around the principal, requiring the EPOs to prevent the crowd from overwhelming the principal. This is the time, when full physical force is necessary to shove the crowd back, but still keeping touch with the principal, not allowing anybody inside the circle and checking and pushing the hands away.

Always watch the faces, eyes and especially the hands of those in the crowd.

In those circumstances, nothing will happen unless those hands in the crowd are holding any type of weapon which could harm the principal. Besides guns or knives the EPO should also be aware of pepper spray or any type of chemicals which could be thrown to the face of the principal or rubbed on the hands of the principal. Everything imaginable can be used as a weapon-the EPO must look out for everything. The face and especially the eyes are the first to signal any action-that is the focus point for the EPO to detect an early warning. The EPO has to look for the contradicting actions and reaction in a crowd; for example in a friendly and cheerful crowd, look for the person who is sad, or even angry looking. That person might try to get closer as the time approaches. That person does not need to stay in the first row, but the way he/she is working through the crowd to get closer to the intended target is the signal for the EPO to be ready. As one may observe from media footages all over the world, EPOs are as much in the spotlight as the principal and their appearance might be as much criticized as that of the person they protect. The EPO should dress appropriately to the occasion and should make a good appearance when working the principal in the crowd.

The EPO's Appearance

Dressing appropriately and for the occasion, like in this instance to work in a crowd, is a "special" challenge to the EPO. Looking good and looking professional at all times is important, but to ruin an expensive suit by a hysteric crowd reveals to be very hazardous to one's wallet and credit card limit. Here is some advise: -only buy a designer suit, designer shirts, designer ties, designer shoes, designer socks and designer underwear if instructing to do so (in that case the client most likely will cover for the expense). Anyway, instead of buying an expensive designer suit (average cost $ 850-$ 1,500), one should consider to purchase a suit, made of exactly the same material, the same style as the original, but without the designer's label. It would still look expensive but for a fraction of the price. The same goes for shoes, shirts and ties. If you are a person, who is used to wearing an expensive wrist-watch, golden rings with stones and golden bracelets, then if you to, wear them only when off duty. First, those accessories easily get lost, especially when with a crowd. Second, a ring or bracelet, even a watch can get caught, and it is not the first time that someone lost a finger or got the wrist cut because of that. Besides, if an EPO is more concerned about the jewelry they wear, he/she cannot protect the principal properly. The only item we cannot dispense is a watch. A black watch with a tactical nylon band and Velcro fastener is the most appropriate. Glasses, as well as sunglasses should be secured in a way to prevent them from falling off. Sunglasses, by many bodyguards are often used just to "enhance" their image and if asked, they might not be able to tell, what those glasses are good for. Sunglasses a practical and very useful. And as the term itself describes, they are made to be used outdoors. Sunglasses are reducing glare and prevent someone from seeing exactly where the EPO is looking. Once entering a building, the sunglasses should be removed allowing the eyes to adapt to the change of the lighting condition. Leaving the building, the glasses should be put on just before exiting, permitting the eyes to adjust to the new lighting conditions.

The Protective Team

The one-man protection "team" is more like a mix between a security guard and a bad paid house-keeper and butler. Probably an au-pair would be more adequate. Protection is a twenty-four hour a day security coverage. This cannot be efficiently done by one single person alone. Considering, that after the principal retires for the night, which might be very late, the EPO has still some hours, in which he/she has to make certain that all the arrangements for the next day are in place. Flights and flight schedules are checked and confirmed and whatever else on administrative duties is attended to. Finally he/she can get their well-deserved sleep. In the morning, the EPO must be up and ready to go at least one hour before the principal and make sure everything is properly prepared for the day. This includes arrangements for the principal's breakfast, security check on the vehicle, instructions to the driver, any last minute change in schedule, last minute information on situations developed, which could impact the safe movement of the principal. Whether a one-man protection was chosen by the client with the budget in mind or because the hired EPO convinced the client that he can do the job all by himself–the result can never be an effective protection. Unfortunately, the one-man protective team is a very common arrangement.

There are factors, which clients and EPOs alike have to take in consideration when working on a protection assignment. A few years back for example, a client was seeking protection services. The client, a bank executive was going on a trip to the Philippines and he required a team of two EPOs for protection. Apparently the client was sure and determined about his needs and expectations, not leaving any room for professional advice. According to his plan he intended to stay for two weeks in Manila and another week in Cebu City. Both EPOs were expected to wait for him at the arrival area of the Ninoy Aquino International Airport (which for local regulations and security reason is not possible). Despite the fact, that he did not have any knowledge of the expected environment, he rejected any advance work (which he considered a waste of time and money). Both EPOs were expected to provide a twenty-four hour coverage. He insisted that both EPOs have to be around him all the time and that working in shifts was not acceptable. As the conversation went on, he explained that he was a hard working man and intended to make the best of this trip, which included the exploration of the Manila nightlife. This client was expecting that both EPOs, after a full day's coverage (with a temperature of 39° C and a humidity level of 80%) would still be fresh and be alert to provide a full night protection coverage. Based on previous experience, this type of assignment would leave the EPOs with just a few hours of sleep (if any); their capabilities and alertness would rapidly deteriorate–a condition, which for a hot spot like the Philippines is unacceptable. Under those circumstances the responsibility, fully resting on the EPOs is not justified.

Assignments, which are based on one EPO or a two-man protective team are providing the base for a closer and more personal contact with the principal. Such a very close relationship might give the wrong impression to the principal, which results in duties expected from the EPO, which are beyond any protective responsibilities. There are thousands of small things, but errors, which a principal might insist to be done. Tasks, which are **not** within the EPO's responsibilities: delivering the morning newspaper, carrying shopping bags or luggage to the vehicle, making appointments for manicure and hairdresser, picking up the suit from the dry cleaner, or even walking the dog. No matter how many officers are assigned to the principal.

These tasks or favors have nothing to do with security and/or personal protection. Clients should not insist, neither expect that an EPO is performing such task. As much as it could be considered important for improving the working relationship, as much it could be seen as a negative effect on the relationship.

The Checkpoint

Checkpoint is the access point to a restricted area; probably the busiest post in the protection program. Through this post are only entering and admitted persons with clearance and an authorized purpose to the restricted zone. The post checks and controls the people in the restricted area of the principal and limits their movement within the zone. Every person must be cleared by the security personnel who guard the post. Any suspicious looking or acting person is screened and marked. Any suspicion is reason to prevent entry. The checkpoint is usually established at a strategic location which permits a unique access to a designated restricted area, where all people can be checked and pass through. Depending on the circumstances, availability and need of personnel one or two EPOs should staff the checkpoint to verify identification and invitations and to inspect all entrants for weapons. When working with a host committee, the checkpoint should staffed by one or two EPOs, enforced by a local police officer (uniformed or plain clothes). Depending on the size of the event, the checkpoint should be equipped with hand-held metal detectors, metal detector portals, x-ray scanner and portable explosives trace detectors. Everybody must pass through, all bags, backpacks, cameras, packages and/or other hand-held items must be manually searched and physically examined.

The Security Posts

It should be clear by now, that the executive protection business is less action loaded, than what is pictured in the movies. Actually some of the assignments and especially post duty can get much boring (depending on the placement and the event) -but that is security all about. One of those assignment is the security post duty. Security posts are part of the second and the third concentric circle of protection around the principal. There are several types of security posts with a wide spectrum of functions. The security post is an established area of responsibility assigned to an EPO as a check and screening point. The EPO on post duty observes, checks, regulates and clears the authorized access into the secured area/s. Executive protection post duties are not much different from those in the military. In this sense the EPO on post duty is bound to follow the same rule. **Do not** leave your post until properly relieved. The assigned EPO has to remain at his/her post until he or she is properly relieved and only than can the EPO leave the post.

Never leave the assigned post—never abandon the principal

The EPO should not leave the post until directed by a supervising EPO, unless of course it is in response to an emergency to shelter the principal. Many times principals are committing the mistake when they see an EPO "hang" around and obviously not doing anything, to direct the EPO to perform some tasks for them. In such a delicate situation the EPO has to be very tactful and decline very diplomatically, while offering to communicate with the EPO in charge or someone else, able to comply. Under no circumstances should the EPO compromise the post and/or the security area. Even if the principal or any other security member insists, the EPO will not abandon the security post. In the event a fire, shooting, or any other disturbance occurs, only the EPO/s working close proximity should respond to the principal. The EPO on post duty must hold the post until directed to leave. The quarrel or whatever the disturbance may be nothing except a ruse to distract a post agent so an assault can be initiated.

The Observation Posts

To observe a specific area and people within that designated area the EPO has to establish observation posts. The observation posts have to pay particular attention to anything that could be suspicious, abnormal, unusual, out of place, harmful or simply embarrassing to the principal. In case something was seen or detected that could have an impact on the welfare of the principal, it must either be resolved by reporting. Report to the command post or an EPO team member, who can respond and investigate the circumstance. The EPO on observation post duty never leaves the post.

This observation post manned by an EPO is part of the second concentric circle of security. The post is established within a secured sector, usually within areas where the principal will be present. The secured zone or area is established, marked and limited by ropes, barricades and/or locked doors. Once the secured area is established, it is scanned and searched for electronic listening and video devices, explosive devices and other things, which are not belonging in that area and are considered potentially hazardous. If something is discovered, it must be removed. The observation EPO assumes the post and becomes operational as the search gets under way. EPOs escorting the principal assume their stationary observation posts in the immediate vicinity of the principal.

The observation posts consist of two types:

The Mobile Observation Post:

This post patrols by foot, car, boat or helicopter (depending on size of the area) the entire secured area. This post's assignment is of no particular nature, except to observe all people and things and to respond whenever required to assist the stationary posts. If in a car patrolling the perimeter of the secured area, the EPO will make contact with any suspicious person/s or investigate any unusual activity.

The Stationary Observation Post:

This post is fixed and can be positioned anywhere within the secured zone. His/her duty is to observe and maintain the integrity of the secured zone. This post can be inside the building, at the entrance to a room, a corridor of a hotel for example, or in the open on a roof, balcony or terrace. The EPO on stationary duty is placed at strategic locations wherever the principal will be present.

The EPO assigned and assuming observation post has to know the EPO in charge, who the principal and his/her family is and must be able to recognize them. He/she should also know and recognize members of the principal's immediate staff. Being aware of the principal's schedules, knowing when he/she arrives and departures and where the principal's exact location is within the secured area are details the observation post EPO must be aware of. The responsibility of the command post is to notify all other posts of any movements of the principal and to keep the posts informed of the principal's location. The EPO on post duty must know and recognize the type and form of immediate identification used by other EPOs and authorized persons cleared to enter the secured area for that particular location. This can be a recognizable badge pin, ID badge, picture identification card or any temporarily for that purpose issued type of identification. The EPO must further know the exact location/s of the other observation posts and any activities planned for the adjacent posts as well as for his/her own responsible observation area. Each observation post has its own specific instructions and equipment, which is unique to each particular post. The EPO on post duty must be familiar with his post directives and the operation of all emergency equipment. The EPO on duty **never** leaves the assigned post unless directed by the command post or until properly relieved by another officer. When relieved by another EPO, he/she must fully brief the relief EPO about the post coverage, operation, and any incidents.

Special Duties

When an EPO is working with the principal, he/she will have certain special duties and assignments to take care of. The strict and responsible execution of these duties is as much important to the security of the principal, as any assignment the entire protection program. Those duties and responsibilities are related to:

Protective Response

If the checkpoint or observation post is detecting any suspicious person or threat, the EPO on post duty will under no circumstance leave the post but notify the protective response officer. The notified EPO will immediately respond to the call, interview the suspicious person, investigate and if possible eliminate the threat and/or if required, escort the person out of the premises. Once the situation is back to normal, the EPO on post duty can return to his normal duties.

Relief

The shift supervisor or the advance man (depending on the assignment) has to determine the number and position of posts. To assure a flawless operation, he/she should determine a number of EPOs needed as relief personnel. Those relief EPOs have to be briefed on the requirements of each post and must able to fill in on a routine or emergency basis. Relief is an essential thing, allowing the EPOs on post duty to have a break, either for meals, refreshment or physical needs. When not relieving a post the EPO should be available in the security room or in the command post able to assist if necessary at any location.

Security Room

This is a designated room, where the EPOs, while not on post duty, can take a break. This room serves also to store spare equipment, meals and drinks. The security room may or may not be staffed at all times. If the room is not permanently staffed, than it has to be secured.

Luggage Check

Prior to departure from the residence, every piece of luggage and bags must be locked and a distinctive seal or sticker should be placed over the opening and the locks. In case a bag was opened, the sticker/seal is broken and provides a good and quick indicator of a possible tampering. All, the principal's and EPO's baggage must be escorted and constantly monitored until the luggage is placed within the control of the airline crew. When retrieving the luggage at the destination, the seals on the luggage should be physically checked before leaving the airport. Bags showing signs of tempering or opening must be x-rayed if possible, physically examined and searched to make sure that nothing was either placed in or removed from the bag.

The Command Post

The command post is the command and control center of the entire protective operation. This post is manned and is twenty-four hours a day operational. During an event, the command post's location is centrally fixed in a mobile unit, which is able to communicate and monitor, provide equipment, information, tactical support and directives to the security areas. The command post is gathering all information and channels the operation related information to all the appropriate sectors.

The post should be operated by an EPO, which is experienced and familiar with the entire procedure. Once briefed by the advance EPO, the command post EPO should have a complete picture and be familiar with the posting and with particular problems the follow EPOs on post duty are likely to face. On command post duty, the EPO will monitor, direct, relay and coordinate the entire security operation with all the other elements of the protective assignment. He/she will be in communication with the host committee, staff, support personnel and local law enforcement and the fire department. The command post EPO may also have a direct contact with the principal if the situation requires. The duty officer is keeping the principal's movements, communication and inquiries logged in the radio log. The command post officer is in his/her supervising function responsible for the successful execution and smooth operation of the executive protection assignment.

The command post is generally equipped with everything necessary to assure and maintain the security and safety of the principal. The equipment and resources may include but certainly is not limited to CCTV monitor; Cellular-(satellite-) phone; folder with phone numbers and directories; first aid emergency kit and resuscitator. Further, maps and diagrams; folders with special orders, directives, photos of the principal, family, staff; duplicate car and room keys; flashlights and radios; spare batteries and chargers. Emergency lighting; binoculars (nightvison); laptop computer, scanner, video cameras; emergency toolbox; spare mags with ammo, flares. The mobile unit itself is equipped with jammers of various frequencies, nightvision cameras, strobe lights, on-board power converter, radio and computer. (see Fig. 29)

Fig. 29

Should it be necessary to locate the command post near the temporary residence of the principal, for example in a hotel, than the post should be close to the principal's suite but never (if possible) next to it. The command post should be located between the principal's residence and the general traffic, but never away from the traffic. Also expect that the principal will pay a visit at any time. Any maid or room service should have access to the command post, but only at an arranged time, so that their activities can be monitored. Is hotel staff present, than all operation sensitive material should be locked and conversations concerning the principal or any other security personnel should be avoided. The command post is a professional place, which is extremely vital for a successful administration and operation of the executive protection program. Personal effects, valuables, passports, and so on of each EPO should be placed in special envelopes, which are sealed and marked with the officer's name. All officer's envelopes are locked safe and stored in the command post along with briefcases, equipment, luggage and other items necessary for the operation.

The Advance

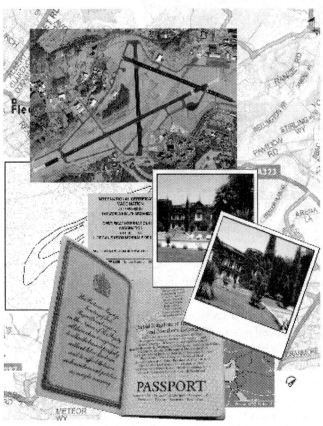

- Timing and Planning

- Anticipating

- Preparing

- Advance Survey Report

- Advance Duties

In many traditions, the person assigned as *Advance* duty moves before others to prepare the way for them. For a businessperson, the advance man will set up appointments and/or even conclude a precontract/presell for him/her and when the person arrives, he/she can complete the deal.

Then, we have the man or even group of people who travels in advance of the appearance of a musician, actor, entertainer or politician. In this instance, the advance man or team's job is to make clear the expectations and desires of the celebrity are smoothly attended. The advance's only importance is to makes everything going smooth regarding each particular needs of the person who follows.

In other occasions, politicians are using the advance man to proceed during their campaigning and make sure, that whatever is required is in place and taken care of for their arrival. The use of this highly specialized craft of the advance men, not so much mentioned in Presidential campaigns before the 1960, became a public awareness in the campaign fight between John F. Kennedy and Richard M. Nixon. The effectiveness of the advanced men in the Kennedy campaign could not be described better than by the author Theodore H. White in his book *The Making of the President, 1960*: [18]

> "Advance men-the small teams of agents who arrange the tours of major candidates-are practitioners of one of the most complicated skills in American politics. A good advance man must combine in himself the qualities of a circus tout, a carnival organizer, an accomplished diplomat and a quartermaster-general."

Traveling for many, like businesspeople, politicians, and diplomats is part of the job; for others, such as celebrities and wealthy people, it is part of the lifestyle. Most of those people are experienced and frequent travelers. They have plenty of knowledge regarding cities, local attractions, hotels, nightclubs, golf and other types of entertainments. But a simple business trip to a less familiar, new destination on a predefined schedule to various locations can reveal to be a very unpleasant and stressful experience. While at home or at work, everybody can be more relaxed and free of any stress. Their vulnerability to threats and risks is reduced to a minimum level by implementing psychological and physical barriers (alarm systems, CCTVs, checkpoints, walls, fences, etc.). But their vulnerability to threats and exposure to stress will increase rapidly to its maximum during a trip (no matter how distant and for how long). It is quite clear, that under such aspects, no businessman or businesswomen is able to concentrate and do proper business. Celebrities and VIPs alike use their advance staff to prepare and look after their travel arrangements, events, and any other non-security related needs. Event organizers, security companies, and professional protection agencies caught up and established especially tailored security related services.

The advance officer's duties are the careful personal inspection of every single area, the principal intends to visit. The advance EPO determines which and how facilities are available, the potential problem areas, possible restrictions, the secured and unsecured sectors. The advance EPO will meet with personnel directly involved with the visit, like the host committee for example. As a specific and detailed part of the security and protection program and it should be carried out by an experienced advance EPO.

It is the responsibility of the advance EPO to take care of the situation and to make sure, that the principal can concentrate on his/her business within a secure environment and less stress. The EPO (or EPO team, depending on need and availability) assigned to the advance duty will gather and predetermine all the necessary information and anticipate the appropriate arrangements for any scheduled appointment, meeting or event. The advance officer is the person, which answers all the questions to the traveling dignitary, accompanying EPOs, staff and even the dignitary's family. The advance officer takes care of all the detailed travel arrangements, hotel reservations, theater reservations and if needed the menu for a special dinner. As much he/she is taking rigorously care of those non-security related needs, as much is the advance officer taking care of the full security preparations.

The advance security planning and preparations can make the big difference between a well organized, pleasant and secure trip and a journey filled with serious threats. Only the carefully planning of the traveling dignitary's movements, the anticipation of all possible adverse events which could occur and taking the right measures to counter those possibilities is the solid foundation for a sound security plan. Such deep and thorough analysis of the potential problems and the liaison with the appropriate host personnel and/or agencies is forming a mobile protective shield prepared by a skilled and experienced advance EPO.

Timing and Planning

The first stage of the advance is to obtain the full outline of itinerary from the principal. The advance officer must make certain, to obtain the principal's schedule with all the details. His/her responsibility is to carefully review this schedule and to determine whether or not sufficient information is available, to make all the required and complete advance arrangements. This should include the places to be visited, dates and time of travel and length of each of the planned visits. Further, the expected time of departure and arrival and the types of transportation. And whether it is a business or a pleasure trip, the names, addresses and phone numbers of all the local contacts and the officials and media to be expected at the locations.

As in many cases, the required information might not be as complete as one is expecting, than it is in the hands of the advance officer to obtain further details. As experience shows certain details and/or additional information is only obtainable when conducting the advance. The advance officer should also expect, that certain information might be subject to a last minute change. Those alterations, when caused by the principal, are usually part of his/her routines and a good EPO should be aware of it and while working as advance officer, should be prepared for minor but important changes.

Even if a trip or visit is scheduled to a location which was visited in the past, does not guarantee, that everything will be at present as it was in the past. The advance officer must review previous advance reports and obtain all the information and adjust those details with finds of the recent advance work. A successful security is based on revision, elaboration and updating of plans, which has been in usage by advance teams at previous operations.

Airport and Airline

If the principal chooses to travel by a commercial airline, special arrangements have to be made with the airline's local supervisor or an airline representative in charge of VIP services at the airport. Making certain, that check-in procedures, boarding and security check can be executed without contact with other passengers. The airline VIP-service representative can assist in all required procedures, permitting the principal and party to proceed smoothly from the vehicle, through the boarding area to the VIP lounge. There he/she can wait and be boarded before or after the regular passengers. The seat for the principal must be selected and reserved in advance. Choosing a seat, as well as all other arrangements regarding the principal, any wishes and/or preferences must be considered, but security has to be priority at all times. The principal's luggage is taken to the airport in due time and checked in; any special instructions as well as request should be discussed there with the airline representative, prior to the principal's arrival at the airport.

The advance EPO should equally get in touch with Airport security, especially when the team accompanying the principal are carrying firearms (local and international airline and airport regulations regarding the carrying and transport of firearms apply always). In situations, where armed personnel is boarding with the principal special procedures must be followed and all the respective forms must be completed. All firearms must be unloaded, stored in a locked container and secured in the traveler's check-in luggage. Each state, county and country has its own laws and regulations regarding the carrying of a firearm. These regulations, in many countries and states have been changed to meet the new security standards. As mentioned earlier, each country has its own firearm regulations and laws, which most likely can present small variations from state to state. Carrying a firearm from one state to another, in the U.S. for example, is legal only if the state visited accepts and recognizes the license from the issuing state. However, this might not correspond to airports and airlines. In some states, law changes are considered, forbidding the carrying of weapons into an airport. On the international level, these regulations might be even more complex. The advance EPO's responsibility is to ascertain all the legal and correct procedures well in advance of the principal's departure.

The principal should be seated by the window with his/her family, the accompanying protection personnel and/or other staff member seated beside, in front and/or behind the principal. Always remember the concept of the concentric circles, maintain a buffer circle or area of security around the principal. Ideally a team with several EPOs would provide a full coverage of the plane, allowing EPOs seating at different locations throughout the entire plane. Each EPO's responsibility is to monitor the other passengers and to act immediately should a situation reveal to be a threat.

Based on experience, terrorists will spread out and mingle with other passengers and maintain a low profile, never revealing themselves at the onset of a skyjacking. Like a terrorist, the EPOs not assigned to close proximity of the principal will take their respective seats and act as they were average passengers or frequent travelers. These EPOs will keep a low profile, while observing and being alert to anything irregular without revealing their real presence as the assigned protective personnel of a dignitary.

There are standard check-in, boarding and security procedures at all regional, national, and international airports which have to be followed, but one might encounter slight variations of those procedures from airports to airport and airline to airline. Embarrassment and possible trouble can be avoided by memorizing the layout of the airport and the various stations and clear all required formalities prior to the arrival at the airport. Based on experience, a professional and polite request to the airport security can be of a great assistance and smooth things at the security screening point. Depending on the position and status of the principal, airport security might assist and escort him/her to the boarding area or even recommend a more direct and private route to board the aircraft.

Once the team with the principal arrived at the destination airport, it is the job of the advance EPO to have the prearranged ground transportation ready and the baggage picked up. Assuring, the principal can proceed without delay to a waiting vehicle-allowing to leave the airport as quick as possible. One of the EPOs should be assigned to retrieve and transport the baggage to the final destination. The airline representative as well as the airport security department can be of great assistance in making things go smoothly.

Transportation

The advance EPO is responsible to arrange transportation for the principal and the team (whatever applies). In those situations it is always the best to have another EPO designated to drive the principal's vehicle. This is not a matter of convenience–the EPO assigned is not only familiar with the principal, the family and the staff, but he/she is trained in executive protection and is an experienced driver. Another reason to assign an EPO is, that he/she is not easily intimidated and is at ease with the principal's status and position.

Sometimes, the situation might not permit to have one of the own team available to be assigned to drive the principal and the best solution is contract a local qualified EPO or a retired, or off-duty law enforcement officer. It is very important for an EPO to have a good relationship with other executive protection and law enforcement professionals and maintain a regular contact with those. Ideally and based on many years in this business, one will be able to many reliable contacts in many countries and cities. The great advantage in hiring a local professional is in knowledge of the surroundings, the streets, the city and its social atmosphere, the restaurants, etc. This local professional is also a vital source to provide and obtain protective intelligence, based on his/her familiarity with local sources which can be and might need to be contacted.

The most common thing, which is the least desire one, is to rent a car with a driver at a local car and limousine rental service. The driver from a local service of course has knowledge of the city, the streets and locations and most likely has local contacts, which might be useful, but he/she has probably no idea of the security and protection concept. Further the driver has most likely average driving experience, but nothing comparable with what is needed and he/she will consider that his/her priorities are above any security concerns. Besides, under the circumstances of such an important position, the driver might become careless and use the influence to impress others, or discuss the job, schedule, itinerary, etc. with friends or anybody-becoming a risk factor, which can be avoided. If there is no other option, use the services of a driver only with caution and never discuss any confidential information in the presence of this driver. Another aspect. When contracting a driver from a local car rental or limousine service, there is the risk of hiring or having assigned someone, which might have an alcohol problem, a psychotic behavior or even a criminal record. Having someone working with the principal on a temporary basis and as often practiced on a short notice, especially without any security profession background is always a great risk, which should (if possible) be avoided-at least considered with reservations. In any circumstance, the advance EPO has to make sure, that the responsible of the respective company is providing all the vital information regarding the driver (e. g. name, date and place of birth, social security number, ID number, driver's license number). In many countries, professional drivers are obliged to have a physical and psychological exam made on a regular basis, the driver's license might be especially marked to be a professional license. In addition, the driver's traffic record (similar to a criminal record) provides information about the conduct of the driver. Depending on the country, drivers of armored vehicles have to provide a certification for operating such a vehicle. It is the responsibility of the EPO to get all these data and if possible copies of the original papers. The rented vehicle has to be physically checked and the identification number of the vehicle (VIN Code) (see Fig. 30) as well as the license plate have to verified and compared. If possible obtain a copy of the documents for the file and as a backup. At the moment the driver reports in, all the documents, such as driver's license etc., have to be checked and compared with the data obtained from the company. The EPO has to make sure that the vehicle assigned is the same, which was previously inspected.

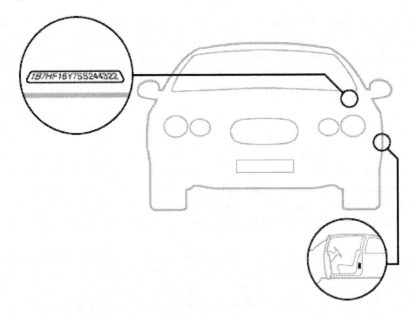

Fig. 30

When renting an armored vehicles, the EPO has to verify if the indicated armor meets the standard armoring protection level/s. (see Fig. 31)
Should for any reason, someone other than the expected assigned driver is reporting for duty, the EPO has to check the identification and driver's license immediately, than call the car rental service and get an explanation and confirmation. If there is any doubt in regard of the driver and/or the service, dismiss the driver at once. Never use a phone number provided by the new driver, but use the phone number directly obtained from the company representative.

The contracted driver has to be thoroughly briefed about the specific duties and responsibilities of the assignment. The EPO has to make clear, that the assigned job is driving and observation only. The driver should remain in the vehicle unless otherwise instructed. The driver should always keep the doors locked and must always have the vehicle immediately ready for the principal.

Levels of Armoring Protection

CAV Levels	Other Standards	Bullet Type	Velocity FPS	Grain	Example
II	B3, NIJ 2				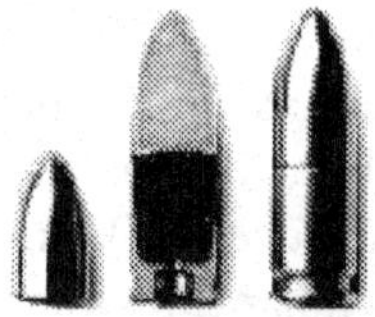
		9 mm FMJ	1120	124	
		.357 Mag SP	1450	240	
		.38 Super Auto FMJ	1280	130	
III	B4, NIJ 3A				
		.44 Mag SWC	1475	240	
		.30 Carbine	1990	110	
		12 Gauge Slug	1575	7/8 oz	
IV	B6, NIJ 3				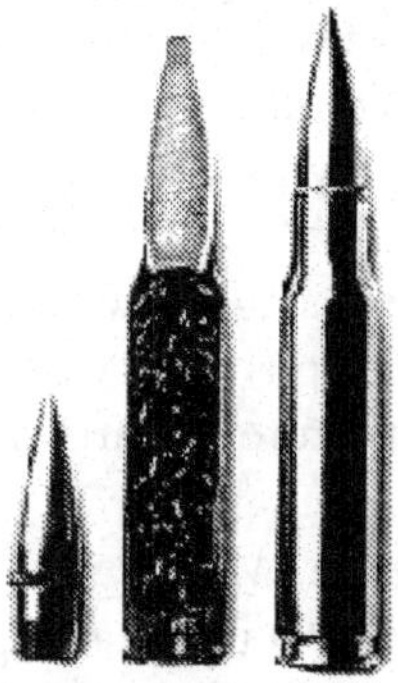
		.30 Cal SP	2794	180	
		7.62 x 51 NATO	2700	147	
		5.56(.223) FMJ	2920	55	
		7.62 x 39 FMJ	2550	123	
		30.06 SP	2410	220	
V	B7, NIJ 4				
		5.56 (.223) AP	2920	55	
		7.62 x 51 NATO AP	2700	147	
		30.06 AP	2410	220	
		7.62 x 39 AP	2550	123	

Abbreviations:
FMJ = Full Metal (Copper) Jacket
SWC = Semi-wad Cutter, Gas Checked
SP = Soft (Lead) Point
NATO = FMJ with Lead Core
AP = Armor Piercing (FMJ with Special Core)

Fig. 31

The EPO has to conduct a visual and physical search of the vehicle, scanning for any hidden recording, electronic tracking devices or explosive. Such a complete search must be conducted each time the car and/or the driver has been away from the assignment-for example temporarily away to a garage or overnight. The advance EPO has to be aware of any possible changes (and those are happening even with the best of planning) must include in the planning any possible eventuality. That means, the advance EPO will be able to anticipate anything and everything what could happen.

Hotel and Residence

By the time the protection team with the principal arrives at the hotel, all necessary check-in procedures have been taken care of by an advance EPO. The principal can be quickly and smoothly be escorted to his accommodations. Depending on preferences, circumstances and availability, the hotel should provide an underground garage, permitting a direct access and an easy exit, especially in the event of an emergency evac. The advance EPO will have the room key ready and the principal can proceed without entering the lobby area directly to the room or suite. The hotel security should have been notified prior to the arrival. Emergency and Fire escape plans, as well as fire extinguishers should be located. All necessary phone numbers, such as emergency services, fire, police and ambulance should be in the hands of the advance EPO. Any additional instructions regarding the hows and whens for room service, chambermaid, bellman and other services should be properly discussed with the hotel manager.

Staying at a rented house, designated as temporary residence of the principal, the advance EPO must first determine the routes to the neighborhood and means of ingress and egress of the residence. This should include all routes, which serve as an alternative of entry and exit. The parking areas must be determined, to avoid any disruption which affects the neighborhood. The local regulations for street parking have to be predetermined as well. In closed communities (resort areas for example), parking is only permitted to residents and only between a given time during the day and/or the night. In other instances, city laws might allow or forbid one-sided parking, parking in marked areas, or during certain hours. The EPO must make certain, that the local parking regulations are followed and if required and/or possible, a special permit should be obtained prior to arrival. The advance EPO should also make certain, that the temporary residence is located in a disaster low risk area (e. g. earthquake, flood), and the building is constructed according to the latest standards and building codes. The advance EPO has to make certain that every single piece of documentation (licenses, permits, reservations) and every single procedure during the trip is taken care of prior to departure. This starts at the principal's residence, to and at the airport of departure, the arrival at the destination airport, to the hotel or temporary residence.

Events, Meetings and other Locations

Whether meeting preparations for a hotel, residence, events or restaurant, the procedures for the advance EPO are always the same. Always select the most direct, yet safest routes to the destination. Always check, locate, select and reserve a parking area or at best a parking facility near the location. Always make sure that the best entrance-and exit-points (emergency and alternative exits as well) to and from the building are memorized. Always make sure to contact with the representatives or in case of an event, the host committee of the location, which will be visited by the principal. Determine the name or names of the people who will meet with and greet the principal. Surveillance as well as the access control post/s must be efficiently and strategically placed. This includes and requires the establishing of personnel needs, procedures and the formulation of post orders for the officers assigned for the operation of the security posts. Any equipment for surveillance and security post/s must be taken care of. The advance EPO has to contact with the responsible of the committee, so that all required and available equipment can be placed at the exact location and checked for operational readiness. The EPOs assigned to the equipment will need time to get familiar with it and to assure a smooth operation during the event. Further, the advance EPO also needs to establish liaison with and to formulate any special planning with the law enforcement, fire-, and paramedic department.

While staying inside rooms, one single rule has to be understood and followed by all, including the principal-the principal should never be allowed to stay or to be placed in front of or near windows. Windows are in general are the perfect access point for any sniper. The target can easily be hit through the window with a high-power sniper rifle. While on the ground floor, bombs, grenades or Molotovs can easily be thrown through the window from the street. The principal should be seated, where he/she is shielded from the view as well as protected in case a bomb is thrown through a window. Ideally, rooms for meetings and events should be in the center of the building without any window. If the room has windows and the principal could at any time be in a position, that he could be seen from the outside, it is advisable to have the windows covered with opaque curtains, blinds or fabric.

It is more easier for the advance EPO to anticipate any probable consequences if he/she has as much information collected and ready available as possible. One has to be capable to anticipating (almost) everything, including illness, injury, accident, activities, human loss and even natural disasters. Countering any threat and assuring a safe environment for the principal is the daily routine of any assigned advance EPO. The anticipation is predicated based on the information (intelligence gathering), the analyzing of data and executing the correct assumptions. Nobody in with risks involved, such as the executive protection business, where protection is provided for an individual, a family, company, agency or other entity is leaving anything to chance and surprises are the least accepted. Any and every possible conceivable scenario has to be clear visualized, everything must be searched and scanned, every closed door has to be opened to reveal what is behind it and than be locked again. All available countermeasures have to be used, every single person must be checked, verified and cleared. An advance EPO has to anticipate and detect any possible occurrences before they happen and immediately has to take preventive action to preserve a safe environment for the principal.

The EPO has to access protective (threat) intelligence and must determine the potential threat level; a risk assessment. For example, the advance EPO has to access and determine:
How much publicity and/or public interest is generated already about the principal and his/her visit. Was there any thing published prior to the principal's visit, specifically related to the itinerary and/or the lodgings. Was there any reports related to any threats (verbal or written) received. What should or could be expected regarding any potential violent attempts or any embarrassing situations.. Is there any report related to expected (pro or contra) demonstrations. Is there any unrelated activity planned which could have impact on the principal's security and itinerary. Any gathering of people, a parade, sport event or public celebration could affect any planned and chosen routes, although not related to the principal or his/her itinerary, could cause significant disruption, detour, delay and/or revision of plans.

Some years ago, a Japanese client needed a full security survey on a building complex in Nagano, to where he intended to move part of his financial offices. Because of the size the assignment, we decided and with the consent of the client, that the survey is conducted together with a colleague, an electronics and surveillance expert. During our survey we noticed that the building was occupied by another "company". Nothing unusual, but somehow and for some reason this company was different and did not fit into the picture. It could have been those strange business hours, the type of clientele, or the number and placement of security guards-but no. What caught our attention was a detector we carried with us, which started to act like crazy-each time we turned around a corner or opened a door the detector's acoustic signal was shrieking in our earpiece. Before completing our report, a trusted contact at the police department was consulted and based on our find, he promised to look into it from a different angle. Finally our survey report was presented to the client, highlighting our finds, suspicions and our anticipated recommendations. A meeting with the board, were our report was presented, analyzed and discussed among other board members, concluded that the report (including us) was exaggerated. A few days later, a call from our police contact confirmed our suspicion-the "company", suspected to belong to a ring of organized crime was already under police surveillance for some time. Even the client a few days later, witnessing the police search at that "company", realized that our survey report was not exaggerated, but professionally anticipated. Which reminds me of the Chinese philosopher Lao Tsze, who once said: "*Anticipate the difficult by managing the easy.*"

Protective intelligence originates from many different sources. Where to find those sources and get the information? The best and quickest way to get information is nowadays via the Internet. The information available however is a more general type. To get a more detailed and specific information, the advance EPO when arriving at his destination will get fresh local information directly from local daily newspaper, radio and TV. Local news is providing what might describe local situations and problems the principal may encounter. In this way, the EPO is aware of any risks locally and can avoid that the principal is confronted with a situation, he/she has nothing to do with. Further the information will allow the EPO to anticipate and to plan, when facing possible road problems, constructions, sport events, public gatherings or celebrations. The advance EPO will also extract from the news any information about local trouble spots, festivities, celebrations, local holidays and crime areas. In pubs and other places of social activity, the EPO will find first hand information about gossips, controversial issues, political matters and social conditions.

Depending on the position and public status of the principal, the advance EPO should contact the local law enforcement authorities, especially the district police, where the visit is taking place. The EPO should inquire if they have any information about threats, demonstrations, person or group/s that could pose a danger to the principal. The local police can be of great assistance when planning the route and to control traffic and crowd if necessary. Even if a police assistance is not required for an assignment, a good policy is always to advise the police that a certain dignitary will be in their jurisdiction.

The advance EPO has to locate the hospital and ambulance service/s and determine the best routes to and from the location/s, the principal intend to visit. It is at the discretion of the advance EPO whether to make prior contact with hospital administration and ambulance management. As the advance EPO is aware of, the entire EPO team should know the special medical conditions and concerns (if any) of the principal and the principal's blood type. Should more people or family members travel with the principal, the team should know their personal details as well. The advance EPO has to determine if there are adequate medical facilities, capable, equipped, and supplied to treat the principal and his/her party should the circumstances demand. The hospital (name, addresses and map coordinates), the name of the person/s to be contacted in the event of a problem should be included in the advance survey report.

The advance EPO has to establish liaison with the host committee/organization or their representing contact person. The advance EPO must work very closely with the representing official as well as with the host committee itself. Usually one person is responsible and in charge of itinerary planning, reception and event coordination. Either that same person is in charge of non-security and security arrangements, or another person is designated by the committee to handle those issues. The presented program by the host committee is the foundation for the advance EPO to work within those parameters and ensure the principal's security–preserving the concept and intent of the event scheduled. Changes in the program will and must be suggested by the advance EPO only, if the principal's security is compromised by the proposed event concept or if any part of the event might interfere and affect the security arrangements. The EPO has to obtain a schedule of the event/s and a list with the names of the participants, special guests, and officials invited and involved in the program. Further, the EPO has to ensure by interviewing the host committee and the assisting staff members about any anticipated problems. He/she has to brief and advise them, that if aware of any (even unconfirmed) rumors about potential problems, threats or any uncommon incident/s, the information should be reported to the advance EPO without delay.

The advance EPO's duty is also to look for facilities which concern the personal comfort and convenience of the principal. These include food, water and refreshments, rest and lavatory, phone and internet, leisure and entertainment. The advance EPO has to determine and make arrangements for the principal's "holding area". The holding area should be located somewhere between the arrival point and the principal's destination point.

The holding area is usually a convenience room at a designated location, used for final preparations before the principal's public appearance. This room should be a secured area, but with its integrity maintained intact. In case the principal arrives earlier that scheduled, he/she will be able to wait in the room until the appointed presentation time. If required, the room can be equipped with a monitor, connected to CCTV/s, which will cover the event in the venue and where the principal will be appearing. Usually, the holding room is the appropriate place for the principal, where he/she can be briefed about the event for the last time and where the principal can meet and greet the event representatives. The advance EPO should also anticipate any wishes of the principal and have information ready and available about local events, like theater, local points and places of interest.

Preparing

Once all the security preparations are completed, the principal and one of his/her representatives (if so required) will be presented with a limited advance survey report. The Report contains detailed description of the itinerary, relevant phone numbers, special instructions, hotel room assignments and additional information important for the principal is included. This survey report must be explicit and each item must be in detail, for example information about the names and phone numbers of people the principal is to meet. The EPO must make certain, that not even the tiniest detail is left out-the entire security will depend on it. The copy of the report for the principal's representative does not need and should not include any information related to the security preparations and the EPOs instructions.

The next phase of the advance is to determine the positioning of the security posts and the security personnel assignment. The advance also determines the routes from and to the location/s (including the principal's movement on foot), the location itself and whether everything else is in position. Once this is completed the advance EPO should physically and mentally walk through the entire operation and search for every possible element, tiny indicators of what could go wrong. The EPO must check and look for places, like high grounds, where a sniper could wait in position for his mark to appear. The EPO looks for any weaknesses in the crowd control and should time and measure every step of the principal. Things which could appear as normal, might reveal to be a surprise, ever single detail (like traffic lights, street crossings, railroad crossing, ferry, schedules of garbage trucks, etc.), must be checked, if necessary double-checked. Working advance is like sensing the unpredictable and solve it before it happen. Small things, such as sun, snow, rain are as much important, as the entire protective operation. There is nothing more embarrassing, than watching a VIP sliding and falling on an icy sidewalk, while the protective team, eager to safe the VIP, is crashing on the ground one by one.

An advance EPO must be aware and in control of everything. The EPO has to consider the positioning of the sun, so it will not interfere with the position of the principal and the security personnel, which would be ineffective if blinded by the bright sun. Any cables or carpets must be tightly fixed to the ground. Any walkway used by the principal has to be inspected for possible cracks, loose stones, holes, tubes or grids, preventing the principal to stumble and fall. Now that everything is in place and nothing can wrong anymore-the EPO should walk through the entire sequence and locations (if time allows) again. This time taking the place of the principal and the other EPOs, observing the environment from the viewpoint of everyone else involved. The final stage is to assume mentally the role of an attacker and attempting to anticipate the means and methods of an attack. Even though it seems that the job of the advance EPO is completed, he/she can only rest when the visit is over and the principal has been safely moved. Once the final survey report (a debriefing or after action report) is prepared the advance is completed. One should never forget-an attacker is well prepared and any attack is equally well planned. The attacker/s is always in an advantage by selecting the time, the place and the method of the attack. An advance EPO will deter if possible a most determined attacker and reduce the vulnerability of the principal to a more favorable and safer level. A well planned security response and countermeasures are the difference between life and death. An elaborate protection plan will save the life of the principal and most likely that of the security personnel.

Advance Survey Report

Once the advance EPO is returning from his assignment, a full report, the advance survey report is presented to the EPO in charge (if working with a team) for further preparations and planning. If the EPO is working independently, the report will either be presented to the client or kept as reference for further planning.

Advance Report Format

Since there is no standard format for the survey report, companies and/or agencies working in the security and executive protection business adapted formats, which reflects the company's policies. No matter, whether one is working for a company or independently, form and appearance of the report might be different from case to case, but the content should be as follows:

Advance Report Purpose and Reason

The purpose of the advance survey report is to provide a record of the advance. The report is serves to present details of the assignment to the protective personnel and to provide a tool to formulate the necessary assignments, special instructions and to resolve anticipated problems. The more informative and detailed the report is, the better the chances are for deterring any adverse activity. Anybody outside, not related to the protective network should not receive a copy of the advance report. It is advisable however, to provide the principal (and/or representative) with a sanitized version related only to the event, additional instructions and logistics, which are of interest to the principal. The reason for compiling a detailed report is to avoid any problems and to co-ordinate the entire operation. Allowing other security personnel arriving at a location with or immediately prior to the principal's arrival have a good orientation to the location. Furthermore, a full record of the advance will provide permanent and full detail of the security preparations in the event a hostile or adverse action occurs. The survey report is also a source of information for future advances and trips to the same location. The report details information for points of contact and access, provides general information that would be relevant to concerned and necessary personnel. The survey report as well as other security related documents must be treated as "confidential" or as (depending on the protection level) "classified" material.

Advance Type

This part of the advance report is providing details about:
- the advance EPO, name and service number (if applicable) etc.
- the reason/s of the advance (for the tour of Miss (principal's name) and band (names of the band members) etc.
- the location/s (name/s of city, places etc.)
- the date/s (date and time of the event/s)
- dates (start of advance and completion date)

Advance Intelligence

This section is listing and analyzing any information regarding threats, potential danger points, descriptions (including photos taken at locations) of persons who may pose a problem and risk assessment. This part may also provide special instructions about persons to contact or ways of dealing with the perceived and anticipated problem.

Itinerary Details and Time Table

The proposed and scheduled times of the principal's movements include arrival and departure dates and times, locations dates and time. The name/s of person/s which will meet the principal, details about travel and transportation-car, plane (commercial or charter), ship, limousine service and driver, etc. This itinerary can cover several days and locations, depending on the principal's schedule.

Routes

In this section of the report, the EPO provides the exact time and distance between each location and the directions for the motorcade. This narrative map gives details of any expected detours, the anticipated traffic conditions, railroad crossings or anything of an unusual nature the motorcade might encounter. Copies of maps and amplified map sections are attached to the report.

Transportation and Logistics

The logistics is giving detailed information on how and when personnel, equipment and other items are moved from and to each location and given time table. Logistics is also including provisions for refreshments, meals and lodging as well as instructions and any special transportation requirements.

Instructions and Special Advise

This part of the report contains all the information pertaining to anything relevant to the safe conduct of the principal. The information which will be necessary for the protective personnel (radio frequencies, location of fire extinguishers, bomb disposal, special eating provisions, breaks, and so on).

Post Assignments

Each assignment of the protective personnel is listed by name, location and time of relief. The post assignments also include the operation and location of the command post, from where the control the operation is supervised and be the logistical center for all communications and equipment.

Identification

This section provides samples and description of any special identification and type, such as badges, tags, logos, Service ID Cards, Lapel pins. Identifications, which might be worn by persons and personnel, in need of entering the secured areas or have close-proximity access clearance to the principal.

Phone Numbers

This section of the report provides the names and phone numbers (fixed and mobile), pager and fax numbers (where still in use) of contacts and emergency personnel. Law Enforcement, Fire and Paramedic information is especially important and should be highlighted and listed separately.

Emergency

The emergency medical facilities and hospitals section includes the names, locations (street addresses with map coordinates), emergency and administration phone numbers and the person/s to contact.

Media and Press

Here provisions are made to accommodate the media and for the control entrance to the press area, credentials, clearances, names and other provisions such as movement of the press.

Advance Duties

A good advance EPO has to consider many other concerns and not just for a good security or perfect protection of the principal. He/she must be able to answer whatever question or have whatever solution for all types of situations. The advance EPO is prepared to answer professionally, not only to the principal and family, but to other security personnel, the police and even to host committee members.
The EPO must have all the answers and solutions to any and all questions that may arise. Included in the duties of the advance is also to prepare sections of maps, which will show only those highlights, important to the protection team members and the principal. Depending on availability and budget, the EPO should also acquire satellite images of those areas and sections of the location/s which are important for the mission. The principal might ask for a map, to get an orientation on the city layout, especially if it is a foreign place and first time visit. The EPO should provide with the map a legend in which special places of interests are highlighted (e. g. fashion designer shops, jewelry shops, entertainment, sports, sightseeing attractions). For example, if the principal is a passionate collector, the EPO would highlight places or shops for this particular hobby. The advance EPO should be familiar with the culture and religion of the principal and the family, so he/she can easily accommodate special wishes and any special needs. The advance EPO can be considered as the most critical and vital element in the entire protective team.

The advance EPO is responsible for all the planning and the conduct of the protective functions. He/she must anticipate every and any possible scenario and threat, any attacker could think of and prepare the proper countermeasures before an attack can materialize. The EPO must also anticipate every desire and wishes of the principal and be able to have a solution immediately at hand.

The advance EPO is not only responsible to the principal, but also the other members of the protective team and any questions they may have. The advance EPO is the person who acts as liaison between the protection team, the host committee and the support units, such as police, fire, paramedics. The advance EPO has to be aware of and to know everything and be the solution to everyone.

The Protective Duty at Home and Office

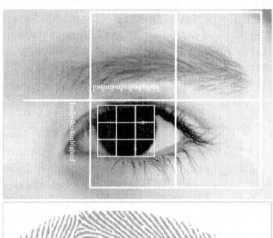

- **Security at Home**

  - **Security Planning**
  - **Protective Barriers**
  - **Security Systems**
  - **The Residence**
  - **Security Procedures**
  - **People**

- **Security at the Office**

  - **Access Control**
  - **Corporate and Industrial Espionage**
  - **Computer Security**
  - **Security Awareness**
  - **Safety Consciousness**
  - **Emergencies and Natural Disasters**
  - **Emergency Plan**

Physical security is defined as that part of security concerned with physical measures designed to safeguard personnel; to prevent unauthorized access to equipment, installations, material and documents; and to safeguard against espionage, sabotage, damage and theft. As such, all security operations are facing new and complex physical security challenges across the full spectrum of operations. Challenges relative to physical security include the use of physical security assets as a versatile protection multiplier.

From the private security sector as well from the clients point of view, reductions in manpower and funding are critical challenges to physical security. Manpower to support any physical security activities is reduced through deployments and cutbacks. The rapid evolution of physical security equipment technology also lends to physical security challenges, which are exponentially multiplied by the introduction of the information age.

Those physical security challenges must be understood and measures must be taken to minimize them to enhance the overall protection. The security industry, as well as security officer must be aware of the human dimension factors and ensure that their security personnel does not become complacent. Human errors rather than modern technology have caused so many lives. Complacency has become a challenge to physical security.

It is essential and in the best interest of security that each installation, residential or office, temporary or permanent is provided and uses a detailed physical security plan. This plan should include at least special and general guard orders (if applicable), access, material and equipment control, protective barriers, lighting systems, alarm systems, intrusion detection and monitoring systems and locks. All physical security plans have the potential of being classified documents and must be treated accordingly.

Security at Home

There was a time, when the old meaningful phrase *"My House is my Castle"* was a proud expression used by many property-, house owners and landlords. Things have changed and the well known Spanish phrase *"mi casa es su casa"* (my house is your house), commonly used as an expression for hospitality, can easily have a new meaning for criminal elements.

The estimated 2.1 million burglaries committed in the United States in 1999, for example, account for approximately 18 percent of reported serious crime. Two of every three burglaries in 1999 were committed in houses, apartments, or other residential dwellings. The majority of residential burglaries, sixty percent occurred during daylight hours, while nonresidential burglaries occurred primarily at night. In 1999, while the average loss for both residential and nonresidential property burglaries declined from the previous year, victims still experienced an estimated total loss of $3.1 billion. That is an average dollar loss of $1, 441.00 per residential burglary and $1, 490.00 for nonresidential burglaries. Burglary is expensive to the victim.[19]

The physical protection of any building, room or area should be designed in accordance with the level of potential risk to that specific area. Meaning, that no design, refurbishment or redevelopment of the premises should be planned without a current security risk assessment. The risk is depending on many factors and vary considerably from location to location, depending mainly on the nature of the current local criminal or other threats, trends and characteristics and status of the owner.

The boundary of any premises is frequently defined by a fence or wall and depending on the nature of the site there may be multiple entry/exit points. This is and acts as the first line of defense against any illegal incursion to a site. The security design of the perimeters should include lighting, access control, barriers, CCTVs, perimeter alarms, fencing, etc..

A residential building should be visualized as a secure box with all sides (including roof and foundation) given equal security protection according to the current threats. Windows and doors in the building are to be considered the weak points and appropriate security measures must be taken to secure these. Any security design of the building must include access control, windows, doors, internal living and working areas and so on. Robberies and burglaries (so-called "home invasions") are the most common threats to a residence.

In addition a continuing and constant threat of stalkers, terrorists, kidnappers and/or assassins ensures that the physical environment of homes is reversed similar to the Middle Ages. To a time, when fortifications with thick walls and guards armed to the teeth were a familiar sight. Nowadays, executives and alike will seek homes and properties, which are located in gated and guarded communities instead of an isolated and idyllic surrounding. Entrance to those communities is guarded by a uniformed security personnel and access granted by personal identification numbers and/or magnetic key cards. Vehicles can access by opening the gates with infrared or Bluetooth devices–in case of a suspicious action, access is denied and crossing-bars raised. High walls and/or bushes with foliage surround the perimeter of the property, monitored with high-definition IR-cameras.

The principal's residence or estate should be a target most difficult to penetrate and the safest place where a he/she and the family members can relax and less worries concerning any kidnapping, invasion or any other threats. However, there are no guarantees-like in any security program, there can only be the best attempts with strong deterrent efforts in keeping out any unauthorized intrusion. Like in personal security, the aim of physical security at an estate is to shift and control the odds of transgression more in favor of the resident (the principal). It is accomplished by maintaining the same concept of the concentric circles. Those circles include planning, people, procedures, systems (alarms) and physical and psychological barriers. There are only two factors limiting physical security-imagination and finance.

Modern technology as available today provides the very highest and most sophisticated electronic protection possible. For the exterior and grounds surrounding the estate seismic sensor alarms can be placed into the ground-triggered by footsteps the sensors can detect any movement on the ground. Photoelectric lenses and microwave emitters can be placed in various patterns to trigger an alarm when disturbed by an intruder. Motion sensors and alarms can be combined with cameras; and search/spotlights, turning on instantly to detect and to monitor movements of anyone walking, crawling or running on the property. CCTV cameras are connected to computer software, which is recording in 24-hour periods. All the recorded data, duly marked with camera number, date and time are stored and retained on hard disk or CDs/DVDs for at least a week and available for review should the need arise. Simultaneously to the video recording, snapshots are taken from each frame and stored with date and time in a separate folder for identification purposes. Special designed software allows analyzation of any video recording or snapshot instantly, and if required it can enhance each section of the frames or search and match with previous recording or the database for identification purposes. A good security system to be effective should have a powerful combination of sound (loud screaming sirens) and light (strong blinding strobe lights)–an intruder will be totally disoriented and paralyzed.

Security hardware and software (CCTV cameras, computer/s, sensors and detectors, monitors, power supply, etc.), is very expensive to purchase and to install-the costs can reach into the thousands of dollars easily. Therefore when planning and designing the security system/s, the costs must be taken into serious consideration to assure that the system/s being integrated provides maximum coverage but a minimum of costs. Providing protection around a residence or estate is based on the same principle of the concentric circles as used to protect the principal. The security system/s and the entire physical security of the residence is arranged in layers to form a greater factor of deterrence. The security system expert has to conceive a target, which is difficult to penetrate, reducing the chances for an authorized or unwanted person to gain access. Physical security of a residence is a series of layers consisting of planning, security system/s, security procedures, physical and psychological barriers, people.

Security Planning

A thorough security survey has to be conducted, all possible weaknesses, vulnerabilities and possible points of penetration and infiltration must be identified and acknowledged before a security planning starts. As much as conditions are constantly changing so the survey has to be of a constant and ongoing process. Many things can change or just simply malfunction or deteriorate–burned-out light bulbs and fuses, loose cables causing short circuits, tired material and equipment.

Once not properly maintained and staying undetected, these type of things will eventually develop into a possible weakness, which is the perfect invitation for any person with bad intentions.

The security survey should begin with a physical inspection of everything belonging to estate–the grounds, premises and the residential building itself. Starting the inspection at the property boundary line perimeter one is checking for holes and gaps in the fence, overhanging tree branches or hedge shrubbery.

Continuing with the inspection one is walking in ever tightening circles around the property–the inspecting EPO determines the areas which require attention and notes the best possible positioning and installation of security system hardware.

Next step is the electrical wiring, phone and communication lines, plumbing system and connection points-safeguards must be addressed and every connection protected with tamper-proof housings or placed securely underground. All the lines and plumbing, if possible and if permitted should be underground with locked control boxes in a secure area. An alternative power source, generator with fuel storage should be considered and located in a secured area. The power generator must be test run on a schedule routine basis and sufficient fuel stored in safe containers. All doors, gates, locks, fences and windows must if necessary be repaired or reinforced and protected with bars where appropriate.

The security survey continues with interviews and/or conversations with each family member, household, secretary and other staff members to determine routines and to solicit any particular areas of concern. This type of conversation not only provides the EPO with vital information but also assures that the security system/s and related security procedures are being fully integrated in the lifestyle of all the household members.

All the required information has been obtained and it is time to analyze the data and to formulate the overall physical security plan. The security plan materializes with integration of alarms, lights, motion and proximity sensors, cameras (night and day) and any additional security measures necessary based on the needs established in the security survey.

The Physical Security Plan

Security planning is a continuous process carried out in advance of, and concurrent with, security and protection operations. Normally, planning for security and protection operations will fall within the patterns, often used by security planners, I. e. the estimate, the equipment, the requirements and compliances, the plan and implementation in the installation and administration. The security estimate with its analysis of the mission and situation (the course of action and decision) provide the basis for the physical security plan. Each estate, building and organization (residence, office, corporate building) requires an individual physical security plan. The principal's activity physical security plan will be integrated into the estate security plan.

It is essential and in the best interest of security that every secured property and/or unit maintains and uses a detailed physical security plan. The plan should include at least special and general guard orders, access and material control, protective barriers/lighting systems, locks and IDSs (**I**ntrusion **D**etection **S**ystem).

The intent of the physical security plan is to clearly identify how the security personnel conducts the day-to-day security duties as well as how it responds to security incidents. The plan should reflect the detailed implementation of the established protection and security policy at the estate/activity and should not be philosophical or an exact reiteration of any previous directive or manual. The physical security plan should be included as an annex or appendix in the protection procedures of the estate. The physical security plan should be based on the findings and recommendations of the security.

The physical security plan is subject to be reviewed on a fixed period of time and in conjunction with filed security incident reports. Any physical security plans has the potential of being classified material and must be treated accordingly. The following depicts a sample of a physical security plan which can be used for a residence as well as for office buildings:

Physical Security Plan

Estate Blueprint Reference: Copy No.:

Address: Issued by:
                                                                        Issued at:
                                                                        Date:

A. Purpose   (Stating the plan's purpose)

B. Area Security   (Definition of areas, building/s and other structures considered
                                    critical; establish priorities for their protection)

C. Control Measures   (Defining and establishing restrictions on access and movement into
                                    critical areas)

- ❖ Categorizing all and any restrictions as to personnel, material and vehicles
  - ▪ Personnel Access:
    - Establishment of controls pertinent to each area and/or structure
      - Authority for access
      - Criteria for access
        - Owner and family (including other family related persons)
        - Visitors
        - Maintenance Staff
        - Household Staff
        - Security Personnel
        - Emergency response teams (police, fire, ambulance, etc.)
    - Identification and control
      - Description of the system to be used in each area. For example if an ID badge system is used, a complete description of all aspects should be used in order to disseminate the requirements for ID and control of personnel conducting business on the estate.
      - Application of the system:
        - Owner and family
        - Visitors to restricted areas
        - Visitors to working and administrative areas
        - Vendors, delivery and so forth
        - Security personnel
        - Maintenance and household staff
        - Fail safe procedures during power outages
  - ▪ Material Control
    - Incoming
      -Requirements for admission of material and supplies
      -Search and inspection of material for possible sabotage hazards
      -Special controls on delivery of supplies or personal deliveries in restricted areas
    - Outgoing
      -Control required

- Vehicle Control
  - Policy on search of private vehicles
  - Policy on search of delivery vehicles
  - Parking regulations
  - Controls for entrance into restricted and administrative areas
    -Owner's vehicles
    -Private and delivery vehicles
    -Emergency vehicles
    -Vehicle registration
- ❖ Indicate the manner in which the following security aids will be implemented on the installation.
  - Protective Barriers:
    - Definition
    - Clear zones
      -Criteria
      -Maintenance
    - Signs
      -Types
      -Location
    - Gates
      -Hours of operation
      -Security requirements
      -Lock security
      -Barrier plan
  - Protective lighting system/s:
    - Use and control
    - Inspection
    - Action taken in case of commercial power failure
    - Action taken in case of failure of alternate power source
  - Emergency lighting system:
    - Stationary
    - Portable
  - Intrusion Detection Systems:
    - Security classification
    - Inspection
    - Use and monitoring
    - Action taken in case of alarm conditions
    - Maintenance
    - Alarm logs or registers
    - Tamper proof provisions
    - Monitor panel locations
  - Communications:
    - Locations
    - Use
    - Tests
    - Authentication
  - Security Personnel:
    General instructions that would apply to all security personnel (fixed and mobile).

Detailed instructions such as special orders and SOP (Standing Operating Procedure) information should be attached as annex. Security personnel facets include:

- Composition and organization
- Duty
- Essential posts and routes
- Weapons and equipment
- Training
- Use of SD (Security Dog) teams
- Method of challenging with signs and countersigns
- Alert Unit:
  - Composition
  - Mission
  - Weapons and equipment
  - Location
  - Deployment concept
- Contingency plans:
  Required actions in response to various emergency situations. Detailed plans for situations (terrorism, bomb threats, hostage negotiations, disaster, fire, etc.), should be attached as annex.
  - Individual actions
  - Alert unit actions
  - Security personnel actions
- Use of other surveillance means
- Coordinating instructions. Matters that require coordination with law enforcement and other civil agencies.

The coordination/interaction allows for an exchange of intelligence information on security measures being used, contingency plans and any other information to enhance local security. Applicable provisions shall be included in, or be an appendix to this plan. This plan contains definite assignment of physical security responsibilities.

Procedures for authorization and ID of individuals to receipt for and physically secure the property. The purpose of such coordination is protection in depth. Authority, jurisdiction and responsibility must be set forth in a manner that ensures protection and avoids duplication of effort.

Signed by the EPO in charge

Physical Security Plan Annex

Physical Security Plan

Annex

Annex to the plan should include, but are not limited to the following.

- Annex A: The installation threat statement (intelligence).

- Annex B: Bomb threat plan. The bomb threat plan should provide guidance for:
  -Control of the operation
  -Evacuation
  -Search
  -Finding the bomb or suspected bomb
  -Disposal
  -Detonation and damage control
  -Control of publicity
  -After action report

- Annex C: An installation closure plan.

- Annex D: A natural disaster plan. This plan will be coordinated with natural disaster plans of local agencies. The natural disaster plan should provide guidance for:
  -Control of the operation, Evacuation, Communication, publicity
  -After action report

- Annex E: A civil disturbance plan. It is the responsibility of the EPO in charge to formulate a civil disturbance plan based on local threats.

- Annex F: A resource plan to meet the minimum essential physical security needs for the estate or activity.

- Annex G: A communication plan. This plan is required to establish communications with local law enforcement agencies to share information about possible threats. The communications plan should address all communication needs for annex B through F above.

- Annex H: A list of designated secured and restricted areas.

- Annex I: A list of installation OEVAs (Operation Essential or Vulnerable Area)

- Annex J: A contingency plan. In most instances, it will be necessary to increase security for residence and other sensitive property, assets, and facilities during periods of natural disasters, natural emergencies or increased threat from terrorists or criminal elements. Therefore, contingency plans should include provisions for increasing the physical security measures and procedures based on the EPO in charge's assessment of the situation. Such contingencies may include hostage negotiations and special reaction teams. These provisions should be designed for early detection of an attempted intrusion, theft, or interruption of normal security conditions.

Protective Barriers

Protective barriers include every type of physical obstacle,, which is able to delay, detour an intruder from gaining access or entrance. The outer concentric circle, the perimeter, consists of fences and gates, walls and hedges, trees etc.. The fences should be of a type and structure able to prevent someone from entering through or over the fence. Trees, plants, shrubbery and hedges might be planted alongside the fence, adding a certain air of privacy and keeping security less visible. Any plants or bushes should be of the kind, which have thorns, spikes and briers, such as rose, cactus and berry bushes-making a climb over the fence or through the hedge more difficult. Barbed wire and barbed tape (Concertina) are very effective and can be camouflaged in the shrubbery (local laws and regulations for use and application of barbed wire/tape apply).

The property should have one entrance only. The design of the entrance gate should be reinforced to prevent ramming with a vehicle, further should it be of two sections (one for people, one for cars). At the outside of the gate an intercom with video camera should be installed, which any visitor whether on foot or with a vehicle has to approach for identification. The camera should have tilt/zoom capability, permitting a close-up view of the person and for a better identification process. Visitors and/or vehicles are recorded and still frames stored separately in a database, providing a permanent record of each visitor and vehicle (by vehicles, the images should zoom in on the license plates) and for further identification purposes. With a database of identified images, the EPO in the command post, monitoring approaches on the gate, will be able to compare the new images with existing images. Some software on the market allow a comparison of images, using biometric details and facial recognition, within seconds. The EPO in the command post is able to decide quickly and whether to allow or deny access and/or to proceed according to his/her security instructions and call law enforcement.

Once the EPO has identified and determined that the visitor is permitted entrance (visual identification and voice through the speaker phone), the EPO opens the gate by remote and allowing access. The gate has to be closed immediately to prevent any tailgating of an unauthorized person/vehicle. Depending on the property, the design and layout of the entrance and access it might be necessary to have a security officer physically present at the gate to identify visitors and to control the gate opening and closing.

A landscape modified strategically to meet the security plan is providing excellent spots to hide cameras; motion sensors can be installed permitting detection beams to overlap, forming protection sections. Any part of the landscape and environment can provide simple barriers (e. g. trees, shrubs, pool garden furniture etc.), to make it more difficult for an intruder to approach and easier to detect the intrusion.

Based on experience, a good combination of physical and psychological barriers proof to be more reliable and more effective than most expensive state of the art systems. A property with a wide open lawn and a driveway can be easily transformed to be an intruder's worst nightmare. Installing a few well hidden CCTVs (day/night capability) with incorporated motion sensors and connected to strong search lights (triggered by motion and directional) have an excellent deterrent effect. Those will dissuade all but the most determined and skilled attempting to cross through specific zones. High-tech state of the art security equipment is what most professionals are looking for when taking on protection assignment-but budget limitations and the client's own idea about security can easily make those dreams vanish. Therefore, any EPO should be able to improvise, using all available resources to create a unique and most effective security system. Psychological and physical barriers should be combined into an effective and intimidating deterrent, so no one, regardless of the intent would attempt to violate.

Security Systems

There is no better security element than a well trained and experienced security professional. However, the professional human element, many times reduced in number and quality because of cuts in manpower and costs has been supplemented with high-tech security gadgets. There is no limit to the hardware, neither the configuration capabilities or the application possibilities of those state-of-the-art systems. But no matter how sophisticated these systems are, whether they include seismic-, motion-, or proximity sensors, whether the beams are visible, infrared or laser, whether search lights are motion triggered or the cameras have day and night capability-the human element is the core of any security system and that makes it so effective.

No matter what equipment and/or configuration is installed and used, the principles of security remain the same at all times. No matter what size the estate has and what equipment or how many systems are installed, protection should be designed in an overlapping pattern-meaning, that one system overlaps the other and the areas and premises covered should be zoned. Zoning means-if an alarm is triggered, the monitoring security officer at control unit is able to register the exact location, where a potential security breach took place. Zoning also permits to disable selectively certain sectors, allowing the residents and staff members movement and freedom. The overlapping and integration of the systems increases its own capability and is used to support another and extending and increasing the effectiveness of the system as whole.

The Residence

Unless the residence was designed and conceived by a team of architect, engineer and security design professional, all weaknesses of the building have to be checked. Doors, windows and locks have to be in perfect functional condition and must be secured. Each and any opening, like doors and windows must be wired with sensors and detectors. If space is available and the landscape design is permitting it, thorny bushes should be planted near and under the windows. Anything, which could be used to assist and intruder by climbing to the second floor through a window must be removed. Nicely forged window bars are perfect as protection, as long as the design and structure is not serving as a ladder. Balconies have to be secured in a manner to make it difficult or impossible for an intruder to climb. Balcony doors, even though considered exterior doors have in most cases the structure of an interior door only -extra precautions have to be made.

Protecting the building from an intrusion is only part of the security plan-heat, smoke and fire is the other priority which needs to be taken care of. Detectors for smoke, heat and fire should be strategically installed and linked to the monitoring unit at the command post. An experienced firefighter can be of assistance when selecting the best location for the smoke and heat detectors. Most of the times detectors are wrongly placed and unable to detect smoke, heat and fire in due time.

Secure Room

Depending on the design of the residence and security interest of the home owner, the building might have or should have a secure room. The secure room is a fortified and reinforced room in the center interior of the residence. This room should contain emergency equipment, as well as a food and water supply. It should have an independent air conduct, electricity source, lighting system and toilet. A CCTV camera should be installed on the inside and contain a cellular phone, medication for family members, a first aid kit and a radio.

The secure room should be monitored by an EPO from an off-site command post (depending on the location) such as the principal's office place. The secure room is also an ideal place to install a safe, where important family papers, valuables, etc., can be stored. The entrance to the room should be camouflaged-difficult to detect by an intruder. The entrance and exit should be connected to an alarm system and the room should be secured whenever none of the family is present. This room serves the principal and family as a safe and secure refuge should the residence be under attack. The room should also provide a hidden escape (location and space apply).

Security Procedures

Security procedures is one of the invisible yet effective circle of personal protection. The method of permitting admittance to the estate or residence has a determined and very deterrent affect on any unauthorized "visitors". The EPO, working with the principal has to establish a set of regulations and guidelines regarding the reception of visitors, guests, deliveries, service and repair personnel, mail, packages, etc.. It is part of the procedures to keep a log where the entry and exit of all visitors is registered. Any unexpected delivery person or visitors has to wait outside the gate until identification, purpose and intent is verified and access cleared. The procedures must be enforced strictly (no exceptions), has to reviewed frequently and reconsidered in order to assure the effectiveness of the procedures. Every person responsible for the enforcement of the admittance procedures must remain alert to suspicious looking and acting people and to those attempting to gain entrance without an authorized reason. Whenever there is an unusual occurrence or incident, like an attempted penetration, a report describing the incident must be prepared and filed. Any such events and/or person/s must be investigated thoroughly to determine any potential risk. Any repeated occurrence could mean a planned attack of some nature against the principal or his/her family.

People

The principal and his/her intimate surrounding constitutes the innermost circle. The family, friends, business associates, business and domestic staff are a very important and forming an integral part of the internal security program. Awareness and alertness to strangers, to people asking too many questions about the principal, the security and the principal's schedule and every unusual occurrences are very crucial for the effectiveness of the protection program. Anything that arouses attention and/or suspicion should immediately be reported to the executive protection officer. Therefore a friendly, open dialogue and communication with family and staff members must be a priority for the security officers. All the protective personnel must establish a good working relationship with the domestic staff and the business staff. All the staff members are a great source of pertinent information which otherwise might not be communicated to the security personnel.

The executive protection team, which is working within all these circles and layers is without a doubt the most crucial factor of all. The EPO team or protection personnel provides the element, which is tying it all together. Protective and security personnel must be stationed around the residence and estate at strategic selected locations, where each of them can keep a full physical surveillance of the residence, without depending and relying only on the high tech equipment. The security personnel is placed where each of them is able to respond readily and neutralize any suspicious activity or to move immediately into the principal proximity. The EPO usually operates from a centrally located command post (a room which should be provided by the principal), where he/she is able to monitor and respond to the entire security and alarm systems. From there he/she can enforce established regulations and procedures for admittance and provide whatever assistance the principal might need. The command post, constantly occupied, should be kept clean, functional and maintained as a professional working station. The post is usually equipped with alarm systems control panels, CCTV monitors, phones and radios (charger and extra batteries). Further emergency and rescue equipment (fire extinguishers, first aid kit, etc.), secure locker for firearms and ammo, the operations and security procedure manuals, computer and other office equipment.

Security at the Office

No matter how big or small a office building or business complex is, the principles of protection are similar to those applied for the principal's residence. The concept of insulating the principal as a deterrent proofs to be as effective at the workplace as it is at the residence or on a trip. Physical and psychological barriers and procedures as many as practical and possible to implement should be between the potentially target, the principal and an intruder. The secure environment, similar to the residence starts at the entrance to the office/business property. This is usually an underground parking facility or a reserved parking lot at the entrance to the building. This type of parking arrangements are most common among companies, corporations and agencies and most appreciated by executives and employees. However, as convenient as those parking facilities are, the fact that most are with a free access to the public makes them vulnerable and equally easy to access for any criminal or terrorist. Unfortunately, several years ago we had to learn how easy it is for a terrorist group enter and to plant a bomb in such an open and free access facility:

> *February 26, 1993, World Trade Center, New York-a car bomb was detonated by Arab terrorists in the underground parking garage below Tower One of the WTC. The attack was planned by Ramzi Yousef, Sheik Omar Abdel-Rahman, El Sayyid Nosair, Mahmud Abouhalima, Mohammad Salameh, Nidal Ayyad, Ahmad Ajaj and Abdul Rahman Yasin. The financing came from al-Qaeda member Khaled Shaikh Mohammed, Yousef's uncle. The 1,500 lb (680 kg) urea nitrate-fuel-oil explosive device generating a pressure estimated over one GPa and opening a 30 meter wide hole through four sublevels of concrete. The detonation velocity of this bomb was about 15,000 ft/s (4.5 km/s). The bomb exploded in the underground garage at 12:17 P.M., killing six and injuring 1,042 people. It was intended to devastate the foundation of the North Tower, causing it to collapse onto its twin.*

Security for an individual should not be restricted to the workplace only. Unfortunately, the security policy of many companies (especially internationally operating corporations), is either relaxed or irrational restrictive. They are limiting physical and protective security to certain areas within the working environment of the person, but not including the access and/or parking area-ideal circumstances for any threat. Those limitations are reflected on the protective assignments, where the EPO is only responsible for the safety and well being of the executive while she/he is within the office environment. Reason might be, that a threat is only "expected" from former employees-expecting that they would not know the private address of the executive. Or because an employee chooses the workplace, because he/she is familiar with the habits of the target and the environment, which makes it easier to close in on the victim and to attack.

Therefore, at least one (if available several) officers of the protective team should be positioned in the parking area prior to the expected arrival of the principal. Giving time to monitor not only the arrival of the principal, but also the parking of the employees and others in the facility. If the circumstances permit, the principal should have a designated parking space reserved and easily accessible and clearly visible. The protective assignment should be pre-positioned with one, ideally two, EPOs in the vicinity of the designated parking place. As the principal arrives in the parking lot, the EPO/s will meet the principal and escort him/her to his office or respective areas of activities. The entire protective personnel must be alert and anticipate, that someone could suddenly get up in a car or move from the trunk of a vehicle with any type of weapon (knife, firearm, explosive device) ready to attack. The parking facility should provide continuous monitoring either by the physical presence of security personnel or by CCTVs. Artificial lighting in most underground parking facilities is not sufficient. The protective personnel has to make sure, that the principal's car is parking in an area, where the light is efficiently reducing and eliminating any shadowy and possible hiding places.

Access Control

Monitoring and controlling all access points to an office area or business place in general will reduce, if not deter any intention or act of violence from a former employee or even an outsider. Access control and monitoring is physically presenting to employees and outside people that security in the company is taken serious and given high priority. CCTV cameras should be installed everywhere, where people is circulating (main entrances, reception area, elevators, stairwells, fire and emergency exits, corridors, etc.). Based on the building plan, visitors to the building should be channeled to the reception, where they have to speak with a receptionist or a security officer before proceeding and gaining access. Employees with clearance are issued ID cards (SmartCard), containing the employee's biometric data and the areas to which the employee is authorized to enter. The employee is gaining access to his/her sector by placing the card on the card reader. Additional security measure (e. g. iris-, or fingerprint scanner) can and should be installed (based on the financial structure of the company). Visitors to the building after clearing the identification will be issued an ID card, clearly marked "VISITOR", which is programmed for the sector to visit only. The card and the person bearing it can be tracked via Bluetooth technology, permitting to monitor each and every move of the visitor. The reception area should be secured and isolated from the main business area. Each visitor's image, identification and visitor card details is filed and stored in a visitor's database.

The access to the executive's area should be isolated from the remaining offices with separate doors. One EPO should be positioned near the principal's office. Depending on the risk and threat level, additional EPOs should be stationed near the elevator/s, the reception area and/or the main entrance. Generally speaking, all entrances and exits to the office premises should have monitored and restricted access, either via CCTVs, electronic locking systems and/or uniformed security personnel. In case a threat has been made, by a former employee for example or any other suspect, a full physical description with photo (if available) has to be distributed at once to all the protective and security personnel. Any information regarding threats from former employees should be available from the human resources department. Gathering information about former employees is part of the EPO's job, even if the assignment (some clients, for whatever reason, feel more safe at their office and do not want any EPO around) excludes a protective duty within business premises.

The essential part of the EPO's duty is to control the access and to monitor any and all incoming personnel, being extremely alert for suspicious people and/or designated threats. In public buildings, the focus of attention must be placed closer to the principal because of any potential threats. The EPO must conduct a security and risk survey and even an overall review of the premises and procedures will permit to acknowledge any indicator/s of possible vulnerabilities. The EPO conducting the survey must direct his/her recommendations to the person in charge in order to have the necessary corrections and changes executed accordingly.

Corporate and Industrial Espionage

Foreign economic espionage directed against U. S. defense contractors is on a rise, according to a recent article in the *C⁴ISR Journal*. The article refers to a report of the Pentagon's Defense Security Service (DSS), in which 106 countries were involved in U. S. targeted espionage in 2005 and 90 countries in 2004. Further, according to the Office of the National Counterintelligence Executive (NCIX), the illegal outflow of technology imposed huge costs on the U. S. economy in 2005. One such cases was the former Northrop-Grumman employee, Noshir Gowadia, which provided classified export controlled infrared signature suppression technology (which he helped develop for the B-2 Bomber) to China and other countries. According to the U. S. Defense Security Service, the top items on the "shopping list" are information systems, laser and optics, aeronautical technology, sensors, armaments and energetic materials, electronic technology, space systems, marine systems, material and processing acquisition and signature control.[20]

In the corporate environment, industrial espionage is sometimes nothing else than an innocent exchange of conversation at a reception, a lunch with colleagues or after work at a pub. Places where naïve and less security conscious employees engage in talks, which might reveal vital business and/or even classified information to whoever might be listening.

An innocent conversation in a public places, such as cafeteria, restaurant or elevator about company internal affairs can quickly turn into a major security problem. Just simple personnel gossip or rumors are the subject of interest to a competitor. Any bits and pieces represent vital and valuable information to those who are in need. Company employees, especially corporate executives are more vulnerable, when traveling. Common practices, such as luggage searches and surreptitious explorations of laptops, as well as confiscated and stolen business and personal equipment, such as PDAs, cell phones and notebook computers are the constant threat while traveling. Traveling contractors and employees can easily fall for the warm welcome and assistance offered by foreign company representatives, hotel staff. Rooms and equipment provided by hosts can easily contain hidden monitoring and recording devices (microphones and cameras in the room, scanning devices in copiers, shredders, software which records keystrokes, e-mail traffic, used files content). Trade shows with the entire organizational arrangements are common playground for "information collectors"-where else can one get firsthand information, samples and product specific data. According to the DSS, among the nations reputed to "collect" aggressively at trade shows are France, Israel, India, South Korea, Taiwan and Russia. [20]

It is not the job of the EPO to keep an eye on employees, which might steal company property or secretes. However, an EPO in execution of his protective duty, while monitoring the CCTV feeds might detect a suspicious acting employee or even discover company theft in progress. In this case the EPO should report the incident to the person in charge without disrupting any of his/her assigned duties. The person in charge, based on the report and the CCTV footage of the incident can proceed accordingly.

Recommendations for correction and alternative procedures should be provided to stop further incidents. In many cases, the mere presence of EPOs, which were assigned to provide protection to various executives of different departments within a company caused a decrease of incidents of company theft.

Computer Security

As much as any vulnerability is taken in consideration when conducting a security survey, as much attention must be given to any computer system. No matter if this is a single personal computer (PC), laptop, notebook computer or a computer network. Computer security gained as much importance in executive protection, as has the security system, physical barriers and access control, etc., at the business or the residence premises. Security systems, access control systems, verifications and recognition systems, as well as personnel are held on databases and are controlled either by a single station computer or connected to an entire network. Since computer technology is getting complex every day and the number of hackers and other criminal elements, taking advantage of this technology is multiplying by the hour, the vulnerability of computers is an essential part of any security survey. Hackers and alike gain easily access and infiltrate most commercial and even military systems, stealing, manipulating, destroying and/or corrupting codes and information stored. The majority of computer (personal or business wise) are all equipped with network adapters and compatible software, allowing the user to connect to other computers either via a local computer network or the worldwide network-the Internet. The level of vulnerability, possibilities of penetration and the opportunity of data theft is only measurable by the type and effectiveness of the countermeasures installed. Computers containing confidential and/or operation critical data should never be left unattended. The EPO conducting the security survey has not only the responsibility to provide recommendations for the security of the computer system. The EPO has to make sure, that any computer or computerized equipment used for protective duty is equally secure and equipped with the latest security software. An EPO assigned to conduct a full security sweep and physical inspection in a residence or business premises, will soon find out that a great number of computers are left on while unattended and even overnight. A common mistake, even banks and government agencies have to face. A lot of computers, when unattended are not only left on and connected to the network, but also display the last opened files and other data on the monitor screen.

Some of the computers may display a professionally designed screensaver with a company logo, secured by a password, which do not even require a professional hacker to crack. Careful screening and checking on employees does not guarantee absolute security and protect from misuse of critical information stored on the computer system. Therefore critical information must be protected and allowed access to trusted employees only, with access level restriction limited to a need-to-know basis; this will greatly reduce the possibility and risks of any unauthorized usage. The computer access to specific data must be protected and controlled by password management and administration software, using high level encryption. The computers should be configured to shut down automatically after several access attempts were unsuccessful or any other security breach or unauthorized access has been detected.

Security Awareness

Security awareness starts with responsibility. Every executive to a certain extend is as responsible for his/her own safety and security, as for that of the family, friends, associates, staff safety and security-and the EPOs/EPO team. The EPOs are the professionals, responsible to take the initiative, assuming leadership in the common objective-keeping the principal safe and alive. A clear common sense and well developed security awareness are the tools to achieve that goal. With a proper security awareness one is able to prevent and to shield off a great deal of trouble. An EPO on the other hand is expected to be conscious of security risks and fully alert of any threats at all times, capable of taking a preemptive action or any necessary reactive measures. Bearing this in mind, the principal (family, friends, staff, employees included) as a responsible part can extremely enhance the protective detail's efforts and be aware of and follow certain precautions. Security awareness is not only a matter of training, but of education, attitude and responsibility. With some responsibility, effort, thought and awareness, principals as well as others can greatly reduce the risks of being involved in a harmful and endangering security incident. Whenever the opportunity presents itself, EPOs should encourage the principal to learn some of the basics of protection and security awareness. The initial security briefing of the principal, family and staff members is the starting point of a security awareness training and education. Everybody present should be briefed and advised about security awareness-covering relevant security precautions, things to be expected in relation to security functions and operation and how each one's cooperation and involvement can strengthen the security effort as a team. With the right and positive attitude toward the security and the executive protection in particular, all efforts could be carried over to all who are concerned about the well being of the principal. Everybody in the immediate surrounding, including the principal should have a positive and collaborative attitude toward the protective concepts and its consequences. A number of factors require a constant concern for the principal's and other's security. Those factors include circumstances, which might result in new threats. Ever changing schedules, last minute changes of itineraries and unscheduled events and visits could place the principal in harm's way through the negligence of someone oblivious to the security and protective concerns. To avoid any possible security incidents, a principal should at least:

- Always avoid any predictable pattern of activity or movement. It is vital to vary as much as possible the departure and arrival times (home, office and travel). Take a moment and look around in the immediate environment. Try to identify anything which is out of the ordinary (any strange acting or looking person or vehicle) before leaving the safe location (home, office, hotel, bar, restaurant) for good. A person should never leave a protected or secure area, if something seems out of place or appears to be wrong.
- Always avoid wearing or carrying extravagant jewelry, clothing, or other distinguishable and expensive accessories in an unprotected or unknown environment.
- Always try to use an alternate route and avoid as much as possible routes which form natural choke points, bottlenecks and/or delays in traffic (e. g. traffic lights with long waiting periods, constructions, narrow and sparsely used roads.

Avoid if possible rush-hour traffic and use the most speedy and direct route. Keep updated frequently on current traffic and conditions, via radio stations and GPS systems. Always drive with the doors locked and the windows closed. Have a monitoring system and alarm installed in the vehicle.

- Always park the car in a secured and if possible CCTV-monitored parking zone-whenever possible vary the parking spaces and locations. Never use a reserved parking lot, which displays the name or license plate of the user. Never use any personalized license plates.
- Before entering the vehicle, make a quick physical inspection of the car. Check the ground in the immediate proximity of the car for scratch marks, leakage or other unusual signs. Make certain, that nobody is hiding inside the car, determine that nothing has been placed inside the gas intake opening, the wheel wells or inside the exhaust pipe. Always remember, if anything looks out of the ordinary or abnormal, never try to remove it or to start the vehicle. Just walk away quickly and call immediately for assistance.
- Always carry a cellular phone with preprogrammed speed-dial numbers of the emergency services, which can be utilized quickly in the event of a crisis. Also make sure, that home and office are informed and aware of departure or arrival. In case of an incident or emergency, it is much easier to track the possible whereabouts.

Safety Consciousness

One should not just take the fact and assume that safety is present. The EPO as part of his/her responsibility has to make a routine survey of the working environment at a daily basis before starting the shift. Further he/she has to look for security risks and must be alert for any safety problems that could cause injury and take if possible the immediate and necessary steps to correct it. Safety hazards can be small things (like oil, grease or other spills, which can make a floor slippery) or more complex things (like poorly isolated electrical wires, cracked or broken plugs, slippery sidewalks and driveways). Whatever the extend of the danger, it is important to take note, report and/or correct safety hazards as soon as they are noticed and prevent any accidents and/or tragic consequences. Many of those dangers are found in any type of job, others might be more specific to this type of activity, in any case the EPO has to be aware of any eventual danger and safety hazard. It is also the job of the EPO to verify and to make sure that fire doors and emergency exits are kept clear, unlocked and duly marked. He/she is responsible to correct anything that could be a potential physical hazard to the principal or expose the principal to civil liability should someone else be injured. Accidents are unplanned but can be prevented. The EPO's duty is not only to prevent that the principal is getting intentionally injured, but to keep the same high level of alertness, awareness and attention to detail to prevent accidental injuries. The EPO's responsibility is also to safeguard the principal and/or his/her business from unintentional injury. Meaning, the EPO must protect the principal and his/her (business) assets from liabilities, which could result from safety violations and hazards or physical injury. Safety concerns are part of the security survey. Any safety risk is not only placing the principal's well-being in jeopardy, but also others. The EPO has to keep informed and updated on developments which may impact the safety and security of the principal, the business environment and working place.

Emergencies and Natural Disasters

Another of the EPO's responsibilities is the adequate and proper response to natural and/or man-made disasters. Nobody is able to predict or control the angry, sometimes violent and capricious behavior of nature. The variety of disasters, *Mother Nature* is using to surprise human beings, range from "simple" floods, tornadoes, hurricanes and snowstorms to earthquakes and volcano eruptions, just to name a few.

Even though, nothing can be done to control natural disasters and forecasts (in some cases) are the only means of alerting. The best solution is to be prepared and to be in a state of constant readiness, so that lives and property can by saved. Man-made disasters (explosions, acts of war, arson, etc.), are not predictable, but preparedness should remain at the same high level. EPOs are expected and should have emergency operation and evacuation plans ready and in force for any natural and/or man-made disaster.

Emergency Plan

The EPO's might be solicited by the principal, his/her representative or corporate emergency planner/s to assist (or volunteer) with his/her expertise to program and elaborate an emergency operations plan to protect the corporate employees and assets. This emergency plan should allow enough flexibility and effective for whatever type of emergency, but still be specific on the identification of the respective responsibilities and related procedures.

The following steps are a guideline for the preparation of an emergency plan:

- A person must be designated and held responsible within each department/section for preparing and monitoring the emergency plan. In large businesses, offices/departments with an existing safety staff, this duty is normally assigned to one of the safety personnel. In smaller businesses/offices, this duty can be assigned as a collateral duty to one of the senior staff members or if available a trained employee. Primary and alternate designees should be specifically noted, trained, and drilled in their reactive responsibilities.

- A warning system should be installed for all personnel. Emergency drills should be conducted and practiced monthly. Alarm notification systems, such as sirens and so on, should be installed and located at strategic points throughout the premises.

- Additional duties are assigned to designated employees, which will be responsible for the overall plan and the designated areas:

  - Reporting emergencies:
    Although all employees can and should immediately report emergencies, persons should be designated to ensure that emergency personnel (such as law enforcement officials and the fire department) have been contacted. These persons will further be responsible for directing emergency personnel to the area of the emergency.
  - Accounting for employees:
    Persons should be designated as responsible for accounting for all employees at the assembly area following evacuation of the work area. These persons should further be responsible for alerting emergency personnel to the last known location of any missing employees.

  If applicable, specific persons should also be designated for the following duties:
  - First Aid and Firefighting:
    Although there is no requirement that every department/office has first aid or firefighting trained personnel available, it is highly recommended. First aid and firefighting trained personnel should be identified to the other employees.
  - Critical operations:
    The work area should be surveyed for critical operations which should be discontinued, if possible, before the area is evacuated.

Such critical operations would include industrial operations which could help propagate a fire or areas containing restricted materials. If such areas are identified, a person should be designated to attempt to discontinue the operation or secure the areas with restricted materials. Under no circumstances should these persons endanger any person (or themselves) by entering a dangerous area.

- Evacuation procedures have to planned and implemented. Evacuation routes must be diagrammed and should be placed visibly (even during blackouts) throughout the offices and near the elevators and stairwells. The elevators should not be used in the event of fire or any emergency with temporary power failures. Every personnel must be familiar with the primary and the secondary (alternative) evacuation routes.

- A training and education program for all employees has to be established and should include emergency medical response, emergency situation reaction and behavior and disaster and emergency preparedness. Training should be provided for all employees to adequately ensure the effectiveness of the program. On employment and at least yearly, all employees should be trained in the general requirements of the plan. Including location of the master plan, evacuation policy, methods of emergency notification, escape procedures and exit routes, methods of reporting emergencies and designated assembly areas following evacuation. This training for employees designated for specific duties should include the following:

  - Reporting emergencies:
    Those individuals designated in the plan as responsible for ensuring that outside emergency personnel have been contacted should be familiarized with all of the current emergency reporting numbers. They should also be instructed as to their duties to coordinate with these outside emergency personnel at the scene.
  - Accounting for employees:
    Those individuals designated in the plan as responsible for ensuring an orderly evacuation, conducting a roll call of employees and reporting any missing employees should be instructed as to their duties.
  - Rescue and First Aid:
    The first aid skills of any person assigned to provide such care should be updated and certified at least yearly.
  - Firefighting:
    If certain employees are designated to operate fire extinguishers, those persons must be trained in the proper use of the extinguishers and that training must be updated at least annually.
  - Critical operations:
    If critical operations are identified, this should be discontinued, if possible, during an emergency. Those persons responsible for deactivating the operations should be trained in those specific operations and in conditions when it will not be possible to deactivate the operations.

- A plan for mobilization, control of critical supplies and security of all personnel, records, and sensitive material has to be developed and in place. A crisis management team or specifically designated and trustable personnel should be assigned.

- Designate and activate an emergency control center. The control center should be located in a safe environment with effective communication capabilities. It is advisable to have this site at a location away from the primary position.

Arrangements must be made for the rapid relocation of personnel, critical equipment, and sensitive material.

- An assembly area has to be designated to be used in case of an emergency. These areas should be located outside of buildings and far enough from the building so that employees will not be exposed to any further dangers. Avoiding interference with the activities of emergency personnel, such as law enforcement or the fire department. All employees have to be informed of the assembly area.

- A shelter and relocation area has to be planned and designated, where the injured can receive medical assistance and a personnel count can be maintained.

- Prepare and allocate emergency kits at strategic locations (duly marked) containing food, water, tools (shovels, axes, ropes, etc.), medical supplies, lights, blankets, generators, and emergency communications equipment, spare batteries, candles, matches and so on. Designated personnel should know the locations and have access to the equipment supply.

- It is most important to keep an ongoing liaison with local governmental and nongovernmental emergency authorities. This should include local civil defense and Red Cross units, gas-, water-, electricity providers, hazardous material agency, fire, police, emergency services, hospitals, etc..

- The entire plan has to be reviewed at least on an annual basis to ensure that all information contained in it is current and accurate. The work areas should also be surveyed at this time to ensure that routes of exit are not blocked and that all required information is posted and current. This annual review of the plan is also an excellent time to ensure that all training is current.

As any corporate office/department develops its own emergency plan, it must consider its relationships with other departments or organizations which may affect portions of the plan. Smaller companies, or incorporated office sections might not have effective control of or responsibility for items such as the sprinkler system, smoke detectors, designating emergency numbers or designating building escape routes. These items might be within the control and responsibility of associated entities, which might have an overall responsibility for a building/facility. The smaller offices/sections must be aware of these items, however and it is the responsibility of the EPO and/or the person/s in charge of the emergency planning to properly include those in the plan.

It is very important that the entity responsible for the overall emergency plan for the building and the individual offices located in the same building/facility coordinate their plans to ensure that the plans are in agreement. Further, some duplication of effort may be saved by coordinating items such as training.

The entity responsible for the overall emergency plan for the building/facility should contact each of the individual offices and provide them with a copy of the master emergency plan. Further specific instructions about the building evacuation routes and appropriate emergency phone numbers. Individual offices should contact the entity responsible of the building and request information on items such as alarm systems, building evacuation routes and appropriate emergency phone number.

The Vehicle and Driving

- **The Vehicle Security**

- **The Motorcade**

- **The Lead**

- **The Follow-Up**

- **The Driving Techniques**

Rule number one-get familiar with the vehicle. Rule number two-even handling the vehicle as it is your own, it still is the property of the principal. The major part of professional EPOs do offer a certain amount of experience with all types of cars. Some might even have passed and qualified from a professional driving school-but will that be enough when confronted with an exotic concept car. Driving a vintage model can sometimes turn into a real adventure. This of course can easily change into a traffic nightmare, especially when one is used to drive on the "wrong" side of the road. No matter what make or model it is, or either it belongs to the principal or is a rental, the EPO is designated to drive (there is no time for explanations nor excuses). Any EPO confronted with an unfamiliar model or make should approach the principal in a professional manner and explain, that he/or she needs some time to get familiar with the vehicle. The principal will understand, because he/she depends on the driving skills of the EPO in case of an emergency. The EPO has not only the responsibility and duty to familiarize with the car in means of driving, but also to get familiar with the car's behavior in different situations. The mechanical and functional part is also important, and sometimes a bit of mechanical and car engine knowledge can save the day. The EPO must make sure, that he/she knows each and every button and the respective functions-this can be live saving.

The Vehicle Security

Criminals, gangs and terrorists are operating like predators-always choosing the weakest prey or the easiest mark to attack. Everybody, not only the professional trained EPO, should be security conscious at all times and increase the odds that these predators choose someone else. The following points are general security recommendations, which can be easily implemented while in and/or around the vehicle. These security recommendations are the first line of defense.

- Vary the times and routes to and from work or other frequently visited locations. Avoid fixed routines.
- Have a thorough knowledge of the area.
- Avoid getting stuck in traffic.
- Always park in a way to have a fast exit from the parking space.
- Never stop for anyone.
- Drive on major roads and main streets, if possible.
- Know the shortest routes to police stations, hospitals, military outposts, etc.
- Check rear-view mirrors frequently.
- Inform someone of your destination and estimated time of arrival.
- Be alert of groups and/or men in some type of uniform (jogging suits, overalls, etc.).
- Never trust anyone with the car key.
- Avoid constructions, blockages, traffic jams etc..
- Always keep the gasoline tank at least half full, and carry a reserve canister in the trunk.
- If the car has been left alone, check thoroughly for tampering before entering and driving.
- If suspicious people are spotted around the vehicle-avoid it.
- Always and if possible, keep a low profile.

While on driving duty, an EPO when working alone might have to leave the principal's vehicle unattended. This can also happen to an entire team, depending on the situations and circumstances. If this is not avoidable, than it is vital to take certain security precautions. All vehicles, part of the motorcade must be equipped with an alarm systems, which is programmable and able to alert the command post and the EPO via visual and audible signal. Parking the vehicles in a closed parking environment or the secured garage at the residence does not mean that precautions should be lessened–the vehicles must be locked and the alarm activated.

In addition small remote CCTV cameras can be installed around the vehicles, allowing the control center a close visual. During the night and if not in a closed garage, the vehicles should be parked in an area with good lighting.

Whenever the vehicle/s are left unattended, the EPO has to carry out a visual check under and around the vehicle/s-from the exhaust pipe and gasoline intake, to the wheel wells and under the hood. The EPO has to look for any unusual devices or signs of tampering, check the immediate surrounding for any unusual material (tape, pieces of wire, fluids) before entering the car and/or starting the engine. Many limo drivers, while waiting for their passenger have this "strange" habit to clean and polish their vehicle. Leaving the vehicle with a very thin almost invisible coating of dust is a perfect condition for detecting any tempering.

All openings, like the hood, trunk and gasoline tank intake cover (as by most current models and makes) should be locked and unlocked from the inside the vehicle. The maintenance and servicing of the vehicle should be done by a trusted and reliable dealer and service station (background check of the owner/s and employees). A service logbook should be kept and the personnel servicing the vehicle/s should always (if possible) be the same. Each time, a vehicle is returning from service, an EPO has to conduct a thorough physical inspection on the vehicle/s (ideally one of the EPOs with some mechanical knowledge would stay with the vehicle).

When on the road, the EPO's responsibility, when driving the principal is to keep the doors locked and the windows shut. The EPO assigned to drive the principal, as well as the other vehicles of the EPO team must be alert for any vehicle which is closing in or appear to be following the motorcade. Besides changing the route and the travel schedule constantly every day, the driver has to know every location of the emergency services (fire, medical and law enforcement) in the area. He/she must avoid any congested areas as much as possible, keeping updated via GPS or radio stations. A designated driver should never stop to assist or pick up any stranded person on the road. In many countries, a driver is obliged by law to stop and to assist another person in an emergency (car accident). In order to avoid any legal consequences, the driver (without stopping) can call and give exact the coordinates of the accident to the emergency services. Or depending on the seriousness of the circumstances and availability of sufficient personnel, detach one EPO for immediate assistance. A communication link between the drivers via two-way radio has to be kept, so anything unusual can be reported immediately. In such situation, the drivers should speed to the nearest police station or any public area, where the "package" can be secured and the authorities notified.

The Motorcade

The following is a simple outline of the procedures which is of prime importance to assure the passengers' (principal, family associates, guests) and EPO team members' safety. And to assure, the EPOs are able to execute their duty without harming other motorists and/or people on the street. Each element of the team within the motorcade plays an important part to assure that the principal has a safe and timely travel. A motorcade usually consists of a *lead vehicle* (Lead), the *principal's vehicle/s* and a *follow-up vehicle* (Follow-up). The first step in assuring the safety of the motorcade is a careful and thorough planning. The designated EPO, when planning the motorcade, has to gather all elements available. Key pieces of information for the planning include:

- Time of the event and time needed (departure to arrival)
- Distance between home base and event/s
- Number of vehicles in the motorcade
- Make and model of each vehicle
- Cruising speeds of each vehicle
- Fuel capacity and range of each vehicle
- Primary and secondary route

- Road conditions, road cover material, weather condition
- Refueling required (coordinates of gas stations)
- Long distance (coordinates of refreshing facilities)

Probably the most important part of the planning is the selection of the primary route and as an alternative the secondary route. There are many factors to consider when selecting the right route. The EPO's responsibility and priority is to get the motorcade with passengers safe and without interference from point A to point B. Traveling smooth and comfortable will be considered as a pleasant extra. When planning the route, the EPO has to consider and to line up every single detail from departure point to arrival point. Any stops required between those points (depending on the distance to travel), necessary turns (left or right turns), intersections, railroad crossings, traffic lights have to be taken in consideration. No detail should left out. Get the latest reports on road conditions and traffic from the responsible agencies or traffic police departments. Congested city streets with many stops and starts should (if possible) be avoided. If for whatever reason stops for refreshment are necessary, than the EPO has to make sure that the selected location has a parking facility for all the vehicles. Fuel stops should be avoided, however it depends on the circumstances and the distance the motorcade has to travel. In that case, the EPO has to make sure that the facility chosen has the fuel type used for the vehicles and is able to refuel several vehicles in the same time. This short stop can be used to check engine oil, water, tires, lights and to clean the windshields.

Once everything is included in the plan and all the details have been registered, the EPO needs to get the entire plan checked by driving the planned route, using the exact driving speed as the motorcade. The EPO will leave the departure point at the scheduled time, preferably on the same day of the week, the motorcade is planned for. The EPO drives at the same route as planned, taking note of anything unusual, any problems with traffic (construction, schools, shift changes). Whatever the EPO will find now, will be noted and passed on to the drivers during the briefing prior to departure. Even if the EPO is familiar with the route, he/she has to advance the route and check and take note of anything unusual.

Before departure each driver should inspect the vehicle according to the security procedures and check oil, water, lights and tires on the vehicle they are driving. Depending on the number of vehicles, a scout vehicle might be used to advance and to secure section of the route. The lead vehicle (Lead) will drive at the point of the motorcade, followed by the principal's vehicle/s and secured from the rear by the follow-up vehicle. (see Fig. 32)

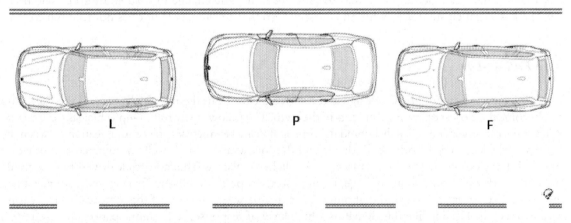

Fig. 32

The lead vehicle is indicating the speed for the entire motorcade, which is keeping a close but safe distance between each other vehicle. Visibility, road conditions, and distance to the principal's car are main factors, the driver of the lead vehicle has to consider and adjust the speed accordingly. All vehicle drivers have to keep visual contact with each other and keep radio contact at all times.

Even with the most accurate planning, anything can happen-a malfunction of one of the cars, flat tire, bad gasoline quality, etc. The lead driver has to be aware of everything and has to be able to react immediately. Flashing LED warning lights (if the vehicles have permission) are of a great help and will assist the motorcade to clear the road. But remember, the use of flashing headlights does not give the right to disrespect others in traffic. Drivers of official motorcades (whether with or without police escort), tend to become superhuman when on the road. A reckless and dangerous driving is not the exact image a VIP (no matter president, diplomat or corporate executive), not EPOs should be proud of. Whatever the circumstances are, no matter how serious the situation is, an EPO has to keep a perfect balance between professional protective duty and the law.

In the event of a forced and unplanned stop because of mechanical failure, a designated EPO responsible for small maintenance should check the cause of the problem and make a decision as to how to proceed. All drivers, principal (family, etc.), must remain in their vehicles, remaining members of the team secure the area. Once the problem is solved, or proper decisions are made, the motorcade continues according to plan.

The Lead

Prior to departure the designated motorcade leader (usually the EPO responsible for the planning and motorcade advance) should have a short briefing with all drivers. During the briefing the drivers will receive final details, such as motorcade speed, updates on road and weather-conditions and specific travel detail. The established speed should be based on road and traffic conditions.

Each driver will receive final instructions regarding the respective position within the motorcade. The driver will receive radio frequency and call sign and the motorcade leader has to make sure that all participants are aware of all necessary details and procedures for any unplanned stop or an emergency. The motorcade leader's responsibility is also to inspect each vehicle (fuel, water, lights, braking lights, warning lights, windshields and mirrors). If, for whatever reasons (official events, committees, group of foreign dignitaries), the motorcade consists of more than three vehicles, it is advisable to split the motorcade into two or more elements. Under these conditions the elements are raveling a few miles apart from each other in order to prevent traffic congestion and to reduce the target size.

Once the motorcade is underway, the designated leader has to keep a watchful eye on all the vehicles, that they are moving together, as well as to look ahead for any change in road and traffic conditions. He/she has to anticipate traffic lights and crossings, so that a changing light does not split the convoy.

The Follow-Up

While on the road, the EPOs designated to drive the lead car, the principal's car and the follow-up car, become the closest operating elements in the team. The follow-up or follow-up vehicle is the designation for the car driven immediately behind the principal's car. Teamwork and communication between the scout vehicle, lead vehicle, principal's driver and the follow-up must be well coordinated and function smoothly like clockwork. There is no place for the slightest mistake. The motorcade drivers have to think, react and perform as one. At an average driving speeds as permitted by traffic laws and with just a few meters between each car (to avoid that other cars come between and cut off the motorcade), there is no room for errors. Driving like this demands a high level of response, reflex, anticipation and awareness from each driver.

When the driver of the lead vehicle signals for a stop, change of lane, or for a turn, the next following vehicle, the principal's car is repeating the same signals, so that the follow-up driver can initiate any maneuver. Any signal must be given enough in advance, so that the follow-up driver has time enough to check the rear (avoiding to cause any danger to oncoming traffic) and to maneuver accordingly.

If, for example the lead vehicle gives the order by radio to change to another lane, the principal's car will wait for the follow-up vehicle to change the lane first. The follow-up will make sure, that it is safe for the oncoming traffic and move the vehicle diagonally into the other lane. As soon as the follow-up driver completes the maneuver, blocking the traffic from the rear, he/she will signal and confirm that the lane is secure and it is safe to change. The principal's vehicle and the lead vehicle initiate the change to the new lane. (see Fig. 33)

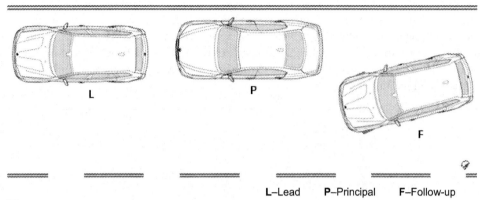

L–Lead   P–Principal   F–Follow-up

Fig. 33

The same applies when making turns at intersections. The follow-up will execute a wide turn to block traffic and to provide a safe turn buffer zone and to prevent another car from ramming into the exposed side of the principal's car. The follow-up vehicle's driver has to be alert and observing all sides of the car. Most importantly, he/she must keep the eyes on the principal's car and be able to react to any sudden move or unexpected changes. The driver must keep an eye on the traffic from both sides and the rear, preventing anybody is overtaking and/or closing in on the principal's vehicle. (see Fig. 34) Once the maneuver is completed, the lead car will be the follow-up and the follow-up the lead till the next intersection.

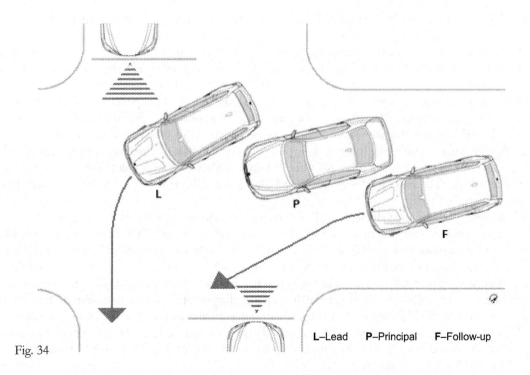

L–Lead   P–Principal   F–Follow-up

Fig. 34

If for some reason another vehicle is coming alongside or too close, the follow-up is blocking any further attempt of getting closer to the principal. The distance between the follow-up and the principal (or the vehicle in the front) is depending on the traffic conditions and circumstances, but should never allow, that another car could squeeze itself between. The follow-up should always drive in a position to allow the driver a clear view ahead, not only to the principal's vehicle (or the car in front), but also the lead vehicle. This allows the driver to react at any given moment and to execute any necessary maneuver to prevent other cars from passing.

Driving the motorcade on a multilane road or in heavy traffic is basically the same initial maneuver as used for a lane change. The follow-up vehicle keeps approximately one half of a car length behind the principal's vehicle and approximately half a car width to the right (or left depending on the position in traffic). In this manner, preventing any other car from getting between the vehicles and coming too close from the side. (see Fig. 35)

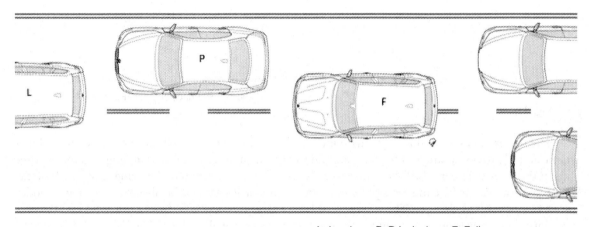

L–Lead   P–Principal   F–Follow-up

Fig. 35

The EPO operating on his/her own does not need to plan or organize any of the motorcade elements, since he/she most likely will drive the principal personally or ride in the principal's vehicle. Whatever the arrangements are, the EPO must take time to plan and advance the route exactly as it would be done for a full motorcade. If circumstances demand, resources and manpower permit, an additional vehicle is the designated follow-up vehicle. In this case the follow-up will have to execute a variety of functions. One of the functions of the follow-up and the lead vehicle is the transportation of the EPO team. Each team member is assigned a specific sector and is seated accordingly, allowing to exit the follow-up rapidly and to fall into position whenever required. For example, EPO-One is responsible for the left rear door, EPO-Two for the right rear door of the principal's vehicle. EPOs-Three and Four are assigned to cover the rear left and right of the principal's car. Additional team members will cover the front left and right of the vehicle. The EPO in charge (senior EPO) and/or EPO team leader is usually seated in the right front passenger seat.

While rapidly leaving the vehicle, the EPOs have to watch their steps and make sure, that they break away from the vehicle clean and position themselves with finger-contact distance to the principal's car. Making a safe and quick exit. Jumping from the car to the pavement, not entangling with the coat or jacket on the car door or sliding on the pavement. These are small things the EPO has to bear in mind when preparing for the exit. Being careless might result in injuries, if not embarrassment. As soon as the principal's car and the follow-up approach the destination, the principal's car stops exactly at the spot designated by the advance EPO, where the principal can step out directly onto the walkway. To make sure, that all EPOs leave the vehicle/s in a disciplined and synchronized manner, the EPO in charge usually will give the command "Get ready!" Receiving the all-clear from each member, the EPO will than command "One and Two go!" Followed by "Three and Four go!" The EPOs will move quickly into their designated positions and secure the area. (see Fig. 36)

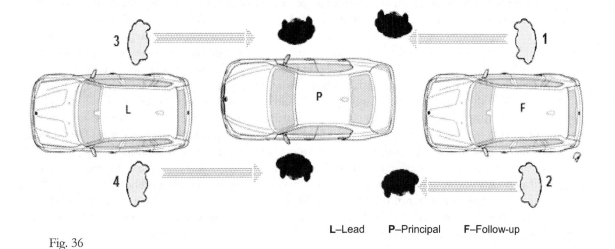

L–Lead   P–Principal   F–Follow-up

Fig. 36

The lead and follow-up vehicle is parked approximately a half meter to the rear and about half a car width to into the traffic lane. The main object is to prevent attempts of others car to park between the two vehicles. If there is another EPO vehicle-it should be parked in the traffic lane beside the principal's car, covering the rear door area.

The vehicles with their engines running are waiting till the principal is safely moved away from the motorcade. Once the principal arrived at his final destination safely, the drivers have to reposition the vehicles for departure. Another function of the follow-up vehicle (as well as of the lead vehicle-if available), is to transport the equipment for the EPOs. Depending on availability and assignment, each of the vehicles (lead and follow-up) should carry the same EPO equipment. Depending on the activities of the principal, most of the assignments might be carried out in rented vehicles. This is the main reason, why the EPO equipment should be mobile; functionally stored within drawers and compartments in lockable aluminum boxes which can be placed for quick and easy access in the trunk any vehicle. (see Fig. 37) The protective equipment in the follow-up should cover everything from emergency, fire and safety, to tactical, convenience and weapons. Another function given to the follow-up vehicle is that of a mobile command post. Each storage box should be marked according to the equipment stored in it.

Fig. 37

The drawers and compartment are fir with separators and contain emergency equipment such as first aid kit, fire extinguisher, shuffle, bolt cutter and crowbar. Further equipment includes gasmasks, towels, blankets, flares, flashlights (extra batteries), mobile and radio charger with car adapter, bad weather gear, spare batteries, battery jumper cables and weapons with ammunition.

The follow-up should contain route maps and specific area maps, radio communication system, jamming equipment and computer with operation specific hardware and software. A voltage converter which can easily be plugged into the cigarette lighter socket is useful for 220V-240V equipment (laptop computer, etc.). Since the follow-up vehicle has many functions, mainly that of a defense vehicle (blocking of the traffic and the protection of the principal's car on turns). Second, it serves as a mobile command post, which makes the selection of the right vehicle as a follow-up so important.

The vehicle designated to be the follow-up car should be an SUV with a powerful engine, capable of high speeds and compatible with the principal's car. Further it should have enough storage space for all equipment and passenger capacity for a small EPO team. A follow-up vehicle of choice must fit the needs and purposes of the EPOs and the protective assignment. Ideally the follow-up should be fast, powerful, all terrain worthy with a large payload capacity and resistant to withstand possible ramming. Some operation specific modifications and adjustments should be considered even with a brand-new vehicle. This ideal condition is unfortunately not the rule and EPOs most likely have to be happy and satisfied with whatever transportation means is available for the assignment. The same selection criteria apply as much as possible in the case of a rental vehicle.

The Driving Techniques

There are three main conditions an EPO designated driver has to rely on-a good mental preparation, lot of experience and a car in excellent mechanical condition. Protective driving, leading, driving in and following-up a motorcade is like formation flying in the Air Force. Departure preparation, route, gasoline consumption, travel speed, distance between vehicles, vehicle formation, arrival procedures and emergency procedures are carefully planned and executed with precision. The vehicles have to be in top condition. The responsibility of the drivers is to know the routes, the turns and the timing. Another EPO, next to the driver (if available) will indicate the exact directions, the marked distance between turns and describe the turns whether as left or right, the stop and halting distance. The entire route will be divided into checkpoints, allowing the driver of the motorcade in progress, to report locations and checkpoints.

Whether driving in a motorcade or just the principal's vehicle, the principal is extremely vulnerable while in the car. The designated driver must concentrate on a smooth drive and be on a constant alert-visually scanning the road to the front, the sides and to the rear via the mirrors. Wide-angle minicameras (with IR capability), mounted on the roof of the vehicle and connected to a small monitor on the dashboard is of great use. The driver can focus entirely on the road (still observing what is going on around the vehicle via the monitor, which is in the same line of view). In this way the driver will be under less stress, especially when driving on highways, where staring at the divider-lines and the monotonous surrounding might cause a hypnotic effect, leading to sleepiness. A second EPO (if available) can take over the task of checking the monitor and provide the driver with precise updates.

The EPO must constantly check and be aware of vehicles which might attempt to cut off and stop the principal's car. A sudden backing out or pulling out of a vehicle from a driveway may be the initiation of a cut-off, ambush, kidnap or assassination attempt. The EPO has to assume instantly, whether the other driver was careless, not paying attention or that an attack is underway and therefore has to take immediate evasive action, by either increase speed or altering immediately the direction.

The EPO designated driver must always anticipate conditions, which could lead to an ambush and therefore he/she must make sure that the vehicle has ample maneuvering space to avoid and/or counter such conditions. But danger is not always coming in form of a suspicious looking car or bike, but in form of debris and other hazardous material littering the road or highway. It is important, that the driver pays attention to sudden changes in the traffic conditions and hazards, such as oil spills, potholes, shredded tire pieces, mufflers, sand, stones or anything else which could cause and accident. The driver (whether principal's car, lead or follow-up) is responsible for the car.

Cleaning and proper equipping is part of the duty. Fire extinguisher, as well as first aid kit should be placed accessible in the passenger compartment, where it can be used by the driver, should an emergency occur. Never store those in the trunk of the vehicle. All the vehicles, whether in case of an emergency or in the event, they are needed in the middle of the night, must be ready and refueled always. This means, whenever the fuel gauge reaches between one half and three quarters of a tank, the vehicle has to be refueled.

Another important factor in protective driving is the selection of the cars-the one to be used for the principal and those used for the EPO team. As mentioned earlier, there are certain criteria, when selecting a vehicle-while payload, speed and SUV characteristics are considered main criteria, application and the capabilities are equally important for an EPO when selecting a vehicle for protective duty. Ideally a security conscious client should consult with the EPO prior to purchasing a vehicle. In situations where a client anticipated decisions or where an EPO accepts an assignment with an existing fleet of vehicles, the EPO should have the possibility of selecting and improving existing cars by his/her professional criteria.

Vehicle Selection and Improvements

When selecting the car for protective duty, the EPO should be aware of a few general aspects. There is the Jeep-type vehicle–very effective off-road and stylish looking, but completely unsuitable for the job. Their tendency to tip over during turns is famous.

Many clients would prefer American cars instead of foreign makes, but when it comes to cars and their protective abilities, one should leave all national preferences behind and take the best. Among those rank the German made cars. There are some notable exceptions, but American and Japanese cars in general are not well known for their handling and performance qualities. Most are made to give a soft and smooth ride and that's all. If it has to be one of these, than the small economy type and the over-sized battleship-type should be avoided. What should be avoided at all costs are exotic European cars, like Ferrari, Lamborghini, Lotus, etc.. From the driver's point of view, they are a true pleasure, but they are like painted prime targets.

Once the vehicle/s has been selected (even newly purchased ones), a few improvements and modifications might be necessary in order to enhance both the performance and reliability of the vehicle. Some of those modifications will also serve as deterrents in the event of an attack:

- Tires
  Only the best tires should be used. Radial tires offer increased durability, allow a superior handling, and have a better gas mileage than other tires. All four tires should be slightly over-inflated and filled with run-flat foam.
- Heavy-duty shock absorbers and springs
  The best tires will be of no use without the proper top quality shocks and springs. Heavy-duty shock absorbers and springs are items, where the price is indicating the quality and those in combination with the tires will improve the car's handling.
- Heavy-duty radiator
  A heavy-duty radiator will help to prevent an overheated engine caused by hard driving, hot weather and rough terrain.
- Stainless steel brake-lines
  Stainless steel brake-lines are used in racing competition and are recommended particularly to those living in rural and mountainous areas. Standard brake-lines may sometimes swell and flex and cause the brakes to fade.
- Heavy-duty battery
  A heavy-duty battery is a must, if additional lights and communication systems are to be installed in the car.

- Headlights

  Replace the standard sealed beam headlights with *Halogen* or *Xenon* headlights. These are providing twice as much light than standard bulbs and with a clear far visibility one can drive much faster at night.

- Flashing warning lights and sirens

  Flashing LED warning lights can either be fit within the front grill of the car or used inside the vehicle on the dashboard or sun visor. The installation and usage of flashing lights might require a special permit, which depends and is regulated by each country's law. The same applies for sirens.

  However, in case of a motorcade, which has been announced to the local police or is escorted by law enforcement elements, a temporary permission for the usage might be granted.

  (Clear white, flashing LEDs in an emergency are warning as well and cannot be mistaken as those of police or other emergency services-most laws do not have provisions for the color white)

- Independent switches

  Additional independent switches are useful and allow an independent control for each light on the vehicle. Adding or eliminating several lights at night is altering the appearance of the vehicle (appearing at a distance like a bike) and is very useful to lose any possible pursuer.

- Tank cap lock

  A gas cap lock prevents anyone from using the gas tank as a receptacle for explosives.

- Tailpipe bolt

  A thick heavy bolt placed through the tailpipe on one or two locations and welded into place will prevent that a bomb can slide into the exhaust system.

- Bumper reinforcement for ramming

  The front and rear bumpers should be reinforced by extra supports from the vehicle frame to the bumper in addition to a welded two-inch metal pipe on the vehicle frame, placed right at the back of the bumper. A necessary reinforcement for ramming situations.

Defensive and Evasive Driving

Defensive or evasive driving is a technique which requires skill and knowledge. This technique is not something one can learn from a video or a book–only a professional school can provide the required knowledge and space to practice to its perfection. Most protective assignments might not even have the level of risk or "opportunity" to use these driving skills in its full perfection-it could proof to be a real lifesaver one day.

Defensive and evasive driving is part of every professional EPO. The EPO must make sure the acquired skills are practiced frequently and improved via professional seminars. Never try to use the principal's car for practice purposes. Never try to show off your skills with the principal around, not even if he/she is demanding it. The following should provide a brief overview on the aspects and variety of maneuvers used as defensive and evasive driving technique.

Turning and Cornering

It is a common mistake to believe, that bends and corners could be handled best, when speeding through them. Three things have to be considered; one, the speed at which a corner is taken; two, the speed, at which the car is leaving a corner and three, whether the car has front-, back-, or 4-wheel traction.

Other details to consider by turns and corners are as follows:

- The Apex Point

    The apex point is that point at which the wheels are closest to the inside edge of the bend. Choosing a relatively late apex point, allows the car to exit a corner at a greater speed than choosing the apex point at an earlier stage.

- The 90-degree Turn

    A 90 degree turn is the most common type of turn in urban areas. This turn is initiated as far to the outside as possible. The maneuver has to be adjusted for the turn if there is heavy traffic. In that case, one has to drive as far to the outside as possible and within the confines of the lane. When approaching the corner, the braking pressure has to increased gradually (avoid a blocking of the brakes), downshift (manual transmissions only) and decrease braking pressure at the first third of the turn. From here gradually increase the speed to full acceleration when coming out of the turn.

The chances of taking full advantage of all lessons and skills are always reduced by the fact, that an EPO, when pursued by another car is most likely driving in an unfamiliar area. Not being familiar with the area and the turns, heavy traffic in all directions and pedestrians strolling around makes a proper cornering technique difficult to execute, if not useless. The EPO has to take full advantage of any opportunity (specialized courses and seminars) and practice those maneuver to perfection.

- 180-degree *"Bootlegger"* Forward Turn

    A famous maneuver, which allows changing the direction 180 degrees without stopping and within the space of a two-lane road. This maneuver works perfectly in cars with automatic transmission and a handbrake. (see Fig. 38)

    At a speed of approximately 25-30 mph, the driver is getting off the gas and turns the steering wheel either to the left or to the right ¼ to ½ of a full turn. Depending on which side of the road one is driving. Simultaneously, the driver applies the emergency brake (cars with manual transmissions will need to depress the clutch as well).

    The moment the vehicle reaches an approximate 90 degrees position, the driver releases the handbrake, steps on the gas and straightens the steering wheel (cars with manual transmission need to let the clutch back out when hitting the gas).

    Note: It is easier to execute the maneuver, if the emergency (hand or foot type) brake catch is rendered inoperative. In order to avoid any damage to the tires, the pressure of all tires should be adjusted to 40 lbs psi.

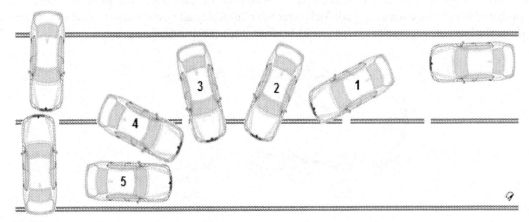

Fig. 38

- 180-degree *"Moonshiner"* Reverse Turn

  Similar to the previous, this turn is a reversed bootlegger turn, which allows the driver to change direction 180 degrees within the space of a two-lane road while going backwards. The perfect maneuver to avoid roadblocks and ambushes. (see Fig. 39)

  The driver reverses at a speed of approximately 20-30 mph, gets off the gas and turns the steering wheel all the way to the left (or right) as fast as possible.

  The moment the car reaches a 90 degrees position, the driver shifts into low gear, hits the gas and straightens the steering wheel.

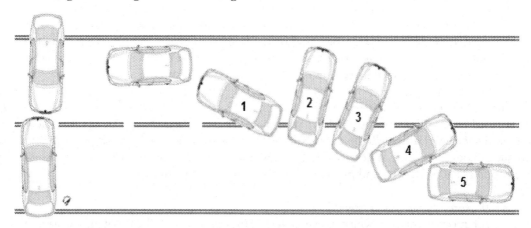

Fig. 39

A stationary roadblock is the most common type of vehicle ambush. This type of attack is executed with one or two vehicles, which are lined up across the road and blocking the victim's path. The attackers usually position themselves with automatic weapons either alongside or behind the blockade-vehicles. Facing such a situation, the EPO might not have time or proper space to initiate an evasive maneuvers, like the bootlegger turn. The only option will be to ram the blockade vehicle/s at their weakest areas and drive through. (see Fig. 40)

The ramming maneuver is relatively safe, as long as the seatbelt is properly fastened and the headrest is in the proper position. Tests have found that the best ramming speed is approximately 25-35 mph. A slower speed will not provide enough power to push through the blocking vehicle and a higher speed may cause the ramming vehicle driver to lose control. The ram must be done squarely with the front or the back of the ramming vehicle. A smash will not be powerful enough to push aside the attacker's car and it could send the ramming car into a spin or totally out of control. The driver and principal must be mentally prepared to ram the car into a roadblock, which is countering all normal instincts. They must be prepared for the impact, because of the physical shock of impact on the other vehicle.

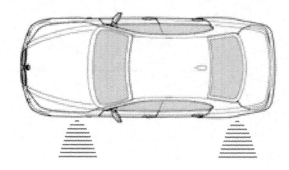

Fig. 40

Ramming however is not a perfect solution and might render the vehicle inoperable after the collision-it must be considered as the last resort. If it is possible at all the EPO in such a situation should always try to drive around, rather than through a roadblock.

Depending on the region and the specifics of the assignment, an EPO might easily face a situation, where an attacker attempts to ram or to crash into the EPO's car. If the road condition and traffic allows, the EPO has to maneuver the vehicle by speeding and braking to get behind the attacker's vehicle. To get the attacker off the road, the EPO has to hit in an angle the vehicle's bumper (right front bumper on left rear bumper), with a speed of 20 mph faster than the attacker's car. This will cause the vehicle to spin and slide sideways. It is important to hit the rear bumper, not push the opponent's vehicle. The enemy's vehicle will slide sideways until the tires regain traction. Using the opportunity, the EPO will slam into the rear wheel section, causing the car to spin off the road. After impact, the EPO has to hit the brakes and counter steer to break contact.

A common method of attack in Central American and Asian countries is to pull the car (in Asia motorcycles) alongside the victim's car and fire away at everybody inside. A proper defense maneuver against this type of attack is to hit the brakes and keep the car steady-the attack vehicle will overshoot its target, allowing time to execute a bootlegger or moonshiner turn (depending on space and traffic). If the attack is executed with a motorcycle, the EPO is simply smashing into it and ends the threat.

Terrorism

- **Definition of Terrorism**
- **Terrorist Motivation**
- **Terrorist Methods**
- **Terrorist Weapons**
- **Profiling the Terrorists**

Definition of Terrorism

Terrorism, as we experience it nowadays, is a form of warfare that relies principally on inflicting fear to its targets-societies, citizens and people and to deliver its deadly and horrifying message. The targets of this controlled violence often go beyond the immediate victims. Its ultimate goal for the terrorists` point of view, a very well orchestrated and theatrical one, the "World Theater" of terrifying and vicious acts. This proves to be more a reality, especially today with all the varieties of television news programs, broadcasting images of the terrorist events with gruesome close-ups and fear inducing background sounds. All that, even before any senior official have had time to assess any extend of the event and outcome of the situation itself. This, together with the advent of cell phones, computer networks and Internet, has led to a "just-in-time decision making"-a new phenomenon in managing and approaching a crisis situation. In most recent years, we have witnessed a never-ending flood of bombings, suicide attacks, assassinations, hostage executions and incidents, where hostages were taken. With every new threat spawning, a new countermeasure has to be developed, and every new counter-measure resulting in a new form of threats. While terrorists are unlikely to give up the concepts of truck bombs or spectacular suicide missions that afford them instant gratification and fame among their ranks. A new cadre of terrorists has been born. This new generation of terrorists may look far beyond, to more nontraditional tactics and weapons and operations. The new terrorist generation of today proved to be computer savvy, with accomplished education, training and possess degrees from a higher education, which is bringing a whole new level of sophistication and flexibility to the battlefield.

Computer technology and the Internet are being used increasingly and more frequently for the planning of terrorist activities, recruiting, fund-raising and operational transmissions. While terrorists can afford the latest technological equipment and seemingly unlimited funds-law enforcement and other officials more often find themselves lagging behind, making it difficult for them to keep up with the terrorists. Further complicating the terrorism warfare formula is the possibility that cyber-attacks against critical infrastructures may be used as a force multiplier to extend the deadliness of an attack. The target of the attack, the critical infrastructures, mainly owned and operated primarily by the private sector, brings a whole new group of players into the terror game. To the contrary of the Cold-War-period, when terrorist groups were mainly motivated by political reasons, the most prominent groups operating today use religious motivation. This makes them particularly dangerous, because the only entity they supposedly need to justify such actions to is God, in whose name they carry out any suitable acts of violence. Politically motivated groups traditionally looked for targets of symbolic value: a soldier, a government official. Religious groups, on the other hand, feel that any form of attacking the infidel is legitimate, even if it means killing innocent civilians. Anyone, anywhere, anytime can become a target. [21]

The *Rand Corporation* has defined terrorism as -the use or threatened use of force designed to bring about political change. The Federal Bureau of Investigation (FBI) has defined terrorism as -the unlawful use of force or violence against persons or property. To intimidate or coerce a government, the civilian population, or any segment of it, in furtherance of political or social objectives.

The three most serious types of conflict short of nuclear war are identified as:

- Conventional warfare
- Guerrilla warfare
- International warfare: Terrorism

In the first two types of conflicts, the noncombatants are usually able to distinguish themselves from combatants. This is not to say that noncombatants are never killed, because they are. It is just that these are isolated or unusual incidents, because in both guerrilla and conventional warfare the major focus of killing is, one armed force against another.

Conflicts can be either highly intense, or of low intensity in nature. There are more than 93 confrontations currently taking place around the globe involving everything from former republics of the Soviet Union and former colonies of European countries to ages-old ethnic hatreds and narcotics trafficking. However, the exploitation of noncombatants (I. e. their suffering and death) is the essence of international terrorism. Because of the covert nature of the activity, terrorist attacks are carried out by a small cohort of operatives who receive financial and logistical support from radical political and activist organizations, which can include governments of rogue nations. Political and other activist groups may be suspected of acting in support of terrorist goals, if not actually fostering and furthering those goals. Questions have been raised, and continue to be concerning the integrity of some persons and groups or whether, in fact, they are being exploited or misused.

The U. S. Department of Defense has described terrorism as a phenomenon in transition and indicated that the nature of the terrorist threat has changed dramatically. The Defense Department attributed these changes to five factors, which is not being shared by everybody and opinions are even considering those factors being understated:

- Collapse of the Soviet Union
- Changing motivations of terrorists
- Proliferation in technologies of mass destruction
- Increased access to information and information technologies
- Accelerated centralization of vital components of the national infrastructure, which has increased vulnerability to terrorist attack

Much of the thrust of terrorism will continue to be directed toward U. S. targets, whether in North America or overseas. The attacks will be concentrated in urban locations, perpetrated by those acting on behalf of religious and ethnic causes and, as in the past, political points of view.

A clear definition however, according to the UNODC (UN Office on Drugs and Crime) is still a question which is clouding the debate among member states for decades. First attempts to reach an internationally acceptable definition was made under the League of Nations, but unfortunately the convention drafted in 1937 never came into existence. The UN Member States still have no definition where to agree on. Terminology consensus would, however, be necessary for a single comprehensive convention on terrorism. The lack of agreement on a definition of terrorism has been a major obstacle to meaningful international countermeasures. Cynics have often commented that one state's "terrorist" is another state's "freedom fighter". If terrorism is defined strictly in terms of attacks on nonmilitary targets, a number of attacks on military installations and soldiers' residences could not be included in the statistics. Terrorism expert A. Schmid suggested in 1992 in a report for the then UN Crime Branch that it might be a good idea to take the existing consensus on what constitutes a "war crime" as a point of departure. If the core of war crimes-deliberate attacks on civilians, hostage taking and the killing of prisoners-is extended to peacetime, we could simply define acts of terrorism as "peacetime equivalents of war crimes".

The proposed definitions of terrorism are according to:

1. League of Nations Convention (1937):
   All criminal acts directed against a State and intended or calculated to create a state of terror in the minds of particular persons or a group of persons or the general public.
2. UN Resolution language (1999):
   1) Strongly condemns all acts, methods and practices of terrorism as criminal and unjustifiable, wherever and by whomsoever committed;
   2) Reiterates that criminal acts intended or calculated to provoke a state of terror in the general public, a group of persons or particular persons for political purposes are in any circumstance unjustifiable. Whatever the considerations of a political, philosophical, ideological, racial, ethnic, religious or other nature that may be invoked to justify them.

3. Short legal definition proposed by A. P. Schmid to United Nations Crime Branch (1992):
   Act of Terrorism = Peacetime Equivalent of War Crime
4. Academic Consensus Definition:
   Terrorism is an anxiety-inspiring method of repeated violent action, employed by (semi-) clandestine individual, group or state actors, for idiosyncratic, criminal or political reasons, whereby-in contrast to assassination-the direct targets of violence are not the main targets. The immediate human victims of violence are generally chosen randomly (targets of opportunity) or selectively (representative or symbolic targets) from a target population, and serve as message generators. Threat-and violence-based communication processes between terrorist (organization) (imperiled) victims, and main targets are used to manipulate the main target (audience). Turning it into a target of terror, a target of demands, or a target of attention, depending on whether intimidation, coercion, or propaganda is primarily sought" (Schmid, 1988). [22]

Another definition of terrorism according to *Patterns of Global Terrorism.* (Department of State, 2001) reads as follows:

No one definition of terrorism has gained universal acceptance. For the purposes of this report, however, we have chosen the definition of terrorism contained in Title 22 of the United States Code, Section 2656f (d). That statute contains the following definitions:

- The term "terrorism" means premeditated, politically motivated violence perpetrated against noncombatant (1) targets by sub-national groups or clandestine agents, usually intended to influence an audience.
- The term "international terrorism" means terrorism involving citizens or the territory of more than one country.
- The term "terrorist group" means any group practicing, or that has significant subgroups that practice, international terrorism.

The U. S. Government has employed this definition of terrorism for statistical and analytical purposes since 1983. Domestic terrorism is probably a more widespread phenomenon than international terrorism. Because international terrorism has a direct impact on U. S. interests, it is the primary focus of this report. However, the report also describes, but does not provide statistics on, significant developments in domestic terrorism.

(1) For purposes of this definition, the term "noncombatant" is interpreted to include, in addition to civilians, military personnel who at the time of the incident are unarmed and/or not on duty. For example, in past reports we have listed as terrorist incidents the murders of the following U. S. military personnel: Col. James Rowe, killed in Manila in April 1989. Capt. William Nordeen, U. S. defense attaché killed in Athens in June 1988. The two servicemen killed in the La Belle disco bombing in West Berlin in April 1986; and the four off-duty U. S. Embassy Marine guards killed in a cafe in El Salvador in June 1985. We also consider as acts of terrorism attacks on military installations or on armed military personnel when a state of military hostilities does not exist at the site, such as bombings against U. S. bases in Europe, the Philippines, or elsewhere.

Terrorist Motivation

In an attempt to explain terrorist motivation and to answer questions such as, who becomes a terrorist and what kind of individuals join terrorist groups and commit public acts of shocking violence, one has to use a political science and sociology approach, as well the discipline of psychology. Although there have been numerous attempts to explain terrorism from a psychiatric or psychological perspective, Wilkinson notes that the psychology and beliefs of terrorists have been inadequately explored.

Most psychological analyzes of terrorists and terrorism, according to psychologist Maxwell Taylor, [23] have attempted to address what motivates terrorists or to describe personal characteristics of terrorists, on the assumption that terrorists can be identified by these attributes. However, although an understanding of the terrorist mindset would be the key to understanding how and why an individual becomes a terrorist, numerous psychologists have been unable to adequately define it. Indeed, there appears to be a general agreement among psychologists who have studied the subject that there is no one terrorist mindset. This view, however, itself needs to be clarified.

The topic of the terrorist mindset was discussed at a Rand conference on terrorism coordinated by Brian M. Jenkins [24] in September 1980. The observations made about terrorist mindsets at that conference considered individuals, groups, and individuals as part of a group. The discussion revealed how little was known about the nature of terrorist mindsets. Their causes and consequences, and their significance for recruitment, ideology, leader-follower relations, organization, decision making about targets and tactics, escalation of violence, and attempts made by disillusioned terrorists to exit from the terrorist group. Although the current study has examined these aspects of the terrorist mindset, it has done so within the framework of a more general tasking requirement. Additional research and analysis would be needed to focus more closely on the concept of the terrorist mindset and to develop it into a more useful method for profiling terrorist groups and leaders on a more systematic and accurate basis. Within this field of psychology the personality dynamics of individual terrorists, including the causes and motivations behind the decision to join a terrorist group and to commit violent acts, have also received attention.

Other small-group dynamics that have been of particular interest to researchers include the terrorists' decision-making patterns, problems of leadership and authority, target selection, and group mindset as a pressure tool on the individual.

Attempts to explain terrorism in purely psychological terms ignore the very real economic, political, and social factors that have always motivated radical activists. And the possibility that biological or physiological variables may play a role in bringing an individual to the point of perpetrating terrorism. Although this study provides some interdisciplinary context to the study of terrorists and terrorism, it is concerned primarily with the socio-psychological approach.

Knutson, [25] Executive Director of the International Society of Political Psychology until her death in 1982, carried out an extensive international research project on the psychology of political terrorism. The basic premise of terrorists whom she evaluated in depth was "that their violent acts stem from feelings of rage and hopelessness engendered by the belief that society permits no other access to information-dissemination and policy-formation processes."

The social psychology of political terrorism has received extensive analysis in studies of terrorism, but the individual psychology of political and religious terrorism has been largely ignored. Relatively little is known about the terrorist as an individual, and the psychology of terrorists remains poorly understood, despite the fact that there have been a number of individual biographical accounts, as well as sweeping sociopolitical or psychiatric generalizations. A lack of data and an apparent ambivalence among many academic researchers about the academic value of terrorism research have contributed to the relatively little systematic social and psychological research on terrorism. This is unfortunate because psychology, concerned as it is with behavior and the factors that influence and control behavior, can provide practical as opposed to conceptual knowledge of terrorists and terrorism.

A principal reason for the lack of psychometric studies of terrorism is that researchers have little, if any direct access to terrorists, even imprisoned ones. Occasionally, a researcher has gained special access to a terrorist group, but usually at the cost of compromising the credibility of her/his research. Even if a researcher obtains permission to interview an incarcerated terrorist, such an interview would be of limited value and reliability for the purpose of making generalizations. Most terrorists, including imprisoned ones, would be loath to reveal their group's operational secrets to their interrogators. Not even to journalists or academic researchers, whom the terrorists are likely to view as representatives of the "system" or perhaps even as intelligence agents in disguise. Even if terrorists agree to be interviewed in such circumstances, they may be less than candid in answering questions.

For example, most imprisoned Red Army Faction members reportedly declined to be interviewed by West German social scientists.

Few researchers or former terrorists write exposés of terrorist groups. Those who do could face retaliation. For example, the LTTE shot to death an anti-LTTE activist, Sabaratnam Sabalingam in Paris on May 1, 1994 to prevent him from publishing an anti-LTTE book. The LTTE also murdered Dr. Rajani Thiranagama, a Tamil, and one of the four Sri Lankan authors of *The Broken Palmyrah*, which sought to examine the "martyr" cult.

Individuals who become terrorists often are unemployed, socially alienated individuals who have dropped out of society. Those with little education, such as youths in Algerian ghettos or the Gaza Strip, may try to join a terrorist group out of boredom. Or a desire to have an action packed adventure in pursuit of a cause they regard as just. Some individuals may be motivated mainly by a desire to use their special skills, such as bomb-making. The more educated youths may be motivated more by genuine political or religious convictions.

The person who becomes a terrorist in Western countries is generally both intellectual and idealistic. Usually, these disenchanted youths both, educated or uneducated, engage in occasional protest and dissidence. Potential terrorist group members often start out as sympathizers of the group.

Recruits often come from support organizations, such as prisoner support groups or student activist groups. From sympathizer, one moves to passive supporter. Often, violent encounters with police or other security forces motivate an already socially alienated individual to join a terrorist group. Although the circumstances vary, the result of this gradual process is that the individual, often with the help of a family member or friend with terrorist contacts, turns to terrorism. Membership in a terrorist group, however, is highly selective. Over a period as long as a year or more, a recruit generally moves in a slow, gradual fashion toward full membership in a terrorist group.

An individual who drops out of society can just as well become a monk or a hermit instead of a terrorist. For an individual to choose to become a terrorist, he or she would have to be motivated to do so. Having the proper motivation, however, is still not enough. The would-be terrorist would need to have the opportunity to join a terrorist group. And like most job seekers, he or she would have to be acceptable to the terrorist group, which is a highly exclusive group. Thus, recruits would not only need to have a personality that would allow them to fit into the group, but ideally a certain skill needed by the group, such as weapons or communications skills.

The psychology of joining a terrorist group differs depending on the typology of the group. Someone joining an anarchistic or a Marxist-Leninist terrorist group would not likely be able to count on any social support, only social opprobrium. On the other hand, someone joining an ethnic separatist group like ETA or the IRA would enjoy considerable social support and even respect within ethnic enclaves.

Psychologist Eric D. Shaw[26] provides a strong case for what he calls "The Personal Pathway Model," by which terrorists enter their new profession. The components of this pathway include early socialization processes, narcissistic injuries, escalatory events, particularly confrontation with police, and personal connections to terrorist group members. The personal pathway model suggests that terrorists came from a selected, at risk population, who suffered from early damage to their self-esteem. Their subsequent political activities may be consistent with the liberal social philosophies of their families, but go beyond their perception of the contradiction in their family's beliefs and lack of social action. Family political philosophies may also serve to sensitize these persons to the economic and political tensions inherent throughout modern society. As a group, they appear to have been unsuccessful in obtaining a desired traditional place in society, which has contributed to their frustration.

The underlying need to belong to a terrorist group is symptomatic of an incomplete or fragmented psychosocial identity. Interestingly, the acts of security forces or police are cited as provoking more violent political activity by these individuals and it is often a personal connection to other terrorists which leads to membership in a violent group (shared external targets?). Increasingly, terrorist organizations in the developing world are recruiting younger members. The only role models for these young people to identify with are often terrorists and guerrillas.

Abu Nidal, for example, was able to recruit alienated, poor, and uneducated youths thrilled to be able to identify themselves with a group led by a well-known but mysterious figure.

During the 1980s and early 1990s, thousands of foreign Muslim volunteers; angry, young, and zealous and from many countries, including the United States-flocked to training camps in Afghanistan, the Pakistan-Afghan border region to learn the art of combat. (14, 000 according to *Jane's Intelligence Review*). They ranged in age from 17 to 35. Some had university education, but most were uneducated, unemployed youths without any prospects.

Deborah M. Galvin[27] notes that a common route of entry into terrorism for female terrorists is through political involvement and belief in a political cause. The Intifada, for example, radicalized many young Palestinians, who later joined terrorist organizations. At least half of the Intifada protesters were young girls. Some women are recruited into terrorist organizations by boyfriends. A significant feature that Galvin feels may characterize the involvement of the female terrorist is the "male or female lover/female accomplice ... scenario." The lover, a member of the terrorist group, recruits the female into the group. One ETA female member, "Begona" told that was how she joined at age 25: "I got involved (in ETA) because a man I knew was a member."

A woman who is recruited into a terrorist organization on the basis of her qualifications and motivation is likely to be treated more professionally by her comrades than one who is perceived as lacking in this regard. Two of the PFLP hijackers of *Sabena Flight 517* from Brussels to Tel Aviv on May 8, 1972, Therese Halsa, 19, and Rima Tannous, 21, had completely different characters. Therese, the daughter of a middle-class Arab family, was a nursing student when she was recruited into Fatah by a fellow student and was well regarded in the organization. Rima, an orphan of average intelligence, became the mistress of a doctor who introduced her to drugs and recruited her into Fatah. She became totally dependent on some Fatah members, who subjected her to physical and psychological abuse.

Various terrorist groups recruit both female and male members from organizations that are lawful. For example, ETA personnel may be members of Egizan (Act Woman), a feminist movement affiliated with ETA's political wing. Or the Henri Batasuna (Popular Unity) party or an amnesty group seeking release for ETA members. While working with the amnesty group, a number of women reportedly tended to become frustrated over mistreatment of prisoners and concluded that the only solution was to strike back, which they did by joining the ETA.

Terrorist Methods

Terrorist attacks begin long before the actually execution. An terrorist attack is planned and prepared weeks, months or even years in advance. A target is selected based on whatever reasons and the preparations begin most likely with the stage of surveillance and intelligence gathering. Terrorists are better informed about their potential target, than most of their counterparts, the law enforcement agencies and as in this case the executive protection officer.

The intelligence gathering is the obtaining of all the data possible regarding the target. During a period of weeks, perhaps months, the terrorists and/or collaborating sympathizers will gather all possible data via site visits individually or within a group on a public tour posing as visitors and/or tourists. During such tours, they will take photos, obtain maps and access blueprints via public sources, such as the internet, or pose as officials and obtain copies from respective services. All their research is very detailed and includes all type of sources, such as news reports, public records and sometimes if possible personal conversations with the appropriate person/s, people like employees, neighbors, security staff and associates. Actually all these pre-attack procedures and planning will allow the terrorist to exactly mimic the activities of the EPO. The terrorist will follow closely the movements of his/her prey, determining the routes, timing, patterns, lifestyle, weak points, habits and strong points. The terrorist will also follow the activities of the deployed security personnel and the security arrangements. Similar to the activities and planning of the EPO, the terrorist will plan, prepare and anticipate every single move for his/her attack.

After the surveillance information, intelligence material is obtained and carefully analyzed, the planning of the attack is put in action. The terrorist ascertains that his/her surveillance and intelligence feed is frequently updated, allowing last minute changes, whether in the itinerary and routines of the target right up to the moment of the attack. As meticulous an EPO should prepare and plan on the security measures, as meticulous is a terrorists in planning the assault. Like the EPO, terrorists leave nothing to chance. Nothing is overlooked, everything is checked and double-checked. Plans, routes, methods, equipment, everything, even alternatives will be considered and included in the final plan. Those preparations are executed with military precision and involve briefings, rehearsals, walking-throughs, weapons acquisition, false identifications, passports, the right clothing, uniforms and if required the training with special equipment.

Furthermore, terrorist cells are conducting risk analysis, which are similar to the preparation and planning of the EPOs. Selecting the potential target, a terrorist will immediately balance the outcome and benefits against the costs and risks of the operation. Most likely an attack will only be executed if the outcome and especially the benefits outweigh or at least balance the risks and the costs. The accomplishment of specific goals, realized as a direct result of the attack is the benefit, the terrorist is seeking. Those goals might be of political or religious nature, publicity, money, an increase of followers and sympathizers and/or the release of prisoners. While the EPO focuses on the risk levels and potentials for an attack from the defense or deterrence point of view, the terrorist concentrates on the risks from an angle of success as an attacker. The risks a terrorist will face are the elimination of the cell/group/organization by death or capture of the members, adverse publicity, loss of support.

The coordination and well-executed terrorist attacks will have a high percentage of success simply because the planner/s of the operation are most likely anticipating every relevant contingency. This includes of course a full risk analysis and/or assessment, operational management, synchronized timing, reliable communication, equipment, leadership and operators, escape routes and methods. The coordinated plan of a terrorist attack anticipates, that something might and will go wrong, especially if the security personnel of the target has accomplished their job properly. The goal of the EPO is to reduce the chances of success by an effective security plan and program, resulting in the crippling, delay or even cancellation of any attack.

Terrorist Weapons

The future may see a time when such a (nuclear) weapon may be constructed in secret and used suddenly and effectively with devastating power by a willful nation or group against an unsuspecting nation or group of much greater size and material power.

US Secretary of War Henry Stimson to Harry Truman

The element of surprise is one of the most effective terrorist weapons. Surprise provides the terrorists the required initial advantage. The attacker is choosing the time, the place and the circumstance of the strike. Terrorists unfortunately are well trained and organized and have most of the time all the contingencies meticulously planned and prepared. Most of their selected targets are in majority undefended or presenting weak security measures. Terrorist attacks are executed with violence, speed and surprise, assuring the suddenness without the chance of a warning and not allowing the target/s or unprepared security personnel time for an effective respond.

The element of fear is another effective terrorist weapon. The sudden appearance of a group of heavy armed, violent terrorists is causing instant fear and can be disastrous to the people at the target zone and the defending personnel. Shooting, explosives, fire and smoke can even affect highly trained combative personnel, rendering those caught up by fear and surprise (at least momentarily) helpless-providing the attackers the intended advantage.

The terrorists' physical arsenal is rather conventional and includes bombs and all makes and models of automatic weapons. Small, medium-, and heavy-sized, semi-, and full-automatic weapons are used in assassinations, for sniping, large scale armed attacks and massacres. All types of grenades, ranging from hand grenades to rocket-propelled grenades are also part of the terrorist weaponry. In recent years car- and truck-bombs revealed to be very powerful weapons, especially in suicide attacks. Explosive bombings, incendiary bombings (e. g. Molotov cocktails), letter and parcel bombs are also favored by the terrorists. Missiles (surface-to-air shoulder-fired) are known to be used a few groups to bring down helicopters, fighter aircrafts and civilian airliners.

Firearms

Terrorists use both "manufactured" and "improvised" weapons. Manufactured, is a designation for those arms made professionally by arms manufacturers. Improvised, describes those weapons which are manufactured by nonprofessional arms manufacturers and/or by illicit workshops.

The manufactured firearms are divided into subcategories:

Small Arms:
Most firearms under the level of medium machine guns, or as a loose rule, belt-fed machine guns. They include pistols (which are now all self-reloading or semi-automatic), revolvers, rifles, submachine guns and light machine guns. Small arms also include so-called assault rifles, which are in fact either submachine gun mechanisms or mechanisms providing the same firing facilities in the body, stock or woodwork of a short rifle or carbine. The handguns (pistols and revolvers) are sometimes known as sidearms.

Medium-size (Infantry) Weapons:
Medium-sized machine guns (many of which are belt-fed), smaller sized mortars, rocket-propelled grenades and smaller caliber wire-guided missiles.

Heavy Infantry Weapons:
Heavy caliber machine guns, heavy caliber mortars, larger caliber wire-guided missiles, shoulder-held antitank missile launchers and some rockets below the category of artillery.

The improvised firearms:

These weapons include any of the above which are made outside professional and legal arms factories. Not all types of the above weapons have been privately manufactured or improvised. But weapons such as the AK-47 Kalashnikov assault rifle or the M-60 heavy machine gun are within the manufacturing capabilities of local arms workshops (e. g. border areas of Turkey-Iraq, north-west border areas of India). Primitive mortars and rocket launchers are also sometimes manufactured by different entities.

Considerable quantities of commercial weapons, including shotguns are diverted into illicit black markets because of the large number of commercial manufacturers. Examples for such diversions are:

AK-47
The AK-47 (Soviet rifle) was accepted as the standard rifle for the Soviet Army in 1949 and retained that status until it was succeeded by the AKM. During the Cold War, the USSR supplied arms to anti-Western insurgent terrorists. The AK-47 became a symbol of left-wing revolution. Between 30-55 million copies and variations of the AK-47 have been produced globally, making it the most widely used rifle in the world.

RPG-7

The RPG-7 (Rocket Propelled Grenade) was issued to forces of the former USSR, the Chinese military and North Korea, and was used in many countries receiving weapons and training from the former Warsaw Pact members. The RPG-7 proved to be a very simple and functional weapon, effective against fixed emplacements and playing an antivehicle/antiarmor role. Its effective range is thought to be approximately 500 meters when used against a fixed target, and about 300 meters when fired at a moving target. The RPG-7 is being used extensively by terrorist organizations in the Middle East and Latin America and is thought to be in the inventory of many insurgent groups. The RPG-7 is available in illegal international arms markets, particularly in Eastern Europe and the Middle East.

FIM 92A

The FIM 92A "Stinger", is an US-made, man-portable infrared guided shoulder-launched Surface-To-Air Missile (SAM). It proved to be highly effective in the hands of Afghan Mujahedeen guerrillas during their insurgency against the Soviet intervention. Its maximum effective range is approximately 5, 500 meters. Its maximum effective altitude is approximately 5, 250 meters. It has been used to target high-speed jets, helicopters and commercial airliners.

SA-7

The SA-7 "Grail", is sold by the thousands after the demise of the former Soviet Union, the SA-7 "Grail" uses an optical sight and tracking device with an infrared seeking mechanism to strike flying targets with great force. Its maximum effective range is approximately 6, 125 meters and maximum effective altitude is approximately 4, 300 meters. It is known to be in the stockpiles of several terrorist and guerrilla groups.

Bombs

Only a few of military bombs (other than those dropped by aircraft) are currently manufactured on the scale and with the diversity found in World War II. An exception to this generalization is the mine, both the antipersonnel and the antitank mine. Mines can be easily adapted and modified without any difficulty and with an average combat-engineer experience. Approximately 320 different types of mines are buried under the soil, killing tens of thousands every year. Most of those bombs assembled by terrorists are improvised. The raw material required for explosives, is stolen from military or commercial blasting supplies or alternatively made from fertilizer and other readily available household ingredients. Such assembled "bombs" are known as Improvised Explosive Devices (IEDs). The IEDs have a main charge, which is attached to a fuse. The fuse is attached to a trigger. In some types of IEDs, these three components are almost integrated into a single component. The trigger is the part which activates the fuse. The fuse ignites the charge and causes the explosion. The explosion consists of a violent pulse of blast and shock waves. The effects of the IEDs are often worsened by the addition of material, such as scrap iron, nails or ball-bearings. The trigger is in most cases not the only component that activates the fuse, therefore to avoid handling and moving an anti-handling device, which triggers the fuse is installed as a backup. The main purpose of the IEDs is to kill or to inflict as much damage as possible. Some IEDs, incendiary types are intended to cause damage or destruction by fire. The type of the charge in some IEDs (some have no casing to contain the components of the IED) can be shaped or directional-rendering a measure of control over the explosion. Antipersonnel mines and other types of mines have been adapted by terrorists to suit their specific purposes.

Explosive charges mainly in use by the terrorists are:

- Semtex (H and A)
  A general-purpose odorless plastic explosive. First made by the Semtín Glassworks (later called VCHZ Synthesia).

It is used in commercial blasting, demolition and in certain military applications. Semtex H contains 50. 2 % of RDX and 49. 8 % of PETN. Semtex A contains 5. 7 % of RDX and 94. 3 % of PETN.

- RDX (Cyclotrimethylenetrinitramine)

  Also known Cyclonite, Hexogen and T4, is an explosive nitrosamine widely used in military and industrial applications. As an explosive it is usually used in mixed form with other explosives and plasticizers or desensitizers. It is stable in storage and is considered one of the most powerful of the military high explosives. It forms the base for a number of common military explosives. Composition A (wax-coated, granular explosive consisting of RDX and plasticizing wax). Composition A5 (mixed with 1.5% stearic acid). Composition B (castable mixtures of RDX and TNT). Composition C (a plastic demolition explosive consisting of RDX, other explosives, and plasticizers). Composition D, HBX (castable mixtures of RDX, TNT, powdered aluminum, and D-2 wax with calcium chloride), H-6, Cyclotol and C4. RDX is also used as a major component of many plastic bonded explosives usually applied in nuclear weapons.

- PETN (Pentaerythritol Tetranitrate)

  Also known as Penthrite, is one of the most powerful high explosives known, with a relative effectiveness factor (R. E. factor) of 1. 66. It is more sensitive to shock or friction than TNT and it is never used alone as a booster. It is primarily used in booster and bursting charges of small caliber ammunition, in upper charges of detonators in some land mines and shells and as the explosive core of detonation cord. PETN was also used by the German army in World War I.[28]

- C-4 (Composition C-4)

  Is a common variety of military plastic explosive. The term composition is used for any stable explosive. Composition A and Composition B are other known variants. C-4 is 1. 34 times as explosive as trinitrotoluene (TNT). The explosive material in C-4 is cyclotrimethylene-trinitramine, commonly called RDX (Research Development Explosive). The additive material is made up of the binder (polyisobutylene) and the plasticizer (di (2-ethylhexyl) sebacate). That is the element that makes the material malleable. It further contains a small amount of SAE10 motor oil and some DMDNB (2, 3-dimethyl-2, 3-dinitrobutane), a chemical identifier.

- TNT (Trinitrotoluene)

  TNT is the most common explosive for military and industrial purposes. It is valued because of its insensitivity to shock and friction, which reduces the risk of unexpected detonations. TNT melts at 80° C (180° F), far below the temperature at which it will spontaneously detonate, allowing it to be poured as well as safely combined with other explosives. TNT neither absorbs nor dissolves in water, which allows it to be used effectively in wet environments.

- Fertilizer (ammonium nitrate)

  As a strong oxidizing agent, ammonium nitrate makes an explosive mixture when combined with a fuel such as a hydrocarbon, usually diesel fuel (oil) or sometimes kerosene. Because ammonium nitrate-fuel oil (ANFO) are readily available in bulk, ANFO mixtures are the most used components for improvised bombs. Urea nitrate is also considered a type of fertilizer-based explosive, although, in this case, the two constituents are nitric acid (one of the ten most produced chemicals in the world) and urea. A common source of urea is the prill used for deicing sidewalks.

Urea can also be derived from concentrated urine. This is a common variation used by terrorists in South America and the Middle East.

- Dynamite (Titadyn 30 AG)
  Also known as Titadine is a type of compressed dynamite used in mining. The explosive comes in the form of colored tubes of a range of diameters, from 50 mm to 120 mm. It is very powerful and fast-burning. This explosive was widely used by the Basque separatist group ETA and the Islamist resistance group Hamas.

The methods/triggers used to detonate an IED are:
- Pressure activated (physical)
- Pressure activated (water or atmospheric)
- Electronic Signal (remote control)
- Electronic Signal (radio frequency)
- Electronic Pulse (detonator box)
- Photo Electric Cell ("when dawn breaks")
- Motion Detector
- Heat Detector
- Radiation Trigger
- Circuit Connection (anti-handling device)
- Time Switch (electronic)
- Time Switch (acid activated)
- Fuse Wire

Examples of IEDs are as follows:

Pipe Bomb
This is the most common type of terrorist bomb and usually consists of low-velocity explosives inside a tightly capped piece of pipe. Pipe bombs are very easily made using gunpowder, iron, steel, aluminum or copper pipes. They are sometimes wrapped with nails to cause even more harm and damage.

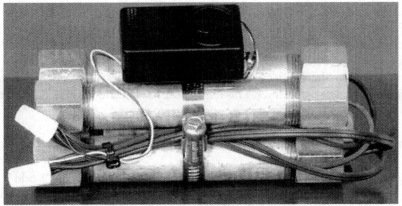
Pipe Bomb

Molotov Cocktail
This improvised weapon-first used by the Russian resistance against German tanks in World War II is used by terrorists world-wide. Molotov cocktails are extremely simple to make and can cause considerable damage. They are usually made from easily obtainable materials like gasoline, diesel fuel, kerosene, ethyl or methyl alcohol and turpentine.

The explosive material is placed in a glass bottle, which breaks on impact. A piece of cotton serves as a fuse, which is ignited before the bottle is thrown at the target.

Fertilizer Truck Bomb

Fertilizer truck bombs consist of ammonium nitrate. Hundreds of kilograms may be required to cause major damage. The Irish Republican Army, Tamil Tigers, some Middle Eastern and homegrown terrorist groups are using the ammonium nitrate bomb.

Barometric Bomb

One of the more advanced weapons in the terrorist's arsenal. It works via a process that involves not one but two explosions; the first uses an explosive known as PETN which releases a lethal cloud of chemicals, ammonium nitrate and aluminum silicate. This cloud is energized with what is described as a "high potential electrostatic field." A few seconds later there follows another blast using an explosive called PDTN that ignites the cloud created with a much greater force than TNT.

Weapons of Mass Destruction (WMD)

In recent years, some analysts have perceived a dangerous trend toward an inflicting of high casualties in terrorist actions. So far, the use of weapons of mass destruction by terrorists has largely been confined to one factor, that the terrorists want a lot of people with fear and watching and not a lot of people dead. This might indicate that the risk that terrorist will use weapons of mass destruction is low. The consequences of using such weapons are far-reaching. Tens of thousands, if not hundreds of thousands of people could be killed in one single strike in several incidents-the need to monitor any shifts in this direction is priority. Until now, terrorist incidents by non-state operators have killed several hundred people in a single attack, with a few exceptions.

In order to kill masses of people, terrorists do not need any sophisticated weapons. In 1994, the Hutus in Rwanda for example used mainly machetes and killed 800, 000 Tutsis and moderate Hutus in less than three months time. Only until World War I, for the first time, weapons of mass destruction were used in form of chemical weapons. World War II became witness of the use of both biological and nuclear weapons. Another still untested WMD is the radiological weapon. Since the Persian Gulf War of 1991, the threat of attack by rogue states such as Iraq using biological or chemical weapons has brought the specter of state-sponsored terrorism to new heights. There is the potential for rogue nations to arm its own operatives with these weapons, as well as to supply terrorist groups elsewhere. The most publicized use of a chemical weapon in a terrorist attack was by a Japanese religious cult, which in the 1990s, unleashed sarin-gas into the Tokyo subway system. Nuclear threats can involve more than surprise attacks. In the low-intensity conflict that for decades has involved India, Pakistan, and Bangladesh, the participant states have developed nuclear capabilities. This might raise the likelihood that nuclear weapons could be involved in a first strike, or in a retaliatory response to terrorism.[21]

Chemical Weapons

Chemical weapons for the first time deployed demonstrated their lethality in World War I, when chlorine-and mustard gas caused 1 million casualties, 90, 000 of those were fatal. In World War II, Zykon-B gas was used against Jews, Gypsies (Roma), political prisoners, prisoners of war and others. The Internet and the access to an enormous amount of information combined with large numbers of physicists, chemists, engineers and biologists has facilitated access to critical information about the production not only of explosives but poisons and lethal chemical weapons.

Precursor chemicals are relatively easy to obtain, conceal and transport. Delivery of chemical as well as biological weapons is greatly facilitated by public access to GPS (Global Positioning System), which can guide a small manned plane or unmanned drones with its deadly freight to the selected target area.

The Japanese cult *Aum Shinrikyo* [21] tried to employ Sarin nerve gas, VX, mustard gas in several attacks on individuals and the general public around Japan. In 1995, the group released Sarin into the Tokyo subway-system, killing 12 and injuring more than 5, 500 people. When the Japanese police raided the Aum properties two days later, they found enough chemicals to kill 4 million people.

Biological Weapons

Unfortunately, till this very day, there is no way to distinguish easily between a bioterrorism attack and an emerging disease causing microbe (pathogen). Virtually every single human pathogen is something that can be used as a bioterrorism weapon. Biological warfare weapons caused the death and injury of hundreds of thousands of people in China during World War II. The potential of a bacteriological weapon could easily surpass that of a thermonuclear weapons:

Plague
A disease transmitted from rodent to human, emerged from India and caused the first plague epidemic in China in 1330. In 1346, Mongol Tatars catapulted plague-infested corpses into the besieged Crimean city of Caffa. Pestilence broke out. The few survivors escaped by boat to Genoa, where rats from the ship spread the plague.
By 1349, one quarter of the European population had died of plague, the *Black Death*.

Smallpox
Caused by the highly contagious variola virus kills some 20 percent of all people contracting it. Although the disease was eradicated worldwide in 1977, laboratory samples still exist and could be reactivated or fall into the hands of the wrong people. The majority of people today are vulnerable to smallpox, since young people were never vaccinated and older people lost their immunity after about 20 years. Advances in genetic biotechnology have increased the possibility of ethnic targeting whereby only one race is affected by a biological weapon.
A panel of the British Medical Association recently concluded that weapons that can distinguish between ethnic groups by exploiting tiny genetic or cellular differences could be a reality within 10 years. Such a development would take away one of the chief obstacles to using biological weapons: the risk of infecting one's own group. Microorganisms tailored to detect differences in the DNA of ethnic groups could offer racists and terrorists of the future a new means of carrying out "ethnic cleansing".

Nuclear Weapons

Since the end of the Cold War, a nuclear black market has emerged in and around the former Soviet Union. Facilities in the new republics where weapons-grade nuclear materials are stored are poorly guarded and there have reportedly been many cases of smuggling of nuclear materials to unknown buyers outside Russia, usually by transnational criminal organizations. Impoverished guards and insiders can steal and try to sell radioactive material and might be able to steal entire warheads.

Russian law enforcement authorities reportedly have investigated and solved approximately 25 cases of theft of fissile materials, but there are constant reports of individuals offering and couriers carrying small vials of material via their usual routes. The potential market for nuclear materials is found not only among what are in some quarters referred to as rogue states, but also among desperate national liberation movements and suppressed ethnic groups.

There are currently approximately 295 armed conflicts of varying intensity going on in the world. These often involve mercenaries, militias, death squads and terrorist groups. In addition to Russia, there are still significant quantities of weapons-grade material in Belarus, Georgia, Latvia, Ukraine, Uzbekistan and Kazakhstan.

Radiological weapons combine conventional high explosives and radioactive materials such as plutonium and can contaminate an area with radioisotopes. While radiological weapons have a long-term contamination potential, their short-term lethality is presumably low. There have been no recorded uses so far. A radiological bomb is not the same as a nuclear fusion or fission bomb, but it can create panic. It would hardly cause mass casualties unless state actors with large quantities of plutonium got involved.

Profiling the Terrorists

The new terrorists are global citizens, resourceful and meticulous, skilled with technology and with the patience to wait years for the opportunity to attack. They are ready to die, without the need to plan an escape route and they are ready to sacrifice teams to force their way through the layers of defense around their targets. They operate in a globalized world in which borders and distance offer little protection to potential victims. This new generation of terrorists have used aircraft as weapons and public transports to kill indiscriminately. They are skilled to make and improvise bombs from obtainable materials used in farming and mining. They have made advances in experimenting with chemical and biological weapons. There capabilities are limited only by imagination and opportunity.

The modern terrorists get around opponents' military superiority by using small teams whose operations are relatively cheap-but detecting, tracking and deterring them is expensive. The small, scattered teams or cells work semi-isolated with their leaders, using modern high-tech communications equipment and systems and public statements to send and receive instructions. Funds are channeled electronically and the use of the internet is to keep in contact, to gather information about their targets and to publicize their threats. Their loose structures allow these teams, in the case a network leader is killed, to survive, operate independently and tap into another part of the network. Most of those modern terrorists are very intelligent, highly educated and skilled at planning, tactics and logistics.

Target and plans, considered impractical in the past, can thanks to the increase of new resources be revisited. If possible new individuals, groups and/or networks, unknown to the intelligence agencies are deployed. Many of those terrorists have lived in a countries they target, allowing them detailed knowledge about customs, culture, security. In many cases local converts to Islam are used to arouse less suspicion. They do not depend on any sponsorship of a friendly nation and do not fear any conventional deterrents. Those constantly evolving networks have the ability to regenerate and to adapt after suffering losses and their resources were put in place years before an attack.

Poverty, lack of education and chronic unemployment were once considered to be the main factors and driving force behind the terrorist recruitment. Over the past few years, however, it become more evident, that these factors may not represent a true picture of the terrorist profile, because most of the terrorists have a good family background, higher education and employment. It also clear now, that the real driving force are the Islamic ideologues, which seek easy targets in those with a desperate need of spiritual guidance. Their only intention shrouded by their own distorted religious beliefs and their misleading teachings is to impose a brutally repressive society upon the world. Their ultimate goal-the establishment of a global caliphate, where terror and fear is the constitution and public flogging, stoning, amputations, decapitations and gang rape is interpreted to be a legal punishment.

For the purpose of anticipating any terrorist activity and how to defend against it, the EPO must be able to recognize and classify the terrorists. The EPO must be able to establish a profile corresponding with the interests the principal might provide as a target. Protective strategies are fundamental in all planned responses it is vital to know the psychology or mind set of those the EPO is assigned to protect against. A principal might be more susceptible to an attack from one group than from another. A principal, based on profession and/or position might not belong to the target group of any political, religious or fundamentalist terrorists. But he/she most likely becomes a target for a criminal attack, such as robbery, extortion or even kidnapping.

The EPO must recognize, prepare and be ready for any attack, whether from the ideologically, politically, or religiously motivated and fanatic terrorists, to the inspired and radical activists or the simply opportunistic criminal. Terrorism has no restriction nor limitations, the victims may be children in schools, airline passengers, travelers on ocean liners, commuters on trains or subways, tourists, businesspeople, political leaders, diplomats, corporate executives, military personnel or humanitarian volunteers. Anyone is potentially a target-everyone can be a victim at any time.

The person/s providing protective services have the duty and responsibility to have a thorough understanding of the factors, characteristics, motivations and interests of individuals or groups, intending to cause embarrassment, to harm, injure, kidnap or assassinate the principal. An effective defense against any type of terrorism begins with research and knowledge regarding the person and/or group/s of people, their operations and activities, which may target a principal, institution or organization. The EPO has to develop intelligence resources, able to provide any information and detailed intelligence, which permits an improvement and enforcement of the safety and resulting well-being of a principal. It is important for the EPO to know how and by which means groups or individuals have carried out previous attacks. All the data is analyzed and becomes part of the risk assessment.

Kidnapping and Bombs

- **Kidnapping**

- **Types of Kidnappers**

- **Kidnap/Extortion Response**

- **Hostage Negotiations**

- **Bombs, IEDs and Boobytraps**

- **Bombers**

- **Bomb Threat**

- **Bomb Delivery**

- **Threat Response/Evacuation**

- **Bomb Search**

- **Crisis Management Team**

Kidnapping

Kidnapping, in a less sophisticated form, but significantly, with all its characteristics and criminal flavors is found throughout history:

- 1356
  The French King John II was captured and kept hostage by the English. In exchange for a ransom and other hostages he was released. When one of the hostages escaped, he willingly returned to captivity in England.
- 1682
  The English verb "*to kidnap*" was first recorded and used with a reference to the practice of taking -"*napping*". Children -"*kids*", where used as slaves or laborers (usually in British colonies).
- 1748
  Two British peers were sent to France as a pledge that the island of Cape Breton would be returned to the French by the English who governed nearby Novia Scotia. (It is said that this was the last traditional use of a hostage exchange).
- 1949
  The Geneva Convention forbids the taking of civilian hostages.

Kidnapping is another favored weapon in the arsenal of terrorists. Kidnapping can be effective as a weapon and very useful as a fund-raising tool. The crime can be used as a multipurpose device in the form of ransom payment, for extortion by trading the release of the victim for some specific goal or action. Or it is simply used for "publicity", to thrust the kidnappers' organization and cause into the headlines and onto television screens. Terrorists groups in Italy, Ireland, Central, South America and Middle East have especially favored kidnapping. Corporations, individuals and even governments are willing to spend millions of dollars to protect against the possibility of kidnapping of personnel.

Second generation terrorist groups also tend to make frequent use of kidnapping. These are groups who may trace their origins to a political cause or an ethnic/national freedom effort, but have since lost their ideological orientation-though not necessarily the rhetoric-and have become merely self-indulgent criminal terrorists. In Colombia, narco-terrorist gangs have been engaging in wholesale kidnapping, seizing large numbers of victims from the same company or group of companies. After certain sums are paid, a few victims are released and more ransom demanded. In Africa, large numbers of U. N. personnel have been captured and held for ransom by rebel forces. Ransom demands include everything from supplies to the removal of U. N. troops from a certain territory. In India, a dissident group kidnapped a nationally popular film actor, in order to force the government to yield to its demands.

Kidnappings are sometimes also the result of attacks, where remaining victims are being held as hostages. In many cases however, the victim of a kidnapping is an individual, which some reason is snatched off a public street or area-most likely within a distance of a few miles of the victims home. The principal, the potential victim and the accompanying EPO/s must be on a constant alert for any unusual potential menacing activity in the immediate surrounding. Regardless of the fact that the EPO is in familiar surrounding, he/she has to be vigilant at all times. An often observed mistake committed by EPO teams is, that they start to relax (because of tiredness and constant readiness) as the motorcade is "feet try" and in the approach of the home area. This is an unacceptable condition and should never happen-because when the guard is down, the attacker, kidnapper most certainly will strike. A kidnapper or criminal group with the intent to commit a kidnapping is attacking the victim by means of a vehicle ambush, which proved in past cases to be extremely successful. The technique is simple; the victim is forced to halt the car either by the blockade or by an attacker's vehicle, which has been placed into a position to cause the victim's car get of the road or to stop. The stop is sudden and swift-the victim caught by surprise, because the first impression is that the action might be caused by another driver resulting in a traffic jam or mishap.

The ambush isolates the victim and he/she is quickly pulled from the vehicle and forced into the kidnapper's car for their escape or the victim is killed on the spot. The victim and the protective detail in situations like this are in disadvantage. One, the attackers use the element of surprise in as much as they control the location, the time, the method and the escape mode-further, killing or kidnapping the victim becomes an option. In addition the attackers are in a mentally aggressive state with a high physical readiness, the weapons at ready and probably would not hesitate to use them. Two, the EPO must acknowledge and react to the attack. Either he/she maneuvers the vehicle out of the situation or responds with a limited firepower (which might put in risk innocent bystanders) -besides, attackers do not have that kind of concerns.

An EPO has to be aware of such elements and shield against them-both, EPO and the potential victim (the principal, family) have to be mentally prepared for any surprise in form of a vehicle ambush. Mental preparedness and physically attentiveness can prevent to become an easy victim. Most people have difficulty to psychologically accept and recognize such situations and/or circumstances. It is hard for them to deal with what is really happening to them-or they simply do not know how to react and what to do under those circumstances (even trained EPOs might experience a certain degree of difficulty). An instantaneous acceptance of the event as it unfolds and with a determination to resist, accompanied by a positive countermeasure is the only acceptable condition. Other potential hazards which can end up in a vehicle attack are mechanical failure, improper and poor driving skills and/or improper timing. It is vital and the exclusive responsibility of the EPO to have the vehicle and any equipment in perfect working condition (a good replacement is better than poor repairs). He/she must be mentally prepared for any confronting activity at all times. Kidnapping, for whatever reason or purpose is increasing worldwide. It is in the best interest of any principal to have an executive protection program planned, programmed and implemented, which emphasizing on the prevention and preparedness for response and aftermath of a kidnapping. There are many things, a potential kidnap victim can do in the absence of an EPO, EPO team and/or an effective executive protection program to deter a possible kidnapping. Standard target hardening procedures and a low profile lifestyle are the key elements, in addition:

- home phone numbers should be unlisted
- keep names off mailboxes and front doors
- avoid any exposure in newspapers and tabloids
- vary daily routines, such as departure and arrival times, travel routes, etc.
- security alarm systems and (hidden CCTV systems) should be installed
- always report threatening phone calls and/or letters
- watch out for any suspicious activity (which could be a type of surveillance)
- compile personal data and profiles on family members and staff (including physical descriptions, photographs, medical histories, etc.) to be used by the authorities in case of an emergency and/or kidnapping (lock the files in a secure safe or vault)
- it is important to determine how family members and staff are reacting in a stressful emergency situation;
- a CMT (crisis management team) should be formed
- written contingency plans should be filed for situations like bomb threats, kidnappings or hostage situations and any other terrorist acts

An EPO can and should develop further contingency plans and obtain the cooperation of family members and associates, rendering the business and living environment as safe and free from adverse action as possible. Living and working in high-threat areas and high-risk theaters demands very close attention to the details of target hardening, threat assessment and preventive measures. Avoiding a payment of kidnap ransom with a life or money, is the best way of make a potential target look unappealing or unreachable to any kidnapper.

Types of Kidnappers

Kidnappers, according to criminal justice experts, criminologists and social scientists are identified and grouped into four categories. Any of the classifications may show patterns which often overlap. The four categories of kidnappers are:

- Criminal
- Professional
- Political
- Domestic (Confrontational or emotionally disturbed persons)

Criminal

Criminal kidnappings-are committed by persons, attempting a one-shot effort to extricate a large sum of money from the family, friends, associates, employer of a wealthy or well-connected individual. Kidnappings falling into this category include the Lindbergh baby in the 1930s. Or the December 1968 case involving Barbara Mackle, daughter of a wealthy Florida real estate developer and the abduction of Reg Murphy, the publisher of the Atlanta Constitution newspaper. The kidnapper is apt to be rational and the only desire is to demand and receive a monetary payment or freedom in exchange for the safe release of the hostage/victim. Kidnappers of this category, no matter how stable or rational they might appear, in most cases do not keep up with their promises.

Professional

Professional kidnappings are carried out by more or less organized groups, which use kidnapping as a source of revenue. The Mafia in Sicily and other parts of Italy, guerrilla groups in Latin America, and the Irish Republican Army have all operated in this way. Often the victims are employed by or are principals of large, usually foreign, corporations who are kidnapped in the hope that the company will pay a huge ransom. One of the distinguishing characteristics of a professional kidnapping is that the victim is almost always returned alive. As professionals, these kidnappers expect to keep doing business and keep their credibility by releasing victims in exchange for ransom. Professional operatives do not always limit their activities to people, abducting and holding for ransom everything.

Among the areas where professional kidnapping is prevalent is the island of Sardinia off the west-coast of Italy. Here the per capita rate of kidnapping is the highest in the world. Criminal groups in Sardinia research the financial resources of potential victims, and ransom demands are scaled according to the family's ability to pay. The amount is high enough to make the enterprise worthwhile, but still low enough that the family has little trouble meeting the demand. If there is an initial resistance to meeting the demand, a finger or ear of the victim may be severed and sent to the family as an inducement to pay the ransom. A curious side effect of the success of the Sardinian kidnappers and the political kidnappings of the Red Brigade in the 1970s and 1980s was, that the Mafia became active in organizing the "kidnapping industry" on mainland Italy. They tried to streamline procedures and codify behavior.

Political

Political kidnappings are designed to create incidents, which put pressure on governments or political parties, and are usually conducted by terrorist gangs, adept at exploiting the accompanying media coverage. The kidnappings can be accomplished with either long-term or short-term gains in mind. In Madras, India, on August 3, 2000, there was a political kidnapping of the popular film star Rajkumar by Tamil kidnappers who were led by a man named Veerappan. In addition to demands for amnesty and $ 12 million, the abductors also included political demands such as referring territorial disputes involving

Tamil Nadu to the International Court of Justice and making Tamil the sole language used in schools in the Indian state of Tamil Nadu.

Long-term kidnapping has been used to a large extent by Islamic fundamentalists in Lebanon. They have at various times kidnapped Americans, British, French, and West German nationals and held them for long periods of time, stockpiling them, so to speak, to be used as bargaining chips at some future time. It has been reported that Libyan leader Muomar Khaddafy would attempt to buy kidnap victims from Lebanese-based terrorists. Most victims of political kidnappings have been released in order to affect specific propaganda ends, although a number have been killed for the same purpose. The effectiveness of this tactic was demonstrated in 1988 when the French government, in order to win release of three French nationals being held in Lebanon, agreed to at least three conditions.

Short-term political kidnappings include such notorious crimes as the abduction and murder of Italian politician Aldo Moro by the Red Brigade. The kidnapping and killing of Hans-Martin Schleyer, head of the West German Federation of Industries by the Baader-Meinhof gang and the kidnapping of U. S. Army Gen. William Dozier in Italy. The Moro kidnapping was a classic terrorist operation. Although Moro was held for 54 days and wrote more than 50 letters during his captivity before being killed, the terrorists failed in their goal of preventing the trial of 49 members of the Red Brigade and their release.

Likewise, the abduction and murder of Hans-Martin Schleyer failed to win terrorists what they said was their stated goal: the releases of jailed members of the Baader-Meinhof gang. The General Dozier kidnapping proceeded even worse, as far as the terrorists were concerned, for he was rescued, somewhat beleaguered but otherwise unharmed, mainly through the cooperation of various Italian police agencies and U. S. armed forces intelligence units. (One of the reasons kidnapping occurred with such frequency in Italy during the 1970s and 1980s was the organizational chaos created by interagency squabbles among various units handling the Red Brigade, as well as other terrorists and kidnappings. It is a negative case in point on the importance of pre-incident interagency liaison). The treatment of General Dozier offers another insight into what terrorist kidnappers will do to a political victim. During his incarceration, the general was kept in a tent that had been pitched inside an apartment, all in an effort to disorient him. He was also forced to wear headphones, through which loud music was blasted at all times, so he would be unable to pick up ambient sounds which might help him identify his location or his captors.

Domestic

Disputes involving spouses sometimes escalate into kidnappings. Statistical data indicate that there are more than 3, 000 cases of parental kidnapping of children when the other spouse has been awarded legal custody. In some instances, the marriage is between persons of significantly different cultures with conflicts and difficulties exacerbating normal marital differences. Often children in such cases are removed from one country to another. In many cases there are no reciprocal agreements and marital disputes are considered so low level in importance as to be lost in diplomatic channels. Abductions of infants from hospital maternity wards are most often carried out by persons, with an emotional disturbance, such as a woman who either never had a child or had a child who died. The motivation in these cases may be understandable, but the action is still illegal.

Kidnapping is a criminal activity and because many of the kidnaps are unreported (estimates indicate that only one in ten is reported) there are only few comprehensive studies from which to get some workable data. Further, kidnapping reports are most of the time collected under reviews of terrorism. Therefore the following figures should only provide an overview on kidnapping in the world:

- 8, 000   - annual kidnappings worldwide
- 3, 000   - annual kidnappings in Mexico only. Until recently, Mexico was considered second in the world for kidnappings. A position which has been taken by Iraq.
- 10   - kidnappings per day in Columbia

- $ 5, 000 -100 million   - the range of ransom demands
- $ 500 million   - annual global "income" of the kidnap industry
- 100 %   - increase in kidnapping around the world over the last six years
- 90 %   - of all kidnap victims are locals and not foreigners. Example: 400 foreigners were kidnapped in Iraq-in the same period 30, 000 Iraqis were also kidnapped
- 21 %   - of hostages in Latin America do survive rescue attempts
- 40 %   - of kidnap victims are released safely after payment of a ransom
- 11 %   - of kidnap victims are released without a ransom being paid, either through negotiation or because the kidnappers realize that no one is going to pay
- 3 %   - of kidnappers caught in Columbia are convicted (compared with the U. S. 95 %)

Kidnap/Extortion Response

Kidnapping, like bombing, is often used to make a statement or to register protest. The victim may be a symbolic one (I. e. associated with a government, corporation, or organization that is somehow associated with the wrong side of the kidnapper's cause). Or the victim may be virtually unknown to the public but still valuable to a government, corporation, or other organization and thus might have high ransom value. It is difficult to determine why kidnapping has not been used to a very great extent by terrorists and radicals operating inside the United States. Most likely, U. S. terrorists have alternative means of achieving publicity aims and raising funds. In addition, the mystique of the FBI's success in tracking down kidnappers may serve as a deterrent. In Europe, Middle East, Latin American, and Pacific Rim countries, kidnapping may be a more popular terrorist tactic because there are fewer publicity opportunities for terrorists to call attention to themselves. As for fund-raising, banks in most countries are much more security conscious than in the United States, where the banks are very consumer oriented and emphasize customer service over security. In addition, outside the United States, relatively fewer opportunities exist to rob armored cars or retail establishments with large amounts of cash.

It is not unreasonable for the family, friends, or associates of a kidnap victim to request verification that the person is actually being held. More often than not, this request will be met. When the first report of kidnapping reaches the business associates, family, and friends of the victim, there is a sense of disbelief, quickly followed by fear and panic. These are part of the tactics, kidnappers employ. They want a quick, emotional response to their demands. The first realization should be, however, that it is quite possible the victim is already dead. Or, if no request is made for verification, the victim may be dispatched as a matter of convenience. It is always wise to request to speak to the victim. Any pretext is acceptable, including the guise that it is assurance that ransom payments will be made to the correct individuals. In addition and to verify that the victim is being held and is still alive, speaking on the telephone helps keep the line of communication open longer, which may prove useful in a subsequent investigation. Even when verification is accomplished with videotape or a Polaroid photograph, where the victim holds up a newspaper to indicate the date, various opportunities present themselves for the gathering of information, as well as evidence for future prosecution.

The decision whether or not to pay ransom is strictly up to the family, business, or to whomever the demand has been made. Neither the local police nor the FBI will advise one way or the other. If the decision to pay is made, however, most law enforcement agencies will do what they can to assist in accumulating the funds and dropping off the ransom payment. If a large sum of money is involved, be mindful that the perpetrators or some independent criminal might rob the people moving or holding the ransom. In the case of Exxon executive Sidney Resso, the oil-company had actually delivered $18. 5 million in cash to his home.

After it had been there almost a day, someone called attention to the lack of security for such a large sum and eventually an FBI tactic team was assigned to protect it. In international kidnapping, terrorist or otherwise, it is the policy of the U. S. government not to pay ransom to anyone. There have been instances, however, when unofficial logistical assistance has been rendered by government agencies.

The EPO has to establish a kidnap/extortion response policy, which is formulating exact guidelines to be followed in the event of a kidnapping of the principal, family members, and so on. The EPO assigned to assist and advise, should be experienced and devise a procedural plan for kidnap and extortion incidents. The guideline should provide a detailed response policy relative to payments of kidnap ransom and extortion fees. The guideline should also emphasis on designating and to name the responsible person/s and authorities in charge for crisis decisions. To avoid any interruption of business, respective provisions have to be in place. Any contingency plans should be frankly discussed with the potential victim (principal and family) and business partners/associates regarding what has to be done in the event of a kidnapping. These contingency plans must be reviewed on a regular basis, updated if necessary and specific code words should be arranged and understood by those, most vulnerable to kidnapping.

Should the kidnappers get in contact and communicate with the family and for the victim to speak, the pre-established code words and duress signals are a useful tool to pass on a hidden message. Any important discussions with the principal (the potential kidnapping victim) and other members of family or associates must be made in advance and have to be defined in detail. One of those decisions is, who has to be notified in the event of a kidnapping. A decision which partly depends on circumstances, the condition of the threat, the actual crisis and the content of the communications from the kidnapper/s.

Terrorists and terrorist groups by habit, use the news and other media to communicate and/or to broadcast proudly their achievements, for example a kidnapping-obviously a guaranteed maximum of publicity. In situations like that the law enforcement and other agencies can be contacted immediately and without risking any further danger to the victims. Criminal groups or individuals, kidnapping for ransom, may demand secrecy and the exclusion of the police under the penalty of death. In such extreme cases, a crisis manager (EPO, director of security or designated person of the family/business associates) must send the pre-established signal to notify the responsible law enforcement agency. Despite warnings received from the kidnappers, the notification (if any) must be as discreet as possible and no other agency or individuals should be involved. In most cases, the victim's home and family will be under surveillance by the kidnappers and the telephone could be monitored. The kidnapper, most likely after his initial communication, will dial the number several times and check if the line is busy (meaning, that the authorities might have been notified-not respecting the warning). Any kidnap situation demands the utmost caution and a clear judgment when notifying the predetermined personnel and/or authorities.

Hostage Negotiations

Hostage negotiations must be conducted by a skilled, experienced and professional hostage negotiator. The key to successful negotiations is communications among the negotiator, hostage taker and the law enforcement authorities. A professional negotiator has to know and understand about the mental state of the hostage-taker. Time is should be on the side of the negotiator, the negotiation process cannot be hurried or stay in a state of panic. Negotiations have to be conducted in a calm and collected manner. Any established kidnap and hostage contingency plan has to identify an expert negotiators, which must be quickly available and respond on a very short notice. The negotiator must be familiar with the background of the victim and the situation as it developed. The negotiators must have the authority (he/she needs to work with the crisis management team and the police) to make decisions and should be able to convey those to the hostage-taker/s.

Individuals likely to become targets of terrorist or kidnap activities include those people of high wealth or status, travelers to politically unstable areas of the world, and particularly, corporate executives and overseas employees. Individuals in the latter two groups are at an even higher risk if they are associated with companies that have a poor corporate image vis-à-vis terrorist groups.

They are at a similar risk, if they trade with the "wrong" countries or the "wrong" side in an internal political dispute. Other persons with above average chances of becoming hostages or kidnap victims are employees of unincorporated American organizations, such as schools, foundations, and the U. S. government, as well as U. S. citizens living abroad for whatever reasons. Just being aware of these risk categories is the first step in an individual's defense plan to avoid being taken captive. Traveling is one of the highest risk activities for individuals who are potential terrorist targets.

During the negotiations, an exact phrasing of statements by a negotiator to a hostage-taker is extremely important and can avoid misunderstanding and misinterpretations. Nonjudgmental words and phrases are preferred. In an effort to eliminate frustration from a hostage situation, the negotiator must eliminate the word "no" from his/her working vocabulary. Rather than saying "no" or using negatives, the negotiator has to replace them with such phrases as "let me see what I can do" or "I will work on it". Even when the request cannot possibly be granted, such as one for weapons for example, never use the word, no. Were the response to a request "no", this could close off the option of problem-solving and force the subject into the aggressive behavior part of the equation. Aggression in these situations can be focused in either of two ways: internalized or externalized. Carried to logical extremes, internalized aggression could result in suicide externalized aggression however to murder. The dynamics are interchangeable; suicide and homicide are two sides of the same coin.

Aggression, like love and hate, is a two-sided coin, and it is difficult to predict which type of behavior a perpetrator will exhibit. Sometimes it is both: if homicide does not satisfy, a suicide may ensue. Persons who could commit homicide could commit suicide and vice versa, as strange as that may sound. Many persons that had committed homicide when incarcerated, hang themselves in their cells. Experienced homicide detectives, when faced with a list of three or four possible suspects of apparently equal culpability, will research whether any of the suspects has a history of suicide attempts. Such as a series of self-destructive incidents such as driving off the side of a road, driving into a wall, and similar one-car accidents. Negotiations are conducted in order to avoid confrontation, which almost invariably leads to violence. The question of confrontation in a hostage situation is a perplexing one for most law enforcement agencies. No one wants to be responsible for precipitating violence, yet police cannot sit back and watches as the bodies of hostages are being thrown out of a building one by one. The determination must be made, however, whether these killings are made during a panic reaction on the part of the perpetrator, on a deadline, or perhaps for some other reason.

Bombs, IEDs and Boobytraps

The bomb has been a favorite weapon of terrorists since the invention of explosives, and currently enjoys particular favor among such groups because of every day and global media coverage of such events every hour. In general, bomb incidents fall into three categories:

- Bomb threat
- Suspicious package or actual explosive device
- Explosion

The most difficult of the three to deal with in terms of planning and developing procedures for a bomb defense plan is the bomb threat. The threat embraces so many variables that there is virtually no guaranteed defense against it. More often than not, the intended target will receive notification that a bomb or explosives have been planted, with the target then informing a law enforcement agency. It is difficult to assess the risk of a bomb threat. Overreacting can be expensive, disruptive, and play right into the hands of those responsible for the threat. Underreacting, however, can be even more costly in terms of time, money, and worst, human life. Dealing with suspicious packages or actual explosive devices in a defense plan and the procedures involved should be much more concrete and specific.

It makes no difference, in fact, whether a suspicious package turns out to be harmless or a live device. Once a package -be it a box, briefcase, backpack, pocketbook, or another other kind of container -is deemed suspicious, it should be treated as though it were an explosive device. Then the trained bomb technicians take over.

Never touch a suspicious package unless you have been fully trained or are a certified bomb technician. The determination of a suspicious package as an explosive device and the removal and disposal of explosive devices are jobs for qualified bomb technicians. Qualified bomb technicians are available from the local law enforcement agency, county, state, or federal agencies, or even the military. Planning and crisis response in the event of an explosion is the same whether the explosion is accidental or bomb related. Only after the determination has been made whether or not an explosion was accidental or intentional do the procedures vary. The use of weapons of mass destruction (WMD), other than explosives such as gases or chemicals, requires different procedures. Explosive devices can come in all shapes, sizes and containers. The frightening thing about a bomb is the fact, that it can be placed in anything, anywhere and go off at any time-injuring, hurting and killing anybody in its proximity. EPOs which could in any way be exposed to a bomb threat either as victims, targets or as bomb searchers at the workplace should be familiar with bombs. This means, the EPO must know how they are build, how they are delivered and how and by which means they explode. Bombs and other explosive devices became a common method of delivering fear and political unrest. To build a bomb is very easy. Bomb construction manuals are available to the public via the Internet. The material used for the bomb can be purchased around the corner. The Oklahoma City bombing and similar incidents revealed the destructive and devastating power of a common fertilizer. Like the old saying goes "Opportunity is making a thief", specialized warehouses, constructions sites, mines and military facilities are more than inviting to be "visited" by criminals, militants and terrorists. Explosive material and missiles are the favored items on the "shopping list" of every international terrorist. A terrorist's bomb making abilities are limited only by the required knowledge about material, explosives, supplies, tools and most importantly-targets. Improvised explosive devices (IEDs) and boobytraps are especially dangerous.

Improvised Explosive Devices (IEDs) and Booby Traps

Improvised Explosive Device:

An IED can be almost anything with any type of material and initiator. It is a "homemade" device that is designed to cause death or injury by using explosives alone or in combination with toxic chemicals, biological toxins, or radiological material. IEDs can be produced in varying sizes, functioning methods, containers, and delivery methods. IEDs can utilize commercial or military explosives, homemade explosives or military ordnance and/or ordnance components. IEDs are unique in nature because they are built by improvisation—only with the materials at hand. Designed to defeat a specific target or type of target, they generally become more difficult to detect and protect against, as they become more sophisticated.

There are three types of categories of IEDs:
- Package Type IED
- Vehicle-Borne IEDs (VBIEDs)
- Suicide Bomb IED

Varying widely in shape and form, IEDs share a common set of components, consisting of:
- Initiation system or fuse
- Explosive fill
- Detonator;
- Power supply for the detonator
- Container

Improvised devices are characterized by the variety of employment techniques. In most of the techniques, the unexploded ordnance (UXO) can easily be engineered to replace an explosive device using one of the several techniques (just to mention a few):

- Coupling
  Coupling is a method of linking one explosive device to another, usually done with a detonating cord. When the first device is detonated, it also detonates the linked explosive. (Military: This technique is often used to defeat countermine equipment, such as mine rollers, etc.)
- Boosting
  Buried explosive devices (or mines, UXOs or others) are stacked on top of one another. The device buried deepest from the surface is fused. Fusing only the deepest ordnance helps mask no- and low-metal explosive hazards placed near the surface. This reduces the probability of detection by metal detectors, and it increases the force of the blast.
- Daisy chaining
  Explosive devices may be used in daisy chains, linked with other explosive hazards (mines, etc.). The explosive devices are linked together with trip wire or detonating cord. When the initial device is detonated, the others explosives devices may detonate. This also creates a large and lethal area.

Booby traps:

Booby traps and IEDs are similar to mines in that they are designed to kill or incapacitate personnel. They are also emplaced to avoid detection and improve effectiveness. Most are victim-activated, but some may involve remote or command detonation concepts.

The use of booby traps is limited only by the imagination of the adversary. Booby traps are victim-activated devices intended to create casualties and terror and may or may not be found in areas of tactical significance.

Booby traps:
- are usually explosive in nature.
- are usually activated when an unsuspecting person disturbs an apparently harmless object
- are designed to kill or incapacitate.
- cause unexpected random casualties and damage.
- create an attitude of uncertainty and suspicion, in effect lowering morale and inducing a degree of caution, restricting or slowing any activity or movement.
- assume that a suspicious object is booby-trapped

It cannot be repeated enough-only well trained and experienced bomb disposal specialists or explosive ordnance disposal personnel should handle any suspicious device, which could be or has the appearance of a bomb. An EPO (unless a qualified bomb disposal/demolition expert) should **never** attempt to defuse or move a bomb.

Bombers

George Metesky

On December 2, 1956-Paramount Movie Theater in Brooklyn, New York. It was a day like all the others-people came their afternoon shopping excursions or work in the offices with the intention to escape for a couple of hours from the worries and stress of the day.

Than at 7: 55 pm, a bomb ripped apart the Paramount Movie Theater and when the smoke and panic cleared, six people were injured; three of which were serious.

Everyone knew whom to blame for the attack-"The Mad Bomber" (F. P., as he signed his mysterious, paranoid letters). He had been planting bombs in New York City for sixteen years. Unfortunately, neither the public nor the police believed he would be stopped before someone was killed. The bomber's competence made tracing his devices nearly impossible. Years of traditional police work had broached few leads. But everyone from city officials to the local media were asking why the police had come up with nothing. Inspector Finney, head of the investigation decided to consult the criminal psychiatrist, Dr. James Brussel [29, 30] and asked him to establish a profile of the "Mad Bomber". Finally, the "Mad Bomber" identified as George Metesky, a Slavic man who lived at Number 17, Fourth Street, in Waterbury, Connecticut could be arrested. During his arrest, he pleasantly and politely confessed to be the bomber. He revealed that F. P. stood for "Fair Play".

Dr. Theodore John Kaczynski

Dr. Theodore John Kaczynski was born May 22, 1942. He is an American anti-leftist anarchist infamous for his campaign of mail bombings that killed three and wounded 23. He sent bombs to several universities and airlines from the late 1970s through early 1990s. He became known as the "Unabomber" (result of an FBI codename). [31]

Forensic sketch of the Unabomber
by Jeanne Boylan

Before his real identity was known, the FBI used the handle "UNABOM" ("**Un**iversity and **A**irline **Bom**ber"), which resulted in variants such as *Unibomber*, and *Unabomber*, when the media started using the name. The Unabomber was the target of the most expensive manhunt in the FBI's history. Agents arrested Kaczynski on April 3, 1996, at his remote cabin outside Lincoln, Montana.

Timothy James McVeigh

Born April 23, 1968 in Pendleton, New York, Timothy James McVeigh, commonly referred to as the "Oklahoma City Bomber", was convicted of eleven federal offenses. He was ultimately executed as a result of his role in the Alfred P. Murrah Federal Building bombing on April 19, 1995, in Oklahoma City. The bombing, which claimed 168 lives, was the deadliest act of terrorism in the U. S. history until the 9/11 attack on the World Trade Center in New York, and remains the deadliest incident of domestic terrorism in United States history. According to the Oklahoma City Memorial Institute for the Prevention of Terrorism (MIPT), more than 300 buildings were damaged.

A variety of reasons and motivations might cause a person to construct and to plant improvised explosive devices and to become a bomber-but each of those bombers is found in one of the four groups:

- Amateur
- Professional
- Psychopathic
- Suicidal

The Amateur

The Amateur bomb-makers can best be described as experimenters. For the most part, the devices amateurs construct, are crude and unsophisticated. They are usually delivered against targets of inconsequential value or targets of opportunity, meaning those with low levels of security awareness. Amateurs also begin in their youth to experiment with fireworks and explosive devices fashioned with material found in school chemistry labs, the laundry room, and the garden shed. Amateur devices may have sophisticated firing mechanisms, but usually employ only a small amount of main charge explosives, which is usually a propellant explosive, such as smokeless powder, black powder, or common fireworks powder. What these substances have in common is that they are relative easy to obtain. In many instances, the amateur bomber may be a copycat bomber, such as a teenager looking for excitement or an attention-seeking individual.

The Professional

The Professional bomber, whether a terrorist, a mercenary who builds or bombs or does both for profit, or an operative in an organized crime syndicate, is distinguished from an amateur by the higher quality of his or her operational techniques. The devices are more sophisticated and reconnaissance, including the use of strict timetables, is an integral part of the operation. The placement of the device is done to assure inflicting maximum damage on the intended target. With time and study, the professional bomber can attack almost any target, using devices that are sufficiently sophisticated to exact a considerable toll.

The Psychopathic

The Psychopathic bomber act without reason. There is little or no predictability to his or her actions. Equally unpredictable is the construction of the explosive device or the rationale behind target selection. The types of devices constructed by these individuals may range from extremely crude to very sophisticated. The sobriquet "mad bomber" has been applied to several different individuals, including Theodore Kaczynski. As a bomb maker, Kaczynski ranked among the best. Many of the components were handmade, including some of the fasteners and the wood boxes in which the devices were placed. Among the subjects that Kaczynski railed against was technology, yet his devices were products of sophisticated technology and handiwork. He was highly educated, yet a reclusive loner. Dr. John M. Oldham, chief medical examiner of the New York State Office of Mental Health, speculated that Kaczynski's behavior might be a mix of two personality styles run amok. He theorized that the Unabomber displayed a loner personality that became schizoid, while his vigilant side drove him to paranoia.

The Suicidal

The Suicidal bombers have emerged as a major attack weapon in recent years, particularly among Islamic terrorist groups. Little in the way of scientific study has been done on the training and motivation of suicide bombers, though speculation leads to parallels with the kamikaze bombers employed by Japan during World War II. However, similarities between both profiles might be found, motivations are differing. Even though the Kamikaze has been branded in history books as being suicidal the deep-rooted motivation of the Japanese mentality and loyalty to ones superior is far from being a suicidal character or pattern. As on the other hand, suicide bombers as we know them from recent events are highly motivated by their religious backgrounds, which are willingly distorted by brainwashing and suggestive methods used by their leaders and commanders. Most of the well-publicized suicide bomb attacks have been attributed to the Hamas organization, carried out against Israeli and Western targets. The attacks are carried out by a shahid, or martyr apparently carrying out a religious mission after having been assured, that eternal life in paradise and the chance to see Allah's face await them on completion of the mission. The profile that has emerged of suicide bombers is one of a male between the ages of 18 and 27, high school educated, from a poor family, and a student of fundamentalist Islamic beliefs. Suicide attacks are usually vehicle-borne improvised explosive devices [IED] packed in or on trucks, vans, cars, and even bicycles. The largest IED to date was delivered by an Islamic suicide bomber against the U. S. Marine Corps barracks in Beirut, Lebanon. It is estimated that the exploded device was the equivalent of about 15, 000 pounds of high explosives, which is equivalent to a payload of 7 BSU-50/B and 2 MK-82 general purpose bombs. In a more recent suicide bombing, that of the naval destroyer U.S.S. Cole in Aden Harbor in Yemen, in October 2000, the bombers employed a Zodiac motorized raft carrying a charge that was estimated at approximately 400 pounds of high explosives.

Bomb Threat

Although threats may be communicated in a number of ways, the most commonly employed medium by far is the telephone. The telephone affords the caller a great deal of anonymity, with public pay phones used to thwart caller identification systems. Even though the bomb threat is a tactic often employed by terrorists and radicals, the fact is that bomb threats are more often perpetrated by nonterrorists. These would be the threats received from individuals wanting to disrupt activities at the target or seeking the thrill of precipitating an emergency response to the threat.

The number of terrorist bombings in the United States has decreased in recent years, but the threat of bombings is still a major concern of law enforcement agencies as well as facilities managers in both the private and public sectors. Work locations, schools, theater, arenas, and stadiums, and centers of public transportation such as airports, train depots, and bus stations are favorite targets of bomb threats, because of the considerable disruption and media attention they can create. Even in instances where no explosives have actually been placed, the threat alone became an instrument of harassment and disruption. A single telephone call can result in the evacuation of thousands of people from a named target location. In 1985, the Toronto, Canada, subway system was severely disrupted when a bomb threat was received. It was purported that an Armenian terrorist organization had placed a bomb in the system to protest the Canadian government's refusal to release several Armenians being held in connection with an earlier hostage situation at the Turkish Consulate. The threat, although real and believable, produced no explosive device.

Several years later, however, a radical terrorist group in Japan released sarin-gas in the Tokyo subway system, in this case, not bothering to issue a forewarning. Statistically speaking, any given bomb threat is probably the work of a prankster, an emotionally disturbed person, someone looking for thrills or sexual fulfillment, or someone seeking revenge for some or imagined grievance. However, and this is an important consideration, any given bomb threat may also be the real thing. The caller may, in fact, have actual knowledge that an explosive device or some other WMD has been placed, or will be placed, at the announced location, and for whatever reason wants to share that information. No threats should be taken lightly. Threats should, however, be evaluated in the context in which they are made so that appropriate responses can be implemented.

It is essential that the person or operator receiving a bomb threat, remain calm and obtain as much information as possible from the caller. A standard *Bomb Threat Report Form* (see Appendix: Useful Forms) for determining the details of the threat should be readily available to telephone operators, receptionists and others in a position where they can receive the threat. They must be familiar with the contents of the form and be prepared to register all information as stated by the caller. The receiver of the calls should start a new form each time the person calls. The receiver who is talking to the caller should be cautious not to volunteer any information about the offices or personnel. Immediately on hearing the caller's threat and/or demand, the person handling the incoming threat should signal an available person to call the building security office, the police, fire department, any other indicated authority. Or just follow the predetermined course of action as prescribed by the company emergency plan.

Bomb Delivery

IEDs can be delivered depending on the shape and size by many means at any time and placed either hidden or visible in any designated target area. The most common tactic is that one or more perpetrators gain or have access to the target area or target object by posing as service or maintenance personnel, vendors, clients, visitors and place and activate the bomb. In other occasions, the delivery and/or placing of the bomb is done by perpetrators, which have access to the target as legally employed personnel (for instance airport personnel). Bombs might also be delivered and placed by accomplices or by the bomber personally to make sure the IED is placed in the exact position and to prevent a premature explosion. Airports and other transport terminals seem to be perfect "playgrounds" for bombers; bombs, hidden in a piece of luggage can be left unattended or even checked-in by someone else. If this is observed, the public is asked to report it without hesitation and the police or respective authorities will confiscate it. The public is also asked not to accept or carry any luggage or any packages from strangers or anyone not flying on the same flight.

Receptionists and other personnel coming into contact with visitors (Office buildings, hotels, etc.), should be cautioned to remind those individuals who appear to forget a briefcase or similar package. If a visitor ignores persists in leaving the object behind, this should be considered a possible bomb and treated accordingly. Sometimes bombs are delivered in the mail, package delivery or by a courier services. Any suspicious package or letter should be treated as a potential bomb. Package and letter bombs (see Fig. 41) can be easily delivered and accepted without causing immediate suspicion during a period when packages are expected, such as Christmas or birthdays.

During the period December 1996 to January 1997, sixteen letter bombs disguised as holiday greeting cards were delivered through the mail to recipients in the United States and the United Kingdom.

Thirteen of the letter bombs were received at the offices of the Al Hayat newspaper in New York City, Washington, D.C., and London, United Kingdom. One bomb exploded in London, seriously injuring two innocent people.

Three other letter bombs were discovered in the United States at the federal penitentiary in Leavenworth, Kansas. All the letter bombs bore a December 21, 1996 Alexandria, Egypt postmark and contained no return address. These bombs were in plain white envelopes, with computer-generated addresses.

Letter and Package Bombs

Recognition:
- Excessive Postage
- Incorrect Titles
- Titles but no Names
- Misspellings of Common Words
- Oily Stains or Discolorations
- No Return Address
- Excessive Weight

- Rigid Envelope
- Lop-sided or Uneven Envelope
- Protruding Wires or Tinfoil
- Visual Distractions
- Foreign Mail, Airmail and Special Delivery
- Restrictive Markings such as Confidential, Personal, etc.
- Handwritten or Poorly Typed Addresses
- Excessive Securing Material such as Masking Tape, String, etc.

Precautions:
- Never accept mail, especially packages, at your home in a foreign country.
- Make sure family members and clerical staff know to refuse all unexpected mail at home or office.
- Remember: It May Be A Bomb. Treat it as suspect.

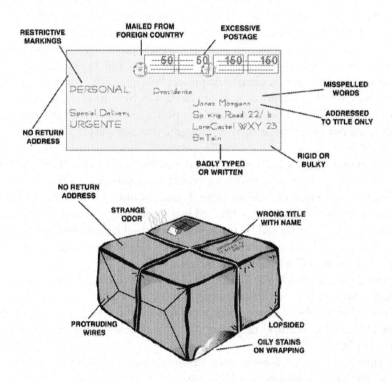

Fig. 41

If a return address is not familiar or if a package or letter appears unusual in any way, it should be suspect. With regard to letter bombs, they are often identified as being slightly thicker and/or heavier than the usual brochure or advertising packet. A spring release or a mercury switch usually detonates them when the envelope is opened or its contents are removed. Therefore, incoming mail to offices and to executive's homes can be considered potentially dangerous. Anything of a suspicious origin or appearance should not be dumped in water, tossed or handed around, or opened until it has been X-rayed or fluoroscoped and declared benign by well trained personnel. Anyone receiving similar letters should exercise extreme caution and should not handle the envelopes in any way. These envelopes should only be opened by qualified explosives technicians.

There is no perfect set of measures to prevent any bombing or other acts of terrorism. Every EPO must use their expertise and own untainted judgment to implement and execute the proper measures. As a reaction to the 9/11 attack and in an attempt to make the air transportation sector safer, all the airports and airlines were submitted to a long needed, but very costly restructuring, upgrading and improvement process. Did it improve the transportation sector's security? No. Well, at least traveling should be much safer now, thanks to implementations of high-level, complex recommendations and the installation of all the expensive high-tech equipment. No, it is not. Even though, there was no further terrorist activity in this sector, does not mean that it is secure or safe. The security sector and especially, those responsible for security should have learned from the past and study the present very carefully. The old generation of terrorists, such as the IRA, Baader-Meinhof Gang, Red Brigade, were planning and operating in a single-layer environment. This new breed of terrorists is planning and operating in a multilayer environment-whatever defense and protection measure is installed, it is just a new and ridiculous challenge for the advanced terrorist. In order to defeat the enemy, one has to think and operate like the enemy. [32] Perhaps than, incidents like Pan American Flight 103 over Lockerbie, Scotland in 1988 and 9/11 on the World Trade Center, New York in 2001 and others would have been prevented.

Threat Response/Evacuation

Locks, security barriers and well trained security personnel are the first line of defense to deter any possible bomb attack. However, if an unexploded bomb is discovered, the best protection is to gain distance from the bomb area as quickly as possible. Every corporate facility, small or large, must have a bomb evacuation plan and procedures in place. Evacuation procedures are similar to any other emergency. Bomb threats can come from virtually any quarter. All bomb-threats (even anonymous threats) must be treated as the real thing until determined otherwise.

There are certain parameters or risk profiles that can assist in assessing the likelihood of a bomb threat being serious or frivolous. Much of the work in determining a credibility index, however, must be completed prior to the threat being received. This reinforces the need for any pre-incident planning. In developing a risk profile of a potential target, there are several points to be considered:

- How tight is security at the target, particularly with respect to a potential bomb attack?
- What is the target's previous experience with bomb threats or bomb attacks or both?
- What is the current climate of terrorist or radical activity?
- Has there been an incident that could inspire copycat activity?
- Does the warning call fit any of the known methods of terrorist activity currently or in the recent past?
- Is this intelligence up-to-date and reliable?
- Is the target involved in labor contract negotiations, or has it been involved in labor/management confrontations in the past?
- To whom was the threatening call made and what was the exact wording of the message?
- Did the caller indicate knowledge of the threatened area?
- Evaluate distinctive traits in the caller's voice or speech mannerism:
- Was the speech slurred; did it contain accents, stutters, or other speech impediments?
- Was the caller rambling or excessive to the point of indicating alcohol or drug influences?
- Was there identifiable background noise such as street sounds, laughter, or music?
- Has any employee of the target recently been discharged or disciplined to the extent that it might precipitate a bomb threat?
- Could the target have caused the alienation of a consumer, member of the public, a special interest group, or a radical organization?

Consider how specific the wording of the threat is. The more specific the details, without being excessive, the greater the need to take the caller seriously. If a person is malicious enough to place an explosive device, or even threaten placement of such a device, there is no guarantee that they will tell the truth about the time or place a bomb will explode. Yet the caller may be telling the truth.

Both possibilities must be considered. Bomb threats, even obvious hoaxes, cannot be totally ignored. If nothing else, a violation of law has been committed by the mere fact of a threat being made. In addition, if there is a series of calls or a pattern of harassment, serious criminal charges may be lodged when the callers are apprehended. In all cases, in addition to reporting the threat to the appropriate law enforcement agency, a search of the affected area should be conducted. (see "Bomb Searches)

Evacuation Options

When a bomb incident results in evacuation of a building or other specific area, tight control must be exercised during the procedures. While a fire evacuation (drill or actual) calls for a speedy evacuation, a bomb evacuation must be more controlled to reduce risk of injury in the event of a premature detonation.

There are three options in handling a bomb threat:

1. Evacuation
2. Partial evacuation of the affected area
3. No evacuation

Which option is employed will depend upon the tactical demands of the situation, including the size of the suspected device. A letter bomb, for example, may require the evacuation of only the immediate area and not the entire building. In other cases, a suspected device may be placed in a location that does not allow a complete evacuation to proceed safely. Perhaps the warning call indicated only a certain area of the building has been targeted. In some situations, a full evacuation may not be possible. For example in a high-rise building where people may have to be evacuated upward from the area rather than descending a stairway past the floor where the suspected device is located. The size of the device dictates the distance required for the safety. Construction, age of the building, and building materials must also be considered.

A bomb threat evacuation is entirely different from a fire evacuation. Primary evacuation routes must be searched prior to ordering an evacuation, and evacuees must be removed a distance sufficient to assure they will not be injured by blast effects or fragmentation in the event of detonation. Some of the most powerful bombs, "weapon of choice and delivery" used in terrorist attacks have been delivered in vehicles parked outside the target, thus damaging not only the intended building or facility, but also much of the immediate vicinity. The use of fire alarms is not recommended to give notice to evacuate for a bomb threat, since fire alarms elicit an automatic response and do not allow for a controlled evacuation.

Additionally, when dealing with explosive devices, doors and windows should be left open in order to ventilate the area. An explosion follows the path of least resistance and open doors and windows will allow the explosive force to vent and, thus, somewhat reduce the amount of damage from the blast. In fire drills, doors and windows are usually closed to reduce drafts and the amount of oxygen available to feed the fire. Another reason for not using the fire alarm is that occupants of the building may assume there is an unannounced fire drill and, without the presence of smoke or fire, linger about or ignore the alarm altogether.

Evacuation Procedures

Anticipated or designated evacuation routes must be searched prior to giving an evacuation order. In many buildings and locations, there are many possible evacuation routes, making it time consuming to search each one individually, even with sufficient personnel. To reduce pre-evacuation search time, specific bomb evacuation routes should be predetermined and searched immediately on receiving a bomb threat, even before the decision has been whether or not to evacuate.

Then, should the evacuation order be given, the escape routes will be clear for safe passage. To reinforce the importance of searching the evacuation route -bear in mind that a number of terrorist organizations that were operating in the United States in the last third of the 20th century used fire stairwells as locations for their planted explosive devices. Fire stairs were used because of their accessibility and lack of traffic during normal business hours. Damage control in a bomb incident differs from that used during a fire. As mentioned above, during a fire, the usual procedure is to shut windows and doors to reduce oxygen that could feed the fire. With bombs, it is desirable to ventilate the explosion. Also with bombs, lights, electrical devices, and office equipment should be turned off. If there is time, gas and fuel lines should be shut down. Even when an evacuation has been initiated, it may be necessary to keep a minimum workforce at a location in order to continue essential services. Contingency plans of high-risk companies and agencies should be reviewed and updated on a regular basis so that minimum operating requirements can be met with a maximum of automation. In some instances, remote or off-site backup systems may be employed on a short-term basis to maintain essential operations. To facilitate safe and orderly evacuations, an Evacuation Officer should be appointed. The primary function of an evacuation officer is to assure that all people are removed from the affected area as quickly as possible. It is preferable to have supervisory or management personnel as officers, because they command respect and possess enough authority to have their instructions carried out without argument. In additional, such personnel are more likely to have a better knowledge of whom is assigned where, assuring that all employees are accounted for. The number of evacuation wardens needed depends upon the size and layout of the areas that could be affected and the number of people occupying these spaces at any one time. In cases in which many officers are required, an evacuation team coordinator should be designated. All those actually carrying out evacuation duties must be under the coordinator's direction. The coordinator need not be a member of the risk assessment team, because the evacuation is primarily a mechanical function.

Bomb Search

In the previous chapters we discussed bomb threats and other types of bomb incidents, building evacuations, and bombers and their motivations. Let's have a look at the mechanics of conducting searches for bombs. Regardless of the advances terrorists make in constructing explosive devices, the methods of conducting a search remain fairly constant. There are four types of searches that a security professional or law enforcement officer typically conducts:

- The building search, where the premises may or may not be occupied at the time the search is conducted
- The search of a suspicious vehicle
- The VIP or pre-incident security bomb sweep of locations or vehicles or both
- The use of explosive-detection canines

Unless extenuating circumstances exist, two general rules should always be followed when conducting a bomb search:

- All searches should begin from the outside and gradually work inward to the interior.
- Once inside, start with the lowest level and work upward, unless the search is in the basement of a building, where the converse is true, begin at the entry level and search downward from there.

The operative's philosophy here is to never let an explosive device get between the searchers and a point of egress.

Searching in Buildings

Traditionally, building searches usually were conducted as a result of a bomb threat notification being received, but currently, many searches are done as part of routine security procedures, particularly where sensitive personnel or locations are involved. Targeted buildings for the most part are multistoried structures or large, sprawling buildings, including schools, transportation facilities, government facilities, commercial office buildings and in some cases, private residences. When private industrial or corporate buildings become the subjects of an anonymous bomb threat, a search will often be conducted by the company's security personnel or a volunteer employee search team, assisted by a security officer or law enforcement personnel.

Searching the Exterior

The number of teams or individuals required to properly search the exterior portion of any location will depend on the size of the building, the area of the grounds, and the degree of experience of the searchers. A general rule for exterior search team assignments is that about 25% of the total personnel involved on each team should be assigned the task of conducting the exterior search.

The initial search should be concentrated on the area closest to the building and extending out from the building line for a distance of about 20 to 25 feet, depending upon the physical layout. Special attention should be given to shrubbery, window ledges, loading docks, waste containers, entranceways, and any indication of loose ducts, ventilation grills, freshly dug dirt, or anything else out of the ordinary. Search time can be reduced and safety enhanced by a regular program of maintenance. That includes keeping the area free of unnecessary obstructions and shrubbery well-trimmed, removing accumulated trash, and generally reducing the chances of providing a hiding place for an explosive device.

Searching the Interior

The interior of a building should be divided into two distinct segments for searching:

- *Public access areas*:   Areas to which the public or other outsiders have general access
- *Restricted access areas*: Areas within the building, which have a restricted access or to which access is limited in any way

Public Access Areas

Those areas are most vulnerable to the covert placement of an improvised explosive device and, therefore, should be searched by the most experienced and best-trained members of the search team. Public access areas include lobbies, rest rooms, unlocked maintenance and utility closets, hallways, fire or other stairwells, and reception and storage areas. Areas where outside delivery or other vendors have access should also be considered public access areas for search purposes.

Restricted Access Areas

These are places where the public does not have regular access which are usually under employee observation, supervision, or control. Even though these areas are supervised, they may still be vulnerable to bomb attacks by determined terrorists willing to attempt penetration. They might pose as repair technicians, messengers and the like. The U. S. Navy was reminded of this when the *U.S.S. Cole* entered the port of Aden in Yemen. An explosives-laden skiff, apparently part of the harbor fleet helping to moor the ship on a refueling call, was able to approach the vessel to inflict considerable damage.

The members of the search team assigned to restricted areas should be those most familiar with these areas because they would be aware of an item or object out of place or out of the ordinary. It is here, then, that non-security personnel will be more helpful in staffing search teams. A word of caution; when employees or volunteers are used in conducting a search for IED s, it should be an "eyes only" search. Searchers must refrain from probing or physically disturbing any areas or objects of a suspicious nature or which otherwise cause concern. Training must stress that the search team members are concerned only with locating the obviously out-of-place item or package that is deemed suspicious.

A suspicious package should **not** be touched or moved under any circumstances. **Only** a trained bomb technician should conduct further examination.

Bomb Search Procedures

Remind all personnel not to touch a suspected item that could be the bomb.

A. All persons make a preliminary search around their immediate area for suspicious items.
B. All persons, as they leave, will remove those items that they brought in (I. e. briefcases, thermos bottles, lunch bags, etc.), turn off radios and unplug office machines.
C. Windows and doors will be left open to help dissipate any explosive force.
D. All cabinets and drawers will be left unlocked (classified cabinets may be an exception) to make it easier for the searchers.
E. When evacuation of a building is accomplished, only authorized personnel are permitted entry until the threat is resolved.
F. Personnel evacuated from a building will be removed to a distance of at least 100 meters.
G. All personnel will be accounted for, usually by section heads and reported to the senior person and a contact point established in case an item cannot be verified as belonging in the area.
H. Personnel conducting search must be familiar with bomb search technique and should be familiar with the area to be searched, I. e. what should be there as opposed to what is obviously out of place or does not belong.
I. Areas will be marked immediately after search so as not to cause another search by other personnel.
J. If an item is found, and suspected of being a bomb, handle as above and continue to search the facility until the entire facility has been searched.
K. All areas will be searched inside and search will include the outside perimeter of building, consider vehicles, etc., parked in close proximity.

DO NOT:

A. DO NOT key radios and transmit.
B. DO NOT handle bomb or suspect package once determined to be a possible bomb.
C. DO NOT permit personnel access to near proximity of the bomb except for official business in connection with the handling of the incident.
D. DO NOT try to move the bomb or enclose it to minimize effects of explosion.
E. DO NOT open container. Open windows and doors, etc., to minimize effects of explosion and release force of explosion.

Crisis Management Team

The crisis management is a process by which an organization reacts to when facing any consequential event that could have an adverse effect on the personnel, property, reputation and/or financial welfare of a company or person. It is clearly a function of management but involves all others, who may have a vested expertise, skill and/or knowledge in damage control relative to the matter causing the emergency. An EPO or CMO (crisis management officer) is a vital figure in the overall operation and planning of the crisis management function, when particular attention is given to the prospect of bomb threats, kidnap/extortion threats and terrorist activities. In the event that the corporation has no readily available or preconceived emergency plan, the EPO should make proper recommendations to establish a crisis management team (CMT), plan and policy, which can be followed in case of an emergency. The CMT should include individuals and personnel, which have the authority to implement all procedures according to the established crisis management plan.

It is vital, based on the selected corporate authorities, the executive protection team included, to pre-establish a policy relating to crisis situations and to disseminate all related information to other corporate employees as deemed necessary and appropriate. The formulation of the crisis policy should include anticipation of all possible scenarios, ways and means to prevent or respond to the event and preparations required and applicable for any special instructions, information, training, equipment, etc. The EPO must work closely with the designated administration officer, in order to assume responsibility for organizing the company's CMT and to take appropriate measures-including training and response evaluation. All crisis team members should be chosen very carefully and provide the ability to work long hours under stress and fatigue. The principal, under general circumstances, might appoint or select the members of the CMT. However, the EPO should have considerable input in selection and/or qualifications of the personnel assigned to this special team. The CMT must be available to devote full time and attention and have the ability to deal with authorities, the media, members of a victim's family, as well as to participate directly in negotiations with kidnappers/hostage-takers. The CMT members must be absolutely loyal, discreet, react calmly under stress and should possess an extraordinary good and clear judgment. Members of the CMT should be briefed by an EPO on a weekly basis, regarding responsibilities in the event of a bomb threat, executive kidnapping, fire, hostage situation, major crime or any other crisis situation. Other crisis situations include natural disasters, etc.. The CMT briefing should include evacuation procedures, operation of fire-fighting equipment, emergency first aid and corporate policy relating to situations, which demand special prearranged management decisions (acts of terror, kidnapping/extortion). Testing of the established procedures and updated recommendations should be made on a regular basis. Each team members should receive a copy of the emergency plan (which should be prepared by the EPO/EPO team). Each CMT member has to become familiar with the contents of the plan. The EPO working with the designated administration officer should assume the responsibility for any necessary updates, modifications or changes deemed necessary for the emergency plan and the briefing of all company employees when and where appropriate.

The EPO cannot be limited to the prevention of a kidnapping or bombing incident. The EPO's role is very important in advising management in the formulation of policies to be followed in the event a kidnapping or bombing is anticipated or carried out. As part of the CMT, the EPO must be familiar with all established procedures, anticipate any adverse action, plan to prevent and prepare for the resolution and control of the situation.

The First Aid

- **Bleeding**

- **Shock**

- **Soft Tissue Injuries**

- **Bones, Joints and Muscles**

- **Environmental Injuries**

- **Medical Emergencies**

- **The Trauma Kit**

As an immediate responder, the EPO plays a vital role in the emergency medical care of the principal and/or anybody else in his/her care. Perhaps the most important reason the EPO's role is so crucial is that he/she is responsible for the first few minutes with the principal. The Emergency Medical Service (EMS) system depends on the responder's action during this time to set the foundation for the remainder of the call. It is during this time that correcting a breathing problem or stopping bleeding will actually save a life. The EPO will also help to prevent further injury, perform the proper assessments, gather a medical history and prepare for the arrival of the Emergency Medical Technician (EMT) or paramedics.

The time may come when the EPO must instantly apply his/her knowledge of lifesaving and first aid measures, possibly under stress or other adverse conditions. Any EPO observing an unconscious and/or ill, injured or wounded person must carefully and skillfully evaluate the casualty to determine the first aid measures required to prevent further injury or death. He should seek help from medical personnel as soon as possible, but must NOT interrupt his evaluation or treatment of the casualty. A second person may be sent to find medical help. One of the cardinal principles of treating a casualty is that the initial rescuer must continue the evaluation and treatment, as the tactical situation permits, until he is relieved by another individual. If, during any part of the evaluation, the casualty exhibits the conditions for which the EPO is checking, he/she must stop the evaluation and immediately administer first aid. After providing first aid, the EPO must proceed with the evaluation and continue to monitor the casualty for further medical complications until relieved by medical personnel. The following procedures are part of an entire First Aid program, of which every EPO has to qualify from. Every qualified EPO should be able to handle any of the following emergencies-car accidents, heart stroke, massive injuries (explosion), knife and gun shoot wounds, fire and smoke inhalation injuries, etc..

Further information about First Aid/CPR see "Appendix: The EPO's Assistant, Section: V."

Bleeding

Bleeding (hemorrhage) is the escape of blood from capillaries, veins, and arteries. Capillaries are very small blood vessels that carry blood to all parts of the body. Veins are blood vessels that carry blood to the heart. Arteries are large blood vessels that carry blood away from the heart. Bleeding can occur inside the body (internal), outside the body (external) or both. Blood is a fluid that consists of a pale yellow liquid (plasma), red blood cells (erythrocytes), white blood cells (leukocytes), and platelets (thrombocytes).

Plasma is the fluid portion of the blood that carries nutrients. Red blood cells give color to the blood and carry oxygen. White blood cells defend the body against infection and attack foreign particles. Platelets are disk shaped and assist in clotting the blood, the mechanism that stops bleeding. There are three types of bleeding. Capillary bleeding is slow, the blood "oozes" from the (wound) cut. Venous bleeding is dark red or maroon, the blood flows in a steady stream. Arterial bleeding is bright red, the blood "spurts" from the wound. Arterial bleeding is life threatening and difficult to control. In small wounds, only the capillaries are damaged. Deeper wounds result in damage to the veins and arteries. Damage to the capillaries is usually not serious and can easily be controlled with a Band-Aid. Damage to the veins and arteries are more serious and can be life threatening. The adult body contains approximately 5 to 6 quarts of blood (10 to 12 pints). The body can normally lose 1 pint of blood (usual amount given by donors) without harmful effects. A loss of 2 pints may cause shock, a loss of 5 to 6 pints usually results in death. During certain situations it will be difficult to decide whether the bleeding is arterial or venous. The distinction is not important. The most important thing to remember is that all bleeding must be controlled as soon as possible.

External Bleeding

While administering first aid to a casualty who is bleeding, you must remain calm. The sight of blood is an emotional event for many, and it often appears severe. However, most bleeding is less severe than it appears. Most of the major arteries are deep and well protected by tissue and bone.

Although bleeding can be fatal, you will usually have enough time to think and act calmly. There are four methods to control bleeding: direct pressure, elevation, indirect pressure, and the use of a tourniquet.

Direct Pressure

Direct pressure is the first and most effective method to control bleeding. In many cases, bleeding can be controlled by applying pressure directly to the wound. Place a sterile dressing or clean cloth on the wound, tie a knot or adhere tape directly over the wound, only tight enough to control bleeding. If bleeding is not controlled, apply another dressing over the first or apply direct pressure with your hand or fingers over the wound. Direct pressure can be applied by the casualty or a bystander. Under no circumstances is a dressing removed once it has been applied.

Elevation

Raising (elevation) an injured arm or leg (extremity) above the level of the heart will help control bleeding. Elevation should be used together with direct pressure. Do not elevate an extremity if you suspect a broken bone (fracture) until it has been properly splinted and you are certain that elevation will not cause further injury. Use a stable object to keep elevation. Placing an extremity on an unstable object may cause further injury.

Indirect Pressure

In cases of severe bleeding when direct pressure and elevation are not controlling the bleeding, indirect pressure must be used. Bleeding from an artery can be controlled by applying pressure to the appropriate pressure point. Pressure points are areas of the body where the blood flow can be controlled by pressing the artery against an underlying bone. Pressure is applied with the fingers, thumb, or heel of the hand. Pressure points should be used with caution. Indirect pressure can cause damage to the extremity because of inadequate blood flow. Do not apply pressure to the neck (carotid) pressure points, it can cause cardiac arrest. Indirect pressure is used in addition to direct pressure and elevation. Pressure points in the arm (brachial) and in the groin (femoral) are most often used, and should be thoroughly understood. The brachial artery is used to control severe bleeding of the lower part of the upper arm and elbow. It is located above the elbow on the inside of the arm in the groove between the muscles. Using your fingers or thumb, apply pressure to the inside of the arm over the bone. The femoral artery is used to control severe bleeding of the thigh and lower leg. It is located on the front, center part of the crease in the groin. Position the casualty on his or her back, kneel on the opposite side from the wounded leg, place the heel of your hand directly on the pressure point, and lean forward to apply pressure. If the bleeding is not controlled, it may be necessary to press directly over the artery with the flat surface of the fingertips and to apply additional pressure on the fingertips with the heel of your other hand.

Tourniquet

A tourniquet should be used only as a last resort to control severe bleeding after all other methods have failed and is used only on the extremities. Before use, you must thoroughly understand its dangers and limitations. Tourniquets cause tissue damage and loss of extremities when used by untrained individuals. Tourniquets are rarely required and should only be used when an arm or leg has been partially or completely severed and when bleeding is uncontrollable. The standard tourniquet is normally a piece of cloth folded until it is 3 or more inches wide and 6 or 7 layers thick. A tourniquet can be a strap, belt, neckerchief, towel, or other similar item. A folded triangular bandage makes a great tourniquet. Never use wire, cord, or any material that will cut the skin. To apply a tourniquet, do the following:

- While maintaining the proper pressure point, place the tourniquet between the heart and the wound, leaving at least 2 inches of uninjured skin between the tourniquet and wound.
- Place a pad (roll) over the artery.
- Wrap the tourniquet around the extremity twice, and tie a half-knot on the upper surface.
- Place a short stick or similar object on the half-knot, and tie a square knot.

- Twist the stick to tighten, until bleeding is controlled.
- Secure the stick in place.
- Never cover a tourniquet.
- Using lipstick or marker, make a "T" on the casualty's forehead and the time tourniquet was applied.
- Never loosen or remove a tourniquet once it has been applied. The loosening of a tourniquet may dislodge clots and result in enough blood loss to cause shock and death.

Do not touch open wounds with your fingers unless absolutely necessary. Place a barrier between you and the casualty's blood or body fluids, using plastic wrap, gloves, or a clean, folded cloth. Wash your hands with soap and warm water immediately after providing care, even if you wore gloves or used another barrier.

Internal Bleeding

Internal bleeding, although not usually visible, can result in serious blood loss. A casualty with internal bleeding can develop shock before you realize the extent of their injuries. Bleeding from the mouth, ears, nose, rectum, or other body opening (orifice) is considered serious and normally indicates internal bleeding. The most common sign of internal bleeding is a simple bruise (contusion), it indicates bleeding into the skin (soft tissues). Severe internal bleeding occurs in injuries caused by a violent force (automobile accident), puncture wounds (knife), and broken bones. Signs of internal bleeding include:

- Anxiety and restlessness.
- Excessive thirst (polydipsia).
- Nausea and vomiting.
- Cool, moist, and pale skin (cold and clammy).
- Rapid breathing (tachypnea).
- Rapid, weak pulse (tachycardia).
- Bruising or discoloration at site of injury (contusion).

If you suspect internal bleeding, do the following:
- Bruise (contusion) -Apply ice or cold pack, with cloth to prevent damage to the skin, to reduce pain and (edema) swelling.
- Severe internal bleeding:
  - Call local emergency number or medical personnel.
  - Monitor airway, breathing, and circulation (ABCs).
  - Treat for shock.
  - Place casualty in most comfortable position.
  - Maintain normal body temperature.
  - Reassure casualty

Nosebleed

Nosebleeds (epistaxis) can be caused by an injury, disease, the environment, high blood pressure, and changes in altitude. They frighten the casualty and may bleed enough to cause shock. If a fractured skull is suspected as the cause, do not stop the bleeding. Cover the nose with a loose, dry, sterile dressing and call the local emergency number or medical personnel. If the casualty has a nosebleed because of other causes, do the following:

- Keep the casualty quiet, sitting with head tilted forward.
- Pinch the nose shut (if there is no fracture), place ice or cold packs to the bridge of the nose, or put pressure on the upper lip just below the nose. Inform the casualty not to rub,

blow, or pick his or her nose. Seek medical assistance if the nosebleed continues, bleeding starts again, or bleeding is because of high blood pressure.

If the casualty loses consciousness, place them on their side to allow blood to drain from the nose and call the local emergency number or medical personnel.

Foreign bodies in the nose usually occur among children. First aid consists of seeking professional medical attention. Nasal damage and the possibility of pushing the object farther up the nose can result from searching and attempts at removal by unqualified personnel. Casualties with severe external bleeding and suspected internal bleeding must be seen by medical personnel as soon as possible. All casualties with external and internal bleeding should be treated for shock.

Shock

Shock, is the failure of the heart and blood vessels (circulatory system) to maintain enough oxygen-rich blood flowing (perfusion) to the vital organs of the body. There is shock to some degree with every illness or injury; shock can be life threatening. The principles of prevention and control are to recognize the signs and symptoms and to begin treating the casualty before shock completely develops. It is unlikely that you will see all the signs and symptoms of shock in a single casualty. Sometimes the signs and symptoms may be disguised by the illness or injury or they may not appear immediately. In fact many times, they appear hours later. The usual signs and symptoms of the development of shock are:

- Anxiety, restlessness and fainting.
- Nausea and vomiting.
- Excessive thirst (polydipsia).
- Eyes are vacant, dull (lackluster), large (dilated) pupils.
- Shallow, rapid (tachypnea), and irregular breathing.
- Pale, cold, moist (clammy) skin.
- Weak, rapid (tachycardia), or absent pulse.

Hypovolemic Shock

Hypovolemic shock is caused by a decreased amount of blood or fluids in the body. This decrease results from injuries that produce internal and external bleeding, fluid loss because of burns, and dehydration due to severe vomiting and diarrhea.

Neurogenic Shock

Neurogenic shock is caused by an abnormal enlargement of the (vasodilation) blood vessels and pooling of the blood to a degree that adequate blood flow cannot be maintained. Simple fainting (syncope) is a variation, it is the result of a temporary pooling of the blood as a person stands. As the person falls, blood rushes back to the head and the problem is solved.

Psychogenic Shock

Psychogenic shock is a "shock like condition" produced by excessive fear, joy, anger, or grief. Shell shock is a psychological adjustment reaction to stressful wartime experiences. Care for shell shock is limited to emotional support and transportation of the casualty to a medical facility.

Anaphylactic Shock

Anaphylactic (allergic) shock occurs when an individual is exposed to a substance to which his or her body is sensitive. The individual may experience a burning sensation, loss of voice, itching (pruritus), hives, severe swelling, and difficulty breathing.

The causative agents are injection of medicines, venoms by stinging insects and animals, inhalation of dust and pollens, and ingestion of certain foods and medications. Individuals with known sensitivities carry medication in commercially prepared kits.

Prevention and Treatment of Shock

While administering first aid to prevent or treat shock, you must remain calm. If shock has not completely developed, the first aid you provide may actually prevent its occurrence. If it has developed, you may be able to keep it from becoming fatal. It is extremely important that you render first aid immediately. To provide first aid for shock, do the following:

- Maintain open airway -Head-tilt/chin-lift or jaw-thrust.
- Control bleeding -Direct pressure, elevation, indirect pressure, or tourniquet if indicated.
- Position casualty -Place the casualty on his or her back, with legs elevated 6 to 12 inches. If it is possible, take advantage of a natural slope of ground and place the casualty so that the head is lower than the feet. If they are vomiting or bleeding around the mouth, place them on their side, or back with head turned to the side. If you suspect head or neck injuries, or are unsure of the casualty's condition, keep them lying flat.
- Splint -Suspected broken and dislocated bones in the position in which they are found. Do not attempt to straighten broken or dislocated bones, because of the high risk of causing further injury. Splinting not only relieves the pain without the use of drugs but prevents further tissue damage and shock. Pain and discomfort are often eliminated by unlacing or cutting a shoe or loosening tight clothing at the site of the injury. A simple adjustment of a bandage or splint will be of benefit, especially when accompanied by encouraging words.
- Keep the casualty comfortable, and warm enough to maintain normal body temperature. If possible, remove wet clothing and place blankets underneath the casualty. Never use an artificial means of warming.
- Keep the casualty as calm as possible. Excitement and excessive handling will aggravate their condition. Prevent the casualty from seeing his or her injuries, reassure them that their injuries are understood and that professional medical assistance will arrive as soon as possible.
- Give nothing by mouth -Do not give the casualty anything to eat or drink because it may cause vomiting. If the casualty complains of thirst, wet his or her lips with a wet towel.
- Request medical assistance -Ask bystanders to call the local emergency number or medical personnel.

Soft Tissue Injuries

The most common injuries (trauma) seen in a first aid setting are soft tissue injuries with bleeding and shock. Injuries that cause a break in the skin, underlying soft tissue, or other body membrane are known as a wound. Injuries to the soft tissues vary from bruises (contusion) to serious cuts (lacerations) and puncture wounds in which the object may remain in the wound (impaled objects). The two main threats with these injuries are bleeding and infection.

Classification of Wounds

Wounds are classified according to their general condition, size, location, the manner in which the skin or tissue is broken, and the agent that caused the wound. It is usually necessary for you to consider some or all of these factors in order to determine what first aid treatment is appropriate.

General Condition

If the wound is new, first aid consists mainly of controlling the bleeding, treating for shock, and reducing the risk of infection. If the wound is old and infected, first aid consists of keeping the casualty quiet, elevating the injured part, and applying a warm wet dressing. If the wound contains foreign objects, first aid may consist of removing the objects if they are not deep. Do not remove impaled objects or objects embedded in the eyes or skull.

Size of Wounds

Generally, large wounds are more serious than small ones and they usually involve severe bleeding, more damage to the underlying tissues and organs, and a greater degree of shock. However, small wounds are sometimes more dangerous than large ones: they may become infected more readily due to neglect. The depth of a wound also is important because it may lead to a complete (through and through) perforation of an organ or the body, with the additional complication of an entrance and exit wound.

Location of Wounds

Since a wound can cause serious damage to deep structures, as well as to the skin and tissues below it, the location is an important consideration. A knife wound to the chest is likely to puncture a lung and cause difficulty breathing. The same type of wound in the abdomen can cause a life-threatening infection, internal bleeding, or puncture the intestines, liver, or other vital organs. A bullet wound to the head may cause brain damage, but a bullet wound to the arm or leg, may cause no serious damage.

Types of Wounds

As the first line of defense against most injuries, soft tissues are most often damaged. There are two types of soft tissue injuries: open and closed. An open wound is one in which the skin surface has been broken, a closed wound is where the skin surface is unbroken but underlying tissues have been damaged.

Closed Wounds

A blunt object that strikes the body will damage tissues beneath the skin. When the damage is minor, the wound is called a bruise (contusion). When the tissue has extensive damage, blood and fluid collect under the skin causing discoloration (ecchymosis), swelling (edema), and pain. First aid consists of applying ice or cold packs to reduce swelling and relieve discomfort. To guard against frostbite, never apply ice or cold packs directly to the skin. Hematomas are the result of a severe blunt injury with extensive soft tissue damage, tearing of large blood vessels, and pooling of large amounts of blood below the skin. With large hematomas, look for broken bones, especially if deformity is present. First aid consists of applying ice or cold packs to reduce swelling and relieve pain, direct pressure (manual compression) to help control internal bleeding, splinting, and elevation. When large areas of bruising are present, shock may develop.

Open Wounds

In open soft tissue injuries, the protective layer of the skin has been damaged. This damage can cause serious internal and external bleeding. Once the protective layer of skin has been broken, the wound becomes contaminated and may become infected. When you consider the way in which the skin or tissue has been broken, there are six basic types of open wounds: abrasions, amputations, avulsions, incisions, lacerations, and punctures. Many wounds are a combination of two or more of these types.

Abrasions

Abrasions are caused when the skin is rubbed or scraped off. Rope burns, floor burns, and skinned knees or elbows are common examples of abrasions. Abrasions easily can become infected, because dirt and germs are usually ground into the tissues. There is normally minimal bleeding or oozing of clear fluid.

Amputations

Amputations (traumatic) are the non-surgical removal of the fingers, toes, hands, feet, arms, legs, and ears from the body. Bleeding is heavy and normally requires a tourniquet, to control the blood flow. There are three types of amputation:

- Complete–Body part is completely torn off (severed).
- Partial–More than 50% of the body part is torn off.
- Degloving–Skin and tissue are torn away from body part.

If the casualty has an amputation, do the following:
- Establish and maintain the airway, breathing, and circulation (ABCs).
- Control bleeding with direct pressure, elevation, indirect pressure, or tourniquet only as a last resort, never remove or loosen a tourniquet once it has been applied.
- Apply dressing to the stump with an ace wrap to replace direct pressure.
- Treat for shock.
- Request medical assistance immediately.

Avulsions

An avulsion is an injury in which the skin is torn completely away from a body part or is left hanging as a flap. Usually, there is severe bleeding. If possible, obtain the part that has been torn away, rinse it in water, wrap it in a dry sterile gauze, seal it in a plastic bag, and send it on ice with the casualty. Do not allow part to freeze and do not submerge in water. If the skin is still attached, fold the flap back into its normal position.

Incisions

Incisions, commonly called cuts, are wounds made by sharp cutting instruments such as knives, razors, or broken glass. Incisions tend to bleed freely because the blood vessels are cut cleanly, without ragged edges. The wound edges are smooth and there is little damage to the surrounding tissues. Of all the classes of open wounds, incisions are the least likely to become infected.

Lacerations

Lacerations are wounds that are torn, rather than cut. They have ragged, irregular edges and torn tissue underneath. These wounds are usually made by a blunt, rather than a sharp, object. A wound made by a dull knife is more likely to be a laceration than an incision. Many of the wounds caused by machinery accidents are lacerations, often complicated by crushed tissues. Lacerations are frequently contaminated with dirt, grease, or other materials that are ground into the wound; they are very likely to become infected.

Punctures

Punctures are caused by objects that enter the skin while leaving a surface opening. Wounds made by nails, needles, wire, knives, and bullets are normally punctures. Small puncture wounds usually do not bleed freely; however, large puncture wounds may cause severe internal bleeding. The possibility of infection is great in all puncture wounds, especially if the penetrating object is contaminated. Perforation (through and through) is a variation, it is the result of a penetrating object entering, passing through, and exiting the body.

Treatment of Wounds

First aid treatment for all wounds consists of controlling the flow of blood, treating for shock, and preventing infection. When providing first aid to casualty with multiple injuries, treat the wounds that appear to be life-threatening first. Since most of the body is covered by clothing, carefully examine the entire body for bleeding. When necessary, tear or cut clothing away from the wound because excessive movement of the injured part will cause pain and additional damage.

Bleeding

After establishing an adequate open airway, the main concern will be to control bleeding, by direct pressure and elevation. Indirect pressure and the use of a tourniquet should be used only if direct pressure and elevation do not control the bleeding. A protective covering (dressing) that is properly applied should adequately control the bleeding. In cases of severe bleeding, you may need to double the dressing. Never remove a dressing that is soaked with blood to replace it with another; just place the new dressing over the old one.

Shock

Shock may be severe in a casualty who has lost a large amount of blood or suffered a serious injury.

Infection

Infections can occur in any wound. Infection is a hazard in wounds that do not bleed freely; in wounds where tissue is torn or the skin falls back into place and prevents the entrance of air; and in wounds that involve the crushing of tissue. Incisions, in which there is a free flow of blood and relatively little crushing of tissues, are the least likely to become infected. The signs of infection are tenderness, redness, heat, swelling, and a discharge. Serious infections develop red streaks that lead from the wound to the heart. Infections are dangerous, especially in the area of the nose and mouth. From this area, infections spread easily into the bloodstream, causing blood poisoning (septicemia), and into the brain, causing a collection of pus (abscess) and infection. Small wounds should be washed immediately with soap and water, dried, and treated with an application of a mild, nonirritating antiseptic. Apply a dressing if necessary. Make no attempt to wash a large wound and do not apply an antiseptic. Cover the wound with a dry, sterile dressing. Further treatment of large wounds should be conducted by medical personnel. All puncture wounds must be evaluated by medical personnel.

Foreign Bodies

Many wounds contain foreign bodies. Wood or glass splinters, bullets, metal fragments, wire, fishhooks, nails, and small particles from grinding wheels are examples of materials that are found in wounds. In most cases, first aid will include the removal of this material if the wound is minor and the object is near the surface and exposed. However, first aid does not include the removal of deeply embedded objects, powdered glass, or any scattered material. Never attempt to remove bullets, examine the casualty to find out whether the bullet remains in the body by looking for both an entrance and exit wound. The general rule is: Remove foreign objects from a wound ONLY when you can do so easily and without causing further damage.
Do not attempt to remove an object that is embedded in the eye or that has penetrated the eye.

Treatment of Specific Conditions

It is impossible to list all wounds in simple categories. Some require special treatment and precautions. You may see wounds that are not described in this course, but most wounds can be treated by calmly remembering the general treatment of wounds.

Head Wounds

Injuries to the head (scalp) can occur as a result of diving, automobile accidents, falls, blunt trauma, knives, bullets, and many other causes. Head wounds can be open or closed. In open head wounds there is an obvious injury in which there is normally a lot of bleeding. Closed head wounds may not be obvious, many times you will have to treat the casualty based on how the accident happened. You may see only the delayed symptoms, such as a seizure, confusion, or personality changes. Head wounds must be treated with particular care, since there is always the possibility of brain damage. If you suspect the casualty has suffered a head injury, look for the following:

- Depressions, lacerations, deformities, bruising around the eyes (Raccoon's Sign) or behind the ears (Battle's Sign).
- Never touch a wound, examine a wound to determine depth, separate the edges of a wound, or remove impaled objects.
- Check the eyes: Are the pupils (constricted) small (dilated), large, equal, or unequal?
- Blood or clear (cerebrospinal) fluid dripping from the nose or ears. (Cover loosely with a sterile dressing to absorb but not stop the flow).

If you suspect a head injury, do the following:
- Position the casualty flat, stabilize the head and neck as you found them by placing your hands on both sides of the head.
- Establish and maintain open airway using the jaw-thrust maneuver. Note that the head is not tilted and the neck is not extended. Check the airway, breathing, and circulation (ABC's).
- Finger sweep to remove any foreign bodies from the mouth.
- Maintain a neutral position of the head and neck and, if possible, apply a cervical collar or improvised (towel) collar.
- Control bleeding using gentle, continuous pressure. Never apply direct pressure if the skull is depressed or bone fragments are seen.
- Apply dressing–Do not use direct pressure or tie knots over the wound. Apply ice or cold packs with cloth to prevent damage to the skin.
- Treat for shock–Casualties with suspected head and neck injuries are to remain flat. Do not raise the casualty's feet. If casualty is vomiting or bleeding around the mouth, place them on their side keeping the neck straight. Do not give anything to eat or drink.
- Request medical assistance immediately -Time is critical.

Facial Wounds

Facial wounds are treated, generally, like other flesh wounds. However, ensure that the tongue or soft tissue does not cause an airway obstruction. Keep the nose and throat clear of all foreign material and position the casualty so that blood will drain out of the mouth and nose. Facial wounds and scalp wounds bleed freely. Any casualty that has suffered a facial wound that involves the eye, eyelids, or the tissues around the eye must receive professional medical attention as soon as possible. First aid for other facial wounds is the same as head wounds.

Bones, Joints and Muscles

Accidents cause many different types of injuries to bones, joints and muscles. When rendering first aid, you must be alert for signs of broken bones (fractures), dislocations, sprains, strains, and bruises (contusions). Injuries to the joints and muscles often occur together, and it is difficult to tell whether the injury is to a joint, muscle, or tendon. It is difficult to tell joint or muscle injuries from fractures. When in doubt, always treat the injury as a fracture. The primary process of first aid for fractures consists of immobilizing the injured part to prevent the ends of broken bones from moving and causing further damage to the nerves, blood vessels, or internal organs. Splints are also used to immunize injured joints or muscles and to prevent the enlargement of severe wounds. Before learning first aid for injuries to the bones, joints, and muscles, you need to have a general understanding of the use of splints.

Splints

In an emergency, almost any firm object or material will serve as a splint. Thus, umbrellas, canes, rifles, sticks, oars, wire mesh, boards, cardboard, pillows, and folded newspapers can be used. A fractured leg can be immobilized by securing it to the uninjured leg. Whenever possible, use ready-made splints such as the pneumatic or traction splints. Splints should be lightweight, padded, strong, rigid, and long enough to reach the joint above and below the fracture. If they are not properly padded, they will not adequately immobilize the injured part. Articles of clothing, bandages, blankets, or any soft material may be used as padding. If the casualty is wearing heavy clothes, you may be able to apply the splint on the outside, allowing the clothing to serve as a part of the required padding. Fasten splints in place with bandages, adhesive tape, clothing, or any suitable material.

One person should hold the splints in position while another person fastens them. Splints should be applied tight, but never tight enough to stop the circulation of blood. When applying splints to the arms or legs, leave the fingers or toes exposed. If the tips of the fingers or toes turn blue or cold, loosen the splints or bandages. Injuries will probably swell, and splints or bandages that were applied correctly may later be too tight.

Fractures

A break or rupture in a bone is called a fracture. There are two basic types; open and closed. A closed fracture does not produce an open wound in the skin, also known as a simple fracture. An open fracture produces an open wound in the skin, also known as a compound fracture. Open wounds are caused by the sharp end of broken bones pushing through the skin; or by an object such as a bullet that enters the skin from the outside. Open fractures are usually more serious than closed fractures. They involve extensive tissue damage and are likely to become infected. Closed fractures can be turned into open fractures by rough or careless handling of the casualty. Always use extreme care when treating a suspected fracture.

It is not easy to recognize a fracture. All fractures, whether open or closed, can cause severe pain or shock. Fractures can cause the injured part to become deformed, or to take an unnatural position. Compare the injured to the uninjured part if you are unsure of a deformity. Pain, discoloration, and swelling may be at the fracture site, and there may be instability if the bone is broken clear through. It may be difficult or impossible for the casualty to move the injured part. If movement is possible, the casualty may feel a grating sensation (crepitus) as the ends of the bones rub against each other. If a bone is cracked rather than broken, the casualty may be able to move the injured part without much difficulty. An open fracture is easy to see if the end of the bone sticks out through the skin. If the bone does not stick out, you might see a wound but fail to see the broken bone. It can be difficult to tell if an injury is a fracture, dislocation, sprain, or strain. When in doubt, splint. If you suspect a fracture, do the following:

- Control bleeding with direct pressure, indirect pressure, or tourniquet only as a last resort.
- Treat for shock.
- Monitor the airway, breathing, and circulation (ABCs).
- Remove all jewelry from the injury site, unless the casualty objects. Gently cut clothing away so that you don't move the injured part and cause further damage.
- Check the distal pulse of the injured part, if pulse is absent, gently move injured part to restore circulation.
- Cover all wounds with sterile dressings, including open fractures. Do not push bone ends back into the skin. Avoid excessive pressure on the wound.
- Apply splint -Do not attempt to straighten broken bones.
  - Apply and maintain traction until the splint has been secured.
  - Wrap from the bottom of the splint to the top, firmly but not too tight.
  - Check the distal pulse to ensure that circulation is still present. If the pulse is absent, loosen the splint until circulation returns. Do not move the casualty until the injury has been splinted.

- Request medical assistance -All suspected fractures require professional medical treatment.

Fracture of the Forearm

There are two long bones in the forearm, the radius and the ulna. When both are broken, the arm usually appears to be deformed. When only one is broken, the other acts as a splint and the arm retains a more natural appearance. Fractures usually result in pain, tenderness, swelling, and loss of movement. In addition to the general procedures above, apply a pneumatic (air) splint if available; if not, apply two padded splints; one on the top (backhand side), and one on the bottom (palm side).

Make sure the splints are long enough to extend from the elbow to the wrist. Once the forearm is sprinted, place the forearm across the chest. The palm of the hand should be turned in with the thumb pointing up. Support the forearm in this position with a wide sling and cravat bandage. The band should be raised about 4 inches above the level of the elbow.

Fracture of the Upper Arm

There is one bone in the upper arm, the humerus. If the fracture is near the elbow, the arm is likely to be straight with no bend at the elbow. Fractures usually result in pain, tenderness, swelling, and loss of movement. In addition to the general procedures above, do the following: If the fracture is in the upper part of the arm, near the shoulder, place a pad or folded towel in the armpit. Bandage the arm securely to the body, and support the forearm in a narrow sling. If the fracture is in the middle of the upper arm, you can use one well padded splint on the outside the arm.

The splint should extend from the shoulder to the elbow. Secure the arm firmly to the body and support the forearm in a sling. If the fracture is at or near the elbow, the arm may be either bent or straight. Regardless what position you find the arm, do not attempt to straighten or move it. Gently splint the arm in the position in which you find it.

Fracture of the Rib

Make the casualty as comfortable as possible so that the chances of further damage to the lungs, heart, or chest wall is minimized. A common finding in all casualties with fractured ribs is pain at the site of the fracture. Ask the casualty to point to the exact area of pain to assist you in determining the location of the fracture. Deep breathing, coughing, or movement is usually painful. The casualty should remain still and may lean toward the injured side, with a hand over the fracture to immobilize the chest and ease the pain. Simple rib fractures are not bound, strapped, or taped if the casualty is comfortable.

If the casualty is more comfortable with the chest immobilized, use a sling and swathe. Place the arm on the injured side against the chest, with the palm flat, thumb up, and the forearm raised to a 45-degree angle. Immobilize the chest, using wide strips of bandage (ace wrap) to secure the arm to the chest.

Fracture of the Thigh

There is one long bone in the upper leg between the kneecap and the pelvis, the femur. When the femur is fractured, any attempt to move the leg results in a spasm of the muscles that causes severe pain. The leg is not stable, and there is complete loss of control below the fracture. The leg usually assumes an unnatural position, with the toes pointing outward. The injured leg is shorter than the uninjured one because of the pulling of the thigh muscles. Serious bleeding is a real danger since the broken bone may cut the large (femoral) artery. Shock usually is severe.

In addition to the general procedures above, gently straighten the leg, apply two padded splints, one on the outside and inside the injured leg. The outside splint should reach from the armpit to the foot, the inside splint from the groin to the foot.

The splint should be secured in five places: (1) around the ankle, (2) over the knee, (3) just below the hip, (4) around the pelvis, and (5) just below the armpit. The legs can then be tied together to support the injured leg. Do not move the casualty until the leg has been splinted.

Fracture of the Lower Leg

There are two long bones in the lower leg, the tibia and fibula. When both are broken, the leg usually appears to be deformed. When only one is broken, the other acts as a splint and the leg retains a more natural appearance. Fractures usually result in pain, tenderness, swelling, and loss of movement. A fracture just above the ankle is often mistaken for a sprain. In addition to the general procedures above, gently straighten the leg, apply a pneumatic (air) splint if available; if not, apply three padded splints, one on each side and underneath the leg. Place extra padding under the knee and just above the heel. The splint should be secured in four places: (1) just below the hip, (2) just above the knee, (3) just below the knee, and (4) just above the ankle. Do not place the straps over the area of the fracture. A pillow and two side splints also work well. Place a pillow beside the injured leg, then gently lift the leg and place it in the middle of the pillow. Bring the edges of the pillow around to the front of the leg and pin them together. Then place one splint on each side of the leg, over the pillow, and secure them in place with a bandage or tape.

Fracture of the Collarbone

The collarbone is also known as the clavicle. When standing, the injured shoulder is lower, and the casualty is unable to raise the arm above the shoulder. The casualty attempts to support the shoulder by holding the elbow. This is the typical stance taken by a casualty with a broken collarbone. Since the collarbone lies near the surface of the skin, you may be able to see the point of fracture by the deformity and tenderness. In addition to the general procedures above, gently bend the casualty's arm and place the forearm across the chest. The palm of the hand should be turned in, with the thumb pointing up. Support the arm in this position with a wide sling. The hand should be raised about 4 inches above the level of the elbow. A wide roller bandage (or any wide strip of cloth) may be used to secure the casualty's arm to the body.

Fracture of the Jaw

The lower jaw is also known as the mandible. The casualty may have difficulty breathing, difficulty in talking, chewing, and swallowing, and have pain of movement of the jaw. The teeth may be out of line, and the gums may bleed, and swelling may develop. The most important consideration is to maintain an adequate open airway. In addition to the general procedures above, apply a four-tailed bandage, be sure the bandage pulls the lower jaw forward. Never apply a bandage that forces the jaw backward, since this may interfere with breathing. The bandage must be firm enough to support and immobilize the lower jaw, but it must not press against the casualty's throat. The casualty should have scissors or a knife to cut the bandage in case of vomiting.

Fracture of the Skull

The skull is also known as the cranium. The primary danger is that the brain may be damaged. Whether or not the skull is fractured is of secondary importance. The first aid procedures are the same in either case, and the primary intent is to prevent further damage. Some injuries that fracture the skull do not cause brain damage. But brain damage can result from minor injuries that do not cause damage to the skull. It is difficult to determine whether an injury has affected the brain, because symptoms of brain damage vary. A casualty who has suffered a head injury must be handled carefully and given immediate medical attention. Signs and symptoms that may indicate brain damage include:

- Wounds of the scalp, deformity of the skull.
- Dizziness, weakness, conscious or unconscious.
- Pain, tenderness, or swelling.
- Severe headache, nausea and vomiting.
- Restlessness, confusion, and disorientation.
- Paralysis of the arms, legs, or face.
- Unequal pupils, abnormal reaction to light.

- Blood or clear fluid from the ears, nose, or mouth.
- Pale, flushed skin.
- Bruising behind the ear (Batlle's Sign).
- Bruising under or around the eyes in the absence of trauma to the eyes (Raccoon's Sign).

If you suspect a head injury, do the following:
- Position the casualty flat, stabilize the head and neck as you found them by placing your hands on both sides of the head.
- Establish and maintain an open airway -jaw-thrust maneuver. Note that the head is not tilted and the neck is not extended. Check the airway, breathing, and circulation (ABCs).
- Finger sweep to remove any foreign bodies from the mouth.
- Maintain neutral position of head and neck and, if possible, apply a cervical collar or im-provised (towel) collar.
- Apply dressing -Do not use direct pressure or tie knots over the wound. Apply ice or cold packs if available. (For blood or clear fluid from the nose or ears, cover loosely with a ster-ile dressing to absorb but not stop the flow).
- Treat for shock -Casualties with suspected head and neck injuries are to remain flat. Do not raise the casualty's feet. If they are vomiting or bleeding around the mouth, place them on their side keeping the neck straight. Do not give anything to eat or drink.
- Request medical assistance immediately -Time is critical. Head and neck injuries should be treated by professional medical personnel, if possible. Do not attempt procedures that you are not trained for.

Fracture of the Spine

The spine is also known as the backbone or spinal column. If the spine is fractured, the spinal cord may be crushed, cut, or damaged so severely that death or paralysis may occur. If the fracture occurs in a way that the spinal cord is not damaged, there is a chance of complete recovery. Twisting or bending of the neck or back, whether due to the original injury or careless handling, is likely to cause irreparable damage.

The primary symptoms of a fractured spine are pain, shock, and paralysis. Pain may be acute at the point of fracture and radiate to other parts of the body. Shock is usually severe, but the symptoms may be de-layed. Paralysis occurs if the spinal cord is damaged. If the casualty cannot move the legs, the injury is probably in the back; if the arms and legs cannot move, the injury is probably in the neck. A casualty who has back or neck pain following an injury should be treated for a fractured spine. If you suspect a frac-tured spine, do the following:

- Position the casualty flat, stabilize the head and neck as you found them by placing your hands on both sides of the head.
- Establish and maintain an open airway -jaw-thrust maneuver. Note that the head is not tilted and the neck is not extended. Check the airway, breathing, and circulation (ABCs).
- Finger sweep to remove any foreign bodies from the mouth.
- Maintain neutral position of head and neck and, if possible, apply a cervical collar or im-provised (towel) collar.
- Keep the casualty comfortable and warm enough to maintain normal body temperature.
- Treat for shock -Casualties with suspected spinal injuries are to remain flat. Do not raise the casualty's feet. If the casualty is vomiting or bleeding around the mouth, place them on their side keeping the neck straight. Do not give anything to eat or drink.
- Request medical assistance immediately -Time is critical. Do not move the casualty unless it is absolutely necessary. Do not bend or twist the casualty's body. Do not move the head forward, backward, or sideways. Do not allow the casualty to sit up.

Fracture of the Pelvis

Fractures often result from falls, heavy blows, and crushing accidents. The greatest danger is damage to the organs that are enclosed by the pelvis. There is danger that the bladder will be ruptured or that severe internal bleeding may occur, due to the large blood vessels being torn by broken bone.

The primary symptoms are severe pain, shock, and loss of the ability to use the lower part of the body. The casualty is unable to sit or stand and may feel like the body is "coming apart." Treat for shock, but do not raise the casualty's feet. Do not move the casualty unless absolutely necessary. Request medical assistance immediately.

Dislocations

A dislocation occurs when a bone is forcibly displaced from its joint. Many times the bone slips back into its normal position; other times, it becomes locked and remains dislocated until it is put back into place (reduction). Dislocations are caused by falls or blows and occasionally by violent muscular exertion. The joints that are most frequently dislocated are the shoulder, hip, finger, and jaw. A dislocation may bruise or tear muscles, ligaments, blood vessels, and tendons.

The primary symptoms are rapid swelling, discoloration, loss of movement, pain, and shock. You should not attempt to reduce a dislocation. Unskilled attempts at reduction may cause damage to the nerves and blood vessels or may fracture a bone. You should leave this treatment to professional medical personnel and concentrate your efforts on making the casualty comfortable. If you suspect a dislocation, do the following:

- Loosen clothing from around the injury.
- Place the casualty in the most comfortable position.
- Support the injured part with a sling, pillow, or splint.
- Treat for shock.
- Request medical assistance as soon as possible.

Sprains

A sprain is an injury to the ligaments that support a joint. It usually involves a sudden dislocation, with the bone slipping back into place on its own. Sprains are caused by the violent pulling or twisting of the joint beyond its normal limits of movement. The joints that are most frequently sprained are the ankle, wrist, knee, and finger. Tearing of the ligaments is the most serious aspect of a sprain, and there is a considerable amount of damage to the blood vessels.

When the blood vessels are damaged, blood may escape into the joint, causing pain and swelling. If you suspect a sprain, do the following:

- Splint to support the joint and put the ligaments at rest. Gently loosen the splint if it becomes so tight that it interferes with circulation.
- Elevate and rest the joint to help reduce the pain and swelling.
- Apply ice or cold packs, with cloth to prevent damage to the skin, the first 24 hours, then apply warm compresses to increase circulation.
- Request medical assistance as soon as possible.

Treat all sprains as fractures until ruled out by x-rays.

Strains

A strain is caused by the forcible over-stretching or tearing of a muscle or tendon. They are caused by lifting heavy loads, sudden or violent movements, or by any action that pulls the muscles beyond their normal limits. The primary symptoms are pain, lameness, stiffness, swelling, and discoloration. If you suspect a strain, do the following:

- Elevate and rest the injured area to help reduce the pain and swelling.
- Apply ice or cold packs, with cloth to prevent damage to the skin, the first 24 hours, then apply warm compresses to increase circulation.
- Request medical assistance as soon as possible.

Treat all strains as fractures until ruled out by x-rays.

Contusions

A contusion (bruise) is an injury that causes bleeding into or beneath the skin, but it does not break the skin. The primary symptoms are pain, tenderness, swelling, and discoloration. At first, the injured area is red due to local irritation; as time passes the characteristic "black and blue" (ecchymosis) mark appears. Several days after the injury, the skin becomes yellow or green in color. Usually, minor contusions do not require treatment. If you suspect a contusion, do the following:

- Elevate and rest the injured area to help reduce the pain and swelling.
- Apply ice or cold packs, with cloth to prevent damage to the skin, the first 24 hours, then apply warm compresses to increase circulation.

Environmental Injuries

Exposure to temperature extremes, whether heat or cold, causes injury to the skin, tissues, blood vessels, vital organs, and in some cases, the entire body. Burns, heat cramps, heat exhaustion, and heatstroke are caused by exposure to heat. Hypothermia (general cooling), frostbite, and (trench foot) immersion foot are caused by exposure to the cold.

Burns and Scalds

Burns are caused by dry heat, and scalds are caused by moist heat. Treatment is the same for both. Contact with an electric current also causes burns, especially if the skin is dry. The seriousness of the burn can be determined by its depth, extent, and location and by the age and the health of the casualty. You must take all these factors into consideration when evaluating burns. Burns are classified according to their depth as first-degree, second-degree, and third-degree.

First-Degree Burns

First-degree burns involve only the first (epidermal) layer of the skin. The skin is red, dry, warm, sensitive to touch, and turns (blanches) white with pressure. Pain is mild to severe, swelling (edema) may occur. Healing occurs naturally within a week.

Second-Degree Burns

Second-degree burns involve the first and part of the second (dermis) layer of the skin. The skin is red, blistered, weeping, and looks (spotted) mottled. Pain is moderate to severe, swelling often occurs. Healing takes 2 -3 weeks, with some scarring and depigmentation.

Third-Degree Burns

Third-degree burns involve all layers (full thickness) of the skin, penetrating muscle, connective tissue, and bone. The skin may vary from white and lifeless to black and charred. Pain will be absent at the burn site if all the nerve endings are destroyed and the surrounding tissue will be painful. There is considerable scarring, and skin grafting may be necessary. Third-degree burns are life threatening.

It is important to remember that the extent (size) of the burned area is more important than the depth of the burn. A first-degree burn that covers a large area of the body is usually more serious than a small third-degree burn.

The "rule of nines" is used to give a rough estimate of the surface area burned and aids in deciding the correct treatment. Shock can be expected in adults with burns over 15 percent or in small children with burns over 10 percent of the body surface area (BSA). In adults, burns involving more than 20 percent of the body surface area endanger life and 30 percent burns are usually fatal if adequate medical treatment is not received. The third factor in burn evaluation is the location: burns of the head, hands, feet, or genitals may require hospitalization. The causes of burns are classified as thermal (heat), chemical, electrical, or radiation.

Thermal Burns

Thermal (heat) burns are caused by exposure to hot solids, liquids, gases, or fire. If the casualty has thermal burns, do the following:

- Monitor the airway, breathing, and circulation (ABC's). Always expect breathing problems when there are burns around the face or if the casualty has been exposed to hot gases or smoke.
- Control bleeding using direct pressure, elevation, indirect pressure, or tourniquet if indicated.
- Remove all jewelry from the area, unless the casualty objects. Swelling may develop rapidly.
- Apply cool water to the affected area or submerge in cool water. Do not use ice or ice water.
- Remove clothing gently from the burned area. Do not remove clothing that is sticking to the skin.
- Cover area with dry, sterile dressings, if possible. Cover large areas with clean, dry sheets. Do not break blisters or apply ointments of any kind.
- Treat for shock -Keep the casualty comfortable and warm enough to maintain normal body temperature. Elevate the burned area above the heart.
- Request medical assistance for all burns. If possible, before transport, inform medical personnel of the degree, location of the burn, and percentage of the body area affected.

Chemical Burns

When acids, alkalines, or other chemicals come in contact with the skin, they can cause injuries that are generally referred to as chemical burns. These injuries are not caused by heat but by direct chemical destruction of the tissues. The areas most often affected are the arms, legs, hands, feet, face, and eyes. Alkali burns are usually more serious than acid burns; alkalines generally penetrate deeper and burn longer. If the casualty has chemical burns, do the following:

- Flush area immediately with large quantities of fresh water, using an installed deluge shower or hose, if available. Avoid excessive water pressure. Continue to flush the area for at least 15 minutes while removing the clothes, including shoes, socks, and jewelry. Dry lime powder (alkali burns) creates a corrosive substance when mixed with water; keep the powder dry and remove it by brushing it from the skin. Acid burns caused by phenol (carbolic acid), should be washed with alcohol. Then wash the area with large quantities of water. If alcohol is not available, flush the area with large quantities of water. Cover chemical burns with a sterile dressing.
- If available, follow the first aid procedures provided in the Material Safety Data Sheet (MSDS) for the chemical.
- Flush the eyes with fresh water immediately using an installed emergency eye/face bath or hose on low pressure for at least 20 minutes. Ask casualty to remove contact lenses. Use your hands to keep the eyelids open. Never use a neutralizing agent, mineral oil, or other material in the eyes.
- Monitor the airway, breathing, and circulation (ABCs).

- Warning -Do not attempt to neutralize any chemical unless you are sure what it is and what substance will effectively neutralize it. Further damage may be done by a neutralizing agent that is too strong or incorrect. Do not apply creams or other materials to chemical burns.
- Treat for shock -Keep the casualty comfortable and warm enough to maintain normal body temperature.
- Request medical assistance for all chemical burns. If possible, before transport, notify medical personnel of the name and other pertinent information about the chemical involved, location of the burn, and percentage of the body area affected. Send the container to medical personnel with the casualty.

Sunburn

Sunburn results from prolonged exposure to the ultraviolet rays of the sun. First-and second-degree burns similar to thermal burns may develop. Treatment is essentially the same as for thermal burns. Unless a major percentage of the body is affected, the casualty will not require more than first aid attention. Commercially prepared sunburn lotions and ointments may be used. Prevention through education and the proper use of sunscreens and sunblocks is the best way to avoid this condition.

Heat Exposure

Excessive heat affects the body in a variety of ways. When a person exercises in a hot environment, heat builds up inside the body. The body automatically reacts to get rid of this heat through the sweating mechanism. If the body loses large amounts of water and salt from sweating, heat cramps and heat exhaustion may develop. If the body becomes too overheated, the sweat control mechanism of the body malfunctions and shuts down. The result is heatstroke (sunstroke). Heat exposure injuries are a threat in any hot environment, especially in desert or tropical areas and in the boiler rooms of ships.

Heat Cramps

Heat cramps are muscular pains and spasms resulting from the loss of water and salt from the body. Excessive sweating may result in painful cramps of the muscles of the abdomen, legs, and arms. Heat cramps also may result from drinking ice water or other cold drinks either too quickly or in too large a quantity after exercise. Heat cramps are often an early sign of approaching heat exhaustion. Signs and symptoms of heat cramps include:

- Muscle pain and cramps.
- Faintness or dizziness.
- Nausea and vomiting.
- Exhaustion and fatigue.

If you suspect heat cramps, do the following:
- Move the casualty to a cool or air-conditioned area.
- If the casualty can drink, give him or her one-half glassful of cool water every 15 minutes. If the casualty vomits, stop giving water. Do not give salt tablets.
- Gently stretch or massage the muscle to relieve the spasm.
- Request medical assistance if the casualty has other injuries or does not respond to the above procedures.

Heat Exhaustion

Heat exhaustion is caused by the excessive loss of water and salt (sweating). It is the most common condition from exposure to hot environments. Signs and symptoms of heat exhaustion include:

- Pale, cool (clammy), moist skin.

- Large (dilated) pupils.
- Normal or below normal temperature.
- Rapid and shallow breathing.
- Headache, nausea, loss of appetite.
- Dizziness, weakness or fainting.

If you suspect heat exhaustion, do the following:
- Move the casualty to a cool area, apply cold, wet compresses, and fan the casualty.
- Treat for shock.
- Remove the casualty's clothing, do not allow the casualty to become chilled.
- If the casualty is conscious and can drink, give him or her one-half glassful of cool water every 15 minutes. If the casualty vomits, stop giving water. Do not give salt tablets.
- Request medical assistance for heat exhaustion casualties as soon as possible.

Heatstroke

Heatstroke, also known as sunstroke, is a life-threatening emergency. It is not necessary to be exposed to the sun for it to develop. It is less common but more serious than heat exhaustion. The casualty experiences a breakdown of the sweating mechanism and is unable to eliminate excessive body heat. If the body temperature rises too high, the brain, kidneys, and liver may be permanently damaged. Signs and symptoms of heatstroke include:

- 105 degrees F (41 degrees C) or higher temperature.
- Hot, wet, or dry and reddish skin.
- Small (constricted) pupils.
- Headache, nausea, dizziness, or weakness.
- Deep and rapid breathing at first, then shallow and almost absent.
- Fast and weak pulse.

If you suspect heatstroke, do the following:
- Move the casualty immediately to a cool area, place them in a cold water bath. If this is not possible, give a sponge bath by applying wet, cold towels to the entire body. If available, place cold packs around the neck.
- Monitor the airway, breathing, and circulation (ABCs).
- Treat for shock.
- Remove the casualty's clothing, do not allow the casualty to become chilled.
- If the casualty is conscious and can drink, give him or her one-half glassful of cool water every 15 minutes. If the casualty vomits, stop giving water. Do not give salt tablets.
- Request medical assistance for heatstroke casualties as soon as possible.

Cold Exposure

When the body is exposed to extremely cold temperatures, the blood vessels constrict and body heat is gradually lost. As the body temperature falls, tissues are easily damaged. The extent of damage depends on such factors as wind speed, temperature, type and duration of exposure, and humidity. Fatigue, smoking, drugs, alcohol, stress, dehydration, and the presence of other injuries increase the harmful effects of the cold.

General Cooling (Hypothermia)

Hypothermia, an abnormally low body temperature, is a medical emergency. It is caused by continued exposure to low or rapidly falling temperatures, cold moisture, snow, or ice. Individuals exposed to low temperatures for long periods may suffer harmful effects, even if they are protected by clothing, because cold affects the body slowly, almost without notice. Signs and symptoms of hypothermia include:

- Several stages of progressive shivering (an attempt by the body to generate heat).
- Dizziness, numbness, and confusion.
- Unconsciousness may follow quickly.
- Signs of shock.
- Extremities (arms and legs) freeze.

If you suspect hypothermia, do the following:

- Move the casualty immediately to a warm place.
- Monitor the airway, breathing, and circulation (ABCs).
- Rewarm by applying external heat to both sides of the casualty. Natural body heat (skin to skin) from two rescuers (buddy warming) is the best method. Do not place heat source next to bare skin. Since the casualty is unable to generate body heat, placing him/her under a blanket or in a sleeping bag is not sufficient.
- If the casualty is conscious and can drink, give warm liquids. Do not give hot liquids, coffee, or alcohol or allow casualty to smoke.
- Request medical assistance for hypothermia as soon as possible.

Immersion Hypothermia

Immersion hypothermia, is the lowering of the body temperature due to prolonged immersion in cold water. It is often associated with limited motion of the extremities and water-soaked clothing. Temperatures range from just above freezing to 50 degrees F (1O degrees C). Signs and symptoms of immersion hypothermia include:

- Tingling and numbness of affected areas.
- Swelling of the legs, feet or hands.
- Bluish discoloration of the skin and painful blisters.

If you suspect immersion hypothermia, do the following:
- Move the casualty immediately but gently to a warm, dry area.
- Monitor the airway, breathing, and circulation (ABC's).
- Remove wet clothing carefully, keep casualty warm and dry. Do not rub or massage affected area.
- Do not rupture blisters or apply ointment to affected area.
- If the casualty is conscious and can drink, give warm liquids. Do not give hot liquids, coffee, or alcohol or allow casualty to smoke.
- Request medical assistance for immersion hypothermia as soon as possible.

Frostbite

Frostbite is damage to the skin due to continued exposure to severe cold. It occurs when ice crystals form in the skin or deeper tissue after exposure to a temperature of 32 degrees F (0 degrees C) or lower. The areas most commonly affected are the hands, feet, ears, nose, and cheeks. Frostbite is classified as incipient, superficial, or deep.

Superficial Frostbite

Superficial frostbite affects the surface of the skin and the tissue beneath. The skin will be firm and white, but the underlying tissue will be soft. The affected area may become blue, tingle, swell, and burn during thawing. Move the casualty to a warm area.

Hands can be rewarmed by placing them under the armpit, or against the abdomen. Feet can be rewarmed by using a buddy's armpit or abdomen, other areas can be rewarmed by immersing in warm water. Do not rub or massage affected areas. Frostbite requires professional medical attention as soon as possible.

Deep Frostbite

Deep frostbite is a medical emergency that affects the entire tissue layer. The skin feels hard and is white to blue in appearance. The purpose of first aid is to protect the affected area from further damage, to thaw the affected area, and to monitor the airway, breathing, and circulation. Move the casualty to a warm area.

Rewarm affected areas-immersing in water at 100 degrees F to 105 degrees F (30 degrees C to 41 degrees C). Gently dry the area with a soft towel, place cotton between the toes and fingers to avoid their sticking together. Do not rub or massage affected areas. Frostbite requires professional medical attention as soon as possible. Do not allow the affected area to be exposed to the cold.

Medical Emergencies

Medical emergencies are defined as an unexpected or sudden occasion; an accident; an urgent or pressing need.

Fainting

Fainting, also known as syncope is a temporary loss of consciousness. It is the result of blood pooling in large (dilated) veins, which reduces the amount of blood being pumped to the brain. Causes include getting up too fast, standing for long periods with little movement, and stressful situations. Fainting also may result from an underlying medical problem such as diabetes, stroke, or heart problems. Signs and symptoms of fainting include:

- Dizziness, nausea, and visual problems.
- Sweating, paleness, weakness, and rapid pulse.

As the body collapses, blood returns to the head and consciousness is quickly regained. If the casualty has fainted, do the following:

- Perform an initial assessment.
- Place the casualty on his or her back, with legs elevated 6 to 12 inches. Do not allow casualty to sit up.
- Monitor the airway, breathing, and circulation (ABCs).
- Loosen restrictive clothing, at the neck, waist, and chest.
- Check the casualty for injuries suffered during the fall.
- Request medical assistance for fainting as needed.

Chest Injuries

All chest injuries must be considered serious, because they can cause difficulty breathing (dyspnea) and severe bleeding. Any casualty complaining of difficulty breathing without signs of an airway obstruction must be examined for either an open or closed chest injury. The most serious chest wound that requires immediate first aid is a sucking chest wound (Open Pneumothorax). This is a penetrating injury that makes a hole in the chest cavity, causing the lung to collapse, which prevents normal breathing. This condition is a medical emergency that will result in death if not treated quickly. Signs and symptoms of a sucking chest wound include:

- Difficulty breathing and sharp chest pain.
- Bluish skin color and anxiety.

If the casualty has a sucking chest wound, do the following:
- Immediately seal the wound with your hand or any airtight (I. D. Card) material available. The material must be large enough so that it will not be sucked into the wound when the casualty breaths.
- Firmly tape the material in place with adhesive tape leaving one corner untaped to prevent a pressure buildup. The purpose of the dressing is to keep air from going in through the wound. If the casualty's condition deteriorates, remove the seal immediately.
- Lay the casualty on his or her affected side.
- Treat for shock -Place the casualty in a semi-sitting position, to help them breath easier.
- Do not give the casualty anything to eat or drink. If the casualty complains of thirst, wet his or her lips with a wet towel.
- Request medical assistance immediately.

Flail Chest

A medical emergency in which two or more ribs are broken, each in at least two places; or a fracture or separation of the ribs from the breastbone producing a free-floating segment. This segment is called the "flail area", its motion is opposite the rest of the chest. The area between the fractures moves in the opposite direction of the rest of the chest during ventilation. This condition can be life-threatening because it may bruise the lung beneath the flail area. The bone ends may also puncture a lung and cause severe bleeding, which can produce shock. It may be difficult to detect a flail chest in an obese or muscular casualty. Signs and symptoms of flail chest include:

- Difficulty breathing that causes severe pain.
- Swelling at site of injury.
- Casualty will splint his/her chest wall with hands and arms.

If the casualty has a flail chest, do the following:
- Establish and maintain the airway, breathing, and circulation (ABC's).
- Gently feel the chest to locate the edges of the flail area.
- Stabilize the flail area with a pad of dressings or a pillow and secure with wide cravats.
- Position the casualty with the flail area against an external object in a semi-sitting position or lying on the injured side.
- Treat for shock.
- Request medical assistance immediately.

Abdominal Injuries

Abdominal injuries are caused by severe blows, gunshots, and stabbings. They can easily become a medical emergency because of the vital organs that may be damaged. Most injuries to the abdomen require surgery to repair the internal damage.

Closed Abdominal Injuries

Closed abdominal injuries are caused by a severe blow or crushing injury, where the skin remains intact. Death is usually caused by bleeding into the abdomen. A complication known as peritonitis, usually the result of a rupture of the intestines, is not seen immediately but develops later and can be fatal. Signs and symptoms of (closed) abdominal injury include:

- Intense pain, nausea, vomiting, and spasm of the abdominal muscle.
- Tenderness, distention, muscle rigidity, and shock.

- Casualty lies with legs pulled up, protecting the abdomen.

If the casualty has a (closed) abdominal injury, do the following:
- Establish and maintain the airway, breathing, and circulation (ABC's).
- Place casualty in the most comfortable position.
- Carefully remove enough clothing to get a clear idea of the extent of the injuries.
- Treat for shock.
- Give nothing by mouth.
- Request medical assistance immediately.

Open Abdominal Injuries

Open abdominal injuries are caused by gunshots, stabbings, and penetrating wounds where the skin is broken. Always suspect that damage has occurred to internal organs, even if signs and symptoms are not immediately present. Extensive lacerations may allow some of the internal organs to stick out, a condition known as evisceration. Signs and symptoms of (open) abdominal injury include:

- Signs and symptoms of (closed) abdominal injury.
- Lacerations, puncture wounds, and vomiting blood.
- Back pain (kidney damage).

If the casualty has an (open) abdominal injury, do the following:
- Establish and maintain the airway, breathing, and circulation (ABC's).
- Carefully remove enough clothing to get a clear idea of the extent of the injuries.
- Place casualty in the most comfortable position.
- Treat for shock.
- Control bleeding and apply a dry sterile dressing.
  - If organs are sticking out (protruding), do not touch or replace them. Apply a sterile compress, moistened with sterile water. If sterile water is not available, use clean drinking water. Do not use material that clings, such as paper towels, cotton, or toilet paper. Apply aluminum foil or plastic wrap over the compress keeping the area moist and warm. Hold the compress in place with a bandage, do not apply more pressure than is necessary to hold the bandage.
- Give nothing by mouth.
- Request medical assistance immediately.

Diabetic Emergencies

Diabetes also known as diabetes mellitus, is a disease that impairs the ability of the body to use sugar and causes sugar to appear abnormally in the urine. The two basic types of diabetes are:

Type I:	Insulin-dependent (juvenile), usually begins in childhood, controlled by daily insulin injections.
Type II:	Noninsulin-dependent (adult-onset), begins in adulthood, controlled by diet or oral medication. Sometimes insulin injections are required.

Diabetic Coma

Diabetic coma, also known as hyperglycemia, is a condition in which the body does not have enough insulin and has too much sugar. Causes include stress, not enough insulin injections, and eating too much sugar. Signs and symptoms of diabetic coma include:

- Fruity odor on breath and very thirsty.
- Dizziness, drowsiness, and confusion.

- Rapid, weak pulse and rapid breathing.
- Nausea, vomiting, and abdominal pain.

If you suspect diabetic coma, do the following:
- Establish and maintain the airway, breathing, and circulation (ABCs).
- Lay casualty flat, slightly elevating the head and shoulders.
- Do not give the casualty candy or soft drinks.
- Treat for shock.
- Request medical assistance immediately.

Insulin Shock

Insulin shock, also known as hypoglycemia, is a condition in which the body does not have enough sugar and has too much insulin. Causes include skipping meals, too much insulin, strenuous exercise, and changes in diet. Signs and symptoms of insulin shock include:

- Headache, dizziness, and irritability.
- Pale, moist skin, and excessive sweating.
- Muscle weakness, hunger, and normal to rapid pulse.

If you suspect insulin shock, do the following:
- Ask casualty or family member these two questions.
  - Has the casualty eaten today?
  - Has the casualty taken his or her insulin?

If the answer is "yes" to the first question and "no" to the second, the casualty is probably in a diabetic coma.
- Establish and maintain the airway, breathing, and circulation (ABC's).
- Lay casualty flat, slightly elevating the head and shoulders.
- Give the conscious casualty candy or soft drinks to increase blood sugar level.
- Treat for shock
- Request medical assistance immediately.

Stroke

Stroke, also known as cerebrovascular accident, is a condition in which one or more of the blood vessels to the brain become blocked or rupture, causing part of the brain to die of lack of oxygen. Causes include arteries blocked by a clot (thrombus), ruptured blood vessels (hemorrhage) in the brain, or a clot that travels (embolus) to the brain from another part of the body. Signs and symptoms of stroke include:

- Onset is sudden, with little or no warning.
- Weakness or paralysis of one side of the body.
- Loss of facial expression and drooping mouth on one side.
- Double vision, stuttering, and severe headache.
- Difficulty speaking, and understanding speech.
- Unequal pupils, nausea, and vomiting.

If you suspect a stroke, do the following:
- Lay casualty flat, slightly elevating the head and shoulders.
- Establish and maintain the airway, breathing, and circulation (ABCs).
- Keep the casualty quiet and warm.
- Give nothing by mouth.
- Request medical assistance immediately.

Heart Attack

Heart attack, also known as myocardial infarction, is a condition in which blood flow to part of the heart is blocked, causing that part of the heart muscle to die of lack of oxygen. Most heart attacks are caused by cardiovascular disease. Risk factors are things that are related to getting cardiovascular disease. Casualties may deny that they are having a heart attack. Suspect heart attack in adults with chest pain until proven otherwise.

- Risk factors that you cannot change:
  - Heredity (family history of cardiovascular disease)
  - Sex (males have a greater risk)
  - Age

- Risk factors that you can change:
  - Smoking
  - High blood pressure
  - High blood cholesterol
  - Obesity
  - Lack of exercise
  - Stress
  - Uncontrolled diabetes

Signs and symptoms of a heart attack include:

- Severe, under the breastbone (substernal) chest pain (crushing, squeezing, or like somebody is standing on my chest).
- May spread to the jaw, shoulders, arms, neck, or back.
- Difficulty breathing.
- Pale, moist skin, and excessive sweating.
- Anxiety, nausea, and vomiting.
- Weakness and light-headed.

If you suspect a heart attack, do the following:
- Establish and maintain the airway, breathing, and circulation (ABCs).
- Place the casualty in the most comfortable (sitting or semi-sitting) position.
- Keep the casualty quiet, and warm.
- Loosen restrictive clothing, at the neck, waist, and chest.
- Be prepared to give CPR.
- Request medical assistance immediately.

Seizures

Seizures, also known as convulsions, are a twisting of the body caused by violent, involuntary muscle contractions. Causes include epilepsy, head injury, infection, disease, and fever. The casualty will be drowsy and disoriented after the seizure. Signs and symptoms of a seizure include:

- A sensation or feeling (aura) usually visual, sound, taste, or smell).
- Crying out or moan from casualty.
- Partial or total loss of consciousness and muscle rigidity.
- Jerking (spasm) of the arms and legs.
- Frothing from the mouth.
- Possible loss of bowel and bladder function.

If the casualty has a seizure, do the following:

- Lay the casualty flat, protecting him or her from injury.
- Move all objects out of the way to prevent further injuries.
- Don't force anything between the teeth or restrain the casualty in any way.
- Loosen restrictive clothing, at the neck, waist, and chest.
- Calm and reassure the casualty.
- Establish and maintain the airway, breathing, and circulation (ABC's).
- Give nothing by mouth.
- Request medical assistance immediately.

Alcohol Intoxication

Alcohol is the most widely used and abused drug today. Alcohol intoxication, also known as drunkenness, is so common that it fails to receive the attention and respect it deserves. Ethyl alcohol (ethanol), is the primary ingredient in wine, beer, and liquor. Ethanol is classified as a drug because it depresses the central nervous system, affecting physical and mental activities. Alcohol is addictive. What starts out as social drinking may, and frequently does, result in alcoholism.

Alcohol affects the body in stages. First, there is a feeling of relaxation and well-being, followed by a gradual disruption of coordination, resulting in an inability to accurately and efficiently perform normal duties and activities. Continued drinking depresses body functions enough to cause difficulty breathing, loss of consciousness, coma, and death. Withdrawal from alcohol can result in delirium tremens (DTs), identified by anxiety, confusion, restless sleep, nausea, vomiting, depression, hallucinations, and seizures. If you choose to drink, do so in moderation. If you can't control your drinking, get help before it's too late. Signs and symptoms of alcohol intoxication include:

- Smell of alcohol on breath.
- Staggering, loss of balance, and slurred speech.
- Nausea, vomiting, and flushed face.

These signs and symptoms may indicate an illness or injury (e. g. diabetes, head injury) other than alcohol abuse. If you suspect alcohol intoxication, do the following:

- Sit or lay the casualty down, protecting him or her from further injury.
- Establish and maintain the airway, breathing, and circulation (ABCs).
- Perform an initial assessment.
- Observe closely, casualty may become unconscious.
- Don't criticize, be firm with casualty.
- Never leave an intoxicated casualty alone.
- Request medical assistance as soon as possible.

Psychiatric Emergencies

A psychiatric emergency is a sudden onset of behavioral or emotional responses that, if not responded to, may result in a life-threatening situation. Probably the most common is the suicide attempt. This may range from verbal threats and suicide gestures to successful suicide. Always assume that a suicide threat is real, do not leave the individual alone. In all cases, the main consideration is to keep them from inflicting harm to themselves and getting them under the care of a medical professional.

Drowning

Drowning is suffocation by immersion in water or other liquid. Causes include diving accidents, drinking alcohol prior to or during swimming, getting trapped under the water, and becoming exhausted while swimming. Fluid rarely enters the lungs because upon contact with fluid, spasms of the windpipe occur which seal the airway from the mouth and nose. If a drowning has occurred, do the following:

- Reach the casualty without putting yourself in danger.
- Establish and maintain the airway, begin mouth-to-mouth or mouth-to-nose breathing while in the water.
- Don't remove the casualty from the water until a backboard or other rigid device is available.
- Maintain a neutral position of the head and neck, apply a cervical collar or improvised (towel) collar.
- Be prepared to give CPR.

After removal from the water.
- Keep the casualty warm enough to maintain normal body temperature.
- Request medical assistance immediately.

An apparently lifeless casualty who has been in cold water for a long period of time may still be revived with rescue breathing. The body reduces the need for oxygen and protects the vital organs in water below 68 degrees F.

The Trauma Kit

It is not always possible to respond to a medical emergency with all the equipment necessary to treat every type of injury or illness. It is not expected that a layperson such as an EPO will have access to some of the more exotic equipment, such as defibrillators, but the more common supplies should be readily and available. As with all medication, sprays, disinfectants, and ointments, keep away from children and be aware of the expiration date. A well-stocked emergency medical kit should include, as a minimum requirement, the following:

The trauma kit should contain the following items:

- Multitrauma dressing (12" x 30")
- CPR mask
- Sterile burn dressing
- Triangular bandage
- Extrication collar
- Gauze (4" x 4")
- Sterile water for sterilization and rinsing
- Paramedic scissors
- Blankets
- Adhesive tape
- Oval eye pads
- Sterile alcohol wipes
- Instant ice pack
- Gauze bandage
- Sterile gloves
- Vaseline gauze (5" x 9")
- Stabilizing splints (full leg and full arm)
- Oxygen tank
- Wound disinfectant

Remember:

Emergency medical training needs of an EPO are as essential as all the rest of specialized training. Medical personnel will not always be readily available, the non-medical EPO will have to rely heavily on the own skills and knowledge of life-sustaining methods to assist the ones under his/her protection to surviv. First aid measures are for all life-threatening situations and intended for both, self-treatment and aid to others. More importantly, it is the prompt and effective action in sustaining life and preventing or minimizing further suffering. First aid is the emergency care given to the sick, injured and/or wounded before they can be treated by medical personnel.

First aid is defined as "urgent and immediate lifesaving and other measures which can be performed for casualties by nonmedical personnel when medical personnel are not immediately available." Nonmedical personnel, including EPOs must have received basic first aid training and should remain skilled in the correct procedures for giving first aid. The next step is to qualify as medical personnel-Paramedic. Paramedics are trained to provide a more complex emergency care.

Legal Status

- **Public and Private Sector Cooperation**

- **Regulations for Private Security Sector**

- **Article 25**

- **Private Security Services Code**

- **Private Security Act 2004**

- **International and Regional Regulations**

According to a report produced by *Ohlhausen Research*,[33] based on the 2004, *National Policy Summit*, the law enforcement agencies, since September 11, 2001 has been under tremendous pressure to conduct their traditional crime prevention and response activities. In addition a large quantum of homeland security work, in a time of tight city, county and state budgets was added. Private security organizations have been under similar pressure to perform their traditional activities to protect people, property and information. Adding their contribution to the nationwide effort to protect the homeland from external and internal threats, all while minding the profitability of the businesses they serve.

Despite their similar interests in protecting the people of the United States, the two fields have rarely collaborated. In fact, through the practice of community policing, law enforcement agencies have collaborated extensively with practically every group but private security. By some estimates, 85 percent of the country's critical infrastructure is protected by private security. The need for complex coordination, extra staffing, and special resources after a terror attack, coupled with the significant demands of crime prevention and response, absolutely requires boosting the level of partnership between public policing and private security.

Public and Private Sector Cooperation

In the interest of both, private and public sector need to work together. For example, law enforcement agencies can prepare private security to assist in emergencies (in many cases, security officers are the first responders) and coordinate efforts to safeguard critical infrastructure. A vast majority of which is owned by the private sector or protected by the private security industry. They could obtain free training and services and gaining additional personnel resources and expertise, benefiting from private sector knowledge specialization (in cyber crime, loss prevention, close protection) and its advanced technology. Gathering better knowledge of incidents (through reporting by security staff) and obtain intelligence, reducing the number of calls for service. Private security also has much to gain from this cooperation. Coordinating plans with the public sector, in advance, regarding evacuation, transportation, food and other emergency issues. Gaining information from law enforcement regarding threats and crime trends. Developing relationships, so that practitioners know whom to contact when they need help or want to report information. Building a law enforcement's understanding of corporate needs (such as confidentiality) and boosting law enforcement's respect for the security field. Currently, the public and private cooperation takes many forms, ranging from local-level, national-level to perhaps international-level in the future. Based on the summit participants, only 5-10 percent of law enforcement chief executives are actually participating in partnerships with the private security sector. The on emergency response exercises, which tend to include police, fire, public health and other governmental authorities, but leaving out the private security sector.

Law enforcement's capacity to provide (homeland) security may be more limited than is generally acknowledged. For the most part, the public sector tends to have the threat information, while the private sector tends to have control over the vulnerable sites. Therefore (homeland) security, including protection of the critical infrastructure, depends partly on the competence of private security practitioners. Thus, building partnerships is essential for effective (homeland) security. Other factors increase the importance of public and private cooperation. Examples include computer-and high-tech crimes, private security in traditional law enforcement roles, the globalization of business, increased international operation by law enforcement and the interdependence of critical infrastructures.

There are certain similarities of law enforcement (public) and executive protection (private) and the general security industry, which provides a sound foundation for a cooperation of both sectors. While the private sector has developed executive protection and protection of individuals into a highly professional business, EPOs unfortunately do still not benefit from a legal status as their counterparts with similar post in government agencies. Government agents have a peace-officer status and therefore also the power to arrest-EPOs in the private sector do not have that or similar power and have to refrain from making arrests. (Exceptions might be applied, but depend highly on existing laws in each country, especially if and where a "Citizen's arrest" law is practiced).

Law enforcement is by law and definition a confrontational force; executive protection and the security sector in general is a nonconfrontational force, not by definition but by effectiveness. While law enforcement is reactive in their actions to serve and protect, executive protection is operating overtly, preventing and deterring in order to protect. The EPO's only obligation is a moral and legal responsibility to report any violation to a police agency.

The EPO, even working side by side with the police and many times depending on the law enforcement support, the EPO is operating without any official mandate or full authority. Without the cooperation of the law enforcement or any other authority, the job of the EPO can be a nightmare and a challenging demonstration of all tricks and abilities. For instance-organizing and escorting a motorcade on a highway (looks great and easy in movies-in real life it can be a pain). Another example-trying to park a full motorcade at locations, which, for the average citizen is already impossible.

In certain areas for example, the executive protection profession is not even regulated by law or is covered under the general category "Security Guard". In other areas, executive protection is regulated by special laws, which permit a person to operate as an EPO only if he/she can provide evidence of a previous experience in law enforcement.

Regulations for Private Security Sector

Most U. S. states and counties require a license to work as a security guard, although 10 states require no licensing. Of the licensing states, 19 do not require any training and many have minimal training requirements. This license may include a criminal background check and/or training requirements. Most security guards do not carry weapons and have the same powers of arrest as a private citizen, called a "private person" arrest, "any person" arrest, or "citizen's arrest." If weapons are carried, additional permits and training are usually required. Normally armed security guards are used (in the USA) to protect sensitive sites such as government and military installations, banks or other financial institutions, and nuclear power plants. However, armed security is quickly becoming a standard for vehicle patrol officers and on many other non-government sites. Armed private security is very rare in many European and other countries. In conflict areas and war-torn countries, armed security is often composed of former military personnel and used to protect corporate and other sensitive assets. In British Columbia, Canada contract security guards are not armed. They are not permitted to carry a firearm and/or any other type of defensive weapon. They are not even allowed to carry handcuffs or other restraint devices-"In-House" security personnel however is not restricted in regards to handcuffs or restraint devices. As a requirement of the Private Security Industry Act 2001, the U. K. now requires all contract security guards to have a valid SIA (Security Industry Authority) license. Licenses are valid for three years and require the holders to undergo formal training, also to pass mandatory Criminal Records Bureau checks. In Canada for example, private security falls under the jurisdiction of Canada's ten provinces. The laws in all provinces require that contract security companies and their employees be licensed. The requirements for licensing vary but many provinces require that security guards either successfully complete a training program before being issued a license or have previous experience as a peace officer (I. e. a police officer). In British Columbia contract Security Businesses, and Employees must be licensed, while "In-House" security organizations and employees are exempt from Provincial Legislation. The following examples of California, Virginia (USA) and Victoria (Australia) should provide a brief look at the requirements and regulations an EPO might have to deal with when applying for a local license, or a temporary license abroad:

- Article 25: Regulations For Private Protection and Security Services
- Private Security Services Code
- Private Security Act 2004

Article 25-Regulations For Private Protection and Security Services
(City and County of San Francisco, U.S.A.)

Sec. 1750. Registration of Fixed Patrols, Street Patrols and Private Watchman.

Unless registered as hereinafter provided, it shall be unlawful for any person, either for himself or for any other person, firm or corporation, to manage, conduct or carry on the business of a fixed patrol, street patrol, or serve as a private watchman service in the City and County of San Francisco, or willfully to hire the services of a private watchman, fixed patrol, or street patrol, unless said private watchman, fixed patrol, or street patrol is registered as hereinafter defined. (Added by Ord. 312-72, App. 11/2/72)

Sec. 1750.1. Fixed Patrol Defined.

For the purpose of this Article, the term "Fixed Patrol" shall mean a person, firm or corporation licensed by the State of California, who or which agrees to furnish, or furnishes, a watchman, guard, patrolman or other person to protect persons or property or to prevent theft, unlawful taking, loss, embezzlement, misappropriation or concealment of any goods, wares, merchandise, money, bonds, stocks, notes, documents, papers or property of any kind, remains at a fixed location and does not utilize the public streets during the course and scope of such employment, except for incidental use of the streets by a fixed patrol operator, or his employee, solely for the purpose of traveling from one location owned or operated by a client to another location owned or operated by the same client, or for the purpose of supervising employees of a fixed patrol operator, or for incidental use of the streets reasonably necessary to accomplish the purpose of the fixed patrol service. (Added by Ord. 312-72, App. 11/2/72)

Sec. 1750.2. Street Patrol Defined.

For the purpose of this Article the term "Street Patrol" shall mean any person, firm or corporation who furnishes or agrees to furnish, for any consideration whatsoever, any of the services enumerated in Section 1750.1 of this Article and utilizes the public streets to perform such services and is licensed by the State of California to perform such services or is employed by a person so licensed. (Added by Ord. 312-72, App. 11/2/72)

Sec. 1750.3. Private Watchman Defined.

For the purpose of this Article the term "Private Watchman" shall mean a person who is appointed a Special Police Officer pursuant to the provisions of Section 3.535 of the Chapter, and is directly employed by one person, firm or corporation to perform any of the services enumerated in Section 1750.1 of this Article, and who shall, in the performance of his duties, remain on or immediately adjacent to the property of his employer. (Added by Ord. 312-72, App. 11/2/72)

Sec. 1750.3.1. Person.

For the purpose of this Article the term "Person" shall mean any individual, corporation, co-partnership, firm, association, joint stock company or combination of individuals of whatever form or character acting as a unit. (Added by Ord. 312-72, App. 11/2/72)

Sec. 1750.4. Method of Registration of Street Patrol and Fixed Patrol Services.

Persons required to register by Sections 1750.6 and 1750.7 of this Article for Street Patrol or Fixed Patrol Services shall do so with the Chief of Police on application forms provided therefore. The application shall be verified and shall contain the following information:

(a) The true name and address of the applicant and of all persons financially interested in the operation of the fixed patrol or street patrol business.
(b) The date, place of birth and citizenship of all such persons.
(c) The past criminal record, if any, of all such persons.
(d) The fingerprints of all such persons.
(e) The area of the City and County of San Francisco, or the portion thereof, in which the applicant proposes to provide street patrol service.
(f) The number and description of motor vehicles proposed to be used by applicant.
(g) The description and serial number of the firearms to be used by applicant and his employees.
(h) Proof of insurance coverage as provided in Section 1750.14 of this Article.
(i) Whether the applicant requests a street patrol registration, a fixed patrol, or private watchman registration.
(j) If the applicant is a corporation, the application shall set forth the name of the corporation exactly as shown in its articles of incorporation; the names and residence addresses of each of the officers, directors, and each stockholder owning more than 10 percent of the stock of the corporation. If the applicant is a partnership, the application shall set forth the name and residence address of each of the partners, including limited partners. If one or more of the partners is a corporation, the provisions of this Section pertaining to a corporate applicant shall apply.
(k) Subsection (d) of this Section shall not apply to any of the following:
   1) A corporation, the stock of which is listed on a stock exchange in the State of California or in the City of New York, State of New York.
   2) A bank, trust company, financial institution, or title company to which application is made or to whom a license is issued in a fiduciary capacity.
   3) A corporation which is required by law to file periodic reports with the Securities and Exchange Commission.

Upon receipt of an application, the Chief of Police shall conduct such investigation as he may deem necessary and proper as to the character and morals of the applicant and persons financially interested in the fixed patrol service or street patrol service for which registration is sought and as to the proposed territory of the City and County of San Francisco, or portions thereof, within which the street patrol service is to be conducted. (Added by Ord. 312-72, App. 11/2/72)

Sec. 1750.5. Review of Registration Application.

The Chief of Police may refuse registration if it is found that the applicant or any person financially interested in the operation of the fixed patrol business or street patrol business is a person of bad moral character. For this purpose the Chief of Police may, in his discretion, consider any facts or evidence which he believes is relevant and will reflect on the moral fitness and reputation of those who will be in charge of such fixed patrol or street patrol business. Should the Chief of Police refuse registration, the applicant for a street patrol business or private patrol business may appeal in the same manner as provided for revocation in Section 1750.12 of this Article. Upon granting the registration application, the Chief of Police, or the Police Commission on appeal, shall designate the portion or portions of the City and County of San Francisco within which such street patrol business may be carried on, and shall specify therein such other reasonable additional requirements imposed upon applicant as are necessary to meet local needs and are not inconsistent with the provisions of the California Business and Professions Code; provided, however, that no person shall be allowed to register as a fixed patrol business or a street patrol business who is not licensed under the provisions of said Code. Such registration shall be disapproved where the territory sought has been allocated to a patrol special officer appointed pursuant to Section 3.536 of the Charter of the City and County of San Francisco; provided, however, such patrol special officer shall not be licensed as a fixed patrol operator. (Added by Ord. 312-72, App. 11/2/72)

Sec. 1750.6. Registration of Employees of Street Patrol Business.

Upon granting the registration application, the registrant shall furnish the Chief of Police with the names of those who are or will be engaged in street patrol, on a form provided therefore. The form shall contain the following information:

(a) The true name and address of the employee.
(b) The date of birth and citizenship of such person.
(c) The past criminal record, if any, of such person as stated by the employee, including a signed statement of the employee that the information in (a), (b) and (c) is true and correct.
(d) The fingerprints of such person.
(e) The serial number and description of each firearm owned by such employee and carried in the course and scope of his duties.
(f) Such other information as may be deemed relevant by the Chief of Police or Police Commission.
(g) Recent photograph of such employee.

Upon receipt of the names of the employees who will be engaged in street patrol service, the Chief of Police shall conduct such investigation as he may deem necessary and proper as to the character and morals of the employee. Should the Chief of Police, after a noticed hearing, find that the character and morals of such employee are such as to constitute a danger to the public if said employee were to be utilized in street patrol services, the registrant shall not thereafter utilize such employee for street patrol service. Any applicant for registration under this Section who is dissatisfied with the decision of the Chief of Police may file an appeal with the Secretary of the Police Commission within five days. The Police Commission shall thereupon fix a date for hearing the appeal which date shall not be more than 10 days from the date of filing said appeal. The Police Commission may affirm, modify or reverse the decision of the Chief of Police. (Added by Ord. 312-72, App. 11/2/72)

Sec. 1750.7. Registration of Employees of Fixed Patrol Business.

Upon granting the registration application, the Chief of Police shall require the registrant to furnish the names of employees of the registrant who are or will be engaged in fixed patrol on a form provided therefore and shall contain the same information as required in Section 1750.6 of this Article. Upon receipt of the names of the employees who will engage in fixed patrol services, the Chief of Police shall conduct such investigation as he may deem necessary and proper as to the character and morals of the employee. Should the Chief of Police, after a duly noticed hearing, find that the character and morals of such employee would constitute a danger to the public if said employee were to be utilized in fixed patrol services, the registrant shall not thereafter utilize such employee for fixed patrol service. Any applicant for registration as a fixed patrol employee who is dissatisfied with the decision of the Chief of Police may appeal as provided in Section 1750.6 of this Article. A fixed patrol business registered under this Article may utilize an employee without complying with Section 1750.7 of this Article for a period not exceeding two weeks where, because of any event described in Section 409.5 of the Penal Code of the State of California or because of an extensive public gathering, the services required of the fixed patrol business cannot be performed without an immediate increase of personnel. Such fixed patrol business shall, not later than completion of the employee's first tour of duty, notify the Chief of Police in writing of the names of the employees so utilized and justification of their use without complying with Section 1750.7 of this Article. (Added by Ord. 312-72, App. 11/2/72)

Sec. 1750.8. Registration of Private Watchman.

Private Watchman as defined in Section 1750.3 of this Article shall register with the Chief of Police and shall furnish the Chief of Police, in writing, the name, address and telephone number of his employer and his hours of duty. Each private watchman shall immediately notify the Chief of Police, in writing, of the termination of his employment. No person, firm, corporation or partnership shall hire a private watchman unless such watchman is appointed by the Chief of Police under authority of Section 3.535 of the Charter. (Added by Ord. 312-72, App. 11/2/72)

Sec. 1750.9. Issuance of Identification Card.

Should the Chief of Police or Police Commission have no objection to the employment of an employee of a street patrol business, a fixed patrol business, or as a private watchman, the Chief of Police shall furnish the employer within 15 calendar days of approval of the application, Sundays and holidays excluded, an employee's identification card, which shall contain a photograph of the employee, with the registration number in figures plainly discernible. The Chief of Police shall determine the manner and form of any other information that may be placed upon such identification card, which must be in the possession of the employee at all times during his hours of employment, and shall be produced for inspection upon request of the Chief of Police or his duly authorized representative. (Added by Ord. 312-72, App. 11/2/72)

Sec. 1750.10. Notice of Termination of Employee.

The registrant, within 10 days after the termination of any employee engaged in street patrol services or fixed patrol services, shall notify the Chief of Police in writing of such termination and the employee shall immediately deliver his identification card to the Chief of Police. (Added by Ord. 312-72, App. 11/2/72)

Sec. 1750.11. Use of Police or Sheriff Titles and Similar Subterfuges.

No person shall, in connection with the operation of a fixed patrol business, street patrol business, or any private watchman, either as a registrant or employee:

(a) Titles. Knowingly use the title, "S. F. Police Officer," "Police Officer," "Special Police or Special Officer," "Sheriff," "Deputy Sheriff," or any other title or designation whatever, which is calculated to indicate an official connection with the Police Department or Sheriff's Office of the City and County of San Francisco, or with the police force of any other government or governmental agency.

(b) Operation. Knowingly represent himself, or falsely represent another, to be a member of the Police Department or the Sheriff's Office of the City and County of San Francisco or use any sign, word, language or device, which is calculated to induce a false or mistaken belief that he is acting or purporting to act on behalf of said department or office of the City and County within the scope or any real or purported duty thereof.

(c) Collections. Knowingly use any sign, badge, title or designation, or make any express or implied representation, which is calculated to induce the belief that he is a member of the Police Department or the Sheriff's Office of the City and County, or connected therewith in any way, in connection with any activity directed toward the collection of any money or debt, or the repossession, recovery or taking of anything of value, or for any purpose of private gain whatsoever.

(d) Uniforms. Knowingly wear any uniform designed to resemble so closely the uniform worn by the Police Department, Sheriff's Office or the California Highway Patrol as reasonably to induce the belief that he represents or is employed by the Police Department, the Sheriff's Office or the California Highway Patrol.

(e) Vehicles. Knowingly use any vehicle which is colored or has affixed thereon any sign, badge, title or device that would reasonably induce the belief said vehicle was being operated by the Police Department, Sheriff's Office, California Highway Patrol, or any agency or local, State or Federal government. (Added by Ord. 312-72, App. 11/2/72)

Sec. 1750.12. Revocation or Refusal of Registration.

The Chief of Police may revoke any registration issued hereunder after a notice of hearing when the applicant or registrant is in violation of any of the provisions of this Article, or of the Business and Professions Code of the State of California, or any rules promulgated by the Chief of Police regulating fixed patrol business, street patrol business or private watchmen. In the event that any registration is revoked, or is refused by the Chief of Police, an appeal may be filed with the Police Commission within 30 days after date of said decision. Notice of said revocation or refusal shall be served upon the registrant or applicant by depositing a true copy thereof, with postage fully paid, in the United States mail addressed to the registrant at his last known address, within three days from the date of action of the Chief of Police. Any appeal must be in writing filed with the Secretary of the Police Commission and served personally or by mail upon the Chief of Police, or his duly authorized representative appointed for said purpose, by the registrant or applicant.

The Police Commission shall by resolution fix a date for hearing said appeal and designate the time and place where such hearing is to be held, which date shall be not more than 14 days from the date of the filing of the appeal. The Secretary of the Police Commission shall give notice of said hearing to the registrant or applicant in the same manner as required for notice of revocation or refusal of registration, but not less than 10 days prior to the date of said hearing. The registrant so notified of the revocation hearing may continue to operate the fixed patrol or street patrol business pending the revocation hearing before the Police Commission, unless in the judgment of the Chief of Police such operation would adversely affect the public interest, in which event the order of the Chief of Police will be effective five days from the date of service of such order.

At any such hearing, the registrant or applicant shall be given the opportunity to defend himself, and may call witnesses, be represented by counsel and present evidence in his behalf. The Chief of Police or his representative shall attend the hearing. It shall require a majority vote of the membership of the Police Commission to overrule the decision of the Chief of Police. (Added by Ord. 312-72, App. 11/2/72)

Sec. 1750.13. Matters to be considered by Chief of Police.

The Chief of Police may disregard any conviction for which the applicant was required to register pursuant to Section 290 of the Penal Code of the State of California if he finds that the applicant has fully completed any sentence imposed because of such conviction and complied with any conditions imposed because of such conviction, that the completion of said sentence, probation, parole, or any conditions whatsoever as a result of such conviction, has occurred at least three years prior to the date of application and that the applicant has not subsequently been convicted of any of the crimes herein mentioned or suffered any subsequent felony convictions of any nature whatsoever. (Added by Ord. 312-72, App. 11/2/72)

Sec. 1750.14. Insurance Coverage.

The applicant, prior to registering as a fixed patrol business, or a street patrol business, or any firm, person, partnership or corporation hiring more than two private watchmen as defined in Section 1750.3 of this Article, must present evidence of insurance in the following amounts:

1) Workmen's Compensation and Employers' Liability Insurance to cover the applicant's employees, as required by the Labor Code of the State of California.
2) Comprehensive bodily injury and property damage liability insurance, including automobile liability and including liability for assault and battery, false arrest, false imprisonment, malicious prosecution, libel and slander, and invasion of privacy. This insurance shall provide limits of liability of not less than $ 200, 000 for injury to each person and $300,000 for each occurrence and $ 50, 000 for property damage. Any comprehensive bodily injury and property damage liability insurance policy or policies shall include the City and County of San Francisco, its officers and employees as an additional named insured, in the event any person shall charge or allege that the City and County of San Francisco, its officers or employees are liable or responsible for any act or conduct of the fixed or street patrol business whether by respondent superior or any other legal theory, and shall contain the following endorsement:
"Not withstanding any other provision in this policy, the insurance afforded hereunder to the City of San Francisco shall be primary as to any other insurance or reinsurance covering or available to the City of San Francisco, and such other insurance or reinsurance shall not be required to contribute to any liability or loss until and unless the appropriate limit of liability afforded hereunder is exhausted."

Each of said policies of insurance shall contain a clause substantially in the following words: "It is hereby understood and agreed that this policy may not be canceled, nor the amount of the coverage reduced, until ten days after receipt by the City Attorney of the City and County of San Francisco of a written notice of such cancellation or reduction of coverage, as evidenced by receipt of a registered letter." All certificates of insurance must be approved as to form by the City Attorney of the City of San Francisco. (Added by Ord. 312-72, App. 11/2/72)

Sec. 1750.15. Registration Fee.

Every person, firm, or corporation registering as a fixed patrol business or as a street patrol business shall pay to the Tax Collector a registration fee of $100 annually, payable in advance. The registration fee prescribed in this Article is due and payable on a yearly basis, starting January 1, 1973. Fees for new registrations issued after the first day of January, 1973, or in any subsequent calendar year, shall be prorated with regard to the calendar year on a monthly basis. For each employee registered, a fee of $6 shall be paid to the San Francisco Police Department to cover costs of investigation; provided, however, that the Chief of Police may waive the provisions of Sections 1750.6 and 1750.7, of this Article for employees previously registered. (Added by Ord. 312-72, App. 11/2/72)

Sec. 1750.16. Exemptions.

This Article does not apply to private investigators as defined in Section 7521(a) of the Business and Professions Code of the State of California, to insurance adjusters as defined in Section 7521(d) of the Business and Professions Code of the State of California, or to repossessors as defined in Section 7521(e) of the Business and Professions Code of the State of California. (Added by Ord. 31-272, App. 11/2/72)

Sec. 1750.17. Severability.

If any section, subsection, subdivision, paragraph, sentence, clause, or phrase of this Article or any part thereof, is for any reason held to be unconstitutional or invalid or ineffective by any court of competent jurisdiction, such decision shall not affect the validity or effectiveness of the remaining portions of this Article or any part thereof. The Board of Supervisors hereby declares that it would have passed each section, subsection, subdivision, paragraph, sentence, clause, or phrase thereof irrespective of the fact that any one or more sections, subsections, subdivisions, paragraphs, sentences, clauses, or phrases be declared unconstitutional or invalid or ineffective. (Added by Ord. 312-72, App. 11/2/72)

Sec. 1750.18. Effective Dates.

The provisions of Section 1750 of this Article shall not be effective for 60 days from the effective date of this Article as it relates to registration of a fixed patrol business or street patrol business. (Added by Ord. 312-72, App. 11/2/72)

Sec. 1750.19. Drawing of Handguns.

It shall be unlawful for any armed guard, while in any place in the City and County of San Francisco, to draw or exhibit other than in a holster any handgun except in lawful response to an actual and specific threat to person and/or property. (Added by Ord. 582-81, App. 12/10/81)

Sec. 1750.20. Permitting Drawing of Handguns.

It shall be unlawful for any person, corporation, partnership, or association which employs or utilizes armed guards to require, allow or permit any such guard, while in any place in the City and County of San Francisco, to draw or exhibit other than in a holster any handgun except in lawful response to an actual and specific threat to person and/or property. In any prosecution for violation of this Section proof that such person, corporation, partnership, or association did not, at the time a guard unlawfully drew or exhibited a handgun, have a written rule prohibiting such acts, shall be *prima facie* evidence that such person, corporation, partnership or association required, allowed or permitted such conduct. (Added by Ord. 582-81, App. 12/10/81)

Private Security Services Code (Virginia-USA)
(Relating to Private Security Services, Effective July 1, 2004)

§ 9.1-138. Definitions.

In addition to the definitions set forth in § 9.1-101, as used in this article, unless the context requires a different meaning:

"Alarm respondent"
means an individual who responds to the signal of an alarm for the purpose of detecting an intrusion of the home, business or property of the end user.

"Armed"
means a private security registrant who carries or has immediate access to a firearm in the performance of his duties.

"Armed security officer"
means a natural person employed to (I) safeguard and protect persons and property or (ii) deter theft, loss, or concealment of any tangible or intangible personal property on the premises he is contracted to protect, and who carries or has access to a firearm in the performance of his duties.

"Armored car personnel"
means persons who transport or offer to transport under armed security from one place to another, money, negotiable instruments or other valuables in a specially equipped motor vehicle with a high degree of security and certainty of delivery.

"Business advertising material"
means display advertisements in telephone directories, letterhead, business cards, local newspaper advertising and contracts.

"Central station dispatcher"
means an individual who monitors burglar alarm signal devices, burglar alarms or any other electrical, mechanical or electronic device used (I) to prevent or detect burglary, theft, shoplifting, pilferage or similar losses; (ii) to prevent or detect intrusion; or (iii) primarily to summon aid for other emergencies.

"Certification"
means the method of regulation indicating that qualified persons have met the minimum requirements as private security services training schools, private security services instructors, compliance agents, or certified detector canine handler examiners.

"Compliance agent"
means an individual who owns or is employed by a licensed private security services business to ensure the compliance of the private security services business with this title.

"Courier"
means any armed person who transports or offers to transport from one place to another documents or other papers, negotiable or nonnegotiable instruments, or other small items of value that require expeditious services.

"Detector canine"
means any dog that detects drugs or explosives or both drugs and explosives.

"Detector canine handler"
means any individual who uses a detector canine in the performance of private security duties.

"Detector canine handler examiner"
means any individual who examines the proficiency and reliability of detector canines and detector canine handlers in the detection of drugs or explosives or both drugs and explosives.

"Detector canine team"
means the detector canine handler and his detector canine performing private security duties.

"Electronic security business"
means any person who engages in the business of or undertakes to (I) install, service, maintain, design or consult in the design of any electronic security equipment to an end user; (ii) respond to or cause a response to electronic security equipment for an end user; or (iii) have access to confidential information concerning the design, extent, status, password, contact list, or location of an end user's electronic security equipment.

"Electronic security employee"
means an individual who is employed by an electronic security business in any capacity which may give him access to information concerning the design, extent, status, password, contact list, or location of an end user's electronic security equipment.

"Electronic security equipment"
means (I) electronic or mechanical alarm signaling devices including burglar alarms or holdup alarms used to safeguard and protect persons and property; or (ii) cameras used to detect intrusions, concealment or theft, to safeguard and protect persons and property. This shall not include tags, labels, and other devices that are attached or affixed to items offered for sale, library books, and other protected articles as part of an electronic article surveillance and theft detection and deterrence system.

"Electronic security sales representative"
means an individual who sells electronic security equipment on behalf of an electronic security business to the end user.

"Electronic security technician"
means an individual who installs, services, maintains or repairs electronic security equipment.

"Electronic security technician's assistant"
means an individual who works as a laborer under the supervision of the electronic security technician in the course of his normal duties, but who may not make connections to any electronic security equipment.

"Employed"
means to be in an employer/employee relationship where the employee is providing work in exchange for compensation and the employer directly controls the employee's conduct and pays some taxes on behalf of the employee. The term "employed" shall not be construed to include independent contractors.

"End user"
means any person who purchases or leases electronic security equipment for use in that person's home or business.

"Firearms training verification"
means the verification of successful completion of either initial or retraining requirements for handgun or shotgun training, or both.

"General public"
means individuals who have access to areas open to all and not restricted to any particular class of the community.

"License number"
means the official number issued to a private security services business licensed by the Department.

"Natural person"
means an individual person.

"Personal protection specialist"
means any individual who engages in the duties of providing close protection from bodily harm to any person.

"Private investigator"
means any individual who engages in the business of, or accepts employment to make, investigations to obtain information on (I) crimes or civil wrongs; (ii) the location, disposition, or recovery of stolen property; (iii) the cause of accidents, fires, damages, or injuries to persons or to property; or (iv) evidence to be used before any court, board, officer, or investigative committee.

"Private security services business"
means any person engaged in the business of providing, or who undertakes to provide, armored car personnel, security officers, personal protection specialists, private investigators, couriers, security canine handlers, security canine teams, detector canine handlers, detector canine teams, alarm respondents, central station dispatchers, electronic security employees, electronic security sales representatives or electronic security technicians and their assistants to another person under contract, express or implied.

"Private security services instructor"
means any individual certified by the Department to provide mandated instruction in private security subjects for a certified private security services training school.

"Private security services registrant"
means any qualified individual who has met the requirements under this article to perform the duties of alarm respondent, armored car personnel, central station dispatcher, courier, electronic security sales representative, electronic security technician, electronic security technician's assistant, personal protection specialist, private investigator, security canine handler, detector canine handler, unarmed security officer or armed security officer.

"Private security services training school"
means any person certified by the Department to provide instruction in private security subjects for the training of private security services business personnel in accordance with this article.

"Registration"
means a method of regulation whereby certain personnel employed by a private security services business are required to register with the Department pursuant to this article.

"Registration category"
means any one of the following categories: (I) unarmed security officer and armed security officer/courier, (ii) security canine handler, (iii) armored car personnel, (iv) private investigator, (v) personal protection specialist, (vi) alarm respondent, (vii) central station dispatcher, (viii) electronic security sales representative, (ix) electronic security technician, (x) electronic technician's assistant, or (xi) detector canine handler.

"Security canine"
means a dog that has attended, completed, and been certified as a security canine by a certified security canine handler instructor in accordance with approved Department procedures and certification guidelines. "Security canines" shall not include detector dogs.

"Security canine handler"
means any individual who utilizes his security canine in the performance of private security duties.

"Security canine team"
means the security canine handler and his security canine performing private security duties.

"Supervisor"
means any individual who directly or indirectly supervises registered or certified private security services business personnel.

"Unarmed security officer"
means a natural person who performs the functions of observation, detection, reporting, or

notification of appropriate authorities or designated agents regarding persons or property on the premises he is contracted to protect, and who does not carry or have access to a firearm in the performance of his duties.

§ 9.1-139. Licensing, certification, and registration required; qualifications; temporary licenses.

A. No person shall engage in the private security services business or solicit private security business in the Commonwealth without having obtained a license from the Department. No person shall be issued a private security services business license until a compliance agent is designated in writing on forms provided by the Department. The compliance agent shall ensure the compliance of the private security services business with this article and shall meet the qualifications and perform the duties required by the regulations adopted by the Board. A compliance agent shall have either a minimum of (I) three years of managerial or supervisory experience in a private security services business; with a federal, state or local law-enforcement agency; or in a related field or (ii) five years of experience in a private security services business; with a federal, state or local law-enforcement agency; or in a related field.

B. No person shall act as private security services training school or solicit students for private security training in the Commonwealth without being certified by the Department. No person shall be issued a private security services training school certification until a school director is designated in writing on forms provided by the Department. The school director shall ensure the compliance of the school with the provisions of this article and shall meet the qualifications and perform the duties required by the regulations adopted by the Board.

C. No person shall be employed by a licensed private security services business in the Commonwealth as armored car personnel, courier, armed security officer, detector canine handler, unarmed security officer, security canine handler, private investigator, personal protection specialist, alarm respondent, central station dispatcher, electronic security sales representative, electronic security technician's assistant, or electronic security technician without possessing a valid registration issued by the Department, except as provided in this article.

D. A temporary license may be issued in accordance with Board regulations for the purpose of awaiting the results of the state and national fingerprint search. However, no person shall be issued a temporary license until (I) he has designated a compliance agent who has complied with the compulsory minimum training standards established by the Board pursuant to subsection A of § 9.1-141 for compliance agents, (ii) each principal of the business has submitted his fingerprints for a National Criminal Records search and a Virginia Criminal History Records search, and (iii) he has met all other requirements of this article and Board regulations.

E. No person shall be employed by a licensed private security services business in the Commonwealth unless such person is certified or registered in accordance with this chapter.

F. A temporary registration may be issued in accordance with Board regulations for the purpose of awaiting the results of the state and national fingerprint search. However, no person shall be issued a temporary registration until he has (I) complied with, or been exempted from the compulsory minimum training standards established by the Board, pursuant to subsection A of § 9.1-141, for armored car personnel, couriers, armed security officers, detector canine handlers, unarmed security officers, security canine handlers, private investigators, personal protection specialists, alarm respondents, central station dispatchers, electronic security sales representatives, electronic security technician's assistants, or electronic security technicians, (ii) submitted his fingerprints to be used for the conduct of a National Criminal Records search and a Virginia Criminal History Records search, and (iii) met all other requirements of this article and Board regulations.

G. A temporary certification as a private security instructor or private security training school may be issued in accordance with Board regulations for the purpose of awaiting the results of the state and national fingerprint search. However, no person shall be issued a temporary certification as a private security services instructor until he has (I) met the education, training and experience requirements established by the Board and (ii) submitted his fingerprints to be used for the conduct of a National Criminal Records search and a Virginia Criminal History Records search. No person shall be issued a temporary certification as a private security services training school until (a) he has designated a training director, (b) each principal of the training school has submitted his fingerprints to be used for the conduct of a National Criminal Records search and a Virginia Criminal History Records search, and (c) he has met all other requirements of this article and Board regulations.

H. A licensed private security services business in the Commonwealth shall not employ as an unarmed security officer, electronic security technician's assistant, unarmed alarm respondent, central station dispatcher, electronic security sales representative, or electronic security technician, any person who has not complied with, or been exempted from, the compulsory minimum training standards established by the Board, pursuant to subsection A of § 9.1-141, except that such person may be so employed for not more than 90 days while completing compulsory minimum training standards.

I. No person shall be employed as an electronic security employee, electronic security technician's assistant, unarmed alarm respondent, central station dispatcher, electronic security sales representative, electronic security technician or supervisor until he has submitted his fingerprints to the Department to be used for the conduct of a National Criminal Records search and a Virginia Criminal History Records search. The provisions of this subsection shall not apply to an out-of-state central station dispatcher meeting the requirements of subdivision 19 of § 9.1-140.

J. The compliance agent of each licensed private security services business in the Commonwealth shall maintain documentary evidence that each private security registrant and certified employee employed by his private security services business has complied with, or been exempted from, the compulsory minimum training standards required by the Board. Before January 1, 2003, the compliance agent shall ensure that an investigation to determine suitability of each unarmed security officer employee has been conducted, except that any such unarmed security officer, upon initiating a request for such investigation under the provisions of subdivision 11 of subsection A of § 19.2-389, may be employed for up to 30 days pending completion of such investigation. After January 1, 2003, no person shall be employed as an unarmed security officer until he has submitted his fingerprints to the Department for the conduct of a National Criminal Records search and a Virginia Criminal History Records search. Any person who was employed as an unarmed security officer prior to January 1, 2003, shall submit his fingerprints to the Department in accordance with subsection B of § 9.1-145.

K. No person with a criminal conviction for a misdemeanor involving (I) moral turpitude, (ii) assault and battery, (iii) damage to real or personal property, (iv) controlled substances or imitation controlled substances as defined in Article 1 (§ 18.2-247 et seq.) of Chapter 7 of Title 18.2, (v) prohibited sexual behavior as described in Article 7 (§ 18.2-61 et seq.) of Chapter 4 of Title 18.2, or (vi) firearms, or any felony shall be (a) employed as a registered or certified employee by a private security services business or training school, or (b) issued a private security services registration, certification as an unarmed security officer, electronic security employee or technician's assistant, a private security services training school or instructor certification, compliance agent certification, or a private security services business license, except that, upon written request, the Director of the Department may waive such prohibition.

L. The Department may grant a temporary exemption from the requirement for licensure, certification, or registration for a period of not more than 30 days in a situation deemed an emergency by the Department.

M. All private security services businesses and private security services training schools in the Commonwealth shall include their license or certification number on all business advertising materials.

N. A licensed private security services business in the Commonwealth shall not employ as armored car personnel any person who has not complied with, or been exempted from, the compulsory minimum training standards established by the Board pursuant to subsection A of § 9.1-141, except such person may serve as a driver of an armored car for not more than 90 days while completing compulsory minimum training standards, provided such person does not possess or have access to a firearm while serving as a driver.

Private Security Act 2004 (Victoria-Australia)
Version incorporating amendments as at 1 July 2006

The Private Security Act 2004 commenced operation in 2005. The Act regulates the activities of:
- security guards
- crowd controllers
- bodyguards
- investigators
- security equipment installers
- security advisers.

The objective of the Private Security Act 2004 is to regulate the private security industry to ensure community safety. The Act is designed to protect innocent third parties, clients and consumers of security services from harm and to provide confidence in the industry's operations.

Act No. 33/2004 Page 51
Part 3-Licensing Private Security Operators

66. Temporary overseas bodyguard visitor permit
    1) A person who ordinarily resides outside Australia may apply to the Chief Commissioner for a permit to act as a bodyguard in Victoria if-
       (a) the person produces evidence to the satisfaction of the Chief Commissioner that the person is licensed or registered or otherwise authorized in his or her country of residence to act as a bodyguard; or
       (b) if the law of the country in which the person is resident does not require a person to be licensed or registered or otherwise authorized to act as a bodyguard, the Chief Commissioner is satisfied as to the suitability of the person to act as a bodyguard.
    2) The holder of a permit under this section does not commit an offense against section 7(b) or 8(b) while acting under and in accordance with the permit.

67. Overseas bodyguard with temporary interstate or Territory permit
    A person who-
       (a) ordinarily resides outside Australia; and

(b) holds a permit that authorizes that person to act as a bodyguard issued under the law of another State or a Territory of a kind specified in the regulations-does not commit an offense against section 7(b) or 8(b) while acting under and in accordance with the permit.

68. Procedure for applications for permits
   1) A person may apply for a permit under this Division in the form and manner approved by the Chief Commissioner.
   2) An application for a permit must be accompanied by proof of identity of the applicant, being, if the Chief Commissioner so requires proof by way of the specified identification method.
   3) In considering an application for a permit the Chief Commissioner may do any one or more of the following-
      (a) take into account any known information about the applicant, that is relevant to the application;
      (b) conduct any investigation or make any inquiry that he or she thinks fit;
      (c) require an applicant to-
         (I) provide any information, relevant to the application and verified by a statutory declaration; or
         (ii) produce any document relevant to the application-that in the opinion of the Chief Commissioner relates to the applicant;
      (d) require a full set of the applicant's fingerprints to be provided to the Chief Commissioner if-
         (I) there is reasonable doubt as to the identity of the applicant for the permit; and
         (ii) proof of the identity of the applicant cannot be obtained by any other reasonable means.
   4) The Chief Commissioner may refuse to issue a permit if a requirement under sub-section (3)(c) or (3)(d) is not complied with.
   5) Section 22(3) and (4) applies to the provision of any set of fingerprints under subsection (3)(d).
   6) The Chief Commissioner may issue a permit to a person who has applied for a permit under subsection (1).

69. Fees for permits
   1) The prescribed application fee for an application for a permit under this Division must be paid by the person applying for the permit.
   2) The prescribed permit fee for a permit under this Division must be paid by the holder of the permit.

70. Limitations and conditions on permits
   1) A permit under this Division must not be issued for any purpose other than for the duration of a special event or events that are specified in the permit and must not continue in force for a period that is greater than the duration of the event or events for which it is issued.
   2) The Chief Commissioner may impose any conditions on a permit under this Division that the Chief Commissioner thinks fit.
   3) The holder of a permit under this Division must comply with any condition imposed on the permit under subsection (2).

The security industry is generally regulated and the executive protection sector is somehow integrated in most countries by the same regulations as applied for security companies in general. International or cross-border regulations are either missing or still a problematic issue. With a few exceptions, most national laws still ignore the existence of the private security industry and related branches. [34] Another rapidly growing international industry-that of private military companies or PMCs is just a recent addition to the already dense regulation jungle.

A report by A. Richards and H. Smith, published by "Saferworld" is giving a closer look at the problematic of this issue. Enforcement of regulations can be problematic in the absence of mutually reinforcing regulatory frameworks at the regional and international levels, even where extraterritorial legislations exist. For example, although South Africa has a system of extraterritorial legislation, if a South African registered PSC is operating abroad, any misdeed cannot practically be addressed by the South African authorities until the individuals' return to South Africa. Unless there is a regulatory system in the host country, or indeed, there is a regional or international framework. It is therefore important that practitioners in this area promote such frameworks, as they present a clear opportunity to ensure more effective control.

At present, however, it is unclear which international laws apply to the industry, partly as a result of the ambiguous legal status of PSCs under existing international treaties. For example, the activities of personnel employed by such firms are not governed by the *1989 International Convention against the Recruitment, Use, Financing and Training of Mercenaries*. Those efforts that are currently underway to remedy the situation should therefore continue. Another example is the initiative by the government of Switzerland to agree an international code of conduct for PMCs/PSCs and similar work by the Confederation of European Security Services. In addition, governments should work towards the formation of regional regulatory instruments as a bridge between the national and international levels. In the European arena for example, this means the pursuit of discussions within the EU, NATO and OSCE on common standards for the industry. Any such agreement could in turn inform future global standards. [35]

Every EPO, no matter, where he/she is licensed must meet the requirements of the city, county, state or country-and this is not just for weapons, but also for the assignment in general. In the performance of their duty, EPOs shall respect and protect human dignity and maintain and uphold the human rights of any persons. EPOs shall not use firearms against persons except in self-defense or defense of others against the imminent threat of death or serious injury. In order to prevent the perpetration of a particularly serious attack involving grave threat to life, or to deter a person presenting such a danger. In any event, intentional lethal use of firearms may only be made when strictly unavoidable in order to protect life (any EPO has to act and operate within the rule of law even when assigned to protect a principal).

Archangel Michael

Mîkhā'ēl (Hebrew: מיכאל)

Mikha'il (Arabic: ميكانيــل)

Mikhaíl (Greek: Μιχαήλ)

Archangel Michael is the patron of the police officers,
soldiers, paratroopers and protection officers.

O glorious Archangel Michael,

Defend us in battle. Watch over us during life.
Defend us against the assaults of the demon and
assist us especially at the hour of death.
Be our protection against the
wickedness and snares of Evil. Thrust
into hell Satan and all evil spirits, who
wander through the world for the ruin
of souls. Obtain for us a favorable
judgment and the happiness of
beholding God face to face.
For all eternity

Amen

Appendix

Abduction
See also: *Kidnapping*

Advance
Preparations and arrangements made prior to and in anticipation of a principal's arrival:
-security advance relating to matter of principal's security
-staff or political advance pertaining to non-security arrangements

Advance Officer
Executive protection officer responsible for security arrangements on route and at site to be visited by the principal.

Advance Car
Security vehicle that precedes the motorcade by approximately two to five minutes. Usually used by a local police officer or EPOs to identify potential problem areas and advance observation for probable attack or ambush situations. The advance car has direct communication to the command post and principal's vehicle. See also: *Pilot Car*.

Advance Survey
Inspection of particular area/s, site/s or location/s for principal's visit. Checks for vulnerabilities, points of ingress and egress, facilities, parking, security posts and location and/or anything else that could impact or temper with the safe arrival and departure of the principal.

Alarm System
System with a series of motion, movement or presence sensors and detectors, which connected to a central panel transmit signals, resulting in the notification of an intrusion by a loud siren or a silent signal of a flashing light.

Ammunition
-*Ball*
Is a round-nosed metal jacketed ammunition. It is used for self-loading firearms like pistols. All military pistol-and rifle-ammunition uses full metal jacket bullets. Synonyms for ball include *FMJ* (= Full Metal Jacket), *MC* (= Metal Case) and *TMJ* (= Totally Metal Jacketed-a term used only by the ammunition maker CCI). Ball-rounds do not expand and are always the worst choice in a defensive round. The military uses ball-rounds because it feeds well (rarely jams), penetrates far, and the military is required to use ball-rounds under the Geneva Convention.

-*Wadcutter* and *Semi-Wadcutter*
Is a sharp-shouldered revolver bullet with an odd cylindrical appearance.

-*Jacketed Soft-Point*
Is a jacketed bullet with exposed lead at the tip. JSP make poor defensive rounds for handguns but may be effective for rifles, due to the latter's high velocity.

-*Jacketed Hollow-Points*
It is the best choice for handguns and most rifles. JHP rounds have a hollow cavity in the nose and usually expand (and stop) in the body of an attacker-transferring all their kinetic energy

for maximum stopping power. They are the safest and best bullets available. JHP bullets are always best for self- defense.

-Round Nose Lead
Is generally a revolver bullet without any metal jacket around the bullet. RNL are worthless for self-defense.

Armored car
A vehicle reinforced with a bulletproof and/or protective material with capability of withstanding minor and medium attacks.

Baggage Team
Protective officer/s responsible for the safe transit of the principal's and his/her entourage's luggage (from pickup point to the loading onboard a plane or other transport and the safe retrieval and delivery of it to the final destination).

Blending in
Blending into the environment and providing protective services without being obvious.

Body armor
A bulletproof Kevlar-vest also known as protective gear worn in high-threat situations.

Bodyguard
Professional providing personal security to an individual.
This somehow outdated term was replaced by *Personal Protection Specialist* or *Close Protection Expert*.

Bug/Bugging
Hidden listening and video and other devices, placed to gain information about a person or business.

Call Sign
Or codename which is used during radio communications.

Checkpoint
A manned, monitored post control the access to restricted areas limited to authorized personnel only.

Chokepoint
A narrow passageway-a passage point where a principal is very vulnerable.

Client
The person being protected. See also: *Principal.*

Close Proximity
Area closest to the principal-within the principal's inner circle.

Close Protection
Being in close proximity to the principal and providing protective services.

Command post
Centralized communication center where all information and equipment for a protective detail is coordinated and disseminated. It is staffed by senior and/or experienced personnel with authority to make decisions.

Concentric Circles
Circles of security set up around the principal and his environment. It should consist of a minimum of three circles and includes people, procedures, and equipment.

Confidential/Confidentiality
The secret keeping of certain matters and issues.

Corporate and Family
The personnel, staff and immediate members of the principal's family and his business.

Countermeasures
Electronic sweeping and physical search including telephone lines for listening devices and video surveillance (debugging) of premises and/or business; preventive action in anticipation of an attack. Procedures taken to counter any adverse activity.

Cover and Evacuate
Immediate response to a principal in the event of a present danger. Protective officer will shield the principal with their own bodies and remove him/her to a safer location and away from the danger.

Covert Action (Operation)
Undercover activities-action or operation taken in secret.

CPR
Cardio-**P**ulmonary **R**esuscitation

Crisis Management
Specific duties and responsibilities executed by designated personnel during an emergency situation, such as a terrorist attack, kidnapping of corporate personnel, natural disaster, or any other catastrophic condition disrupting the natural flow of business.

Designated Person
See also: *Principal*.

Detail
Team working for the protection of a client. Details vary in size according to the threat level and principal's profile. See also: *Protective Detail*.

Detail Leader
Senior ranking officer or officer in charge (OIC) of the protective assignment. Usually operates in close proximity to the principal.

Discretion
Using a good judgment and in the best interest of the principal-sometimes secrecy or confidentiality.

Dressing Down
Wearing casual clothing.

Dressing Up
Wearing a suit or tuxedo.

Dress Code
Dressing accordingly-guidelines on what to dress and when

Duress Signal
Silent alarm sent by the principal and received by the command post to be responded to as an emergency situation by protective personnel. Can be a secret, specific spoken or written code word in case of trouble as part of a plan to alert others to the danger or threat.

EAR
Expired Air Resuscitation

ECC
External Chest Compressions

EOD
Explosive ordnance disposal-the "bomb squad". Personnel trained to remove or neutralize an explosive device.

Escape Route
Secondary or predetermined route of escape in an emergency during the course of an event or motorcade-evacuation to safety. See also: *Cover and Evacuate.*

Escort
A term used for a bodyguard, whether armed or unarmed. This term is also applied for accompanying security vehicles within a motorcade.

Etiquette
Behavior and manners-differing by countries and cultures. See also: *Protective Protocol.; Protocol.*

Event Site
A location, scheduled for visit by the principal.

EP-Cocktail
Nonalcoholic drink carried and to be consumed by an executive protection officer while blending into a social gathering or party.

Executive protection officer (agent or specialist)
A professional trained in the fine art of providing a secure environment to a principal. A trained and knowledgeable individual with expertise in all aspects of close personal protection.

Final survey report
Written report in narrative form, made after an event or completion of an assignment. It should contain all the highlights, such as unusual incidents, contact telephone numbers, changes in the original survey (advance) report, emphasizing on any difficulties encountered, their solution and should outline recommendations for future similar assignments

Follow-up Vehicle
Special vehicle with protective agents and equipment assigned to drive immediately behind the principal's car. It provides defensive measures for the principal's vehicle.

Formation
Positioning of the officers in close proximity to the principal while walking.

Hardening a Target
Making a potential attacker's center of interest (the target) more difficult to penetrate.

A defensive posture incorporating technological systems, procedures, awareness and readiness.

Hardware
Weapons used on a protective detail. The equipment comprising alarm systems, including closed-circuit television (CCTV), monitors, control panel and computers (Laptop).

High Profile
Obvious security, maximum protection, a show of force, a well-known and highly placed person.

High Threat Level
Verified threat likely to occur; possible imminent danger to the principal. It requires full alert, total awareness, and maximum close protection.

Holding Room
Specific and secured room expressly reserved for the private use of the principal.

Hostage
Person taken against his/her will and being held for satisfaction of demands by the kidnapper (s).

Hostage Negotiator
Person skilled, trained and experienced in negotiating and securing the safe release of hostages.

Identification Pins
Small badge like lapel pins, worn by the protective team members, serving as instant recognition and identification purposes.

Inspection Mirror
Small mirror with flashlight attached to a long handle, which allows the officer to inspect and search for bombs, listening or recording devices under a vehicle or in hard-to-reach places.

Intelligence
Analyzed data with conclusive projections obtained from raw information relative to the safety and the concern of the principal:
   -Strategic Intelligence and Tactical Intelligence

Kidnapping
The illegal capture or detention of a person against their will, regardless of age for ransom or settlement of demands.

Kidnapping/Ransom Insurance
A special insurance purchased by large corporations for their key personnel.

Lead Vehicle
Vehicle immediately ahead of the principal's vehicle. It is usually a marked police car with a local police officer and a senior advance officer.

Letter Bomb
Letter or large sized envelope containing an explosive charge that detonates on breaking the seal or removing the contents.

Loose Element
An officer who is not necessarily a team player, following his/her own rules and is very likely

disregarding any proper protocol.

Low Profile
Protective officers who are blending in with the environment.

Low Threat Level
No actual threats known or no indications of any potential threats. Any person known to the EPO.

Medical Protocol
Defines specific procedures for attending to medical emergencies.

Medium Threat Level
This is the most common type of the protective detail. Potential danger, but no actual threats received or determined-reception of possible harassing telephone calls or letters.

Motorcade
Organized group of vehicles in formation traveling in a controlled manner. Can consist of three or more vehicles. Motorcade formation can be as follows: pilot or scout car, lead car, principal's car, follow-up car, staff car, other necessary vehicles and tail car.

Movement
The principal changing locations-traveling or moving from one location to another.

Off Duty
Not in a service related status.

Off the Air
Radio is turned off-no radio communication.

Officer
Title or designation for a security person assigned to protective detail providing for the safety and security of a principal.

Overt operation
Plain open visible operation-High profile.

Packed
Carrying a concealed weapon.

Paparazzo (Italian; pl. paparazzi)
A freelance photographer who doggedly pursues celebrities to take candid pictures for sale to magazines and newspapers. (named after "Signor Paparazzo", a character in "La Dolce Vita", a Federico Fellini film)

Panic button
Device carried by or placed within reach of a principal. It is used in the event of an emergency requiring immediate response by the protective officers. The device transmits a silent alarm to a central location or to an officer's receiver to alert him of the emergency.

Personal Protection Specialist
Person highly trained in the profession of close personal protection.

Personal Security Officer
Individual providing close proximity protection to a principal. This position is usually assumed by the detail leader or senior officer.

Physical Barrier
Anything which is building a barricade that prevents direct access-this might be a door, a wall, trees, etc.

Pilot Car
A marked police car preceding the motorcade by approximately a quarter of a kilometer. Its job is to scan the areas for potential immediate problems, obstructions, dangerous activity, etc.

Point Man
Officer assuming the lead in a protective movement formation; protects the principal to the front.

Portfolio
Confidential case file of the principal, including pertinent information and photos

Post Orders
The specific instructions regarding the operation of a security post.

Press Area
Designated area for members of the press. Only credentialed press members are allowed into this area.

Principal
The person receiving the protective service.

Principal's Car
Vehicle designated to carry the principal.

Private Sector
Not related to a government agency; private firms or individuals providing protective services. Private enterprise, which may be an individual or a major corporation.

Professional
Highly trained officer or agent, dedicated to provide the very best protective services available-knowledgeable in every aspect of his business.

Profile
Characterization and reference to the risk potential-the way a person, a situation, or a protective detail is viewed.

Protective Protocol
Accepted and recommended behavior and attitude toward the principal, his family, staff, business, and his property. See also: *Protocol; Etiquette.*

Protection
Physical security of a principal. Prevention of any harm to the principal, which includes home, travel, leisure, work and business environment.

Protective Detail
A general term given to the group of officers, assigned to provide protective services to a client-or a protective responsibility.

Protective Intel
Intelligence, Data, information, and even rumors regarding potential threats to the principal.

Protective Intel Car
A car with at least one protective officer and a plain-clothes local police officer, assigned to the approximate area of an event to respond and resolve any activity of possible threats or disruptions. Usually applied on a large-scale protection operation.

Protocol
Rules, regulations and codes which are given and implemented for official dealings and certain activities. Examples are the correct procedures for displaying a country's flag, receiving high-ranking political and social figures, etc.

Psychological Obstacles
Obstacles, which do not present any difficulty of physical penetration, but cause a psychological challenge for the intruder, e. g. multilevel alarm systems, electronic eye scan, fingerprint scan, open spaces, etc..

Risk Analysis
The evaluation of information and intelligence available regarding the potential problems and the degree of danger posed against the principal.

Risk Factor
The potential factor of danger and the probability of its occurrence.

Route Car
Mobile team of executive protection officers in an unmarked car, depending on the size and operation accompanied by a plain-clothes local police officer. Used to scan the principal's motorcade route for any traffic problems, crowd buildup, buildings that could house a possible problem, or any obstruction jeopardize the progress of the motorcade. See also: *Advance Car*.

Route Survey
The selection of primary and alternative routes for the principal's travel movement. It includes time (morning, noon, evening, night) and distance, directions, anticipated traffic problems, locations of emergency medical facilities, etc..

Routine
Is a repetitious activity performed in a usual manner-an unvaried schedule, a habit.

Sabotage
Deliberate act to cause damage to the property of another. Also actions designed to counter the efforts of a protective detail.

Secure Room
A reinforced, secure room, which is easily and quickly accessible to the principal and his family in case of emergency. A safe room is usually equipped with emergency rations, lighting, audio and video communication equipment.

Secure Area
A location that has been surveyed and cleared of any suspicious, unauthorized persons and objects and is continuously monitor and secured by established security post assignments within and around the location.

Security Advance
Prior arrangements of a security-related nature in anticipation of the arrival of a principal. See also: *Advance*.

Security perimeter
Established boundary that involves the placement and utilization of security personnel, alarms, barricades, and other devices to provide protection, surveillance, and intelligence information; the area and the people within the perimeter have been cleared for security purposes.

Security Post
Area of the security network-also known as a "post". It can be a fixed surveillance post, a checkpoint or a special assignment.

Security Room
Security personnel (protective officers, police, fire personnel, paramedics) break-and/or relief room.

Site Survey
Security inspection and subsequent security planning for a given or specific location. See also: *Advance*.

Stalker
A Person who constantly pursues and preys on the attention or affection of another person against his/her will.

Stalking
A form of repeated invasion of a person's privacy. Such an invasion in a manner of repeated harassment causes fear to the target.

Strategic Intelligence
Information and planning for a long-termed time factor. See also: *Intelligence*.

Surveillance
Activity of observing and monitoring the activities of another.

Sweep
Specific method of searching an area explosive, electronic listening or surveillance audio and video devices.

Tactical Intelligence
Intelligence and planning for the immediate use and implementation. See also: *Intelligence*.

Tail Car
The closing car, the last one in a motorcade, which is usually a marked police car.

Tail Man
Agent protecting the rear of a principal, while in a protective movement formation.

Team
Group of agents working together to provide protective services to a protectee. See also: *Detail; Protective Detail*.

Team leader
See also: Detail Leader.

Terrorism
Acts of violence, usually bombing and/or kidnapping, based on political or religious reasons. Terror created and directed toward a principal and his family or the business for the purpose of causing fear, major disruption or elimination.

Terrorist
One who plans, coordinates and participates in terrorist activities for political, religious, or ideological reasons.

Threat Level
See also: *Risk Analysis; Risk Factor.*

Trustworthy
Primary requisite for a protective officer-can be entrusted with top secret and intimate information, money and valuables.

Venue
Location or site of an event.

VIP
See also: *Principal*

Visual Protection Area
Area assigned to each officer of the protective detail, providing a sector-scanning ability with a minimum amount of head movement.

Zone
Selective sectors of an alarm system, independent of other sectors for the purpose of easy identification of the location where an alarm is triggered. Also used to provide capability to deactivate portions of the system, while allowing the remaining system to stay active.

Zone Car
Mobile teams assigned to a specific sector (zone) adjacent to a motorcade route or visit site for surveillance and intelligence purposes.

Footnotes

1 K. K. Kienlen, et al.   *A comparative Study of psychotic and non-psychotic stalking*
                                 J Am Acad Psychiatry Law 25:3:317-334 (1997)

2 P. E. Mullen, M. Pathé   *Study of Stalkers*
   R. Purcell, G. W. Stuart   The American Journal of Psychiatry, 156 (8): 1244-1249,Aug. 1, 1999

3 P. E. Mullen, M. Pathé   *A Study of Women Who Stalk*
   R. Purcell   Am J Psychiatry 158:2056-2060 (2001)

4 CE Novell   *The Old Man of the Mountain*, in Speculum, xxii (1947), 497-519

5 W. Ivanow   *A brief survey of the evolution of Ismailism*, Leiden 1952

6 J. N. Hollister   *The Shi'a of India*, London, 1953

7 Ed Sanow   *What Are The Best Loads For Defense?*
                                 July 1995 issue of Petersen's Handguns Magazine

8 W. Howe, S. V. Hart   *Selection and Application Guide to Personal Body Armor*
                                 NIJ Guide 100-01, November 2001

9 F. Jackson, K. M. Earle   *Blunt head injuries incurred by Marine recruits in hand-to-hand combat*
   Y. Beamer, R. Clark   Military Medicine. 132: 803-808 (1967)

10 S. Wos, J. Puzio,   *Post-traumatic internal carotid artery thrombosis following karate blow*
   G. Opala   Polski Przeglad Chirurgiczny, 49: 1271-1273 (1977)

11 E. R. Serina, D. K. Lieu   *Thoracic injury potential of basic competition taekwondo kicks*
                                 Journal of Biomechanics, 24: 951-960 (1991)

12 M. R. Yeadon   *Comments on 'Thoracic injury potential of basic competition Taekwondo kicks'*
                                 Journal of Biomechanics, 25: 1247-1248 (1992)

13 J. D. Cantwell,   *Karate chops and liver lacerations*
   J. T. King Jr.   Journal of the American Medical Association, 224: 1424 (1973)

14 G. Y. Berkovich, et al   *Renal vein thrombosis after martial arts trauma*
                                 J Trauma, 2001 Jan; 50 (1): 144-5

15 L. A. Geddes,   *Evolution of our knowledge of sudden death due to commotio cordis*
   R. A. Roeder   Am J Emerg Med. 2005 Jan; 23(1): 67-75

16 M. Oler, W. Tomson,   *Morbidity and mortality in the martial arts: a warning*
   H. Pepe, D. Yoon   J Trauma. 1991 Feb;31(2):251-3

17   *World Security Services to 2010*
                                 The Freedonia Group, Nov. 2006

18 Theodore H. White   *The Making of the President 1960*
                                 Buccaneer Books, April 1999

19   *Statistics from the FBI Uniform Crime Reports for the United States 1999*
                                 Release: October 15, 2000

20 Richfield, P.   *Spies among us-How foreign intelligence targets American industry's secrets.*
                                 C4ISR Journal, May 2007, Page 22-25

21 Hunsicker A.   *Understanding International Counter Terrorism*: A Professional's Guide to
                                 the Operational Art
                                 Universal Publishers, 2006

22 Schmid A.P.   *Academic Consensus Definition of "Terrorism"*
                          UNODC (United Nations Office on Drugs and Crime), 1992

23 Taylor, Maxwell   *The Terrorist*
                          London: Brassey's, 1988

24 Jenkins, Brian M.   *High Technology Terrorism and Surrogate Warfare: The Impact of New Technology on Low-Level Violence.* Santa Monica, California: Rand, 1975

    Jenkins, Brian M.   *International Terrorism: A New Mode of Conflict.* In David Carlton and Carolo Schaerf, eds., International Terrorism and World Security. London: Croom Helm, 1975

    Jenkins, Brian M.   *Terrorists at the Threshold.* In E. Nobles Lowe and Harry D. Shargel, eds., Legal and Other Aspects of Terrorism. New York: 1979

25 Knutson, Jeanne N.   *Social and Psychodynamic Pressures Toward a Negative Identity.* Pages 105-52 in Yonah Alexander and John M. Gleason, eds., Behavioral and Quantitative Perspectives on Terrorism. New York: Pergamon, 1981

    Knutson, Jeanne N.   *The Terrorists' Dilemmas: Some Implicit Rules of the Game .* Terrorism, 4, 1980, 195-222

    Knutson, Jeanne N.   *Toward a United States Policy on Terrorism.* Political Psychology, 5, No. 2, June 1984, 287-94

    Knutson, Jeanne N.   *Handbook of Political Psychology.* San Francisco: Jossey-Bass, 1973

26 Shaw, Eric D.   *Political Terrorists: Dangers of Diagnosis and an Alternative to the Psychopathology Model.* International Journal of Law and Psychiatry, 8, 1986, 359-68

27 Galvin, Deborah M.   *The Female Terrorist: A Socio-Psychological Perspective,* Behavioral Science and the Law, 1, 1983, 19-32

28 Stettbacher, A.   *Die Schiess-und Sprengstoffe,* Barth, 1933, 459

29   *Crimes and Punishment, "The Mad Bomber"*
                          The Symphonette Press, 1974

30 Brussel, J., M.D   *The Casebook of Crime Psychiatrist*
                          Bernard Geis Associates, 1968

31 Graysmith, R.   *Unabomber: A Desire To Kill*
                          Pocket Books, 2000

32 Sun Tzu   *The Art Of War* (translated by Lionel Giles, M.A., 1910)
                          El Paso Norte Press, March 21, 2005

33 Ohlhausen Research   *National Policy Summit: Private Security/Public Policing Partnerships*
                          Report produced by Ohlhausen Research, 2004

34 Caroline Holmqvist   *Private Security Companies-The Case for Regulation*
                          SIPRI Policy Paper No. 9, January 2005

35 Richards, A., Smith, H. *Addressing the Role of Private Security Companies within Security Sector Reform Programmes*
                          Report published by SAFERWORLD, January 2007

- *International Child Abduction*
  Published by Hague Conference on Private International Law (www.hcch.net)

- *The School Shooter: A Threat Assessment Perspective* by Mary Ellen O'Toole, PhD
  Published by FBI Academy/FBI Publications

- *Warriors of Medieval Japan* by Stephen Turnbull
  Published by Osprey 2005

- *Bernard of Clairvaux: In Praise of the New Knighthood* translated by M Conrad Greenia
  Published by Cistercian Publications 1977, rev edn 2000

- *The Assassins -A Radical Sect in Islam* by Bernard Lewis
  Published by Phoenix/Orion Books Ltd., London, 2003

- *The Secret Order of Assassins:*
  The Struggle of the Early Nizari Isma'ilis Against the Islamic World by Marshall G S Hodgson
  Published by Pennsylvania Pb, 1955, reprint 2005

- *Serial Killers-The Method and Madness of Monsters* by Peter Vronsky
  Published by Berkleys Publishing Group/Penguin Books Ltd., 2004

- *The Serial Killer Files* by Harold Schechter
  Published by The Random House Publishing Group, 2003

- *Security Consulting* by Charles E. Sennewald
  Published by Elsevier Science Inc., 2004

- *A Family Resource Guide on International Parental Kidnapping* by O. J. J. D. P.
  Published by the Office of Juvenile Justice and Delinquency Prevention, 2002

- *US Army Special Forces Medical Handbook* by U. S. Army
  Published by U. S. Army Institute for Military Assistance, 1982

- *Atlas of Emergency Medicine, 2nd ed.* by Kevin J. Knoop, Lawrence B. Stack, Alan B. Storrow
  Published by McGraw-Hill, 2002

- *The Seirin Pictorial Atlas of Acupuncture* by Yu-Lin Lian, Chun-yang Chen, M. Hammes
  Published by Könnemann Verlagsgesellschaft, 1999

- *Acupuncture, Meridian Therapy and Acupunture Points* by Li Ding
  Published by Foreign Languages Press, 1991

- *Crime Scene Investigation: A Reference for Law Enforcement Training* by US Department of Justice
  Published by NACDL Publications Service, 2004

- *World Security Services to 2010*
  Published by The Freedonia Group, Nov. 2006

- *The Psychology of Group Aggression* by Arnold P. Goldstein
  Published by John Wiley & Sons, 2002

- *The World Factbook*
  Published by CIA Publications, 2007

- *Handbook of International Law* by Anthony Aust
  Published by Cambridge University Press, 2005

- *Principles and Practice of Travel Medicine* by Jane N. Zuckerman
  Published by John Wiley & Sons, 2001

- *Special Air Service Survival Guide* by John Wiseman
  Published by Harper Collins Publishers, 1993

- *Selection and Application Guide to Personal Body Armor*
  Published by The National Institute of Justice's National Law Enforcement and Corrections
  Technology Center, 2001

- *US Army Survival Manual (FM 21-76)* by US Departmen of Defense
  Published by Apple Pie Publishers, 1992

- *Encyclopedia of Terrorism* by Dr. Harvey Kushner
  Published by Sage Publications, 2003

- *The Directory of International Terrorism* by George Rosie
  Published by Paragon House, 1987

- *The United Kingdoms Legal Responses to Terrorism* by Michael Joachim Bonell
  Published by Transnational Publisher, 2003

- *Handbook of Face Recognition* by S.Z. Li and A.K. Jain
  Published by Springer Verlag, 2005

- *Sun Tzu–The Art of War* by Samuel B. Griffith, B. H. Liddell Hart
  Published by Oxford University Press, 1971

- *Understanding International Counter Terrorism: A Professional's Guide* by A. Hunsicker
  Published by Universal-Publishers, 2006

- *Fundamentals of Physical Surveillance* by Raymond P. Siljander
  Published by Charles C. Thomas Publishers, 1977

The *EPO's Assistant* is designed to assist and to provide the EPO with a quick, detailed step-by-step reference for the executive protection duty, assuring a successful and safe security service. In this easy to use format it becomes a practical tool and quick reference for the novice and an advance check-list for the experienced professional.

Each section is covering different topics with exact details of procedures. The EPO on duty can easily access a section in question and conduct the assignment accordingly. The practical content serves for advance planning as well as debriefing purposes.

In order to enjoy all the benefits of this extremely useful quick-reference-tool and to have it at hands at all times, you are encouraged to have the following section *"Executive Protection Officer's Assistant"* copied to a pocket-size format (11cm x 15cm), laminated and spiral bound. (see example below)

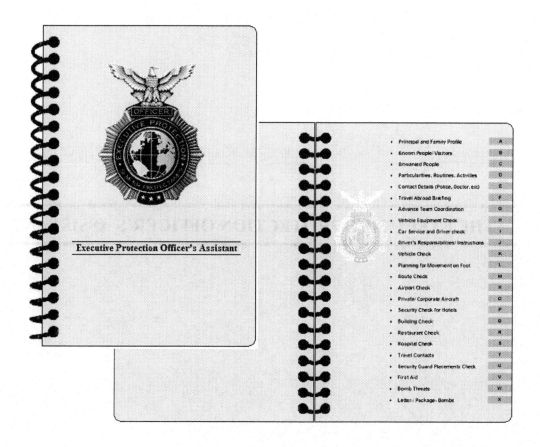

Executive Protection Officer's Assistant

- Principal and Family Profile — A
- Known People/ Visitors — B
- Unwanted People — C
- Particularities, Routines, Activities — D
- Contact Details (Police, Doctor, etc) — E
- Travel Abroad Briefing — F
- Advance Team Coordination — G
- Vehicle Equipment Check — H
- Car Service and Driver check — I
- Driver's Responsibilities/ Instructions — J
- Vehicle Check — K
- Planning for Movement on Foot — L
- Route Check — M
- Airport Check — N
- Private/ Corporate Aircraft — O
- Security Check for Hotels — P
- Building Check — Q
- Restaurant Check — R
- Hospital Check — S
- Travel Contacts — T
- Security Guard Placements Check — U
- First Aid — V
- Bomb Threats — W
- Letter-/ Package- Bombs — X

THE EXECUTIVE PROTECTION OFFICER'S ASSISTANT

- **Principal and Family Profile** — A
- **Known People/Visitors** — B
- **Unwanted People** — C
- **Particularities, Routines, Activities** — D
- **Contact Details (Police, Doctor, etc)** — E
- **Travel Abroad Briefing** — F
- **Advance Team Coordination** — G
- **Vehicle Equipment Check** — H
- **Car Service and Driver check** — I
- **Driver's Responsibilities/Instructions** — J
- **Vehicle Check** — K
- **Planning for Movement on Foot** — L
- **Route Check** — M
- **Airport Check** — N
- **Private/Corporate Aircraft** — O
- **Security Check for Hotels** — P
- **Building Check** — Q
- **Restaurant Check** — R
- **Hospital Check** — S
- **Travel Contacts** — T
- **Security Guard Placements Check** — U
- **First Aid** — V
- **Bomb Threats** — W
- **Letter-/Package-Bombs** — X

Principal and Family Profile

A

- Title/Degree/Rank/Honors
- Full Name (including pseudonyms)
- Address (private and business)
- Additional address ("unofficial")
- All phone numbers used by principal/family
- Physical description of principal (incl. Scars, beard, mustache, eyeglasses, contacts, etc.)
- Photo
- Video recording with voice sample
- Handwriting sample, including signature
- Fingerprints

- Physical disabilities and conditions

  - Blood Type
  - Allergies and chronic conditions
  - Stress and treatment related conditions (diabetes, cardiovascular etc.)
  - Diets

- Banks, Bank Officers, direct numbers
- Credit cards, numbers, names and bank contact
- Principal's Physician and Dentist contact info

- Full Name of spouse (including maiden name)
- Particularities, routines, social activities of spouse
- Children (names, details, schools, friends, sports, other activities)
- Children: Emergency contact arrangements
- Routes to and from school
- Special arrangements for boarding school/college
- Names, addresses and contact numbers of relatives

- List, description and location of all vehicles used by principal and family
- List and storage location of all firearms owned by principal and family
- List, location maps and blueprints of all houses owned by the principal and family

- Existing arrangements regarding divorce
- Reports on any past threat made against the
- Principal or family members (type, how, when, police reported)

Known People/Visitors/Contacts

(Known people who you or the principal have had contact with at the residence, the company, or during social event)

❖ *Build for each person a separate file with the following data:*

- Person checklist should include:

  - File Number

  - Name, Address, Phone numbers (home, job)

  - Position, Title, Rank, others

  - Special Interests

  - Additional Observations (behavior, etc.)

  - Corporate executives and others at company

  - Government officials, secretaries, couriers

  - People your principal had social contact at the residence, club, etc.

  - Service and staff members, drivers etc.

  - Special interests/activities of those people (tennis, gambling, dancing, horse race, etc.)

Unwanted People

Differentiate between a casual visitor or one who appears to have a certain interest in the principal.

C

- Interview the person at a secure location, whenever you have a chance
- ALWAYS assume such a person to be dangerous
- How does the person appear, behave, dress
- Calm, nervous, agitated, easy irritated, etc.
- Clothing is casual, well dressed, clean, dirty, worn clothing, etc.
- Hair and beard clean cut and trimmed or uncut and untrimmed
- Hands are manicured, clean, dirty, cigarette stains
- Overall appears

- Details to obtain during interview:

  - Name
  - Age
  - Where is he/her from
  - How did he/her get to your principal's residence/office
  - Is he/her alone or with other people, if so how many and where are they

- Ask for an Identification and check the ID very carefully
- Check if the person is known by the principal, spouse, children. staff
- Be polite at all times, and apologize if necessary

- Use a casual conversation type to ask your questions:

  - Sorry, what your name again?
  - Where did you say you are coming from?
  - Do you know the owner of this building?

❖ *Allow the person to talk as long and as much as he/she likes. It is the best way to get answers.*

- During the conversation and according to your questions, check for reactions, signs of anger, evasion, avoidance, irritation and observe the body movement and body language (eye contact, hands etc).
- Get acquainted with local laws regarding restraining orders, threats and psychological unstable cases
- Keep a file on each such encounter
- Follow up with local law enforcement and people contacted by suspicious person
- Try to get a photo of that person

❖ *ALWAYS*-Communicate such encounters to the principal, principal's family, security staff, and service staff

Particularities, Routines, Activities

Differentiate between a casual visitor or one who appears to have a certain interest in the principal.

- Interview the person at a secure location, whenever you have a chance

❖ *ALWAYS*-assume such a person to be dangerous

- How does the person appear, behave, dress
- Calm, nervous, agitated, easy irritated, etc.
- Clothing is casual, well dressed, clean, dirty, worn clothing, etc.
- Hair and beard clean cut and trimmed or uncut and untrimmed
- Hands are manicured, clean, dirty, cigarette stains
- Overall appears

- Details to obtain during interview:

  - Name
  - Age
  - Where is he/her from
  - How did he/her get to your principal's residence/office
  - Is he/her alone or with other people, if so how many and where are they

- Ask for an Identification and check the ID very carefully

- Check if the person is known by the principal, spouse, children. staff

Contact Details (Police, Doctor, etc)

- Physicians

  - Principal's Physician
  - Name, Title, address, phone, direct mobile
  - Other medical contacts used by the principal
  - Specialty
  - Name, Title, address, phone, direct mobile

  - Family Physicians if other than principal's
  - Name, Title, address, phone, direct mobile

- Emergency

  - Observations for emergency procedures
  - Shortest routes, pre-assigned codes, additional contacts and numbers

- Hospitals

  - Local Hospital
  - Address, phone numbers, shortest routes for emergencies
  - Ambulance service, phone numbers

- Police

  - Local Police
  - Courtesy visit with proper introduction
  - Ranks, names, contact numbers of commanding officers
  - Pre-assigned codes for emergency procedures

E

Travel Abroad Briefing

- Country of destination
- Physical characteristics
- Location, terrain, climate, health, laws
- Language requirements
- Currency (sufficient cash for emergency)
- Visa requirements and restrictions
- Local laws, regulations, restrictions
- Interpreter names and contacts
- Educational system
- Country Analysis Report by the U. S. Dep. State
- Warnings, recommendations, crime statistic
- Health
- Vaccination and immunization required
- Hygiene, water, sanitation conditions
- Names, addresses and contacts of English speaking physicians (medical training where)
- Where to find special medication
- Arrangements and procedure for evacuation and/or medevac
- Contact numbers for evacuation
- Cultural and religious background of country of destination
- Local Hospital
- Address, phone numbers, shortest routes for emergencies
- Ambulance service, phone numbers
- Other sensitive information
- Female acceptance in society (female security agents, driver)
- Usage and carrying of weapons, type and caliber regulations and restrictions, etc.
- Photographic equipment usage
- Local restricted areas
- Socio-political background
- Parties, unions and fraction of the local political arena
- Type of government
- Acceptance or rejection of foreign nations
- Security Concerns
- Awareness briefing to principal and family
- Security measures/procedures while traveling
- Principal's self-protective program
- Vehicle Security (boat, airplane, car, jeeps)
- Emergency contact names, numbers at the diplomatic mission abroad
- Once arrived at destination check in with diplomatic mission and local police/law enforcement
- Emergency contact numbers of hospital and medical emergency units
- Further and other specific problems in the area of destination
- Additional security support and contacts abroad

F

Advance Team Coordination

The following is vital for the travel arrangements and can determine the outcome: success or failure

- Itinerary must include:

    - Number of principals participating
    - Date and time (daylight/night)
    - Contacts and phone numbers (home, work, others)
    - Time schedules
    - Transportation type: car, boat, plane etc.
    - Lodging
    - Additional special arrangements set by the principal/s

- Revision and confirmation of the itinerary

    - Divide it into sections
    - Business, pleasure or otherwise
    - Flight time, time changes, possible transiting
    - Special needs, clothing, etc.
    - Check and reconfirm airline and hotel reservations, seat and room allocation in plane and hotel
    - Possible last minute problems
    - Reconfirm itinerary with secretary, staff supervisor

- Check advance files from the past

    - Itinerary related details (destination, routes, car service, plane/s, hotel/s)
    - Contacts (verify if data needs update)
    - Differences encountered between old file and new data
    - Any event, problems registered in the past

- Any contact you have in the area of destination

    - Expertise of contact (contact detail recheck)
    - Availability of this contact-any replacement if needed
    - Replacement has same or similar experience and language skills

- Intelligence

    - Geographical location, potential problems, overall socio-political atmosphere, possible threats or hot spot to be avoided.
    - Weather, terrain, temperatures, known but noticeable climate changes
    - Special requests (golf, fishing, theater, receptions, etc.)
    - Contact numbers of airline, hotel, car rental, limousine-service, etc.
    - Overseas trip with/without multiple border crossing:

G

- Passport, validity/renewal, visa, WHO-vaccination pass, departure/arrival tax (vaccines/immunization in due time)
- Diplomatic mission abroad and diplomatic missions of countries to be visited
- Contact persons and numbers
- Customs restriction, regulations for firearms, photographic, electronic equipment
- Local taboos and special dates, public holidays

- Material available for further research

  - Newspapers, travel reports, books, magazines, library, internet
  - U. S. Department of State, embassies, consulate
  - Airport Guide, Medical Handbook for Travelers, Hotel and Tourist Guide

G

- Appointments

  - Take note of each call made: contact name, number, time and date
  - Make appointments with:
  - Airport, Airline, Hotel, Limousine service, Police, diplomatic mission/s, event organizer

- Weapons permit

  - Local, interstate, international
  - Special arrangements with authorities abroad

- Weapons Check and procedure

  - Domestic and international airport
  - Office buildings
  - Government buildings and agencies
  - Police stations
  - Get a written clearance from the country of destination through their diplomatic mission
  - What type of weapon, type and caliber of ammo is allowed
  - Request that your pickup at the airport of destination has a weapon permit

- Advance Person's items list

  - Itinerary proposed for the trip
  - Proposed contact names, addresses and phone numbers
  - Copies of reservations, e. g. hotel, car, real estate, etc.
  - Letter of Mandate (authorization should depend on position and status) notarized and issue by the principal (should be translated in language of destination as well)

- Airline Tickets
- Passport and notarized copy of passport (keep in safe place)
  Note: A copy of your passport notarized in your own country is useless in a foreign country with foreign language; better get one from the country's embassy/consulate as well.
- Cash in various currencies (destination currency included) (foreign currency import regulations)
- Copies of passports, photos and details of all persons participating in the trip
- Credit cards, business cards
- Numbers and copies of all credit cards should be kept at safe place at home
- Emergency details and profile of the principal
- Photo, physical status, emergency numbers, prescriptions, etc.

- First Aid Kit

  - Medical Kit for principal

- All license numbers and car details (motorcade)
- Traveling nonstop shall not be an excuse for not looking professional
- Appearance is everything, so dress unless otherwise instructed in a professional manner
- The way you dress should not impede your functions and actions
- When traveling with more than one piece of luggage, make sure that you have the essentials, like change of clothes, shaving utensils, etc. in a carry-on bag.
- Small tool kit, batteries, camera, PDA, Laptop computer, GPS, accessories and chargers, mobile/satellite phone

- Electronic and electrical equipment

  - Because of different voltage, you might need power converters for your equipment

Vehicle Equipment Check

- Radios, spare batteries, spare radios
- Mobile phones with precharged batteries
- Satellite phone and accessories
- Maps and satellite images relevant to the area

- Fire extinguisher
- First Aid kit and medication (if applicable) for principal
- Gasmasks
- Portable Oxygen equipment

- Flashlights with spare batteries
- Strong spotlight (flashlight size with 25 + bundled LEDs)

H

- Spare tires, jack set,, tool set
- Jumper cables
- Car keys and spare keys
- Towing rope and snow equipment
- Spare fuses, electric tape, wire

- Emergency tools (hammer, crowbar, bolt cutter, spade)
- Blankets, Gloves, Umbrella
- Drinking Water
- Spare Gasoline (Diesel or high-octane gasoline) spare motor oil and water for car

- Metal detector
- Telescopic mirrors and autozoom night vision monocular

- Flash-bangs, smoke grenades, flares (if feasible)
- Body armor (Kevlar Vests)
- Backup weapons and ammo

- Cleaning Kit, Paper towels, Toilet paper, etc.

Car Service and Driver check

- Company name, address, phone numbers
- Company background check

- Owner name, address, phone numbers
- Owner background check

- How long in business
- References/recommended by
- How are drivers checked, level of driving skills

- Driver's Profile
- Dress code and clothes for driver/s
- Copies of driver's license
- Driver's license check where applicable

- Interview the driver/s

- Type of Vehicles used (limousine, van, sedan, etc.)
- Number and technical condition of vehicles in fleet
- Per hour charge and any discounts for the vehicles used
- How long will it take to get a back-up vehicle
- Any extra equipment within the vehicle (phone, reading light, standard emergency kit, toolbox with small tools, radio, television)

- Remind the service to provide the driver with two sets of keys

Driver's Responsibilities/Instructions

The following list is by far not complete and each driver has to use it by his best judgment as the situation arises.

- Contact with the head of security if there is any question or doubt.
- The vehicle's tank has to be full at all times, never below half of the tank
- Driver must show up at least 30 minutes prior to departure for last minute briefing.
- The driver has one set of keys, the other is with the security escort in the car
- The vehicle should have appropriate inside temperature (time of year) before arrival of the principal
- The radio should be off, unless otherwise indicated
- Driver should await the principal standing outside the car, ready to open the door
- Doors locked once all persons are seated
- Respect and obey all traffic rules
- Drive on highway in a secure manner that no traffic can pass on the principal's side. Change lane (if required) fluently
- Use horn according to local regulations and only in emergencies
- Do not eat, nor smoke while driving or with the principal inside
- Do not play the radio unless requested
- Only speak with principal, if conversation is initiated by principal
- The car phone shall not be used for personal calls
- The driver stays with the car at all times. Unless instructed otherwise.

- The security escort is brief and drill the driver on:

  - Entering and exiting the vehicle
  - Standing at ready by the car, to open the door when needed
  - Driver is staying behind the steering wheel, if principal is entering or exiting the vehicle escorted by security.
  - Evacuation and take-down drills
  - What should be expected

❖ *Note:* Driver, security and principal should work out an emergency code.

Vehicle Check

Make sure the car is always clean before leaving-use clear tape for doors, hood, etc..

- Vehicle type:
  - Model, Type, number of doors, year
  - License Number
  - Country, State, location of security check
  - Search date, time, search start, search end
  - Signature of searching officer

- Exterior search-scanning only:
  - Visible signs of forced entry
  - Visible signs of tampering-scratches, fingerprints, any fluids on or around vehicle, any free hanging or exposed wires
  - Check the areas around each tire
  - Check tapes for breakage, doors, hood, trunk, external spare wheel cover

- Check vehicle undercarriage:
  - The right front engine compartment and suspension area
  - The left front engine compartment and suspension area.
  - The rear engine compartment right side
  - The rear engine compartment left side
  - Transmission, gearbox, drive shaft, oil filter, muffler, tailpipe
  - The rear axle and rear suspension
  - Around, below and above fuel tank and fuel tank lit
  - Wheels, tires, valves

- Interior search-physical search-rear area:
  - Doors and door panel
  - Under floor mats
  - Seats and armrests
  - Storage compartments
  - Headrests. Pillows, ashtrays, bar, speakers, interior lights and light switches
  - Rear window inside
  - Back of front seat

- Interior search-physical search-front area:
  - Doors and door panel
  - Under floor mats, pedals, switches, steering wheel, glove compartment, fuse box
  - Under front seats, front seats, dashboard, radio, speakers, vents and air-ducts, cigarette lighter, sun-visors, reading lights, switches and headrests

- Trunk search-physical search:
  - Mats, spare tire if in trunk, back of the rear seats
  - Tool compartment. Toolbox, electrical wiring, the underside of the rear window
- Check the fuel tank cap, engine (entire compartment), check the fuel tank and engine oil, water level

K

Planning for Movement on Foot

- What is the degree of exposure

- Is it formal or informal

- Is the selected route the shortest

- Route and timing-predictable

- Does an alternative route exist and is it acceptable for a formal movement

- What are the risk areas and hot spots from A to B

- What is the best route for evacuation

- Can one official car follow along the route to provide a safe area

- If not, is a safe and secure area on the route-on the alternative route

- What is the direct route to a medical facility

- Do any other hazards exist, such as bad terrain, vicious animals, etc.

- Establish number, type and location of security posts

- Is there any need or support from other services, and what type of support

- Is there any need to control the crowd and is the personnel sufficient or is extra personnel required

- Security personnel shall be strategically posted along the route

- Check for:

  - Suspicious objects, unexpected roadwork, trash cans, garbage bags, new construction

Route Check

- Country. City, District, Date, time

- Movement time (morning, afternoon, etc)

- Departure and Arrival point

- Movement Type-single, with escort, in foot, with vehicle/s

- Status in case of an emergency

- Road conditions (pavement type, holes, gravel, etc.) -on road, or off road

- Traffic density and flow during weekdays:

  - Sparse, light, moderate, heavy, time

- Traffic density and flow during weekends/holidays:

  - Sparse, light, moderate, heavy, time

- Bridges (type), open or closed for water traffic

- Highway overpasses:

  - Are overpasses open, shielded or closed, can objects be hidden or thrown from it

- Tunnels-illumination type, light and visibility conditions

- Railroad crossings-protected or unprotected, visibility, etc.

- Buildings, schools, monuments along the route

- Traffic lights and stop signs, school zones along the route

- Hospital, police, fire and emergency response

- Alternative route check

- Route checks and checkpoints selection and code assigned, safe areas designated

Airport Check

- Airport name, airport abbreviation code, location, check done by, date and time

- Floor Plans and location diagram

- Exact location of airport emergency response units

- Overall condition of the airport, number of terminals, public terraces

- Airport security and passenger organization

- Open and closing time of airport

- FAA reports and warnings

- Time from arrival to luggage retrieval, Customs to exit

- Condition and location of departure and arrival gates

- Traffic regulation outside the airport building at departure and arrival gates

- Establish on floor plans with color codes the location of:

  - Security Office, Police, First Aid, security checkpoints, customs office
  - Telephones, Rest rooms, information desk, observation deck
  - Car Rentals, VIP Lounge, Check-in, departure lounge, luggage retrieval, restaurant, newsstand, duty-free shop
  - Airline and airline counters
  - Exchange office

- Any additional observation which might be unusual

N

Private/Corporate Airport Facilities

- Airport name, airport abbreviation code, location, check done by, date and time

- Address, contact numbers and route to access facility

- Hours of operation (opening and closing, by emergencies)

- Emergency response units location

- Night landing restrictions and equipment

- Noise and aircraft types restrictions

- Facility is independently operating or as part of local airport

- Length and number of runways

- Hangar, mechanics, fuel supply, catering and security

- Restaurant, conference facilities, rest rooms, telephones, other facilities

- Parking facilities

- Snow and ice removal, deicing facilities

- Jurisdiction of police, customs

- Hospital and trauma-facility, direct route

- Traffic conditions from airport to hospital, distance and time

- Any difficulties or problems encountered

- Unusual observations

- Additional observations and comments

N

Private/Corporate Aircraft

- Aircraft model, make, year, owner, registration number

- Total of flight hours
- Last and next maintenance
- Where is aircraft based
- Previous registered incidents with the aircraft
- Technical data, flight range, etc.
- Capacity for passengers and cargo

- Flight crew, position and how many
- Pilot and co-pilot qualifications and experience
- Flight crew details-names, address, contact numbers-background check
- Had the flight crew security training before
- Previous incidents registered, with one of the flight crew members

- Aircraft interior design layout-phone, bathroom, bed, couch, satellite phone, TV, VCR, internet, kitchen, tables, couch

- Hotel facilities for the flight crew

- Flight and travel preparations:

  - Departure info-site and time, arrival time of pilots and crew prior to departure, weather check for departure, en-route and at destination, catering arrangements
  - Flight and arrival time, pilot radio contact 20 minutes to touchdown
  - Contacts and phone numbers

O

Security Check for Hotels

This advance check should be made at a time of the day, when the arrival is expected. Be aware of shift changes in advance.

- Date, Time, Checked by

- General check
  - Name, address and all contact numbers of the hotel
  - Confirmation in writing of room and service reservation
  - Security facilities of the hotel security
  - Meeting arrangement with hotel manager, security director, Maitre'd, cook, door attendant and bell captain
  - Names, addresses, contact numbers and photos of the above personnel
  - Location of cameras and other security checks

- Hotel Manager
  - Location of rooms, floors, emergency needs and risks
  - Room numbers
  - Billing and payment arrangements
  - Special events during visit
  - Other requirements related to room personnel,, cleaning, room service, etc.
  - Security arrangements of any other VIP guests at the hotel (what type of VIP and related risk level)

- Director of Security
  - Any security breach in the past of the hotel (theft, assault, threats, etc.)
  - Location of safe-deposit boxes
  - Security phone 24 hours
  - Blueprint and specific needs during stay
  - Name, addresses, contact number of director
  - Local regulations regarding armed security personnel (available alternative such stun gun, etc.)

- Door attendant and Bell Captain
  - Name and any particulars
  - Advise the door attendant to be at ready when vehicle of principal arrives
  - Arrangements for vehicle parking and security
  - Checking of parking and surrounding area and vehicles
  - Check outdoor attendant assistants if any
  - Name of bell captain and particulars
  - Check and arrange the order how the luggage has to be delivered to the rooms

- Maitre' d
  - Name and particulars
  - Table arrangements. requirements and choice

P

- Specific food requirements-diets, others
- Inform how the principal has to addressed
- Specific beverage requirements, arrangements

- Hotel Inspection
  - Location of all hotel entrances and exits, including underground garage and roof level
  - Location of rest rooms, conference rooms and phones
  - Location and check of all staircases, elevators, fire extinguishers and fire detectors
  - Type of fire detection system
  - Fire alarm sound check and response time

- Hotel Services offered and available
  - Telephone, Fax, Internet, secretarial and notary public services
  - Safe-deposit boxes
  - Money Exchange
  - Valet and laundry services
  - Beauty parlor, room service, newspapers (names of papers)
  - Cable, satellite access
  - Recreational facilities, sauna, pool, solarium (type and access)

- Room Inspection
  - Room number/s
  - Emergency exits near to the room/s
  - Door and window locks
  - Fire, smoke detector and sprinkler system
  - Air-condition and heating system
  - Television, lights, phone, plugs
  - Bathroom, lights, plugs, etc.
  - Minibar, bottled water, ice compartment
  - Any hazardous items in rooms
  - Avoid rooms near to elevators, stairs, or any other noisy areas (ice dispenser, shoe polisher, etc.)

- Restaurant and Kitchen Inspection
  - Name of cook, particulars
  - Location of kitchen and number of restaurants
  - Bar and rest room location
  - Table location
  - Copy of menu (food variety and cooking style-French, Chinese, Italian etc.
  - Wine and beverage list
  - Restaurant opening times
  - Dress code

P

- Inspection of recreational facilities
  - Type of facilities available (Masseuse, Gym, Sauna, Pool, Tennis, Golf, etc.)
  - Access conditions: hotel guest, membership

- Police, Fire, Ambulance
  - Department chief name
  - Location, name, address, contact numbers
  - Response time

- Other points of consideration (condition of hotel and personnel, any problems found, language problems)

P

Building Check

- Date, Time, Checked by
- Name of building (if any), address, district, surrounding area and neighborhood (other businesses, stores, etc.), intersections, stops, general appearance
- Building type and construction characteristics
- Number of entrances, exits, floors, terraces, fire and emergency exit types
- Number of apartments, offices, workers, occupants
- Unused areas, floors
- Access to garage (access cards required)
- Roof access, roof structure and condition for Helicopter
- Roof Condition and details
  - Any access to a higher level from the roof
  - Roof type (straight-flat, peaked-slanted, etc.)
  - Roof cover material
  - Illumination and visibility to street and route
  - Other access/exit to and from roof
  - Roof height compared to other buildings
  - Access from roof to other buildings

- Building owner/s, name/s, address and contact number/s (day/night)
- Person in charge of building, name, address, contact number (day/night)
- Storage areas and dangerous material on roof
- Any generator or air-condition system housing
- Requirements for access Identification
  - Personnel
  - Vehicles
  - Principal
  - Visitors
- Special arrangements for armed personnel
- Location of security cameras and other security equipment (type and condition)
- Name and contact numbers of building security supervisor
- Visibility check of route from:
  - Roof, Terrace/s, balcony/s, Windows
- Is any of the following dangerous material stored in or around the building and how are they secured
  - Flares, explosive material, fuel, ammo, firearms

- Placement of personnel (armed, unarmed)
  - Roof
  - Garage entrance
  - Entrance and exits
  - Lobby
  - Drop and Pick-up location

- Nearest emergency services, police, hospital, contact numbers
- Emergency services response time
- Any additional requirements, attentions, arrangements

Restaurant Check

This advance check should be made at a time of the day, when the arrival is expected. Be aware of shift changes in advance.

- Date, Time, Checked by

- General check

- Name, address and contact restaurant

- Is a reservation required (how much time in advance)

- Name of restaurant manager, contact

- Restaurant and kitchen inspection

- Name of cook, particulars

- Location of kitchen, entrance/exit points

- Bar, rest room, phone, private rooms location

- Table location

- Copy of menu (food variety and cooking style-French, Chinese, Italian etc.

- Wine and beverage list

- Restaurant opening and closing times

- Dress code

- Payment arrangements (advance payment, cask or credit card)

- Extra services

- Smoking/Nonsmoking areas

- Arrangements for seating and tables

- Other events during time and day of visit

- Emergency services (Police, hospital, ambulance) contact numbers and location

R

Hospital Check

This advance check should be made at a time of the day, when the arrival is expected. Be aware of shift changes in advance.

- Date, Time, Checked by

- Name, address and contact numbers

  - Characteristics (affiliation, religious or not, special treatment or disease oriented, etc.)

- Names, position an contacts of administration staff members

- Contact numbers of emergency admission and ambulance service

- Helicopter landing facility

  - Address and coordinates, lighting, approach path, wind indicator

- Security specific:

  - Is protection personnel permitted to stay with Principal till discharge (24-hour duty)
  - What is the hospital policy for carrying weapons

- Contact numbers and names of hospital security department

- Number of qualified medical staff-for which units. If not available-what will be the response time

- Medical qualifications of the unit chiefs

- Check statistics for emergency, trauma and common treatments over a period of time

- Lab, diagnostic specific equipment, blood bank

- Private accommodations for patients (with/without family members)

- In case of need, is there any transfer protocol in place and for which situations and to where

- Address and contact numbers of the transfer location

- Details of the transfer location (same procedures)

- Procedures of billing and payment terms

Travel Contacts

- Country, region, city, country and local prefix

- Residence, hotel address, phone and fax numbers, e-mail address
- Persons to contact for reservations
- Confirmation for additional items, services

- Facilities available at location (computer, internet access, copy and shredding facilities, after hour service)

- Reservations were made and confirmed by principals, secretary, security or travel agents

- Hotel information, contact numbers, manager (refer to the *Hotel Check*-section for details)

- Airport information and confirmation

  - Travel/airline agent, contact numbers
  - Contact person at agency
  - Restrictions and regulations (security related)
  - Border/immigration authorities and Customs
  - Vaccination and visa
  - Time from airport to hotel
  - Car Rental service
  - Rental agency name, contact numbers
  - If a driver is contracted, name, license number, contact numbers
  - Type, make and model of car (luggage and passenger capacity)
  - Car phone number
  - Billing and payment arrangements

- Additional transportation arrangements:

  - Helicopter charter:

    - Company, Owner, phone numbers
    - Pilot, phone numbers, license number
    - Company and helicopter base
    - Pickup airport or pre-assigned location
    - Make, model, capacities, range of Helicopter

- Police and other security authorities

  - Commanding officer
  - Full address
  - Phone numbers
  - Special concerns and arrangements
  - Support and in which form

T

- Emergency Services

  - Hospital, name, address, phone numbers
  - Doctor, specialty, name, address, phone numbers
  - Dentist, name, address, phone numbers
  - Pharmacy, Drugstore, names, address, phone numbers

- Businesses and people to be visited

  - Names, addresses, phone numbers, particularities

- Restaurants, Bars, Clubs

  - Addresses, contact person, phone numbers, reservations
  - Other Observations

Security Guard Placements Check

- General Information
  - Show picture of principal with his/her particulars to the protection personnel
  - Picture and details of principal entourage
  - Purpose of visit, location and arrival time
  - Expected departure time and pick-up location

- Threat Analysis and other intelligence
  - Information about the possible threats from individuals/groups

- Guard posts and placement
  - ✓ Chain of command
  - ✓ Specific posts and the assigned individuals by name
  - ✓ Placement of Identification checking personnel (ID Scanner) outside special event location

- Relief and Report time
- Transport to and from posts
- Communication
  - Communication type
  - Radio frequency
  - Call sign assignment
  - Cell phone numbers

- Floor plan with floor assignments and posts
- Assignment of safe areas-designation on each floor
- Post assigned individual must familiarize with surroundings

- Required equipment:
  - Listing and posting each and every equipment piece required by name and quantity
  - Weapons other than the side-arms
  - Equipment type assigned to (name and post)

- ID System in use and the time schedule for change

- Protective Personnel
  - Support personnel
  - Room, Suite or residence
  - Guests (rooms)
  - Additional security personnel
  - Special personnel assigned

- Location of key box/locker
- Key Logbook
- ID Logbook

U

First Aid

❖ *Note:* This section is just a reminder of the basic rules of First Aid. The first minutes of a medical emergency situation are vital and every EPO and security officer must attend and qualify in a formal First Aid/CPR training.

❖ **Stay calm at all times-access the situation**

☐ Breathing Assessment

A person who is having difficulty breathing is in **respiratory distress**. A person who is not breathing is in **respiratory arrest**. A person in respiratory arrest needs **EAR** (**E**xpired **A**ir **R**esuscitation). When a person is in respiratory arrest, the heart may still be beating. Without expired air resuscitation, the heart will stop beating soon after breathing stops. In some instances the heart may stop beating first, and then breathing stops immediately. This casualty needs **CPR** (**C**ardio-**P**ulmonary **R**esuscitation), which combines expired air resuscitation with **ECC** (**E**xternal **C**hest **C**ompressions) to circulate the blood. Properly performed CPR can keep a casualty's vital organs supplied with oxygen-rich blood until ambulance personnel arrive to provide advanced care.

- The First Aid Process known as **DRABC**

- **D**–DANGER
Ensure the area is safe for you as the first aid provider, the casualty/s and any by-standers. If it is unsafe and you cannot secure the area without putting yourself at risk, call for assistance and the emergency services. If the area is safe, proceed with:

- **R**–RESPONSE
Gently touch the casualty to try to establish some sort of response. If the casualty responds, ask their name and if they have any injuries, pain etc. Check their vital signs and get an ambulance for the casualty if that is what is required. If the casualty does not respond the casualty is unconscious.
Immediately roll the casualty into the lateral position keeping their head, neck and spine in alignment in case of spinal injury. Once in the lateral position proceed with:

- **A**–AIRWAY
Position the casualty's chin at an angle downward, open the mouth and check for material which may cause an obstruction. Scoop the material out of the mouth using your fingers. Once the airway is clear, continue with:

- **B**–BREATHING
Open the casualty's breathing passage by putting the head in backward tilt. Bend over the casualty placing your hand on the rib cage and your ear over the mouth and nose.
LOOK, LISTEN AND FEEL FOR BREATHING.

V

If the casualty is breathing, ensure a safe lateral position and continue to observe the pulse and breathing. If the casualty is not breathing, commence EAR immediately.

- **C–CIRCULATION**
  Placing your fingers on the casualty's chin, drag down the throat halfway and move to the groove on either side of the throat. By checking in this manner it will ensure you are directly over the carotid artery. Check pulse for 10 seconds. If a pulse is present, recheck the breathing.
  If the casualty is **NOT breathing** continue/commence *EAR*. If the casualty does **NOT HAVE A PULSE** immediately commence CPR.

- ☐ Position of Casualty for EAR

  Roll the casualty back onto their back. Tilt the head back to open the airway and pistol grip the jaw to move the tongue from the back wall of the mouth. Open the mouth and get ready to provide mouth-to-mouth.

  Begin by giving **5 full breaths in 10 seconds**. After each breath turn your head to the side to ensure the chest rises and not the stomach, also you can listen for air being exhaled. If air goes into the stomach by mistake, reposition the casualty's head with more tilt and ensure you have a good pistol grip on the jaw.

❖ **Do not stop** EAR unless one of the following occurs:

  - The casualty starts to breath on their own
  - The casualty's pulse is not present-Commence *CPR*
  - Someone else arrives on the scene and can take over
  - The ambulance arrives and take over
  - You are physically exhausted and unable to continue

- EAR for Adults (9 years plus):

  - Open airway with full head tilt and jaw support
  - Make a "pistol grip" with your hand and apply to the chin
  - Other hand is applied to the top of the head
  - Give five (5) full breaths in ten (10) seconds
  - Check breathing and pulse
  - If no change continue EAR at the rate of one (1) breath every four (4) seconds (15 breaths per minute)
  - After the first minute (15 breaths) Check breathing and pulse
  - If no change, continue as required for two (2) minute periods. After each two (2) min period check breathing and pulse

- EAR for Child (1-8 years)
  EAR varies somewhat for a child (1 to 8 years of age) to take into account the size of the child and also the fact that children breathe at a faster rate and have a faster heart rate than do adults. Follow the same sequence as for an adult, with the following exceptions:

  - Head tilt will vary according to the development of the child
  - Gently breath air into the child using just enough pressure to make the chest rise
  - If the breath does not go in, check that the airway is open. More head tilt may be needed to open the airway.

  Because children breath faster than adults, give **1 breath every 3 seconds (20 breaths per minute) for a child**.
  Once the child begins to breathe on their own, position them into the lateral position and continuously monitor their pulse and breathing.

- EAR for Infants (<1 year)
  The head on an infant is unstable and must be supported continuously. Because the infant's tongue is proportionally larger it is more likely to block the airway, so be sure the airway is open when you give EAR.
  The breathing rate is the same as for children:
  1 puff every 3 seconds (20 puffs per minute).
  The EAR technique is similar to that for children with the following differences:

  - Steady the infant's head continuously because it is unstable
  - **Do not tilt back the head**, but support the jaw
  - Avoid putting any pressure on the soft tissues under the infant's chin because this could obstruct the airway
  - For EAR, cover both the infant's mouth and nose with your mouth
  - **Check** for the pulse in the arm at the brachial artery or listen over the chest.

- Mouth to Nose EAR
  Reasons for use:
  - Rescuer's choice
  - Jaw clenched tight
  - When resuscitating in deep water
  - Major mouth/jaw injuries

  Technique:
  - close the casualty's mouth with the hand that is supporting the jaw
  - apply head tilt and seal the lips with the thumb
  - blow into the casualty's nose
  - turn your head to the side, look, listen and feel

V

- Providing EAR for a casualty with a possible head, neck or back injury
  If you suspect a casualty has sustained a head, neck or back injury, you should try to minimize movement of the head and neck and spine as much as possible. If your casualty is not breathing EAR must still be performed and, if possible, you should **use jaw thrust** and not head tilt and jaw support.

- Providing EAR via the Mouth to Mask Technique
  The mouth-to-mask avoids mouth-to-mouth contact between the first aid provider and the casualty.

  Whenever available, this method should be used as it is more hygienic.

Resuscitation should not be delayed whilst waiting for the mask to arrive.

Method:

Position yourself at the head of the casualty facing the feet. Ensure a firm seal over both mouth and nose. Maintain head tilt, jaw thrust and breathe into the mask. Remove your mouth from the mask, move your head to the side keeping your eyes on the chest to check for inflation and also allow the casualty to exhale.

- Mouth to Stoma Method of EAR
  You may at some stage encounter a casualty who has had an operation to remove all or part of the upper end of the windpipe. After such an operation, the person must breathe through an opening called a stoma in the front of the neck. You may not see the stoma immediately. You will probably notice the opening in the neck as you tilt the head back to open the airway. If you see a tube in the stoma, always keep it in place to keep a hole open for breathing and resuscitation.
  If you see a valve closing the tube, you must remove the valve before giving EAR to allow the air to enter.

  When providing air through the stoma you must ensure:

  - your mouth is sealed around the stoma
  - the stoma or tube is not blocked
  - closure over the mouth and nose to prevent air escaping.

- Distension of the stomach
  This may occur when air enters the stomach instead of the lungs. This is usually due to too much air being blown into the lungs causing over-inflation or the head is not positioned properly using enough head tilt. If the stomach does become distended **DO NOT APPLY PRESSURE TO THE STOMACH** as this may cause regurgitation.

V

- CPR (**C**ardio-**P**ulmonary **R**esuscitation)

  Always commence with:
  Danger
  Response
  Airway
  Breathing (no breathing, give 5 breaths in 10 seconds)
  Circulation (no pulse, commence CPR immediately).
  Remember, chest compressions on a beating heart, which are not needed, may cause harm. Always check for a pulse for up to 10 seconds.

- CPR for Adults 9 years plus

  For chest compressions to be effective there are some important points to keep in mind:
  - the casualty should be lying flat on a firm surface
  - kneel beside the casualty directly opposite their shoulder
  - position your hands into the middle of the lower half of the sternum

Only the heel on one hand should have contact with the chest, fingers parallel with the ribs and up off the rib cage. The other hand supports the first hand which is in contact with the chest

  - depress the sternum 1/3 of the casualty's depth of chest, keeping compressions very smooth and rhythmical
  - **compress the chest 15 times, then provide 2 effective breaths**
  - repeat this sequence 4 times in a minute
  - at the end of the first minute check the pulse and breathing
  - if no change continue as above for two (2) minute blocks.

  - CPR for Children (1-8years) and Infants
    (0-1year) CPR for infants and children is exactly the same whether one (1) or two (2) operators, however you must take into consideration the following:

- *for children:*
  - breaths should be enough to make the chest rise
  - compressions are still at 1/3 of the depth of chest
  - compressions are conducted with one (1) hand only
  - partial head tilt with jaw support

- *for infants:*
  - support the jaw without tilting the head
  - compressions are still at 1/3 of the depth of the chest
  - compressions are conducted with two (2) fingers on the lower half of the sternum
  - use PUFFS of air instead of breaths

V

- When to cease performing CPR
  Once you commence CPR it is necessary to continue to ensure you circulate oxygenated blood around the body. You do not stop resuscitation unless one of the following occurs:

  - someone else arrives at the scene and takes over CPR for you
  - the ambulance arrives
  - the casualty responds
  - the area becomes dangerous and it is not safe to continue
  - you are unable to continue because of exhaustion.

☐ **Trauma Kit**

The trauma kit should contain the following items:

- Multitrauma dressing (12" x 30")
- CPR mask
- Sterile burn dressing
- Triangular bandage
- Extrication collar
- Gauze (4" x 4")
- Sterile water for sterilization and rinsing
- Paramedic scissors
- Blankets
- Adhesive tape
- Oval eye pads
- Sterile alcohol wipes
- Instant ice pack
- Gauze bandage
- Sterile gloves
- Vaseline gauze (5" x 9")
- Stabilizing splints (full leg and full arm)
- Oxygen tank
- Wound disinfectant

❖ **Every EPO must obtain qualified training to handle the following emergencies:**

  ❖ Car accidents, heart stroke, massive injuries (explosion), knife and gun shoot wounds, fire and smoke inhalation injuries.

V

Bomb Threats

Procedure:

❖ Be calm. Be courteous. Listen. Do not interrupt the caller. Notify supervisor/security officer of your element by prearranged signal while caller is on the line.

- Date and Time the call started
- Date and Time the call ended
- Exact words of person placing call

❖ Questions to ask:

1. When is the bomb going to explode?
2. Where is the bomb right now?
3. What kind of bomb is it?
4. What does the bomb look like?
5. What will cause it to explode?
6. Why did you place the bomb?
7. What is your name and address?

❖ Try to determine the following:

- **Caller's identity**: Male, Female, Adult, Juvenile, Age
- **Voice**: Loud, Soft, High-pitched, Deep, Intoxicated, Other
- **Accent**: Local, Foreign, Region (description)
- **Speech**: Fast, Slow, Distinct, Distorted, Stutter, Slurred, Nasal
- **Language**: Excellent, Good, Fair, Poor, Foul, Other
- **Manner**: Calm, Angry, Rational, Irrational, Coherent, Incoherent, Deliberate, Emotional, Righteous, Laughing, Intoxicated
- **Background noise**: Office machines, Factory machines, Bedlam Trains, Animals, Music, Voices, Airplanes, Street-Traffic, Mixed, Party-Atmosphere, Other
- Additional Information

❖ Receiving telephone number, Person receiving call

❖ Report Call immediately to authorities.

❖ Ensure that this can be accomplished on a second independent line.

W

Letter-/Package-Bombs

Characteristics:

- ❖ Foreign mail, airmail, special delivery

- ❖ Excessive postage

- ❖ Special markings such as "Confidential", "Personal", "Classified material"

- ❖ Poorly handwritten or typed addresses

- ❖ No sender address

- ❖ Incorrect title, name spelling

- ❖ Missing or misspelled parts in name and/or address

- ❖ Smell

- ❖ Discoloration

- ❖ Oily stains

- ❖ Excessive weight compared with type of package

- ❖ Uneven envelope

- ❖ Tinfoil or wires are protruding

- ❖ Excess in packaging material, such as tape, strings, etc.

X

NOTES

The following forms can be adapted for use as needed.

- ❏ **Fingerprint Form**

- ❏ **Vehicle Search/Location/Installation Report**

- ❏ **Aircraft Search Report**

- ❏ **Building Search/Location/Installation Report**

- ❏ **Bomb Threat Report Form**

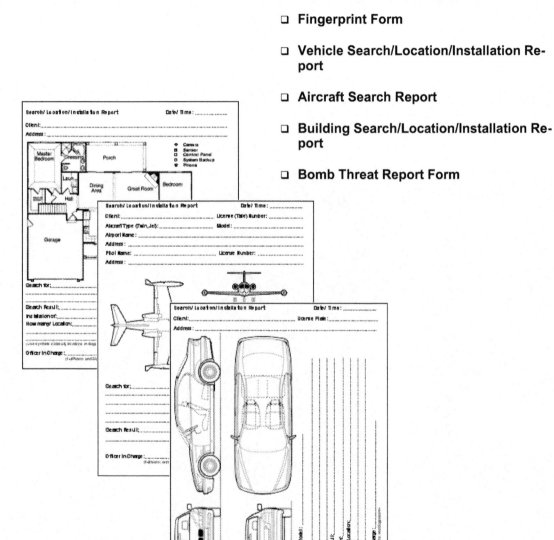

Fingerprint Form -Child

- A -

Child's Name: _____ Date Photo was Taken: _____

Place of Birth: _____ Date of Birth: _____ Age at time of photo: _____

Sex: **M ( ) F ( )** Race: _____ Height: _____ Weight: _____ Hair: _____ Eyes: _____

Blood Type: _____ Scars, Birthmarks, Piercing, Tattoos: _____

Address: _____ Phone Number: _____

Father's Name: _____ Home Phone: _____ Work Phone: _____ GSM: _____

Mother's Name: _____ Home Phone: _____ Work Phone: _____ GSM: _____

School Child attends (name): _____ Address: _____

Phone Number: _____ Room Number: _____ Teacher's Name: _____ Principal's Name: _____

Doctor's Name: _____ Phone Number: _____ GSM: _____

Dentist's Name: _____ Phone Number: _____ GSM: _____

Additional Information (habits, hobbies, sports): _____

Special Medication: _____

Person to notify in case of emergency: _____ Address: _____

Phone: _____ GSM: _____

PHOTO

Place "X" on figures to indicate location of moles, scars, piercing, tattoo or birthmark

Front

1. _____
2. _____
3. _____
4. _____
5. _____
6. _____

Back

1. _____
2. _____
3. _____
4. _____
5. _____
6. _____

Fingerprinted by: _____ Date Fingerprinted: _____

363

R. Thumb	R. Index	R. Middle	R. Ring	R. Little

L. Thumb	L. Index	L. Middle	L. Ring	L. Little

Fingerprint Form -Child   - B -

Right Four Fingers Taken Simultaneously

Left Four Fingers Taken Simultaneously

Fingerprint Form -Adult

- A -

Name (last): _____ First: _____ Middle: _____

Place of Birth: _____ Date of Birth: _____ Date Photo was Taken: _____

Age at time of photo: _____

Sex: **M ( ) F ( )** Race: _____ Height: _____ Weight: _____ Hair: _____ Eyes: _____

Blood Type: _____ Scars, Birthmarks, Piercing, Tattoos: _____

Address: _____ Phone Number: _____

GSM: _____ Social Security Number: _____ Company Name: _____

Work Address: _____ Work Phone: _____

Doctor's Name: _____ Phone Number: _____ GSM: _____

Dentist's Name: _____ Phone Number: _____ GSM: _____

Additional Information (habits, hobbies, sports): _____

Special Medication: _____

Person to notify in case of emergency: _____ Address: _____

Phone: _____ GSM: _____

PHOTO

Front

1. _____
2. _____
3. _____
4. _____
5. _____
6. _____

Place "X" on figures to indicate location of moles, scars, piercing, tattoo or birthmark

Back

1. _____
2. _____
3. _____
4. _____
5. _____
6. _____

Fingerprinted by: _____ Date Fingerprinted: _____

Fingerprint Form -Adult - B -

R. Thumb	R. Index	R. Middle	R. Ring	R. Little
L. Thumb	L. Index	L. Middle	L. Ring	L. Little

Right Four Fingers Taken Simultaneously

Left Four Fingers Taken Simultaneously

Search/Location/Installation Report   **Date/Time:** _____

Client: _____ License Plate: _____

Address: _____

Car Make/ Model: _____

Search for: _____

Search Result: _____

Installation of: _____

How many/ Location: _____

Officer in Charge: _____
(Full Name and Signature)

Use the above form for a vehicle search, or the location and installation of security and camera systems. (Replace the blueprint with your own diagram. Any car dealer can provide corresponding blueprints for model and make).

Search/Location/Installation Report   **Date/Time:** _____

Client: _____ License (Tale) Number: _____

Aircraft Type (Twin, Jet): _____ Model: _____

Airport Name: _____

Address: _____

Pilot Name: _____ License Number: _____

Address: _____

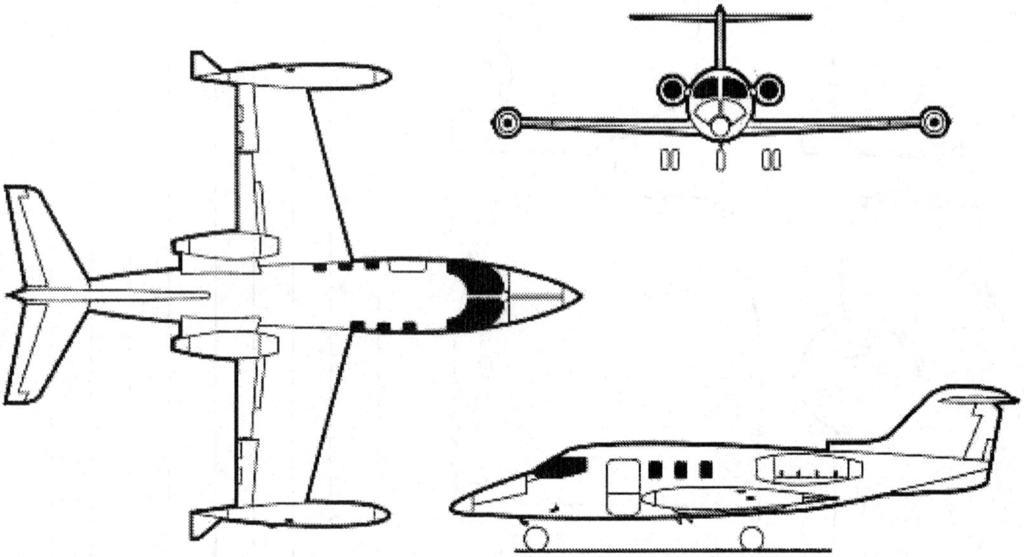

Search for:_____

_____

_____

_____

_____

Search Result:_____

_____

Officer in Charge:_____
                      (Full Name and Signature)

Use the above form for an aircraft search. (Replace the blueprint with your own diagram. Any aircraft dealer can provide corresponding blueprints for model and make).

Building/Construction Blueprint Familiarization

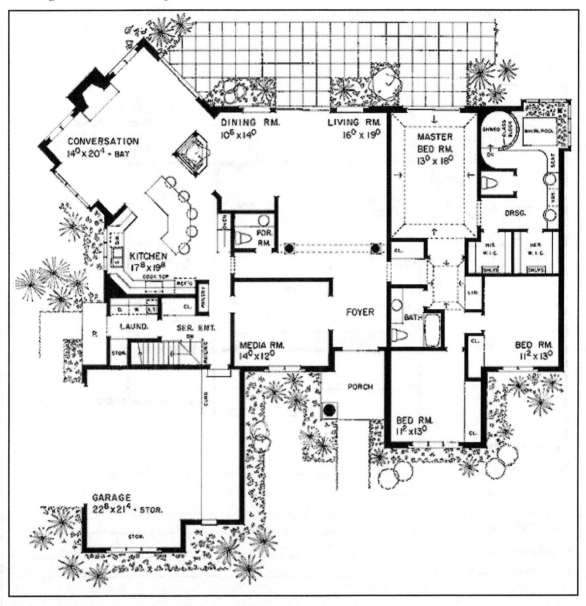

Many people have a certain difficulty in reading and understanding a construction diagram of a building, including house owners. The above is a simple standard blueprint of the type of house one might be confronted with, while on assignment as an EPO.

Familiarization with the appearance, terminology and the symbols of a blueprint is part of the job. Symbols, measurements and presentation of a blueprint are slightly different, depending on a country's standards. The Internet is the best source to get advance information and further details on standards in the country of operation.

Search/Location/Installation Report **Date/Time:** ___________

Client: ____

Address: ____

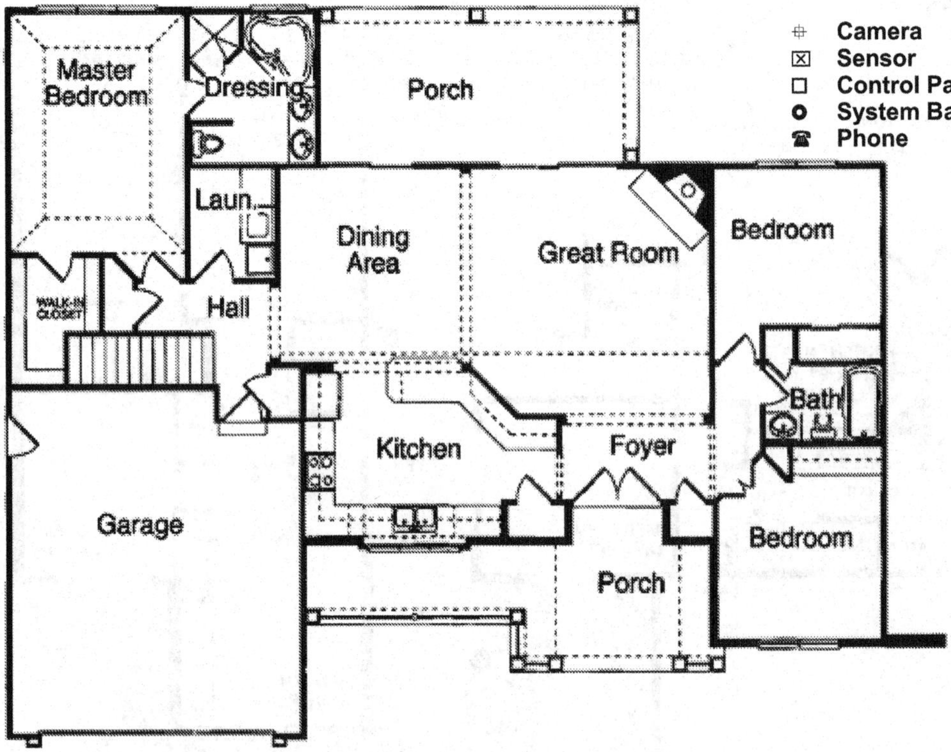
Camera
Sensor
Control Panel
System Backup
Phone
Master Bedroom
Dressing
Porch
Laun.
Dining Area
Great Room
Bedroom
Walk-in Closet
Hall
Bath
Kitchen
Foyer
Garage
Bedroom
Porch

Search for: ____

____

____

Search Result: ____

Installation of: ____

How many/Location: ____

____

____

(Use symbols to identify locations in diagram)

Officer in Charge: ______________________________
(Full Name and Signature)

Use the above form for a building search, or the location and installation of security and camera systems. (Replace the blueprint with your own diagram).

BOMB THREAT REPORT FORM

INSTRUCTIONS:
Be calm. Be courteous. Listen. Do not interrupt the caller. Notify supervisor/security officer of your element by prearranged signal while caller is on the line.

DATE: _____   TIME: _____

Exact words of person placing call: _____

_____

QUESTIONS TO ASK:

1. When is the bomb going to explode? _____
2. Where is the bomb right now? _____
3. What kind of bomb is it? _____
4. What does the bomb look like? _____
5. What will cause it to explode? _____
6. Why did you place the bomb? _____
7. What is your name and address? _____

Try to determine the following:
(circle as appropriate)

Caller's identity:

Male	Female	Adult	Juvenile	Age _____	years

Voice: Loud Soft High-pitched Deep Intoxicated Other _____

Accent: Local Foreign Region (description) _____

Speech: Fast Slow Distinct Distorted Stutter Slurred Nasal_____

Language: Excellent Good Fair Poor Foul Other _____

Manner: Calm Angry Rational Irrational Coherent Incoherent
Deliberate Emotional Righteous Laughing Intoxicated

Background noise: Office machines Factory machines Bedlam Trains Animals
Music Voices Airplanes Street-Traffic
Mixed Party-Atmosphere Other

ADDITIONAL INFORMATION:

_____

_____

_____

_____

_____

_____   _____
Receiving Telephone Number   Person Receiving Call

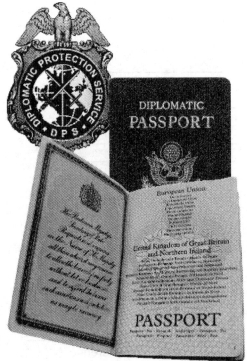

- Vienna Convention on Diplomatic Relations

- Vienna Convention on Consular Relations

- Documents used in the Diplomatic Service

- Definitions of Diplomatic Security Terms

- Diplomatic/Consular Privileges and Immunity from Criminal Jurisdiction

Vienna Convention on Diplomatic Relations
Done at Vienna on 18 April 1961

The States Parties to the present Convention,

Recalling that peoples of all nations from ancient times have recognized the status of diplomatic agents,

Having in mind the purposes and principles of the Charter of the United Nations concerning the sovereign equality of States, the maintenance of international peace and security, and the promotion of friendly relations among nations,

Believing that an international convention on diplomatic intercourse, privileges and immunities would contribute to the development of friendly relations among nations, irrespective of their differing constitutional and social systems,

Realizing that the purpose of such privileges and immunities is not to benefit individuals but to ensure the efficient performance of the functions of diplomatic missions as representing States, affirming that the rules of customary international law should continue to govern questions not expressly regulated by the provisions of the present Convention,

Have agreed as follows:

Article 1

For the purpose of the present Convention, the following expressions shall have the meanings hereunder assigned to them:

(a) The "head of the mission" is the person charged by the sending State with the duty of acting in that capacity;

(b) The "members of the mission" are the head of the mission and the members of the staff of the mission;

(c) The "members of the staff of the mission" are the members of the diplomatic staff, of the administrative and technical staff and of the service staff of the mission;

(d) The "members of the diplomatic staff" are the members of the staff of the mission having diplomatic rank;

(e) A "diplomatic agent" is the head of the mission or a member of the diplomatic staff of the mission;

(f) The "members of the administrative and technical staff" are the members of the staff of the mission employed in the administrative and technical service of the mission;

(g) The "members of the service staff" are the members of the staff of the mission in the domestic service of the mission;

(h) A "private servant" is a person who is in the domestic service of a member of the mission and who is not an employee of the sending State;

(i) The "premises of the mission" are the buildings or parts of buildings and the land ancillary thereto, irrespective of ownership, used for the purposes of the mission including the residence of the head of the mission.

Article 2

The establishment of diplomatic relations between States, and of permanent diplomatic missions, takes place by mutual consent.

Article 3

1. The functions of a diplomatic mission consist, inter alia, in:

    (a) Representing the sending State in the receiving State;
    (b) Protecting in the receiving State the interests of the sending State and of its nationals, within the limits permitted by international law;
    (c) Negotiating with the Government of the receiving State;
    (d) Ascertaining by all lawful means conditions and developments in the receiving State, and reporting thereon to the Government of the sending State;
    (e) Promoting friendly relations between the sending State and the receiving State, and developing their economic, cultural and scientific relations.

2. Nothing in the present Convention shall be construed as preventing the performance of consular functions by a diplomatic mission.

Article 4

1. The sending State must make certain that the *agreement* of the receiving State has been given for the person it proposes to accredit as head of the mission to that State.

2. The receiving State is not obliged to give reasons to the sending State for a refusal of *agreement*.

Article 5

1. The sending State may, after it has given due notification to the receiving States concerned, accredit a head of mission or assign any member of the diplomatic staff, as the case may be, to more than one State, unless there is express objection by any of the receiving States.

2. If the sending State accredits a head of mission to one or more other States it may establish a diplomatic mission headed by a chargé d' affaires ad interim in each State where the head of mission has not his permanent seat.

3. A head of mission or any member of the diplomatic staff of the mission may act as representative of the sending State to any international organization.

Article 6

Two or more States may accredit the same person as head of mission to another State, unless objection is offered by the receiving State.

Article 7

Subject to the provisions of articles 5, 8, 9 and 11, the sending State may freely appoint the members of the staff of the mission. In the case of military, naval or air attachés, the receiving State may require their names to be submitted beforehand, for its approval.

Article 8

1. Members of the diplomatic staff of the mission should in principle be of the nationality of the sending State.

2. Members of the diplomatic staff of the mission may not be appointed from among persons having the nationality of the receiving State, except with the consent of that State which may be withdrawn at any time.

3. The receiving State may reserve the same right with regard to nationals of a third State who are not also nationals of the sending State.

Article 9

1. The receiving State may at any time and without having to explain its decision, notify the sending State that the head of the mission or any member of the diplomatic staff of the mission is persona non grata or that any other member of the staff of the mission is not acceptable. In any such case, the sending State shall, as appropriate, either recall the person concerned or terminate his functions with the mission. A person may be declared non grata or not acceptable before arriving in the territory of the receiving State.

2. If the sending State refuses or fails within a reasonable period to carry out its obligations under paragraph 1 of this article, the receiving State may refuse to recognize the person concerned as a member of the mission.

Article 10

1. The Ministry for Foreign Affairs of the receiving State, or such other ministry as may be agreed, shall be notified of:

   (a) The appointment of members of the mission, their arrival and their final departure or the termination of their functions with the mission;
   (b) The arrival and final departure of a person belonging to the family of a member of the mission and, where appropriate, the fact that a person becomes or ceases to be a member of the family of a member of the mission;
   (c) The arrival and final departure of private servants in the employ of persons referred to in subparagraph (a) of this paragraph and, where appropriate, the fact that they are leaving the employ of such persons;
   (d) The engagement and discharge of persons resident in the receiving State as members of the mission or private servants entitled to privileges and immunities.

2. Where possible, prior notification of arrival and final departure shall also be given.

Article 11

1. In the absence of specific agreement as to the size of the mission, the receiving State may require that the size of a mission be kept within limits considered by it to be reasonable and normal, having regard to circumstances and conditions in the receiving State and to the needs of the particular mission.

2. The receiving State may equally, within similar bounds and on a non-discriminatory basis, refuse to accept officials of a particular category.

Article 12

The sending State may not, without the prior express consent of the receiving State, establish offices forming part of the mission in localities other than those in which the mission itself is established.

Article 13

1. The head of the mission is considered as having taken up his functions in the receiving State either when he has presented his credentials or when he has notified his arrival and a true copy of his credentials has been presented to the Ministry for Foreign Affairs of the receiving State, or such other ministry as may be agreed, in accordance with the practice prevailing in the receiving State which shall be applied in a uniform manner.

2. The order of presentation of credentials or of a true copy thereof will be determined by the date and time of the arrival of the head of the mission.

Article 14

1. Heads of mission are divided into three classes, namely:

    (a) That of ambassadors or nuncios accredited to Heads of State, and other heads of mission of equivalent rank;
    (b) That of envoys, ministers and internuncios accredited to Heads of State;
    (c) That of charges d' affaires accredited to Ministers for Foreign Affairs.

2. Except as concerns precedence and etiquette, there shall be no differentiation between heads of mission by reason of their class.

Article 15

The class to which the heads of their missions are to be assigned shall be agreed between States.

Article 16

1. Heads of mission shall take precedence in their respective classes in the order of the date and time of taking up their functions in accordance with article 13.

2. Alterations in the credentials of a head of mission not involving any change of class shall not affect his precedence.

3. This article is without prejudice to any practice accepted by the receiving State regarding the precedence of the representative of the Holy See.

Article 17

The precedence of the members of the diplomatic staff of the mission shall be notified by the head of the mission to the Ministry for Foreign Affairs or such other ministry as may be agreed.

Article 18

The procedure to be observed in each State for the reception of heads of mission shall be uniform in respect of each class.

Article 19

1. If the post of head of the mission is vacant, or if the head of the mission is unable to perform his

functions a chargé d' affaires ad interim shall act provisionally as head of the mission. The name of the chargé d' affaires ad interim shall be notified, either by the head of the mission or, in case he is unable to do so, by the Ministry for Foreign Affairs of the sending State to the Ministry for Foreign Affairs of the receiving State or such other ministry as may be agreed.

2. In cases where no member of the diplomatic staff of the mission is present in the receiving State, a member of the administrative and technical staff may, with the consent of the receiving State, be designated by the sending State to be in charge of the current administrative affairs of the mission.

Article 20

The mission and its head shall have the right to use the flag and emblem of the sending State on the premises of the mission, including the residence of the head of the mission, and on his means of transport.

Article 21

1. The receiving State shall either facilitate the acquisition on its territory, in accordance with its laws, by the sending State of premises necessary for its mission or assist the latter in obtaining accommodation in some other way.

2. It shall also, where necessary, assist missions in obtaining suitable accommodation for their members.

Article 22

1. The premises of the mission shall be inviolable. The agents of the receiving State may not enter them, except with the consent of the head of the mission.

2. The receiving State is under a special duty to take all appropriate steps to protect the premises of the mission against any intrusion or damage and to prevent any disturbance of the peace of the mission or impairment of its dignity.

3. The premises of the mission, their furnishings and other property thereon and the means of transport of the mission shall be immune from search, requisition, attachment or execution.

Article 23

1. The sending State and the head of the mission shall be exempt from all national, regional or municipal dues and taxes in respect of the premises of the mission, whether owned or leased, other than such as represent payment for specific services rendered.

2. The exemption from taxation referred to in this article shall not apply to such dues and taxes payable under the law of the receiving State by persons contracting with the sending State or the head of the mission.

Article 24

The archives and documents of the mission shall be inviolable at any time and wherever they may be.

Article 25

The receiving State shall accord full facilities for the performance of the functions of the mission.

Article 26

Subject to its laws and regulations concerning zones entry into which is prohibited or regulated for reasons of national security, the receiving State shall ensure to all members of the mission freedom of movement and travel in its territory.

Article 27

1. The receiving State shall permit and protect free communication on the part of the mission for all official purposes. In communicating with the Government and the other missions and consulates of the sending State, wherever situated, the mission may employ all appropriate means, including diplomatic couriers and messages in code or cipher. However, the mission may install and use a wireless transmitter only with the consent of the receiving State.

2. The official correspondence of the mission shall be inviolable. Official correspondence means all correspondence relating to the mission and its functions.

3. The diplomatic bag shall not be opened or detained.

4. The packages constituting the diplomatic bag must bear visible external marks of their character and may contain only diplomatic documents or articles intended for official use.

5. The diplomatic courier, who shall be provided with an official document indicating his status and the number of packages constituting the diplomatic bag, shall be protected by the receiving State in the performance of his functions. He shall enjoy person inviolability and shall not be liable to any form of arrest or detention.

6. The sending State or the mission may designate diplomatic couriers ad hoc. In such cases the provisions of paragraph 5 of this article shall also apply, except that the immunities therein mentioned shall cease to apply when such a courier has delivered to the consignee the diplomatic bag in his charge.

7. A diplomatic bag may be entrusted to the captain of a commercial aircraft scheduled to land at an authorized port of entry. He shall be provided with an official document indicating the number of packages constituting the bag but he shall not be considered to be a diplomatic courier. The mission may send one of its members to take possession of the diplomatic bag directly and freely from the captain of the aircraft.

Article 28

The fees and charges levied by the mission in the course of its official duties shall be exempt from all dues and taxes.

Article 29

The person of a diplomatic agent shall be inviolable. He shall not be liable to any form of arrest or detention. The receiving State shall treat him with due respect and shall take all appropriate steps to prevent any attack on his person, freedom or dignity.

Article 30

1. The private residence of a diplomatic agent shall enjoy the same inviolability and protection as the premises of the mission.

2. His papers, correspondence and, except as provided in paragraph 3 of article 31, his property, shall

likewise enjoy inviolability.

Article 31

1. A diplomatic agent shall enjoy immunity from the criminal jurisdiction of the receiving State. He shall also enjoy immunity from its civil and administrative jurisdiction, except in the case of:

    (a) A real action relating to private immovable property situated in the territory of the receiving State, unless he holds it on behalf of the sending State for the purposes of the mission;

    (b) An action relating to succession in which the diplomatic agent is involved as executor, administrator, heir or legatee as a private person and not on behalf of the sending State;

    (c) An action relating to any professional or commercial activity exercised by the diplomatic agent in the receiving State outside his official functions.

2. A diplomatic agent is not obliged to give evidence as a witness.

3. No measures of execution may be taken in respect of a diplomatic agent except in the cases coming under subparagraphs (a), (b) and (c) of paragraph 1 of this article, and provided that the measures concerned can be taken without infringing the inviolability of his person or of his residence.

4. The immunity of a diplomatic agent from the jurisdiction of the receiving State does not exempt him from the jurisdiction of the sending State.

Article 32

1. The immunity from jurisdiction of diplomatic agents and of persons enjoying immunity under article 37 may be waived by the sending State.

2. Waiver must always be express.

3. The initiation of proceedings by a diplomatic agent or by a person enjoying immunity from jurisdiction under article 37 shall preclude him from invoking immunity from jurisdiction in respect of any counter-claim directly connected with the principal claim.

4. Waiver of immunity from jurisdiction in respect of civil or administrative proceedings shall not be held to imply waiver of immunity in respect of the execution of the judgment, for which a separate waiver shall be necessary.

Article 33

1. Subject to the provisions of paragraph 3 of this article, a diplomatic agent shall with respect to services rendered for the sending State be exempt from social security provisions which may be in force in the receiving State.

2. The exemption provided for in paragraph 1 of this article shall also apply to private servants who are in the sole employ of a diplomatic agent, on condition:

    (a) That they are not nationals of or permanently resident in the receiving State; and

    (b) That they are covered by the social security provisions which may be in force in the sending State or a third State.

3. A diplomatic agent who employs persons to whom the exemption provided for in paragraph 2 of this article does not apply shall observe the obligations which the social security provisions of the receiving

State impose upon employers.

4. The exemption provided for in paragraphs 1 and 2 of this article shall not preclude voluntary participation in the social security system of the receiving State provided that such participation is permitted by that State.

5. The provisions of this article shall not affect bilateral or multilateral agreements concerning social security concluded previously and shall not prevent the conclusion of such agreements in the future.

Article 34

A diplomatic agent shall be exempt from all dues and taxes, personal or real, national, regional or municipal, except:

    (a) Indirect taxes of a kind which are normally incorporated in the price of goods or services;

    (b) Dues and taxes on private immovable property situated in the territory of the receiving State, unless he holds it on behalf of the sending State for the purposes of the mission;

    (c) Estate, succession or inheritance duties levied by the receiving State, subject to the provisions of paragraph 4 of article 39;

    (d) Dues and taxes on private income having its source in the receiving State and capital taxes on investments made in commercial undertakings in the receiving State;

    (e) Charges levied for specific services rendered;

    (f) Registration, court or record fees, mortgage dues and stamp duty, with respect to immovable property, subject to the provisions of article 23.

Article 35

The receiving State shall exempt diplomatic agents from all personal services, from all public service of any kind whatsoever, and from military obligations such as those connected with requisitioning, military contributions and billeting.

Article 36

1. The receiving State shall, in accordance with such laws and regulations as it may adopt, permit entry of and grant exemption from all customs duties, taxes, and related charges other than charges for storage, cartage and similar services, on:

    (a) Articles for the official use of the mission;

    (b) Articles for the personal use of a diplomatic agent or members of his family forming part of his household, including articles intended for his establishment.

2. The personal baggage of a diplomatic agent shall be exempt from inspection, unless there are serious grounds for presuming that it contains articles not covered by the exemptions mentioned in paragraph 1 of this article, or articles the import or export of which is prohibited by the law or controlled by the quarantine regulations of the receiving State. Such inspection shall be conducted only in the presence of the diplomatic agent or of his authorized representative.

Article 37

1. The members of the family of a diplomatic agent forming part of his household shall, if they are not nationals of the receiving State, enjoy the privileges and immunities specified in articles 29 to 36.

2. Members of the administrative and technical staff of the mission, together with members of their families forming part of their respective households, shall, if they are not nationals of or permanently

resident in the receiving State, enjoy the privileges and immunities specified in articles 29 to 35, except that the immunity from civil and administrative jurisdiction of the receiving State specified in paragraph 1 of article 31 shall not extend to acts performed outside the course of their duties. They shall also enjoy the privileges specified in article 36, paragraph 1, in respect of articles imported at the time of first installation.

3. Members of the service staff of the mission who are not nationals of or permanently resident in the receiving State shall enjoy immunity in respect of acts performed in the course of their duties, exemption from dues and taxes on the emoluments they receive by reason of their employment and the exemption contained in article 33.

4. Private servants of members of the mission shall, if they are not nationals of or permanently resident in the receiving State, be exempt from dues and taxes on the emoluments they receive by reason of their employment. In other respects, they may enjoy privileges and immunities only to the extent admitted by the receiving State. However, the receiving State must exercise its jurisdiction over those persons in such a manner as not to interfere unduly with the performance of the functions of the mission.

Article 38

1. Except insofar as additional privileges and immunities may be granted by the receiving State, a diplomatic agent who is a national of or permanently resident in that State shall enjoy only immunity from jurisdiction, and inviolability, in respect of official acts performed in the exercise of his functions.

2. Other members of the staff of the mission and private servants who are nationals of or permanently resident in the receiving State shall enjoy privileges and immunities only to the extent admitted by the receiving State. However, the receiving State must exercise its jurisdiction over those persons in such a manner as not to interfere unduly with the performance of the functions of the mission.

Article 39

1. Every person entitled to privileges and immunities shall enjoy them from the moment he enters the territory of the receiving State on proceeding to take up his post or, if already in its territory, from the moment when his appointment is notified to the Ministry for Foreign Affairs or such other ministry as may be agreed.

2. When the functions of a person enjoying privileges and immunities have come to an end, such privileges and immunities shall normally cease at the moment when he leaves the country, or on expiry of a reasonable period in which to do so, but shall subsist until that time, even in case of armed conflict. However, with respect to acts performed by such a person in the exercise of his functions as a member of the mission, immunity shall continue to subsist.

3. In case of the death of a member of the mission, the members of his family shall continue to enjoy the privileges and immunities to which they are entitled until the expiry of a reasonable period in which to leave the country.

4. In the event of the death of a member of the mission not a national of or permanently resident in the receiving State or a member of his family forming part of his household, the receiving State shall permit the withdrawal of the movable property of the deceased, with the exception of any property acquired in the country the export of which was prohibited at the time of his death. Estate, succession and inheritance duties shall not be levied on movable property the presence of which in the receiving State was due solely to the presence there of the deceased as a member of the mission or as a member of the family of a member of the mission.

Article 40

1. If a diplomatic agent passes through or is in the territory of a third State, which has granted him a passport visa if such visa was necessary, while proceeding to take up or to return to his post, or when returning to his own country, the third State shall accord him inviolability and such other immunities as may be required to ensure his transit or return. The same shall apply in the case of any members of his family enjoying privileges or immunities who are accompanying the diplomatic agent, or traveling separately to join him or to return to their country.

2. In circumstances similar to those specified in paragraph 1 of this article, third States shall not hinder the passage of members of the administrative and technical or service staff of a mission, and of members of their families, through their territories.

3. Third States shall accord to official correspondence and other official communications in transit, including messages in code or cipher, the same freedom and protection as is accorded by the receiving State. They shall accord to diplomatic couriers, who have been granted a passport visa if such visa was necessary, and diplomatic bags in transit, the same inviolability and protection as the receiving State is bound to accord.

4. The obligations of third States under paragraphs 1, 2 and 3 of this article shall also apply to the persons mentioned respectively in those paragraphs, and to official communications and diplomatic bags, whose presence in the territory of the third State is due to force majeure.

Article 41

1. Without prejudice to their privileges and immunities, it is the duty of all persons enjoying such privileges and immunities to respect the laws and regulations of the receiving State. They also have a duty not to interfere in the internal affairs of that State.

2. All official business with the receiving State entrusted to the mission by the sending State shall be conducted with or through the Ministry for Foreign Affairs of the receiving State or such other ministry as may be agreed.

3. The premises of the mission must not be used in any manner incompatible with the functions of the mission as laid down in the present Convention or by other rules of general international law or by any special agreements in force between the sending and the receiving State.

Article 42

A diplomatic agent shall not in the receiving State practice for personal profit any professional or commercial activity.

Article 43

The function of a diplomatic agent comes to an end, inter alia:

(a) On notification by the sending State to the receiving State that the function of the diplomatic agent has come to an end;
(b) On notification by the receiving State to the sending State that, in accordance with paragraph 2 of article 9, it refuses to recognize the diplomatic agent as a member of the mission.

Article 44

The receiving State must, even in case of armed conflict, grant facilities in order to enable persons enjoying privileges and immunities, other than nationals of the receiving State, and members of the families of such persons irrespective of their nationality, to leave at the earliest possible moment. It must, in particular, in case of need, place at their disposal the necessary means of transport for themselves and their property.

Article 45

If diplomatic relations are broken off between two States, or if a mission is permanently or temporarily recalled:

(a) The receiving State must, even in case of armed conflict, respect and protect the premises of the mission, together with its property and archives;

(b) The sending State may entrust the custody of the premises of the mission, together with its property and archives, to a third State acceptable to the receiving State;

(c) The sending State may entrust the protection of its interests and those of its nationals to a third State acceptable to the receiving State.

Article 46

A sending State may with the prior consent of a receiving State, and at the request of a third State not represented in the receiving State, undertake the temporary protection of the interests of the third State and of its nationals.

Article 47

1. In the application of the provisions of the present Convention, the receiving State shall not discriminate as between States.

2. However, discrimination shall not be regarded as taking place:

(a) Where the receiving State applies any of the provisions of the present Convention restrictively because of a restrictive application of that provision to its mission in the sending State;

(b) Where by custom or agreement States extend to each other more favorable treatment than is required by the provisions of the present Convention.

Article 48

The present Convention shall be open for signature by all States Members of the United Nations or of any of the specialized agencies Parties to the Statute of the International Court of Justice, and by any other State invited by the General Assembly of the United Nations to become a Party to the Convention, as follows: until 31 October 1961 at the Federal Ministry for Foreign Affairs of Austria and subsequently, until 31 March 1962, at the United Nations Headquarters in New York.

Article 49

The present Convention is subject to ratification. The instruments of ratification shall be deposited with the Secretary-General of the United Nations.

Article 50

The present Convention shall remain open for accession by any State belonging to any of the four categories mentioned in article 48. The instruments of accession shall be deposited with the Secretary-General of the United Nations.

Article 51

1. The present Convention shall enter into force on the thirtieth day following the date of deposit of the twenty-second instrument of ratification or accession with the Secretary-General of the United Nations.

2. For each State ratifying or acceding to the Convention after the deposit of the twenty-second instrument of ratification or accession, the Convention shall enter into force on the thirtieth day after deposit by such State of its instrument of ratification or accession.

Article 52

The Secretary-General of the United Nations shall inform all States belonging to any of the four categories mentioned in article 48:

    (a) Of signatures to the present Convention and of the deposit of instruments of ratification or accession, in accordance with articles 48, 49 and 50;

    (b) Of the date on which the present Convention will enter into force, in accordance with article 51.

Article 53

The original of the present Convention, of which the Chinese, English, French, Russian and Spanish texts are equally authentic, shall be deposited with the Secretary-General of the United Nations, who shall send certified copies thereof to all States belonging to any of the four categories mentioned in article 48.

IN WITNESS WHEREOF the undersigned Plenipotentiaries, being duly authorized thereto by their respective Governments, have signed the present Convention.

DONE at Vienna this eighteenth day of April one thousand nine hundred and sixty-one.

* * * * * *

Vienna Convention on Consular Relations
Done at Vienna on 24 April 1963

The States Parties to the present Convention,

Recalling that consular relations have been established between peoples since ancient times,

Having in mind the Purposes and Principles of the Charter of the United Nations concerning the sovereign equality of States, the maintenance of international peace and security, and the promotion of friendly relations among nations,

Considering that the United Nations Conference on Diplomatic Intercourse and Immunities adopted the Vienna Convention on Diplomatic Relations which was opened for signature on 18 April 1961,

Believing that an international convention on consular relations, privileges and immunities would also contribute to the development of friendly relations among nations, irrespective of their differing constitutional and social systems,

Realizing that the purpose of such privileges and immunities is not to benefit individuals but to ensure the efficient performance of functions by consular posts on behalf of their respective States,

Affirming that the rules of customary international law continue to govern matters not expressly regulated by the provisions of the present Convention,

Have agreed as follows:

Article 1
Definitions

1. For the purposes of the present Convention, the following expressions shall have the meanings hereunder assigned to them:

(a) "consular post" means any consulate-general, consulate, vice-consulate or consular agency;

(b) "consular district" means the area assigned to a consular post for the exercise of consular functions;

(c) "head of consular post" means the person charged with the duty of acting in that capacity;

(d) "consular officer" means any person, including the head of a consular post, entrusted in that capacity with the exercise of consular functions;

(e) "consular employee" means any person employed in the administrative or technical service of a consular post;

(f) "member of the service staff" means any person employed in the domestic service of a consular post;

(g) "members of the consular post" means consular officers, consular employees and members of the service staff;

(h) "members of the consular staff" means consular officers, other than the head of a consular post, consular employees and members of the service staff;

(i) "member of the private staff" means a person who is employed exclusively in the private service of a member of the consular post;

(j) "consular premises" means the buildings or parts of buildings and the land ancillary thereto, irrespective of ownership, used exclusively for the purposes of the consular post;

(k) "consular archives" includes all the papers, documents, correspondence, books, films, tapes and registers of the consular post, together with the ciphers and codes, the card-indexes and any article of furniture intended for their protection or safe keeping.

2. Consular officers are of two categories, namely career consular officers and honorary consular officers. The provisions of Chapter II of the present Convention apply to consular posts headed by career consular officers, the provisions of Chapter III govern consular posts headed by honorary consular officers.

3. The particular status of members of the consular posts who are nationals or permanent residents of the receiving State is governed by article 71 of the present Convention.

CHAPTER I.
CONSULAR RELATIONS IN GENERAL
SECTION I.   ESTABLISHMENT AND CONDUCT OF CONSULAR RELATIONS

Article 2
Establishment of consular relations

1. The establishment of consular relations between States takes place by mutual consent.

2. The consent given to the establishment of diplomatic relations between two States implies, unless otherwise stated, consent to the establishment of consular relations.

3. The severance of diplomatic relations shall not ipso facto involve the severance of consular relations.

Article 3
Exercise of consular functions

Consular functions are exercised by consular posts. They are also exercised by diplomatic missions in accordance with the provisions of the present Convention.

Article 4
Establishment of a consular post

1. A consular post may be established in the territory of the receiving State only with that State's consent.

2. The seat of the consular post, its classification and the consular district shall be established by the sending State and shall be subject to the approval of the receiving State.

3. Subsequent changes in the seat of the consular post, its classification or the consular district may be made by the sending State only with the consent of the receiving State.

4. The consent of the receiving State shall also be required if a consulate-general or a consulate desires to open a vice-consulate or a consular agency in a locality other than that in which it is itself established.

5. The prior express consent of the receiving State shall also be required for the opening of an office forming part of an existing consular post elsewhere than at the seat thereof.

Article 5
Consular functions

Consular functions consist in:

(a) protecting in the receiving State the interests of the sending State and of its nationals, both individuals and bodies corporate, within the limits permitted by international law;

(b) furthering the development of commercial, economic, cultural and scientific relations between the sending State and the receiving State and otherwise promoting friendly relations between them in accordance with the provisions of the present Convention;

(c) ascertaining by all lawful means conditions and developments in the commercial, economic, cultural and scientific life of the receiving State, reporting thereon to the Government of the sending State and giving information to persons interested;

(d) issuing passports and travel documents to nationals of the sending State, and visas or appropriate documents to persons wishing to travel to the sending State;

(e) helping and assisting nationals, both individuals and bodies corporate, of the sending State;

(f) acting as notary and civil registrar and in capacities of a similar kind, and performing certain functions of an administrative nature, provided that there is nothing contrary thereto in the laws and regulations of the receiving State;

(g) safeguarding the interests of nationals, both individuals and bodies corporate, of the sending States in cases of succession mortis causa in the territory of the receiving State, in accordance with the laws and regulations of the receiving State;

(h) safeguarding, within the limits imposed by the laws and regulations of the receiving State, the interests of minors and other persons lacking full capacity who are nationals of the sending State, particularly where any guardianship or trusteeship is required with respect to such persons;

(i) subject to the practices and procedures obtaining in the receiving State, representing or arranging appropriate representation for nationals of the sending State before the tribunals and other authorities of the receiving State, for the purpose of obtaining, in accordance with the laws and regulations of the receiving State, provisional measures for the preservation of the rights and interests of these nationals, where, because of absence or any other reason, such nationals are unable at the proper time to assume the defense of their rights and interests;

(j) transmitting judicial and extra judicial documents or executing letters rogatory or commissions to take evidence for the courts of the sending State in accordance with international agreements in force or, in the absence of such international agreements, in any other manner compatible with the laws and regulations of the receiving State;

(k) exercising rights of supervision and inspection provided for in the laws and regulations of the sending State in respect of vessels having the nationality of the sending State, and of aircraft registered in that State, and in respect of their crews;

(l) extending assistance to vessels and aircraft mentioned in subparagraph (k) of this article, and to their crews, taking statements regarding the voyage of a vessel, examining and stamping the ship's papers, and, without prejudice to the powers of the authorities of the receiving State, conducting investigations into any incidents which occurred during the voyage, and settling disputes of any kind between the master, the officers and the seamen insofar as this may be authorized by the laws and regulations of the sending State;

(m) performing any other functions entrusted to a consular post by the sending State which are not prohibited by the laws and regulations of the receiving State or to which no objection is taken by the receiving State or which are referred to in the international agreements in force between the sending State and the receiving State.

Article 6
Exercise of consular functions outside the consular district

A consular officer may, in special circumstances, with the consent of the receiving State, exercise his functions outside his consular district.

Article 7
Exercise of consular functions in a third State

The sending State may, after notifying the States concerned, entrust a consular post established in a particular State with the exercise of consular functions in another State, unless there is express objection by one of the States concerned.

Article 8
Exercise of consular functions on behalf of a third State

Upon appropriate notification to the receiving State, a consular post of the sending State may, unless the receiving State objects, exercise consular functions in the receiving State on behalf of a third State.

Article 9
Classes of heads of consular posts

1. Heads of consular posts are divided into four classes, namely

    (a) consuls-general;
    (b) consuls;
    (c) vice-consuls;
    (d) consular agents.

2. Paragraph 1 of this article in no way restricts the right of any of the Contracting Parties to fix the designation of consular officers other than the heads of consular posts.

Article 10
Appointment and admission of heads of consular posts

1. Heads of consular posts are appointed by the sending State and are admitted to the exercise of their functions by the receiving State.

2. Subject to the provisions of the present Convention, the formalities for the appointment and for the admission of the head of a consular post are determined by the laws, regulations and usages of the sending State and of the receiving State respectively.

Article 11
The consular commission or notification of appointment

1. The head of a consular post shall be provided by the sending State with a document, in the form of a commission or similar instrument, made out for each appointment, certifying his capacity and showing, as a general rule, his full name, his category and class, the consular district and the seat of the consular post.

2. The sending State shall transmit the commission or similar instrument through the diplomatic or other appropriate channel to the Government of the State in whose territory the head of a consular post is to exercise his functions.

3. If the receiving State agrees, the sending State may, instead of a commission or similar instrument, send to the receiving State a notification containing the particulars required by paragraph of this article.

Article 12
The exequatur

1. The head of a consular post is admitted to the exercise of his functions by an authorization from the receiving State termed an *exequatur*, whatever the form of this authorization.

2. A State which refused to grant an *exequatur* is not obliged to give to the sending State reasons for such refusal.

3. Subject to the provisions of articles 13 and 15, the head of a consular post shall not enter upon his duties until he has received an *exequatur*.

Article 13
Provisional admission of heads of consular posts

Pending delivery of the *exequatur*, the head of a consular post may be admitted on a provisional basis to the exercise of his functions. In that case, the provisions of the present Convention shall apply.

Article 14
Notification to the authorities of the consular district

As soon as the head of a consular post is admitted even provisionally to the exercise of his functions, the receiving State shall immediately notify the competent authorities of the consular district. It shall also ensure that the necessary measures are taken to enable the head of a consular post to carry out the duties of his office and to have the benefit of the provisions of the present Convention.

Article 15
Temporary exercise of the functions of the head of a consular post

1. If the head of a consular post is unable to carry out his functions or the position of head of consular post is vacant, an acting head of post may act provisionally as head of the consular post.

2. The full name of the acting head of post shall be notified either by the diplomatic mission of the sending State or, if that State has no such mission in the receiving State, by the head of the consular post, or, if he is unable to do so, by any competent authority of the sending State, to the Ministry for Foreign Affairs of the receiving State or to the authority designated by that Ministry. As a general rule, this notification shall be given in advance. The receiving State may make the admission as acting head of post of a person who is neither a diplomatic agent nor a consular officer of the sending State in the receiving State conditional on its consent.

3. The competent authorities of the receiving State shall afford assistance and protection to the acting head of post. While he is in charge of the post, the provisions of the present Convention shall apply to him on the same basis as to the head of the consular post concerned. The receiving State shall not, however, be obliged to grant to an acting head of post any facility, privilege or immunity which the head of the consular post enjoys only subject to conditions not fulfilled by the acting head of post.

4. When, in the circumstances referred to in paragraph 1 of this article, a member of the diplomatic staff of the diplomatic mission of the sending State in the receiving State is designated by the sending State as an acting head of post, he shall, if the receiving State does not object thereto, continue to enjoy diplomatic privileges and immunities.

Article 16
Precedence as between heads of consular posts

1. Heads of consular posts shall rank in each class according to the date of the grant of the *exequatur*.

2. If, however, the head of a consular post before obtaining the *exequatur* is admitted to the exercise of his functions provisionally, his precedence shall be determined according to the date of the provisional admission; this precedence shall be maintained after the granting of the *exequatur*.

3. The order of precedence as between two or more heads of consular posts who obtained the *exequatur* or provisional admission on the same date shall be determined according to the dates on which their commissions or similar instruments or the notifications referred to in paragraph 3 of article 11 were presented to the receiving State.

4. Acting heads of posts shall rank after all heads of consular posts and, as between themselves, they shall rank according to the dates on which they assumed their functions as acting heads of posts as indicated in the notifications given under paragraph 2 of article 15.

5. Honorary consular officers who are heads of consular posts shall rank in each class after career heads of consular posts, in the order and according to the rules laid down in the foregoing paragraphs.

6. Heads of consular posts shall have precedence over consular officers not having that status.

Article 17
Performance of diplomatic acts by consular officers

1. In a State where the sending State has no diplomatic mission and is not represented by a diplomatic mission of a third State, a consular officer may, with the consent of the receiving State, and without affecting his consular status, be authorized to perform diplomatic acts. The performance of such acts by a consular officer shall not confer upon him any right to claim diplomatic privileges and immunities.

2. A consular officer may, after notification addressed to the receiving State, act as representative of the sending State to any intergovernmental organization. When so acting, he shall be entitled to enjoy any privileges and immunities accorded to such a representative by customary international law or by international agreements; however, in respect of the performance by him of any consular function, he shall not be entitled to any greater immunity from jurisdiction than that to which a consular officer is entitled under the present Convention.

Article 18
Appointment of the same person by two or more States as a consular officer

Two or more States may, with the consent of the receiving State, appoint the same person as a consular officer in that State.

Article 19
Appointment of members of consular staff

1. Subject to the provisions of articles 20, 22 and 23, the sending State may freely appoint the members of the consular staff.

2. The full name, category and class of all consular officers, other than the head of a consular post, shall be notified by the sending State to the receiving State in sufficient time for the receiving State, if it so wishes, to exercise its rights under paragraph 3 of article 23.

3. The sending State may, if required by its laws and regulations, request the receiving State to grant an *exequatur* to a consular officer other than the head of a consular post.

4. The receiving State may, if required by its laws and regulations, grant an *exequatur* to a consular officer other than the head of a consular post.

Article 20
Size of the consular staff

In the absence of an express agreement as to the size of the consular staff, the receiving State may require that the size of the staff be kept within limits considered by it to be reasonable and normal, having regard to circumstances and conditions in the consular district and to the needs of the particular consular post.

Article 21
Precedence as between consular officers of a consular post

The order of precedence as between the consular officers of a consular post and any change thereof shall be notified by the diplomatic mission of the sending State or, if that State has no such mission in the receiving State, by the head of the consular post, to the Ministry for Foreign Affairs of the receiving State or to the authority designated by that Ministry.

Article 22
Nationality of consular officers

1. Consular officers should, in principle, have the nationality of the sending State.

2. Consular officers may not be appointed from among persons having the nationality of the receiving State except with the express consent of that State which may be withdrawn at any time.

3. The receiving State may reserve the same right with regard to nationals of a third State who are not also nationals of the sending State.

Article 23
Persons declared "non grata"

1. The receiving State may at any time notify the sending State that a consular officer is persona non grata or that any other member of the consular staff is not acceptable. In that event, the sending State shall, as the case may be, either recall the person concerned or terminate his functions with the consular post.

2. If the sending State refuses or fails within a reasonable time to carry out its obligations under paragraph 1 of this article, the receiving State may, as the case may be, either withdraw the *exequatur* from the person concerned or cease to consider him as a member of the consular staff.

3. A person appointed as a member of a consular post may be declared unacceptable before arriving in the territory of the receiving State or, if already in the receiving State, before entering on his duties with the consular post. In any such case, the sending State shall withdraw his appointment.

4. In the cases mentioned in paragraphs 1 and 3 of this article, the receiving State is not obliged to give to the sending State reasons for its decision.

Article 24
Notification to the receiving State of appointments, arrivals and departures

1. The Ministry for Foreign Affairs of the receiving State or the authority designated by that Ministry shall be notified of:

(a) the appointment of members of a consular post, their arrival after appointment to the consular post, their final departure or the termination of their functions and any other changes affecting their status that may occur in the course of their service with the consular post;

(b) the arrival and final departure of a person belonging to the family of a member of a consular post forming part of his household and, where appropriate, the fact that a person becomes or ceases to be such a member of the family;

(c) the arrival and final departure of members of the private staff and, where appropriate, the termination of their service as such;

(d) the engagement and discharge of persons resident in the receiving State as members of a consular post or as members of the private staff entitled to privileges and immunities.

2. When possible, prior notification of arrival and final departure shall also be given.

SECTION II.
END OF CONSULAR FUNCTIONS

Article 25
Termination of the functions of a member of a consular post

The functions of a member of a consular post shall come to an end, inter alia:

(a) on notification by the sending State to the receiving State that his functions have come to an end;

(b) on withdrawal of the exequatur;

(c) on notification by the receiving State to the sending State that the receiving State has ceased to consider him as a member of the consular staff.

Article 26
Departure from the territory of the receiving State

The receiving State shall, even in case of armed conflict, grant to members of the consular post and members of the private staff, other than nationals of the receiving State, and to members of their families forming part of their households irrespective of nationality, the necessary time and facilities to enable them to prepare their departure and to leave at the earliest possible moment after the termination of the functions of the members concerned. In particular, it shall, in case of need, place at their disposal the necessary means of transport for themselves and their property other than property acquired in the receiving State the export of which is prohibited at the time of departure.

Article 27
Protection of consular premises and archives and of the interests of the sending State in exceptional circumstances

1. In the event of the severance of consular relations between two States:

(a) the receiving State shall, even in case of armed conflict, respect and protect the consular premises, together with the property of the consular post and the consular archives;

(b) the sending State may entrust the custody of the consular premises, together with the property contained therein and the consular archives, to a third State acceptable to the receiving State;

(c) the sending State may entrust the protection of its interests and those of its nationals to a third State acceptable to the receiving State.

2. In the event of the temporary or permanent closure of a consular post, the provisions of subparagraph (a) of paragraph 1 of this article shall apply. In addition,

(a) if the sending State, although not represented in the receiving State by a diplomatic mission, has another consular post in the territory of that State, that consular post may be entrusted with the custody of the premises of the consular post which has been closed, together with the property contained therein and the consular archives, and, with the consent of the receiving State, with the exercise of consular functions in the district of that consular post; or

(b) if the sending State has no diplomatic mission and no other consular post in the receiving State, the provisions of subparagraphs (b) and (c) of paragraph 1 of this article shall apply.

CHAPTER II.
FACILITIES, PRIVILEGES AND IMMUNITIES RELATING TO CONSULAR POSTS, CAREER CONSULAR OFFICERS AND OTHER MEMBERS OF A CONSULAR POST
SECTION I. FACILITIES, PRIVILEGES AND IMMUNITIES RELATING TO A CONSULAR POST

Article 28
Facilities for the work of the consular post

The receiving State shall accord full facilities for the performance of the functions of the consular post.

Article 29
Use of national flag and coat-of-arms

1. The sending State shall have the right to the use of its national flag and coat-of-arms in the receiving State in accordance with the provisions of this article.

2. The national flag of the sending State may be flown and its coat-of-arms displayed on the building occupied by the consular post and at the entrance door thereof, on the residence of the head of the consular post and on his means of transport when used on official business.

3. In the exercise of the right accorded by this article regard shall be had to the laws, regulations and usages of the receiving State.

Article 30
Accommodation

1. The receiving State shall either facilitate the acquisition on its territory, in accordance with its laws and regulations, by the sending State of premises necessary for its consular post or assist the latter in obtaining accommodation in some other way.

2. It shall also, where necessary, assist the consular post in obtaining suitable accommodation for its members.

Article 31
Inviolability of the consular premises

1. Consular premises shall be inviolable to the extent provided in this article.

2. The authorities of the receiving State shall not enter that part of the consular premises which is used exclusively for the purpose of the work of the consular post except with the consent of the head of the consular post or of his designee or of the head of the diplomatic mission of the sending State. The consent of the head of the consular post may, however, be assumed in case of fire or other disaster requiring prompt protective action.

3. Subject to the provisions of paragraph 2 of this article, the receiving State is under a special duty to take all appropriate steps to protect the consular premises against any intrusion or damage and to prevent any disturbance of the peace of the consular post or impairment of its dignity.

4. The consular premises, their furnishings, the property of the consular post and its means of transport shall be immune from any form of requisition for purposes of national defense or public utility. If expropriation is necessary for such purposes, all possible steps shall be taken to avoid impeding the performance of consular functions, and prompt, adequate and effective compensation shall be paid to the sending State.

Article 32
Exemption from taxation of consular premises

1. Consular premises and the residence of the career head of consular post of which the sending State or any person acting on its behalf is the owner or lessee shall be exempt from all national, regional or municipal dues and taxes whatsoever, other than such as represent payment for specific services rendered.

2. The exemption from taxation referred to paragraph 1 of this article shall not apply to such dues and taxes if, under the law of the receiving State, they are payable by the person who contracted with the sending State or with the person acting on its behalf.

Article 33
Inviolability of the consular archives and documents

The consular archives and documents shall be inviolable at all times and wherever they may be.

Article 34
Freedom of movement

Subject to its laws and regulations concerning zones entry into which is prohibited or regulated for reasons of national security, the receiving State shall ensure freedom of movement and travel in its territory to all members of the consular post.

Article 35
Freedom of communication

1. The receiving State shall permit and protect freedom of communication on the part of the consular post for all official purposes. In communicating with the Government, the diplomatic missions and other consular posts, wherever situated, of the sending State, the consular post may employ all appropriate means, including diplomatic or consular couriers, diplomatic or consular bags and messages in code or cipher. However, the consular post may install and use a wireless transmitter only with the consent of the receiving State.

2. The official correspondence of the consular post shall be inviolable. Official correspondence means all correspondence relating to the consular post and its functions.

3. The consular bag shall be neither opened nor detained. Nevertheless, if the competent authorities of the receiving State have serious reason to believe that the bag contains something other than the correspondence, documents or articles referred to in paragraph 4 of this article, they may request that the bag be opened in their presence by an authorized representative of the sending State. If this request is refused by the authorities of the sending State, the bag shall be returned to its place of origin.

4. The packages constituting the consular bag shall bear visible external marks of their character and may contain only official correspondence and documents or articles intended exclusively for official use.

5. The consular courier shall be provided with an official document indicating his status and the number of packages constituting the consular bag. Except with the consent of the receiving State he shall be neither a national of the receiving State, nor, unless he is a national of the sending State, a permanent resident of the receiving State. In the performance of his functions he shall be protected by the receiving State. He shall enjoy personal inviolability and shall not be liable to any form of arrest or detention.

6. The sending State, its diplomatic missions and its consular posts may designate consular couriers ad hoc. In such cases the provisions of paragraph 5 of this article shall also apply except that the immunities therein mentioned shall cease to apply when such a courier has delivered to the consignee the consular bag in his charge.

7. A consular bag may be entrusted to the captain of a ship or of a commercial aircraft scheduled to land at an authorized port of entry. He shall be provided with an official document indicating the number of packages constituting the bag, but he shall not be considered to be a consular courier. By arrangement with the appropriate local authorities, the consular post may send one of its members to take possession of the bag directly and freely from the captain of the ship or of the aircraft.

Article 36
Communication and contact with nationals of the sending State

1. With a view to facilitating the exercise of consular functions relating to nationals of the sending State:

(a) consular officers shall be free to communicate with nationals of the sending State and to have access to them. Nationals of the sending State shall have the same freedom with respect to communication with and access to consular officers of the sending State;

(b) if he so requests, the competent authorities of the receiving State shall, without delay, inform the consular post of the sending State if, within its consular district, a national of that State is arrested or committed to prison or to custody pending trial or is detained in any other manner. Any communication addressed to the consular post by the person arrested, in prison, custody or detention shall be forwarded by the said authorities without delay. The said authorities shall inform the person concerned without delay of his rights under this subparagraph;

(c) consular officers shall have the right to visit a national of the sending State who is in prison, custody or detention, to converse and correspond with him and to arrange for his legal representation. They shall also have the right to visit any national of the sending State who is in prison, custody or detention in their district in pursuance of a judgment. Nevertheless, consular officers shall refrain from taking action on behalf of a national who is in prison, custody or detention if he expressly opposes such action.

2. The rights referred to in paragraph 1 of this article shall be exercised in conformity with the laws and regulations of the receiving State, subject to the proviso, however, that the said laws and regulations must enable full effect to be given to the purposes for which the rights accorded under this article are intended.

Article 37
Information in cases of deaths, guardianship or trusteeship, wrecks and air accidents

If the relevant information is available to the competent authorities of the receiving State, such authorities shall have the duty:

(a) in the case of the death of a national of the sending State, to inform without delay the consular post in whose district the death occurred;

(b) to inform the competent consular post without delay of any case where the appointment of a guardian or trustee appears to be in the interests of a minor or other person lacking full capacity who is a national of the sending State. The giving of this information shall, however, be without prejudice to the operation of the laws and regulations of the receiving State concerning such appointments;

(c) if a vessel, having the nationality of the sending State, is wrecked or runs aground in the territorial sea or internal waters of the receiving State, or if an aircraft registered in the sending State suffers an accident on the territory of the receiving State, to inform without delay the consular post nearest to the scene of the occurrence.

Article 38
Communication with the authorities of the receiving State

In the exercise of their functions, consular officers may address:

(a) the competent local authorities of their consular district;

(b) the competent central authorities of the receiving State if and to the extent that this is allowed by the laws, regulations and usages of the receiving State or by the relevant international agreements.

Article 39
Consular fees and charges

1. The consular post may levy in the territory of the receiving State the fees and charges provided by the laws and regulations of the sending State for consular acts.

2. The sums collected in the form of the fees and charges referred to in paragraph 1 of this article, and the receipts for such fees and charges, shall be exempt from all dues and taxes in the receiving State.

SECTION II.
FACILITIES, PRIVILEGES AND IMMUNITIES
RELATING TO CAREER CONSULAR OFFICERS AND
OTHER MEMBERS OF A CONSULAR POST

Article 40
Protection of consular officers

The receiving State shall treat consular officers with due respect and shall take all appropriate steps to prevent any attack on their person, freedom or dignity.

Article 41
Personal inviolability of consular officers

1. Consular officers shall not be liable to arrest or detention pending trial, except in the case of a grave crime and pursuant to a decision by the competent judicial authority.

2. Except in the case specified in paragraph 1 of this article, consular officers shall not be committed to prison or be liable to any other form of restriction on their personal freedom save in execution of a judicial decision of final effect.

3. If criminal proceedings are instituted against a consular officer, he must appear before the competent authorities. Nevertheless, the proceedings shall be conducted with the respect due to him by reason of his official position and, except in the case specified in paragraph 1 of this article, in a manner which will hamper the exercise of consular functions as little as possible. When, in the circumstances mentioned in paragraph 1 of this article, it has become necessary to detain a consular officer, the proceedings against him shall be instituted with the minimum of delay.

Article 42
Notification of arrest, detention or prosecution

In the event of the arrest or detention, pending trial, of a member of the consular staff, or of criminal proceedings being instituted against him, the receiving State shall promptly notify the head of the consular post. Should the latter be himself the object of any such measure, the receiving State shall notify the sending State through the diplomatic channel.

Article 43
Immunity from jurisdiction

1. Consular officers and consular employees shall not be amenable to the jurisdiction of the judicial or administrative authorities of the receiving State in respect of acts performed in the exercise of consular functions.

2. The provisions of paragraph 1 of this article shall not, however, apply in respect of a civil action either:

    (a) arising out of a contract concluded by a consular officer or a consular employee in which he did not contract expressly or impliedly as an agent of the sending State; or

    (b) by a third party for damage arising from an accident in the receiving State caused by a vehicle, vessel or aircraft.

Article 44
Liability to give evidence

1. Members of a consular post may be called upon to attend as witnesses in the course of judicial or administrative proceedings. A consular employee or a member of the service staff shall not, except in the cases mentioned in paragraph 3 of this article, decline to give evidence. If a consular officer should decline to do so, no coercive measure or penalty may be applied to him.

2. The authority requiring the evidence of a consular officer shall avoid interference with the performance of his functions. It may, when possible, take such evidence at his residence or at the consular post or accept a statement from him in writing.

3. Members of a consular post are under no obligation to give evidence concerning matters connected with the exercise of their functions or to produce official correspondence and documents relating thereto.

They are also entitled to decline to give evidence as expert witnesses with regard to the law of the sending State.

Article 45
Waiver of privileges and immunities

1. The sending State may waive, with regard to a member of the consular post, any of the privileges and immunities provided for in articles 41, 43 and 44.

2. The waiver shall in all cases be express, except as provided in paragraph 3 of this article, and shall be communicated to the receiving State in writing.

3. The initiation of proceedings by a consular officer or a consular employee in a matter where he might enjoy immunity from jurisdiction under article 43 shall preclude him from invoking immunity from jurisdiction in respect of any counterclaim directly connected with the principal claim.

4. The waiver of immunity from jurisdiction for the purposes of civil or administrative proceedings shall not be deemed to imply the waiver of immunity from the measures of execution resulting from the judicial decision; in respect of such measures, a separate waiver shall be necessary.

Article 46
Exemption from registration of aliens and residence permits

1. Consular officers and consular employees and members of their families forming part of their households shall be exempt from all obligations under the laws and regulations of the receiving State in regard to the registration of aliens and residence permits.

2. The provisions of paragraph 1 of this article shall not, however, apply to any consular employee who is not a permanent employee of the sending State or who carries on any private gainful occupation in the receiving State or to any member of the family of any such employee.

Article 47
Exemption from work permits

1. Members of the consular post shall, with respect to services rendered for the sending State, be exempt from any obligations in regard to work permits imposed by the laws and regulations of the receiving State concerning the employment of foreign labor.

2. Members of the private staff of consular officers and of consular employees shall, if they do not carry on any other gainful occupation in the receiving State, be exempt from the obligations referred to in paragraph 1 of this article.

Article 48
Social security exemption

1. Subject to the provisions of paragraph 3 of this article, members of the consular post with respect to services rendered by them for the sending State, and members of their families forming part of their households, shall be exempt from social security provisions which may be in force in the receiving State.

2. The exemption provided for in paragraph 1 of this article shall apply also to members of the private staff who are in the sole employ of members of the consular post, on condition:

   (a) that they are not nationals of or permanently resident in the receiving State; and

(b) that they are covered by the social security provisions which are in force in the sending State or a third State.

3. Members of the consular post who employ persons to whom the exemption provided for in paragraph 2 of this article does not apply shall observe the obligations which the social security provisions of the receiving State impose upon employers.

4. The exemption provided for in paragraphs 1 and 2 of this article shall not preclude voluntary participation in the social security system of the receiving State, provided that such participation is permitted by that State.

Article 49
Exemption from taxation

1. Consular officers and consular employees and members of their families forming part of their households shall be exempt from all dues and taxes, personal or real, national, regional or municipal, except:

(a) indirect taxes of a kind which are normally incorporated in the price of goods or services;
(b) dues or taxes on private immovable property situated in the territory of the receiving State, subject to the provisions of article 32;
(c) estate, succession or inheritance duties, and duties on transfers, levied by the receiving State, subject to the provisions of paragraph (b) of article 51;
(d) dues and taxes on private income, including capital gains, having its source in the receiving State and capital taxes relating to investments made in commercial or financial undertakings in the receiving State;
(e) charges levied for specific services rendered;
(f) registration, court or record fees, mortgage dues and stamp duties, subject to the provisions of article 32.

2. Members of the service staff shall be exempt from dues and taxes on the wages which they receive for their services.

3. Members of the consular post who employ persons whose wages or salaries are not exempt from income tax in the receiving State shall observe the obligations which the laws and regulations of that State impose upon employers concerning the levying of income tax.

Article 50
Exemption from customs duties and inspection

1. The receiving State shall, in accordance with such laws and regulations as it may adopt, permit entry of and grant exemption from all customs duties, taxes, and related charges other than charges for storage, cartage and similar services, on:

(*a*) articles for the official use of the consular post;
(*b*) articles for the personal use of a consular officer or members of his family forming part of his household, including articles intended for his establishment. The articles intended for consumption shall not exceed the quantities necessary for direct utilization by the persons concerned.

2. Consular employees shall enjoy the privileges and exemptions specified in paragraph 1 of this article in respect of articles imported at the time of first installation.

3. Personal baggage accompanying consular officers and members of their families forming part of their households shall be exempt from inspection. It may be inspected only if there is serious reason to believe

that it contains articles other than those referred to in subparagraph (*b*) of paragraph 1 of this article, or articles the import or export of which is prohibited by the laws and regulations of the receiving State or which are subject to its quarantine laws and regulations. Such inspection shall be carried out in the presence of the consular officer or member of his family concerned.

Article 51
Estate of a member of the consular post or of a member of his family

In the event of the death of a member of the consular post or of a member of his family forming part of his household, the receiving State:

(a) shall permit the export of the movable property of the deceased, with the exception of any such property acquired in the receiving State the export of which was prohibited at the time of his death;

(b) shall not levy national, regional or municipal estate, succession or inheritance duties, and duties on transfers, on movable property the presence of which in the receiving State was due solely to the presence in that State of the deceased as a member of the consular post or as a member of the family of a member of the consular post.

Article 52
Exemption from personal services and contributions

The receiving State shall exempt members of the consular post and members of their families forming part of their households from all personal services, from all public service of any kind whatsoever, and from military obligations such as those connected with requisitioning, military contributions and billeting.

Article 53
Beginning and end of consular privileges and immunities

1. Every member of the consular post shall enjoy the privileges and immunities provided in the present Convention from the moment he enters the territory of the receiving State on proceeding to take up his post or, if already in its territory, from the moment when he enters on his duties with the consular post.

2. Members of the family of a member of the consular post forming part of his household and members of his private staff shall receive the privileges and immunities provided in the present Convention from the date from which he enjoys privileges and immunities in accordance with paragraph 1 of this article or from the date of their entry into the territory of the receiving State or from the date of their becoming a member of such family or private staff, whichever is the latest.

3. When the functions of a member of the consular post have come to an end, his privileges and immunities and those of a member of his family forming part of his household or a member of his private staff shall normally cease at the moment when the person concerned leaves the receiving State or on the expiry of a reasonable period in which to do so, whichever is the sooner, but shall subsist until that time, even in case of armed conflict. In the case of the persons referred to in paragraph 2 of this article, their privileges and immunities shall come to an end when they cease to belong to the household or to be in the service of a member of the consular post provided, however, that if such persons intend leaving the receiving State within a reasonable period thereafter, their privileges and immunities shall subsist until the time of their departure.

4. However, with respect to acts performed by a consular officer or a consular employee in the exercise of his functions, immunity from jurisdiction shall continue to subsist without limitation of time.

5. In the event of the death of a member of the consular post, the members of his family forming part of his household shall continue to enjoy the privileges and immunities accorded to them until they leave the receiving State or until the expiry of a reasonable period enabling them to do so, whichever is the sooner.

Article 54
Obligations of third States

1. If a consular officer passes through or is in the territory of a third State, which has granted him a visa if a visa was necessary, while proceeding to take up or return to his post or when returning to the sending State, the third State shall accord to him all immunities provided for by the other articles of the present Convention as may be required to ensure his transit or return. The same shall apply in the case of any member of his family forming part of his household enjoying such privileges and immunities who are accompanying the consular officer or traveling separately to join him or to return to the sending State.

2. In circumstances similar to those specified in paragraph 1 of this article, third States shall not hinder the transit through their territory of other members of the consular post or of members of their families forming part of their households.

3. Third States shall accord to official correspondence and to other official communications in transit, including messages in code or cipher, the same freedom and protection as the receiving State is bound to accord under the present Convention. They shall accord to consular couriers who have been granted a visa, if a visa was necessary, and to consular bags in transit, the same inviolability and protection as the receiving State is bound to accord under the present Convention.

4. The obligations of third States under paragraphs 1, 2 and 3 of this article shall also apply to the persons mentioned respectively in those paragraphs, and to official communications and to consular bags, whose presence in the territory of the third State is due to force majeure.

Article 55
Respect for the laws and regulations of the receiving State

1. Without prejudice to their privileges and immunities, it is the duty of all persons enjoying such privileges and immunities to respect the laws and regulations of the receiving State. They also have a duty not to interfere in the internal affairs of the State.

2. The consular premises shall not be used in any manner incompatible with the exercise of consular functions.

3. The provisions of paragraph 2 of this article shall not exclude the possibility of offices of other institutions or agencies being installed in part of the building in which the consular premises are situated, provided that the premises assigned to them are separate from those used by the consular post. In that event, the said offices shall not, for the purposes of the present Convention, be considered to form part of the consular premises.

Article 56
Insurance against third party risks

Members of the consular post shall comply with any requirements imposed by the laws and regulations of the receiving State, in respect of insurance against third party risks arising from the use of any vehicle, vessel or aircraft.

Article 57
Special provisions concerning private gainful occupation

1. Career consular officers shall not carry on for personal profit any professional or commercial activity in the receiving State.

2. Privileges and immunities provided in this chapter shall not be accorded:

   (a) to consular employees or to members of the service staff who carry on any private gainful occupation in the receiving State;
   (b) to members of the family of a person referred to in subparagraph (a) of this paragraph or to members of his private staff;
   (c) to members of the family of a member of a consular post who themselves carry on any private gainful occupation in the receiving State.

CHAPTER III.
REGIME RELATING TO HONORARY CONSULAR OFFICERS AND CONSULAR POSTS HEADED BY SUCH OFFICERS

Article 58
General provisions relating to facilities, privileges and immunities

1. Articles 28, 29, 30, 34, 35, 36, 37, 38 and 39, paragraph 3 of article 54 and paragraphs 2 and 3 of article 55 shall apply to consular posts headed by an honorary consular officer. In addition, the facilities, privileges and immunities of such consular posts shall be governed by articles 59, 60, 61 and 62.

2. Articles 42 and 43, paragraph 3 of article 44, articles 45 and 53 and paragraph 1 of article 55 shall apply to honorary consular officers. In addition, the facilities, privileges and immunities of such consular officers shall be governed by articles 63, 64, 65, 66 and 67.

3. Privileges and immunities provided in the present Convention shall not be accorded to members of the family of an honorary consular officer or of a consular employee employed at a consular post headed by an honorary consular officer.

4. The exchange of consular bags between two consular posts headed by honorary consular officers in different States shall not be allowed without the consent of the two receiving States concerned.

Article 59
Protection of the consular premises

The receiving State shall take such steps as may be necessary to protect the consular premises of a consular post headed by an honorary consular officer against any intrusion or damage and to prevent any disturbance of the peace of the consular post or impairment of its dignity.

Article 60
Exemption from taxation of consular premises

1. Consular premises of a consular post headed by an honorary consular officer of which the sending State is the owner or lessee shall be exempt from all national, regional or municipal dues and taxes whatsoever, other than such as represent payment for specific services rendered.

2. The exemption from taxation referred to in paragraph 1 of this article shall not apply to such dues and taxes if, under the laws and regulations of the receiving State, they are payable by the person who contracted with the sending State.

Article 61
Inviolability of consular archives and documents

The consular archives and documents of a consular post headed by an honorary consular officer shall be inviolable at all times and wherever they may be, provided that they are kept separate from other papers and documents and, in particular, from the private correspondence of the head of a consular post and of any person working with him, and from the materials, books or documents relating to their profession or trade.

Article 62
Exemption from customs duties

The receiving State shall, in accordance with such laws and regulations as it may adopt, permit entry of, and grant exemption from all customs duties, taxes, and related charges other than charges for storage, cartage and similar services on the following articles, provided that they are for the official use of a consular post headed by an honorary consular officer: coats-of-arms, flags, signboards, seals and stamps, books, official printed matter, office furniture, office equipment and similar articles supplied by or at the instance of the sending State to the consular post.

Article 63
Criminal proceedings

If criminal proceedings are instituted against an honorary consular officer, he must appear before the competent authorities. Nevertheless, the proceedings shall be conducted with the respect due to him by reason of his official position and, except when he is under arrest or detention, in a manner which will hamper the exercise of consular functions as little as possible. When it has become necessary to detain an honorary consular officer, the proceedings against him shall be instituted with the minimum of delay.

Article 64
Protection of honorary consular officers

The receiving State is under a duty to accord to an honorary consular officer such protection as may be required by reason of his official position.

Article 65
Exemption from registration of aliens and residence permits

Honorary consular officers, with the exception of those who carry on for personal profit any professional or commercial activity in the receiving State, shall be exempt from all obligations under the laws and regulations of the receiving State in regard to the registration of aliens and residence permits.

Article 66
Exemption from taxation

An honorary consular officer shall be exempt from all dues and taxes on the remuneration and emoluments which he receives from the sending State in respect of the exercise of consular functions.

Article 67
Exemption from personal services and contributions

The receiving State shall exempt honorary consular officers from all personal services and from all public services of any kind whatsoever and from military obligations such as those connected with requisitioning, military contributions and billeting.

Article 68
Optional character of the institution of honorary consular officers

Each State is free to decide whether it will appoint or receive honorary consular officers.

CHAPTER IV.
GENERAL PROVISIONS

Article 69
Consular agents who are not heads of consular posts

1. Each State is free to decide whether it will establish or admit consular agencies conducted by consular agents not designated as heads of consular post by the sending State.

2. The conditions under which the consular agencies referred to in paragraph 1 of this article may carry on their activities and the privileges and immunities which may be enjoyed by the consular agents in charge of them shall be determined by agreement between the sending State and the receiving State.

Article 70
Exercise of consular functions by diplomatic missions

1. The provisions of the present Convention apply also, so far as the context permits, to the exercise of consular functions by a diplomatic mission.

2. The names of members of a diplomatic mission assigned to the consular section or otherwise charged with the exercise of the consular functions of the mission shall be notified to the Ministry for Foreign Affairs of the receiving State or to the authority designated by that Ministry.

3. In the exercise of consular functions a diplomatic mission may address:

    (a) the local authorities of the consular district;
    (b) the central authorities of the receiving State if this is allowed by the laws, regulations and usages of the receiving State or by relevant international agreements.

4. The privileges and immunities of the members of a diplomatic mission referred to in paragraph 2 of this article shall continue to be governed by the rules of international law concerning diplomatic relations.

Article 71
Nationals or permanent residents of the receiving State

1. Except insofar as additional facilities, privileges and immunities may be granted by the receiving State, consular officers who are nationals of or permanently resident in the receiving State shall enjoy only immunity from jurisdiction and personal inviolability in respect of official acts performed in the exercise of their functions, and the privileges provided in paragraph 3 of article 44. So far as these consular officers are concerned, the receiving State shall likewise be bound by the obligation laid down in article 42. If criminal proceedings are instituted against such a consular officer, the proceedings shall, except when he

is under arrest or detention, be conducted in a manner which will hamper the exercise of consular functions as little as possible.

2. Other members of the consular post who are nationals of or permanently resident in the receiving State and members of their families, as well as members of the families of consular officers referred to in paragraph 1 of this article, shall enjoy facilities, privileges and immunities only insofar as these are granted to them by the receiving State. Those members of the families of members of the consular post and those members of the private staff who are themselves nationals of or permanently resident in the receiving State shall likewise enjoy facilities, privileges and immunities only insofar as these are granted to them by the receiving State. The receiving State shall, however, exercise its jurisdiction over those persons in such a way as not to hinder unduly the performance of the functions of the consular post.

Article 72
Non-discrimination

1. In the application of the provisions of the present Convention the receiving State shall not discriminate as between States.

2. However, discrimination shall not be regarded as taking place:

    (a) where the receiving State applies any of the provisions of the present Convention restrictively because of a restrictive application of that provision to its consular posts in the sending State;

    (b) where by custom or agreement States extend to each other more favorable treatment than is required by the provisions of the present Convention.

Article 73
Relationship between the present Convention and other international agreements

1. The provisions of the present Convention shall not affect other international agreements in force as between States Parties to them.

2. Nothing in the present Convention shall preclude States from concluding international agreements confirming or supplementing or extending or amplifying the provisions thereof.

CHAPTER V.
FINAL PROVISIONS

Article 74
Signature

The present Convention shall be open for signature by all States Members of the United Nations or of any of the specialized agencies or Parties to the Statute of the International Court of Justice, and by any other State invited by the General Assembly of the United Nations to become a Party to the Convention, as follows: until 31 October 1963 at the Federal Ministry for Foreign Affairs of the Republic of Austria and subsequently, until 31 March 1964, at the United Nations Headquarters in New York.

Article 75
Ratification

The present Convention is subject to ratification. The instruments of ratification shall be deposited with the Secretary-General of the United Nations.

Article 76
Accession

The present Convention shall remain open for accession by any State belonging to any of the four categories mentioned in article 74. The instruments of accession shall be deposited with the Secretary-General of the United Nations.

Article 77
Entry into force

1. The present Convention shall enter into force on the thirtieth day following the date of deposit of the twenty-second instrument of ratification or accession with the Secretary-General of the United Nations.

2. For each State ratifying or acceding to the Convention after the deposit of the twenty-second instrument of ratification or accession, the Convention shall enter into force on the thirtieth day after deposit by such State of its instrument of ratification or accession.

Article 78
Notifications by the Secretary-General

The Secretary-General of the United Nations shall inform all States belonging to any of the four categories mentioned in article 74:

(*a*) of signatures to the present Convention and of the deposit of instruments of ratification or accession, in accordance with articles 74, 75 and 76;

(*b*) of the date on which the present Convention will enter into force, in accordance with article 77.

Article 79
Authentic texts

The original of the present Convention, of which the Chinese, English, French, Russian and Spanish texts are equally authentic, shall be deposited with the Secretary-General of the United Nations, who shall send certified copies thereof to all States belonging to any of the four categories mentioned in article 74.

IN WITNESS WHEREOF the undersigned Plenipotentiaries, being duly authorized thereto by their respective Governments, have signed the present Convention.

DONE at Vienna this twenty-fourth day of April, one thousand nine hundred and sixty-three.

* * * * * *

British Honduras
Ministry of Foreign Affairs

Belmopan, British Honduras

December 16, 2001

     I have the honor to acknowledge the receipt of your embassy's note (T/SK-951/94) datedNovember 11, 2001, informing the Ministry of Foreign Affairs of the appointment of Mr. XYZ as Honorary Consul of Eastern Samoa at Belmopan.

     In compliance with the request contained in the embassy's note, recognition is accorded Mr. XYZ in the above-mentioned capacity.

Accept, Excellency, the renewed assurances of my highest consideration.

For the Minister of Foreign Affairs: XXX XXX XXXXX.

His Excellency
ABC
Ambassador to Eastern Samoa

Copy to:
The Honorable Mr. XYZ, Consul of Eastern Samoa

(Sample of a Professional Courier Letter)

British Honduras
Ministry of Foreign Affairs

Belmopan, British Honduras

No.: 234

TO ALL WHOM THESE PRESENTS SHALL COME, GREETING:

I, the undersigned, Minister of Foreign Affairs of British Honduras, hereby request all those whom it may concern to afford all such facilities as may be necessary to permit

XYZ XXXXX
Diplomatic Courier

the bearer of official property of British Honduras between the Ministry of Foreign Affairs at Belmopan, British Honduras and the Embassies and Consulates of British Honduras, to pass safely and freely in fulfillment of this mission without examination of the official property in question which is under seal, and in case of need, to provide all lawful aid and protection.

I further request all whom it may concern to extend to the holder all privileges and immunities which may expedite passage on this urgent mission with which said Diplomatic Courier has been charged on behalf of British Honduras.

This courier letter is issued only to individuals regularly employed as Diplomatic Couriers and is given solely for the purpose herein before indicated. This letter is valid for a period of three years from date of issue, with the expressed understanding that it will be returned to the Ministry of Foreign Affairs for cancellation on the termination of the bearer's employment.

In the event of an emergency concerning this courier, please contact the Ministry of Foreign Affairs, DCS Department, Belmopan, British Honduras; telephone: (xx)(xxx) xxx-xxxx.

Given under my hand and seal of the Ministry of Foreign Affairs of British Honduras at Belmopan this third day of March in the year of our Lord, Two Thousand and one.

Minister of Foreign Affairs
of British Honduras

-SEAL -

(Sample of a Non-Professional Courier Letter)

Embassy of the
British Honduras

No. 244

TO ALL WHOM THESE PRESENTS SHALL COME, GREETING:

I, the undersigned Ambassador of British Honduras, hereby request all whom it may concern to permit Mr. XXX XXXX acting as ad-hoc diplomatic courier between the Embassy of British Honduras and the Ministry of Foreign Affairs at Belmopan, British Honduras, bearer of official property of the Government of British Honduras, to pass safely and freely in fulfillment of this mission without examination of the official property in question which is under seal, and in case of need, to provide all lawful aid and protection.

I further request all whom it may concern to extend to Mr. XXX XXXX any or all privileges or facilities that may expedite passage of this urgent mission.

This letter is authorized solely for the single journey indicated herein and issued with the expressed understanding that it must be surrendered to the DCS Department, Ministry of Foreign Affairs for cancellation. This courier letter is valid for a period of seven days from date of issue.

In the event of an emergency concerning this courier, please contact the nearest Embassy or Consulate of British Honduras or the Ministry of Foreign Affairs, DCS Department, Belmopan, British Honduras; telephone: (xx)(xxx) xxx-xxxx.

Given under my hand and seal of the British Honduras Embassy, at Embassy this second day of April in the year of our Lord, Two Thousand.

XXX XXXX
Ambassador
British Honduras

-SEAL -

Definitions of Diplomatic Security Terms

A

Access:
The ability and the means necessary to read, store, or retrieve data, to communicate with, or to make use of any resource of an automated information system.

Access control:
The process of limiting access to the resources of a system only to authorized programs, processes, or other systems (in a network). Synonymous with controlled access and limited access.

ACR:
Acoustic Conference Room, an enclosure which provides acoustic but not electromagnetic emanations shielding. ACR are no longer procured. TCR are systematically replacing them.

Advisory Sensitivity Attributes:
User-supplied indicators of file sensitivity that alert other users to the sensitivity of a file so that they may handle it appropriate to its defined sensitivity. Advisory sensitivity attributes are not used by the AIS to enforce file access controls in an automated manner.

Agency:
A Federal agency including department, agency, commission, etc..

Areas to be accessed:
Embassy areas to be accessed are defined in two ways. Controlled Access Area (CAA) are spaces where classified operations/discussions/storage may occur. Non-controlled access areas are spaces where classified operations/discussions/storage do not occur.

ASE:
Acoustic Shielded Enclosure.

Audit log/trail:
Application or system programs when activated automatically monitor system activity in terms of on-line users, accessed programs, periods of operation, file accesses, etc.

Authenticate:
(1) To verify the identity of a user, device, or other entity in a computer system, often as a prerequisite to allowing access to resources in a system; and
(2) To verify the integrity of data that otherwise have been stored, transmitted, or exposed to possible unauthorized modification.

Authorized access list:
A list developed and maintained by the information systems security officer of personnel who are authorized unescorted access to the computer room.

Automated Information System (AIS):
An assembly of hardware, software, and firmware used to electronically input, process, store, and/or output data. Examples include: main frames, servers, desktop workstations, laptops, and Personal Electronic Devices (PED), such as Personal Digital Assistants (PDA). Typically, system components

include, but are not limited to: central processing units (CPUs), monitors, printers, and removable storage media, such as flash drives. An AIS may also include nontraditional peripheral equipment, such as networked digital copiers, and cameras and audio recording/playback devices used to transfer data to or from a computer.

B

Black:
In the information processing context, black denotes data, text, equipment, processes, systems or installations associated with unencrypted information that requires no emanations security related protection. For example, electronic signals are "black" if bearing unclassified information.

Building passes:
Those passes the Department/Secretariat of Diplomatic Security (DS) issues to permanent Ministry of Foreign Affairs/Department of State employees possessing a security clearance and a minimum of career-conditional status. To DS-cleared contractors and other individuals (such as members of the press, or employee family members), with a legitimate need to enter Ministry of Foreign Affairs/Department of State facilities on a regular basis. Each pass has the bearer's photograph, an individual identification number, expiration date, microchip and may provide access through an electronically operated gate or other entrance.

C

Carve-out-contract:
A classified contract issued in conjunction with an approved Special Access Program (SAP) wherein the designated cognizant SAP security office retains inspection responsibility, in whole or in part.
While the term "carve-out" technically only applies to the security function, it may also be used to designate contract administration services, audit, review, and other functions that are performed by groups other than those who normally accomplish these tasks.

Central Department of Record (CDR):
The Department element which keeps records of accountable COMSEC material held by accounts subject to its oversight.

Classification:
The determination that certain information requires protection against unauthorized disclosure in the interest of national security, coupled with the designation of the level of classification: *Top Secret*, *Secret*, or *Confidential*.

Classification authority:
The authority vested in an official of an agency to originally classify information or material which is determined by that official to require protection against unauthorized disclosure in the interest of national security.

Classification guides:
Documents issued in an exercise of authority for original classification that include determinations with respect to the proper level and duration of classification of categories of classified information.

Classified information:
Information or material, herein collectively termed information that is owned by produced for or by, or under the control of the Government, and that has been determined pursuant to prior orders to

require protection against unauthorized disclosure, coupled with the designation of the level of classification.

Classifier:
An individual who makes a classification determination and applies a security classification to information or material. A classifier may either be a classification authority or may assign a security classification based on a properly classified source or a classification guide.

Clear mode:
Unencrypted plain text mode.

Cleared citizen:
A citizen of the nation who has undergone a background investigation by an authorized Government Agency and been issued a Confidential, Secret, or Top Secret security clearance in accordance with implementing guidelines and standards of the country.
Abroad-Cleared citizens are required to have minimum a Secret-level clearance.

Code room:
The designated and restricted area in which cryptographic operations are conducted.

Communication protocols:
A set of rules that govern the operation of hardware or software entities to achieve communication.

Communications security (COMSEC):
(1) The protection resulting from the proper application of physical, technical, transmission, and cryptologic countermeasures to a communications link, system, or component.
(2) Combined Security measures

Communications system:
A mix of telecommunications and/or automated information systems used to originate, control, process, encrypt, and transmit or receive information. Such a system generally consists of the following connected or connectable devices:
(1) Automated Information Equipment (AIS) on which information is originated
(2) Central Controller (i. e., CIHS, C-LAN) of principal access rights and information distribution
(3) Telecommunications Processor (i. e., TERP, IMH) which prepares information for transmission
(4) National level devices which encrypt information (COMSEC/CRYPTO/CCI) prior to its transmission via Diplomatic Telecommunications Service (DTS) or commercial carrier.

Composite Threat List:
A Department of State threat list intended to cover all localities operating under the authority of a chief of mission and staffed by direct-hire personnel. This list is developed in coordination with the intelligence community and issued by the Department of Diplomatic Security (DS).

Compromise:
Loss of security enabling unauthorized access to classified information. Affected material is not automatically declassified.

Compromising emanations:
Intentional or unintentional intelligence bearing signals which, if intercepted and analyzed, disclose national security information transmitted, received, handled, or otherwise processed by any information

processing equipment. Compromising emanations consist of electrical or acoustic energy emitted from within equipment or systems (e. g., personal computers, workstations, facsimile machines, printers, copiers, typewriters) which process national security information.

Computer Incident Response Unit (CIRU):
The functional office within the Department of Diplomatic Security (DS) that is the central point for reporting and resolving cyber incidents. The CIRU analyzes incidents to determine their severity and technical ramifications.

COMSEC account:
The administrative entity, identified by an account number, used to maintain accountability, custody and control of COMSEC material.

COMSEC custodian:
The properly appointed individual who manages, controls, and is accountable for COMSEC material charged to the facility account. Only Department of State personnel will be appointed.

COMSEC facility:
Space employed for the purpose of generating, storing, repairing, or using COMSEC material.

COMSEC material:
The term which nominally covers any means or method used to apply COMSEC security. It includes, but is not limited to:
(1) Key;
(2) Equipment;
(3) Devices;
(4) Firmware;
(5) Software;
(6) Controlled Cryptographic Items (CCI);
(7) Material marked CRYPTO; and
(8) Any other items developed or produced to perform COMSEC functions.

COMSEC Material Control System (CMCS):
The logistics and accounting system through which COMSEC material is distributed, controlled, and safeguarded.

COMSEC officer:
The properly appointed individual responsible to ensure that COMSEC regulations and procedures are understood and adhered to, that the COMSEC facility is operated securely, that personnel are trained in proper COMSEC practices, and who advises on communications security matters. Only Ministry of Foreign Affairs/Department of State personnel will be appointed.

Confidential-cleared citizen:
A citizen of the nation who has undergone a background investigation by an authorized Government Agency and been issued a Confidential security clearance in accordance with implementing guidelines and standards.

Construction security certification:
Certification/confirmation is required from the Department if any new construction or major renovation is undertaken in the controlled access area (CAA). A site security plan must be submitted prior to commencing work.

Consumer electronics:
Any electronic/electrical devices, either AC-or battery-powered, which are not part of the facility infrastructure. Some examples are radios, televisions, electronic recording or playback equipment, PA systems, paging devices (see also electronic equipment).

Controlled Access Area:
Controlled access areas are specifically designated areas within a building where classified information may be handled, stored, discussed, or processed.

Controlled Cryptographic Item (CCI):
Secure telecommunications or information handling equipment, or associated cryptographic components, which are unclassified but governed by a special set of control requirements.

Controlled shipment:
The transport of material from the point at which the destination of the material is first identified for a site, through installation and/or use, under the continuous 24-hour control of Secret-cleared citizen or by DS-approved technical means and seal.

Courier:
See "Nonprofessional courier," and "Professional courier."

CRYPTO:
A marking or designator identifying COMSEC keying material or devices used to secure or authenticate telecommunications carrying classified or sensitive national security or national security-related information.

Cryptographic access:
The prerequisite to, and authorization for, access to crypto-information, but does not constitute authorization for use of crypto-equipment and keying material issued by the Department.

Cryptographic access for use:
The prerequisite to and authorization for operation, keying, and maintenance of cryptographic systems and equipment issued by the Department/Secretariat.

Cryptographic material:
All COMSEC material bearing the marking "CRYPTO" or otherwise designated as incorporating cryptographic information.

Cryptography:
The principles, means, and methods for rendering information unintelligible, and for restoring encrypted information to intelligible form.

Crypto Ignition Key (CIK):
The device or electronic key used to unlock the secure mode of crypto equipment.

Custodian:
An individual who has possession of or is otherwise charged with the responsibility for safeguarding and accounting for classified information.

Cyber infrastructure:
The unclassified cyber infrastructure comprises the interconnected AIS hardware (including peripheral,

networked and networking devices, and cabling) and software that enables automated information processing and communication across the enterprise, e. g. Open-Net.

Cyber security incident:
A failure to protect the unclassified cyber infrastructure from potential damage or risk.

Cyber security infraction:
One subset of a cyber security incident that contravenes computer security policy but does not result in damage to cyber infrastructure.

Cyber security violation:
The second subset of a cyber security incident, which is more serious than an infraction because it results in damage or significant risk to the cyber infrastructure due to an individual's failure to comply with established computer security policy.

D

Declassification:
The determination that particular classified information no longer requires protection against unauthorized disclosure in the interest of national security. Such determination shall be by specific action or automatically after the lapse of a requisite period of time or the occurrence of a specified event. If such determination is by specific action, the material shall be so marked with the new designation.

Declassification event:
An event which would eliminate the need for continued classification.

Decontrol:
The authorized removal of an assigned administrative control designation.

Degauss:
To apply a variable, Alternating Current (AC) field for the purpose of demagnetizing magnetic recording media. The process involves increasing the AC field gradually from zero to some maximum value and back to zero, which leaves a very low residue of magnetic induction on the media.

Department:
Applies to the Diplomatic Service, but not to its domestic field offices in the country; the term "post/s" applies to Foreign Service posts throughout the world and diplomatic missions to international organizations, except those located in the country.

Derivative classification:
A determination that information is in substance the same as information currently classified, coupled with the designation of the level of classification.

Diplomatic courier:
See "Professional courier."

Diplomatic pouch:
A properly documented, sealed bag, briefcase, envelope, or other container. It is used to transmit approved correspondence, documents, publications, and other articles for official use between the Department and post and between posts.

Diplomatic Security Control Officer (DSCO):
An individual in DS, who oversees the shipment of controlled/unclassified, nonpouched material from the Department to its posts worldwide. The DSCO must remain with the assigned material until it is delivered or properly secured in temporary storage.

Distributed system:
A multiwork station, or terminal system where more than one workstation shares common system resources. The work stations are connected to the control unit/data storage element through communication lines.

Document:
Any recorded information regardless of its physical form or characteristics, including, without limitation, written or printed material. Data processing cards and tapes; maps; charts; paintings; drawings; engravings; sketches. Working notes and papers, reproductions of such things by any means or process. Sound, voice, or electronic recordings in any form.

Downgrading:
The determination that particular classified information requires a lesser degree of protection or no protection against unauthorized disclosure than currently provided. Such determination shall be by specific action or automatically after lapse of the requisite period of time or the occurrence of a specified event. If such determination is by specific action, the material shall be so marked with the new designation.

Duration of visit or assignment:
Duration of visit or assignment is described as short-term or long-term assignment. Short-term visits are one-time visits up to and including thirty (30) days or intermittent visits within a thirty-day period. Long-term visits are visits in excess of thirty days or short term intermittent visits occurring beyond a thirty-day period.

E

Encrypted text:
Data which is encoded into an unclassified form using a nationally accepted form of encoding.

Encryption:
The translation of plain text into an unintelligible form in order to render the information meaningless to anyone who does not possess the decoding mechanism.

Escort:
A cleared citizen at post who assists couriers with arrivals and departures.

F

Foreign government information:
   (1) Information provided to the country by a foreign government or international organization of governments in the expectation, express or implied, that the information is to be kept in confidence;
   (2) Information, requiring confidentiality, produced by the country pursuant to a written joint arrangement with a foreign government or international organization of governments. A written joint arrangement may be evidenced by an exchange of letters, a memorandum of understanding, or other written record of the joint arrangement.

I

Identification media:
A building or visitor pass.

Information security:
Safeguarding information against unauthorized disclosure; or, the result of any system of administrative policies and procedures for identifying, controlling, and protecting from unauthorized disclosure, information the protection of which is authorized by order or statute.

Information systems:
A combination of AIS and communications equipment, software, and related devices.

Intelligence method:
The method which is used to provide support to an intelligence source or operation. This, if disclosed, is vulnerable to counteraction that could nullify or significantly reduce its effectiveness in supporting the foreign intelligence or foreign counterintelligence activities of the country. This would, if disclosed, reasonably lead to the disclosure of an intelligence source or operation.

Intelligence source:
A person, organization, or technical means which provides foreign intelligence or foreign counterintelligence. This, if its identity or capability is disclosed, is vulnerable to counteraction that could nullify or significantly reduce its effectiveness in providing foreign intelligence or foreign counterintelligence to the country. An intelligence source also means a person or organization which provides foreign intelligence or foreign counterintelligence to the country only on the condition that its identity remains undisclosed.

International organization:
An organization of governments.

L

Least privilege:
Principle requiring that each subject be granted the most restrictive set of privileges needed for the performance of authorized tasks. Application of this principle limits the damage that can result from accident, error, or unauthorized use of an information system.

Logged on but unattended:
A workstation is considered logged on but unattended when the user is:
   (1) Logged on but is not physically present in the office; and
   (2) There is no one else present with an appropriate level of clearance safeguarding access to the workstation. Coverage must be equivalent to that which would be required to safeguard hard copy information if the same employee were away from his or her desk. Users of logged on but unattended classified workstations are subject to the issuance of security violations.

Logically disconnect:
Although the physical connection between the control unit and a terminal remains intact, a system enforced disconnection prevents communication between the control unit and the terminal.

Lost pouch:
Any pouch out of control which is not recovered.

M

Message stream:
The sequence of messages or parts of messages to be sent.

Modular Treated Conference Room (MTCR):
A second-generation design of the treated conference room (TCR), offering more flexibility in configuration and ease of assembly than the original TCR, designed to provide acoustic and RF emanations protection.

N

National security:
The national defense or foreign relations of the country.

National security information:
Information specifically determined under executive order criteria to require protection against unauthorized disclosure.

Network device:
An external device that can be connected to a network, including but not limited to a hub/concentrator, switch, router, printer, scanner or digital photocopier. This excludes internal network interfaces since internal network interfaces are considered part of an Automated Information System (AIS).

Nonprofessional courier:
Any direct-hired, citizen employee of the government, other than a professional diplomatic courier, who possesses a top secret clearance and who has been provided with official documentation to transport properly prepared, addressed, and documented diplomatic pouches or controlled/unclassified material in country, in emergencies, or when the diplomatic courier cannot provide the required service. (Clearance is preferred, but not required for handling unclassified material.)

Nonrecord material:
Extra and/or duplicate copies that are only of temporary value, including shorthand notes, used carbon paper, preliminary drafts, and other material of similar nature.

O

Object:
From the Orange Book definition, "A passive entity that contains or receives information. Access to an object potentially implies access to the information it contains. Examples of objects are: records, blocks, pages, files, directories and programs, as well as bits, bytes, words, fields, keyboards, clocks, printers, network nodes, etc."

Object reuse:
The reassignment to a subject (e. g., a user) of a medium that previously contained an object (e. g., a file). The danger of object reuse is that the object may still contain information that the subject may not be authorized to access. Examples are magnetic tapes that haven't been erased or workstations that hold information in local storage.

Off-hook:
A station or trunk is off-hook when it initializes or engages in communications with the Computerized

Telephone Switch (CTS) or with another station or trunk using a link established through the CTS.

Official information:
That information or material which is owned by, produced for or by, or under the control of the Government.

Original classification:
An initial determination that information requires protection against unauthorized disclosure in the interest of national security, and a designation of the level of classification.

Original classifier:
An authorized individual in the executive branch who initially determines that particular information requires a specific degree of protection against unauthorized disclosure in the interest of national security and applies the classification designation "Top Secret", "Secret", or "Confidential."

OSPB:
The Overseas Security Policy Board (OSPB) is an interagency group of security professionals from the foreign affairs and intelligence communities who meet regularly to formulate security policy for missions abroad. The OSPB is chaired by the Director for Diplomatic Security.

P

Paraphrasing:
A restatement of text in different phraseology without alternation of its meaning.

Password:
A protected string of characters that authenticates a user, specific resource, or access type.

PCC:
Post Communications Center.

Plain text:
Information, usually classified, in unencrypted form.

Post security officer:
A citizen employee of the Foreign Affairs Service who is designated to perform security functions. At posts where regional security officers are located, they will be assigned this duty.

Pouch:
See "Diplomatic Pouch."

Pouch out of control:
Refers to any pouch over which cleared citizen control is interrupted for any period of time making outside intervention and compromise of its contents a possibility.

Product certification center:
A facility which certifies the technical security integrity of communications equipment. The equipment is handled and used within secure channels.

Professional courier (or diplomatic courier):
A person specifically employed and provided with official documentation by the Ministry of Foreign

Affairs/Department of State to transport properly prepared, addressed, and documented diplomatic pouches between the Department and its Foreign Service posts and across other international boundaries.

Protected distribution system (PDS):
A wire line or fiber-optic communications link with safeguards to permit its use for the distribution of unencrypted classified information.

Protection schema:
An outline detailing the type of access users may have to a database or application system, given a user's need-to-know, e. g., read, write, modify, delete, create, execute, and append.

R

RDCO:
The Regional diplomatic courier officer (RDCO) oversees the operations of a regional diplomatic courier division.

Record material:
All books, papers, maps, photographs, or other documentary materials, regardless of physical form or characteristics, made or received by the Government in connection with the transaction of public business and preserved or appropriated by an agency or its legitimate successor as evidence of the organization, functions, policies, decisions, procedures, or other activities of any agency of the Government, or because of the informational data contained therein.

Red:
It denotes encrypted/classified data, text, equipment, processes, systems or installations associated with information that requires emanations security protection. For example, wiring that carries unencrypted classified information either exclusively or mixed with unclassified is termed "Red" wiring.

RED/BLACK Concept:
The separation of electrical and electronic circuits, components, equipment, and systems which handle classified plain text (RED) information in electrical signal form from those which handle unclassified (BLACK) information in the same form.

Red-Black separation:
The requirement for physical spacing between "Red" and "black" processing systems and their components, including signal and power lines.

Redundant control capability:
Use of active or passive replacement, for example, throughout the network components (i. e., network nodes, connectivity, and control stations) to enhance reliability, reduce threat of single point of failure, enhance survivability, and provide excess capacity.

Regional security officer:
A professionally trained officer who has been designated to administer the security program for a specific area or post.

Remote diagnostic facility:
An off-premise diagnostic, maintenance, and programming facility authorized to perform functions on the Department computerized telephone system via an external network trunk connection.

Restricted area:
A specifically designated and posted area in which classified information or material is located or in which sensitive functions are performed, access to which is controlled and to which only authorized personnel are admitted.

Restricted data:
All data/information concerning:
      (1) Design, manufacture, or utilization of atomic weapons;
      (2) The production of special nuclear material;

RF shielding:
The application of materials to surfaces of a building, room, or a room within a room, that makes the surface largely impervious to electromagnetic energy. As a technical security countermeasure, it is used to contain or dissipate emanations from information processing equipment, and to prevent interference by externally generated energy.

Risk:
A measurement of the likelihood of compromise of information, and the damage to U. S. interests that would result. Risk is determined by threat, vulnerability, and sensitivity of the information stored or processed at post.

S

Sanitize:
The degaussing or overwriting of information on magnetic or other storage media.

SCI:
Sensitive Compartment Information, a category of highly classified information which requires special protection governed by the Director of Intelligence Agency.

Secret-cleared citizen:
A citizen of the nation who has undergone a background investigation by an authorized Government Agency and been issued a Secret-security clearance in accordance with orders, implementing guidelines and standards.

Secure room:
Any room with floor to ceiling, slab to slab construction of some substantial material, i. e., concrete, brick,. Any window areas or penetrations of wall areas over 15.25 cm must be covered with either grilling or substantial type material. Entrance doors must be constructed of solid wood, metal, etc., and be capable of holding a DS-approved three-way combination lock with interior extension.

Secure voice:
Systems in which transmitted conversations are encrypted to make them unintelligible to anyone except the intended recipient. Within the context of Department security standards, secure voice systems must also have protective features included in the environment of the systems terminals.

Secured domestic Foreign Affairs facility:
Any building or other location in the country or its territories staffed or managed by the Ministry of Foreign Affairs/Department of State which the Department of Diplomatic Security (DS) determines as warranting restricted entry.

Security anomaly:
An irregularity possibly indicative of a security breach, an attempt to breach security, or of noncompliance with security standards, policy, or procedures.

Security classification designations:
Refers to "Top Secret", "Secret" and "Confidential" designations on classified information or material.

Security domain:
The environment of systems for which a unique security policy is applicable.

Security equipment:
Protective devices such as intrusion alarms, safes, locks, and destruction equipment which provide physical or technical surveillance protection as their primary purpose.

Sensitive intelligence information:
Such intelligence information, the unauthorized disclosure of which would lead to counteraction:
> (1) Jeopardizing the continued productivity of intelligence sources or methods which provide intelligence vital to the national security;
> (2) Offsetting the value of intelligence vital to the national security.

Sensitive unclassified information:
Information which, either alone or in the aggregate, meets any of the following criteria and is deemed sensitive by the Department and must be protected in accordance with the magnitude of its loss or harm that could result from inadvertent or deliberate disclosure, alteration or destruction of the data:
> (1) Medical, personnel, financial, investigative or any other information the release of which would result in substantial harm, embarrassment, inconvenience, or unfair treatment to the Department or any individual on whom the information is maintained;
> (2) Information relating to the issuance or refusal of visas or permits to enter the country;
> (3) Information which may jeopardize the physical safety of Department facilities, personnel and their dependents, as well as citizens abroad;
> (4) Proprietary, trade secrets, commercial or financial information the release of which would place the company or individual on whom the information is maintained at a competitive disadvantage;
> (5) Information the release of which would have a negative effect on foreign policy or relations;
> (6) Information relating to official travel to locations deemed to have a terrorist threat;
> (7) Information considered mission-critical to an office or organization, but which is not national security information; and
> (8) Information which could be manipulated to commit fraud.

Sensitivity attributes:
User-supplied indicators of file sensitivity that the system uses to enforce an access control policy.

Special Agent:
A special agent in the Diplomatic Security Service (DSS) is a sworn officer of the Department of State or the Foreign Service, who has been issued special agent credentials by the Director of the Diplomatic Security Service to perform those specific security enforcement duties.

Special Investigator:
Special investigators are contracted by the Department. They perform various noncriminal investigative functions in Diplomatic Security (DS) head office, field, and resident offices. They are not members of the Diplomatic Security Service (DSS) and are not authorized to conduct criminal investigations.

Spherical zone of control:
A volume of space in which noncleared personnel must be escorted.

Storage object:
A data object which is used in the system as a repository of information.

System accreditation:
The official authorization granted to an information system to process sensitive information in its operational environment based on a comprehensive security evaluation of the system's hardware, firmware, and software security design, configuration and implementation and of the other system procedural, administrative, physical, personnel, and communications security controls.

System certification:
The technical evaluation of a system's security features that established the extent to which a particular information system's design and implementation meets a set of specified security requirements.

T

Technical penetration:
An unauthorized Radio Frequency (RF), acoustic, or emanations intercept of information. This intercept may occur along a transmission path which is:
    (1) Known to the source;
    (2) Fortuitous and unknown to the source;
    (3) Clandestinely established.

Technical surveillance:
The act of establishing a technical penetration and intercepting information without authorization.

Telecommunications:
Any transmission, emission, or reception of signs, signals, writings, images, sounds, or information of any nature by wire, radio, visual, or other electro-magnetic, mechanical, or optical means.

Tenant agency:
A Government department or agency operating overseas as part of the Foreign Affairs community under the authority of a chief of mission. Excluded are military elements not under direct authority of the chief of mission.

Threat:
In the security technology context, the likelihood that attempts will be made to gain unauthorized access to information or facilities.

Top Secret-cleared citizen:
A citizen of the country who has undergone a background investigation by an authorized Government Agency and been issued a Top Secret security clearance in accordance with orders, implementing guidelines and standards.

Treated Conference Room (TCR):
A shielded enclosure that provides acoustic and electromagnetic attenuation protection.

Trusted Computing Base (TCB):
The totality of protection mechanisms within an AIS (including hardware, firmware and software), the

combination of which is responsible for enforcing a security policy. A trusted computing base consists of one or more components that together enforce a unified security policy over a product or AIS. The ability of a trusted computing base to correctly enforce a security policy depends solely on the mechanisms within the trusted computing base and on the correct input by system administrative personnel of parameters (e. g., a user's clearance) related to the security policy.

U

Unauthorized disclosure:
The compromise of classified information by communication or physical transfer to an unauthorized recipient. It includes the unauthorized disclosure of classified information in a newspaper, journal, or other publication where such information is traceable to an agency because of a direct quotation or other uniquely identifiable fact.

Unit security officer:
A citizen employee who is a nonprofessional security officer designated with a specific or homogeneous working unit to assist the office of security in carrying out functions prescribed in these regulations.

Upgrading:
The determination that particular unclassified or classified information requires a higher degree of protection against unauthorized disclosure than currently provided. Such determination shall be coupled with a marking of the material with the new designation.

User's identification:
A character string which validates authorized user access.

V

Vienna Convention:
The Vienna Convention on Diplomatic Relations, which sets forth law and practice on diplomatic rights and privileges. Couriers must follow these guidelines to ensure that diplomatic rights and privileges are not infringed upon.

Visa fraud:
The fraudulent procuring, forging, or fraudulent use of visas or other entry documents.

Visitor:
Any person not issued a permanent building pass, who seeks to enter any Department facility for work, consultation, or other legitimate reason.

Visitor passes:
Passes of limited duration which DS issues to visitors at designated facilities. These also include conference or other special function passes.

Vulnerability:
The susceptibility of a facility, system or equipment to penetration by technical means.

Diplomatic and Consular Privileges and Immunities from Criminal Jurisdiction

Summary of Law Enforcement Aspects

	Category	May be arrested or detained	Residence may be entered subject to ordinary procedures	May be issued Traffic Citation	May Be subpoenaed as witness	May be prosecuted	Recognized family member
Diplomatic	Diplomatic Agent	No [1]	No	Yes	No	No	Same as sponsor (full immunity and inviolability)
	Member of Administrative Technical Staff	No [1]	No	Yes	No	No	Same as sponsor (full immunity and inviolability)
	Service Staff	Yes [2]	Yes	Yes	Yes	No- for official acts. Otherwise Yes [2]	No immunity or inviolability [2]
Consular	Career Consular Officer	Yes, if for felony and pursuant to a warrant [2]	Yes [4]	Yes	No- for official acts. Testimony may not be compelled in any case	No- for official acts. Otherwise Yes [2]	No immunity or inviolability [2]
	Honorary Consular Officer	Yes	Yes	Yes	No- for official acts. Yes, in all other cases	No- for official acts. Otherwise Yes	No immunity or inviolability
	Consular Employee	Yes [2]	Yes	Yes	No- for official acts. Yes, in all other cases	No- for official acts. Otherwise Yes [2]	No immunity or inviolability [2]
International Organizations	International Organizations Staff [3]	Yes [3]	Yes [3]	Yes	No- for official acts. Yes, in all other cases	No- for official acts. Otherwise Yes [3]	No immunity or inviolability
	Diplomatic Level Staff of Missions to International Organizations	No [1]	No	Yes	No	No	Same as sponsor (full immunity and inviolability)
	Support Staff of Missions to International Organizations	Yes	Yes	Yes	No- for official acts. Yes, in all other cases	No- for official acts. Otherwise Yes	No immunity or inviolability

1 Reasonable constraints, however, may be applied in emergency circumstances involving self-defense, public safety, or the prevention of serious criminal acts.
2 This table presents general rules. Particularly in the cases indicated, the employees of certain foreign countries may enjoy **higher** levels of privileges and immunities on the basis of special bilateral agreements.
3 A small number of senior officers are entitled to be treated identically to "diplomatic agents."
4 Note that consular residences are sometimes located within the official consular premises. In such cases, **only** the official office space is protected from police entry.

Once a decision is made that you have immediate, short-or long-term security needs, it should be determined whether limited or complex security requirements are necessary. Due to the actual global threat, it is strongly recommended, that every corporation, business, institution and private entity undertake security as a long-term and ongoing process. Depending on the nature and complexity of the corporation/institution or private entity, an assessment by security professionals might be required. The term "institution" in this context stands for everything from company, corporation, business to private person or entity. The term "security professional" or "professional" stands for everything from security company/firm to security personnel, security guard, security officer, EPOs.

Immediate, Short-and Long-Term Assignment

Whether security may be required on an immediate, short-and long-term basis, corporations and institutions should obtain competitive bids as soon as possible. It is essential to check with local law enforcement and other community agencies for recommendations. It is essential to clearly define the security professional's scope of work., for which all of the following criteria should be met:

- A concise statement describing the security tasks to be performed, including the number of days and hours that security is needed. This information should be clearly outlined with the security professional before any security (staff) is assigned to the site.

- A detailed set of general and particular special instructions. The importance of these instructions cannot be overstated. The institution should not rely on the security professional only to provide them. These instructions should be discussed with and agreed upon between the decision-makers of the institution and the security professional. Security professionals are to provide supplemental instructions to their personnel.

- Assignment of one person who will be the security personnel's contact and will greet the security personnel throughout the assignment. This liaison will greet the security personnel upon arrival to ensure that the officer understands his/her role and among other requirements, has a neat appearance and proper attitude.

Interactions with Security Professional/Personnel

First impressions are important in determining how the security personnel will perform. It is important to remember that the security professional is present to deter and detect unusual or suspicious activity as well as to safeguard property and people. The following are key points that the institution's contact person should discuss with the security professional/personnel:

- Requirements of the assignment.
- Purpose of security during the prescribed times.
- The security professional will be assessed during the shift for alertness.
- Rules of conduct that enhance effectiveness.
- For example, no smoking, practical joking, fraternizing, etc.
- The scope of work should be explained and written concise expectations presented as soon as the security professional arrives (keeping a copy for yourself):
- Liaison contact and how to immediately reach him/her.

- Layout of the facility.
- Facility security and/or fire regulations.
- Any vulnerable areas.
- Locations of telephones, fire-fighting equipment, fire alarms, emergency exits, etc.
- Location of stairways and doors.
- Clear operational guidelines to be used in the event of an emergency (fire, suspicious package, bomb threat, etc.)

Criteria for Security Professional Selection

As soon as the need for a security has been determined on an immediate, short or long-term basis, a security professional should be selected. Selecting a professional that has valid, current state licenses is essential. You should be certain that a company is reliable and in good standing. All of the following criteria should be met:

- Adequate and current insurance
- Track record/reputation
- Proposal characteristics
- References
- Training
- Equipment
- Costs
- Contract
- Management
- Security professional's qualifications

Insurance

After you have established that a security professional is duly licensed, scrutinize the insurance coverage the security professional provides. Every state licenses and keeps records on security professionals and companies. As such, it is essential to hire a security professional that has a valid, current state license and to determine the reputation of the security professional by investigating any history of complaints reported against it to the state licensing authority. The following insurance criteria should be met prior to hiring a security professional/firm:

- The security professional provides and maintains adequate insurance coverage for your situation.
- Your risk manager (insurance agent) approves of the security professional's coverage.
- Security professional's Broad Form General Liability Insurance covers a minimum of $1 million per incident and $3 million total. The higher the coverage the better. Determine whether the security professional has fidelity bonding and other coverage.
- The security professional's Workers Compensation Insurance is at statutory minimums.
- The security professional should have adequate Automobile Liability Insurance coverage for all vehicles used.
- Security professional's insurance covers sexual harassment through their Professional Liability coverage.
- Liability coverage for special equipment provided (CCTVs, golf carts, computer equipment, watch clocks, monitors, etc.).
- Security professional's insurance carriers name your entity as "Additional Insured" on their liability insurance policies (or at least, obtain certificates of insurance for the security professional). If so, is there an extra charge for this?

- Your insurance adviser does not object to any of the policy "Exclusions."
- Ask for EMR (Employment Modification Rate) for the last three years. The lower the EMR, the better the security professional's safety performance.

Reputation

A security professional's reputation should be examined to ensure that the security professional has maintained a trustworthy and dependable reputation. To determine the quality of past work, ascertain whether there has been a recent history of valid or successful lawsuits or complaints to state agencies against the security professional filed by clients or employees. This can be learned at your local courthouse or through a local attorney. Consider three main factors when researching a security professional's history: negligence, workers compensation claims and experience and management.

Negligence

Determining possible history involving negligence by the security professional is important. Request "Loss Experience" or "Loss Runs" reports from the security professional in order to review its liability insurance claims history. Inquire of the security professional directly whether they ever were involved in any lawsuits and whether there has been any legal incident involving the employees while on a client's property during the last 10 years. Your lawyer or insurance broker can explain the report and advise you on the significance of each case and report.

Workers Compensation Claims

Review the listing of worker compensation claims to determine the possibility of patterns of carelessness or inadequate employee safety practices. This report is available from the security professional and your insurance agent can advise you of the significance of the data. These criteria are important in determining whether a security professional's insurance coverage is sufficient to meet your needs. A security professional must both provide security and be properly insured. Again, ask for EMR (Employment Modification Rate) for the last three years (the lower the EMR, the better the professional's safety performance).

Experience and Management

First and foremost, it is important to recognize that you are hiring a security professional/team. Inquire as to the number of years of service in the security industry, area of operation, special services, regional management and operations management. Although not essential, the security professional should have recently provided security service to an institution/entity similar to yours.

Proposal Characteristics

Carefully analyze the proposal submitted by the security professional. The proposal should address the specific security needs at your site and demonstrate that the security professional has carefully reviewed and considered your needs. The following are key points that the security professional should enumerate in a proposal for you.

Training and Qualifications

The proposal should set the minimum qualification as follows: describe the security related education, training levels, and experience of personnel to be assigned at your institution. Security professionals that provide additional education and training to their staffs are preferable.

Staffing

Staffing may be regular, rotating or temporary and it is important to know beforehand which personnel you will be dealing with. A permanent staff assignment is always best if it can be obtained. However, security firms often have difficulty maintaining regular staff as a result of odd shifts, frequently consisting of less than eight hours. You should research the security professional's history of staff stability and be wary of excessive turn-over or poor relationships with employees. The security professional should also obtain your approval before transferring (or replacing) personnel from your site. It is important to assure that the security professional's needs at other sites should not take precedence over security needs at your site.

Description of Supervision

Does the proposal describe the exact nature of supervision to be provided? Security professionals should be willing to explain clearly how they will monitor and control the quality of security services.

Documentation

In selecting the best quality security professional, the proposal should describe the type and frequency of reports and documentation (daily officer activity logs, incident reports, crime reports, officer time sheets, other special reports, etc.). Consistent and thorough written communication is an important output of contract security services and is an important management control mechanism you have over security services and costs.

Instructions to Security Guard

Carefully analyze whether the proposal includes sample Post Orders or Standard Operating Procedures Manual. This document describes all aspects of job performance at your site including security personnel grooming and decorum, sets the standard of security services and provides the basis of guard discipline. Ultimately, this document becomes the main basis of legal defense in the event of litigation. The security professional should provide a document that is comprehensive and clear both to you and the security personnel.

Emergency Procedures

The security professional's proposal should describe how its personnel will function under various emergency conditions. The proposal should demonstrate an understanding and coherent approach to a wide variety of nonstandard, unusual or crisis situations.

Equipment Issues

If a security guard is expected to patrol your institution/residence when it is closed (holidays, overnight, etc.), he/she should be equipped with a radio/cell phone enabling contact with emergency services if needed. It is important for you to ask what other equipment is standard issue and/or the personnel is certified to use (permits, etc.). For example, will the personnel carry a baton, pepper spray, handcuffs, weapon, etc.?

References

References help identify quality and reputable security professionals. Client references give invaluable insight as to the reliability and performance of a security professional and highlight areas of possible improvement. To secure the most qualified and experienced security firm, use references that:

- Clients verify a security professional's history of relevant experience.
- Past clients' references verify a security professional's history of responsiveness.
- References indicate security professional's employee turnover rate is lower than or equal to that of industry norms.

Costs

Prospective security professionals should address the following issues:

- How frequently will firm bill for services rendered? Weekly? Bi-weekly? Other? Is this convenient for you?
- Will it be a flat monthly rate, a uniform hourly rate for all employees or a unique hourly rate for each individual employee? Generally, paying a unique hourly rate for each guard provides clients with the most economical service.
- Security professional discloses wages to be paid to guards assigned to your site. A good security professional should be willing to discuss openly all cost drivers and the fee or profit margins it expects to earn for the services to be provided.
- Security professional's periodic invoices list wages and bill rates for each guard. Invoice detail provides a good audit trail and shows firm's professionalism.
- How will guard pay increases be handled? Inadequate or stagnant wages are a frequent cause of staff turnover. Wage increases should be proposed in advance by the security professional, based on officer incentive and merit, reflected logically in billing rate adjustment and mutually agreed upon by the security professional and client before implementation.
- Will any additional charges be made for uniforms, equipment, supplies, etc.? Again, these should be proposed, justified, logical and mutually agreed upon.
- Is the total estimated average monthly cost within your budget? Your monthly guard budget can be calculated by multiplying the hourly wage rate.

Contract

The security contract defines the rights and responsibilities between you and the security professional and ensures that the security professional will meet your needs. There are numerous questions and criteria that a security professional should specifically address in order to ensure that the security firm is responsible and dependable. These serve as guidelines to refer to and are listed below:

- Does the security professional indemnify you for all security-related liability for which the firm is responsible? In cases where partial liability is determined by a court of law, does the agreement clearly specify how such indemnifications shall be applied? You should discuss client indemnification of the firm.
- At contract time will there be a price increase? How much? Why?
- Do you retain the right to terminate the agreement at any time and for any reason? Is this right mutual?
- Is the amount of notice required for contract termination-by the security professional or client-reasonable? Thirty days is the standard.
- Is the agreement sufficiently flexible to meet your needs?
- Does it assure fairness to the security professional and adequate control to the client?
- Can you replace a guard if necessary?

Management

You and the security professional must share an understanding of the reasons for entering into the contract. As such, discussion issues should include the following:

- Discuss your desires with the security company management.
- Discuss terms of supervision with the security professional, field and management staff.

The security personnel know, understand, and comply with your site's written policy manual. If a security guard performs below par, it is important to know that the individual will be counseled, disciplined and replaced by the security professional as needed.

- Once the security guards are in place, you will need to monitor them to ensure that they meet high professional standards, project a professional and alert demeanor and respond effectively to security-related concerns. It should be required that all that written materials from the security guard (logs, reports) be clear, complete and usable. You should receive a copy of every report filed by your guard.

Deciding What Kind of Security Should Be Hired

It is important to know that hiring a security professional, whether limited or extensive, armed or unarmed, is a serious business and not to be taken lightly. Different kinds of security professionals are appropriate for different situations. One important issue is whether you would like security at your site to be provided by a uniformed or plain-clothes officers.

- The main goal for hiring a uniformed security professional is deterrence.
- The main goal for hiring a plain-clothes security professional is apprehension.

After deciding what kind of security to hire, you must determine whether the security professional should be *armed* or *unarmed*. There are many costs and benefits to be considered when choosing an armed versus unarmed security professional. The following should help you analyze the issue and determine what is in the best interest of your institution.

Armed Security Guards

It is important to determine if hiring armed security professionals meets your institution's expectations for security.

- Realize that armed security professionals may utilize deadly force.
- Determine the training qualifications the security professionals have with firearms.
- Determine the security professional's policy on the use of weapons with regard to deadly force.
- Keep in mind moral questions when hiring an armed security professional. You should determine whether the members of your corporation/institution will accept an armed security professional on the premises. Please note that special care should be taken if your institution serves many young people. Schools should be particularly concerned with the message an armed security professional conveys to students, parents and staff.
- Consider the cost effectiveness of an armed security professional. They are much more expensive than unarmed security, due to licensing and training requirements.

- Decide whether the presence of a weapon may escalate the possible use of force and violence which otherwise may not occur.
- Insurance may be adversely affected by the presence of an armed guard.

Unarmed Security Guards

- Use of deadly force is neither desired nor required.
- Unarmed security professionals often provide the same deterrent as armed security professionals without the risk of deadly force.
- The protection afforded by unarmed security professionals is less expensive and may incur less liability and insurance.

Checklist for Security Professional Selection

As previously mentioned, when the need for a security professional has been determined on an immediate, short-or long-term basis, a security professional should be selected. The following points will assist you in this process:

- Institution Name
- Security professional/firm Name
- Requested Received Accepted
- Insurance
- Reputation
- Negligence
- Workers Compensation
- Claims
- Experience
- Proposal
- References
- Costs
- Contract
- Management
- Security professionals assigned

CPSIA information can be obtained
at www.ICGtesting.com
Printed in the USA
LVOW03s1039280216
477035LV00006B/154/P